To a precious family friend

Kathy Shuff

with gratitude for your

hospitality – May 2017

(Wordworth)

To my children and grandchildren —
an unceasing source of happiness and inspiration with an
unconditional love for their father and 'Dedi'

Sofia Andreevna Tolstaya and Lev Nikolaevich Tolstoy

TOLSTOY AND TOLSTAYA

A PORTRAIT OF A LIFE IN LETTERS

Translated from the Russian by
John Woodsworth, Arkadi Klioutchanski & Liudmila Gladkova

With a Foreword by
Vladimir Tolstoy

Edited and with an Introduction by
Andrew Donskov

UNIVERSITY OF OTTAWA PRESS
2017

u Ottawa

The University of Ottawa Press gratefully acknowledges the support extended to its publishing list by Heritage Canada through the Canada Book Fund, by the Canada Council for the Arts, by the Ontario Arts Council, by the Canadian Federation for the Humanities and Social Sciences through its Aid to Scholarly Publications Program, and by the University of Ottawa.

Proofreading: Michael Waldin
Layout: Sandra Friesen Design
Cover illustration: Lev Nikolaevich and Sofia Andreevna on their 48th wedding anniversary,
23 September 1910. Photo by S.A. Tolstaya, 1910
Cover design: Martyn Schmoll

LIBRARY AND ARCHIVES CANADA CATALOGUING IN PUBLICATION

Tolstoy & Tolstaya : a portrait of a life in letters / translated from the Russian by John Woodsworth, Arkadi Klioutchanski & Liudmila Gladkova ; edited and with an introduction by Andrew Donskov.

Includes bibliographical references and indexes.
Issued in print and electronic formats.
ISBN 978-0-7766-2471-6 (hardcover).—ISBN 978-0-7766-2472-3
(PDF).—ISBN 978-0-7766-2473-0 (EPUB).—ISBN 978-0-7766-2474-7 (Kindle)

1. Tolstoy, Leo, graf, 1828-1910—Correspondence. 2. Tolstaᶥiʼ,S. A. (Sofʼʼiʼ Andreevna), 1844-1919—Correspondence. 3. Authors,Russian—19th century—Correspondence. 4. Authors' spouses—Russian—Correspondence. I. Donskov, Andrew, 1939-, editor II. Woodsworth, John, 1944-, translator III. Klioutchanski, Arkadi, 1965-, translator IV. Gladkova, Liudmila, 1954-, translator.
Title: Tolstoy and Tolstaya.

PG3379.T65 2017   891.73'3   C2017-902466-3
                                           C2017-902467-1

Printed and Bound in Canada, 2017

Canadä

TABLE OF CONTENTS

ACKNOWLEDGEMENTS
VII

MAP OF EUROPEAN RUSSIA (EARLY TWENTIETH CENTURY)
AND LIST OF RUSSIAN GEOGRAPHICAL NAMES
IX

SELECTED GENEALOGY
XVI

FOREWORD BY VLADIMIR IL'ICH TOLSTOY
XXI

FROM THE EDITOR
XXIII

FROM THE TRANSLATORS
XXXI

CHRONOLOGICAL LIST OF LETTERS 1862–1910
XXXIII

EDITOR'S INTRODUCTION
Leo Tolstoy and Sofia Tolstaya:
A dialogue of two independently minded kindred spirits
LXIX

LEV NIKOLAEVICH TOLSTOY & SOFIA ANDREEVNA TOLSTAYA
CORRESPONDENCE

PART I
Introduction to Part I
LETTERS 1862–1879
3

PART II
Introduction to Part II
LETTERS 1880–1888
83

PART III
Introduction to Part III
LETTERS 1889–1910
199

PART IV
Introduction to Part IV
ELEVEN UNPUBLISHED LETTERS (1864–1905)
313

BIBLIOGRAPHY
341

SELECTED CHRONOLOGY
349

LIST OF PERIODICAL TITLES
with their English equivalents
397

INDEX OF WORKS
by Lev Nikolaevich Tolstoy and Sofia Andreevna Tolstaya
401

INDEX OF NAMES
407

ACKNOWLEDGEMENTS

The present volume — as part of my larger multi-tome project of publishing the entire correspondence between Lev Nikolaevich Tolstoy and Sofia Andreevna Tolstaya in its original Russian — draws upon the support of a number of individuals and scholarly institutions in both Canada and Russia.

My first debt of gratitude is to the Tolstoy Museum in Moscow, its Director, Sergej Aleksandrovich Arkhangelov and Deputy Director Natalija Kalinina, for granting us the exclusive rights of translation and publication in English of these most precious materials and illustrations and their helpful consultations throughout.

I am also indebted to Dr. Marina Shcherbakova, Head of the Russian Classical Division of the Russian Academy of Sciences' Institute of World Literature, for her ongoing support and advice. Thanks especially to Liudmila Gladkova, Senior Researcher and a Deputy Director of the Tolstoy Museum, not to mention a world-renowned specialist on the work of Fyodor Ivanovich Tyutchev. It was my great pleasure to work with her very closely on the annotations, which have indeed enhanced the readers' knowledge of the context of these letters, and her participation in the translation process has been invaluable. With no less enthusiasm I thank our good friend Vladimir Il'ich Tolstoy, Director of the Yasnaya Polyana Tolstoy Museum Estate and great-great-grandson to Sofia Andreevna and Lev Nikolaevich — along with the Museum Estate's Head of Research, Dr. Galina Alekseeva — for their frequent advice and assistance in facilitating access to rare documentary materials. We are also appreciative of Vladimir Il'ich's consent to provide a Foreword to this volume.

On the Canadian side of the Atlantic, I should like to express my heartfelt gratitude to the highly accomplished work of John Woodsworth and Arkadi Klioutchanski, both members of our Slavic Research Group here at the University of Ottawa and laureates of the 2012 Lois Roth Award presented by the Modern Language Association of America for the best translation of a

work into English (in this case, Sofia Tolstaya's *My Life*, published in 2010 by the University of Ottawa Press). John Woodsworth, a member of the Literary Translators' Association of Canada, not only is widely esteemed for his translation of poetry and literary prose from Russian (including Vladimir Megré's popular 9-volume *Ringing Cedars Series*), but has also published his own Russian-language poetry, while Arkadi Klioutchanski, a native speaker of Russian, has produced some excellent scholarly work on Tolstoy and is currently completing a manuscript on Dostoevsky's *The Possessed* [*Besy*]. His participation in the work on the Tolstoy Chronology is much appreciated.

A huge note of thanks is also due my capable assistant Anna Kozlova for her help both in research and in work on the index, mainly in the hallowed halls and archive vaults of the Tolstoy Museum in Moscow, in consultation with notable Tolstoy specialists. I am obliged, too, to Svetlana Astachkina and Tatiana Carter for additional work on the index and manuscript preparation.

In addition, I express my sincere gratitude for the wise counsel and continuing support of Dr. Robert Major, Vice-Rector Academic Emeritus and President of the University of Ottawa Press. To Lara Mainville, Director of the University of Ottawa Press, along with her most capable team Dominike Thomas, Elizabeth Schwaiger, Thierry Black and Sonia Rheault, our appreciation for the enthusiastic assistance they have provided in overseeing all the phases of this challenging undertaking.

Naturally, in a work of this scope, maintaining the delicate balance of fidelity to the original and good English style is a considerable task. I readily acknowledge, however, that the ultimate responsibility for the final product rests on my shoulders alone.

This project has been made possible by the moral and financial support of the Social Sciences and Humanities Research Council of Canada (SSHRC). Finally, I thank my friend and colleague Dr. Juana Muñoz-Liceras, Vice-Dean of Research, Faculty of Arts of the University of Ottawa, for her encouragement of the whole project.

Ottawa, Canada
December 2016

Andrew Donskov, F. R. S. C.
Distinguished University Professor
University of Ottawa

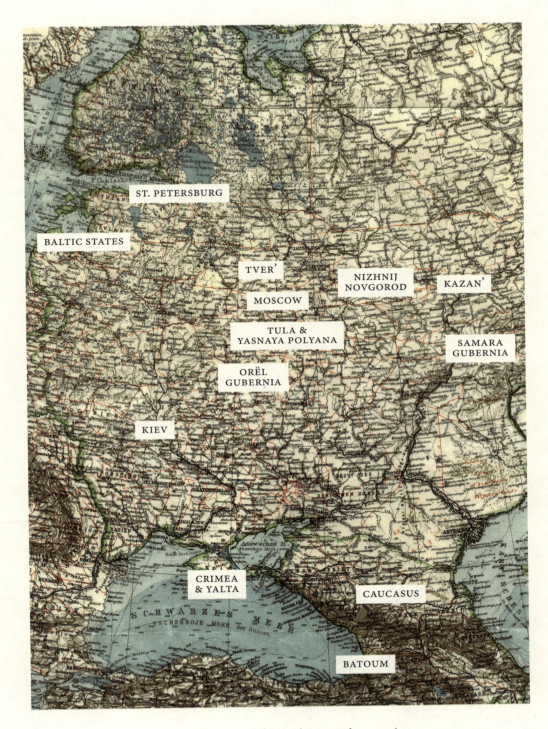

Map of European Russia (early twentieth century)

LIST OF RUSSIAN GEOGRAPHICAL NAMES

appearing in the correspondence

Aleksandrovka[1] *(Aleksandrovskij homestead, a.k.a. Protasovo)* — a small estate owned by LNT adjoining Nikol'skoe-Vjazemskoe

Arkhangel'skoe — see *Blagodatnoe*

Arzamas — regional centre of Arzamas Uezd in Nizhegorodskaja (Nizhnij Novgorod) Gubernia

Astapovo — railway station 95 versts from Yasnaya Polyana where LNT spent the final hours of his life

Atkarsk — regional centre of Atkarsk Uezd in Saratov Gubernia

Baburino — a village located 5 versts from Yasnaya Polyana

Bajdary — settlement in Simferopol' Uezd in the Crimea

Balaklava — a dacha community in the Crimea, about 12 versts from Sevastopol'

Bastyevo — a station on the railway Orël line, not far from Il'ja L'vovich's Grinëvka estate

Begichevka — settlement in Dankov Uezd, Rjazan' Gubernia, also the estate of Tolstoy's friend Ivan Ivanovich Raevskij; this was one of the bases where Tolstoy worked on famine relief

Belaja — a tributary of the River Kama

Belëv — regional centre of Belëv Uezd in Tula Gubernia (western part)

Blagodatnoe (Arkhangel'skoe) — settlement in Tula Gubernia, also a railway station near the Sukhotins' Kochety estate

---

1 Stressed vowels in Russian place names are shown in **boldface** type. The stress on the words *Uezd* and *Gubernia* are indicated at their first occurence only. Note that the letter **ë** (always stressed) has a sound approximating *yo*. A *verst* is equivalent to 1.07 km (see From the Editor).

x

Bogatovo (Bogatoe) — a station on the Orenburg railway line, 65 versts from Samara; the closest station to the Tolstoy's Samara homestead

Bogoroditsk — regional centre of Bogoroditsk Uezd in Tula Gubernia, 70 versts south of Tula

Bol'shoj Irgiz — see *Irgiz*

Borodino — settlement in the Mozhajsk Uezd, Moscow Gubernia, about 115 versts from Moscow (the famous Battle of Borodino in the summer of 1812 was a turning-point leading to · the rout of the Napoleonic forces from Russia)

Borolomka — a stream 3 versts from Yasnaya Polyana, the location of a watermill

Brattsovo (Brattsevo) — a dacha community in Moscow Gubernia, 13 versts from Moscow

Buzuluk — regional centre of Buzuluk Uezd in Samara Gubernia, 140 versts south-east of Samara (now part of Orenburg Oblast) — the Uezd where LNT bought a homestead in 1871

Chepyzh — forest at Yasnaya Polyana

Chern' — regional centre of Chern' Uezd, Tula Gubernia (southwestern part), 75 versts from Yasnaya Polyana

Chernava — railway station in Rjazan' Gubernia, the closest postal station to Begichevka

Dmitrievka — a village in Kaluga Gubernia

Dmitrov — regional centre of Dmitrov Uezd in Moscow Gubernia, 65 versts north of Moscow and 20 versts from the Olsuf'evs' Nikol'skoe-Obol'janovo estate

Dnieper (Russian: *Dnepr*; Ukrainian: *Dnipro*) — a major European river, flowing from western Russia through Belarus and Ukraine (bisecting the city of Kiev) and emptying into the Black Sea

Epifan' — regional centre of Epifan' Uezd, Tula Gubernia, 75 versts south-east of Tula

Gaspra — village in Yalta Uezd on the south shore of the Crimea (location of Sof'ja Vladimirovna Panina's estate, where the Tolstoys recuperated during the winter of 1900–01)

Gavrilovka — Cossack settlement in Samara Gubernia, not far from the Tolstoys' farmstead

Grinëvka — village in Chern Uezd, Tula Gubernia, also the estate of the Tolstoys' son Il'ja

Grodno — administrative centre of Grodno Gubernia, located in what is now western Belarus near the Polish border, about 855 versts west of Moscow

Grumont — village in Krapivna Uezd, Tula Gubernia, 3 versts from Yasnaya Polyana

Ikonskie Vyselki — village in Krapivna Uezd, Tula Gubernia

Irgiz (Bol'shoj Irgiz) — a river flowing into the Volga (the Karalyk is its tributary)

Ivitsy — settlement in Tula Gubernia, also the estate of Tolstaya's maternal grandfather, Aleksandr Mikhajlovich Islen'ev (it was here in August 1862 that LNT proposed to Sof'ja Andreevna Behrs)

Kaluga — regional centre of Kaluga Gubernia, about 180 versts south-west of Moscow

Kama — one of the main tributaries of the River Volga, flowing into it from the north-east

Kameluk (Kamelik) — a tributary of the River Bol'shoj Irgiz in Samara Gubernia

Karalyk (Orlovka) — settlement on the River Karalyk in Samara Gubernia

Kazan' — historic city on the River Volga, administrative centre of Kazan' Gubernia, 820 versts east of Moscow

Kaznacheevo — settlement in Tula Gubernia, 50 versts north-west of Tula

Khar'kov — a major city in what is today eastern Ukraine, about 455 versts east of Kiev

Khitrovo — settlement in Chern Uezd, Tula Gubernia, also the estate of the Barons Delvig, 2 versts from Elizaveta Aleksandrovna Tolstaja's Pokrovskoe estate

Klekotki — a railway station in Rjazan' Gubernia, 30 versts from Begichevka

Kochaki — settlement on the Kochak Stream, 2 versts from Yasnaya Polyana; location of the Tolstoys' family cemetery on the grounds of the Church of St Nicholas the Miracle-Worker

Kochety — settlement in the Novosil'sk Uezd of Orël Gubernia, also the estate of Tat'jana L'vovna's husband Mikhail Sergeevich Sukhotin

Kolodezi — village in Rjazan' Gubernia, close to Begichevka

Kostroma — administrative centre of Kostroma Gubernia, located at the confluence of the Volga and Kostroma Rivers, 345 versts north-east of Moscow

Kovno (Kaunas) — administrative centre of Kovno Gubernia, just under 1,000 versts west of Moscow, now in Lithuania

Kozlovka (Kozlova Zaseka) — a railway station only 4 versts from Yasnaya Polyana

Krapivna — regional centre of Krapivna Uezd in Tula Gubernia, 45 versts from Yasnaya Polyana

Krasnye Dvory — a coaching inn near the Kondyrëvka post office in Chern Uezd, Tula Gubernia

Kronshtadt (Kronstadt) — a port on Kotlin Island in the Gulf of Finland, just west of St. Petersburg

Kurkino — settlement in Tula Gubernia, 20 versts from Begichevka

Kutais (Kutaisi) — administrative centre of Kutais Gubernia in Georgia, 220 versts from Tiflis (Tbilisi)

Kuzmodem'jansk (Koz'modem'jansk) — port on the Volga River and regional centre of Kuzmodem'jansk Uezd in Kazan' Gubernia, 214 versts from Kazan'

Lapashino — village in Mtsensk Uezd, Orël Gubernia, about 1.5 versts from Grinëvka

Lapotkovo — settlement in Krapivna Uezd, Tula Gubernia, a postal station 25 versts from Yasnaya Polyana

Livadija — royal estate 4 versts south-west of Yalta in the Crimea

Malakhovo — a bog in Krapivna Uezd, Tula Gubernia, 10 versts from Yasnaya Polyana

Mocha — river in Samara Gubernia, now known as the Chapaevka, a tributary of the Volga

Morshansk — regional centre of Morshansk Uezd in Tambov Gubernia (south-east of Moscow), on the way to the Tolstoys' farmstead in Samara, located 90 versts north of Tambov

Mozhajsk — regional centre of Mozhajsk Uezd in Moscow Gubernia, 100 versts south-west of Moscow

Mtsensk — regional centre of Mtsensk Uezd, Orël Gubernia, 55 versts north-east of Orël, not far from Turgenev's Spasskoe-Lutovinovo estate

Nikol'skoe-Obol'janovo — settlement in Dmitrov Uezd, Moscow Gubernia, also the estate of the Tolstoys' friends, the Counts Olsuf'evs

Nikol'skoe-Vjazemskoe — settlement in Chern' Uezd, Tula Gubernia, also LNT's estate (100 versts from Yasnaya Polyana) which he inherited from his elder brother Nikolaj in 1860

Nizhnij Novgorod (Nizhnij) — administrative centre of Nizhegorodskaja Gubernia, 400 versts east of Moscow on the Volga (known as Gor'kij 1932–90)

Novoselki — settlement in Mtsensk Uezd, Orël Gubernia, also the estate of the poet Afanasij Fet not far from Tolstoy's Nikol'skoe-Vjazemskoe estate

Obidimo — settlement 16 versts from Tula; a station on the Syzran'–Vjaz'ma railway line

Odessa — port on the Black Sea, regional centre of Odessa Uezd straddling Kherson' and Odessa Gubernias, 450 km south of Kiev

Odoev — regional centre of Odoev Uezd of Tula Gubernia (western part)

Omsk — a city in Eastern Siberia, some 2,600 versts east of Moscow.

Optina pustyn' — monastery of the Russian Orthodox Church situated in Kozel'sk Uezd, Kaluga Gubernia, 150 versts from Yasnaya Polyana, where Tolstoy went for the last time shortly before his death in 1910

Orël — administrative centre of Orël Gubernia, 360 versts south-west of Moscow

Orenburg — administrative centre of Orenburg Gubernia in the southern Urals, at the confluence of the Ural and Sakmara Rivers, 1450 versts south-east of Moscow

Orlovka — settlement in Epifan' Uezd, Tula Gubernia, 8 versts from Begichevka; see also *Karalyk*

Patrovka — settlement in Samara Gubernia 20 versts from the Tolstoys' Samara farmstead

Pavlovsk — suburb of St. Petersburg, approx. 24 versts south of the city centre.

Penza — administrative centre of Penza Gubernia (620 versts south-east of Moscow), where Tolstoy went in 1869 to buy an estate

Petrovskoe-Razumovskoe — dacha community (now in the northern part of Moscow), site (since 1865) of the Petrovskaja Agricultural Academy with a farm and nurseries

Pirogovo — settlement in Krapivna Uezd, Tula Gubernia, also the estate of LNT's brother Sergej Nikolaevich and sister Marija Nikolaevna

Podol'sk — regional centre of Podol'sk Uezd in Moscow Gubernia, 36 versts south of the centre of Moscow on the way to Yasnaya Polyana

Podsolnechnaja — a railway station in Moscow Gubernia, the closest station to the Olsuf'evs' Nikol'skoe-Obol'janovo estate

Pokrovskoe — settlement in Chern Uezd, Tula Gubernia, also the estate of Elizaveta Aleksandrovna Tolstaja

Pokrovskoe-Streshnevo (Pokrovskoe) — dacha community north-west of Moscow, where for many years SAT's father Andrej Evstaf'evich Behrs rented a dacha (it was here on 22 August 1844 that Sofia Andreevna Behrs was born)

Poltava — administrative centre of Poltava Gubernia, in the south of Russia, 290 versts east of Kiev (now in Ukraine)

Rjazan' — administrative centre of Rjazan' Gubernia, 175 versts south-east of Moscow

Rozhnja — village in the Dankov Uezd of Rjazan' Gubernia, not far from Begichevka

Rudakovo — settlement in the Tula Uezd of Tula Gubernia, about 7 versts from Yasnaya Polyana

Rvy — a village about 5 versts from Yasnaya Polyana

Samara — administrative centre of Samara Gubernia, just over 1,000 versts south-east of Moscow on the Volga River, known as Kuybyshev 1935–91 (here in the Gubernia's Buzuluk Uezd LNT bought a homestead in 1871)

Saransk — regional centre of Saransk Uezd in Penza Gubernia, about 500 versts south-east of Moscow

Saratov — administrative centre of Saratov Gubernia, on the Volga, about 800 versts south-east of Moscow

Selivanovo — settlement in Tula Gubernia 20 versts from Yasnaya Polyana

Sergievskoe — settlement in Krapivna Uezd, Tula Gubernia belonging to the Princes Gagarin; also a postal station 40 versts from Yasnaya Polyana

Sevastopol' — military port on the south-west shore of the Crimean peninsula, about 850 versts south of Kiev (it was LNT's participation in the heroic defence of the city during the Crimean War [1853–56] that gave rise to his *Sevastopol' stories*)

Shablykino — settlement in Karachaevsk Uezd, Orël Gubernia, also the estate of Nikolaj Vasil'evich Kireevskij, where LNT often went hunting

Shamordino — settlement in Kozel'sk Uezd, Kaluga Gubernia, location of the Convent of St-Ambrose and Our Lady of Kazan', where LNT's sister Marija Nikolaevna served as a nun

Shilovo (Shilino) — village 19 versts from Gorbatovo, Nizhegorodskaja Gubernia, on the way to Penza Gubernia, where LNT went in 1869 to purchase an estate

Simbirsk — administrative centre of Simbirsk Gubernia, about 840 versts south-east of Moscow, re-named Ul'janovsk in 1924

Simeiz — settlement on the southern shore of the Crimean peninsula, 20 versts south-west of Yalta, featuring parks and cypress groves

Spass-Torbeevo — a village not far from the Troitse-Sergieva Monastery Sergiev-Posad, about 110 versts north of Moscow.

Spasskoe-Lutovinovo — settlement in Mtsensk Uezd, Orël Gubernia, also the estate of writer Ivan Sergeevich Turgenev

Starogladkovksaja (Starogladovskaja) — Cossack village in the Terek region on the River Terek, where Tolstoy lived while serving in the Caucasus (1851–54), described as Novomlinskaja in his narrative *The Cossacks*

Sudakovo — village in Tula Gubernia, 7 versts from Yasnaya Polyana

Tambov — administrative centre of Tambov Gubernia, about 420 versts south-east of Moscow

Tananyk — the dried-up tributary of the River Bobrovka, which flowed into the River Buzuluk in Samara Gubernia

Teljatinki — village in Krapivna Uezd, Tula Gubernia, 2 versts from Yasnaya Polyana, also the estate of Vladimir Grigor'evich Chertkov and his family

Tiflis — administrative centre of Tiflis Gubernia; the capital of Georgia; known today as Tbilisi

Tsarskoe Selo — a town about 22 versts south of St. Petersburg, where one of the royal residences was located

Tula — administrative centre of Tula Gubernia, about 200 versts south of Moscow

Tver' — administrative centre of Tver' Gubernia, 170 versts north-west of Moscow; known as Kalinin (1931–90)

Ufa — administrative centre of Ufa Gubernia, 1,260 versts east of Moscow

Uspenskoe — settlement in Bogoroditsk, Tula Gubernia, also the estate of Vasilij Nikolaevich Bibikov

Uzlovaja — railway station 48 versts south-east of Tula

Voin — estate of Pëtr Petrovich Novosil'tsov in Orël Gubernia, 13 versts south-west of Mtsensk

Vorob'ëvka — estate of Afanasij Afanas'evich Fet in Kursk Gubernia

Voronezh — administrative centre of Voronezh Gubernia, about 500 versts south of Moscow

Voronka — stream located 1 verst from **Ya**snaya Pol**ya**na

Vorotynka — village in Bogoroditsk Uezd, **T**ula Gubernia, originally belonging to the Tolstoys and sold at the beginning of the 1850s

Vsesvjatskoe — settlement on the Petersburg Chaussée north-west of Moscow, close to Nikol'skoe and Pokrovskoe-Streshnevo

Yalta — port in the Crimea on the Black Sea, about 840 versts south of Kiev

Yasenki — postal station 5 versts from **Ya**snaya Pol**ya**na; also, from the late 1860s, a station on the Moscow-Kursk railway line, later re-named Shchëkino

Yasnaya Polyana — the name of LNT's ancestral estate, as well as of a nearby village, located in Krapivna Uezd, 45 versts from Krapivna (the regional centre).

Zemljanki — settlement in Samara Gubernia, 15 versts from the Tolstoys' farmstead

Zhitovo — settlement in the Krapivna Uezd, **T**ula Gubernia, also the Ladyzhenskij family's estate

CHILDREN AND GRANDCHILDREN OF NIKOLAJ IL'ICH TOLSTOY
AND MARIJA NIKOLAEVNA TOLSTAYA

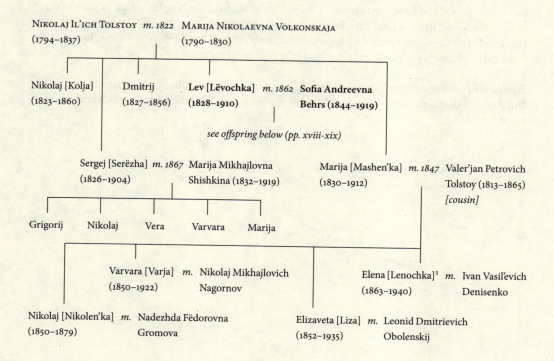

Nikolaj Il'ich Tolstoy *m. 1822* Marija Nikolaevna Volkonskaja
(1794–1837)   (1790–1830)

Nikolaj [Kolja]   Dmitrij   Lev [Lëvochka] *m. 1862* Sofia Andreevna
(1823–1860)   (1827–1856)   (1828–1910)   Behrs (1844–1919)

see offspring below (pp. xviii-xix)

Sergej [Serëzha] *m. 1867* Marija Mikhajlovna   Marija [Mashen'ka] *m. 1847* Valer'jan Petrovich
(1826–1904)   Shishkina (1832–1919)   (1830–1912)   Tolstoy (1813–1865)
                                                                                          [cousin]

Grigorij   Nikolaj   Vera   Varvara   Marija

Varvara [Varja] *m.* Nikolaj Mikhajlovich   Elena [Lenochka][1] *m.* Ivan Vasil'evich
(1850–1922)   Nagornov   (1863–1940)   Denisenko

Nikolaj [Nikolen'ka] *m.* Nadezhda Fëdorovna   Elizaveta [Liza] *m.* Leonid Dmitrievich
(1850–1879)   Gromova   (1852–1935)   Obolenskij

1   By her mother's extra-marital liaison (see *My Life* Part III, Note 435).

CHILDREN AND GRANDCHILDREN[2] OF ANDREJ EVSTAF'EVICH BEHRS AND LJUBOV' ALEKSANDROVNA BERS

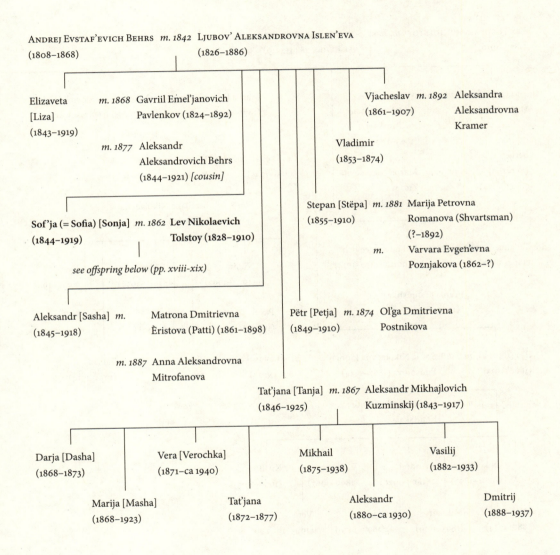

ANDREJ EVSTAF'EVICH BEHRS   *m. 1842*   LJUBOV' ALEKSANDROVNA ISLEN'EVA
(1808–1868)   (1826–1886)

Elizaveta   *m. 1868*   Gavriil Emel'janovich   Vjacheslav   *m. 1892*   Aleksandra
[Liza]   Pavlenkov (1824–1892)   (1861–1907)   Aleksandrovna
(1843–1919)   Kramer
                 m. 1877   Aleksandr
                             Aleksandrovich Behrs   Vladimir
                             (1844–1921) [cousin]   (1853–1874)

Sof'ja (= Sofia) [Sonja]   *m. 1862*   Lev Nikolaevich   Stepan [Stëpa]   *m. 1881*   Marija Petrovna
(1844–1919)   Tolstoy (1828–1910) (1855–1910)   Romanova (Shvartsman)
                                                                                        (?–1892)
see offspring below (pp. xviii-xix)   *m.*   Varvara Evgen'evna
                                                                                        Poznjakova (1862–?)

Aleksandr [Sasha]   *m.*   Matrona Dmitrievna   Pëtr [Petja]   *m. 1874*   Ol'ga Dmitrievna
(1845–1918)   Èristova (Patti) (1861–1898)   (1849–1910)   Postnikova

                    m. 1887   Anna Aleksandrovna
                                Mitrofanova

                                       Tat'jana [Tanja]   *m. 1867*   Aleksandr Mikhajlovich
                                       (1846–1925)   Kuzminskij (1843–1917)

Darja [Dasha]   Vera [Verochka]   Mikhail   Vasilij
(1868–1873)   (1871–ca 1940)   (1875–1938)   (1882–1933)

      Marija [Masha]   Tat'jana   Aleksandr   Dmitrij
      (1868–1923)   (1872–1877)   (1880–ca 1930)   (1888–1937)

2   Grandchildren listed only by Sofia Andreevna Tolstaya and Tat'jana Andreevna Kuzminskaja.

CHILDREN AND GRANDCHILDREN OF LEV NIKOLAEVICH TOLSTOY
AND SOFIA ANDREEVNA TOLSTAYA

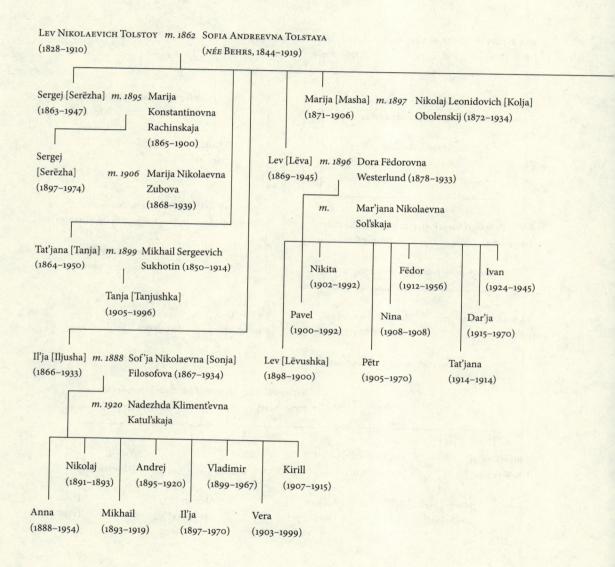

LEV NIKOLAEVICH TOLSTOY *m. 1862* SOFIA ANDREEVNA TOLSTAYA
(1828–1910) (*NÉE* BEHRS, 1844–1919)

Sergej [Serëzha] *m. 1895* Marija
(1863–1947) Konstantinovna
Rachinskaja
(1865–1900)

Marija [Masha] *m. 1897* Nikolaj Leonidovich [Kolja]
(1871–1906) Obolenskij (1872–1934)

Sergej
[Serëzha] *m. 1906* Marija Nikolaevna
(1897–1974) Zubova
(1868–1939)

Lev [Lëva] *m. 1896* Dora Fëdorovna
(1869–1945) Westerlund (1878–1933)

m. Mar'jana Nikolaevna
Sol'skaja

Tat'jana [Tanja] *m. 1899* Mikhail Sergeevich
(1864–1950) Sukhotin (1850–1914)

Nikita
(1902–1992)

Fëdor
(1912–1956)

Ivan
(1924–1945)

Tanja [Tanjushka]
(1905–1996)

Pavel
(1900–1992)

Nina
(1908–1908)

Dar'ja
(1915–1970)

Il'ja [Iljusha] *m. 1888* Sof'ja Nikolaevna [Sonja]
(1866–1933) Filosofova (1867–1934)

Lev [Lëvushka]
(1898–1900)

Pëtr
(1905–1970)

Tat'jana
(1914–1914)

m. 1920 Nadezhda Kliment'evna
Katul'skaja

Nikolaj
(1891–1893)

Andrej
(1895–1920)

Vladimir
(1899–1967)

Kirill
(1907–1915)

Anna
(1888–1954)

Mikhail
(1893–1919)

Il'ja
(1897–1970)

Vera
(1903–1999)

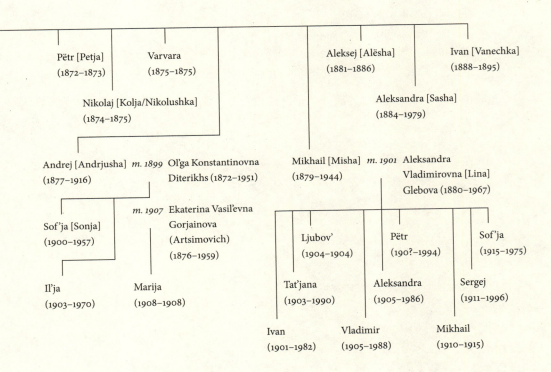

Pëtr [Petja]
(1872–1873)

Varvara
(1875–1875)

Nikolaj [Kolja/Nikolushka]
(1874–1875)

Aleksej [Alësha]
(1881–1886)

Ivan [Vanechka]
(1888–1895)

Aleksandra [Sasha]
(1884–1979)

Andrej [Andrjusha]   *m. 1899*   Ol'ga Konstantinovna
(1877–1916)   Diterikhs (1872–1951)

Mikhail [Misha]   *m. 1901*   Aleksandra
(1879–1944)   Vladimirovna [Lina]
                                Glebova (1880–1967)

m. 1907   Ekaterina Vasil'evna
            Gorjainova
            (Artsimovich)
            (1876–1959)

Sof'ja [Sonja]
(1900–1957)

Ljubov'
(1904–1904)

Pëtr
(190?–1994)

Sof'ja
(1915–1975)

Il'ja
(1903–1970)

Marija
(1908–1908)

Tat'jana
(1903–1990)

Aleksandra
(1905–1986)

Sergej
(1911–1996)

Ivan
(1901–1982)

Vladimir
(1905–1988)

Mikhail
(1910–1915)

FOREWORD

Yasnaya Polyana. It has been the home of the Tolstoys for generations. I myself have spent many days here, paying tribute, along with the thousands of visitors who flock to this idyllic spot each year, to two of my great-great-grandparents — one whom the world knows already, the other who deserves to be better known by the world. I am speaking, of course, of Leo Tolstoy (or Lev Nikolaevich Tolstoy, as he is known around here) and his wife, companion, transcriber, editor and publisher (among other things), Sofia Andreevna Tolstaya. And just as Yasnaya Polyana is now open to the world, so it is high time that the dialogue between my illustrious ancestors likewise receive its share of the world's attention. Which is the essential purpose of setting forth, for the first time as a dialogue in print, the exchange of letters you are about to open and read. It brings the world of Yasnaya Polyana directly to you, wherever you may be on the globe.

It may be said that for two people who loved each other deeply but, for one reason or another, spent so much of their time apart, their mutual correspondence constitutes the best biography of their lives. The book is indeed a chronicle — not only of the life of the two correspondents, but of their family of thirteen children; their extended family of sisters, brothers, aunts, uncles, cousins and in-laws (some of whom enjoyed a prominent reputation among their own professional circles); the celebrated scholars, writers, artists, musicians, philosophers and others who graced the halls of Yasnaya Polyana with their visits; the peasants and servants whose relationship with their employer could be considered practically unique among the aristocratic families of the time; not to mention Russian society as a whole, whose evolving course from monarchial autocracy to worker revolution is by no means excluded from the chronicle presented herein.

But, of course, it is more than a chronicle. It is also a personal dialogue punctuated by constant expressions of mutual love — from the early days when husband and wife shared the same

ideals of life right up to the last days when their divergent ideals of life proved a source of so much conflict between them. Even in his final letter to Sofia Andreevna, on the day of his leaving his beloved estate for good, Lev Nikolaevich could not refrain from expressing his love for her: "Don't think I left because I don't love you. I do love you and I have pity for you with all my heart…" Her letters, too, reciprocate the sentiment.

Yasnaya Polyana itself plays a major role throughout this husband-and-wife correspondence. A great majority of the letters were either written or received right here, by one party or the other. This quiet country estate, which was so dear to both of them in the early years of their marriage, later afforded Lev Nikolaevich the peace and solitude which he so desperately craved as a muse to his writing career. Sofia Andreevna, too, felt at home here, and sometimes found herself quite reluctant to return to their Moscow dwelling for the winter. Yasnaya Polyana provided a stable environment in which to raise their many offspring during their formative years. And today, as a twenty-first-century member of the Tolstoy family, I am pleased to see the events which this grand estate witnessed more than a century ago shared with the outside world through such a far-reaching correspondence, particularly with the many readers who will have access to it for the first time through an English translation.

I might also point out that the current volume is a fitting complement to my great-great-grandmother's extensive autobiography, — a memoir she modestly entitled *My Life*. It was published a few years ago for the very first time in its original Russian and (shortly before that) shared, too, with the English-reading world. I am grateful to the Slavic Research Group at the University of Ottawa, with whom our Tolstoy Museums have had a collaborative and fruitful relationship for many years, for facilitating and publishing (through the University of Ottawa Press) the translation of both these volumes. They will help readers in many parts of the globe become better acquainted with the significant contribution to world culture made by two of my forebears — all through the ups and downs of their personal conjugal life. This book is truly "a portrait of a life in letters".

October 2016
Vladimir Il'ich Tolstoy

FROM THE EDITOR

Recent scholarship has witnessed an outcry over the dispersal, among a multitude of sources, of the Tolstoy/Tolstaya couple's previously published letters to one another. To make this particularly valuable source more accessible and suited for study by scholars and researchers around the world, there has been a strong push to have their entire correspondence published in chronological order. One particular benefit of such a project would be a corrective to inappropriate mislabelling of their complementary roles. For example, in his essay on the Russian version of Sofia Tolstaya's memoir *My Life*, the former director of the L. N. Tolstoy Museum in Moscow, Vitalij Remizov noted the following:[1]

> The notion has taken hold in the popular consciousness that Lev Tolstoy, albeit a genius, was pretty much a cantankerous fellow, difficult to get along with, and therefore his wife, Sofia Andreevna, is entitled to every kind of sympathy and justification. All the published diaries, narratives, excerpts from *My Life*, incline the reader to this very opinion. What to do? True, Tolstoy wrote thirteen volumes of diaries, but he showed himself reluctant to include in them the history of his relations with Sofia Andreevna. The whole complexity of their relationship is no doubt detailed in the couple's exchange of letters, but this has never been published as correspondence. To search through Tolstoy's letters to his wife in the 90 volume edition of his works[1] is an exhausting task, while the collection of Sofia Andreevna's letters to her husband came out in the pre-war years and is not accessible to the general public.[2]

1 The 90-volume Jubilee Edition of Tolstoy's works (Moscow: Gosizdatel'stvo khudozhestvennoj literatury, 1928–58) includes his letters to Sofia Andreevna (in Vols. 83 & 84), but none of her letters to him (except the occasional excerpt in a footnote). The formal Russian title of the Jubilee Edition is *Polnoe sobranie sochinenij [Complete Collected Works]*, and will be designated throughout the footnotes by its Russian abbreviation: PSS.
2 *Pis'ma k L. N. Tolstomu 1862–1910 [Letters to L. N. Tolstoy. 1862–1910]*. Ed. A. I. Tolstaja & P. S. Popov. Intro. P. S. Popov. Moscow & Leningrad: Academia, 1936.

And so the modern reader is left with only one aspect of the problem: the life of the family seen through the eyes of [one] spouse.

Our current edition may be seen as a first step in offering a remedy on a global scale: covering 239 of the couple's letters, it is presented chronologically in a translation annotated specifically for English-speaking readers. In fact, it is part of a much larger project[3] — the publication of the entire Tolstoy/Tolstaya correspondence in its original Russian, containing more than 1,500 letters, in addition to some 500 postscripts attached to the letters of others. I shall be carrying out this project jointly over the next few years with the L. N. Tolstoy Museum in Moscow. The four-volume publication will also feature 201 letters by Sofia Andreevna Tolstaya never published before in any language, save the eleven samples appearing for the very first time in this English edition. A fifth volume will comprise a comprehensive critical study in English of the correspondents' personal (family and acquaintances) and, in particular, professional relationships, based primarily on their letters and postscripts, as well as other archival sources recently made available.

While the publication of just the new letters and postscripts by Tolstaya would represent a noteworthy achievement in itself, it would still lack the dimension of being seen in the context of the larger whole, and would simply add to the dispersal syndrome hinted at in the Remizov reference above.

It is precisely the combination of an integrated, chronological presentation and extensive annotations, many based on archival sources, which lends significance to this English edition and its projected multi-volume Russian counterpart. By illuminating, for example, the points and questions that each were responding to in their respective letters, they will afford the reader the opportunity to study the entire, complex relationship between husband and wife in previously unseen detail. The correspondence is a track record of the whole history of their marital life, from the very beginning of their falling in love to their very last "Forgive me" and "Farewell". Here one may trace the consecutive stages of their expanding circle of love and family life, the potholes and pitfalls in their often stormy journey, not only through time and the trial of raising their many children, but through the ever-changing ethical norms and mores of nineteenth-century Russian society.

The social and political struggle between the traditional lifestyle of the privileged upper class and the poverty of the peasants and other underprivileged segments of the populace — a struggle which was accelerating toward revolution — was aptly mirrored in this husband-and-wife conflict. While Tolstoy was constantly obsessed with his ideals of social justice for the masses, Tolstaya failed to understand why he could not bring himself to put his own family first. While Tolstoy, for better or for worse, missed the Revolution, which occurred just a few years after his death in 1910 (and just two years before his wife's passing in 1919), the social and political events over the fifty-or-so years preceding it are echoed in their own family struggles and well documented in the couple's correspondence. Moreover, the letters include frequent references to friends and acquaintances at all levels of the social spectrum, ranging from local peasants and children's governesses to artistic and literary celebrities (who were often guests in their home), and representatives of the nobility (including the Tsar and his entourage), some of whom they counted among their own relatives.

---

3 Funded by a grant from the Social Sciences & Humanities Research Council of Canada.

The significance of the opportunity to study personal correspondence (in contrast with diaries, autobiographies and other narratives) cannot be overestimated. For one thing, many of these letters were written during periods when their authors did not keep diaries. More importantly, it is the dialogue of personal letters which may offer the sincerest portrayal of their innermost thoughts and convictions, often expressed in response to specific themes and ideas raised by their partner just a day or two (or even hours) before. It should be remembered that while the nineteenth-century Russian postal service could not equal the speed of today's emails, it was considerably quicker than many of its twenty-first century counterparts: a letter posted by Tolstaya in Moscow in the evening would usually reach her husband's hands in Yasnaya Polyana by the following morning, and it was not unheard of to have a letter posted in the morning to arrive at its destination later the same day. Hence the interval between sending and receiving was short enough to keep the exchange fresh and right up to date, yet long enough to allow a bit of a pause for thought before the next exchange (in comparison with the spur-of-the-moment interchange of an oral conversation). And the benefits of being able to study a dialogue that was originally written on paper well over a century ago go without saying.

I am sure the readers of this translated volume will agree that the selection contained herein offers rich opportunity for insight into the thoughts and feelings behind the statements found in the already published accounts of both correspondents. These include Sofia Andreevna Tolstaya's comprehensive memoir *My Life*, published in English by the University of Ottawa Press in 2010. Not only that, but we are also afforded a rare glimpse into the extensive everyday life of two kindred but independently minded thinkers. We learn of causes on which they were united in their efforts, for example, in helping provide famine relief during the drought of 1891–92 through a fund-raising campaign organised by Tolstaya, and her husband's setting up of soup-kitchens in the worst-hit areas. There were also issues on which they were sharply divided. These included religion, where Tolstaya's traditional views in line with Russian Orthodoxy were opposed to Tolstoy's belief (shared by many Russian religious dissidents, especially the Doukhobors) that church organisation mattered little by comparison with each individual finding God within their heart and practising their beliefs in their daily life.

Beyond major issues like these, we also learn of the many people, places and day-to-day events that informed their lives, their thinking and their collective literary output (bear in mind that Tolstaya was a literary author in her own right), and, perhaps most importantly, their relationships with their children. While each marriage partner saw their children as a sounding-board for their own understanding of family values, it was their children, in fact, who put their sets of ideals to the test of real life and showed how each measured up in practice. These are but a few of the considerations worth bearing in mind as one wades through the lifetime of experiences and adventures described in the present book.

It should be pointed out that, like Sofia Tolstaya's extensive autobiographical memoir *My Life*, the concept of the present book draws significantly on my previous research on Tolstoy extending over a period of four decades. Most recently, this has included a collection of eleven books (either authored or edited) known as the "Tolstoy Series", published by the University of Ottawa's Slavic Research Group, of which I served as Founding Director (1998–2012). All of my work on Tolstoy and his circle of family and associates over the past several decades has been generously supported by Canada's national Social Sciences and Humanities Research Council, for which I am most grateful.

A perusal of any or all of my previous works on Tolstoy will enhance the reader's understanding and appreciation of the significance of the publication of this volume; for a partial

listing, see my entries in the Bibliography. At this point I should just like to mention three books in particular which are probably unfamiliar to most readers of the Tolstoys' correspondence, where I have taken the liberty of drawing upon my own introductions in preparing the following essay. These are: (a) *L. N. Tolstoj i S. A. Tolstaja: Perepiska s N. N. Strakhovym / The Tolstoys' Correspondence with N. N. Strakhov* (Tolstoy Series 3, 2000); (b) *Edinenie ljudej v tvorchestve L. N. Tolstogo / The Unity of People in Leo Tolstoy's Works* (Tolstoy Series 5, 2002); (c) *Sofia Andreevna Tolstaya: Literary Works* (Tolstoy Series 9, 2011).

As a general rule, the annotations to the English edition speak for themselves. However, in view of not only the linguistic but terminological and cultural differences between nineteenth-century Russia and the modern Anglophone world, a few additional practical notes are in order, as applied to the text of the correspondence.

It may be noted that the letters (at least those that history has preserved) are not distributed equally by year, either in our translated selection (see Chronological List of Letters below) or, for that matter, taking the whole of the writers' correspondence into account. For example, no known letters passed between them in the year 1873, and only one letter by Tolstoy is extant for 1875 (with no response from Tolstaya).

The bulk of the correspondence dates from the 1880s and 1890s — that is, in the two decades following Tolstoy's spiritual crisis, when his new philosophical views began driving a wedge in their marital relationship. Tolstoy's busiest year was 1885, when he wrote 59 letters to his wife (in comparison to her 22 letters in return), while Tolstaya's letter-writing peaked in 1893, when she penned 47 (to his 32), mostly dealing with her work on the Russian famine.

The lengthiest periods of their correspondence occurred during Tolstoy's trips to Samara and the Crimea, for health reasons, and over the winter months in the 1880s and 1890s, which Tolstaya spent in Moscow with the children during their school years while Tolstoy preferred the solitude of Yasnaya Polyana. After 1900, the frequency of the correspondence diminished considerably; over the whole decade we know only of 89 letters from Tolstoy and 101 from Tolstaya (of which 32 remain unpublished).[4]

As to the criteria we used for the selection of letters to be included in the translated edition, we decided that the chosen letters should

- be a representative sampling of the whole correspondence in terms of both chronology and subject-matter;
- convey the element of dialogue by presenting (in many cases) specific responses to questions and comments one of the spouses had just received from the other;
- feature the correspondents' commentaries both on important events in their own lives and on events of historical significance in Russian society as a whole; and
- highlight key episodes in their interaction with their family, as well as in their joint efforts to get Tolstoy's manuscripts from their first rough draft to their final publication.

* * *

4 These statistics are based on LNT's *Complete Collected Works [PSS]* and on the 1936 volume *Pis'ma* k *L. N. Tolstomu 1862–1910* [Letters to L. N. Tolstoy 1862–1910], edited by A. I. Tolstaja and P. S. Popov (see Bibliography).

GLOSSARY OF TERMS AND ACRONYMS

ADMINISTRATIVE DIVISIONS. The nineteenth-century Russian state was divided into units called a *gubernia* [Russian form: *gubernija*], presided over by a *gubernator* (governor). Each *gubernia*, in turn, was made up of a number of smaller administrative units known as an *uezd* (pron. ʻoo-**yezd**ʼ). The closest English equivalents would be province and county, respectively. They were called after the name of their administrative centre. For example, *Tula Gubernia* (where Yasnaya Polyana was located) was named after its central city, Tula, while *Krapivna Uezd* took its name from its major town, Krapivna (see List of Russian Geographical Names). In the Russian language, in combination with *Gubernia* or *Uezd* the adjectival variant of the city name was used (*Tulʼskaja Gubernia, Krapivenskij Uezd*), but this modification is not reproduced in the English version. Less populated areas were sometimes designated a *kraj* (pron. ʻcryʼ). Cities were divided into districts, each of which was called a *rajon* (pron. ʻrayonʼ).

AREA. Land area in nineteenth-century Russia was commonly measured by a unit known as the *desjatina*, equal to 1.09 hectares. This term has been retained in the text.

CALENDAR DATES. Before February 1918, Russia operated on the old-style (O. S.) *Julian calendar*; by that time most Western countries had adopted the new-style (N. S.) *Gregorian calendar* proclaimed in 1582, designed to reflect more accurately the actual solar year by abolishing the date of 29 February (leap year) for those centenary years not exactly divisible by 400. As a result, by the nineteenth century the old-style calendar was 12 days behind the new-style (13 days in the twentieth century).

For example, Christmas Day (25 December) 1898 in the old-style (O. S.) calendar came on 6 January 1899 according to Western calendars, while on New Years' Day (1 January) 1899 in Russia, it was already 13 January new-style (N. S.) in the West.

In the year 1900, however, another day's discrepancy was added, since the day of 29 February, omitted that year from the Western calendar, continued to be observed in Russia according to the old Julian calendar. Hence New Year's Day 1901 old-style fell on 14 January new-style.

The Bolshevik October Revolution was named from its O. S. date of 25 October 1917, now celebrated on 7 November (N. S.). A few months later, at the beginning of 1918, the new Bolshevik government brought Russia into line with the rest of the world by officially switching the country to the new-style Gregorian calendar. The old Julian calendar, however, continues to be used in the Russian Orthodox Church even to this day.

Unless otherwise noted, the dates in the text of the letters, the accompanying footnotes and the chronology are cited according to the Julian (O. S.) calendar.

AUTHOR ABBREVIATIONS. Throughout the footnotes and supplementary texts, *Lev Nikolaevich Tolstoy* is abbreviated as LNT, while *Sofia Andreevna Tolstaya* is designated by her initials SAT.

CURRENCY. The Imperial Russian rouble (*rublʼ*) in 1899 was either a paper note or silver coin worth approximately one-tenth of a pound sterling, or about 50 cents (Canadian or American), at the time. A kopek coin (Russian: *kopejka*) was a hundredth part of a rouble. The *grivennik* was worth ten kopeks (i.e., one-tenth of a rouble), while the term *pjatak* (or *pjatachok*) referred to a five-kopek copper (or, occasionally, silver) coin. No monetary equivalents are given in the translation — beyond the writers' own notations on the subject. However, to facilitate a better

comprehension, we might mention a few typical average salaries at the beginning of the twentieth century: a *gubernia* (provincial) governor might have made as much as 10,000 roubles per year, a university professor — 2,400 and a police chief — 1,500, all in addition to a food-and-lodging allowance.

DISTANCE. The most common unit of distance measurement in Imperial Russia was the *verstá*, known in English as the verst, roughly the equivalent of 1.07 km. Smaller units of measurement were the *sazhen'*, equal to 2.1 m, the *arshin*, equal to 0.71 m and the *vershok* = 4.45 cm (retained in the text with a metric equivalent).

HONOURARY TITLES. The Russian aristocracy had a hierarchy roughly parallel with those of Western European countries. Tolstoy was officially a Count (Russian: *graf*, a term borrowed from German), and his wife a Countess (*grafinja*) — a title she jealously guarded until her death. The honorary title was frequently added either to the surname (Count Tolstoy) or the first-name-plus-patronymic combination (Count Lev Nikolaevich) as a special mark of respect or politeness. Titles, at times hereditary, were originally bestowed for a particular service to the Tsar, who was also referred to as 'Emperor of all the Russias'. In the nineteenth century, the terms Tsar (Russian: *tsar'*, derived from Latin *Cæsar*) and Emperor (*imperator*) were more or less interchangeable in reference to Russia's supreme ruler, while their wives were called either *tsaritsa* or *imperatritsa*. On occasion the Empress herself might serve as the supreme ruler, as in the case of Empress Catherine the Great (*Imperatritsa Ekaterina Velikaja*) in the second half of the eighteenth century.

One of the highest titles the Tsar could bestow was *knjaz'*, most often translated as 'Prince', although it was actually more the equivalent of 'Duke'. (A prince's wife was known as *knjaginja*, translatable either as 'Princess' or 'Duchess', while a princess by birth was known as *knjazhna* before marriage.) Members of the Tsar's own family, including heirs to the throne, were honoured with the title *Velikij knjaz'* (Grand Prince) or *Velikaja knjaginja* (Grand Duchess).

Apart from honorary titles, the system of both civil and military ranks was extremely important. It was based on the so-called Table of Ranks (*Tabel' o rangakh*) promulgated by Tsar Peter the Great in 1722, which set forth a hierarchy of fourteen ranks through which worthy individuals might advance — and achieve nobility (even hereditary) status — in both the military and civil services. This system continued in force right up to the overthrow of the monarchy in 1917.

LETTER HEADINGS. Readers will note that the letter headings (with date and place of writing) are different for the two authors: LNT's headings are in italics, while SAT's are in Roman type with editorial additions in brackets. Here we have simply reproduced the style of headings we received from the original Russian editors of the correspondence, reflecting the fact that LNT's and SAT's letters have always been published separately, never as a joint dialogue. The designation TTC stands for 'Tolstoy-Tolstaya Correspondence'. PSS = *Polnoe Sobranie Sochinenij* (LNT's *Complete Collected Works*). LSA = *Letters of Sofia Andreevna*.

PARAGRAPH DIVISIONS. In a manner characteristic of informal letter writing of the period, both correspondents made relatively infrequent use of paragraph divisions. As a result, some of the paragraphs in the letters translated here are rather long and rambling, with many unmarked changes of subject within a single paragraph. It has been decided to leave this format intact in the translation, rather than artificially introduce paragraph divisions that are not in the original letters.

RUSSIAN NAMES. Most Russian surnames have both a masculine and feminine variant — a distinction we decided to maintain in the translation. (In Russian this is further complicated by the existence of a separate plural form; indeed, all three of these variants — masculine, feminine and plural — may change according to the function of the word in the sentence, i.e., the grammatical case, of which there are six variations. In addition, many surnames, including *Tolstoj/Tolstaja*, are derived from adjectives rather than nouns, which gives them an entirely different set of case endings.)

The surname (*familija*) comprises the third of three parts of every Russian person's name (although in official documents the surname is placed first). As in most cultures, it is traditionally passed down through the male lineage from generation to generation. The first part (*imja*, or so-called Christian name) is the only one chosen by the parents (or godparents) at the birth of their offspring, and even this (in the pre-Soviet era) was frequently taken from the name of the saint on whose day the birth took place. The middle part, known as the patronymic (*otchestvo*) is invariably derived from the first name of the baby's father, with an ending *ovna* (or *evna*) for female progeny and *ovich* (or *evich*) for males. Hence the patronymic *Andreevna* in Tolstaya's name is derived from her father's name *Andrej*, while the corresponding *Nikolaevich* in *Lev Nikolaevich Tolstoy* is taken from his father's name *Nikolaj*.

In addition, almost every Russian Christian name (*imja*), in its standard form (the form used on birth certificates), gives rise to a host of diminutive (or endearing) forms, both primary (often used by one's colleagues, friends and childhood acquaintances, as well as family) and secondary (generally restricted to use by family members and especially close friends). The standard form *Tat'jana*, for example, yields the primary diminutive *Tanja* and the secondary *Tanechka* (along with *Tanjusha, Tanjukh, Tanjushen'ka* and dozens of other possible variants). From *Lev* come *Lëva, Lëlja, Lëvochka*, etc. These variants may be used to distinguish members of a family having the same Christian name. Lev Nikolaevich was often called *Lëvochka* by his wife and a few others close to him, while his son Lev L'vovich was mostly referred to simply as *Lëva* (or, sometimes, *Lëlja*). Lev L'vovich's own baby son, Lev L'vovich Jr, was dubbed *Lëvushka*. Note that the letter ë in Russian represents a sound similar to *yo* in English, and is always stressed, while the apostrophe indicates a softening of the preceding consonant before another consonant or at the end of a word, and is represented by a separate letter of the Russian alphabet (ь).

It is important to realise that the combination of the first name (in its standard form) and patronymic together constitutes the most common polite form of address among adults acquainted with each other (in preference to the Russian equivalents of Mr. and Ms., which tend to be used only on official occasions). Tolstaya would be known in public as *Sofia Andreevna*, her husband as *Lev Nikolaevich*, and this is how they would feel comfortable being addressed by any acquaintance or stranger (but never as *Sofia* or *Lev* alone). In her writings (including her letters) Tolstaya often calls her husband by his diminutive name *Lëvochka*.

TRANSLITERATION OF RUSSIAN WORDS. This follows a modified academic system (for example, using *ju* and *ja* for the last two letters of the Russian alphabet, *j* for the Russian letter й, but *sh, ch* and *zh* in place of the variants with diacritics). An exception is made in the case of names and terms already possessing a well-established English spelling — for example, *Tolstoy* (rather than Tolstoj) for LNT, *Yasnaya Polyana* (Jasnaja Poljana), *Dostoevsky* (Dostoevskij), *Tchaikovsky* (Chajkovskij), *balalaika* (balalajka). Particularly notable among these exceptions is the name of Tolstaya herself, which for a combination of reasons we have rendered throughout as *Sofia Andreevna Tolstaya* (rather than the normative transliteration Sof'ja Andreevna Tolstaja).

However, for all other male and female persons sharing their surnames, we have used *Tolstoj* and *Tolstaja,* respectively.

WEIGHT. A standard unit of measurement for foodstuffs in Imperial Russia was the *funt,* which at 409.5 g was slightly less than a pound (453.6 g). Larger quantities were measured in a unit known as a *pood*; 1 pood = 40 Russian funts, or 16.38 kg.

WORD-USAGE AND ORTHOGRAPHY. Given the essentially European character of the work — bear in mind that Tolstaya was brought up speaking both French and German (her father's native tongue) as well as Russian, while Tolstoy had a strong exposure to French as a child; both later acquired a very good knowledge of English — word-usage and orthography have been conformed, in the main, to early twentieth-century (British) English. Spelling throughout the text follows the *Oxford English Dictionary,* except for material quoted from a published English-language source, where the original orthography has naturally been retained.

ACRONYMS

LNT   Lev Nikolaevich Tolstoy
LSA   Letters of Sofia Andreevna
N.S.   new-style Julian calendar
O.S.   old-style Julian calendar
PSS   Polnoe Sobranie Sochinenij (*Complete Collected Works*)
SAT   Sofia Andreevna Tolstaya

FROM THE TRANSLATORS

One might think, at first glance, that translating the correspondence between Lev Tolstoy and Sofia Tolstaya would be a rather similar task to our translation of the latter's autobiographical memoir *My Life*, published in 2010. Well, yes… and no.

We started off with the same translation team as before (Arkadi Klioutchanski and myself), under the same editorship (Andrew Donskov), the same publisher (University of Ottawa Press), the same author (Sofia Andreevna Tolstaya), the same geographical settings (notably Moscow and Yasnaya Polyana) and, to a large extent, the same time span in each case (the latter half of the nineteenth century). So what was different?

The first key difference was the introduction of a second author — not just any author, but one who was intimately (in the most literal sense of the word) acquainted with the first author — namely, her husband, Lev Nikolaevich Tolstoy.

The second major difference was the reason for writing in each case, together with the writers' intended audience. Tolstaya wrote her memoirs with the public definitely in mind. In view of the many widespread speculations about her role in her husband's career and potential future misrepresentations of their relationship, she wanted to set the record straight — from *her* point of view. Hence in her memoirs she took a special degree of care in her grammar, writing style, identification of people and places, and so forth. It is also worth noting they were written in retrospect, often years after the events described.

On the other hand, her immediate purpose in writing letters to her husband was to make enquiries and convey information pertinent to the moment, as well as to express personal feelings about their relationship with each other and their family (feelings ranging from love and tenderness to frustration and despair); here the letters they wrote during their physical separations were a natural extension of their conversations when they were together. Tolstoy's reasons for writing were basically the same as his wife's, although he was probably more conscious than

she of how these letters — indeed, of how anything he wrote — might be treated by readers of the future!

But consider the problem this type of writing poses for translators! Just as in their conversations at home, a husband and wife's personal letters do not reflect the same grammatical standards and logical explanations that they might use in preparing a public talk or a journal article on an unfamiliar subject. This couple, in fact, were so well acquainted both with each other and with the subjects of their correspondence that a single sentence — indeed, a single word or phrase — might easily substitute for a whole paragraph of expository prose. A single term (the name of an illness, for instance) might conjure up a whole series of recent occurrences in the mind of either correspondent. And when it came to mentioning mutual acquaintances, only one of the three components of the traditional Russian name — even a single diminutive (see From the Editor above) — was generally sufficient to remind their spouse as to who was being spoken about, even where multiple referents were theoretically possible. For example, Tolstaya's sister Tat'jana Andreevna and the couple's eldest daughter Tat'jana L'vovna might both be identified simply as *Tanja* even in the same paragraph. Similarly, *Serëzha* might alternately refer to Tolstoy's brother Sergej Nikolaevich and their eldest son Sergej L'vovich. In other words, it is not always evident to an outsider who exactly is being referred to by a single component of their name. Apart from that, there were further ambiguities and other apparent gaps in the background to various passages that begged to be filled in, especially for a non-Russian reader in the twenty-first century! Questions like these the Ottawa translators were not always able to decide on their own.

Hence our translation team had to expand to include not only an English literary translator and a classical Russian-language specialist working in Canada, but also a Russia-based scholar with hands-on experience with all the many archival writings associated with the Tolstoys. Liudmila Gladkova, a Senior Researcher and Deputy Director of the Tolstoy Museum in Moscow (the ultimate global repository of all things Tolstoyan) was chosen by our Editor, Andrew Donskov, since, as a member of our Slavic Research Group at the University of Ottawa, she had successfully participated in a number of previous publication projects related to Tolstoy.

The procedure would begin with my draft translation, five letters at a time. The draft would then be emailed to Arkadi, who would review it carefully (on the basis of his familiarity with classical Russian literature) and highlight points for a telephone discussion the following day. Translation questions still not resolved after this consultation would be forwarded to Liudmila in Moscow for her investigation in the Tolstoy Museum archives, and her answers would subsequently be incorporated into the translated text. Only then would it be sent to the Editor for final approval. And all this took place before the customary in-house peer-review procedures, editing and proofreading conducted by the University of Ottawa Press.

In sum, the English translation of a written dialogue between this intimately related Russian literary duo of more than a century ago has proved to be a multi-layered, complex and often daunting task. It has taken the best efforts of an experienced translation team, working under the guidance of an experienced Editor, to render this fascinating dialogue accessible (at least in part) to the vast English-reading segment of the world's population.

John Woodsworth
with Arkadi Klioutchanski and Liudmila Gladkova
Translators

CHRONOLOGICAL LIST OF LETTERS

1862–1910

1862
1. S. A. Tolstaya, 28 August 1862, Pokrovskoe-Streshnevo
2. L. N. Tolstoy, 14 September 1862, Moscow
3. L. N. Tolstoy, 2nd half of October 1862, Yasnaya Polyana

1864
4. L. N. Tolstoy, 22–23 April 1864, Pirogovo
5. S. A. Tolstaya, 23 April 1864, Yasnaya Polyana
6. L. N. Tolstoy, 9 August 1864, Pirogovo
7. L. N. Tolstoy, 9 August 1864, Chern'
8. L. N. Tolstoy, 10/11 August 1864, Novoselki
9. S. A. Tolstaya, 11 August 1864, Yasnaya Polyana
10. S. A. Tolstaya, 22 November 1864, Yasnaya Polyana
11. L. N. Tolstoy, 24 November 1864, Moscow
12. S. A. Tolstaya, 25 November 1864, Yasnaya Polyana
13. L. N. Tolstoy, 25 November 1864, Moscow
14. S. A. Tolstaya, 26 November 1864, Yasnaya Polyana
15. L. N. Tolstoy, 27 November 1864, Moscow
16. L. N. Tolstoy, 1 December 1864, Moscow
17. L. N. Tolstoy, 2 December 1864, Moscow
18. L. N. Tolstoy, 4 December 1864, Moscow
19. S. A. Tolstaya, 5 December 1864, Yasnaya Polyana
20. L. N. Tolstoy, 7 December 1864, Moscow
21. S. A. Tolstaya, 7 December 1864, Yasnaya Polyana
22. L. N. Tolstoy, 11 December 1864, Moscow

1865
23. L. N. Tolstoy, 27 July 1865, Voin
24. S. A. Tolstaya, 28 July 1865, Pokrovskoe
25. L. N. Tolstoy, 27? July 1865, Orël
26. S. A. Tolstaya, 29 July 1865, Pokrovskoe

1866
27. L. N. Tolstoy, 11 November 1866, Moscow
28. S. A. Tolstaya, 11 November 1866, Yasnaya Polyana
29. S. A. Tolstaya, 12 November 1866, Yasnaya Polyana
30. L. N. Tolstoy, 14–15 November 1866, Moscow
31. S. A. Tolstaya, 14 November 1866, Yasnaya Polyana
32. L. N. Tolstoy, 15 November 1866, Moscow

1867
33. S. A. Tolstaya, 17 June 1867, Yasnaya Polyana
34. L. N. Tolstoy, 18 June 1867, Moscow
35. L. N. Tolstoy, 25 September 1867, Moscow
36. L. N. Tolstoy, 27 September 1867, Moscow

1869

37.   L. N. Tolstoy, 1 September 1869, Moscow
38.   S. A. Tolstaya, 4 September 1869, Yasnaya Polyana

1871

39.   L. N. Tolstoy, 11/12 June 1871, Steamship on the Volga
40.   S. A. Tolstaya, 17–18 June 1871, Yasnaya Polyana
41.   L. N. Tolstoy, 23 June 1871, Karalyk
42.   L. N. Tolstoy, 16–17 July, 1871, Karalyk
43.   S. A. Tolstaya, 27 July 1871, Yasnaya Polyana

1872

44.   L. N. Tolstoy, 14 July 1872, Farmstead at Tananyk

1876

45.   S. A. Tolstaya, 4 September 1876, Yasnaya Polyana
46.   L. N. Tolstoy, 5 September 1876, Kazan'

1877

47.   S. A. Tolstaya, 15 January 1877, St. Petersburg
48.   L. N. Tolstoy, 16 January 1877, Yasnaya Polyana
49.   L. N. Tolstoy, 28/29 May 1877, Moscow
50.   L. N. Tolstoy, 26 July 1877, Optina Pustyn'

1878

51.   L. N. Tolstoy, 9 February 1878, Moscow
52.   S. A. Tolstaya, 5 March 1878, Yasnaya Polyana
53.   L. N. Tolstoy, 7–8 March 1878, St. Petersburg
54.   L. N. Tolstoy, 14 June 1878, Steamship on the Volga
55.   S. A. Tolstaya, 18 June 1878, Yasnaya Polyana
56.   L. N. Tolstoy, 18 June 1878, Farmstead on the Mocha

1880

57.   S. A. Tolstaya, 28 August 1880, Yasnaya Polyana
58.   L. N. Tolstoy, 28 August 1880, Moscow
59.   L. N. Tolstoy, 8 October 1880, Moscow

1881

60.   L. N. Tolstoy, 11 June 1881, Krapivna
61.   S. A. Tolstaya, 12 June 1881, Yasnaya Polyana
62.   S. A. Tolstaya, 3 July 1881, Moscow
63.   L. N. Tolstoy, 4 July 1881, Yasnaya Polyana
64.   L. N. Tolstoy, 19 July 1881, Farmstead on the Mocha
65.   S. A. Tolstaya, 27 July 1881, Yasnaya Polyana
66.   L. N. Tolstoy, 31 July 1881, Farmstead on the Mocha
67.   S. A. Tolstaya, 26 August 1881, Moscow
68.   L. N. Tolstoy, 26 August 1881, Yasnaya Polyana

1882

69. L. N. Tolstoy, 3 February 1882, Yasnaya Polyana
70. S. A. Tolstaya, 4 February 1882, Moscow
71. L. N. Tolstoy, 4 February 1882, Yasnaya Polyana
72. S. A. Tolstaya, 6 February 1882, Moscow
73. L. N. Tolstoy, 6 February 1882, Yasnaya Polyana
74. S. A. Tolstaya, 7 February 1882, Moscow
75. L. N. Tolstoy, 2 March 1882, Yasnaya Polyana
76. L. N. Tolstoy, 3 March 1882, Yasnaya Polyana
77. S. A. Tolstaya, 3 March 1882, Moscow
78. S. A. Tolstaya, 8 April 1882, Moscow
79. L. N. Tolstoy, 9 April 1882, Yasnaya Polyana
80. L. N. Tolstoy, 17 May 1882, Yasnaya Polyana
81. S. A. Tolstaya, 18 May 1882, Moscow
82. L. N. Tolstoy, 11 September 1882, Moscow
83. S. A. Tolstaya, 12 September 1882, Yasnaya Polyana

1883

84. L. N. Tolstoy, 21 May 1883, Tula
85. L. N. Tolstoy, 25 May 1883, Samara Farmstead
86. S. A. Tolstaya, 29 May 1883, Yasnaya Polyana
87. L. N. Tolstoy, 29 September 1883, Yasnaya Polyana
88. L. N. Tolstoy, 30 September 1883, Yasnaya Polyana
89. S. A. Tolstaya, 1 October 1883, Moscow
90. L. N. Tolstoy, 10 November 1883, Yasnaya Polyana
91. L. N. Tolstoy, 11 November 1883, Yasnaya Polyana
92. S. A. Tolstaya, 12 November 1883, Moscow

1884

93. L. N. Tolstoy, 28 January 1884, Yasnaya Polyana
94. S. A. Tolstaya, 29 January 1884, Moscow
95. L. N. Tolstoy, 30 January 1884, Yasnaya Polyana
96. S. A. Tolstaya, 31 January 1884, Moscow
97. L. N. Tolstoy, 5 February 1884, Yasnaya Polyana
98. S. A. Tolstaya, 5 February 1884, Moscow
99. L. N. Tolstoy, 21 October 1884, Yasnaya Polyana
100. S. A. Tolstaya, 23 October 1884, Moscow
101. L. N. Tolstoy, 23 October 1884, Yasnaya Polyana
102. S. A. Tolstaya, 25 October 1884, Moscow
103. L. N. Tolstoy, 28 October 1884, Yasnaya Polyana
104. L. N. Tolstoy, 12 December 1884, Yasnaya Polyana
105. S. A. Tolstaya, 13 December 1884, Moscow
106. L. N. Tolstoy, 13 December 1884, Yasnaya Polyana

1885

107. L. N. Tolstoy, 2 February 1885, Yasnaya Polyana
108. S. A. Tolstaya, 21 February 1885, St. Petersburg

109. L. N. Tolstoy, 22 February 1885, Moscow
110. L. N. Tolstoy, 22 February 1885, Moscow
111. S. A. Tolstaya, 22 February 1885, St. Petersburg
112. S. A. Tolstaya, 11 March 1885, Moscow
113. L. N. Tolstoy, 14 March 1885, Bajdary
114. S. A. Tolstaya, 18 August 1885, Moscow
115. L. N. Tolstoy, 12 October 1885, Yasnaya Polyana
116. S. A. Tolstaya, 13 October 1885, Moscow
117. S. A. Tolstaya, 21 October 1885, Moscow
118. S. A. Tolstaya, 22 October 1885, Moscow
119. L. N. Tolstoy, 23 October 1885, Yasnaya Polyana
120. L. N. Tolstoy, 20 November 1885, Moscow
121. S. A. Tolstaya, 21 November 1885, St. Petersburg
122. L. N. Tolstoy, 21 November 1885, Mocow
123. S. A. Tolstaya, 23 November 1885, St. Petersburg
124. L. N. Tolstoy, 15–18 December 1885, Moscow
125. S. A. Tolstaya, 19 December 1885, Moscow
126. L. N. Tolstoy, 21/22 December 1885, Obol'janovo
127. S. A. Tolstaya, 23 December 1885, Moscow
128. S. A. Tolstaya, 24 December 1885, Moscow
129. L. N. Tolstoy, 27 December 1885, Obol'janovo

1886

130. S. A. Tolstaya, 7 April 1886, Moscow
131. L. N. Tolstoy, 9 April 1886, Yasnaya Polyana
132. S. A. Tolstaya, 2 May 1886, Moscow
133. L. N. Tolstoy, 4 May 1886, Yasnaya Polyana

1887

134. S. A. Tolstaya, 3–4 January 1887, Moscow
135. L. N. Tolstoy, 7 January 1887, Nikol'skoe-Obol'janovo
136. S. A. Tolstaya, 10 January 1887, Moscow
137. S. A. Tolstaya, 11 April 1887, Moscow
138. L. N. Tolstoy, 13 April 1887, Yasnaya Polyana
139. S. A. Tolstaya, 14 April 1887, Moscow
140. L. N. Tolstoy, 1 May 1887, Yasnaya Polyana

1888

141. S. A. Tolstaya, 18 April 1888, Moscow
142. L. N. Tolstoy, 23 April 1888, Yasnaya Polyana
143. S. A. Tolstaya, 1 May 1888, Moscow

1889

144. L. N. Tolstoy, 24 March 1889, Spasskoe
145. S. A. Tolstaya, 26 March 1889, Moscow
146. L. N. Tolstoy, 1 April 1889, Spasskoe
147. S. A. Tolstaya, 25 October 1889, Moscow

1891

148. S. A. Tolstaya, 29 March 1891, Moscow
149. L. N. Tolstoy, 1 April 1891, Yasnaya Polyana
150. L. N. Tolstoy, 4 April 1891, Yasnaya Polyana
151. S. A. Tolstaya, 9 September 1891, Moscow
152. L. N. Tolstoy, 27 September 1891, Yasnaya Polyana
153. S. A. Tolstaya, 25 October 1891, Moscow
154. S. A. Tolstaya, 26 October 1891, Moscow
155. L. N. Tolstoy, 29 October 1891, Begichevka
156. L. N. Tolstoy, 2 November 1891, Begichevka
157. S. A. Tolstaya, 4 November 1891, Moscow
158. S. A. Tolstaya, 13 November 1891, Moscow
159. L. N. Tolstoy, 28 November 1891, Begichevka

1892

160. S. A. Tolstaya, 6 February 1892, Moscow
161. L. N. Tolstoy, 12 February 1892, Begichevka
162. S. A. Tolstaya, 16 February 1892, Moscow
163. L. N. Tolstoy, 28 February 1892, Begichevka
164. L. N. Tolstoy, 7 November 1892, Yasnaya Polyana
165. S. A. Tolstaya, 9 November 1892, Moscow

1893

166. L. N. Tolstoy, 3 February 1893, Yasnaya Polyana
167. S. A. Tolstaya, 25 February 1893, Moscow
168. L. N. Tolstoy, 15 September 1893, Yasnaya Polyana

1894

169. L. N. Tolstoy, 28 January 1894, Grinëvka
170. S. A. Tolstaya, 31 January 1894, Moscow
171. L. N. Tolstoy, 3 February 1894, Yasnaya Polyana
172. S. A. Tolstaya, 11 May 1894, Moscow
173. L. N. Tolstoy, 12 May 1894, Yasnaya Polyana
174. S. A. Tolstaya, 11 September 1894, Moscow
175. L. N. Tolstoy, 18 September 1894, Yasnaya Polyana
176. S. A. Tolstaya, 27 October 1894, Moscow
177. S. A. Tolstaya, 31 October 1894, Moscow

1895

178. L. N. Tolstoy, 26 April 1895, Moscow
179. S. A. Tolstaya, 26 April 1895, Kiev
180. L. N. Tolstoy, 3 October 1895, Yasnaya Polyana
181. S. A. Tolstaya, 12 October 1895, Yasnaya Polyana
182. S. A. Tolstaya, 29 October 1895, Moscow
183. L. N. Tolstoy, 2 November 1895, Yasnaya Polyana

1896

184. L. N. Tolstoy, 22 February 1896, Nikol'skoe-Obol'janovo
185. S. A. Tolstaya, 26 February 1896, Moscow
186. L. N. Tolstoy, 3 March 1896, Nikol'skoe-Obol'janovo
187. S. A. Tolstaya, 5 March 1896, Moscow
188. S. A. Tolstaya, 9 September 1896, Moscow
189. L. N. Tolstoy, 26 September 1896, Yasnaya Polyana
190. L. N. Tolstoy, 31 October 1896, Kozlova-Zaseka
191. L. N. Tolstoy, 12 November 1896, Yasnaya Polyana
192. S. A. Tolstaya, 13 November 1896, Moscow

1897

193. L. N. Tolstoy, 1 February 1897, Nikol'skoe-Obol'janovo
194. S. A. Tolstaya, 16 February 1897, Moscow
195. L. N. Tolstoy, 17 February 1897, Nikol'skoe-Obol'janovo
196. S. A. Tolstaya, 6 May 1897, Moscow
197. L. N. Tolstoy, 12–13 May 1897, Yasnaya Polyana
198. L. N. Tolstoy, 19 May 1897, Yasnaya Polyana
199. L. N. Tolstoy, 8 July 1897, Yasnaya Polyana
200. S. A. Tolstaya, 19 November 1897, Moscow
201. L. N. Tolstoy, 26 November 1897, Yasnaya Polyana

1898

202. L. N. Tolstoy, 22 March 1898, Moscow
203. S. A. Tolstaya, 28 April 1898, Yasnaya Polyana
204. L. N. Tolstoy, 30 April 1898, Grinëvka
205. L. N. Tolstoy, 19 October 1898, Yasnaya Polyana
206. S. A. Tolstaya, 9 November 1898, Moscow

1899

207. S. A. Tolstaya, 9 February 1899, Kiev
208. L. N. Tolstoy, 15 February 1899, Moscow

1900

209. S. A. Tolstaya, 23 September 1900, Moscow
210. L. N. Tolstoy, 31 December 1900, Moscow

1902

211. S. A. Tolstaya, 22 April 1902, Sevastopol'

1903

212. L. N. Tolstoy, 2 May 1903, Yasnaya Polyana
213. S. A. Tolstaya, 8 October 1903, Moscow

1904
214. S. A. Tolstaya, 10 January 1904, Moscow
215. S. A. Tolstaya, 17 February 1904, Moscow
216. L. N. Tolstoy, 14 August 1904, Pirogovo

1905
217. S. A. Tolstaya, 15 January 1905, Moscow
218. L. N. Tolstoy, 16 January 1905, Yasnaya Polyana
219. S. A. Tolstaya, 19 January 1905, Moscow

1906
220. S. A. Tolstaya, 14 May 1906, Moscow

1907
221. L. N. Tolstoy, 4 April 1907, Yasnaya Polyana

1908
222. L. N. Tolstoy, 16 May 1908, Yasnaya Polyana

1909
223. S. A. Tolstaya, 18 June 1909, Yasnaya Polyana
224. L. N. Tolstoy, 23 June 1909, Kochety
225. S. A. Tolstaya, 24 June 1909, Yasnaya Polyana
226. S. A. Tolstaya, 13 December 1909, Moscow

1910
227. L. N. Tolstoy, 14 June 1910, Otradnoe
228. L. N. Tolstoy, 14 July 1910, Yasnaya Polyana
229. S. A. Tolstaya, 15 July 1910, Yasnaya Polyana
230. S. A. Tolstaya, 24–25 July 1910, Yasnaya Polyana
231. L. N. Tolstoy, 1 September 1910, Kochety
232. S. A. Tolstaya, 11 September 1910, Kochety
233. S. A. Tolstaya, 14 October 1910, Yasnaya Polyana
234. L. N. Tolstoy, 28 October 1910, Yasnaya Polyana
235. S. A. Tolstaya, 29 October 1910, Yasnaya Polyana
236. S. A. Tolstaya, 30 October 1910, Yasnaya Polyana
237. L. N. Tolstoy, 30–31 October 1910, Shamordino
238. S. A. Tolstaya, 1 November 1910, Yasnaya Polyana
239. S. A. Tolstaya, 2 November 1910, Yasnaya Polyana

LEO TOLSTOY AND SOFIA TOLSTAYA:

A dialogue of two independently minded kindred spirits

ANDREW DONSKOV

…when you're away, your letters help me live, just like your voice when you're around.
— Sofia Andreevna to Lev Nikolaevich (Letter N° 86)[1]

*Your letters reflect not only your mental state, but that of the children, too — [the ones] at home. […]
I use your letter[s] (as though they were a thermometer) to follow the moral temperature of the family
— has it gone up or down?*
— Lev Nikolaevich to SOFIA ANDREEVNA (Letter N° 106)

I have been busy collecting and transcribing as many of my letters as possible to Lev Nikolaevich
over my whole lifetime. What a touching account these letters hold of my love for Lëvochka and my
life as a mother!
— SOFIA ANDREEVNA, *Dnevniki* [Diaries] (11.10)

SETTING THE STAGE

Both Lev Nikolaevich Tolstoy (1828–1910) and his wife Sofia Andreevna Tolstaya (1844–1919) were prolific letter writers. According to records in the Tolstoy Museum archives in Moscow, Lev Nikolaevich wrote approximately 10,000 letters over his lifetime — 840 of these addressed to his wife, as published in volumes 83 and 84 of the Jubilee Edition of his works (1938 and 1949). Tolstaya had earlier compiled and published two editions of her husband's letters to her: the first (1913) contained 656 letters arranged chronologically, the second (1915) included seven more letters, the last dated 31 October 1910, shortly before the writer's death,

---

1   Throughout the notes, the abbreviation LNT designates *Lev Nikolaevich Tolstoy,* while SAT is used in reference to his wife, *Sofia Andreevna Tolstaya.*

as well as some 700 personal annotations.[2] Letters written by (or to) Sofia Andreevna over her lifetime also numbered in the thousands.

When Tolstaya published the letters she received from Lev Nikolaevich, she declined to include any of her 644 letters to him. The absence of half their correspondence has served to obscure the underlying significance of many of his comments to her and occasionally led the reader to wrong conclusions. This problem was only partly resolved when about two-thirds (443) of Tolstaya's letters to her husband were published through Academia (Moscow and Leningrad) in 1936 by the Tolstoys' granddaughter Anna Il'inichna Tolstaja and her husband Pavel Sergeevich Popov in the collection *Tolstaja S. A. Pis'ma k L. N. Tolstomu [S. A. Tolstaya, Letters to L. N. Tolstoy]*.

Tolstaya's remaining 201 letters have never been published in any language, and the University of Ottawa's Slavic Research Group has been granted exclusive rights for publication in Russian, as well as the translation and publication rights in English. Of interest to readers, eleven of these unpublished letters have been included (in both their original form and in English translation) in an appendix to the present volume, though without the extensive annotations that will eventually accompany their appearance in the Russian edition.

In addition to these letters, both Tolstoy and Tolstaya frequently wrote postscripts to letters penned by other people in whose presence they happened to be at the time — for example, children, close relatives, friends and acquaintances. In the case of such additions by Tolstoy, the Jubilee Edition contains only his postscripts, nearly always without the benefit of the context supplied by the original letters, which in many cases provide valuable insights into his remarks. The postscripts (approximately 400–500 of them between the two writers) help us to establish the dates on which the letters were written, gain further insights into the couple's way of life, define their circles of correspondents, and determine the kind of reading they engaged in. When added to the letters, the result will be a total of some 2,000 documents, to be published in their original Russian in a four-volume referential edition, thoroughly comparing all texts with their original sources. The inaccuracies and omissions in earlier editions, stemming mainly from censorship and ideological bias, will be corrected and restored in the new publication.

THE MULTI-VOLUME PROJECT: LOOKING AHEAD

The century which has passed since the deaths of Leo Tolstoy (1910) and Sofia Tolstaya (1919) has seen unceasing scholarly investigation of the former's remarkable works, thought and life, as well as several important studies devoted to the latter. It should not seem surprising, moreover, that the field known as *Tolstoy Studies*, now entering its second century, remains a highly dynamic and evolving academic discipline, producing new ideas and bringing to light new materials and sources.

It is hoped that this particular edition will serve as a reference for years to come, especially since it chronicles and analyses an extensive series of personal and professional exchanges between two significant Russian figures of the turn of the twentieth century: Lev Nikolaevich Tolstoy and his chosen life partner Sofia Andreevna Tolstaya. Cultural historians, gender studies specialists, and humanists in various disciplines may well find fascination in examining such personal (but still topical) exchanges between these two individuals — a literary dialogue sustained over their 48 years of married life. Of particular interest will be the many insights offered by an insider into Tolstoy's world-view and the evolution of his ideas over the period.

---

2   An additional 177 letters had come to light by the time the Jubilee Edition was published.

Tolstaya was an artistically sensitive critic and, at the same time, a pragmatic professional, who played a role more closely integrated than any other human being into all facets of Tolstoy's life, including his inner spiritual development and his constantly evolving career as a writer.

I believe that the projected multi-volume publication, multifaceted as it is in scope, will be a landmark edition, of value to seasoned academics and the next generation of young scholars. It will offer both the academic community and the general public a unique opportunity to become acquainted with a remarkable woman whose fascinating career contributed so significantly both to that of a great writer and to the larger society in which they lived. It will, in addition, lead to a re-evaluation by scholars of some of their previous conclusions regarding Tolstoy and Tolstaya, for their correspondence — especially Sofia Andreevna's 201 unpublished letters — reveals a complexity of much deeper layers in their relationship. It will lead to new corrections on a variety of subjects, ranging from Tolstaya's collaboration and assistance in Tolstoy's creative production to the sometimes bitter accusations and unfair treatment she received from some of his followers (known as "Tolstoyans") — notably his long-time associate, Vladimir Chertkov — not to mention criticism directed at her by her children and, indeed, by her husband himself.

It will be possible to better understand and more accurately evaluate many significant ideas encountered both in Tolstoy's fiction and in his treatises on the basis of Tolstaya's reaction to them in her letters and her husband's subsequent counter-reaction.

The value of these new epistolary materials reveals itself in relation to the overall context of writings, diaries and other correspondence, particularly during the periods in Tolstoy's life when he did not keep a diary. Hence the need to set forth the entire correspondence in an integrated string of chronologically arranged letters that enables readers to follow the epistolary exchange from start to finish.

Another consideration favouring the chronological sequencing of the whole correspondence with no omissions is the opportunity to search for and analyse (with proper dating) the real-life events which Tolstoy later transformed into episodes in his literary works. Nowhere is the connection between the writer's life and his creative process more apparent than in his family letters, which are a more reliable guide than memoirs to real-life experiences (memoirs often being written at a later period, and under the influence of subsequent events).

Furthermore, the sequence of letters reflects the changing patterns and trends of the literary and social atmosphere over five decades. Numerous references over this period allow the reader to trace these changes both in Russia as a whole and in the Tolstoys' relationships with well-known figures of the time (e.g., writers Dostoevsky, Turgenev, Chekhov, Gorky and Fet; painters Kramskoj, Repin and Ge; composers Taneev, Arenskij and Tchaikovsky; philosophers Grot, Lopatin and Strakhov; even the tsars: Alexander II, Alexander III and Nicholas II). Thus the project's scope reaches far beyond the study of two individual correspondents.

Such a multifaceted and interdisciplinary edition, as previewed in the present English translation, will greatly enrich not only the field of Tolstoy studies but provide useful research material for scholars and students in history, sociology, culturology and gender studies, in reference to the five decades of Russian history covered by the correspondence (1860s to 1900s).

Tolstaya's letters and postscripts to her husband, embracing (as they do) the whole period of their married life (from August 1862 to his death in November 1910), written from a consistent point of view and with remarkable clarity of insight, constitute the most important documentary source for Tolstoy scholarship to be published in many years. They provide significant new information that is not to be found in any of her other writings. Indeed, recent scholarship

(notably, Remizov 2011) has seen an outcry over the current dispersal of the couple's letters among so many sources and encouraged the publication of their entire correspondence as a source of particularly valuable information on both Tolstoy and Tolstaya as subjects of scholarly research.

First, these letters and postscripts allow us to peer into the soul, as it were, of this remarkable woman, whose lot it was not only to be married to one of the world's greatest writers, but to take on a number of significant roles in conjunction with his creative output: as a painstaking transcriber of his daily jottings; as a consultant who sometimes contributed to his actual writing; as a publicist and liaison with publishers, printing-houses and the press (later as a publisher herself). She also acted as her husband's advocate and defender in questions of censorship — a task Tolstoy abhorred (on one occasion she even presented a plea on his behalf to the Tsar) — and as his eyes and ears on the social and political scene in Moscow, from where she would report to him through her letters sent back to his preferred abode at Yasnaya Polyana. Her letters confirm and illustrate what she wrote in 1904 in the preface to her memoir *My Life:* "The significance of my forty-two years of conjugal life with Lev Nikolaevich cannot be excluded from his life." In addition, they reflect and illustrate her independent activities as a musician, painter, photographer and writer of her own novels and stories.

Second, letters and postscripts written by both correspondents provide fresh insights into the major works Tolstoy produced over almost a half-century. They help explain and clarify not only the aims of his various novels and treatises, but also the practical procedures involved in their publication and promotion, as well as their reception on the part of contemporary critics. They illustrate the vital link between many of Tolstoy's fictional scenes and characters, and events and personages in his family life, which then in turn consciously or sub-consciously informed these same scenes and characters.

Third, the letters and postscripts chronicle in considerable detail not only the shared experiences and mutual relationship of two individuals, but also members of the extended Tolstoy family and their circles of acquaintances (one of the principal themes running through the correspondence). Beyond that, they serve as a window on the whole of Russian society of the late nineteenth and early twentieth centuries.

APPRAISING A LIFE THROUGH AN EPISTOLARY EXCHANGE

This, however, is a task for the future. The current volume of selected letters presents a continually unfolding dialogue between the Tolstoy-Tolstaya couple for the first time in English translation, and offers substantial and unique insight into the minds of two fascinating individuals over the 48-year period of their conjugal life. Not only do we gain a more multifaceted understanding of these deep-thinking correspondents by penetrating their immediate and extended family life — full of joy and sadness, bliss and tragedy. This dialogue also allows us to observe, as in a generation-spanning chronicle, a variety of scenes from Russian society — from rural peasants working the lands of the Tolstoy estates to lords and ladies of noble birth parading within the walls of the Imperial Court and the Russian Orthodox Church — all of whom both writers were well acquainted with. We learn about Tolstoy's diverse family setting in which he penned a host of stories, novels and philosophical treatises (including two of the world's most famous works of fiction: *War and Peace* and *Anna Karenina*). We learn about Tolstaya's development as a writer, businesswoman and an individual in her own right, including her indispensable (yet all too often overlooked) contribution to the writing, publishing and dissemination of her husband's works. We learn about the far-reaching effects of Tolstoy's spiritual

conversion in 1880 on his marital and family relations, including the events leading up to his final departure from his beloved Yasnaya Polyana in October 1910, and his death which followed shortly afterwards, as well as the devastating effects of these events on Tolstaya as a wife and mother. In sum, this correspondence represents two lifetimes of intertwined creative energy that collectively left their indelible mark on both Russian history and world literature.

It is indeed surprising that no attempt has been made to date to publish the integrated correspondence as an entire or even partial exchange — or to offer a sustained critical study of the particular relationship evident in these letters — especially since a similar edition of letters between Fëdor Mikhajlovich Dostoevsky and his wife Anna Grigor'evna Dostoevskaja was issued in a prestigious academic edition: *F. M. Dostoevskij—A. G. Dostoevskaja: Perepiska [Correspondence]* (1979), including 239 letters by the two correspondents and a critical overview by the editors (pp. 352–88). This fact may serve as yet another illustration of the bias against Sofia Andreevna on the part of those offended by the fact that her often negative criticism of her husband's failings had impugned the idyllic image promoted by the vast majority of his followers and some researchers; this image had permeated both Soviet and post-Soviet Tolstoy research and prevented many scholars from investigating a good deal of obviously important material. The recent first-time publication (in Russian, preceded by an English translation under my editorship) of her major autobiographical work, *My Life,* for example, is a hint that the correction of these errors is very much on the agenda of Slavic scholarship today.

A few Soviet works on Tolstoy and Tolstaya are relevant and should be taken into account. Apart from the annotations to Tolstoy's letters in the Jubilee Edition (1938, 1949) and Tolstaya's letters to Tolstoy in Tolstaja and Popov's 1936 edition, little discussion on the overall exchange of letters is available in Russia. To be sure, every Russian scholar who has written about the husband-wife relationship (e.g., Pavel Birjukov, Vladimir Zhdanov, Vladimir Tunimanov, Nina Nikitina, Tat'jana Komarova) discusses their letters, but not as a dialogue. This includes the brilliant, judicious account of their marriage in Pavel Basinskij's *Lev Tolstoj: begstvo iz raja [Leo Tolstoy: Flight from Paradise]* (2010). Nor do we encounter any more comprehensive treatment of their correspondence in the major biographical works published in the West.

Three recent biographies might be mentioned as particularly pertinent: one of Tolstoy, Rosamund Bartlett's *Tolstoy: A Russian Life* (2011); and the other two of Tolstaya: *Sofja Andrejewna Tolstaja: Ein Leben an der Seite Tolstojs [Sofia Andreevna Tolstaya: A Life at Tolstoy's Side]* (2009) by Ursula Keller and Natalja Sharandak; *Sophia Tolstoy: A Biography* (2010) by Alexandra Popoff.

A notable exception here is the earlier two-volume edition (1978) of Lev Tolstoy's letters to various addressees, translated into English and annotated by Professor Reginald F. Christian of the University of St. Andrews in Scotland, which includes 36 addressed to Sofia Tolstaya but, again, without either her responses or the letters Tolstoy was responding to.

A shorter study with excellent overview and analysis is Hugh McLean's "The Tolstoy marriage revisited — many times" (2011). Also worth noting is Inessa Medzhibovskaya's thorough analysis, *Tolstoy and the Religious Culture of his Time: A Biography of a Long Conversion, 1845–1887* (2008), and Hilde Hoogenboom's conference paper, "The Tolstoy Family: Conflicts in the Literary Field at Home" (2014).

There are lessons, however, suggested by some previously published works. For example, in the Dostoevsky couple's letters mentioned above, the biographical introduction focused almost entirely on Fëdor Mikhajlovich and very little on his wife Anna Grigor'evna. In the current essay, on the other hand, in view of the proliferation of criticism already accorded Lev

Nikolaevich Tolstoy and his writings by world literary scholarship, as well as the obvious significance of Sofia Andreevna Tolstaya's accomplishments, a more appropriate balance in emphasis begs observance.

SOFIA ANDREEVNA TOLSTAYA: THREE PERIODS OF DEVELOPMENT

Sofia Andreevna Behrs was born 22 August 1844 at Pokrovskoe Glebovo-Streshnevo near Moscow. She received her education at home and, in 1861, at the age of seventeen, passed the 'home-teacher' examination at Moscow University. By this time her father, Andrej Evstaf'evich Behrs, had been appointed physician to the Imperial Court — a position which provided him and his family with a private apartment in the Kremlin.

The following year, on 14 September 1862, she was proposed to by Lev Nikolaevich Tolstoy, who had courted her on her grandfather's estate (Ivitsy) near Tula, some fifty kilometres north of Yasnaya Polyana. His proposal contained a caveat, perhaps a hint that the marital journey ahead would not be an easy one: "Tell me *as an honest person*, do you want to be my wife? Only if you can *fearlessly,* from the bottom of your heart, say *yes.* If there is even a shadow of a doubt in your mind, it would be better to say *no*" *(14 September 1862, Letter № 2).*

The wedding took place nine days later on 23 September at the Birth of the Virgin Mary Church [*Tserkov' Rozhdestva Bogoroditsy*] on the Kremlin grounds.

Following the wedding, Sofia Andreevna quickly adapted not only to the role of Tolstoy's wife but also to that of his copyist and literary assistant, starting with his *Polikushka,* a story of peasant life, which was published the following year. It took her significantly longer to accustom herself to the duties of household manager and mother (of what eventually turned out to be a family of thirteen children — five of whom did not survive to adulthood, and not counting several miscarriages). She fulfilled all these roles with a natural ability, efficiency and devotion. She took personal charge of her children's education during their younger years, even devising special readers and grammar books for them. Her busy home schedule left little time for amusement or travel, apart from the occasional trips to St. Petersburg, Kiev and the Crimea. Sadly, despite her early studies in French (in which she was fluent) and later in English and German, she never had the opportunity to travel outside Russia.

She was, however, quite active in community and social affairs, especially during her time in Moscow — including the famine relief efforts of 1891 and 1892, when she set up and managed a campaign to collect funds for famine victims and purchase needed food and other supplies.[3] She also found time to develop her artistic talent for music, painting, photography and writing. Among other painting activities, she would make copies of early portraits of her husband by well-known artists of the day.

One of her greatest legacies was her ongoing support of her husband's unique literary career. She authored the first biographical sketch of Tolstoy to appear in print.[4] During the 1870s she wrote a series of essays on certain aspects of his life (his conflict with Turgenev, for example), as well as his career as a novelist (in particular, his work on *War and Peace* and *Anna Karenina*). During the periods of her husband's illness, she would issue press releases on the true state of his health in an effort to counteract widespread false rumours as to his supposed arrest or even death. She publicly defended him from malicious attacks by his opponents, and did her best to

---

3 This is described in *My Life,* v.129.
4 *Graf Lev Nikolaevich Tolstoj [Count Lev Nikolaevich Tolstoy],* published in St. Petersburg by M. M. Stasjulevich in 1879 as part of his *Russkaja biblioteka* series.

protect him from undesired visits to Yasnaya Polyana either by over-zealous supporters or by those interested primarily in personal gain. And despite her personal and philosophical objections to his later writings such as *The Kreutzer Sonata,* she made a (successful) personal petition to the Tsar himself against their official censorship ban.[5]

With her fluency in French and her better-than-average knowledge of German and English, she frequently found herself translating Tolstoy's works into French as well as translating texts of interest to him from all three of these languages into Russian.[6]

Most importantly, particularly during the later years of their marriage, Tolstaya took an active role in the publication of her husband's writings. This included negotiations with printers and publishers, supervising the editing and proofreading process[7] and even maintaining a warehouse of his books in a wing of their Khamovniki home in Moscow. A major turning-point in this activity came in May 1883, when Tolstoy gave Tolstaya complete charge of the publication of all his writings published before 1881 (including royalties), while he himself renounced his rights to virtually all his later writings (as well as personal property in general). Between 1886 and 1891 she brought out eight different editions of his collected writings as well as republishing fifteen volumes of individual works.

Added to all this is her activity as archivist and documentary historian. It is in good measure thanks to Tolstaya that so many materials (including manuscripts, letters and diaries and a catalogue of her husband's library holdings at Yasnaya Polyana) have been preserved for future generations of scholars. According to senior museum researcher Tat'jana Nikiforova, the S. A. Tolstaya archive in the Manuscript Division of the State L. N. Tolstoy Museum in Moscow numbers 22,000 items,[8] including thousands of letters written by or addressed to her. Her correspondents included many prominent contemporary writers, artists, critics, philosophers, theatre people, lawyers and politicians.

Sofia Andreevna Tolstaya's independent role as editor and publisher of Tolstoy's works is not to be underestimated, certainly not by Tolstoy's biographers, who have provided a good deal of documentation on her life (though sadly neglecting her own literary pursuits).

Until very recently, however, there were very few published objective portrayals of Sofia Andreevna's life and professional activity. Of the comments extant, the vast majority may be divided into two groups: (a) those from Tolstoyans and suchlike, who saw her as authoritarian, intellectually limited, offensive and coarse in her dealings with people; and (b) those from

5 See *My Life,* v.93 and v.94.
6 In 1885–86, for example, she translated the book *Uchenie 12 apostolov [Teachings of the Twelve Apostles]* from German, and in 1888 her translation of Tolstoy's *O zhizni [On Life]* was published in French as *De la Vie.*
7 This she did in close co-operation with Tolstoy's editorial adviser, Nikolaj Nikolaevich Strakhov, who enjoyed a relationship of mutual admiration and respect with both Sofia Andreevna and her husband. See A. A. Donskov (ed.), *L. N. Tolstoj i S. A. Tolstaja: Perepiska s N. N. Strakhovym / The Tolstoys' Correspondence with N. N. Strakhov* (Donskov 2000). This volume contains the complete extant correspondence between Tolstaya and Strakhov: 40 letters written by Strakhov and 47 by Tolstaya, mainly discussing editing and proofreading questions.
8 These comprise documents relating to Tolstaya's biography; her writings (literary works and memoirs); household documents (various accounts, inventories of personal effects in the Moscow and Yasnaya Polyana houses, records of income and expenses, plans of the estate, records of payments to day-workers, orders for flower seeds and fruit-tree saplings for the Yasnaya Polyana orchard etc.); publishing-related materials (order blanks for publishing Tolstoy's writings, correspondence with print-shop owners, subscription notices for regular editions, records of publication income and expenses, distribution lists for the volumes, along with their contents).

visitors to her home and her own regular correspondents, who by and large came to appreciate her talents, her dedication to her family and her invaluable assistance to her husband's writing career. The latter group included many famous names, for example: artists Il'ja Repin and Leonid Pasternak; composers Sergej Taneev and Anton Arenskij; philosophers Nikolaj Grot and Pavel Bakunin; theatre directors Konstantin Stanislavsky and Vladimir Nemirovich-Danchenko; literary critics Nikolaj Strakhov and Vladimir Stasov, plus a large number of writers and publishers, including Afanasij Fet, Ivan Turgenev, Maxim Gorky, Zinaida Gippius and Anna Dostoevskaja.

Her descriptions of these personalities read as a chronicle of the times, affording a unique portrait of late-nineteenth-century and early-twentieth-century Russian society. Together with her other ventures, they also highlight her accomplishments as an author in her own right — a rarity in the largely male-dominated world of the time.

In Part III, Chapter 39 of *My Life,* Tolstaya describes "three significant periods in my life that had a considerable influence on me", namely (a) her first acquaintance with Tolstoy's early works (which led to a subsequent interest in Russian and world literature), (b) her platonic attraction to the Tolstoys' family friend Prince Leonid Dmitrievich Urusov, who introduced her to philosophy, (c) the death of her youngest son, Vanechka, and the subsequent comfort she found in music. This comfort came in particular from the music of pianist-composer Sergej Ivanovich Taneev, and her platonic relationship with him enriched and enhanced her life-long love of music and served as a catalyst for her novel *Song Without Words.* All three of these significant periods left their mark on Tolstaya's career as a writer, and are worth exploring in some detail.

LITERATURE AND LEV NIKOLAEVICH TOLSTOY

In her youth, Tolstaya developed an interest in both Russian and world literature. She describes this experience in Chapter I.22 of *My Life:*

> From the age of fourteen up to eighteen I read through the whole of Russian literature, [including] Grigorovich's *Rybaki [The fishermen]* and *Pereselentsy [The migrants].* I was delighted to read Aksakov's *Semejnaja khronika [A family chronicle].* I also read all of Tolstoy, and Goncharov's *Oblomov,* along with everything that came out in Russian translation — Dickens, and so forth.
>
> We also read a good many French books at random: in the case of Molière, Racine and Corneille we just had to read *everything.* We read George Sand with great enthusiasm, as well as V[ictor] Hugo's *Notre Dame de Paris,* [Paul Henri] Féval's *Le Bossu* and many others.
>
> …in German I was reading Goethe, Schiller and Auerbach, which I quite liked. I was particularly pleased with [Auerbach's] novel *Auf der Höhe [On the Heights].*

She then goes on to recount her exploration of the whole history of Russian literature, likening it to "the growth of a living being" (*ibid.*), and how she was particularly fascinated with Ivan Turgenev (1818–1883). As a university student she participated in a public reading of Turgenev's *Fathers and Sons,* finding "something very appealing and promising for the future" in the character of Bazarov (*Autobiography,* p. 141). She also had a special attraction to Charles Dickens's *David Copperfield* — which she at the time read in Russian translation (later she would become quite proficient in reading original works in English) — growing very attached to the novel's characters, as though they were "the dearest and closest people to me" (*My Life,* I.7).

The greatest pleasure and impact of all, however, came from her reading of two autobiographical novels by Lev Nikolaevich Tolstoy, namely *Childhood [Detstvo]* and *Boyhood [Otrochestvo],* later to be supplemented by the third part of his well-known trilogy, *Youth*

[Junost']. When it came to Tolstoy, she "wasn't content with just reading — I would copy favourite passages and commit them to memory" (*ibid.*). It was in part her reading of these books that inspired her to write her first story, *Natasha*.

Here may be seen the very beginnings of a mutual literary attraction and interaction between Sofia Andreevna and Lev Nikolaevich, which actually preceded their personal relationship and romance.

After their marriage the newly-wed Tolstaya took on the task of transcribing her husband's texts (penned in his notoriously indecipherable handwriting) to make them legible for the typesetters. Because of the author's inevitable dissatisfaction with his initial drafts, this often meant copying the same stories over and over again to incorporate his many corrections and newly minted passages. While initially she found the task daunting — for example, shortly after their marriage she wrote: "I have been transcribing Lëvochka's [i.e., Lev Nikolaevich's] work for days on end, and am so tired" (*My Life*, II.6), — it is clear that she came to relish the opportunity for such close familiarity with her husband's creative process. She confessed in *My Life* (II.14):

> The transcribing of *War and peace* — and indeed, all Lev Nikolaevich's works — was a source of great æsthetic pleasure for me. I fearlessly looked forward to my evening labours, and joyfully anticipated just *what* I would derive from the delight of becoming further acquainted with his work as it unfolded. I was enthralled by this life of thought, these twists and turns, surprises and all the various unfathomable aspects of his creative genius.

And her letters to Lev Nikolaevich confirm the depth of enthusiasm she felt for this work:

> Today I spent practically the whole day transcribing. I didn't get very far ahead, though, as I got distracted. But transcribing *is* pleasant, as though a close friend were sitting [with me] in the same room, and [this friend] doesn't need to be entertained — it's just good that he is here. This is how it is with my copying: I don't have to think, but simply to follow and benefit from the various thoughts of another, one very close to me, and from that comes good. (SAT *to* LNT, *11 November 1866, Letter N° 28*)

> What have you decided as regards our 'shrine' — your novel? I've now started to think of it as your (meaning mine, too) baby, and releasing these sheets of paper comprising your novel to Moscow is literally letting go of a child, and I'm fearful lest it come to any harm. I've really fallen in love with your creation. It's doubtful I'll love anything as much as this novel. (SAT *to* LNT, *14 November 1866, Letter N° 31*)

Thirty years later Sofia Andreevna still had nostalgic thoughts about her fascination with the transcribing of her husband's fiction ("artistic") works ("How silly I was when you were writing *War and Peace* and how smart you were! How delicately — cleverly, with such genius — *War and Peace* was written!" — Letter N° 167.) But her feelings for his post-1880 philosophical writings were entirely different. They would frequently cause her concern that they were a waste of such a talented writer's time and that he should give them up in favour of a return to fiction. Yet, at least with hindsight, in 1894 she could look at his change of literary genre quite philosophically herself:

> I cannot forswear my love for your *artistic* works; and today I suddenly had the clear realisation that this is because I experienced it during the best years of my life together with you — i.e.,

simply in my youth. And [our] daughters in *their* youth are experiencing another side of your literary activity, and will love it above all else. (SAT to LNT, 11 September 1894, Letter № 174)

But Tolstaya's role in her husband's creative endeavours was not long confined to simply transcribing. Her contributions to his *Primer*,[9] as well as to some of the descriptions (especially of women's clothing) in *War and Peace* and *Anna Karenina* have been all too frequently left unsung. The eminent Tolstoy scholar Lidija Gromova-Opul'skaja (2005: 305), for example, states:

> It is well known that during the time *War and peace* was being created, Sofia Andreevna Tolstaya was not just a transcriber, but Tolstoy's first enthusiastic reader and even his assistant. According to Èvelina Zajdenshnur, in both *War and peace* and *Anna Karenina* Sofia Andreevna would redescribe the clothing of Tolstoy's heroines. Zajdenshnur points out, for example, that in Tolstoy's early draft, Natasha and Sonja appeared at their first ball "in muslin dresses with roses on their corsages" [*v kisejnykh plat'jakh s rozami u korsazha*] whereas Tolstaya changed this to: "in gossamer dresses with rose-coloured capes and roses on their corsages" [*v dymkovykh plat'jakh na rozovykh chekhlakh s rozami u korsazha*] — and the change was accepted by Tolstoy.

There are in fact, several instances in which Tolstoy declined to describe his female characters' dress, happily leaving this task to Tolstaya as part of her transcribing duties.[10]

The writer Maxim Gorky, for one, recognised Tolstaya's contribution, declaring:

> We do not know what — or how — Leo Tolstoy's wife spoke to him in those moments when they sat eye to eye as he read to her (before anyone else) the book chapters he had only just finished writing. Mindful of the genius's monstrous intuitive insight, I still think that certain aspects of the images of women included in his great novel [*War and peace*] could only be perceived by a woman, who in turn suggested them to the novelist.[11]

Even earlier, just two years after their marriage, Tolstoy himself had acknowledged his wife's literary acumen in a letter he penned to her on 7 December 1864:

> What a smart girl you are in anything you put your mind to!.. Like a good wife, you think of your husband as yourself, and I remember how you said to me that all my military and historical [scenes] that I've put so much effort into will turn out poorly, while the [parts about] family, the characters' traits and psychological [makeup] will turn out fine. That is so true; nothing could be truer. And I remember your saying that to me, and I remember the whole of you like that. (LNT to SAT, 7 December 1864, Letter № 20)

Indeed, perhaps nowhere more vividly can the interaction between these two literary careers be seen (never mind the fact that one of them was obviously much more widely known than the other) than in the many letters Tolstoy and Tolstaya exchanged throughout their lifetime, which started even before their marriage. A good part of their correspondence centred around

---

9 See Chapter 4.2 in my book *Sofia Andreevna Tolstaya: Literary works*.

10 For example, in one of the drafts of *Anna Karenina* — see PSS 20: 523 — LNT left a marginal notation: "Ask Sonja [= SAT] to describe the outfits".

11 Gorky 1973: XVI: 358–74, cited in the editor's Introduction to *My Life*, p. xxviii. See also *ibid.*, p. xxvi, where SAT is quoted as saying: "for some reason he actually believes and listens to my opinions (much to my pride)".

literary topics, and was actually written in a superb literary style, with sensitive artistic descriptions of nature, which she took personal delight in. Her letters to him were replete with pithy and obviously vivid psychological portrayals of people, capturing a whole image in the brushstrokes of a few sentences — not only providing for highly interesting reading, but making readers even today feel they are living part of her life with her.

Some of her letters contain opinions (occasionally critical) of her husband's works, passing her own judgement on her favourite and not-so-favourite characters (for example, Prince Andrej and Princess Mar'ja — see Letter № 12 of 25 November 1864). Overall, however, she was deeply appreciative of her husband's creative genius. She was particularly moved by his play *The Power of Darkness [Vlast' t'my]* (1886) and expressed enthusiasm over its performance in a number of theatres. She criticised *Resurrection* as "false, spicy, drawn out and even repulsive",[12] at the same time describing *Master and Man [Khozjain i rabotnik]* as "fresh fruit" by comparison.

In a letter to her husband of 29 October 1895, she wrote with complete candour:

> I received your little letter just before I left. It is brief, but again one that lets me feel the whole of you very close to me, and reachable, and kind, and understandable. Besides, I feel quite ashamed and sorry to tell you this, but for some reason I find joy in the fact that you have become disenchanted with your narrative [an early draft of *Resurrection [Voskresenie]*]. I've felt all along that it was *contrived*, and that it did not well up from the depths of your heart and talent. It was something you *composed*, but did not *live*. [...]
>
> How I would like to lift you higher so that when people read you, they might feel they, too, need wings to fly to you, so that their heart might melt, and so that whatever you wrote would offend no one, but make things better, and so that your work might have an *eternal* character and fascination.
>
> (SAT to LNT, 29 October 1895, Letter № 182)

As much as she was put off by Tolstoy's post-1880 philosophical writings, she nevertheless remained a devoted supporter of his belletristic works, and took every opportunity to encourage him to concentrate on the latter at the expense of the former. In a letter of 5–6 March 1882, for example, she wrote him (quoted in *My Life*, III.107):

> What a feeling of joy came over me as I read that you once more feel like writing in an *artistic genre*. You have felt something I've been waiting for and desiring for a long time. Herein lies our salvation and our joy — here is something that will bring us together once more, something that will comfort you and refresh our lives. It is the real work for which you were created, and outside this sphere there is no rest for your soul... May God grant you hold on to this vision, so that this Divine spark may flare up in you once more.

It is evident from a number of places in her correspondence and diary entries that while Tolstaya recognised to some extent her own creative talent, she felt consistently held back by the role dictated by society as a female member of the human race. She felt that, as a woman, opportunities for manifesting that talent and devoting herself more fully to her literary pursuits were constantly being thwarted both by the overwhelming shadow cast by her world-famous

---

12 Letter to SAT's son Lev L'vovich Tolstoj, 12 August 1895 (L. N. Tolstoy Museum archives, unpublished).

husband's public profile, and by the duties imposed on her as a wife and mother (particularly the latter). In a diary entry of 12 June 1898 (1: 388) she mused:

> I was thinking today: why are women not geniuses? There are no [women] writers, artists or composers. Because all the passion and abilities of energetic women are spent on their families, their love, their husbands — and, especially, their children. All other abilities are atrophied, and stay undeveloped in the womb. Once child-bearing and child-raising are over, then their artistic needs awaken — but by then it is already too late to develop anything within themselves.

And as late as 16 September 1908 she wrote:

> …Lev Nikolaevich has been smart and happy his whole life. He has always worked at what *he* enjoys, and not because it was something he had to do. He would write whenever he wanted to. He would be out ploughing whenever he wanted to. Whenever he got tired of something, he would drop it. Would I ever try living like that? What would become of the children, or Lev Nikolaevich himself?" (*Dnevniki,* 11.114)

Still, on the basis of all the information presented both in this current volume and her own writings, especially *My Life,* it is evident that Tolstaya's own writing career was not completely atrophied, that she left to history a (given the constraints on her life) literary legacy worthy of study. Her early youthful jottings, her all too often neglected works of fiction, and above all her lifelong interaction with her celebrated husband's belletristic creativity as described above, point to an observable development of her writing abilities far beyond "the womb". As devoted as she was to caring for the physical and educational needs of her husband and children, she did allow her own inherent genius to shine through, as much as her complex life circumstances would permit.

Indeed, her care of the educational needs of her children[13] also extended, on occasion, to the spheres of writing and sculpture as favourite activities. In a letter to her son, Lev L'vovich, dated 30 June 1897, she admits to an "excellent understanding of the whole creative process", on the basis of which she willingly offered constructive literary advice to a son who had recently celebrated his 28th birthday:

> You say that you are continuing to write. I am afraid that you are taking a too light-hearted approach. Your story "Vorobejchik" [The little sparrow] is simply boring, and the public doesn't like that. It can't like it, and so that's why it was returned. You have to look at it from all sides and record, record, especially your direct impressions or express your moments of inspiration in some kind of form, even if in the most compressed form. I am poor at expressing myself, but I have an excellent understanding of the whole creative process.

To her eldest son Sergej L'vovich she wrote on 26 October 1917 about the difficulty of editing and arranging his father's literary manuscripts, along with the need for a collective approach:

---

13 For example, she compiled a Russian grammar for them, and composed a number of stories which she read to them during periods of extended travel.

...apparently you have clearly not appreciated the enormity and complexity of the task. For example, the manuscripts of *War and peace* were not only [damaged] in a ditch but then ended up being stuffed into a couple of drawers. These are all just clippings and fragments, and it's difficult to come up with a system to put everything in order. Working alone is unthinkable.[14]

Hence it may be seen that Sofia Andreevna's writing legacy, though apparently in competition with her family duties, is intricately bound together with her husband's writing pursuits, and those of her children as well. More than in the case of Tolstoy himself, who, notoriously (at least in his later period), found it difficult to reconcile the ideals of his writing with real-life situations,[15] the ideas underlying Tolstaya's brief writing career *grew out of* real life and were inseparable from it. From *Natasha* to *Who is to blame?*, each of her works may be found to be deeply rooted in her own life experience, which gives them a poignancy and an impression of realism that only enhances their effect on the reader.

Sofia Andreevna summed up her debt to her husband in *My Life* (III.39) as follows: "...as for Lev Nikolaevich, who had opened up the treasure of literature to me through his *Childhood*, I naturally began to poeticise him, to love him as a human being. And, despite all the ups and downs in our lives, I have never stopped loving him."

PHILOSOPHY AND LEONID DMITRIEVICH URUSOV

"The second significant period in my spiritual life," wrote Sofia Andreevna in *My Life* (*ibid.*), "was the time when I learnt to know the beauty of the philosophical thinking of the sages, who afforded me so much by way of spiritual development and even helped me live, simply through their wisdom."

The philosophers on her reading list were many — from Socrates and Plato to Nikolaj Grot and Vladimir Solovëv. As an example of the personal significance they held for her, witness the following passage from her *Autobiography [Avtobiografija]* (p. 156):

> The brilliant style and wealth of thinking of this philosopher [Marcus Aurelius] got me so carried away that I went over his writings twice. After this I read a number of philosophers one after the other, buying [their] books and writing out [their] thoughts and sayings which made an impression on me. I remember how I was struck by Epictetus's thoughts on death. I found Spinoza quite difficult to understand, but his *Ethics* interested me, especially his explanation of the concept of God. I was excited by Socrates, Plato and other philosophers (mainly Greek), and I can say that [such] sages went a long way toward helping me live and think. Later I tried reading newer philosophers, too: I read Schopenhauer and others, but I liked the ancient ones a whole lot better.

Interestingly enough, Sofia Andreevna immediately went on to speak of the philosophical writings of her husband, Lev Nikolaevich, singling out her favourite, *On life [O zhizni]*. She

---

14 Quoted in *Dnevniki* II: 597.

15 As I have mentioned in a number of my publications, even the peasants, with whom Tolstoy himself identified more than with any other social group, were generally represented in his writings as stereotypes or abstractions, rather than as true-to-life individuals. See, for example, my 1979 article "The peasant in Tolstoy's thought and writings" in *Canadian Slavonic Papers*, where I argue that the *grace* that came to Tolstoy's major characters in moments of their most intense spiritual anguish was in the form of peasants, not so much as personalities as the *symbolic qualities* they embody, qualities of sincerity, simplicity and naturalness. Over the course of Tolstoy's post-1880 writings, the peasants may be seen as evolving into vehicles through which, he hoped, everybody could learn a great deal about life.

translated this treatise into French with the editorial assistance of a native French speaker surnamed Tastevin and, in her *Autobiography*, even mentioned seeking help from Grot and Solovëv (*ibid.*), as well as from Lev Nikolaevich himself.

However, there was more to her philosophical attraction than the message of philosophy itself. It turned out she was also deeply attracted to the messenger, in the form of a Tolstoy family friend, the Deputy Governor of Tula Gubernia, Prince Leonid Dmitrievich Urusov, who was largely responsible for introducing her to the study of philosophy. In her introduction to the chapter dealing with the three most significant periods in her life, she said the following about her study of philosophy (*My Life,* III.39):

"It was L. D. Urusov who set me and later guided me along this path. I became quite attached to him, and loved him for a long time because of this,—in fact, I have never really stopped loving him either, even though he has been dead a long time."

Tolstaya repeatedly emphasised the platonic nature of her relationship with Urusov. A page or so following this paragraph in *My Life,* she stated, for example:

"His relationship to me was gentlemanly and courteous, albeit occasionally on the ecstatic side. But we never, either in word or gesture, hinted at anything in the way of a romance between us."

It is fair to say that the philosophical connection that she and Urusov shared satisfied their intellectual desires more fully than any spiritual bond they might have had with their respective spouses. As much as Tolstaya appreciated (and was even, on occasion, enamoured by) her husband's philosophical tendencies, she perceived them as largely taking him mentally away from her and their children. She yearned for an idea-based relationship where family duties played no part, and found it, at this point in her life, in Urusov. The deputy governor, for his part, had found little intellectual interest in common with his wife, Marija Sergeevna (Monja, *née* Mal'tseva), whom Tolstaya describes (*ibid.*) as highly materialistic, "a very unpleasant woman, who had lived almost all her life in Paris, and with a poor reputation to boot".[16] Not only that, but she had taken their four children to live with her in Paris, cutting them off almost completely from any family interaction with their father. It was not surprising, therefore, that the pursuit of common philosophical interests nudged both Tolstaya and Urusov into a special meeting of minds which transcended their personal situations.[17]

This experience necessarily had an effect on Tolstaya's artistic and literary contributions.

MUSIC AND SERGEJ IVANOVICH TANEEV

Music had played a significant role throughout Sofia Andreevna's life, beginning with the final composition she wrote for her teaching certificate in 1861, entitled "Music".[18] During the early part of her marriage she often played four-handed piano pieces with Lev Nikolaevich.[19] She found in music the comfort she needed from the more tedious aspects of child-rearing:

16 Ironically, perhaps, as it turned out, Urusov's wife had a considerable appreciation and respect for Sofia Andreevna and her conjugal relationship to Tolstoy. In a letter to Tolstaya following Leonid Dmitrievich's death, she wrote: "You are your husband's best pupil — you have taken from him everything you need for the perfecting of your marvellous nature" (quoted in *My Life,* v.103).

17 It has been mistakenly assumed that the prototype for the character of the Duke's friend, Dmitrij Bekhmetev, in SAT's *Who is to blame?* was the poet Afanasij Fet. Clearly, the whole text, seen against the background of her letters, notes and diaries, points to Urusov as the prototype.

18 See Editor's introduction to *My Life,* p. xxii.

19 See *ibid.,* p. xxxi.

… and the music, which I have not heard in a long time, has at once taken me out of my own realm of the nursery, diapers and children which I have not taken a single step out of for a long time and transported me somewhere far, far away, where everything is different.[20]

Her diaries and letters mention regular attendance at concerts and musical evenings held at Yasnaya Polyana, along with commentaries about various composers and musicians. She was, in fact, familiar with about as many composers as philosophers.

It was not until in 1895, however, that Sofia Andreevna became fully aware of her absolute dependence on the comforting power of music to carry her through what must have been one of the worst ordeals of her life, namely, the death of her youngest son, Vanechka,[21] the favourite of the whole circle of the Tolstoys' family and friends. This experience she described in her chapter on three significant periods[22] as follows:

> This was the time following the death of my little son Vanechka. I was in a state of extreme despair — the kind that happens only once in a lifetime. Such a state of sorrow is usually fatal, and those that survive are not in a condition to endure such heart-wrenching suffering a second time. But I did survive, and for that I am obliged to chance, as well as to the mysterious medium of … *music.*

Just as with her earlier introduction to philosophy, this particular message of music arrived together with a messenger, in the person of a prominent pianist and composer: "One day in May … I was sitting on the balcony. It was a warm day, and the whole garden had already turned green. Sergej Ivanovich Taneev dropped by…"

As it happened, the well-known composer was looking for a place to live for the summer, and Sofia Andreevna offered to rent him the then-empty annexe on the Yasnaya Polyana estate. She admitted she "was morally reaching out for anything that would take my mind off my life with Vanechka, and the presence of someone who was completely oblivious of my sadness to date — and was a pretty good pianist to boot — seemed quite desirable to me".

This situation continued for two summers, as well as for part of the intervening winter. Sofia Andreevna "became intoxicated by music and got so accustomed to hearing it that I found myself no longer able to live without it". She took out subscriptions to concerts and listened to music at every possible opportunity — not an easy task in an age when musical recordings were not nearly as accessible as they are today.

But it was Taneev's music which affected her most of all:

> It was he who first taught me, through his marvellous playing, to listen to and love music. I made every effort to hear his playing wherever and however I could, and would arrange to meet him just for this purpose — just so that I could ask him to play. Occasionally, when I did not manage to do this for some time, I felt sad, tormented by the burning desire to hear him play once more, or even just to see him.

---

20 SAT to LN, 7 December 1864 (Letter № 21). See also Letter № 206 and № 218.

21 The Tolstoys had already experienced an inordinate number of deaths in their family, but Vanechka's passing affected her with particular grief. Her relation to Vanechka in itself was a catalyst for two of the stories in her collection *The Skeleton-dolls* (see Chapter 4.3 of my 2011 book *Sofia Andreevna Tolstaya: Literary works*), and possibly had an influence on the writing of her final story for Tolstoy's *New primer* (see below).

22 Unless otherwise indicated, all the quotations in this section are from SAT's chapter "Three significant periods" (*My Life*, III.39).

His presence had a beneficial effect on me whenever I started feeling a longing for Vanechka. I would weep and feel the energy drain from my life. Sometimes all it took to calm me down was to meet with Sergej Ivanovich and hear his quieting, dispassionate voice. I had already got accustomed to being calmed by his presence and especially his playing. It was a kind of hypnosis, an involuntary influence on my aching soul — one he was completely unaware of.

It was not a normal state to be in. It happened to coincide with my change of life. For all my moodiness I remained virtually unaffected by Taneev's personality....

For healing my sorrowful soul unintentionally through his music — he didn't even know about it — I have remained forever grateful to him, and I have never stopped loving him. He was the first to *open* the door for me to an *understanding* of music, just as Lev Nikolaevich led me to the understanding of the literary arts, just as Prince Urusov gave me an understanding of and love for philosophy. Once you enter upon these scenes of spiritual delight, you never want to leave them and you constantly come back to them.

Again, just as with Urusov, Tolstaya took pains to deny any kind of romantic relationship with her musical muse:

I refused to entertain such a thought. I would always deny it and was actually afraid of it, even though there was one time when the influence of Taneev's personality was very strong. Once that kind of feeling surfaces, it kills any sense of importance in the music and art. I wrote a long piece on that.

This brings us back directly to Tolstaya's writing pursuits. The "long piece" she mentions was none other than her narrative *Song without words [Pesnja bez slov]*,[23] which is based directly on her experience with the composer Taneev. Just as in real life, one of the distinguishing features of the composer/enchanted-listener relationship in her story is that the music itself is its guiding principle, outweighing any feelings of romance or physical attraction.

Sofia Andreevna's protests of innocence, however, did not serve to mitigate the real feelings of jealousy on the part of Lev Nikolaevich over her obvious attentions to Taneev,[24] and bitter misunderstandings and arguments ensued (her husband even threatened to leave home). She sums up her own and her husband's viewpoints in Chapter VII.16 of *My Life*:

Lev Nikolaevich also began to get irritated by Taneev's presence, even though in the evenings he continued to play chess with him and listen to his music. Whenever they talked, Lev Nikolaevich would get irritated and once even told Taneev: "Only peasants or very stupid people would ever reason like that!" Taneev got up and walked out without saying a word, and later Lev Nikolaevich apologised to him.

Subsequently he wrote in his diary that he didn't like the fact that Taneev had become *le coq du village* in our home. Indeed, everybody liked him, and everybody had a good time with him. He studied Italian together with Tanja and Masha. We would all go for walks together or take a carriage ride. *I* was friendly with Taneev, too — I was very excited about his piano-playing.

All this did not go over well with Lev Nikolaevich, and he was especially angry at me. I couldn't put it down to jealousy; at first that never even entered my head. I was already fifty-two, and

---

23 The title is taken from Mendelssohn's well-known collection *Songs without words* (see Chapter 4.5 in my *Sofia Andreevna Tolstaya: Literary works*).
24 See Letters N° 193 and N° 198.

men as such could not possibly exist for me. Besides, I was too firmly and fervently in love with my husband, and there was absolutely no point in comparing anyone with such a being as Lev Nikolaevich, who was unique in terms of his spiritual beauty and elevation.

In addition to the above, it should also be pointed out that, while always polite, understanding, cordial, and appreciative of Sofia Andreevna, Taneev himself, as a homosexual, never felt any romantic affection for her.

SPIRITUAL SEARCHING, EVALUATION OF SELF

One can trace through the letters how both correspondents change over the decades, how they mature and progress in gaining a more multi-dimensional understanding of themselves and their partner, of their family, of the world around them, as well as of the meaning of life.

The love-stricken Lev Nikolaevich's romantic infatuation with his young bride did not stop him from characterising her and other members of the Behrs family psychologically back in the early years of their marriage. He divided them into two categories with an intentional play on words: black and white Behrs. Sonja, along with her mother, her sister Tanja and her youngest brother Vjacheslav (Slava), fall into the black branch of the Behrs family, those whose mind is dormant but whose emotions run high: "they are capable, but unwilling, and hence comes their confidence (not always à propos) and tact", though "their mind is dormant because they love with great strength" (Letter Nº 20, dated 7 December 1864). The white Behrs, on the other hand, "have a great sympathy for intellectual interests, but their minds are weak and shallow" (*ibid.*).

The first years were happy ones for the married couple, but feelings of depression, mainly on the part of Lev Nikolaevich, began to appear by the end of the decade. Commenting on a letter written to Tolstoy by his great aunt Aleksandra Andreevna (Alexandrine), in which the latter reveals her death-imbued outlook on life resulting from an unhappy love, Tolstaya wonders whether her husband's depression—and her own, though she doesn't make the connection overtly—and might be similarly attributable (see Letter Nº 38 of 4 September 1869).

Fears over depressive mental states resurfaced during Tolstoy's trips to Samara for *koumiss* (fermented mare's milk) treatments, to which he attributed considerable relief: "The feelings of melancholy and indifference I was complaining about have passed" he writes to his wife on 23 June 1871 (Letter Nº 41); "I feel I've entered a Scythian state of mind, where everything is interesting and new."

Following his wife and children's move to the recently purchased Khamovniki Lane house in Moscow in 1882, Lev Nikolaevich spent his winters in solitude at Yasnaya Polyana, filling his days with physical labour (especially ploughing), daily walks and horseback riding. He also spent time conversing with peasants and simple folk, most of whom were living hard lives: "Someone's either begging, epileptic, consumptive, crippled, beating his wife or abandoning his children. And everywhere there's suffering and evil, and people have come to accept that that's the way it ought to be" (Letter Nº 75, 2 March 1882). A similar picture was evident almost three years later in Letter Nº 107 (2 February 1885), though in this case he seemed to be taking some comfort in his viewpoint as an observer and writer above the fray:

I have been having a lot more impressions of poverty and suffering. I see them always and everywhere, but it's easier to spot them in the countryside. Here you see everything down to the last detail. And you see both the cause and the means. And I love it — not actually love it, but feel good — when I can clearly see my own situation amidst other people's.

Sofia Andreevna, on the other hand, initially accepted the arrangement to live apart from her husband as necessary to provide the solitude Lev Nikolaevich needed to fully concentrate on his literary creativity. However, in time she came to suspect that he had ulterior motives. In a letter (Nº 100) dated 23 October 1884 she wrote:

> Yesterday I received your *first* letter, and it saddened me. I see that you have been staying at Yasnaya not for the sake of your intellectual work, which I prize above everything else in life, but for some sort of 'Robinson Crusoe' game. You dismissed [our servant] Adrian, who longed to stay to the end of the month; you dismissed the cook, who would have been happy to do some work in exchange for a stipend, and from morning to night you engage in inappropriate physical labour which in ordinary life is done by young [peasant] men and women. Really, it would be better and more productive [for you] to live with the children. Of course you will say that this kind of life is in accord with your convictions, and that you are feeling so good [about it]. Well, that's another matter, and I can only say "Enjoy!" — and still be upset that such intellectual forces are wasted in chopping wood, putting on the samovar and sewing boots — which are all very fine as a relaxation and a change of pace, but not [at least for you] as professional activities in themselves.

Tolstoy's acute feeling of social injustice, however, did not afford him the opportunity to ensconce himself in a more sedentary life such as his wife hinted at, or to even think of living out *her* ideal: a life based on mutual affection and attention to bringing up their children in accord with the highest standards, while the husband and father devoted his genius to producing finely crafted fictional works complete with penetrating insight into the psychology of Russian society. But that kind of life, along with writing fiction in general, had become inimical to Tolstoy's natural inclinations. His search for the meaning of life was now dictating to him the necessity of radically changing the life of each individual within his sphere of mental outreach, including his family's and his own.

He summed up this new outlook on existence which he was now letting govern his path in life, as well as its incompatibility with the more traditional views of his wife, in a long, far-ranging letter written over several days in mid-December 1885 (Letter Nº 124). The brief excerpt below will convey something of the scope of his personal dilemma:

> Here's the crux of the matter, after all: this concept that I'm occupied with — perhaps one to which I am called — is an issue of moral teachings. And issues of moral teachings are different from all other subjects in that they cannot change, they can't be relegated to [mere] words, that they cannot be obligatory for one but not obligatory for another. — If one's conscience and reason require — and it has become quite clear to me what conscience and reason require — I cannot avoid doing what conscience and reason require and feel at peace — I cannot look at people associated with my love, people who know what reason and conscience require and refuse to do it, and not suffer. —
>
> No matter which way you turn, I cannot help but suffer! living the life we live.

The fundamental discrepancy in their philosophical views of life only deepened over the decades, notwithstanding that the manifestations of these views in the letters were constantly interspersed with news of friends and family, practical day-to-day activities, and expressions of unchanging, undying love for each other.

Another wave of conflict came to a head in November of 1897, with both underlying positions set forth in plainer and plainer terms. After again acknowledging her husband's claim that

solitude was indispensable to his creativity as a major writer for mankind — a claim, she said, that may be well judged true by future generations — she measured what she deemed his professional criteria for success against a more personal perspective:

> But as an individual, as your wife, I am obliged to make a tremendous effort to admit that whether something is written slightly better or worse, or whether the number of articles you have written is lesser or greater — is more important than my personal life, my love for you, my desire to live with you and find happiness in *this* and not *somewhere else*. (SAT to LNT, 19 November 1897, Letter N° 200)

She also acknowledged that, by this point, she had accustomed herself to not getting bored during his absences. In fact, it even seemed to her at times that "when we are physically apart, we are more together in spirit, while when we come together materially, it is as though we drift emotionally apart" *(ibid.)*.[25] Still, she would have preferred to find a way of living together harmoniously, no matter how faint a possibility that seemed to be ("Stay [at Yasnaya] for as long as it seems necessary and pleasant to you; everything here would be vexing to you, and that is harder than separation" — *ibid.*).

Lev Nikolaevich's reply of a week later (Letter N° 201, 26 November 1897) was equally blunt, flatly rejecting both the notion that his rightful place was alongside his wife as head of the family and her suggestion (inspired by reading a biography of Beethoven) that he might actually be under the influence of a latent desire for fame: "Fame may be the goal of a youngster or a very empty person," he countered. "For a serious person, though, especially an older person, the goal of one's activity is not fame, but the very best use of one's abilities." His dismissal of his wife's reasoning as "patently unfair" and his point-by-point refutation of her claims took this position further:

> First, the question is by no means what is more important; secondly, I am living here not just because some essay might turn out to be a little better written; thirdly, my presence in Moscow, as you very well know, could not prevent either Andrjusha or Misha from living badly, if that's what they want. Not even the strictest father in the world can stop people with full beards from living the way they feel is best; fourthly, even if the question lay in what is more important — [(a)] writing what I write or what I at least think and hope (otherwise I wouldn't [bother to] work [at all]) will be read by millions and may have a good influence on millions [of people], or [(b)] living in Moscow without any purpose there, in vanity, nervously and in poor [moral] health — then anyone would decide the question in favour of not going to Moscow. (LNT to SAT, 26 November 1897, Letter N° 201)

THE EVOLUTION OF A KINDRED AND LOVING RELATIONSHIP

Despite some disagreements, especially concerning breast-feeding — which Lev Nikolaevich insisted on (Sofia Andreevna suffered early from mastitis) — and child-rearing in general, most scholars agree that the first two decades of the couple's married life were marked by a strong attachment and love. The letters from this period are replete with words of love, care and concern for each other's well-being — a theme which runs through their entire correspondence. Each of them waited for the other's letters with great impatience, and even temporary absences seemed to cause torment. This remained largely true despite the worsening

---

25 Lev Nikolaevich himself had earlier recognised (Letter N° 56, 18 June 1878) that he felt a high spiritual love for his wife most strongly when they were apart.

conflict over the years regarding their views on life and Christian teachings (as extensively detailed in previous and subsequent sections).

In the meantime, I would like to give the reader a sample of the expressions of mutual love that persist throughout the five decades of their correspondence; theirs was a love that somehow managed to remain constant and unaffected in their later years by the ever-widening philosophical discrepancy between their world-views, brought about in part by external influences (such as Chertkov and the Tolstoyans). It is a personal closeness which transcended the intellectual and their all-too-frequent physical separation.[26] These expressions are presented in chronological order without additional comment — they speak for themselves.

I suggest you don't stay sitting [all day long], but keep walking around — otherwise (if I dare say it) my absence will make you feel sadder. — I'll still keep writing to you every day, as I'm doing now — even if I have to bring you the letters myself, and you, *please do write...* (*LNT to SAT, 22–23 April 1864, Letter N° 4*)

I find it terribly, terribly difficult [being alone], and I'm both miserable and frightened without you. (*SAT to LNT, 23 April 1864, Letter N° 5*)

But, my sweet Lëva, I constantly feel I want to tell and explain everything to you. Lëvochka, make your letters to me a little longer, if you have the time. Even just a few minutes a day would be happy ones with your obvious participation. Otherwise [my life] feels so empty, so lonely. (*SAT to LNT, 29 July 1865, Letter N° 26*)

...your letters are probably more dangerous to me than all the Greek [writers] because of the excitement they arouse in me. Especially since I receive them suddenly. I can't read them without [breaking into] tears; I'm all a-trembling, and my heart beats [fast]. And you write whatever comes into your head, while for me *every word* is significant; I read all of them over and over. (*LNT to SAT, 16–17 July 1871, Letter N° 42*)

Farewell, darling. I still haven't received any letters from you. I try not to think of you while you're away. Yesterday I went over to your desk and jumped back as though I had burnt my fingers, so as to avoid picturing you so vividly. Same thing at night-time — I don't look at your side [of the bed]. (*LNT to SAT, 16 January 1877, Letter N° 48*)

I'm concerned about you, and think [about you] whenever I'm alone. Only God grant that everything may be safe during our time apart, and I love this feeling of special love, the very highest spiritual love toward you which I feel all the stronger when we're apart. (*LNT to SAT, 18 June 1878, Letter N° 56*)

Farewell, my dear friend. As to how to comfort you, my dove, there's only one thing I can do: love and feel sorry for you, but you don't need that any more. What *do* you need? [I'd like] at least to know. Hugs and kisses to you, and I am hastening to send off this letter. (*SAT to LNT, 3 March 1882, Letter N° 77*)

---

26 Letters signify separation, distance, and absence. The sheer volume of their correspondence (some 1,500 letters in total) suggests at least five years, all told, of prolonged absence from each other.

During this past while (I can't say exactly how long — it's been continuing to grow) you've become especially dear and interesting to me, and *dear* in all respects. It seems a new bond is being forged between us, and I worry terribly that it might break. *(LNT to SAT, 29 September 1883, Letter N° 87)*

I had just sent off my letter [to you] yesterday, dear Lëvochka, when I received yours [dated 23 October 1884]. By some strange coincidence, everything you say to me I not only do not object to, but I myself have been thinking exactly the same thing... *(SAT to LNT, 25 October 1884, Letter N° 102)*

You and I are a lot closer in our letters than in our lives. In a letter we remember everything and write down anything that might be of interest, even just a little, while in life we see little of each other... *(SAT to LNT, 1 May 1888, Letter N° 143)*

For the very first time, dear Lëvochka, you wrote me a letter [dated 7 November] in which I could feel your heart, and I at once felt light and cheerful, as though my whole life were once again turned radiant. You were quite right that none of us should feel angry towards one another, especially us oldsters. We need to treat everything calmly and remember that the basis of our relationship is a solid love for one another, — and that's the main thing. *(SAT to LNT, 9 November 1892, Letter N° 165)*

For God's sake, my dove, don't hold anything in, don't think about others, only of yourself. I would be happy to give up a lot for you, but unfortunately I don't need to give up anything here, since coming to see you will be a joy [for me]. *(LNT to SAT, 2 November 1895, Letter N° 183)*

How was your trip and how are you doing now, my friend? Your arrival left such a strong, cheerful and good impression, too good even for me, since I am missing you [now even] more strongly [than before]. *(LNT to SAT, 12–13 May 1897, Letter N° 197)*

Dear Lëvochka, I have not felt so sorry and sad for a long time at parting from you as on this occasion, apart from that concern about leaving you that is constantly with me. *(SAT to LNT, 28 April 1898, Letter N° 203)*

How are you all doing? How is Il'ja Vasil'evich? How are the snowstorms — has anyone been hurt by them? I hope that you are taking care of yourself. Hugs and kisses to you, my greetings to everyone. *(SAT to LNT, 19 January 1905, Letter N° 219)*

If only you could feel how I love you, how I am willing with my whole being to make any kind of concessions, to do anything to serve you. Lëvochka, forgive me, come back to me, *save* me! Don't think these are all just words, *love* me, take pity [on me] once again in your heart... *(SAT to LNT, 30 October 1910, Letter N° 236)*

Don't think I left because I don't love you. I do love you and I have pity for you with all my heart, but I cannot act in any other way. *(LNT to SAT, 30–31 October 1910, Letter N° 237)*

THE EVOLUTION OF TOLSTOY'S INDEPENDENT RELIGIOUS VIEWS

Despite the many expressions of love reflected in the small sample above, even a number of their early letters show hints of more serious issues to come, notably Tolstaya's tendency towards a certain imbalance, sudden outbursts of emotion, exaggerated fears for her children,

a growing criticism of her husband's absences — all of which become more evident and pronounced following their move to Moscow in September 1881.

Tolstoy, on the other hand, was experiencing ever-increasing anger towards government practices (especially perceived injustice in respect to the peasants and especially following the assassination of Tsar Alexander II in March 1881), as well as towards the traditional conservatism of the Russian Orthodox Church (which in turn had given rise to a proliferation of both domestic and foreign religious sects in Russia). Tolstoy was perplexed by his own dissatisfaction with his station in life, and the burning question of "What is the meaning of life that my inevitable death will not destroy?" This query is echoed by the major characters in his fiction.

As early as 1870 — but, especially after completing *Anna Karenina* — he wrote about "pauses in life", old age and the unavoidable transition called death.[27] There are notable pauses in his diary-keeping, too. From 1850 to 1865 he kept a diary fairly regularly, followed by a pause in this activity while he was working on his two major novels. He resumed in 1878, but there are relatively few entries (except for the years 1881 and 1884) until 1888, when he went back to regular diary-keeping, and continued this activity until his death in 1910. It is particularly noteworthy that relatively few entries were recorded during the years of his spiritual crisis (mid-1870s to early 1880s).[28] This makes the personal letters he wrote during this period all the more critical for study and analysis.

In the nineteenth and twentieth centuries the search for the ideal world was reinforced by Russian Christian and Marxist philosophies, accompanied by an increase in the number of treatises on the subject — utopias and dystopias. By the early nineteenth century the idea of the unity of people had already taken on the status of a prominent objective among Russian philosophers.

Most prominent among the unity promoters, however, were Dostoevsky and Tolstoy. The latter, especially, laid great emphasis on the love of goodness, of the other rather than the self. The supremacy of truth and non-violent resistance to evil, discernible even in his early fiction, grew in intensity throughout his literary works, both fiction and treatises. As early as 1855 his proclamation "to work *consciously* for the unification of people through religion" situated the idea of the unity of people within the spiritual and Christian context.

Tolstoy also read widely in the major Western and Eastern philosophies. In the Christian Scriptures, Jesus's Sermon on the Mount was particularly meaningful to him, inculcating in him the idea that life should be a process of moral self-perfection. His treatise *On Life [O zhizni]* (1886–1888) picked up on the Biblical dictum (I John 4:8) of God as *love*, and on love being the only rational activity, along with the concomitant notion of the fundamental opposition between good and evil.[29]

Christianity and its commandments — above all, the law of universal love — serve to counter the evil enemy forces, particularly the revolutionaries (as depicted also in *Resurrection*) aiming to change the world by violence and largely replace the outward forms of societal existence. From Tolstoy's point of view, there was only one thing needed — a social order based "on free agreement and mutual love" (*To political activists [K politicheskim dejateljam]*, 1903). It was in the name of this love that he protested against the punishment of peasants seeking one thing

---

27 This is especially reflected in his letter to his brother Sergej Nikolaevich of 9–10 November 1875 (L. N. Tolstoj, *Perepiska s sestroj i brat'jami* [L. N. Tolstoy: *Correspondence with his sister and brothers*]).

28 Sofia Andreevna, by contrast, kept her diary quite consistently from 1862 almost until her passing in 1919.

29 In his important religious treatise *V chëm moja vera [What I believe]* (1884), Tolstoy sets forth five 'commandments' in summary of his creed: (1) do not be angry; (2) do not lust; (3) do not curse; (4) do not resist evil with violence; (5) love all people without distinction.

only (albeit a necessity for them) through their "disorders" — land — and he was devastated that peaceful, kind Russian peasants were learning so quickly to "make revolution".

The truths he discovered after *Confession* (which he worked on from 1879 to 1880), in which he talked about his spiritual crisis, not only saved Tolstoy from despair but infused his writing activity with considerable new meaning. His sharp criticism of the anti-Christian structure of society led to a confrontation with authority, with the power of the state, the church, and even his own family. The latter conflict was aroused by his outline for the autobiographical drama *I svet vo t'me svetit [And the light shineth in darkness]* (begun in the 1890s, but not published until 1911, posthumously) — which Tolstoy repeatedly called "my drama" — and resulted in his ultimately leaving Yasnaya Polyana. The play can be seen as a ruthlessly condemning philosophical rebuttal of his own teachings in the person of the protagonist, who is aware of the internal discord that his newly acquired faith brings to both his surroundings and to himself, but who is incapable of altering it in any way. As to his argument with the official church, his falling away from it led in part to a rupture with the majority of his beloved Russian peasantry, who traditionally adhered to Orthodoxy, and eventually to his ex-communication from the Russian Orthodox Church in 1901.

The critical pathos evident in Tolstoy's works strengthened the Protestant, disuniting mood in the country, which was marching irrevocably towards revolution, in spite of the postulate of nonviolent resistance to evil, and the conviction that evil could be conquered not through violence but simply through refusal to participate in evil actions. Hence his ardent support of all sorts of sectarian movements, even while realising the limitations and disuniting tendencies inherent in each of them.

It should be pointed out that Russian sects provided a formal expression for social protest in the context of historical circumstances. While some sects dated from the time of the schism [*raskol*] in the 1650s, many saw the peak of their activity during the late nineteenth century, following the emancipation of the peasants in 1861. Progressive elements in Russian society were unable to find any spiritual connection with the people as a whole — witness the failure of the "going to the people" [*khozhdenie v narod*] movement of the 1870s, which attempted to enlighten the peasantry through various educational projects. But such projects only resulted in widening the gap between the peasants and the upper classes, and caused a feeling of distrust and devastation among the former. This was reflected in a number of literary works of the period, such as Gleb Uspenskij's novel *Vlast' zemli* [The power of land] (1882).

The assassination of Alexander II in 1881 by young radicals marked a hardening of government attitudes towards any kind of protest.[30] Similar repressive measures were taken against the many (from both higher and lower classes) who dared voice their disenchantment with the Russian Orthodox Church and affiliate themselves with one of the foreign Christian preachers who had come to Russia in search of new converts.

It was against this political and social background that Tolstoy, after completing *Anna Karenina*, took his search for meaning in life in new directions. A period of spiritual crisis led to the attainment of a newfound faith, based on a harmonisation of his own views with the simple approach to life he observed on the part of those who tilled the land. This new outlook on life was very much in sympathy with ideas expressed by a number of peasant sectarians (e.g.,

---

30 Tolstoy's urgent plea to Alexander III to pardon the guilty fell upon deaf ears; some of the leaders were promptly executed and this plea brought further suspicion upon Lev Nikolaevich on the part of the authorities, not to mention added concern and anger from Sofia Andreevna.

M. P. Novikov, P. V. Verigin, V. K. Sjutaev, T. M. Bondarev and F. A. Zheltov)[31] in their letters to him — a correspondence that continued until the end of his life. He in turn gave them moral encouragement to persevere in the face of persecution — witness his advice to one Tolstoyan, Prince Dmitrij Khilkov, in the summer of 1896:

> …persecution is not only an inescapable condition of establishing truth, but it is a compulsory condition thereof. Don't be concerned about the friction — if there is no friction, I can tell you right from the start that there will be no progress.[32]

Notwithstanding his affinity with the sectarians[33] and the financial assistance he afforded them, Tolstoy persistently rejected one of their principal tenets, the importance of group identity (i.e., the sense of belonging to their own faith), which inherently signified disunity and separation from those of other faiths. On the contrary, he insisted (both in his correspondence and his works) on subjugating such identity to the overarching concept of the unity of people — that is, all people — which alone could provide a true motive power for the moral and spiritual uplifting of mankind.

Tolstoy was able to encourage his brother Sergej to accept his discovery. On 27 September 1899 he wrote to him:

> This is how I understand the meaning of life: establishing the Kingdom of God on the Earth, i.e., to replace people's violent, cruel and hateful co-existence with a loving and brotherly [co-existence]. The means to this end is one's own self-perfection, i.e., the replacement of one's selfish motives by a loving service to others, as is said in the Gospel, in which is all the law and the prophets; to do unto others as ye would that they should do unto you.[34] And in this I see the meaning of life, I see none higher than this, and I myself am far from consistent in living up to this meaning of life, but I often — and the further from my goal the more often I do it — train myself to live up to it, and the more I accustom myself to this, the more joyful, free and independent of anything external my life becomes, and the less I am afraid of death.[35]

After his so-called spiritual crisis, Tolstoy more or less abandoned his literary-artistic pursuits in favour of proselytising his new-found spiritual ideas. This was done through the publishing house *Posrednik* [The Intermediary] founded in mid-1880s, which enabled him to publish his own stories in large circulation, as well as those by peasants themselves, and to offer his own moral instructions based on Christ's teachings. He did this through folk-dramas and stories such as *The first distiller [Pervyj vinokur]*, *Aggej*, *Peter the Publican [Pëtr Khlebnik]*, *God sees the truth, but waits [Bog pravdu vidit, da ne skoro skazhet]*, *What men live by [Chem ljudi zhivy]*,

---

31 See Bibliography.

32 *PSS* vol. 69, pp. 140–41.

33 One of the most notable examples of Tolstoy's financial aid to Christian sectarians was his channelling of proceeds from the sale of his last major novel, *Resurrection [Voskresenie]*, to support the emigration of the persecuted Doukhobors from the Caucasus to Canada in 1899. For more on this fascinating story, see my 2005 book: *Leo Tolstoy and the Canadian Doukhobors: an historic relationship*, as well as my earlier edition (1998) *Sergej Tolstoy and the Doukhobors: a journey to Canada*.

34 See Matth. 22: 40 and Matth. 7: 12.

35 L. N. Tolstoj, *Perepiska L. N. Tolstogo s sestroj i brat'jami [L. N. Tolstoy's correspondence with his sister and brothers]*, p. 431.

and various treatises. The basic aim of these works was to show how to attain inner freedom and spiritual peace through self-denial, meditations about God, good and evil, along with self-less service to one's neighbour.

SOFIA ANDREEVNA'S REACTION TO LEV NIKOLAEVICH'S PHILOSOPHY

Needless to say, all these pre-occupations and activities placed a strain on the couple's relationship, as well as on the family. After 1881, their increasing spiritual separation was exacerbated by physical distance. Sofia Andreevna moved into their newly purchased house in Denezhnyj Lane in Moscow, not only to better provide for their children's advanced schooling, but also to satisfy her innate desire for the sophisticated urban life she had grown up with. Lev Nikolaevich, as an individual who was repulsed by this same urban life, stayed mainly at their Yasnaya Polyana estate which *he* had grown up with, and which offered a solitude much more conducive to his creative success as a writer, though he did make occasional forays to see his wife and family in Moscow. In either place, the situation was not improved by all-too-frequent visitors, or by Lev Nikolaevich's close association with his disciple Vladimir Chertkov (1854–1936) whom Sofia Andreevna looked upon as her arch enemy. She was particularly vexed and distraught, even threatening suicide, over the issue of her husband's diaries and papers being placed in Chertkov's hands, and she insisted on having them returned.

As late as 26 June 1910, she wrote in her diary (*Dnevniki* II.119):

> My life with Lev Nikolaevich is becoming more unbearable by the day because of his heartlessness and cruelty toward me. And this is all the fault of Chertkov, gradually and consistently over a period of time. He has taken hold of this unfortunate old man any way he can, he has separated us from each other, he has killed the spark of artistry in Lev Nikolaevich and kindled the condemnation, hatred and denial which I have sensed in Lev Nikolaevich's articles these past few years, which he had written under the influence of a stupid evil genius.

Incidentally, the 25-year acquaintance and collaboration between Tolstoy and Chertkov resulted in five volumes of Tolstoy's letters and commentaries in the 90-volume Jubilee Edition of Tolstoy's works — a compulsory read for any study of Tolstoy as a thinker (especially a religious thinker).

Chertkov was a Tolstoyan, a member of group that had taken it upon itself to disseminate its revered teacher's words and to practise the kind of life he preached after 1881: non-violent resistance to evil along with condemnation of governments, official churches, law-courts and prevailing laws on private property. As noted above, while such attitudes and practices served to enhance Tolstoy's popularity among the Russian populace at large, they naturally aroused suspicion and negative reaction on the part of government authorities who were generally quite intolerant towards any contrary views. Their activities soon met with harassment, incarceration and exile.

The extreme views and actions provoked by Tolstoy's ideas in his followers, especially Chertkov, also took a huge negative toll on the mental and physical health of Tolstaya, notably evident in her letters to her husband and to other family members. Her expressions of support for Tolstoy must be weighed against the many aspects of his teachings and activities that troubled her: his insistence on applying his abstract faith to everyday life (which she found impractical and insincere), his denigration of her and of women in general, and especially what she saw as his too-cozy relationship with Vladimir Chertkov and the latter's undue influence on

him (especially after 1883). All of this continued to provoke great dissatisfaction and depression in her, right up to the time of her husband's death in 1910.[36]

One of Lev Nikolaevich's earliest sounding-boards for gaining feedback for his evolving ideas on God and religion was his great aunt Aleksandra Andreevna (Alexandrine) Tolstaja, an extremely refined and intelligent woman, a lady-in-waiting to the Imperial Court, and one of his favourite correspondents.

In a letter to her dated 3 May 1859, he confided that while he was a fervent (Orthodox) believer as a child, in a sentimental, unthinking way, at the age of 14 his thoughts about life brought him face to face with religious tenets which did not fit in logically with his own, more pragmatic view of life. He decided to abandon these in favour of his inner discoveries. He wrote to Alexandrine:

> I found that there is such a thing as immortality, such a thing as love, and that one must live for others to be eternally happy. I was surprised at how close these discoveries were to the Christian religion, and instead of exploring them further on my own, I began to search for them in the Gospels, but found little. I found neither God, nor a Redeemer, nor *sacraments*, nothing at all; but I searched with all, all the powers of my soul, and wept, and tormented myself, and wanted nothing but the truth. For God's sake, don't think that my words could give you even the slightest inkling of the whole force and concentration of my searchings of that period. It's one of the great mysteries of the soul which lies in each of us, but I can say that rarely have I encountered in people such passion for the truth as was at that time in me.[37]

Later, after completing his second major novel, *Anna Karenina*, he felt a renewed urge to align himself with the traditional practices of Russian Orthodoxy. His wife noted in her diary of 25 August 1877:

> A religious spirit is taking firmer and firmer root in him. Just as in his childhood, every day he gives himself to prayer, on holidays he goes to mass, where each time he is surrounded by *muzhiks*, asking about the war; he fasts on Fridays and Wednesdays and keeps talking about the spirit of humility, cutting off and silencing, half-jokingly, those who would condemn others. On the 26th of July he took a trip to Optina-Pustyn' [Monastery] and was delighted at the wisdom, education and life of the elder monks there.[38]

Tolstoy's occasional visits to the monastery, however, were not enough to appease his hunger for intellectual answers and bring him spiritual peace. He set about reading Joseph Ernest Renan's *Vie de Jésus* (1863), as well as David Friedrich Strauss's *Der alte und der neue Glaube [The old faith and the new]* (1873). In a commentary to Tolstoy's correspondence with Aleksandra Andreevna Tolstaja, biographer Natal'ja Ivanovna Azarova sums up his search as follows:

---

36 It is noteworthy that no comprehensive study has been made to date of SAT's editions of her husband's works. A substantive article (if not a book), would be a welcome contribution to Tolstoy scholarship. The interested reader is referred, for starters, to Gudzij & Zhdanov 1953; Nikiforova 2004; the articles "Tvorcheskaja istorija povesti «Kholstomer»" [The creative history of the narrative *The Strider*] in Gromova-Opul'skaja 2005: 76–92, and "Nekotorye itogi tekstologicheskoj raboty nad «Polnym sobraniem sochinenij L. N. Tolstogo»" [Some results of a textological study of L. N. Tolstoy's *Complete Collected Works*], *ibid.*: 277–320.

37 *L. N. Tolstoj i A. A. Tolstaja: Perepiska [Correspondence] (1857–1903)*, pp. 158–59.

38 S. A. Tolstaja, *Dnevniki [Diaries]*, I.503.

The truth which he sought for so long and tormentingly was revealed to him in Christ's words to a disciple: "Leave all, and follow me".[39] The desire to forsake the world's glory, hiding in the depths of his heart, became his leitmotif: to live in a Godlike manner meant distancing himself from all the earthly vanities that had tempted him before, cutting himself off from the life of people of his circle, as Tolstoy would later write in *A confession [Ispoved']*.

Tolstoy's way of seeing his surroundings changed. He became impatient towards those who had gone astray, expressing condemnation and even indignation. He beheld, in historical Christianity, evil intent on the part of church officials and came down with passionate fury on those who represented for him the falsehood and deceit of the church.

He began a tremendous undertaking — translating the Gospel texts afresh from the Greek, merging them into a single whole, free from superstition and, as it seemed to him, more understandable to the common people. His goal was to establish a practical religion — a set of ethical teachings based on Christ's Sermon on the Mount. In working on harmonising the Gospel texts, he dispensed with everything irrational constituting the living heart of religion: miracles, the divinity of the Christ, the Trinity of the Godhead, the redeeming sacrifice of the Saviour for the sins of humanity. Not comfort and compassion, but self-perfection was emphasised in his revised teachings. Tolstoy called his treatise *Harmony and translation of the four Gospels [Soedinenie i perevod chetyrëkh Evangelij]*. During the process he experienced such rapture over the revelation that he felt he really had attained that pure Christian religion he had dreamt about as a child, and passionately desired to preach it.[40]

As hinted at earlier, all of this lay heavily on Sofia Andreevna. It is not that she was overly set in her religious beliefs, but she had been brought up in Russian Orthodox ways and practices. She observed religious holidays, fasted, attended church services, took part in communion and genuinely desired to impart Christian values to her children — values which their father increasingly condemned in his writing. Witness her comments in *My Life* (VI.62), in which she made clear her disapproval of his harsh tone in his philosophical writings:

> His book *A criticism of dogmatic theology [Issledovanie dogmaticheskogo bogoslovija]* was written in such a sharp manner that for the very first time I refused to transcribe one of Lev Nikolaevich's works. I was simply bothered by his cursings and railings at everything I was accustomed to hold dear. And in any case I did not understand philosophy in the form of coarse disgruntlement. A philosopher should lay out his thoughts calmly, concisely and wisely.
>
> I recall gathering all the sheets together, bringing them to my husband and declaring that I would no longer do any transcribing for him, that I did not relish criticising him, but it was impossible for me not to criticise this *Criticism of dogmatic theology*. Subsequently Lev Nikolaevich significantly softened his sharpness of expression in this book.

Sofia Andreevna's reaction to her husband's change of literary direction from fiction to philosophical treatise was more than simply a personal antipathy to his new ideas and his less-than-compassionate manner of expressing them. She was concerned that they could actually be harmful — to the Russian reading public of the time, ultimately, but first and foremost to her own children. In a touching letter dated 3 April 1902 to Aleksandra Andreevna Tolstaja, she wrote:

---

39 See, for example, Luke 18: 22.
40 *L. N. Tolstoj i A. A. Tolstaja: Perepiska [Correspondence] (1857–1903)*, p. 667.

To change his spiritual mindset, of course, is impossible. And I often think that perhaps he *has* gone higher and farther than us, and that his approach to God and the next life is clearer than ours. In our approach to spiritual questions there is more tenderness and humility, while in his, perhaps, there is more understanding and elevation, which is not given to me as an ordinary woman to understand.

Most of all I fear for the children. Their father has turned them utterly into unbelievers. Let alone the older ones, he has completely ruined Sasha[41] for me: without having lived any spiritual life whatsoever, she has jumped right away into scepticism and denial. The other day we were travelling with her to Yalta and along the journey I tried to instil the truth in her and point out the errors of her ways. I told her that her father had come through [periods of] both faith in the Church and struggle [against it], that he had read all the sages and the Holy Fathers, and the tenets of all kinds of faiths — and come to his own special, personal, spiritual state of mind. Sasha, by contrast, had read nothing, did little in the way of thinking, engaged in no struggles at all, quit the Church and was left hanging. Her stubbornness and character are inflexible, and I am powerless in the face of her father's iron influence.

CHILDREN IN THE TOLSTOY-TOLSTAYA CORRESPONDENCE

Indeed, much in the couple's correspondence is devoted to their children, whom Lev Nikolaevich accepted on a formal level as a focus of his family duties; for Sofia Andreevna, throughout most of her marriage, they practically constituted the raison d'être of her earthly existence. Naturally, they were *little* children at first, and Sofia Andreevna's detailed description of their early development bubbled over with all the pride and concerns of any new mother. On 22 November 1864 (Letter № 10) she wrote her husband in regard to her first two:

The girl [Tanja] has been quite rebellious, while the boy [Serëzha] has lately been having severe diarrhœa — six times already, though he has been sleeping very well at night. Perhaps it's for the better, but still there's a lot of grief. There's a blush of smallpox starting, but I'm not afraid of smallpox. That's my report on your own children, I've nothing more to say about them.

But even after that uncompromising statement she could not resist a further note of exuberance: "Now they're sleeping like little cherubs…"

By and by new children's names appeared in the letters. The family was growing and expanding. We see a woman involved in child-raising as well as running a household, completely absorbed in her husband and offspring. In Letter № 12 (25 November 1864), she spoke about the downstairs (where the children's rooms were located): "this is my realm, my children, my activities and my life" and later added: "I don't feel like going anywhere outside the nursery".

Lev Nikolaevich, on the other hand, was more ambivalent regarding his parental role. As early as 1 December 1864 (Letter № 16) he wrote his wife:

Along with you and the children (though I still feel my love for them is not very strong) I have a constant love and care for my writing. If I didn't have that, I feel I could definitely not last a day without you, and you understand correctly: writing is to me what the children are no doubt to you.

And ten days later, on 11 December (Letter № 22) he added a clarification of sorts: "Don't say or think that I don't love them… It's just that I don't love them to the same degree that I love you."

---

41 *Sasha* — the Tolstoys' youngest daughter, Aleksandra L'vovna Tolstaja (1884–1979).

As time went on, Lev Nikolaevich found himself increasingly indulging in the solitude he craved for his first love — that is, his writing career — and spending less and less time with his wife and children. The degree of mental and physical separation between father and family was exacerbated by two major factors: (1) the spiritual crisis Tolstoy experienced, particularly at the beginning of the 1880s (in January 1881 Tolstaya noted in her autobiographical memoir *My Life* [III.73] that her husband's obsession with studying the Gospels had made him "oblivious of life"); and (2) the family's decision to purchase a second house in Moscow (the Arnautov house in Khamovniki Lane) where Sofia Andreevna would live with her children to expose them to a broader range of educational opportunities, while Lev Nikolaevich would continue to spend most of his time in the solitude of Yasnaya Polyana. But this second circumstance, in the very act of driving husband and family apart, also had an unanticipated benefit: it meant that far more of their marital dialogue would be preserved for history through whole archives of written correspondence.

It becomes increasingly apparent from the letters that Tolstoy's much-coveted solitude equalled much-dreaded loneliness for Tolstaya, associated with her growing neurotic troubles. Amid all the purely informative statements about their day-to-day activities in their respective homes — reports on the children's health, on their own health, on the children's upbringing and education, on problems with the children's tutors, governesses and household staff — is sprinkled a liberal dose of disappointments, regrets, accusations and self-justifications. Paramount among these is Sofia Andreevna's oft-expressed feeling that her husband saw good and evil only in the abstract, through the idealism of his writings; she felt he had not the slightest regard for why or how this should be expressed, first and foremost in practical terms within his own family. He in turn saw his fatherly duty from a diametrically opposite point of view. In an extended letter (No 124) dated 15–18 December 1885, he presented his wife with a carefully considered outline of how he perceived the discrepancy in their views on child-raising and education. It is worth quoting a few excerpts here:

> … what I consider good, I consider as such not for myself, but for others and especially for my children.…what you were preparing for them in the form of a refined education with French and English governors and governesses, with music, etc., were temptations of vainglory, exalting one's self over others — [this was] a millstone which we ourselves had placed around our necks.…
>
> Life passed by me. And sometimes (you were wrong about this), you called upon me to participate in this life, you made demands on me, you reproached me for not involving myself in money matters or in the bringing up of our children, as though I were capable of handling money matters, [as though I were capable of] increasing or preserving [our] wealth, so as to increase and preserve the very evil which, in my view, was causing my children to ruin themselves. As though I could involve myself in an upbringing based on pride — isolating one's self from people, secular education and academic degrees, which were identical with what I associated with people's downfall! You, along with our growing children, were moving farther and farther in one direction, and I in quite another. Thus years passed — one year, two years, five years. The children grew, [you] spoilt them as [you] raised them, while the two of us kept growing farther and farther apart, and my situation became more false, more difficult.

A week or so later, Sofia Andreevna countered with her own impression of her children (Letter No 127, 23 December 1885): "I am grateful that my children trust me. And I shall justify their trust, as now that's the only thing I have left."

Lev Nikolaevich's sons (especially Lev L'vovich) tended to be very critical of their father's new ideas. He in turn was critical of what he considered the empty and dissolute lives led by several of his sons (witness the above quotation), Andrej and Mikhail in particular, though, in terms of views on life, he experienced the greatest disagreements with Sergej and Lev.

His daughters, on the other hand, were more supportive and generally took his side. However, he felt quite possessive, jealous and perturbed when they decided to leave home to get married. It is noteworthy that upon his final departure at the end of October 1910, he chose to reveal his whereabouts only to his youngest daughter, Aleksandra (Sasha), and made her promise not to share this information with his wife.

CRITICISM OF TOLSTOY'S IDEAS FROM FAMILY AND FRIENDS

While the attacks on Tolstoy's ideas from official sources (the government and the church) may have been harsh, the writer might well have expected this from those he considered his enemies, and he was able to bear them more or less in stride. Criticism from people close to him — his wife, his children, other family members and dear friends — was actually more hurtful, and he took it more personally.

In addition to personal opposition from his sons, one of the earliest critical responses after his 1880s conversion had come from his great-aunt confidante, Aleksandra Andreevna (Alexandrine) Tolstaja, to whom, as we have already seen, Sofia Andreevna eventually confessed her own misgivings some twenty years later. In a letter to Sofia Andreevna dated 19 July 1882 she gave a rather insightful summary of Lev Nikolaevich's new religious outlook, as follows:

Quite possibly I'm mistaken, but it seems to me sometimes that it is from this exclusive standpoint of belief that Lëvochka [i.e., Lev Nikolaevich] has proceeded step by step to rejecting and breaking no longer just human opinion, but the very Word of God, when it runs counter to his convictions. He has indeed searched for God, but with no humility, and found only *himself*, i.e., some kind of new and distorted code he has thought up himself and which he cherishes and *takes pride in*, precisely because he worked it out himself. This was all done with his usual sincerity (I have no doubt), but without wisdom and without simplicity, and left on him a trace of that anxiety, irritation and moral emptiness that struck me during our visit together in Moscow. I could find in him not a hint of spiritual or mental peace, or more patience, intrinsically and mathematically associated with genuine love or truth. That is why I felt right from the very first time that this was not the truth. The truth is so attractive in itself that the heart accepts it involuntarily, before any rationalisation occurs, but there was nothing like that going on here. In the tempest of Lëvochka's words, in his wild indignation and condemnation of anything that does not fit into his system, I could find nothing comparable to the meekness of Christ, in Whose name he writes and preaches. Darling *Sophie*, you as a woman will catch another feeling I have had. I have felt hurt and ashamed that I did not bring with me from Moscow a single ray of cheer, all the while remembering practically the only long conversation I had with Dostoevsky a week before he died; up until then my heart was swelling and my spirits were being lifted. Dostoevsky was aflame with love for people, as is Lëvochka, but somehow on a broader scale, without limitations, without material details and all those trifles which Lëvochka gives pride of place to. When Dostoevsky spoke of Christ, you could feel that genuine sense of brotherhood which unites us all in one Saviour. I can never forget the expression on his face, nor his words, and I began to understand the tremendous influence that he had on everyone without exception, even on those who were unable to fully understand him. He didn't take

anything away from anyone, but the spirit of his truth animated everyone. — This is what I dream about for our Lëvochka when he stops sitting in his Tower of Babel.

A few years later a similar criticism was voiced by Tolstoy's close friend and literary associate Nikolaj Nikolaevich Strakhov in correspondence with a mutual acquaintance Ivan Sergeevich Aksakov. First, in a letter written 12 December 1884, he declared that "Everything Tolstoy writes concerning his subjective interpretation of Christianity is *very poorly written*."[42] Then, on 17 May 1885, this letter:

> On holiday here in Mshatka I read over the whole *Gospel in brief* with complete attention (and comparison with the [Scriptural] text) and, I must confess, despite my usual position regarding Lev Nikolaevich Tolstoy, I was astounded at the utter hideousness of the writing. It had seemed to me that he would have clung even closer here to his own translation of the Gospel text — the translation I am familiar with, which he keeps at Yasnaya Polyana. As it turned out, his *Gospel in brief* goes beyond all bounds in its departure from the text — it is not even a translation but some kind of paraphrase, just like the content summaries at the beginning of each chapter [of the Gospels]. The whole thing gives the appearance of distortion and deception. These utterly gratuitous departures, by their sheer numbers, take away from those places where there is no departure from the actual text but only from the generally accepted translations, which are indeed precise and significant.
>
> The language is unrestrained, uneven, and sometimes unnecessarily crude. [...]
>
> Then, in the dogmatic sense, of course, he is a huge heretic; in terms of practical teachings he is a Quaker and in terms of the metaphysical he's a Unitarian.[43]

Strakhov didn't shy away from expressing such criticisms directly to Tolstoy, rejecting the latter's unreasonable Christian demands on people's lives and thought patterns, even while he continued to have nothing but admiration for the acknowledged level of artistry shown in his earlier fiction works. A decade later, on 29 October 1894, he wrote to his friend:

> Now I am surprised at how often you forget that people have certain insurmountable needs. "Human affairs must yield to God's," you write, "in matters of everyone's personal life." Oh, without a doubt! You hold on to the true path — the path of personal self-perfection — and the correctness of your steps has always excited me. But you don't realise just how absorbed you are in your inner work and you ask people to do what they are not capable of taking on. *The rejection of all personal will* — that's what it all amounts to; but this rejection is a renunciation of life, and people can't renounce life. Life requires calm, fixed forms, it requires space for one's desires, it requires labour and rest, fun and excitement… and that is something you know perfectly well — you have said it in all your writings.[44]

A final example of criticism from friendly quarters may be found in the memoir of Tolstoy's last private secretary, Valentin Fëdorovich Bulgakov, which he appropriately entitled: *Disputing with Tolstoy [V spore s Tolstym]* (see esp. pp. 6–7). He was particularly sceptical of Tolstoy's

---

42 M. I. Shcherbakova, *I. S. Aksakov — N. N. Strakhov: Perepiska / Ivan Aksakov — Nikolaj Strakhov: Correspondence* (2007): 119–21.
43 *Ibid.*, pp. 134–37.
44 *L. N. Tolstoj — N. N. Strakhov: Polnoe sobranie perepiski / Leo Tolstoy & Nikolaj Strakhov: Complete correspondence*, vol. II, pp. 969–70.

exaggeration of the need for spiritual self-perfection and the emphasis on this aspect of life at the expense of man's material needs — a doctrine he viewed as a deplorable estrangement of the human personality from its firm earthly roots. He took issue with Tolstoy's position that evil was confined within the individual, suggesting instead that more serious attention be paid to the negative pressure exerted by problems in the individual's environment and society at large. In contrast with his employer, he believed that the state indeed had a role in keeping the perverse actions of its citizens in check, since anarchy against the state posed an equal if not greater danger to social well-being. Near the beginning of Part 1, Chapter 2, of *Disputing with Tolstoy* (p. 33), Bulgakov wrote:

> One can demand a harnessing of the spirit and call upon it to hold sway over the corporeal element in our lives, but one cannot maintain, as do Lev Nikolaevich Tolstoy and his disciple, the philosopher Pëtr Petrovich Nikolaev, that there exists *only* the spiritual (!), and that the corporeal is scarcely more than the product of our imagination. All of this betrays a measure of disrespect not only for man, but for the existing world order which is quite independent of our will.

Bulgakov insisted that, in the nature of all living things, the spiritual and corporeal do not exist independently of each other. They only represent two aspects of the same phenomenon. From this perspective, one cannot focus one's educational endeavours on the spiritual and neglect the corporeal. Only the development of the spiritual and material in harmony leads to the ideal embodiment of man.

TOLSTAYA AS TOLSTOY'S ADVOCATE

Despite her antipathy towards her husband's interpretation of Christian teachings, as Tolstoy's wife she was sometimes (reluctantly) pressed into service to defend those very teachings or at least their consequences in terms of the Russian legal system. A case in point was a young man named Aleksej Petrovich Zaljubovskij, who, influenced by Tolstoy's ideas of non-violence, refused to be conscripted into the armed forces and was imprisoned as a result. In a letter to Tolstaya dated 20 November 1885 (Letter N° 120) he enlisted (albeit with an apology: "I'm afraid … that you will get upset with me for piling this matter on top of you") her participation in a campaign to free the young man, and three days later she responded with an outline of what she was willing to contribute. But the tone of her reply and the reservations evident therein are especially significant:

> The only thing I can do — and will do — is to go and petition the war minister [Pëtr Semënovich Vannovskij], while Birjukov will go ask [the Governor-General of Moscow] Grand Prince Sergej Aleksandrovich. — It is difficult for me as your wife, as I am petitioning for the release of your works, to [also] petition for someone who has accepted these teachings. When I think of *what* I shall say to the minister or to whomever I ask, the only thing that comes to me is that I am asking because I have been requested to, and it is painful for me that this young man's convictions, which are probably derived from your teachings of Christ, have not led to any good — i.e., not to the result *you* intended, but to the young man's demise, and that is why I am asking to mitigate his fate. (*SAT to LNT, 23 November 1885, Letter N° 123*)

On several occasions Tolstaya advocated on her husband's behalf in publishing some of his more controversial works, despite her own disagreement with their underlying message. When

The Kreutzer Sonata was banned by the authorities, she went to St. Petersburg in April 1891 and, in a private audience with Tsar Alexander III, won not only a lifting of the ban for publication in Tolstoy's *Complete Collected Works*, but also the Tsar's promise that he alone would be the arbiter of censorship in respect to Tolstoy's future works published by Tolstaya.[45] Tolstaya hoped that her public advocacy for the uncensored release of *The Kreutzer Sonata* would deflect any mistaken impression that its heroine could in any way be identified with her person or her family.

There were a few causes in which not only Sofia Andreevna, but also their sons and daughters, shared Tolstoy's enthusiasm. During the winters of 1891–92 and 1892–93 there was widespread famine in Rjazan' and Samara Gubernias, and Lev Nikolaevich, together with his daughters, his son Lëva and a scattering of his Tolstoyan followers, headed out to both regions to organise soup-kitchens for the famine victims and take other practical measures to alleviate their suffering. Each time, Tolstaya was apparently as moved by the disaster as her husband. She was not content to sit at home, inactive, during these periods. She took it upon herself to organise a publicity campaign — first through personal contact among her wealthy social acquaintances and then, through the newspapers, among the public at large — to raise funds for the actual foodstuffs and equipment needed to establish and maintain the soup-kitchens which had been set up at her husband's initiative.

Her first step was to send Tolstoy's own description ("A frightful question") of the scope of the tragedy to the press, as she confirmed in her letter to him of 4 November 1891 (Nº 157). Here, too, we learn that the editor of *Russkie vedomosti*, Vasilij Mikhajlovich Sobolevskij, considered these articles so important that he decided to come to see Tolstaya the next day with the text already typeset and ready to proofread.

However, her very next sentence in the same letter includes the query: "Did you read my letter to the editor in *Russkie vedomosti* dated 3 November? In just twenty-four hours it brought me in around 1,500 roubles." Her only question at that point pertained to where the collected funds should be sent. She then proceeded to recount several touching stories about her personal contact with various donors of money and clothing, which brought her as an individual right to the heart of the hunger relief efforts.

Indeed, Tolstoy and the famine victims were not the only beneficiaries of Tolstaya's charitable campaign. As is evidenced by the aforementioned accounts, participating in a social activity of her husband's which she could finally agree with reinvigorated her with a renewed sense of purpose, and helped improve both her mental and physical health. A whole new tone is apparent in the subsequent part of her 4 November letter:

> I don't know how all of you will look at my actions. But I find it tiresome just sitting by without participating in your efforts, and since yesterday I even feel my health has improved; I record [all my transactions] in a notebook, make out receipts, express my thanks, talk with the public, and I am glad that I can help in the expansion of your cause, even if it is through other people's donations.

45 SAT's specific request to the Tsar took this form: "Your Majesty, if my husband should again write in the belletristic genre and I publish his works, it would give me the greatest happiness if the fate of his writings were to be decided by the personal will of Your Majesty." To which the Tsar replied: "I shall be most happy to do so. Send his writings directly to my attention." (*My Life*, v.93). One is perforce reminded of the maxim (attributed by some to Voltaire, by others to English author Evelyn Beatrice Hall): "I wholly disagree with what you say, but will defend to the death your right to say it."

The dialogue on the famine situation and Tolstaya's contribution to its relief continues through a number of subsequent exchanges (Letters № 158–163).

One other point deserves particular mention under the topic of Tolstaya's advocacy of her husband's literary career, despite her personal opposition to most of his post-1881 ideas. When Tolstoy was formally ex-communicated by the Holy Synod of the Russian Orthodox Church in February 1901, she immediately launched a vehement protest against this move in the Russian press of the day, writing that "My sorrow and displeasure [at this decision] know no bounds."[46]

The complete text of Tolstaya's letter to Konstantin Petrovich Pobedonostsev, Senior Procurator of the Russian Orthodox Church, was first published in the Russian Orthodox paper *Tserkovnye vedomosti* [Church Gazette] (which had published the original ex-communication decree) on 25 March 1901. But from there, as she writes in *My Life* (VIII.16), "that letter of mine practically flew around the world. It was translated into all sorts of languages, and garnered flattering reviews of my action and praise for my boldness...." She further claimed that Tolstoy's own *Reply to the Synod [Otvet Sinodu]*, completed 4 April 1901 (PSS 34:245–53), "didn't resonate with the same effect as my impromptu action of a woman defending her husband, which took everyone by surprise". However, in her next edition of Tolstoy's *Complete Collected Works*, she included an article he had written on 15 March 1901 entitled *To the Tsar and his associates [Tsarju i ego pomoshchnikam]*, giving "all sorts of advice and directives as to how to govern Russia". This article was subsequently removed from the twelfth edition by the censors.

TOLSTAYA'S ANNOTATIONS TO HER HUSBAND'S LETTERS

No matter the depth of her personal feelings for Lev Nikolaevich as a husband and a human being, or the extent of her strongly felt opposition to his post-1880 interpretation of Christian teachings, there were times when she could not help but approach his writings, including their 48-year correspondence, through the lens of an editor with an eye on the future history of world literature. Only a few years after his passing, she hastened to publish his letters to her and append hundreds of her own editorial annotations.

The first edition, published in 1913, comprised 656 letters in chronological order, while the second edition of 1915 added seven additional letters. It was entitled *Pis'ma grafa L. N. Tolstogo k zhene, 1862–1910 [Letters of Count L. N. Tolstoy to his wife, 1862–1910]*.

In her preface to the first edition she offered this explanation for the timing:

> Before I leave this life to join my beloved in the spiritual realm to which he has departed, I should like to share with those who love and admire him something he gave me that is very dear to me, namely his letters to me, including details of our conjugal life of forty-eight years together, which was happy almost to the very end...
>
> I was prompted to publish these letters, too, by my concern that after my death, which is probably not far off, people will (as usual) misinterpret and write falsely about our mutual husband-wife relationship. So let them find interest in and base their judgements on true and living sources, and not on conjecture, gossip and invention.
>
> And may they look with compassion on someone who took upon her delicate shoulders something she was possibly not quite ready for at such an early age, namely, the task of being the spouse of a genius and a great man.

---

46 From the text of SAT's letter, reproduced in *My Life*, VIII.16.

One particular copy of the second edition preserved in the Yasnaya Polyana archives is, in fact, a dismantled printer's copy, with a fresh sheet of paper inserted between each page by Sofia Andreevna herself, containing her annotations or commentaries. She began these in January 1919 and continued work on them up to her death in November of that year.

The annotations can be arbitrarily categorised by their themes, listed here in order of importance:

1. Clarifications (apart from proper names)
2. Tolstoy's works
3. Famine relief efforts (1891–93)
4. Friends and acquaintances
5. Personalities (including authors, musicians, artists and government officials)
6. Relatives (both close and distant)
7. Teachers (tutors to the Behrs and the Tolstoy families)
8. Servants (managers and general staff)
9. Peasants (especially those on the Yasnaya Polyana estate)
10. Animals
11. Places (commentaries on geographical place-names)

Some of these are worth noting in particular, as they may serve as a final clarification to the overall relationship reflected in this correspondence. One example is Lev Nikolaevich's letter (№ 88) of 30 September 1883, in which he wrote: "Both [your recent letters] indicate to me that you are in that same lovely good spirit which I left you in, and which you've been in, with minor interruptions, for a long time." On the very same date, Sofia Andreevna notes, in her first commentary concerning their philosophical disagreements, "There was no time to think about how to live better. Life had drained all my strength, and this was not something Lev Nikolaevich wanted."[47]

A FEW CONCLUDING THOUGHTS

Two lives. Two independently minded souls, who were as fervently kindred in love as they were fiercely independent in world-view. No matter how strong the bonds of the soul and heart, they were driven apart mentally and physically as they increasingly felt the need to claim their own solitudes in their individual places of residence. Yet they remained deeply bound by an undeniable affection for each other. Indeed, as Tolstaya herself recognised in her letter (№ 200) of 19 November 1897, the closer their relationship of personal intimacy approached the everyday, mundane world of family and society, the more it was threatened to be torn asunder by the ever-widening gulf between Sofia Andreevna's realism and Lev Nikolaevich's idealism. It was a gulf between differing perceptions of the social mores that had been evolving through the Russian upper classes for centuries — between the 'Tolstayas' who accepted them more or less unquestioningly, and the 'Tolstoys' who, with apparently good reason, were beginning to question their legitimacy.

47 With the exception of a brief note by Tat'jana Komarova — see: T. V. Komarova, "Pometki S. A. Tolstoj na jasnopoljanskom èkzempljare *Pisem grafa L. N. Tolstogo k zhene 1862–1910 gg.*" [SAT's annotations on the Yasnaya Polyana copy of *LNT's letters to his wife 1862–1910*], *Jasnopoljanskij sbornik 1998* (Tula, 1999): 155–58 — these annotations have not been subject to detailed study and analysis. This will constitute part of my investigation into the above-mentioned multi-volume complete correspondence which I am currently engaged in.

Hence the dialogue set forth in this book is much more than a routine exchange of letters between two members of the same family, though the dialogue between practicality and idealism is certainly not unique to this particular couple. What makes it unique and of publishable interest more than a century after its occurrence is twofold. First, there is the fact that the dialogue was carried on between two extremely artistically gifted and intelligent thinkers, both of whom could be described as writers in their own right. Second, this dialogue continued for almost fifty years, not in spontaneous unrecorded oral conversations where words vanish the moment they escape the participants' short-term memories, but in meticulously recorded thought-traces in pen and ink, where each sentence could be parsed and pondered by the respective interlocutors. Through the magic of annotation, translation and publishing, this possibility is now open to thousands of readers in faraway lands and future centuries, many of whom would not have been able to understand the original conversations had they been present.

It is curious — some might even say ironic — that the physical distance that increasingly separated Tolstoy and Tolstaya during their lifetimes became the catalyst for the couple exchanging their thoughts on paper rather than in person. As a result, their exchange was made accessible to a far broader circle of onlookers than those who happened to be within range of their voices at the time.

It is truly a dialogue for the ages, a dialogue across both time and space.

PART I

LETTERS 1862–1879

INTRODUCTION TO LETTERS, PART I

The story narrated in the first part of the correspondence covers two decades: the 1860s and 1870s — very important years in the life of the newly formed Tolstoy family, which happened to coincide with the apogee of Leo Tolstoy's creative activity. At the same time the Russian Empire was undergoing significant social, political and cultural transformations.

The Tolstoys spent most of the time on their Yasnaya Polyana estate, taking occasional trips to Moscow and later to the Bashkir Volga region. It never occurred to Lev Nikolaevich to show the larger world to his wife, whose time was divided between taking care of their growing family, assisting him in running the estate as well as in the creation of his literary works.

It was during the first two decades of their marriage that Tolstoy wrote his two greatest novels: *War and Peace* [*Vojna i mir*] (1863–1869) and *Anna Karenina* (1873–1877). In between, when his artistic genius needed some rest through a change of activity, he revived his old passion for teaching and, with significant input from Tolstaya, prepared the first edition of his *Primer* [*Azbuka*].

During the 1870s, he also attempted to clarify for himself the essence of philosophy, religion and science as "three ways" of pursuing a greater, unifying "truth about the world" that he had always genuinely sought and was now seeking with even greater urgency. Finding significant flaws in all three "ways", he reasoned himself into a desperate moral and philosophical quagmire, which, by the end of the 1870s, resulted in his well-known spiritual crisis.

This bursting intellectual and busy family life in Yasnaya Polyana may have been physically remote but was never completely shielded from the mainstream of external events. During the reign of Emperor Alexander II (1855–1881), Russia lived through a period of profound political and social reforms. The most prominent of these was the 1861 emancipation of peasant serfs from their master-owners, although the failure to provide them with land to call their own meant a significant degree of continuing subordination. Other reforms dealt with finances (1863), education (1863, 1871), local administration (1864 in the countryside, 1870 in the cities), the legal system (1864), transportation (1865) and the military (1874). In the meantime, the empire celebrated the Russian 'Millennium' (1862), concluded its conquest of the Caucasus (1864), began encroaching on Central Asian territories (1865), suppressed a major Polish uprising (1863–64) and won yet another Russo-Turkish war (1877–78).

The upheaval associated with these events agitated, perplexed and greatly perturbed many sectors of Russian society. It gave rise on the one hand to significant conservative resistance to reforms in general and, on the other, to heightened expectations of social progress, even to extreme revolutionary ideas. The latter were seen notably in the populist movement of *khozhdenie v narod* [going to the people], which began in the early 1860s and peaked in 1874, and its transformation into terrorist activities, including numerous attempts on the life of the Emperor (beginning in 1866).

The fermentation of reforms also made itself felt in Russian cultural development. The 1860s, for example, saw the emergence in St. Petersburg of the *Moguchaja kuchka* [Mighty Five] — a group of five composers (Mily Balakirev, Alexander Borodin, César Cui, Modest Mussorgsky and Nikolai Rimsky-Korsakov), who created new patterns in Russian classical music. At the same time Russian art witnessed the rise of its own, and much larger, ground-breaking group, the *Peredvizhniki* [Itinerants] (including Pavel Brullov, Ivan Kramskoi, Isaac Levitan and Ilya Repin).

These two decades were especially noteworthy for the rise in prominence of Russian literature. Apart from Tolstoy himself, those best known in the West were Ivan Turgenev with works like *Fathers and Sons* [*Ottsy i deti*] (1862) and *Virgin Soil* [*Nov'*] (1877), and Fyodor Dostoevsky

with his *Crime and Punishment [Prestuplenie i nakazanie]* (1866) and *The Brothers Karamazov [Brat'ja Karamazovy]* (1879–80). Other writers of the period included Ivan Goncharov, Nikolai Leskov and Alexander Ostrovsky. In the end, Tolstoy, Dostoevsky and Turgenev rose to prominence during this time and established themselves as uncontested stars on the Russian and world literary scene.

Nº 1 – SOFIA ANDREEVNA TOLSTAYA ✍ LEV NIKOLAEVICH TOLSTOY

[LSA 1]

[28 August 1862. Pokrovskoe-Streshnevo][1]

If I were the Empress,[2] I would honour your birthday[3] with a most gracious Imperial rescript. As a mere mortal, however, I can only congratulate you for making your appearance in God's world one fine day, and I hope that for many more days to come — for ever, if that be possible — you will continue to see it through the same eyes as you do now.

Sonja

Nº 2 – LEV NIKOLAEVICH TOLSTOY ✍ SOFIA ANDREEVNA TOLSTAYA

[PSS 83/2]

14 September 1862. Moscow.

Sofia Andreevna!

It's becoming simply unbearable for me. Three weeks have passed, and every day I tell myself: it's time to let everything out, and walk away with the same longing, fear and happiness in my soul. And every night, as at this moment, I am constantly going over the past, torturing myself and telling myself: why didn't I say it, how should I say it, and what should I say? I'm carrying this letter around with me to give to you, in case it should happen again that I'm not able, or can't muster up the courage, to tell you everything in person.

Your family's false opinion of me, as I see it, comes down to their belief that I'm in love with your sister, Liza.[4] *That's uncalled for. Your story[5] has become ingrained in my head,* since, in reading it, I became convinced that, Dublitsky[6] that I am, I'm forbidden to dream of happiness…

1   *Pokrovskoe-Streshnevo (Pokrovskoe)* — dacha community north-west of Moscow, where for many years Sofia's father Andrej Evstaf'evich Behrs rented a dacha; it was here on 22 August 1844 that Sofia Andreevna Behrs — later Sofia Andreevna Tolstaya (SAT) was born. See List of Russian Geographical Names at the beginning of this volume for place-names not explained in a footnote.

2   See Sofia's musings in *My Life* (I.39):
"I recall once we were all having fun and in a rather playful mood. I kept repeating the same silly line over and over: 'When I am Empress, I shall do such-and-such', or 'When I am Empress, I shall issue an order to…'

Near the balcony stood my father's cabriolet, from which the horses had just been unharnessed. I took a seat in the cabriolet and cried:
'When I am Empress, I shall ride in a cabriolet such as this!'
Lev Nikolaevich grasped hold of the shaft and, taking the place of the horse, began pulling me along at a trot, saying:
  'And I shall take my Empress for a ride.'"

3   On 28 August 1862 Lev Nikolaevich Tolstoy (LNT) marked his 34th birthday.

4   Elizaveta Andreevna Behrs (1843–1919) — Sofia Andreevna's elder sister. In the Behrs household it was thought that Tolstoy was courting Liza, and she was greatly distressed when Tolstoy proposed to her sister Sofia. Elizaveta Behrs subsequently married aide-de-camp Gavriil Emel'janovich Pavlenkov (1824–1892); after divorce she married a second husband, her cousin Aleksandr Aleksandrovich Behrs (1844–1921). Elizaveta wrote several books on economics: *O prichinakh razorenija zemledel'cheskoj Rossii* [On the causes of the devastation of agricultural Russia] (St. Petersburg, 1899), *Voprosy nashego vremeni* [Issues of our time] (St. Petersburg, 1906), *Kurs na russkij rubl'* [Russian rouble exchange rate] (Petrograd, 1914). Tolstoy used her as a model for Vera Rostova in *War and Peace*.

5   At age 16 Sofia Behrs wrote a long story, "Natasha", in which she described the first pure love she dreamt about; she endowed her title character with the traits of her younger sister, Tat'jana (Tanja). Sofia gave the story to Lev Nikolaevich Tolstoy (LNT) to read at his request. After reading he wrote in his diary of 26 August 1862: "What energy of truth and simplicity!" (PSS 48: 41)

6   Dublitsky was the leading male character of Sofia Behrs' story, distinguished by an "extraordinarily unattractive appearance" and an "inconsistency in judgement", in which LNT recognised himself.

that your *distinct,* poetic demands of love… that I have never envied and shall never envy anyone you may bestow your love upon. I felt that I should be able to delight in you as I would delight in children.

Back at Ivitsy[7] I wrote: *All too vividly your presence reminds me of my age, and the impossibility of my obtaining happiness, you in particular.*[8]

But even back then, and since, I lied to myself. Back then I would have been able to cut all ties and once more shut myself up in a monastery of lonely labour and concentration on my work. Now I can't do anything. I feel I've thrown your family into a quandary, that my simple, endearing relations with you as a friend, as an honest person, are now lost. I can't leave, and I dare not stay. I implore you, honest person that you are, with your hand on your heart, tell me what to do — but *not to hurry, for God's sake don't hurry.* "He who laughs last, laughs best." I would have died of laughter if someone had told me a month ago that I could suffer the way I'm suffering now, and be happy suffering, this time. Tell me *as an honest person,* do you want to be my wife?[9] Only if you can *fearlessly,* from the bottom of your heart, say *yes.* If there is even a shadow of a doubt in your mind, it would be better to say *no.*

For God's sake, ask yourself the question in all honesty.

I'm terrified of your saying *no,* but I'm prepared for it and shall find within myself the strength to bear it, but if, as a husband, I should never be loved in the same way I myself love, that would be worse.

Nº 3 – LEV NIKOLAEVICH TOLSTOY ⚭ SOFIA ANDREEVNA TOLSTAYA
[PSS 83/3]
Second half of October 1862. Yasnaya Polyana.

I've had tremendous delight from reading all these letters.[10] And I read them *with you.* Read *with me,* too. How marvellous, how precious they [your family] all are! All of them. Better your world than mine, which is wretched, what with workmen and all.[11]

---

7   Ivitsy — settlement in Tula Gubernia, also the estate of Tolstaya's maternal grandfather, Aleksandr Mikhajlovich Islen'ev, located in Odoev Uezd of Tula Gubernia, 50 versts from Yasnaya Polyana (it was here in August 1862 that LNT proposed to Sofia Andreevna Behrs).

8   LNT wrote the initials of the words with chalk on a card-table, and Sofia Behrs guessed all the words right on a hunch. Later she reminisced: "I had a vague awareness that there was something serious and important between him and me — something that was already past the point of no return." *(My Life,* I. 35)

9   LNT wrote an earlier letter with a proposal of his hand and heart on 9 September 1862, but couldn't bring himself to offer it to Sofia Behrs (see PSS 83: 3–4).

10   Letters to SAT in Moscow from her relatives. On 19 October 1862 she wrote to her brother Aleksandr (Sasha) Behrs: "Today I received two whole packets of letters from my family and went wild with joy."

11   After the wedding, which took place 23 September 1862 in Moscow, LNT took his young wife to Yasnaya Polyana, where he plunged into the usual farm activities, the organisation of schools for the peasant children, and the pedagogical journal *Jasnaja Poljana* [Yasnaya Polyana]. It was hard for 18-year-old SAT to share his attentions with them. She reminisced: "Lev Nikolaevich wanted to accustom me to working with the cattle and dairy cows and took me out to the cattle yard. I tried to watch and take account of the milk yield, the butter churning, and so forth. But the smell of manure soon made me choke and vomit, and I was taken home pale and barely able to stay on my feet." *(My Life,* II.5) The newlyweds had their first quarrels.

Nº 4 – LEV NIKOLAEVICH TOLSTOY ✽ SOFIA ANDREEVNA TOLSTAYA

[PSS 83/10]
22–23 April 1864. Pirogovo.

22 April, 10 a.m.

We arrived safe and sound,[12] nothing got torn or broken, and Sasha[13] was pleased with his *seat*. When we reached Pirogovo, before entering the house we went into the stable-yard and it was so sad — *passionately* so! — looking at the stables, which before had been filled with thousands of horses and now sat empty or furnished with cots. — I hadn't been to Pirogovo for four years, and it was terribly heartwrenching, after all its former abundance and luxury, to see such squalor, and amidst the squalor the town house with the paths under the windows strewn with rubble. It turned out that the house was unheated, and we (we, I was freezing, especially sitting on the coach-box) went to the foreman, an astonishingly pitiful and laughable *dummer Junge,* as I mentioned to Këller.[14] On Serëzha's estate there is nothing for me to do, though I feel that I am useful even if only in meaningful conversation with the peasant Elder and the Foreman. Today I made a mistake. They were rounding up some cattle and one of the peasants took it upon himself to take [some of] them away, I frightened him, and he came to ask forgiveness. But this man had no nose and was thus quite pitiful-looking, and I forgave him — not the fine but [any additional] punishment. And now I regret what I did. Sasha and Këller have gone off hunting, and I'm sitting here with the priest, who tells me this fellow lost his nose when he went visiting some 'society ladies'. We're very hungry, but we had our fill of tea, and Serëzhka[15] is cooking us some chicken.

23 April, 4:30 a.m. I awoke at 4, despite going to bed around midnight, and right off I woke up everyone else, ordering [the servants] to put on the samovar and get the horses ready. — The house is literally a cardboard playhouse and is beautifully furnished down to the last detail, but it was so cold that [yesterday] we took our dinner, or rather, supper, in the kitchen. I kept chatting with the priest, while Serëzhka stood right here beside us cooking over the stove.

After supper I took a detailed tour through the whole house and recognised [my brother] Serëzha's things (various and sundry objects) which I hadn't seen in ages, which I knew from 25 years ago, when we were both children, and I became incredibly sad, as though I had lost him for ever. And it was almost true. They [Sasha Behrs and Këller] slept together upstairs, and I below, probably on the same sofa on which Tanja had held his [hands] behind the screens.[16]

---

12 LNT's trip to Pirogovo was connected with the departure of his brother Sergej Nikolaevich (Serëzha) Tolstoj (1826–1904) and his sister Marija Nikolaevna (Masha, Mashen'ka) Tolstaja (1830–1912) out of the country; during their absence LNT looked after their estate. Sister Marija owned Little Pirogovo, and brother Sergej — Great Pirogovo, located in Krapivna Uezd of Tula Gubernia.

13 Aleksandr Andreevich [Sasha] Behrs (1845–1918), Sofia Andreevna's younger brother, an officer of the Preobrazhensk Regiment. His being "pleased with his seat" refers to a joke prevalent in the Behrs family at the time.

14 Gustav Fëdorovich Këller (1839–1904) — a teacher at the Yasnaya Polyana School, a position to which he was invited by LNT when the two met in Weimar in 1861. He also taught German at the Tula *gymnasium* [European-style high school], where he worked for 39 years. In 1862–64 he was tutor to Sergej Nikolaevich's son Grigorij.

15 Sergej Petrovich (Serëzhka) Arbuzov (1849–1904) — a servant who served 22 years in the Tolstoy household; author of the book *Gr. L. N. Tolstoj, Vospominanija S. P. Arbuzova, byvshego slugi grafa L. N. Tolstogo* [Count L. N. Tolstoy, Reminiscences of S. P. Arbuzov, former servant to Count L. N. Tolstoy] (Moscow, 1904).

16 In the summer of 1863 Sofia's younger sister Tat'jana Andreevna (Tanja) Behrs and two of LNT's relatives, were visiting Sergej Nikolaevich at Great Pirogovo when they got caught in a downpour and were obliged to spend the night at his place. The evening's conversation was marked with the first hints of romance between Tanja and Sergej Nikolaevich — an evening that would remain a poetic memory to them both the rest of their lives.

And this sad and poetic story played out vividly in my imagination. Two good people — two kind and beautiful people — the ageing gentleman and the girl barely out of childhood, and now both of them unhappy;[17] and I realise how the memory of that night — alone in that empty, charming little house — will remain for both of them the most poetic recollection of their lives, and because they were both so dear, especially Serëzha. Anyway, lying there on the same sofa, I started feeling sad about them, about Serëzha — especially when I caught sight of the little box of paints — right here in the room — which he used to paint with when he was 13 years old; he was a decent, fun-loving, straightforward lad. He liked to draw all the time, and sang song after song without stopping. And now, it seems that he — *that* Serëzha — is no more.

Later I experienced a ringing in my ears and began to miss you terribly (I'm not missing Serëzha so much yet) and became fearful about how I had left you all alone; then I fell asleep and dreamt about various characters from my novel.[18] — We are continuing our journey on Masha's horses, while Këller is bringing a beekeeper in the cart with my horses; he wasn't able to come earlier since his brother-in-law died the other day. The beekeeper also promised to bring with him a woman cook (along with Këller). I'm afraid Këller might have been offended. I also hired a peasant [a freed serf] named Kondratij [Pimenov] (who lived at Serëzha's and had been dismissed by the Foreman) with the idea of returning him to Serëzha when the latter got back. But according to Këller, Serëzha already has a high estimation of him.

From what can be seen on the surface, Serëzha and Masha's estate is not doing too poorly, and even the cabinet-maker/foreman isn't as bad as he seemed at first. — I beg of you, while I'm gone, please don't let yourself be pulled down (as Tanja influences you), but act the way you did when you went to Myshka's[19] and played the piano and only Serëzha[20] distracts you. (If Serëzha's not well, send for me right away.) I suggest you don't stay sitting [all day long], but keep walking around — otherwise (if I dare say it) my absence will make you feel sadder. — I'll still keep writing to you every day, as I'm doing now — even if I have to bring you the letters myself, and you, *please do write;* but don't send your letter by post, it won't get here. Rather, Saturday evening *send out Jakov,*[21] *if he happens to come and if there is someone [else] to fetch the rest of the horses, then send out Jakov with the horses (shod) to Lapotkovo. He can stay overnight there and on Sunday meander over to Sergievskoe. He can spend the night there, too, if we don't arrive the same day. He'll bring me your letter. At Lapotkovo he can check in at the post station, and in Sergievskoe he can stay with Cherëmushkin.*[22] He can carry 2 measures of oats with him and buy whatever he needs more. Dorka[23] has abandoned you, I'm sure. If she's still there, tell Pëtr Fëdorov[24] not to let go of the rope or the chain holding her *for one second.* Farewell, and my love to my Aunties.[25]

17   The 38-year-old Sergej Nikolaevich proposed to the 17-year-old Tanja, but could not break ties with his common-law wife, the gypsy woman Marija Shishkina, who lived in Tula with their son Grigorij and was expecting another baby. He legitimised this marriage, and the couple exchanged their vows on 7 June 1867.

18   LNT was working on the novel he initially entitled *The Year 1805,* which eventually became *War and Peace.*

19   Ol'ga Rodionovna (Myshka) Egorova (married name: Bazykina) — a Yasnaya Polyana peasant of rather short stature.

20   In this instance *Serëzha* refers to the Tolstoy couple's firstborn son Sergej L'vovich (1863–1947).

21   Jakov Vasil'evich Tsvetkov (1848–1921), a peasant from the village of Vorob'ëka.

22   Boris Filippovich Cherëmushkin (1821–1895) — a merchant, a former serf of the Princes Gagarin.

23   Dorka — a yellow setter, the Tolstoys' favourite dog, named after Dora, David Copperfield's first wife in Dickens' famous novel.

24   Pëtr Fëdorovich Arbuzov — caretaker at Yasnaya Polyana, father to Sergej Petrovich Arbuzov.

25   A reference to Tat'jana Aleksandrovna Ergol'skaja (see Note 33 below) and Pelageja Il'inichna Jushkova.

Nº 5 – SOFIA ANDREEVNA TOLSTAYA ❧ LEV NIKOLAEVICH TOLSTOY
[LSA 2]
23 [April 1864], evening [Yasnaya Polyana]

I also wanted to describe to you — thoroughly and accurately — all that has been going on here with us this past day and a half, but all of a sudden Serëzha started wheezing, his chest was congested, and I was overcome with such fear that as usual I'm starting to feel lost and terrified. And it's worse and even more frightening without you here. I've been using all sorts of remedies for a cold, I hope to God it's not serious. But I find it terribly, terribly difficult, and I'm both miserable and frightened without you. He's asleep now, and so I've decided to describe everything to you. — Yesterday after you left I held myself together and didn't weep. But suddenly it seemed I was overwhelmed by so many things to do, and I ran to and fro in a daze, all in a bother, but ask me now what I did, — I don't know. I kept on fussing over Serëzha and hardly let him out of my hands. I didn't go for any walk, and spent the evening knitting. When I got to my room and I really wanted to lie down, all of a sudden I felt so bored that I sat up for two hours writing, and when that didn't work out, I wept, and hardly got to sleep the whole night long. And when I dozed off, I kept having fearful dreams and took fright and woke up. At five o'clock Dorka roused us. Tanja[26] (she was sleeping in the drawing-room) got up, dressed herself and let her out on a lead. But again there was the same fuss with the dogs, and Tanja picked up Dorka in her arms and carried her into the house. Then she was locked up and taken off to Moscow only at 11 o'clock. It took quite a time as it was hard to get away from the [local] dogs.

After five o'clock I still couldn't get much sleep. I rose at eleven and seemed to be ill, I felt so under the weather. Serëzha was cheerful, and healthy, and just a dear. Over tea I found out that Nikolaj[27] was ill and couldn't even cook. I went to the kitchen and spent the whole morning cooking. Tanja brought me your letter[28] in the kitchen. I was so excited and got all flustered. I read it and simply sighed with delight. In fact, it seems like you left a long time ago. Everything you wrote about [your brother] Serëzha resonated with me so much that I just felt like weeping, and all at once I felt so much love for him that I, too, began to pity him. I'm very glad you thought to write — we didn't make any kind of arrangement [ahead of time], I didn't want to say anything at the time, since it was so difficult to say good-bye as it was. And now it grieves me to write, and I keep avoiding calling you by name, since it's as though I'm talking with you and you're not there, and it's even harder on me. After getting your letter they brought mail from the post office — from S. Gorstkina,[29] from Anetochka,[30] as well as from Islavin[31] and [your brother] Serëzha. These last ones I'm forwarding to you. I'm sure Serëzha's letter will cheer you up. I've been so delighted about him, words fail me. In any case he's morally improved, and it seems I get upset so easily these days that I take everything very much to heart. Don't get angry that we opened the letter. It was a joy for all and that's the only reason I have no regrets — [but] if that displeases you, I do apologise and beg forgiveness. — Serëzha's

26 SAT's younger sister Tat'jana Andreevna.
27 Nikolaj Mikhajlovich Rumjantsev (1818–1893) — cook at Yasnaya Polyana.
28 LNT's letter of 22–23 April 1864 (Nº 4 in the current volume).
29 Sof'ja Mikhajlovna Gorstkina (née Kuzminskaja, 1842–1891) — sister to Aleksandr Mikhajlovich Kuzminskij, who in 1867 would marry SAT's younger sister Tat'jana Andreevna.
30 Anna Karlovna (Anetochka) Zenger (1843–?; married name: Jurgens) — daughter of the chemist appointed to the Imperial Court Karl Petrovich Zenger (1800–1872), a friend of SAT's.
31 Vladimir Aleksandrovich Islavin (1818–1895) — SAT's maternal uncle.

coughing something terrible; I'm beginning to feel out of sorts and tomorrow I'll send for the doctor and let you know if he's not any better.

24 [April]. After lunch.

Everything's cleared up here, and it bothers me that you're still on the road and worrying about us all. I'll be soon telling you everything in person. I'm writing to make the time pass more quickly — and it's still as though I'm chatting with you. What happened to me yesterday? I can't remember at all! Quite unexpectedly, we were sitting down to tea, and all at once Serëzha[32] started coughing. I got up and took a look, and nothing seemed out of the ordinary. Then everything took a turn for the worse; I was writing and then heard another cough. I went into the nursery and there he was starting to choke. I was confused at first, and don't even remember anything about people around me. He sounded as though he were coughing from a barrel and started gasping for breath, but I soon came to my senses, even though I was still weeping. One thing I know: it was very serious and probably dangerous, and everyone, especially Tanja and Tat'jana Aleksandrovna,[33] were very frightened. I feel like boasting that I took good charge of the situation, though if you say I acted wrongly, I'd probably agree with you. I sent for Ivan Ivanovich[34] and asked him to go at once to [fetch] Shmigaro,[35] and if he couldn't come, to bring any doctor. I also ordered Kondratij[36] to join me. And I had Dunjasha[37] make a mustard plaster and a poultice, which I was reminded of by Këller. (Apparently he took it very much to heart.) I gave Serëzha some castor oil and applied the mustard. If you could only see how pitiful he looked. He was crying, gasping for breath, smarting from the mustard. He kept twitching his little legs and grasping hold of my hair, my earrings, my collar, as though he was wanting to crawl right into me and begging me to save him. I kept holding him in my arms and the more he suffered, the more lively his twitchings seemed to be, along with his love for me and all his facial expressions, and I thought he was going to die. I remembered, too, that you would have taken him from me and got angry with me, while I would have given God knows what for you to be with me. In thinking about Serëzha's death, I began to be more fearful in your absence. You just can't imagine the sense of loneliness which I go through when you're away, and which I went through especially yesterday with my sick Serëzha. I started to figure out how I could let you know as quickly as possible. Kondratij arrived. It turned out that on horseback it would have taken him a whole day and night or even longer; and he didn't have any [travel] documents; otherwise I would have sent him on a post-horse. Tanja says: "Send Aleksej."[38] He agreed, and here you can see my report. Thank God, he was sent in vain; it would have been worse if it hadn't turned out to be in vain. I need you terribly, I am so exhausted and there's nobody I can find peace with. Tanja and Auntie Tat'jana Aleksandrovna have been terribly kind. Their loving nature was fully evident. Tanja kept running the whole time: between the

---

32 From now on, unless otherwise indicated, the name *Serëzha* will refer to the Tolstoys' eldest son Sergej L'vovich Tolstoj (1863–1947).

33 Tat'jana Aleksandrovna Ergol'skaja (1792–1874) — LNT's second cousin, once removed, who raised him after his parents both passed on in the 1830s. LNT later wrote about her: "The third most important influence in my life after my father and mother was my Auntie, as we called her, T. A. Ergol'skaja… she taught me the spiritual delight of love" (PSS, 34: 364, 366).

34 Ivan Ivanovich Orlov (1863–1889) — foreman in charge of Tolstoy's Nikol'skoe-Vjazemskoe estate.

35 Sigizmund Adamovich Shmigaro — chief physician at the Tula Arms Factory.

36 Kondrat Pimenov — a former servant of LNT's family, released from employ in 1859.

37 Evdokija Nikolaevna Bannikova (?–1879; married name: Orekhova) — daughter to LNT's personal attendant Nikolaj Bannikov, a maid to Tat'jana Aleksandrovna Ergol'skaja. Nikolaj is described in LNT's *Childhood [Detstvo]*. Evdokija is also known as Avdot'ja.

38 Aleksej Stepanovich Orekhov (?–1882) — *valet de chambre*, later a foreman and manager at Yasnaya Polyana.

servants, the workers, relaying my orders; she didn't get a whole night's sleep, only about three hours, and helped in everything, even though she herself was trembling and crying with fright, and Tat'jana Aleksandrovna was both sprightly and kind, and supported me simply through her genuine sympathetic support. We were all very afraid. I didn't see Auntie Polina.[39] She overate and slept soundly the whole night, only she went to the tent and overindulged in peppermint. Forgive me for being so coarse and malicious towards her.

After the mustard-plaster and the castor oil Serëzha fell asleep, but kept gasping horribly all night long. I continued to apply poultices and he slept the whole night without his bedclothes, he was so touching and dear, in the dearest baby poses. Auntie Tat'jana Aleksandrovna and I — à la lettre — didn't fall asleep even for a moment. I maintained constant watch over him to make sure he didn't suffocate, while Auntie kept dropping by. Nobody got undressed. I continued to rub him with warm oil, but there was no way I could make him perspire. How much I kept going over in my mind that night, how much I loved you, how distinctly I understood and felt what a superb individual you are and how I loved you! I lay on the sofa and kept my ear out for the doctor. Several times I would run out to the porch to see if he were coming, and each time Këller would come out from the study and ask: "Wie geht [es] de[m] Kleine[n]?".[40] He never got undressed either and didn't blow out the candles. Some time between four and five Ivan Ivanovich appeared and with him some chubby blond doctor. I brought the doctor into the nursery and asked Ivan Ivanovich who this might be. Apparently Shmigaro didn't come, and this was Vigand,[41] whom they had some difficulty in persuading to come. He kept making excuses, saying we were Shmigaro's patients and he wouldn't come. On three occasions Vigand gave Serëzha 85 drops of antimony. He applied the mustard plaster not to the boy's chest as we had done, but to his back, and gave him syrup which was quite effective against the coughing. Once again I was in fearful torment: poor Serëzha was terribly flustered; he was nauseous and vomiting; he kept lying against my shoulder and grasping hold of me. You can't imagine what a pitiful sight he was! But he stopped choking, and started breathing more and more normally, and calmly went to sleep. All of us got together for tea, by this time it was six o'clock and already light out. Everybody calmed down, and I saw that the danger had passed, but I was still bothered by his coughing and breathing, and I still have not found my peace about that. He ate well, had a decent sleep and his system was nicely cleared out. But his tenderness towards me is overwhelming. I always feel like crying, my nerves are shot, maybe because of that. He's got thinner and has begun to look even more like you. I don't see you and I keep wishing to recognise your features in his little face and note a resemblance. When the doctor left I lay down and slept about an hour and a half in the nursery. Everything seems so foggy in my mind — last night, Nature, people — you know, how after a sleepless night, and when I thought about you, there was this terrible emptiness, ennui and everything seems like it's not for me, like I've died and only Serëzha's health and you bring me back to life. And this feeling persists even right this moment. Serëzha's been getting better and better, Auntie's been sleeping, Tanja's been running everywhere — into the garden and goodness-knows-where else, and I'm constantly with Serëzha, and always with the most joyful but alarming thoughts about you. Around three o'clock [in the afternoon] we all came alive, washed and dressed; Këller went to Tula, Serëzha actually began playing and laughing and I sat down to have something to eat. Then I was in the nursery again, Serëzha's love for me — I'm very attached to him. Around half-past four we

---

39 Pelageja Il'inichna (Polina) Jushkova (1801–1875).
40 *Wie geht [es] dem Kleine[n]?* = How is the little one doing? *(German).*
41 Èduard Il'ich Vigand (Wiegand; 1826–1903) — a physician in Tula; later Chief Physician of the Tula Arms Factory.

had dinner, and then, with my permission, Ivan Ivanovich went horseback-riding with [his] son and Tanja. The other day they rode out to look for peasants' horses in our meadows, but didn't catch any. Now after dinner I went to Myshka's and again I seemed dead to everything. The weather was magnificent, for a whole hour and a half the sun shone especially brightly on the grass — I couldn't help noticing. Myshka wasn't in. I returned home and met up with Ivan Ivanovich, Tanja and Anatol'.[42] Tanja was simply radiant. A real charmer all fresh and bright-looking in her velvet jacket and hat with multi-coloured little feathers. I felt just a bit envious, and I thought you, too, would be struck by her — it was even a little frightening. Compared to poor me with my scrunched-up face, pitiful looks and such an inelegant gait. — Back home, while Serëzha slept I did a bit of writing, then he called me away, later I started writing again and have been writing right up 'til now. They're putting him to bed, and I shall now dismiss the nurse and stay with him myself until you arrive. I'm definitely waiting for you at night now. Are you coming? I shall probably wait in vain. But how I want to see you, just as soon as possible!

Nº 6 – LEV NIKOLAEVICH TOLSTOY ❧ SOFIA ANDREEVNA TOLSTAYA
[PSS 83/14]
9 August 1864. Pirogovo.

Sunday.

We went by the old road. After we had gone 4 versts I ran into a little bog and made a failed attempt at shooting a snipe. Later, near Pirogovo, at the Ikonsky settlement I killed a snipe and a double snipe as well. Tanja and a bunch of country boys were there and let out a shriek of excitement. At Pirogovo we were met by Mashen'ka,[43] the children, Grisha,[44] and along with them Serëzha [Sergej Nikolaevich] and Auntie [Tat'jana Aleksandrovna]. I tried to persuade Mashen'ka to go and see you. At the moment she can't or doesn't want to. Auntie was the first to mention that we had left you all alone, and said she would go. I urged her to go the following day, but she didn't say when. It would have been all perfectly wonderful, if it hadn't been for the presence of Serëzha and Tanja, which infects all our interactions with tension and insincerity. I find this singing and going out to the balcony and everything terribly annoying. This whole experience is ruining my life. I feel constantly awkward and fearful for both of them. I had hardly managed to have dinner than they started to gather round. Masha offered a cart and a horse, Këller went with me to Vorotynka. That's 12 versts from Pirogovo. That evening we found nothing except for Vasilij Nikolaevich Bibikov[45] who was returning from hunting in the same bog we were heading for. He assured us that there was absolutely no game to be found, but I persuaded him to spend the night with us. We stayed the night at a peasant's [farm]. I had a sound sleep in the barn together with Dorka to keep me warm and with no insects around. At 4 in the morning we were wakened by shots from the bog, which is about a quarter of a verst from the village. There were about five hunters there already. We went, and I shot at one double snipe but missed, later I killed one, as did Këller. Then we went looking farther. And we

42 Anatolij L'vovich Shostak (1842–1914) — son to Lev Antonovich Shostak and Ekaterina Nikolaevna Shostak (*née* Isleneva), who was headmistress of the Nikolaev Institute in St. Petersburg. Anatolij was a second cousin to SAT and her sister Tanja; the latter had a strong romantic infatuation with him. He was the prototype for Anatolij Kuragin in *War and Peace*.

43 LNT's sister Marija Nikolaevna Tolstaja and her children Varvara Valer'janovna (1850–1921; married name: Nagornova), Nikolaj Valer'janovich (1851–1879); Elizaveta Valer'janovna (1852–1935; married name: Obolenskaja).

44 Grigorij Sergeevich (Grisha) Tolstoj (1853–1928) — son of LNT's brother Sergej Nikolaevich Tolstoj.

45 Vasilij Nikolaevich Bibikov (1830–1893) — landowner in Bogoroditsk Uezd, Tula Gubernia.

didn't find anything except hunters — seventeen of them had gathered here in one day, yesterday, from various parts. I should have come two weeks earlier. This bog is famous, and people come here from all around. — By evening we had joined up with another young married Bibikov[46] and the young Marsochnikov,[47] and at this point, on the way home, I found and killed two snipes. It was already after 5 when we approaching Pirogovo. Bibikov (Nikolai) persuaded me to dine at his place (he lives 2 versts from Mashen'ka's). I accepted, took dinner (but the butter was bad) and was about to leave when [my brother] Serëzha appeared. He was completely unaware that we were here; he was simply out for a drive with his 'Zephyrlets'[48] and dropped by. We rode home together. We had our fill of tea and then supper, and I lay down with Dorka in the outbuilding where, they say, are bedbugs, but I had an excellent sleep, and don't know whether there were any around or not. There was something going on between Serëzha and Tanja — I can see the tell-tale signs, and find this extremely annoying. Nothing but grief — and grief for everyone — will come of it. And in no way will there be any good. At the moment I am up, everyone's asleep, and so I've got hold of a notebook and am writing to Sonja — it's hard to live without her. —

Yesterday on my way back to Pirogovo I thought of then going back to Yasnaya; I've been feeling so fearful for you and Serëzha, who I've had dreams about. And it bothered me that Auntie wouldn't go and hasn't gone. But when Auntie announced that she would be going with Tanja the next day, I decided to go to Nikol'skoe[-Vjazemskoe]. I doubt I shall go any farther [than that]. Write [to me] care of the post stations. Possibly I'll find a letter waiting for me at Chern'. — I'm quite out of sorts. You say I'll forget. Not for a moment, especially when I'm with people. When I'm out hunting I may forget — I'm just thinking about double snipes — but around people, with every encounter I think about you once again, and I keep wanting to tell you things that I can't tell anybody else. Now I'm on my way to Nikol'skoe, where I'll spend the whole day tomorrow, and probably won't go anywhere else, and the day after I'll come back. I'll write to you from Chern'.

Nº 7 – LEV NIKOLAEVICH TOLSTOY ❧ SOFIA ANDREEVNA TOLSTAYA
[PSS 83/15]
9 August 1864. Chern'.

I love you so much! My dove, my dear.

The whole way to Chern' I kept thinking: no, there will no doubt be some mix-up with the letters and I shan't receive anything in Chern'. I get there, and Tomas' former foreman[49] — what a dear face this foreman has! — says: Would you care to receive some letters? No. And I was so hungry, I was so busy with my soup I didn't yet ask. What a sweet letter,[50] and how sweet you are. I'm at peace, and by the letter I can see that you're in a very good — if not cheerful — state

---

46 Nikolaj Nikolaevich Bibikov (1840–1906) — landowner in Krapivna Uezd, Tula Gubernia.
47 Semën Nikolaevich Marsochnikov, son of the owner of Teljatinki House near Yasnaya Polyana.
48 *Zephyrlets* [Russian: *Zefiroty*] — a pet name from a legend about a half-bird, half-dolphin as told by Marija Nikolaevna's godmother (a nun named Mar'ja Gerasimovna) — a name which LNT jokingly applied first to SAT and her sister Tanja and eventually to his nieces Varvara Valer'janovna (Varja) and Elizaveta Valer'janovna (Liza).
49 *Tomas' former foreman* — identity unknown.
50 This letter is unknown.

of mind. I'm not thinking of going to see Fet[51] or Kireevskij,[52] à *moins qu'il n'arrive quelque chose d'extraordinaire.* Not to go to Nikol'skoe and return to you as I wanted to would have been shameful, moreover [going to Nikol'skoe] was necessary, and without you there can be no pleasure for me in anything except hunting. I can't hunt at Kireevskij's or Fet's. I've thought this over now. What if I were to go see Kireevskij, I would have to write him in advance and arrive before he headed out. I am not cancelling the date of the 15th, only I shall try to arrive earlier. It's now 7 [p.m.] and I am in Chern'. That means I shan't get to Nikol'skoe before tomorrow. And I have to finally take a look around and get a good familiarity with this estate, which I do not know and have not seen, never mind that I've been living off its proceeds for five years already. Do question Tanja about big Serëzha's [i.e. Sergej Nikolaevich's] mood. Now here's something funny. On my way out from Masha's I ducked into the bog near the roadside. I see Serëzha, Grisha and Këller on their way in. I think to myself: there they are, and I'll meet up with them, talk a bit, only right at that moment I feel the call of Nature, and need to go fast, so I'll be free to meet up with them. I sat down in the bog and… Serëzha comes riding by, all in a huff… "Bye-bye!" "Bye-bye!" I'm quite certain that in this incident he must have seen something out of the ordinary that gave him offence. Either from something in his nature or his relations with Tanja, or from something in my nature, but I've had oh so hard a time relating to him. I keep asking myself these days: is there something wrong with me? — but no, Auntie's been really dear to me. Mashen'ka's exceptionally dear and kind; not to mention the Zephyrlets, but still he constrains me, makes me feel uncomfortable. —

Along the way I met an architect I know and invited him to pay me a visit. He'll come around the 16th. On my own horses I reached Krasnyj Dvor, 18 versts beyond Sergievskoe, and sent them to [Boris Filippovich] Cherëmushkin's to be fed pending my return. Tell Ivan Ivanovich to order someone — maybe Kondratij [Pimenov] — to take care of the horses in the stable. Tell him, too, not to sow two *desjatinas* of the best acreage (the richest in manure), but leave it for the wheat they'll be bringing from Nikol'skoe. As to the choice of acreage, he should ask advice from Timofej[53] the peasant elder. Tell him, too, to take a look at the seed clover — not to spoil it, but to make sure the tips don't get broken off. Also the seed clover beyond the grove needs to be winnowed. [Tell him] to send ten girls and Sonja along with them, as soon as the weather is good, and pinch off the tips, gather them in their aprons, and from the aprons [shake them] into the cart. —

I hope that both Tanjas [Tat'jana Aleksandrovna Ergol'skaja and Tat'jana Andreevna Behrs] are with you, give them a kiss from me. I shan't say anything further about you. This time I feel you closer to me than ever.

---

51 Afanasij Afanas'evich Fet (real surname: Shen'shin (1820–1892) — prominent Russian lyric poet and friend of the Tolstoy family, who dedicated several poems to SAT. He lived on his Stepanovka estate in Mtsensk Uezd, Orël Gubernia, not far from Pokrovskoe-Vjazemskoe.

52 Nikolaj Vasil'evich Kireevskij (1797–1870) — the owner of the Shablykino estate in Karachev Uezd, Orël Gubernia. He often went hunting with LNT.

53 Timofej Mikhajlovich Fokanov (1822–1891) — a Yasnaya Polyana peasant.

Nº 8 – LEV NIKOLAEVICH TOLSTOY ❧ SOFIA ANDREEVNA TOLSTAYA
[PSS 83/16]
10 or 11 August 1864. Novoselki.

An opportune moment again. Fet will bring you my letter. I arrived yesterday at Nikol'skoe at 8 [p.m.]. A frightening event there, which left a horrible impression on me.[54] An elderly cattle-tender dropped a bucket into the well in the stableyard. The well was only 12 *arshins* deep. She sat on a plank of wood and told a peasant to lower her down. The peasant was an elder and a beekeeper, the only one in Nikol'skoe who was near and dear to me. The old woman climbed down and fell off the plank. The peasant elder asked that he himself be lowered down. He got half-way down, then fell off the plank, too. [Those standing around] ran to fetch more people, and in half an hour they pulled them out, [but] both were dead. The well was only three-quarters full of water. They buried them yesterday. I didn't sleep well, the flies were biting. I got up at 10 and received a note saying that Fet was here and would be leaving presently. I went to Borisov's[55] and am writing from his place. Fet is ill and in a gloomy mood. He doesn't want to come and see us. The Nikol'skoe estate is doing very well, but the harvest isn't too good. Tomorrow I'll have a look at the lands [at Nikol'skoe-Vjazemskoe] and shall probably be ready [to return home]. — Pity we weren't able to live together at Nikol'skoe. Fet is sitting [here] and spinning out terrific puns, and is quite entertaining. Borisov will give [us] a [hunting] dog. —

Farewell, my sweet. Now I'll send [a servant] to Chern'. Maybe there is a letter from you waiting there. —

At Borisov's there is an abundance of plums, and Fet says that the people who live here *are very happy* looking for plums.

Hugs and kisses. Tell Serëzha *atàta, atàta.*

10 August.

Nº 9 – SOFIA ANDREEVNA TOLSTAYA ❧ LEV NIKOLAEVICH TOLSTOY
[LSA 4]
[11 August 1864], *Tuesday evening* [Yasnaya Polyana]

Right now I've been feeling so down-and-out, dear Lëvochka,[56] that all my cheerfulness has vanished, and I have such a great longing to see you very, very soon. This all came from your sweet letter,[57] your love for me and the fact that we are living better and better together in this life. I'm saddened that you won't be returning right away; besides, my Serëzha is still not well, and that's because the cow is sick. Her legs are so weak she can't even walk. But all this is happening, it seems, for a reason. He's started to make such a good recovery; and all at once comes such a misfortune! He's having painless bowel movements, without effort, but very fluid and often. He's been enjoying good sleep and eats decent meals. Now he's out and about all day, since the weather is marvellous, warm and calm. My day went like this: I got up, as usual, at

---

54 This occurrence gave LNT the idea for his story *Harmful air [Vrednyj vozdukh]*, which he wrote for his *Primer [Azbuka]*.

55 Ivan Petrovich Borisov (?–1871) — a relative of the poet A. A. Fet and a close acquaintance of LNT's; he lived on his Novoselki estate not far from Nikol'skoe-Vjazemskoe.

56 *Lëvochka* (derived from *Lev*) is SAT's most frequent pet name for her husband. At this stage she sometimes calls him by the shorter variant *Lëva*, but later, as of 1869, this latter form is reserved for their fourth child, Lev L'vovich.

57 Letter Nº 7 of 9 August 1864.

eight o'clock, had a good sleep for the first night [in a long time], since Serëzha slept soundly; then I sent [my sister] Tanja to Yasenki. She brought me your letter, and I spent the whole morning clearing away all the books — yours and ours — dusted them all down, washed the shelves and got exhausted. This is the last time I'm doing any cleaning of clutter before I give birth; it's not easy work. Later I was overtaken by a desire for orderliness and I began clearing away *everything*. Before dinner I did some drawing and it's going rather poorly, but this time I want to hold through and finish what I've started. I had dinner at four o'clock sharp. Our steward has been performing his duties admirably, as have we all. Then I went for a walk with Serëzha through all our gardens. Yesterday the watchman, a [retired] soldier, was drunk and he is most repulsive; the old man Kondratij is constantly drunk — and I've told Ivan Ivanovich [Orlov] to pay attention to this. Pushkin [a Tula merchant] and Kuz'ma [the greenhouse gardener] are peeling pears and plums, and Kuz'ma is very diligent, except when he's working in the vegetable garden. I have conveyed all your instructions to Ivan Ivanovich. Pity that the best acreage has already been sown, your letter took a long time to get here. Tanja checked just last night and there was still no letter. Now I'm going to take a bath and go to bed around nine, since the evenings without you and Serëzha are very sad and long. Serëzha's turned pale again, and he looks so sick and feeble. As for big Serëzha, I've spoken with Tanja. She tells me he said the same thing as you, i.e. that you were somehow worried and anxious, that he wanted to speak with you about some matter, but that you didn't feel up to it; he was wondering whether there might have been some bad news from Yasnaya. But there was nothing wrong with him at Pirogovo and he was cheerful, and nothing wrong with Tanja; she gave me her word that there was nothing wrong, or the slightest hint of anything between them. I've now been having quite a bit of frank conversation with Tanja. She complains a lot about you, saying you have quite a bad opinion of her, that you aren't very nice to her, that you consider her an awful flirt and that she feels very awkward and confused in your presence. Of course she believes this is not completely random, and she's deserved it, but won't admit it. And I've told her straight out what I think and what's in my heart, and she has appreciated my frankness.

Our Auntie [Tat'jana Aleksandrovna Ergol'skaja] keeps walking up and down the pathways with an umbrella and wants to eat everything in sight: peaches, chicken, apples. She's in very good spirits and kind. And now she's been telling us touching tales of old times, about the death of everybody close to her and, as always, you know, her voice has been trembling a little and her feelings are very touching. In the meantime I was drawing, and Tanja, too, was listening [to Auntie]. My dearest Lëva, couldn't you possibly come home right away? I'm already dreaming you'll get this letter at Chern' on your way home. I don't know what you mean when you say you're "not thinking of going to see Fet or Kireevskij, *à moins qu'il n'arrive quelque chose d'extraordinaire*". But what extraordinary thing could happen? Farewell for now; tomorrow morning I'll write some more and send this letter. Kisses to you, my sweet.

N° 10 – SOFIA ANDREEVNA TOLSTAYA ❧ LEV NIKOLAEVICH TOLSTOY [LSA 5]
22 November [1864], Sunday, 10 p.m. [Yasnaya Polyana]

I've just put my little girl[58] to bed, dear Lëvochka, and now I've sat down to write to you before I fall asleep over this letter. The girl has been quite rebellious, while the boy has lately

---

58   Tat'jana L'vovna (Tanja) Tolstaja (1864–1950) — the Tolstoys' second child and eldest daughter. Henceforth the name Tanja will refer to Tat'jana L'vovna unless otherwise indicated.

been having severe diarrhœa — six times already, though he has been sleeping very well at night. Perhaps it's for the better, but still there's a lot of grief. There's a blush of smallpox starting, but I'm not afraid of smallpox. That's my report on your own children, I've nothing more to say about them. Now they're sleeping like little cherubs, while their nanny[59] is on the *lezhanka* [stove-bench] drinking tea. What condition will you be in when this letter reaches you? I don't have great expectations, only that God will give you the strength to bear life as best you can. Tomorrow I'm sending [a servant] to pick up a wire either at [your brother] Serëzha's or at the telegraph office; pity we did not arrange ahead of time as to where your telegram should be sent.[60] Lëva, my dove, please tell me the whole truth; I know that after eight weeks [following your accident] it is very difficult and painful, and probably dangerous to set a bone, but I hope in spite of everything it will turn out all right.

Don't you be thinking about us, but, more importantly, think about yourself, get some good treatment — maybe there are better specialists in Petersburg than in Moscow. You must surely be there by now, if the carriage arrived on time and didn't break down. Our Behrs family must have been happy to see you. I feel I'm mentally with you all now that I can picture you not on the road, but in the Kremlin.[61] I can breathe easier, and I don't feel so sad. This time when you left, I went to see the children, and while I was looking at them in their beds, I felt just a slight twinge of frustration concerning them — the same feeling I had when you and I said goodbye. Our little girl has now woken up, and I've sat [with her] for quite a while, fed her and keep thinking how happy I am thanks to you and how much good you have inspired in me. I did not sleep very well on this sofa, and in the morning I went upstairs, where I got so bored I couldn't sleep. Mashen'ka[62] doesn't want to move into my room. The fear of a draught everywhere, from both the doors and the windows, has so deeply ingrained itself in her that it seems there's a draft through my door and her teeth start to hurt. Let [people] do what they like, but it would be more comfortable for her. She doesn't talk about leaving, thank God. I'm very happy and I'm concerned that she might leave us as she feels uncomfortable [about being a burden]. The children[63] spent the whole day enthusiastically looking at pictures, and I've been transcribing[64] all day long; I hope to finish soon, and am using literally every second of time to write at least one word — it's all coming along nicely. I'll send it [to you] directly I finish. I wanted to remind you of what you yourself said: Don't show your novel to anyone — to anyone who might judge you. Remember you've been thrown off more than once before, and now it's very important that no one say anything silly that you might take to heart. If you need anything transcribed, give it to [my] Mama — she's a terrific scribe, and she will be happy to copy for you. What about Tanja [Tat'jana Andreevna], is she taking care of you? It's sometimes frightening to think about how far away from us you are and how many unpleasantries you might be having to deal with.

Lëva, I've now despatched Jakov [Vasil'evich Tsvetkov], but can you imagine, he didn't comprehend what I said about the infirmary and headed for [your brother] Serëzha's. Serëzha told him: "All right, brother, tomorrow you and I shall go together to the infirmary." I'm very glad about that, and shall tell you what [the doctors] will do to him. Tomorrow they'll bring him

---

59 Tat'jana Filippovna was nanny to LNT himself as a child, later to his nieces and to his eldest son Sergej (Serëzha).

60 On 23 November 1864 LNT sent his wife a telegram concerning the upcoming operation on his arm. On 26 September LNT had fallen from a horse and dislocated his shoulder. The arm was unsuccessfully set in Tula and on 21 November LNT had gone to Moscow to consult with doctors there.

61 In Moscow LNT stayed with SAT's parents: Ljubov' Aleksandrovna and Andrej Evstaf'evich Behrs, who was Physician to the Imperial Court and had an apartment in the Kremlin.

62 LNT's sister Marija Nikolaevna, who was visiting Yasnaya Polyana at the time.

63 Marija Nikolaevna's daughters Varvara and Elizaveta.

64 SAT was transcribing an early draft of LNT's novel *The Year 1805*, which would later become *War and Peace*.

home, I'm sending for him. I want to start my walks again. This constant sitting in the nursery with its stuffiness has deadened me, both emotionally and physically. I've been feeling quite sluggish and numb, and I've been so craving fresh air that I'm going to start my walks again, despite this frosty, clear, snowless weather. I have to get refreshed and lift my spirits. Otherwise, without you I can feel quite down and my loneliness is more difficult to bear.

Last night and the day you left and we said good-bye — all that now seems to me like a dream. I myself have been in such a dream-like state, feeling tense and unnatural. What a good time we've had lately — so happy and friendly — why should we have to experience such misfortune? I feel terribly sad without you and I constantly think: if he's not here, what's the meaning of it all? Why do I need to have dinner, why do the stoves need to be stoked and everything be a bother, and the same bright sun, and the same Auntie, and the Zephyrlets, and all? I've been spending all day downstairs now, writing like mad, and that helps.

Nº 11 – LEV NIKOLAEVICH TOLSTOY ❧ SOFIA ANDREEVNA TOLSTAYA
[PSS 83/21]
24 November 1864. Moscow.
[TELEGRAM]

Countess Tolstaya
Tula
St-Catherine's Day[65] got in the way. [Everything's] postponed until tomorrow. I shall still consult with Inozemstev.[66] My overall health has improved.

Tolstoy.

Nº 12 – SOFIA ANDREEVNA TOLSTAYA ❧ LEV NIKOLAEVICH TOLSTOY
[LSA 6]
25 November [1864], Wednesday. [Yasnaya Polyana] Evening.

I've now received both telegrams,[67] sweet Lëvochka. Yesterday's telegram was received after Semën had left, — the line was busy, and [Gustav Fëdorovich] Këller, to whom they [first] brought it, sent it over this morning, while the second telegram [our servant] Semën just brought me now. I don't know whether I should be delighted or devastated. Of course I'm glad you are avoiding tremendous suffering and even danger, but I feel sad, too, that it's finished; [your] former strength, muscles and freedom of movement — they're all gone. Sad, too, that since you will be getting callisthenics therapy, you won't be allowed to return home for a long time, you have to show [mental] stamina, and consistently, and for a long time. Well, now, those are trifles; what's important is that it is not in vain, but produces results. I'm glad that your overall health has improved — that's the main thing. How boring it's been not having any letters from you until now. I feel your spirit wafting over me when I read your letter and this gives me

---

65 24 November (7 December N. S.) is the Day of the Great Martyr Saint-Catherine of Alexandria, one of the most important winter holidays of the Orthodox world.
66 Fëdor Ivanovich Inozemtsev (1802–1869) — a surgeon living in Moscow. In 1847 he became the first surgeon to perform an operation using æther anæsthesia anywhere in the Russian Empire.
67 These telegrams were sent on 24 and 25 November. For the text of the first of these, see Letter Nº 11. The text of the second telegram reads: "Have decided to follow Rudinskij's advice; he advised not to break, saying it's almost healed and will greatly improve with physical exercise." (PSS, 83: 54)

a great deal of comfort and cheer, even the little details. The main thing is that I find out what the doctors have said, as well as how you are viewing all these troubles with your arm. Does all this give you a lot of bother or not? Serëzha [Sergej Nikolaevich] keeps talking about your arm with some disappointment, but everyone's glad that they will not have to break it. I don't have to ask you to write me about everything in detail, you yourself will certainly not forget me. And here I was yesterday, foolishly accusing you of not sending me a wire.[68] Forgive me, Lëvochka, I was so perturbed and depressed. I spent an altogether wretched night. I did so much thinking that my head became all muddled and heavy. Circumstances separated us. We couldn't help but experience sorrow — we can't be joyous all the time. And this is real sorrow, serious sorrow, which we also must learn to bear. How are you all doing there? Are you yourself all right? Don't think about me, do what cheers you up. Go to the club, and to any acquaintances you like; I feel now so calm about everything, so happy for you and confident about you that I'm not afraid of anything in the world. I say this sincerely and it's pleasant to feel it in my heart. Everything's going along here as before, without the slightest changes. I'm still sitting downstairs, this is my realm, my children, my activities and my life. When I come upstairs, it seems like I'm a guest [in my own home]. When I come in, Serëzha stands up. When I'm not there, he jokes and fibs, but in my presence all's formal and tense, even though he's kind and good to me. I get the feeling I'm a stranger to all of them; it's funny — a stranger to *your* kin; that they all love and cherish each other, but look at me condescendingly and benignly, as though I were a foster child in the house. They're all very kind, and care for me very much, but still something is not as it should be. Without you I'm lost here — such wild thoughts come to me. When you're around I feel like a queen, without you I'm superfluous. Everyone who likes me is now in the Kremlin, and I'm living constantly with you — my whole life, except for the children, is still *there*. Auntie [Tat'jana Aleksandrovna Ergol'skaja] is closest to me and the kindest. She never changes — she's always the same. I'm afraid what I am saying will somewhat displease you, but you, Lëva, are one with me, so it's simple and natural to tell you everything that's in my heart. Don't get me wrong: we are all very friendly with each other here, at least that's the way it seems to me now. I came to see them in the drawing room, they're all sitting in a circle, busy, reading, chatting; Serëzha is lying on the sofa, Liza[69] is sitting at his feet. When I walked in, Serëzha jumped up, we exchanged a few words, — [the conversation was] boring, and I left. I was certainly in their way. — I haven't finished transcribing everything, just been too busy. I'll finish tomorrow for certain.

My little girl has been very restless, she's burning from the smallpox [vaccination]: one lump has appeared on one hand and three on the other. Serëzha, it seems, has not been affected, although the nanny assures me that he will. He is still experiencing rather serious diarrhœa, probably because the vaccination is not taking. This diarrhœa does not alarm me very much. He is quite cheerful, sleeps and eats well, but it purges his [system] up to six times a day and is very obnoxious. I'm not giving him any medicine, only milk and chicken soup, which he has a hard time eating. Overall in the nursery just about everything's in good order, and whatever is not, God grant that it will [soon] pass. Write and tell me, sweet Lëvochka, when you think you might be coming. It seems such a long time ago that you left. How is Papà's health? How

---

68   In a letter dated 24 November (not included in this volume), SAT wrote: "Has it not entered anybody's head that I'll feel terrible if I don't receive a telegram?" (*Pis'ma k L. N. Tolstomu [Letters to L. N. Tolstoy], Moscow, 1936, p. 29*)

69   The reference here is to LNT's brother Sergej Nikolaevich and his 13-year-old niece (daughter of Marija Nikolaevna), Elizaveta Valer'janovna Tolstaja.

is the tube?[70] Pity I don't have the letters you all wrote. I picked up this large sheet of paper, I wanted to write you a long letter, but my hand is so tired from the copying that I can barely move it. You'll no doubt be interested in learning about Jakov. He didn't want to stay in hospital and left. They wanted to cut off his finger, but there was no way he would submit to that. It will be a terrible experience: his whole hand is already swollen and everything's very painful. We're constantly enquiring about his [condition], but have no idea what to do. What silly people — simply a fright! Just wait and see: he'll get St-Anthony's Fire. There's no coping with him without you. Maybe it will pass on its own, but that's unlikely. It's all very bad. I know nothing about your [Yasnaya Polyana] estate. All they will say is that everything's well and good. I saw the elder[71] today — he wanted to buy two axes, and he said the cook had a fight with the German. Grigorij the cabinet-maker made some baseboards, tomorrow they'll buy some felt and paint and, perhaps we'll apply the linoleum without you, if I don't meet any obstacles; I really want [to get this done]. — The health of all us adults is good, only Masha had a toothache, but she's better now. We're all staying as though bottled up inside [the house], [afraid], God help us, even to open the doors. I'm staying indoors because my winter coat isn't ready yet — they'll bring it to me tomorrow, and I'll start going for walks. — How will your callisthenics therapy proceed? It's probably passive rather than active callisthenics, as you can not raise your arm. What did they say about your posterior fossa, the protruding bone in front and the lump I could feel? Did you like the doctors? How I'd like to know all in a bit more detail! What about Tanja — is she carrying out my instructions in regard to you, and taking care of you pretty well? Since [the doctors] decided not to break your arm and you're in the same situation, you're probably out and about; write me the details, as in a diary — where you go, whom you see, etc., etc. Farewell, sweet friend; be healthy, calm, cheerful. I am in a hurry to finish, as my [daughter] Tanja has been tossing and turning. Now, it seems, she's dropped off again.

What you've given me to copy, how good it all is! I do like everything [you've written about] Princess Mar'ja! One can just picture her. And such a glorious, likeable character. I'll still be your critic. — Prince Andrej,[72] I would say, is still not clear. It's hard to tell what kind of a person he is. If he's smart, how is it that he can't understand and explain to himself his relations with his wife? The old prince is very good, too. But the first one — the one you weren't happy with — I like better. On the basis of him I pictured to myself an ideal, which doesn't fit the present prince. The scene of Prince Andrej's departure is very good, and with the image of Princess Mar'ja — excellent. It was a real pleasure for me to transcribe this. Are you writing while in Moscow? Have you been to see Katkov?[73] As regards money matters I advise you not to accept print copies in lieu of payment. *Russkij vestnik* readers do not buy books, and that's the majority of moneyed people who subscribe to the journal. Better to wait, perhaps you'll print it yourself.

This isn't my business, I know — it just popped into my head.

Lëvochka, my dearest friend, when shall I see you? Do you still take delight in thinking about our life at Yasnaya — you haven't been liking it in Moscow? I think not. Without you, Yasnaya itself no longer appeals to me. I don't feel like going anywhere outside the nursery, I

---

70 In October 1864 SAT's father, Andrej Evstaf'evich Behrs, underwent a tracheotomy operation and was given a silver tube as a prosthetic throat.

71 Vasilij Ermilov Zjabrev (1826–1880) — an elder *[starosta]* in Yasnaya Polyana.

72 Princess Mar'ja, Prince Andrej — characters in LNT's novel *War and Peace*, which SAT was transcribing at the time.

73 Mikhail Nikiforovich Katkov (1818–1887) — editor of the journal *Russkij vestnik*, in which LNT published his stories *Family happiness [Semejnoe schast'e]*, *The Cossacks [Kazaki]* and *Polikushka*. LNT was at the time negotiating with Katkov over the publication of his new novel *War and Peace*.

don't feel like doing anything. Only don't think I've let myself go. I'm still very active and cheerful. But now I really must say good-bye. Big hugs and kisses. The next time I write I'll send you the manuscript. That should be this Saturday. God grant you all good! Take care of yourself, for God's sake. Remember us with the children.

Yours, Sonja.

Nº 13 – LEV NIKOLAEVICH TOLSTOY ❧ SOFIA ANDREEVNA TOLSTAYA
[PSS 83/24]
25 November 1864. Moscow.

This morning I sent [you] a third telegram[74] saying there won't be any operation. This is what has transpired.

I stayed home this morning waiting for Rudinskij.[75] Before he came, Vendrikh[76] happened to drop by. They showed him [my arm], and he said it didn't need straightening, though he admitted that the arm was not in place, and described three attempts at straightening old dislocations, all of which turned out unsuccessful. I didn't believe him and waited for Rudinskij, whose word I was pretty much ready to accept and act on, no matter what it might be. — Earlier I had asked Andrej Evstaf'evich [Behrs] not to speak with him before I do but leave me to explain it all by myself. He made a careful observation and decided that there was no need to break [my arm], that there was a fracture (as Popov[77] admitted, too), and that some kind of ligament that had got twisted under the bone might prevent a complete straightening, and, besides, any empty space not occupied by the bones of the arm were already *probably* filled with cartilage (this Popov corroborated, too), and so there was no use trying. He said that the arm was off by very, very little, and that [eventually] I would be able to control it much better than I can right now. The reason I'm not able to control it now is mainly that all my muscles have become weak through inaction, and that the injury caused a stretching of the muscles and a paralytic condition, which might pass all by itself, or through the use of iodine or ointment, which would bring about an external inflammation. That I shall do tomorrow. My main hope is on the callisthenics therapy. Foss[78] assured [me] yesterday that he has known such cases to be healed completely, over the course of about six months. He said that should be done by him alone, consequently in Moscow, which I, of course, would not agree to, but I'm thinking of proceeding this way: starting tomorrow, I shall invite him to visit me every day for exercises, which I shall continue for a week or ten days. Aleksej [Stepanovich Orekhov] will be present and observe; and if I notice an improvement, I shall carry on doing the same thing on his instructions. Unfortunately, today he was to come and see Andrej Evstaf'evich but for some reason didn't make it, so I still haven't had a chance to discuss everything with him. Anyway, whatever will be will be. I shall not be very upset if the arm even stays in its present position with no pain, and if I knew that you were looking at it in the same way, I would be completely calm. Still no letter from you. — This morning I was happy do some writing again. Later the younger

---

74 See Letter Nº 12, Note 67.
75 Orest Ivanovich Rudinskij (1816–1889) — surgeon, professor at the Moscow Military Hospital.
76 Al'fred Fëdorovich Vendrikh — a Moscow surgeon.
77 Aleksandr Petrovich Popov (1816–1886) — professor of surgery at Moscow University.
78 *Foss* — the owner of an exercise gym in Moscow.

Obolenskij[79] arrived — it seems he is desirous to *faire la cour* to Liza,[80] and Sukhotin[81] also came — he has become considerably thinner and looks like an old *valet de chambre*. Both of them were quite boring, later Anke[82] was even more so, sitting through the whole dinner and the entire evening. Andrej Evstaf'evich is also difficult with his ceaseless, tormenting fuss about his health, which would actually be a lot better if only he paid less attention to it and restrained himself more. In the evening we all went again to the Maly Theatre (except for Tanja) to see a new farce, but it was quite a fine [evening] on the whole, only not for me. I'm quite bored here, apart from my work and Tanja's singing. She's not good. She constantly weeps and won't say anything, almost the way she did immediately after her [time with Sergej]. We received a very good letter from Sasha,[83] he just dreams about taking a trip to Yasnaya Polyana. Up until now I was pre-occupied with my arm. Now that that's resolved, tomorrow I'll get an answer from Katkov and start publishing either with him or in a separate book. I've picked up a lot of materials here. How are things going with you? What about the nursery? Farewell, sweet friend. Tomorrow I may add something further, but right now it's 11 o'clock and I'm very tired; since dinner I've been doing callisthenics with my arm. —

Nº 14 – SOFIA ANDREEVNA TOLSTAYA ❧ LEV NIKOLAEVICH TOLSTOY
[LSA 7]
26 November [1864], Late evening. [Yasnaya Polyana]

Here, Lëvochka, dear friend, I am sending you my transcription and I beg forgiveness for being lazy and not doing very much copying. Now I'm sorry that I've finished; I found it so entertaining, all the more so since you said to me on the day of your departure: "You are my assistant." I would be happy to copy from morning 'til night and to assist you. I wrote a letter in care of Serëzha [Sergej Nikolaevich] to Papà, saying that the smallpox didn't take on [our] son Serëzha, but I just had a look now, and it seems it has taken on his healthy hand, probably on his sick hand, too, it seems. Ivan [Alekseevich] has just arrived from Tula and brought no letters from you. I found that rather upsetting. Write to me, dove — this would really comfort me. Tomorrow, Lëvochka, we shall cut out the linoleum and measure everything and make [any necessary] adjustments. We bought some felt today — 6 silver roubles it cost, very expensive, as well as paints for the baseboards. A request from the cabinet-maker.

How is your arm, my dear, sweet Lëva? Is it getting better? Have you been benefited at all by your Moscow trip? Oh Lord, how I'd like to see you, talk with you, sit with you. What are you doing in Moscow? Where do you go? Whom do you see? It's terrible: for so many days I learn about you only in a few words, with no details, and no letters to date. Lëvochka, in any case I'm writing to you on the reverse side a list of what we need from Moscow.[84] If you can ask Tanja and Mamà to buy these. — As to myself there is nothing worth telling you; you know me, you know how much I love you and that I'm lonely without you.

79 Prince Dmitrij Dmitrievich Obolenskij (1844–1931) — a Tula landowner, owner of the Shakhovskoe estate in Bogoroditsk Uezd, 60 versts from Yasnaya Polyana.
80 Elizaveta Andreevna (Liza) Behrs — SAT's elder sister.
81 Sergej Mikhajlovich Sukhotin (1818–1886) — chamberlain, a Tula landowner, married to Dar'ja Alekseevna D'jakova, sister to a friend of LNT's.
82 Nikolaj Bogdanovich Anke — a friend of SAT's father's.
83 Aleksandr Andreevich (Sasha) Behrs — see Letter Nº 3, Note 10.
84 On the reverse a list of needed purchases is written in SAT's hand: a piece of cloth, thin flannel, a lining for LNT's dressing gown, cocoa, soap, a comb, etc.

N° 15 – LEV NIKOLAEVICH TOLSTOY ❧ SOFIA ANDREEVNA TOLSTAYA
[PSS 83/25]
27 November 1864. Moscow.

Yesterday for the first time I missed writing you in the evening of the same day, and now I'm writing in the morning while everyone's still asleep, so as to get to the post office before 9. Please send [the coachman] Kondratij or Serëzhka [Sergej Petrovich Arbuzov] every day. I wasn't able to write you yesterday as I got carried away reading [Mikhail Zagoskin's novel] *Roslavlev*. You see, he is so helpful and interesting to me. Yesterday I didn't go anywhere, waiting for the callisthenics specialist Foss. I tried to write, but there was nowhere I could — too much interference — besides, I wasn't in the mood, it seems. It is not cheerful here — the Kremlin is definitely not a cheerful place. Andrej Evstaf'evich talks of nothing but the disease he finds in his intestines. Liza sits quietly and goes about her own affairs, while Tanja cries for days on end, as she did yesterday morning. About what? You can't tell whether it's all about the same thing, or simply about being bored. It's true. Two or three years ago the whole world was yours and hers, with various infatuations and gay ribbons, and with all the poetry and silliness of youth. Now, all of a sudden, after seeing and admiring our world and after all the disappointments — i.e. feelings — she's experienced, she no longer finds, upon returning home, that world which she had with you. What remains is the virtuous but boring Liza, and here she's been placed face to face — i.e. so close — to her parents, who have become difficult to live with because of [her father's] illness. Anyway, she has got involved in skating, she's made a hat of *merlushka* lambskin, she's gone to concerts, but all that's not very much for her.

Yesterday, despite all that, she burst into tears when she apparently heard through Aleksej[85] that Serëzha was marrying Masha.[86] I had a talk with her, but it's both sad and disheartening to talk with her. Then Ljubimov[87] arrived from Katkov's. He heads up *Russkij vestnik*. You should have heard how he bargained with me continuously over two hours (I think) for 50 roubles per printer's sheet, all the while smiling professorially and foaming at the mouth. I held my ground and am now waiting for a reply. — They very much want, and will probably settle for 300, while I, I must confess, am afraid to publish it myself — including the bother with the printers' and especially with the censors. After him I went over to see Foss. As misfortune would have it, when I wanted to start, he wasn't there for two days in a row. At dinner the doorbell rang — just newspapers. When it rang a second time, Tanja ran down again — it was your letter. They all asked me to read it, but I was loath to share it [at the moment]. It's too good, [I thought,] and they won't understand, and didn't understand. It's had an effect on me like a piece of good music — joyful, sad and pleasant all at the same time. I felt like crying. How clever you are to say that I should never give anyone my novel to read;[88] even if wasn't clever, I would have obeyed because you wished it. — There have been no confrontations between your parents over the corned beef, etc., and after dinner Tanja brightened up (youth claims its own), and it was so pleasant. I got ready to go to the bath-house with Petja and Volodja[89] while Tanja and Mamà went to Kuznetskij Most

85 Aleksej Stepanovich Orekhov, *valet de chambre*.
86 LNT's brother Sergej Nikolaevich was living common-law with a gypsy from Tula, Marija Mikhajlovna [Masha] Shishkina (1829–1919) and had children by her. They legally married only in 1867.
87 Nikolaj Alekseevich Ljubimov (1830–1897) — professor of physics at Moscow University, one of Mikhail Katkov's leading associates.
88 See Letter N° 10 dated 22 November 1864.
89 Pëtr Andreevich (Petja) Behrs (1849–1910) and Vladimir Andreevich (Volodja) Behrs (1853–1874) — two of SAT's younger brothers.

[Street]. After bathing I was given *Roslavlev,* and while listening at tea-time, and conversing, and listening to Tanja's singing, kept reading with a delight which no one save the author could understand. Andrej Evstaf'evich has boiled some cocoa and is relentlessly urging me to have a drink. Farewell. My arm hurts, but I am hopeful. I rubbed it with iodine, and now I will make every effort to track down Foss. Farewell, my sweet; write and check with Tula every day.

Anyway, think about it and explain. The other day Sasha Kupfershmidt[90] was here, and we talked around two hours about hunting. And yesterday I went down to see the nanny and speak with her about the children and various cases; and, believe me, these two conversations were more entertaining than any I have had [to date] during my whole stay in Moscow, including Ljubimov, Sukhotin and Tjutcheva.[91] The more I meet with people now, having grown up, [the more] I'm convinced that I'm quite a unique individual, and am different only in that I no longer have my former vainglory and tomfoolery which a person rarely gets rid of.

Nº 16 – LEV NIKOLAEVICH TOLSTOY ❧ SOFIA ANDREEVNA TOLSTAYA
[PSS 83/28]
1 December 1864. Moscow.

From Lëvochka. —

My health is very good, but my main concern, my arm, is still doubtful. The doctor was just here. He bound it for the third time after the operation, and won't permit me to make the slightest movement. He promises that I shall be able to use my arm again, but admits that, though the bone is in a much better position than before, not everything is yet in its right place. My conscience is clear; I've tried everything I could, and I'm sick and tired of either talking or thinking about it. Now about my life: Tanja wrote to you about yesterday — as to why I didn't write myself, I have no idea. I guess I was tired, and despite its solemnity,[92] the whole day was difficult and tedious for everyone. [It didn't matter] who showed up, or who you talked to. D'jakova,[93] Varin'ka Perfil'eva[94] and Sasha (Aleksandr Mikhajlovich) Kupfershmidt are all good people and extend their sympathy, but — God alone knows why — it was not only tedious, but difficult, as if sitting with them were some sort of punishment. As it's proved true in our experience that we don't need a house, but a simple nursery is enough, so in my adult life I see that we don't need anybody beyond five or six people that are the closest to us. I always used to feel embarrassed and ashamed when you and I spoke of Ljubov' Aleksandrovna (Behrs) — everything about her is good, but you felt I couldn't hide [the fact] that my heart was not terribly inclined towards her. This time, and last evening in particular, when everyone had left, we had a really good conversation, and I found myself loving her very much. We didn't talk about anything out of the ordinary, [just] about [the days of] her youth, the story of the Shidlovskijs,[95] about you all and

90 Aleksandr Mikhajlovich (Sasha) Kupfershmidt (1805–1879) — a musician.

91 Ekaterina Fëdorovna Tjutcheva (1835–1882) — daughter of the poet Fëdor Ivanovich Tjutchev, as of 1867: a lady-in-waiting to the Imperial Court. Some time before his marriage LNT was attracted to her.

92 On 30 November SAT's father, Andrej Evstaf'evich Behrs, celebrated his 'name-day' (i.e. the day of the saint whose name he bears) — in his case, St. Andrew's Day. St. Andrew (Svjatoj Andrej) happens to be the patron saint of Russia, Scotland and a number of European countries.

93 Dar'ja Aleksandrovna D'jakova, *née* Tulub'eva (1830–1867) — wife of LNT's friend Dmitrij Alekseevich D'jakov.

94 Varvara Stepanovna (Varin'ka) Perfil'eva (?–1890) — daughter to Stepan Vasil'evich Perfil'ev (1796–1878), a high-ranked general, and sister to Vasilij Stepanovich Perfil'ev (1826–1890), who was married to LNT's second cousin Praskov'ja Fëdorovna Tolstaja (1831–1887).

95 SAT's maternal aunt Vera Aleksandrovna Islavina and her second husband Vjacheslav Ivanovich Shidlovskij.

about her marital relations, and her eyes were especially sparkling, and it all turned out really fine. I've tended to judge her too harshly as you and I are exceedingly spoilt by being surrounded by exceedingly good people. In fact, she is very, very good, sweet, and, most importantly, a smart woman, which I didn't recognise before.

More fun than anything else yesterday — more fun than Armfeľd,[96] the blancmange and Nikolaj Bogdanovich [Anke]'s pies, was our getting together with Tanja and Petja [Pëtr Andreevich Behrs] in the annexe and all repeating in chorus: "Sa-a-sh Kup-fer-shmidt" (!!!!staccato!!!!), in an unnatural voice. In any case, Sasha Kupfershmidt, Pëtr Gavrilovich,[97] the nanny and a lot of other things I found particularly surprising and pleasant, as they reminded me of you as a little girl, as well as when we were engaged to be married, and that is a good feeling I am experiencing for a second time, staying here in the Kremlin without you. I'm just teasing. How are things with you? After your large envelope[98] I haven't received anything, and sometimes it gets very lonely without you, especially since nothing's been coming to me to write these past two days. I was telling Tanja yesterday why it's been easier to endure the separation than it would have been if I didn't have anything to write. Along with you and the children (though I still feel my love for them is not very strong) I have a constant love and care for my writing. If I didn't have that, I feel I could definitely not last a day without you, and you understand correctly: writing is to me what the children are no doubt to you. Tanja keeps putting her finger to her eye, and is sometimes strange, sometimes unhealthfully cheerful, at other times she will suddenly give a nervous and joyful cry, like yesterday, when Klavdija[99] told about our [midwife] Marija Ivanovna,[100] and a 16-year-old priest's daughter she'd brought into their clinic who gave birth, and all at once Tanja burst into tears. Liza amazes me with her constant activity and sense of duty: she's either studying English, or translating, or working with the children, or looking after me or Papà, but it's all awkward and not terribly appealing. Andrej Evstaf'evich continually complains about his disease, he mopes about, and his family judges him too harshly. He worries about his health, but the situation with this tube [in his throat] is not very pretty; at least lately Ljubov' Aleksandrovna has been very good with him. I am always flattered by praise, and your praise of the character of Princess Mar'ja[101] really gratified me, but now I've been reading over everything you sent, and it all seems rather ugly, and I miss not having a [working] arm. I wanted to do some correcting, crossing out some things out, but I couldn't. I now feel quite discouraged over my talent, especially since yesterday I dictated to Liza some frightful nonsense. I know it's only a temporary mood, which will pass, possibly because my nerves are still weak from the chloroform and generally reduced to an abnormal state by the tight binding across my chest. Anyway, don't think that I am unhealthy; I am eating and sleeping well, and tomorrow I shall definitely go out for a walk or a drive to breathe some pure air. Oh yes, I haven't yet described what has been happening today — really, there is nothing to say — literally nothing. I have been reading Gogol's *confession*[102] (which I had long ago forgotten) along with some French *mémoires*, and I've been playing with Slavochka[103] — he's really such a

---

96 Aleksandr Osipovich Armfeľd (1806–1868) — a professor of forensic medicine at Moscow University, who liked to go hunting with SAT's father.
97 Pëtr Gavrilovich Stepanov (1806–1869) — an actor of the Maly Theatre and a friend of SAT's father's.
98 SAT sent her transcribed manuscripts of the novel *The Year 1805* (i. e., *War and Peace*).
99 *Klavdija* — a midwife, daughter to the nanny of SAT's brothers.
100 Marija Ivanovna Abramovich — a midwife who assisted SAT in childbirth.
101 A character in *War and Peace* (cf. Letter N° 13, Note 72).
102 Nikolaj Vasiľevich Gogol' (1809–1852), *An author's confession [Avtorskaja ispoved']* (1847).
103 Vjacheslav Andreevich (Slava, Slavochka) Behrs (1861–1907) — SAT's youngest brother (eighth child in the family).

dear. He keeps asking me to tell him a "tory" (story), and I tell him about the boy who ate seven cucumbers, etc. And he repeats: Mama, there… there was one boy, he ate seven cucumbers, ha-ha-ha! Their supposed Frenchman I really don't like at all; he quite belongs to the same ilk as Labourdette,[104] but what to do? He is needed, I agree, for poor Ljubov' Aleksandrovna, who is now faced with raising four boys without help from her husband, right at a time when help is most needed. Poor Stëpa[105] feels utterly downtrodden — even this Labourdette hits him from time to time — but he doesn't give up.

Whenever Stëpa enters a room and sees a visitor, an unfamiliar face (as he did yesterday with Sukhotin and D'jakova), he conscientiously bows, so that the visitor feels obliged to respond to the gesture with a particularly pleasant smile and thinks that this is it, but immediately Stëpa becomes even more sensitively and persistently obsequious, as though expecting something else. The visitor smiles again, Stëpa makes another bow, so that everyone in the room feels embarrassed. Yesterday he drove Sukhotin to the point of tender kissing.

Well, farewell, my precious friend. It is frightening to write nonsense; perhaps you don't have time [to read] it: I hope your concerns over me have already dissipated.

Hugs and kisses to all. You forgot to include tea in your list — I shall buy some; Mamà will buy the rest. I managed to pick up some Brahmapootra chickens and shall bring them with me. Whatever money I make from my novel I shall hand over to the Behrs family. As for Jakov [Tsvetkov], he was such a fool to run away from the hospital; do keep an eye on him. What's happening with the farm animals? Have there been any casualties? Is Anna Petrovna[106] still out of sorts? Or has she been spending too much time with her daughter's[107] wedding? Encourage her to give a good watering and feeding to the calves and pigs, and, most importantly, tell the elder to make sure the cattle are doing fine, otherwise two weeks could spoil everything that was done over [the past] year. Farewell, my dove, go for a walk with the Zephyrlets, take a look at the rabbit tracks, and check [for mail] at Tula every day and write to me.

Nº 17 – LEV NIKOLAEVICH TOLSTOY ☙ SOFIA ANDREEVNA TOLSTAYA
[PSS 83/29]
2 December 1864. Moscow. [Preceded by SAT's Unpublished Letter Nº 1U, 1 December 1864]

My dear Sonja, I just received your distressing letter[108] this evening and cannot write or think of anything else but what is happening with you all. I dreamt about you last night and am so afraid for each of you. The main thing is not to give into weakness or despair, keep [Serëzha's] tummy warm, don't give him any medicine, but summon the doctor, summon him without fail, not to give him medicine but to offer you hope and so for you to listen to his comfortings; I know how necessary that is. Send for him without fail, but it may already be too late: four days have gone by already. I shall come soon, I can't live without you, but I shan't leave until I see the end of the diarrhœa which is tormenting me. The smallpox vaccination is nothing [to worry about], that's what our whole family has said. When I think about what might happen, it's horrible, so I try not to think about it. One thing that comforts me is that, judging by the whole

---

104 *Labourdette* — French tutor to the Behrs brothers.
105 Stepan Andreevich (Stëpa) Behrs (1855–1910) — another of SAT's brothers (sixth child in the family).
106 Anna Petrovna Mikhajlova — farmworker in the Tolstoys' employ.
107 Evdokija Nikolaevna Mikhajlova (?–1879) — SAT's maid, who married *valet de chambre* Aleksej Stepanovich Orekhov.
108 On 28 November 1864 SAT wrote about the illness her children Sergej (Serëzha) and Tat'jana (Tanja) experienced after being vaccinated for smallpox (PSS 83: 74; letter not included in this volume).

tone of your letter, you're not quite feeling yourself, and I comfort myself with the thought that you are exaggerating this to yourself and hence inadvertently to me. If only I were certain that with even the worst-case scenario I would be sent a telegram, then I could feel calm, but right now — I can't. I know that they will say: Why hasten to send a report of misfortune? — people always find out about it too early. Give me your solemn, faithful word in advance to keep me informed, whatever happens, otherwise I can't live, can't live. I'm not to blame if you don't receive my letters; right from the start since I got here, I have only missed one day — before the operation. This morning I dictated a little to Tanja, read some books for [my] novel and looked through archival papers,[109] which they bring home as a favour arranged [for me] by Sukhotin. But despite the wealth of materials here, or, specifically because of this wealth, I feel that I am in a daze and nothing is getting written. I have been forcing myself to do some dictating, but Tanya has gone off skating. I got ready to go, too, or drive over to see them, for which I asked the doctor's permission yesterday, but the bandaging and overcoat proved so heavy that I turned back, getting only as far as Mokhovaja Street.[110] While I was gone, Popov came, but I don't regret [missing him]; I really don't need him and he can't do anything right now. I only need the bandaging which his assistant Gaak[111] makes up. I sent him 30 roubles and hope that he won't come over again. By dinner time Obolenskij[112] showed up, and I still can't figure out whom he's ardently in love with; only there's something there, and he's a very dear boy, delicate and modest, and that in itself is a major quality. In the evening I read and grieved over your letter; rode around to the shops with Tanja and Petja — it was a beautiful moonlit night. I wonder what you were doing at the time. If [you] were all in good health, you'd be out for a drive, [too]. Upon our return home, we met Grandfather;[113] he looks the same, but I was sad to see that all the respect which I had for him earlier is now completely gone. He brought along a photo showing Kostin'ka[114] with his moustache, and I was dying to see it, but it's still in an unpacked suitcase. Now the thought has come to me with such clarity and horror: What if a tragedy occurred — and here I went and wrote you this humorous letter yesterday. It is pleasant for me every evening to be with you by dictating a letter, along with a heavy feeling as if in a dream, that someone wants to grasp something and can't.

Farewell, my sweet darling dove. I can't dictate everything. I love you so greatly all this time with all the love [I can muster]. My precious friend! And the more I love, the more afraid I am. — Please give me your word that you will telegraph me about anything [important]. As soon as my arm is unbound — that will be in about five days — I shall see if it's got any better, in which case I shan't stay on here any longer. All this time I shall be doing exercises and getting accustomed to taking drives again; quiet rides in the carriage can't do any harm. Our whole family are very precious and in good health. Andrej Evstaf'evich's health, despite his complaining, has got better since I've been here. Hugs and kisses to all; I'll be sending a reply tomorrow to the dear Zephyrlets. Please write again, dear Zephyrlets.

---

109 *archival papers* — of the Palace intelligence archives. Mikhail Sukhotin (see Letter №13, Note 82) worked in the offices of the Imperial Court. LNT needed these materials for writing his novel *The Year 1805* (i.e. *War and Peace*).

110 Mokhovaja Street runs parallel to the Aleksandrov Gardens in the Kremlin.

111 Fëdor Egorovich Gaak (1836–1875) — a surgeon, assistant in a hospital surgery clinic under Dr. Aleksandr Petrovich Popov (see Letter №13, Note 78).

112 Prince Dmitrij Dmitrievich Obolenskij (1844–1931) — a jurist, a writer on current affairs, and Head of the Nobility in Bogoroditsk Uezd.

113 Aleksandr Mikhajlovich Islen'ev (1794–1882) — SAT's maternal grandfather, a retired military captain.

114 Konstantin Aleksandrovich Islavin (1827–1903) — SAT's maternal uncle, a friend of LNT's.

Nº 18 — LEV NIKOLAEVICH TOLSTOY ✹ SOFIA ANDREEVNA TOLSTAYA
[PSS 83/31]
4 December 1864. Moscow.

My dear Sonja, I was just now at Aksakov's,[115] who, you will remember, caused you so many tears and me such repentance.[116] How I remember the feeling I had when I was riding up to the house and you rushed forth to meet me. The only joy I feel here is what reminds me of you. And today again Aksakov vividly reminded me of the time when you were sitting with Nil Popov[117] on the steps at Pokrovskoe, and I, feigning indifference, was terribly jealous over you, and loved you, only quite differently from the way I do now. Yesterday at the theatre I was explaining this to your dear Anetochka;[118] when she was coming out of our loge, I told her: "I see you're feeling fine", — and in the corridor, never mind the ushers and other people about, she deftly turned to me and replied: "How delightful!" Such a dear thing! I encouraged her not to be afraid that her happiness might fade, or that they will love each other less and less [as time goes on]; [I said] that you love more and more, only in a different way; this indicates the wisdom of the world; but it would be tiresome to always love someone in exactly the same way.

And so Aksakov reminded me — when I had come for information about Austria[119] — he told me it would best of all to contact Nil Popov, who had just returned from there. I shall definitely try to go see him.

I have received letters from you for two days in a row, and so am cheerful and at peace. How clever you are to go for walks, and with the dear Zephyrlet Liza![120] How happy I would be [to be] with you, it seems, but if I came, I suppose we might quarrel over some minor trifle. But now for sure we shan't.

I have some not-so-good news to tell you about my arm. Yesterday Popov and Gaak deliberately came by together, took off the bandaging and, even though they assure me that the bone has moved a little, it seems that there has been little benefit from the operation *per se*. They proposed trying once again, repeating anew that there is one chance in 100. And I was really in a state of uncertainty, but I thought of consulting with Inozemtsev[121] and Nechaev,[122] son of the celebrated bone-setter they were telling me about. This morning I went to see Inozemtsev. At first he said there was no dislocation at all, but that I had an internal disease which he discovered when he examined my tongue through a magnifying glass; then he suggested that I wear a surgical patch, and later said it was worth another attempt at straightening [the arm]. He's completely barmy. Back home I found Vendrikh, who said there was no way I should wear a patch. So judge for yourself. At 2 o'clock Nechaev came by and said that it was absolutely impossible to straighten it, and suggested a steam-bath, ointment and a small patch under my arm, assuring

---

115 Ivan Sergeevich Aksakov (1823–1886) — Slavophile, social activist and writer on topical affairs. See his correspondence with LNT's editorial associate Nikolaj Nikolaevich Strakhov (Shcherbakova 2007).
116 On a previous visit to Moscow LNT spent an evening with Aksakov, promising to pick up his wife later at the Kremlin so they could go home together. But he did not show up until 4 a.m., causing SAT no end of worry and tears (see PSS 83: 79).
117 Nil Aleksandrovich Popov (1833–1891) — a professor of Russian history at Moscow University and a friend of the Behrs family.
118 *Anetochka* (chemist's daughter, a friend to SAT) — see Letter Nº 5, Note 30.
119 *information about Austria* — for the novel *War and Peace*.
120 Elizaveta Valer'janovna (Liza) Tolstaja, daughter to LNT's sister Marija Nikolaevna.
121 Fëdor Ivanovich Inozemtsev — see Letter Nº 11, Note 66.
122 Nikolaj Vasil'evich Nechaev (1818–1877) — a surgeon, resident physician at the Golitsyn Hospital in Moscow.

me that this could almost make it straight; in any case he promised that I would be able to use my arm almost fully. Since his remedies were completely harmless, I decided to give them a try, and now I'm on my way to take a bath. My cherished hope is that I shall once again be able to pick you up with my right arm or use my right hand to punch anyone who offends you.

Now there is still some swelling and feebleness from the break. I can't lift my arm at all, and any pushing causes pain; also, I have not received back from Katkov either the manuscripts or the money and so I am thinking of staying [here] until the end of next week. As for writing, I haven't written anything this whole time — rather, the writing's not coming, or there's simply no time, but I have been getting a lot of things ready for myself and shall continue to do so. Farewell, my sweet friend. How I love you — hugs and kisses. — Everything's going to be fine, and we have no misfortunes, if you love me the way I love you.

Poor, sweet Tanja is still sorrowing and crying. You're quite right: she and Ljubov' Aleksandrovna are the best of them all, and I love them both very much. —

N° 19 – SOFIA ANDREEVNA TOLSTAYA ✒ LEV NIKOLAEVICH TOLSTOY
[LSA 10]
5 December [1864]. Morning. [Yasnaya Polyana]

I've just got home, after spending the whole morning running household errands. Here's a detailed account. First of all I went to see the sheep. Everything's quite fine there, every one in place: the young, the old, the rams, the wethers,[123] all in special enclosures. Only among the young ones I discovered two older sheep; the German chap[124] said they were in poor health, and he wanted to try to make them better. They had feed, very clean. I saw your Rambouillet ram; he's amazingly good, well-fed, and his wool is superb. I told the German to take special care, and he assured me he would take special care, and I really think [he's doing] well. The little English pigs he has are very good and well-fed, and I even felt them with my hands. — Next I went to see Anna Petrovna.[125] Very bad here. The calves, especially the three bull-calves, are so thin that all their ribs are showing. The young bulls, who should have been fed only milk, are trying to eat the hay which is scattered about and being trampled under foot. I gave [Anna Petrovna] a strong reprimand; she was befuddled and wasn't even talking properly. I told her to tie up the milk-feeding bull-calves so that they would stay away from the hay, and to do a better job of nursing, and to put the hay in order. But I think the bull-calves are already ruined and their meat will not be so good and white. Then I headed over to the pigs. It seems to me the pigs are very well-fed and fat, but, again, I saw no feed there. Anna Petrovna kept assuring me that she had already fed them, and that there needn't be feed there every moment. The bull-calf bought from the Kopylovs is also bad. While I was there she gave him a little oats, but the hay was scattered about the whole pen, and he was trampling it with his feet. I gave her a reprimand for that, too. The Pashkovs' calf is very good and well-fed. What a beauty — a charmer! I saw the sick cow, she's already eating well and getting better. There are no other sick ones, they're all healthy. For four days now the cows have had no lees, as the [wine] factory[126] is out of operation

---

123 *wethers* — castrated rams.
124 *the German chap* — here referring to a farmworker at Yasnaya Polyana.
125 Anna Petrovna Bannikova (1807–after 1864) — a farmworker in the Tolstoys' employ.
126 This wine factory at Teljatinki was built by the Tolstoy family in 1863 on a share basis with a neighbouring land-owner, but closed down after operating only a year and a half.

and Anna Petrovna assures me that on account of that they lost weight. In fact, they watered the cows while I was there; but no sooner do they pour out the water than it freezes. The cowshed is clean, there's only oat-straw there, I said they should rake it up — the hay that was brought in was lying about by the gates in a disorderly fashion. I didn't go see the horses, since Kondratij had gone to fetch water, and I don't have any understanding myself. I really liked the Kopylov's [female] calf, such a sweet charmer! Well, next I went to see my bird pens. That doesn't interest you: I'll say only that two of my hens have been laying for more than a week now, come and taste some fresh eggs. These days I feel like a real lady of the house, and am no longer intimidated by or give into the rantings of the various Anna Petrovnas. I forgot to mention that Anna Petrovna claimed that the calves were thin because they had diarrhœa. But she's to blame for that. How would they get diarrhœa if they're in a warm shed and are fed with warm milk? Anna Petrovna further said that the cows aren't drinking water because of the bad smell from the pond. I don't know if that's correct or not, but I told them to take the water from the Voronka [brook]. If that's not right, it won't be for long, God grant the factory will be back in business. When you read all this chit-chat about the estate, you'll probably laugh at me, you'll say: "Look at how competent she's making herself out to be!" I realise that I've been giving myself a few airs, but still I've started to understand a few things, thanks to my walks with you around the stables, pens, cattle yards, etc. Now, as far as the estate goes, *that's it*.

Evening. Serëzha's still sick and weak. His diarrhœa continues and often drives me to despair. He is constantly having liquid bowel movements. It's so fluid and awful. He's grown terribly thin, all his ribs are showing. I keep putting up with it, patiently, and don't know when it will end. I feel saddened that you don't have much love for the children; they are so dear and precious to me. But if that's the way you feel, I shan't keep telling you about them — how they are doing and what's new [with them]. Only it's a pity that Serëzha won't be up and walking by the time you get here. What a time it's been for me without you! But a really sad time. And you, now, dear Lëva, what a world you live in! We've changed places: I'm in yours, and you're in mine. And as for who Sonichka Behrs was in the Kremlin — that is now nothing but a legend, and there isn't even a trace of her. I wish I could now reach my ideal of the perfect housewife, especially being active and capable of doing everything, not to mention taking care of children who appeared all on their own without any effort. My daughter has been, up to now, quite as I had imagined. Exactly the kind of child I wished for: healthy, strong, calm — my offspring. I don't have any problems with her. At this present moment Serëzha is playing around me on the floor, and keeps lying down with his face to the linoleum. It chills the scrofula on his cheeks, and he keeps moving from place to place to find a cool spot. At first, Lëvochka, I kept thinking that all of a sudden you would walk in, but now I've quite lost heart. I'm no longer anticipating your arrival, but there is a constant aching feeling in my soul. Another time, possibly, I shall no longer agree to part from you, my precious friend. I torment myself to the extreme, and what for? Lately I've been sitting upstairs with [Tolstoy's sister] Mashen'ka and the children. We've had some pretty sad conversations. Liza is still ill, and she's been experiencing some dizziness. Mashen'ka's very concerned. She's not even accustomed to living in Russia, let alone the countryside. What's more, to tell the truth, if we lived in the city, your arm would have been already completely healthy, and no matter how you figure it, it's very sad that you still have this deformity. You keep saying: "It's mostly for you that I want my arm to be straightened." Why for me? I shan't love you any less for it — on the contrary, [I shall love you] more. Lëvochka: the gardener's just stopped by and asked me to write you to buy some seeds:

Large pineapple melon.
Large Black Sea melon.
Bukhara melon.
¼ funt of semi-Dutch cucumbers.

Thank you for the Brahmapootras, I'm so happy to have them. I'm just afraid my old woman will let them die of neglect. I think I'll bring them into the kitchen. They'll start laying eggs sooner there and be better fed. Serëzha is always crawling on the floor — he has a lot of room to play — and my heart is glad. Only one [concern] — they didn't stretch the linoleum very smoothly, there are wrinkles in places. There's just one piece that's still intact. It's worth 5 roubles. What to do with it? It might be useful at some point. — This evening, can you imagine, I hear singing! It's Natal'ja Petrovna,[127] Mashen'ka, and the children, who over tea started to sing Mar'ja Gerasimovna's[128] hymn "*svoim dukhom uteshajus'…*" ["I am comforted by my spirit…"] etc. Too bad I couldn't be with them, I was putting my little girl to bed, and now here I am writing to you, my sweet. That is a pleasure for me. It's eight o'clock already, but they still haven't returned from Tula and so no letter yet.

Just now they brought me your letter, my precious Lëva. It's a real treat for me to read what you've scribbled with your sick arm. "With all the loves" — but I for one do not know which of my loves I love you with. Anyway, I'm always reticent to talk about them, since you once said: "Why talk? People don't talk about that." You've become very alarmed about Serëzha; I regret now [telling you,] although I did not exaggerate. I didn't send for the doctor, and still shan't as long as it doesn't get much worse. But now, in any case, he's a little better — he crawls, plays and eats. Of course I would wire you [if anything should happen] — do you think I would leave you in the dark? Don't hurry, my dear friend, we'll be seeing each other; above all, take good care of your arm; you will be sorry later [if you don't]. — Why can't you write [anything]? Such a pity! It's all that wretched chloroform. And the last time it affected the nerves, remember, and you too were discouraged about yourself and were sometimes gloomy and doubted yourself. Don't give in to your nerves, my sweet Lëvochka, they [only] trick you. Your talent is not something for you to judge and it could not suddenly disappear, but the chloroform has ruined everything. Wait a little, and it will all come back. And if you cannot write, we'll go look at the pigs, the sheep, the cows and the Brahmapootras which you'll bring with you; we'll go for a walk in the fresh snow and enjoy Nature; we'll do some reading aloud and have fun with the children. Now everything will seem new once again. You *had a good time* in Moscow. I haven't felt dejected so far, on the contrary, I'm surprised myself at how cheery I've been. I have to admit that, while Serëzha is no less dear and precious to me, it means a lot to me that I have a second child — that gives me considerable support. At the moment Nanny is holding her in her arms; she's laughing and waving her tiny hands. Lëvochka, dear, I'll be seeing you some time, my friend. We'll have quite a different life then. As for the arm, the arm — it's simply a tragedy. As for the young Obolenskij, it would be better for him to go after Tanja — she's more of a match for him; Liza's too serious, besides, she's older than he. Have him come over to see us, if [you find] him a nice person. I am very grateful to Tanja for writing me on your behalf. Give her a heartfelt kiss from me. Lëva, right now I'm busy all day long distributing vouchers for wine to the staff and

127 Natal'ja Petrovna Okhotnitskaja (?–1876) — a poor noblewoman living at the Tolstoys', a companion to Tat'jana Aleksandrovna Ergol'skaja, after whose death she moved to an alms-house set up on Turgenev's Spasskoe-Lutovinovo estate.
128 *Mar'ja Gerasimovna* — a nun, godmother to LNT's sister Marija Nikolaevna Tolstaja.

day-workers. Tomorrow's a holiday, and I shall go look around the estate once again. And the money I give out — I borrowed 100 silver roubles from Masha, but there's no place I can get any more. I give it to them because I can't turn them down, and I feel it doesn't make much difference whether I'm in debt to Masha or the workers. — Well, Lëvochka, my dove, farewell. I've been writing this letter to you the whole day. Still, it's nice and long. I'm enclosing Serëzhka's[129] letter to Aleksej. I laughed so hard when he brought it to me with his smile and asked me to forward it. He's coping very well, and we don't notice Aleksej's absence too much. Farewell; I could go on writing and writing. And it's bedtime; I still have to feed our little daughter. I sleep in the middle of the room on the floor, and that suits me just fine. Hugs and kisses to you, my sweet, and I love you possibly more than you can love me. I have been reading over your letters twenty times; thank you for writing every day. Now Serëzha [Sergej Nikolaevich] has come; I shan't see him, as I'm [already] undressed and need to feed [Tanja].

Nº 20 – LEV NIKOLAEVICH TOLSTOY ✹ SOFIA ANDREEVNA TOLSTAYA
7 December 1864. Moscow.

Yesterday I received your good letter,[130] dear friend. It's already the fourth day [in a row] that the postman's rung regularly, right at dinner time, and brought me your letters.

Remember, darling, I'm counting on your informing me right away if Serëzha takes a turn for the worse. He must have catarrh of the stomach. The remedy is hygiene, warmth and easily digestible food — milk, soup, and Andrej Evstaf'evich strongly recommends calves' legs and sago.[131] I'll bring you some sago. Yesterday I wrote you about my plans, my arm and my melancholy here. The same is exactly true today. Sunday I'm planning to be with you; I'm asking Aleksej to exercise my arm twice a day and I'm wearing a bandage which gives me considerable relief. I can't take care of any business [at the moment]. — Yesterday I was reading an English novel by the author of *Aurora Floyd*.[132] I bought ten volumes of these English novels which I haven't yet read, and very much look forward to reading them with you. You and Liza, after all, could be studying English. Then [I had] another [visit from] the repulsive Aleksandr Mikhajlovich [Kupfershmidt], as well as from Katerina Egorovna[133] and Liza. I couldn't even read — there was no corner [I could retreat to]. I just went for a walk before dinner, and couldn't visit the libraries or the shops, because it was Sunday. After dinner again [I read] [the romance novel] *Pogubil ja svoju molodost'* [*I ruined my youth*],[134] and at 7 o'clock [I went to see] *A Life for the Tsar [Zhizn' za Tsarja]*.[135] It was very good, but monotonous. In the theatre was just a Sunday audience, and so half the interest for me as an observer wasn't there. Still, back home again, we were alone: Ljubov' Aleksandrovna, who is very, very precious and good, Liza, Tanja and Petja, and somehow we managed to have a lot of fun. We reminisced, discussed

---

129 Sergej Petrovich (Serëzhka) Arbuzov (servant) — see Letter Nº 4, Note 15.
130 Letter Nº 19 of 5 December 1864.
131 *sago* — a cereal made out of starch from the sago palm.
132 Mary Elizabeth Braddon (1835–1915) — English writer, author of *Aurora Floyd* (1863). LNT was probably reading one of her two subsequent books: either *Lady Audley's secret* (1862) or *John Marchmont's legacy* (1863), both of which are to be found in his Yasnaya Polyana library.
133 Ekaterina Egorovna Böse — German teacher to the Behrs boys.
134 This phrase is uttered three times by the hero of LNT's story *Two hussars [Dva gusara]*, Count Il'in, in a state of depression and confusion following a huge gambling loss.
135 An opera by the composer Mikhail Ivanovich Glinka (1804–1857), which LNT heard at the Bolshoi Theatre on 6 December 1864.

things. Tanja declared that all she wanted was to live high, high up in a tower with a guitar. Ljubov' Aleksandrovna pointed out that one would need to eat and go to the loo in the tower, whereupon Tanja, nervously but still cheerfully — like the time [she was told] about the priest's daughter — burst into tears, and we all left to go to bed. Besides, Petja was sleeping, or at least pretending, and I recounted how I ought, despite my wife's jealous nature, to confess to my unfortunate incident with Annochka[136] in order to clear my conscience. As I was taking off my dress-coat, I happened to wave my arm just as she was walking past, and my hand landed right on her breast. I can see you making your usual squeamish face [as you read this]… Oh, Sonja, will these five days ever pass? To clear my conscience I want to show my steam-treated arm to Nechaev. From Katkov and Ljubimov I have received no answer or manuscript, and that bothers me. Nevertheless, I really don't feel like going over to see Katkov. In the archives [of the Palace intelligence service] there is nothing useful for me. And now I shall pay a visit to the Chertkov and Rumjantsev Libraries.[137] I feel extremely wretched and bored, especially these past two days. You say I should get out for a drive. I don't feel like going anywhere. [I just have] one thought: how to keep from forgetting to do what is necessary. But, choosing between two indulgences — contriving to talk about intelligent [ideas] or affectations, or shuffling around the rooms in the Kremlin without purpose, the latter alternative looks better and better, especially when Aleksandr Mikhajlovich is away — he, and I'll tell you [in person] why, has become so repulsive to me that I can no longer look on him indifferently, and lately I've been deliberately so cold to him that he will no longer come and see us [at Yasnaya Polyana]. He left yesterday at 5 o'clock. All the blacks[138] in your family are dear and nice to me. Ljubov' Aleksandrovna is terribly much like you. A few days ago she made a lampshade — when you get right down to work, you can't be torn away. You even have similar negative traits in common. I sometimes hear her starting to speak with confidence about something she has no knowledge of, and make positive statements and exaggerate, and I recognise you. But you are good to me in every sort of way. I am writing in a study, and in front of me are your portraits at four different ages. My dove, Sonja. What a smart girl you are in anything you put your mind to!.. That's why I say, too, that you have an indifference to intellectual interests, and not only a lack of limitation, but a mind, and a great mind at that. And that's something shared by all of you, my especially dear black bears. There are black Behrs — Ljubov' Aleksandrovna, you, Tanja; and white [Behrs] — the rest of you. In the black [Behrs] the mind is dormant — they are capable, but unwilling, and hence comes their confidence (not always à propos) and tact. But their mind is dormant because they love with great strength, and also because the foremother of the black bers was undeveloped, i.e. Ljubov' Aleksandrovna. On the other hand, the white Behrs have a great sympathy for intellectual interests, but their minds are weak and shallow. Sasha is multi-coloured,

---

136 *Annochka* — elderly maid to SAT's sisters Liza and Tanja.

137 The Chertkov Library is the collection of the archæologist and numismatist Aleksandr Dmitrievich Chertkov (1789–1858) containing more than 20,000 volumes of books and manuscripts; in 1863 it became the first free and publicly accessible library in Moscow, at the initiative of his son, Grigorij Aleksandrovich Chertkov (1832–1900). The Rumjantsev Library was organised by the prominent political figure Nikolaj Petrovich Rumjantsev (1754–1826), who offered his private collection for public use. From 1924 to 1992 it was known as the Lenin Library; since then it has been known as the Russian National Library, one of the largest in Europe.

138 LNT divided the members of the Behrs family into *blacks* (i.e. brown-eyed, such as Ljubov' Aleksandrovna, SAT, her sister Tanja et al.) and *whites* (or blue-eyed, such as Andrej Evstaf'evich, SAT's sister Liza et al.). He also makes a play on words with the surname *Bers* (Russian, or more commonly Behrs in English), originally a variant of the German word *Bär* [bear]. Later SAT would make a similar distinction among her own children. SAT's siblings mentioned: Liza (Elizaveta [earlier]), Tanja (Tat'jana), Sasha (Aleksandr), Slavochka (Vjacheslav), Stëpa (Stepan), Petja (Pëtr), Volodja (Vladimir). See Editor's Introduction ("Spiritual Searching, Evaluation of Self").

half-white. Slavochka is like you, and I love him. There's something about his upbringing with all the overindulgence and spoiling that grates me the wrong way, but he will surely be a promising lad. Only Stëpa, I fear, will still cause us all much misfortune. He himself is bad for some reason, but his upbringing has been even worse. Yesterday on account of a dispute about the tutor, in which Tanja, Petja and Volodja ganged up on the tutor, Ljubov' Aleksandrovna decided to place them all — except for Petja — in boarding schools. And I say: Fine, at least your conscience will be clear. But it's true that the father is absent. I say: If I am to die [soon], I shall leave one bequest to Sonja, [namely,] that she place Serëzha in a state-run boarding school. And I haven't actually said why I consider you really smart. Like a good wife, you think of your husband as yourself, and I remember how you said to me that all my military and historical [scenes] that I've put so much effort into will turn out poorly, while the [parts about] family, the characters' traits and psychological [makeup] will turn out fine.[139] That is so true; nothing could be truer. And I remember your saying that to me, and I remember the whole of you like that. And, like Tanja, I feel like crying out: "Mamà, I want to go to Yasnaya, I want Sonja." When I began this letter, I wasn't quite myself, but I'm finishing it as quite a different person. My darling soul-mate! Only you love me as I love you, and there's nothing I can't bear, and everything is marvellous. Farewell, it's time for me to get down to business.

Nº 21 – SOFIA ANDREEVNA TOLSTAYA ✿ LEV NIKOLAEVICH TOLSTOY
[LSA 11]
7 December [1864]. Evening. [Yasnaya Polyana]

I'm sitting here in your study, writing and weeping. I'm weeping about my [state of] happiness, about you, [the fact] that you're not here. I'm remembering my whole past, I'm weeping because Mashen'ka[140] has started playing something, and the music, which I have not heard in a long time, has at once taken me out of my own realm of the nursery, diapers and children which I have not taken a single step out of for a long time and transported me somewhere far, far away, where everything is different. I've even become fearful — I have long silenced within myself all those strings which painfully resonated at the sound of music, at the sight of Nature, as well as at everything you seemed to be missing in me — and this sometimes annoyed you. But in this moment I feel everything, and it is both painful and good. It is better we don't have all this as mothers and housewives. If only you could see how I am weeping now, you would be surprised, because I don't know myself what about. I have always regretted that I have so little an understanding of all that is good, and now, at this moment, I wish these feelings had never been awakened in me. To you as a poet and writer such feelings are necessary, but to me as a mother and housewife they are only painful, because I cannot and must not give into them. — Lëvochka, when we see each other [again], never ask what happened to me or why I was crying; right at this moment I can tell you everything, but later on I would [only] feel ashamed. At this moment I am listening to music, all my emotions are uplifted, I am terribly in love with you, I see how beautifully the sun is setting through your windows. At this moment the Schubert melodies I used to be so indifferent to are stirring my whole soul, and I can't restrain myself from weeping the most bitter tears, even though [I feel] good. Sweet Lëvochka, you are going to laugh at me, you will say I'm out of my mind. Now they'll be lighting the candles, they'll be

---

139 The reference here is to LNT's novel *The Year 1905* (later known as *War and Peace*).
140 In this letter *Mashen'ka* refers to LNT's sister Marija Nikolaevna Tolstaya.

calling me to breast-feed [my little girl], and I shall see what a mess Serëzha's managed to make of himself, and my whole mood will be gone at once, as though nothing had ever happened to me. — Mashen'ka is standing by the bedroom window; I just walked by and she's blowing her nose. I think she, too, is weeping. What has happened to us? I didn't approach her, but that's how it seemed to me. — I'm still looking around your study, and still remember how you used to get dressed for hunting over by the gun cupboard, how Dora would leap up so joyfully beside you, how you would sit at your desk and write, and I would come and fearfully open the door, peep in — to make sure I wasn't disturbing you — and you would see how timid I was and say "Come in". But that's all I wanted. I remember how you used to lie on the sofa when you were ill; I remember the difficult nights you had following your bone dislocation, and Agaf'ja Mikhajlovna[141] would be [lying] on the floor, dreaming in the half-light, — and I was so sad — I can't tell you how sad I was. God forbid we should ever part again. All this is a real ordeal. I shan't be seeing you now for almost a week, my sweet dove. I just sent Serëzhka [Arbuzov] to Tula, and he brought me two letters: one from Tanja, the other was yours,[142] with all your reminiscences about the past. It's as though things will never be good for us, that it's all just reminiscences — precisely that right now we are sad and it is very hard to live in this world. I can't even talk of your arm without acute distress. How much trouble and grief, and what's come out of it? It's just the same [as before]. From what I can see, the operation took a lot of time, added a tremendous amount of suffering on the part of both you and me, with hardly any benefit. Most of all I'm afraid that you are starting to feel depressed because you won't be able to control your arm as before. You want to do something or other, and your arm doesn't move the way it should, and you begin to feel despondent. And now it seems [to you] that things are fine at home, at Yasnaya Polyana, but you'll come and settle in, and I'll start to irritate you again; and then there's the diarrhœa, and the children — it will all seem routine. Oh, about Serëzha, I should tell you that the diarrhœa has continued without any change for several days now. He's happy, but he's weak and thin. Our little girl is doing fine, but now all day long she has trouble sleeping and fidgets — it takes up a lot of my time. In spite of that, I've managed now to read in the new *Russkij vestnik* a very silly story called "*Doch' upravljajushchego*" [The manager's daughter][143] and the beginning of the English novel *Armadale*,[144] which I found very interesting, so much so that I spent a pleasant hour [on it]. It's amazing how many English writers there are, and they're all very interesting, while here all sorts are writing silly narratives. I still haven't read [Dickens' novel] *Our Mutual Friend* yet, and I didn't continue reading it, as I gave it to Serëzha [Sergej Nikolaevich]. — Lëva, just imagine, my friend, what grief. Nanny went to a party at Anna Petrovna's and on her way back she fell and injured her leg bone something awful; for a half-hour now her ankle's been frightfully swollen and she's in great suffering — I don't know what to do. We're applying cold compresses, and tomorrow I'll send for the doctor. She can take a few steps, only with great pain. I'm holding up, don't worry about me. I'm healthy, strong, and can do everything. Liza's ill, too — with stomach fever, it seems. We are sending for Dr. Vigand,[145] and now the same woman [bone-setter] is straightening her leg that straightened

---

141 Agaf'ja Mikhajlovna (1808–1896) — former serf, maid to LNT's paternal grandmother Pelageja Nikolaevna Tolstaja.
142 Letter N° 18 of 4 December 1864.
143 A story which was possibly written by Sof'ja Dmitrievna Khvoshchinskaja (1824–1865), published under the pseudonym N in the journal *Russkij vestnik*, N° 10 (1864), pp. 632–75.
144 A novel by the English writer Wilkie Collins (1824–1889), published in Russian translation in *Russkij vestnik*, N° 10 (1864), pp. 676–727. Collins became a close friend to his mentor and collaborator, Charles Dickens.
145 Èduard Il'ich Vigand — see Letter N° 5, Note 41.

your [arm]. If it turns out bad, I'll send for Preobrazhenskij.[146] No matter how much we curse them, we still need them. I have my little girl in my arms, and I'm hastening to write to you, my dear friend. You see, I don't hide anything from you. Now you be sensible and don't be overly concerned, and don't come home if the doctors don't allow it. If something really bad happens, I'll send you a wire. I'm hoping that Nanny has just a bruise and swollen tendons, since she can at least stand on her feet, even though it's painful. What a miserable time this is! All I need now is to have a breakdown! But I'm a fighter. Yesterday my throat started hurting, and now that's passed. The [bone-setter] tells me that Nanny had a dislocation, and that's a shame. Farewell, dear friend. Now my workload has doubled, and I shan't be writing you as much. Big hugs and kisses. What terrible misfortunes have befallen us! Serëzha, unfortunately, refuses to be cuddled, when he is ill, by anyone [except Nanny]. So she will have to lie down and cuddle him in her arms. I shall hand him to her. Don't worry about me. I'll do fine with Dushka's[147] and Dunjasha's[148] help. — The woman has now been doing the straightening, and Nanny assures me that she has got a lot better and has stopped moaning. Maybe it was simply a bruise and she's improved with the cold water and camphor alcohol we applied. How are you doing? How is your unfortunate arm? I imagine you've grown even thinner. Hugs and kisses to dear Tanja for looking after you this way, and for our love to her (yours and mine). And Mamà, too, of course. I don't write her because there's too much I have to tell her. She still knows I love her, and you know that, too. Lëva dear, it is true that in the meantime you and I love each other, we can bear all things, and are strong enough for everything.

Your Sonja.

N° 22 – LEV NIKOLAEVICH TOLSTOY ❧ SOFIA ANDREEVNA TOLSTAYA
[PSS 83/36]
11 December 1864. Moscow.

Sonja, darling. I'm in very good spirits — as good as I can be without you. I have three joys today. 1) This morning I went to take a bath, and, as usual, while in the water, I began to exercise my arm and push the bone back where it ought to be. You can imagine, how surprised I was to notice that the bone is sometimes forward by 1/8 of a *vershok* [about 1/2 cm], and when you push it, it goes back. After pushing it back, I tried raising it. In the water it lifted easily. I got up, and in the air, to my great surprise, I was able to raise it shoulder-height and higher — much higher — than my head. As long as I support the bone with my [other] arm, I can lift my [injured] arm without pain or difficulty. You can imagine how greatly delighted I was by this discovery. The question now is how to keep the bone in this position. The bandaging will hold it, but not completely, and, besides, it constrains my arm. Tomorrow I'll have a visit from Nechaev, to whom I am grateful for the advice regarding the bath, the ointment and the bandaging, and after that I'll still go and see Popov. They can take a look on the spot and see what needs to be done further.

This letter will probably arrive along with me, but I am writing it (apart from [the fact] that I'm feeling fine and wanting to talk with you) just in case I shan't get there by Sunday, so that you will know that some kind of bandage or [doctor's] examination of my arm has delayed me. That probably won't happen. 2) This is not exactly a joy, but, nevertheless, pleasant news. This

---

146 Vasilij Grigor'evich Preobrazhenskij (1839–1887) — a Tula physician.
147 Avdot'ja Ivanovna (Dushka) Bannikova (1852–?) — daughter of farm-worker Anna Petrovna.
148 Avdot'ja Nikolaevna (Dunjasha) Bannikova — maid, later the wife of Aleksandr Stepanovich Orekhov.

morning Ljubimov came to see me from Katkov's, and negotiated for another three hours, and ended up getting me to release to them — i.e. allow them to print — 500 copies (I didn't back away from the price) and making me tell them sharply that they were crude. He left, agreeing to everything, and asked me only to now leave them the manuscript.[149] Hence this matter is now closed. 3) Your letter,[150] candid and long. My darling, I rejoice in your tears, I understand them, I love them very, very, very much. Only it's frightening [to think] they might be mixed in with regret, and isn't there something I could do to make that regret go away? It saddens me that you still can't say that Serëzha's diarrhœa is over. Don't say or think that I don't love them. One of my chief desires is for Serëzha to be completely well. I would ask nothing more, even of a witch-doctor. It's just that I don't love them to the same degree that I love you. —

Another pleasant experience today — very pleasant — was that Zhemchuzhnikov[151] came to see me, and, counter to your advice, I promised to read him several chapters. By co-incidence [Ivan Sergeevich] Aksakov showed up at just the same time. I read to them up to the place where Ippolit tells his story: "one girl"[152] greatly appealed to both of them, especially Zhemchuzhnikov. They said it was charming. And I'm glad, and am more enthusiastic about continuing. It's dangerous when there's no praise or when praise is insincere; still, it is helpful when you feel you've made a strong impression. Under the influence of this delightful feeling we had a good conversation in the bedroom, and I took supper at the table, sitting at the very same place you were waiting for me when I proposed to you, which I recall ever so vividly. How could we not remember? Thank God, both our reminiscences about the past and our dreams of the future are good, and our present will be good, too. How lovely that when we see each other again, I shall behold the especially gladsome face which you make so beautifully at moments like this. I so vividly recalled, too, your terrified face, and your lilac-coloured dress. I kept pointing this place out to [your sister] Tanja, but she couldn't guess [its significance]. —

Kisses to Auntie's hands, and hugs and kisses to Masha, the Zephyrlets, big Serëzha and little Serëzha, and Tanja who's still an infant. If God be willing, I shall bring this letter myself.

N° 23 – LEV NIKOLAEVICH TOLSTOY ✿ SOFIA ANDREEVNA TOLSTAYA
[PSS 83/41]
27 July 1865. Voin.

Sonja! So you can see where I'm writing from.[153] I arrived late yesterday at the Novosil'tsovs'[154] and one way or another couldn't get away any earlier than today at 2 o'clock. —

The old chap started telling me his anecdotes and stories from my good old era of 1812. But his son tormented me, showing off his estate. His house and estate are diametrically opposite

---

149 The novel *The Year 1805* was scheduled to be printed in the February 1865 issue of *Russkij vestnik* (equivalent to the first twenty-eight chapters of the 1886 edition of *War and Peace*).

150 Letter N° 21 of 7 December 1864.

151 Aleksej Mikhajlovich Zhemchuzhnikov (1821–1908) — Russian lyric poet, satirist and humorist.

152 In the final version of *War and Peace* Ippolit tells a joke about a Moscow noblewoman and her maid (Part I, Chapter 5).

153 *Voin* — the name of the Novosil'tsovs' estate 13 versts south-west of Mtsensk in Orël Gubernia (115 versts from Yasnaya Polyana), imprinted in the upper left-hand corner of the first page.

154 Pëtr Petrovich Novosil'tsov (1797–1869) — Privy Councillor, Deputy Governor of Moscow (1838–1851), Governor of Rjazan' (1851–1858), and his son Ivan Petrovich Novosil'tsov (1827–1890) — equerry. Both were hunting partners of LNT's.

to that of the Barons.[155] Everything's for show and vainglory: parks, gazebos, ponds, *points-de-vue*, and it's very good. But Yasnaya is better. And, can you imagine, the sight of his estate has aroused me to something you love and desire, [namely,] to do a thorough cleaning at Yasnaya. At the moment God knows when I shall arrive, but I shall come without stopping. I'll release my horses here, as Baraban[156] has taken ill. I'll buy everything [I need] at Orël. I am happy that they entertained me today, otherwise I would have been sad and greatly worried about you along the way. It's funny to say this, but no sooner had I left than I thought how frightful it was for me to leave you alone. — Farewell, darling, be a good girl and write. Pëtr Petrovich is pacing around me as I write, getting in the way and saying things like "*mettez-moi aux pieds de la Comtesse*". Farewell.

L. Tolstoy.

Nº 24 – SOFIA ANDREEVNA TOLSTAYA ❧ LEV NIKOLAEVICH TOLSTOY
[LSA 14]
28 July 1865. Evening. [Pokrovskoe.]

I've just now come from the Del'vigs', my sweet friend Lëva. I was only two hours there. I drove in the wagon with Pavel,[157] quite apart from everyone else. I can't tell you about their party and the guests. The provincial riff-raff, with pale-skinned ladies, with a provincial lion in a Russian velvet coat and black *peau-de-soie* pantaloons. Not fun at all and not funny. Their *petits jeux* are boring, the cavaliers' jokes are silly and not funny; various jams on saucers, oldsters playing cards and children flitting here and there in gay-coloured dresses and little chiffon pantaloons. The only sweet things there are the host and hostess — the joyous and actually amazingly simple Fionochka, along with the baron himself — kindhearted and actually without any trace of pomposity. I deliberately tried to discover pomp in something, but couldn't. Mashen'ka is highly respected in their circles, and I myself was made quite a fuss over. I didn't want to go in the first place — it was frightening to leave the children even for a couple of hours. Anyway, they are safe and sound. Only Serëzha's come down with a hoarse throat; I'm surprised it hasn't passed yet.

Somehow I've missed telling you about receiving your sweet letter[158] this morning — sweet because you also regretted leaving me, and because I wasn't the only one for whom your departure was sad and painful. I was very happy about that, and your letter was such a delight today that I have been carrying it around with me and reading it over and over again. I wasn't surprised to learn that you stopped over at the Novosil'tsovs'. I'm glad that you had some rest and relaxation. It doesn't matter to me where you are or what you do, as long as you're first of all healthy and, secondly, happy. But you haven't written to me anything concerning your stomach or the noise in your ear. Baraban [the horse] is now getting better and is starting to eat feed; you gave him a real work-out. I wanted to tell you what we did yesterday and today, but I don't remember it very well. The only thing I remember about yesterday is that we spent the morning sewing and beading, then we went bathing twice and ate a lot of gooseberries. Last evening

155 Baron Aleksandr Antonovich Del'vig (1818–1882) and his wife Khionija Aleksandrovna, *née* Chapkina, a friend of LNT's sister Marija Nikolaevna. Aleksandr Del'vig and his brother, poet Anton Del'vig, owned an estate in Chern' Uezd, Tula Gubernia. Anton Del'vig was a friend to the celebrated Russian poet Aleksandr Sergeevich Pushkin (1799–1837).
156 *Baraban* — one of LNT's favourite horses.
157 *Pavel* — coachman to Marija Nikolaevna (Mashen'ka) Tolstaja.
158 Letter Nº 23 of 27 July 1865.

Mashen'ka went to visit the Sukhotins,[159] while the four of us young people all had a nice chat. We were in a poetic mood, and started telling the girls about our childhood and early youth, along with a few stories. Then Mashen'ka arrived, and it was obvious that we had an evening à *confidences*. The girls went off to bed, and she [Mashen'ka] told Tanja and me in detail about her romance with Turgenev, and about her romance abroad.[160] We broke up quite late, and for a long time I couldn't sleep. I kept dreaming about you, half asleep, half awake. It seemed as though you were pointing to a corner where some lights were flickering, and saying: "Look, look…" It was so lonely and frightening. Only my little girl who was sleeping with me comforted and delighted me with her presence.

I got up late this morning and my head ached so. I spent the whole morning dressing Mashen'ka and the girls to go visiting — someone needed a ribbon, another earrings, a third wanted her hair combed. They went early, off to dinner, while I spent the whole time up to six o'clock transcribing for you, and made good progress indeed. At six [p.m.] the children got up and I had dinner with them at home. We had such a good and happy time together. Serëzha ate with an appetite, and was so sweet. It was almost eight by the time I went to see the barons. Tomorrow morning I am sending this letter — there probably won't be any letter from you yet. Various gentlemen and ladies at the barons' were asking for you, and wondering how your writing was coming along. "They're just trying to be nosy," I thought several times. Anyway, God knows who it was, but I'm pleased when they talk about you and praise you. My sweet Lëvochka, where are you right now? I've been thinking these are real hunting days — warm, with a drizzle. God grant you to be well and happy. Farewell, hugs and kisses, darling. Please do write me more often.

Nº 25 – LEV NIKOLAEVICH TOLSTOY ❧ SOFIA ANDREEVNA TOLSTAYA
[PSS 83/42]
27? July 1865. Orël.

I snatched this piece of stationery from the Novosil'tsovs.[161]

I'm writing several more lines from Orël, which I am now departing. I'll reach Shablykino[162] probably after midnight and I guess I'll have to stay the night at a coaching inn. My health is just so-so, although one ear hurts. Travelling is boring, but the time I spent at the Novosil'tsovs' was interesting — and [thus] very pleasant.

I'm going shopping now for some [new] shoes, but I shall probably not be able to send them home. If I did, they would probably not arrive before I got there. I'm getting more and more bored, depressed and frightened.

159 Pavel Ivanovich Sukhotin and his wife Anna Petrovna Sukhotina, who lived on their Parintsevo estate close to Marija Nikolaevna Tolstaja's Pokrovskoe estate.
160 In 1854 the writer Ivan Sergeevich Turgenev was living in exile on his Spasskoe-Lutovinovo estate next door to Marija Nikolaevna Tolstaja's Pokrovskoe estate. They met in October 1854, a year before Turgenev's acquaintance with LNT, and Turgenev was attracted to her. He used her as the prototype for the heroine of his story "Faust". The *romance abroad* refers to the common-law marriage between Marija Nikolaevna Tolstaja with Swedish Viscount Hector de Kleen (1831–1873), whom she met in Switzerland and from whom she bore an extra-marital offspring, Elena (1863–1942; married name: Denisenko). In 1857 Marija Nikolaevna separated from her husband Valer'jan Petrovich Tolstoj, who betrayed her, but her husband did not grant her a formal divorce, and so her marriage to de Kleen was not legitimised.
161 The imprint of Novosil'tsovs' *Voin* seal is visible in the corner. See also Letter Nº 23 above.
162 *Shablykino* — the estate of Nikolaj Vasil'evich Kireevskij (1797–1870) in Karachev Uezd, Orël Gubernia, where LNT was on his way to do some hunting.

I probably shan't find Kireevskij at home and shall spend the 28th chasing after him.

You know, if I can get to hunt on the 29th, 30th and 31st I shall be completely satisfied and could be home on the 2nd [of August], but that's just a guess.

It's turned out that instead of arriving [at Shablykino] this morning, I'll get there tomorrow morning. In any case, I'll be home by the 5th, and I hope and wish it to be earlier.

Never before our [most recent] separation have we been so unemotional as this time, and so I do worry about you. Farewell, darling. Write a detailed account of everything in your diary. At least I'll [be able to] read it when I get home.

L. Tolstoy.

On the fourth page: To her Ladyship the Countess Sofia Andreevna Tolstaja, Chern', Village of Pokrovskoe, [estate of] Countess [Marija Nikolaevna] Tolstaja.

Nº 26 – SOFIA ANDREEVNA TOLSTAYA ❧ LEV NIKOLAEVICH
[LSA 15]
29 July 1865. [Pokrovskoe.]

I never anticipated such happiness, my sweet Lëvochka, that you would send me yet another letter. I've just risen, and Dushka [Avdot'ja Ivanovna Bannikova] has brought me a little note — I wondered who it might be from, and all at once [I saw] it's another one from you. So sorry to hear your health is still not good — you won't believe the constant suffering I've gone through over your health. Again, I was delighted to hear that you are still thinking of me all the time, only what gave you the idea that we were indifferent to each other before you left? I was not indifferent, I was sad that you were leaving, especially since you weren't well. Your indifference, on the other hand, I considered to be a jaundiced, unhealthy attitude in which you hold nothing dear and nothing touches you. It would be good if you came earlier, but I'm afraid to ask you; maybe you'll be happy, but I shouldn't be selfish. But there's still a week to go to the fifth [of August].

Can you just imagine — all day long, whenever someone passes by, I look out the window to see if it's a wagon, maybe you've started to miss me and are coming home. But that's all it is, a silly fantasy. What kind of condition are you in now? Did you find Kireevskij? And the days now are nice and warm, and good for hunting; it would be a shame to waste them chasing after Kireevskij. And every evening I count another day gone by, thank God, and write you before I go to bed. Today again we got up very late — my little girl, who's been inseparable from me, suddenly sat up beside me in the middle of the night, and started in "Ma, Ma, Ma". But the candle had already gone out in the room, I was so surprised. So we stayed up together until almost three a.m. She was so cheerful and lively. Then we [adults] drank coffee in the house, recounting to each other the adventures and the gala day we had at the Barons'. I kept on copying right up until my bath-time, but things went slowly. I no sooner had started transcribing than the children interfered or the flies started biting something terrible — not only that, but then it would get interesting and I would go on reading and begin forming my own opinions about all the characters and scenes of your novel. I really like Dolokhov. But I still feel myself a part of the primitive reading public. We all went bathing, including my children. Serëzhka laughed, and my little girl kept crying "Ma, Ma, Ma!" and crawled to me in the water. After dinner we were all picking berries in the garden, and then I requested Baraban be hitched to the wagon, and Serëzha and I went for a drive just through a field, along a smooth path. At first he was very cheerful, we gave him the reins and he urged the horse on, shouted "Whoa", pointed to Pavel,

laughed and said "Pa". And then all at once he fell asleep. When we got home, he again set out for a walk. I wheeled him around the garden in a wheelbarrow; this really delighted him, and he let out whoops of joy. Just now we've been taking tea, and once I finish this letter, I'll get down to transcribing some more. So that's everything that's happening with me today. Just about everyone else in our community is spending their time this way, too. Everyone's healthy, the children, too. Serëzha still has a hoarse throat. You asked me to write more specifically, so here it is right down to the last detail. Only you told me I shouldn't get angry [over anything]; on this score you can rest assured, I am in the most calm and unexcitable of spirits, though sad without you. It might seem as though it's deliberate, but when you're not around I do make an effort to be better. But it's not deliberate, only that I'm so occupied by the thought of your absence, by your condition and whereabouts and safety, and how soon you'll be home, that I can't be touched or concerned by anything else. — If you saw me, you would probably say, as you always do, with special emphasis: "Don't explain, don't explain!". But, my sweet Lëva, I constantly feel I want to tell and explain everything to you. Lëvochka, make your letters to me a little longer, if you have the time. Even just a few minutes a day would be happy ones with your obvious participation. Otherwise [my life] feels so empty, so lonely. Today Serëzha looked so cheerfully at your portrait, pointed to it with a big smile and said "Papà". He's become even more precious on account of the constant, sincere and genuine love for you that he and I share. After all, nobody taught him to love you, and that must mean it's something he really feels. He's terribly sweet; only today he again cried out something awful — probably just on a whim. That's a pity. You'll say that I'm rather spoilt myself. What to do? On the other hand, my little girl today practically beat me for taking a gooseberry away from her. And who spoilt her? Nobody could have managed to spoil her yet, she's too small. Lizan'ka is surprised that I can write so much to you; if she actually read the trifles I write to you, she would start laughing at me, but I can't possibly stop writing to you. I don't give much thought to how or what I'm writing to you. — Tanja [SAT's sister] sings all the time, she's very much in voice, and very animated — her singing is touching. It seems she can be made to forget the past — that's my impression, though I may be mistaken. Lëvochka, my dove, right at this moment I am simply dying to see you and to take tea together with you under the little windows at Nikol'skoe, and to run over to Aleksandrovka[163] and once again live our sweet life at home. Farewell, darling, precious, huge hugs and kisses. Write and take care of yourself — that is my will.

Your Sonja.

Kisses from [your] elder daughter, your nieces,[164] too, and Mashen'ka says "From me, too!". They wanted to make sure I added that. They are enthusiastically devouring their potatoes at dinner. That's it for now.

I've just come into my lonely room in the bath-house[165] to seal this letter before going to bed — and oh my, what longing, and loneliness, and anxiety! I'm sure you don't feel half the anxiety for me that I do for you.

---

163 Aleksandrovka (Aleksandrovskij homestead, a.k.a. Protasovo) — a small estate owned by LNT adjoining Nikol'skoe-Vjazemskoe.
164 Varvara (Varja) and Elizaveta (Liza, Lizan'ka), daughters to LNT's sister Marija Nikolaevna (Mashen'ka) Tolstaja.
165 SAT was staying with her children and their nanny in the empty bath-house on Marija Nikolaevna's Pokrovskoe estate.

Nº 27 – LEV NIKOLAEVICH TOLSTOY ❧ SOFIA ANDREEVNA TOLSTAYA
[PSS 83/55]
11 November 1866. Moscow.

And so we've arrived, my precious dove. And we've arrived safe and sound and found everyone safe and sound. We drove faster than we had anticipated, so that we reached the court physician's doors[166] before eight o'clock. I don't know where anyone was [before that], but they all met us with the usual screams on the stairs and in the dining room. Andrej Evstaf'evich looks exactly the same as he did last year — he is very happy about the puppy[167] and put it in his room in the annexe. Ljubov' Aleksandrovna looks a little plumper. She's very glad to see Tanja, though I can detect in her eyes and in what she says the hostile *arrière pensée* that Tanja is going off with the D'jakovs[168] [to Italy]. Both parents, as you guessed, stubbornly insist that Tanja can't possibly have consumption —and [they say this] with self-confident rancour, even Ljubov' Aleksandrovna. They are still talking about Tanja's trip in passing, without belabouring the point, as though feeling that this is a topic demanding further discussion. — Petja [SAT's brother Pëtr, 17] has grown up quite a bit since [the last time]. And he's still morose. Volodja [her brother Vladimir, 13] is not well — his throat is sore, and he looks gloomy, but meek. Stëpa [her brother Stepan, 11] is cheerful and happy; he is the third [best pupil] in his class and hopes to make it to the Gold Board. Slavochka [her brother Vjacheslav, 5] is still the same, from what I can see. Liza [her elder sister Elizaveta] is downstairs with Tanja in the big room. Volodja and Stëpa are in your [family's] annexe. Petja is in Nanny's room and I am with him.

At Tanja's suggestion we didn't [stop for] anything to eat the whole way, and thanks to that I arrived quite refreshed, but now I've had my fill of tea, ate some grouse, which Andrej Evstaf'evich carved for me with his sweet, naïve hospitality, and now my face is flushed and I feel tired and lazy. Apart from that, I don't know what else might be of interest. Ljubov' Aleksandrovna is constantly asking after our children. It's actually quite touching. We'll be sending Sasha [Tolstaya's brother Aleksandr] a telegram. Ol'ga Abakumova is going to marry Matveev,[169] *Tanja's "half-loaf, better than none!"* (as Liza said I should write). Liza's thinned down some, she had an awful toothache; they pulled out the tooth, but it was terribly painful.

Tomorrow I'll go to see Bashilov[170] as well as to [Katkov's] printing-house and the Rumjantsev Museum to read about the Masons. Farewell, darling dove, know and remember that I have been thinking of you along the way no less than you [have been thinking of me], I am thinking of you now and shall be thinking of you. Farewell, precious Sonja, Serëzha, Tanja, Iljusha.[171] Kisses for Auntie's hand. 'Til tomorrow.

---

166 LNT had arrived at father-in-law Andrej Evstaf'evich's (the court physician's) home in the Moscow Kremlin along with SAT's younger sister Tat'jana (Tanja). The purpose of his trip to Moscow was to enquire as to the possibility of publishing his novel as a separate volume with illustrations by SAT's cousin Mikhail Bashilov (see Note 171 below).

167 LNT had brought a puppy with him at his father-in-law's request — from the litter of their dog Dorka (see Letter Nº 4, Note 23).

168 Tanja Behrs was about to leave for Italy with LNT's childhood friend Dmitrij Alekseevich D'jakov, who was taking his wife (Dar'ja Aleksandrovna D'jakova) there for medical treatment.

169 No further details are known.

170 Mikhail Sergeevich Bashilov (1820–1870) — an artist and cousin of SAT's, who did the first illustrations for *War and Peace,* according to LNT's instructions.

171 Il'ja L'vovich (Iljusha) Tolstoj (1866–1933) — the Tolstoys' third child — after Sergej (Serëzha) and Tat'jana (Tanja).

N° 28 – SOFIA ANDREEVNA TOLSTAYA ❧ LEV NIKOLAEVICH TOLSTOY
[LSA 17]
11 November 1866. Evening [Yasnaya Polyana]

These past twenty-four hours I have been mentally travelling with you, my Lëva, and now once again I can picture how happy you are, and how happy they all were [in Moscow] to see you [and my sister Tanja], and, I must admit, if it weren't for the cheerful, sweet voices of [my children] Serëzha and Tanja, I would be very sad and even bored by the monotonous snoring of Natasha[172] and Auntie [Tat'jana Andreevna Ergol'skaja], both of whom sleep and doze every evening. Today I spent practically the whole day transcribing. I didn't get very far ahead, though, as I got distracted. But transcribing *is* pleasant, as though a close friend were sitting [with me] in the same room, and [this friend] doesn't need to be entertained — it's just good that he is here. This is how it is with my copying: I don't have to think, but simply to follow and benefit from the various thoughts of another, one very close to me, and from that comes good. Today I got involved in a number of projects, but I still haven't felt the need for activity which always comes upon me in your absence. It's just that everywhere I feel an emptiness and lethargy and dissatisfaction with myself, along with a tinge of animosity towards others. Don't get upset over that — what to do? But I can't help telling you everything that's going on with me, even if it doesn't interest you. What time I have free from the children this evening I'm going to be reading — that's very pleasant in the mood that I'm in right now. I've been looking at Turgenev's *Rudin,* and I even had the impression that I, too, have outgrown it. I simply didn't like it.

Tanja and Iljusha are the same as yesterday — quite cheerful, and coughing only in the morning, and Serëzha has mild diarrhœa, which will probably be over by tomorrow. I'm still in doubt. I want to send for the Englishwoman but am still hesitant. I'm very grateful to you for your note from Tula.[173] I think the [two] of you must have travelled on a fairly good road to the end. It was warm, and I think the dog must have bothered you. Just now [little] Tanja came over to me and said: "Take Papasha down from the wall and I shall take a look", and this morning Serëzha was asking: "Why isn't Papasha come?" They take note of your absence. How could anyone not notice it? This morning, just think, I get a letter addressed to you from Pirogovo from Egor Mikhajlovich.[174] He writes that the Countess needs a carriage to send him to Khitrovo[175] — i.e. to the Baron. Of couse, Ljubochka[176] will come and *spout all sorts of nonsense,* and Masha no doubt intends to stay on longer at Pirogovo. I must say I've actually started to feel quite annoyed and disagreeable. I'm not bothered too much about the mode of transport — he'll get there even in a gipsy cart — but I feel very sympathetic towards the girls [Marija Nikolaevna's daughters Liza and Varja].

How are things with all of you, how is Tanja [Tolstaja's sister], how is her health, how will the doctors and her parents find her? I am living with the lot of you with all my heart, and am still asking myself "When will you rise [spiritually]?" I so do want to rise above this boredom and nastiness. Now my reply to Tanjusha would be: "No, I'm nasty." Do write me a little more,

---

172 Natal'ja Petrovna (Natasha) Okhotnitskaja — see Letter N° 19, Note 127.

173 In a letter from Tula dated 10 November 1866 (not included here), LNT had written that one of their carriage wheels had broken and that they had had to wait an hour and a half for repairs (PSS 83: 114).

174 Egor Mikhajlovich — manager of Marija Nikolaevna's estate. LNT used him as a prototype for the foremaan Egor Mikhajlovich in *Polikushka.*

175 *Khitrovo* — the estate of the Barons Del'vig (see Letter N° 23, Note 155).

176 Ljubov' Antonovna (Ljubochka) Del'vig — sister to the poet Anton Antonovich Del'vig.

Lëvochka. I love you so much, my sweet, and without you I am such an insignificant creature. Ever since we parted yesterday, I keep reminiscing and thinking how lovely it will be to see each other again. And now I send you a kiss, my sweet friend, stay healthy. I'm not trying to hurry you, because I know that it will be very sad for Papà and the whole Behrs family, and I know that you yourself will be in haste to get home. Farewell, darling. Serëzha hasn't slept today, and I keep hearing him fooling about, and it's late already. Farewell.

N° 29 – SOFIA ANDREEVNA TOLSTAYA ✿ LEV NIKOLAEVICH TOLSTOY
[LSA 18]
12 November [1866]. Saturday evening [Yasnaya Polyana]

My sweet friend Lëva, just think, before dinner today the L'vovs' tall Englishwoman[177] came by with her sister — *our* Englishwoman. I was even thrown all into a heat, and even now all my thoughts are muddled, and still my head aches from excitement. Well, how to describe all this to you? She's just as I had expected her to be. Very young, quite sweet, a pleasant face, quite nice, really, but our ignorance of each other's language is abysmal. Her sister is staying with us tonight, so she can act as our interpreter, but what will happen after that, God knows. I'm completely lost, especially when you're not here, my sweet friend. This time I remembered your rule, about how we should think how light and insignificant it's all going to seem a year from now. But now I'd even say it's extremely difficult. The children have been coping, Tanja has been sitting in her arms, looking at pictures, and saying something to her on her own. Serëzha went running with her, said "She like plays with me!". Then Tanja in the nursery imitated the English-woman's voice, and no doubt everything will turn out all right in the end, but for the moment it all seems very unnatural, difficult, awkward and frightening. I keep searching for you in my soul as a support; maybe you're not here, but in that case we might get through it even sooner. One thing is simply dreadful — that we can't understand each other at all. I thought I would be able to understand better than I do. Her sister, that is, the L'vovs' Englishwoman, looks at everything with some suspicion and animosity, while ours, it seems, is kind-hearted and tries to get along. Tomorrow I'll let you know how things go without her sister as interpreter. — My children are healthy, only Iljusha is coughing [now], while Tanja has stopped completely. Everyone's cheerful, they're not fooling about, and they took a nap during the day. I was quite emotional all morning; I felt very nervous, but now all that's changed, and all the threads of my mind and heart are concentrated on the Englishwoman.

For some time now I have been getting a tremendous emotional uplift from your novel. Just as soon as I sit down to transcribe, I am carried away into some kind of poetic world, and it even seems to me that it is not so much that your novel is good (of course it instinctively seems that way), but that I'm so smart. Please don't laugh at me, but my head aches so much I can't even lie because of it. Only, I swear to God, I'm not lying at all, I'm trying so hard to express everything with accuracy. — Lëvochka, now I'm going to write you about something you don't like, but, indeed, I have to. The thing is, you left me 50 roubles and I've spent almost all of it on string, a sleigh, salaries, travelling to Moscow, etc. And still they say: "The Count has ordered it, it is absolutely necessary." And so [soon] I shall have nothing to live on, and

---

177 Englishwoman Jenny Tarsey served as a governess in the family of LNT's friend, Tula landowner Evgenij Vladimirovich L'vov (1817–1896). Her sister Hannah Tarsey (ca1845–?) looked after the Tolstoys' children from 1866 to 1872, then went with the Kuzminskijs to Kutais (in Georgia) to be governess to SAT's sister Tanja's children, until she married a local prince Dmitrij Georgievich Machutadze in 1874.

the Count has supposedly ordered wheat to be sent when the new workers arrive, which, of course, I have seen neither hide nor hair of. I have no idea how I'll pull through. Best you hurry as fast as possible, to get here sooner. I've become so mixed up. The estate, and the children, and the Englishwoman, and all that. The piglets and the butter are being sent first thing tomorrow morning. Here are six bottles of honey fungus and Mamà's butter. I'm not sending a letter with them by cart, as I am writing you every day through the post in any case. Lëvochka, dear, how are you all getting along there? If only I could free myself from all my cares and fly to the Kremlin! I just might receive at least a wee note from you tomorrow, but, not likely — it's still too early. Today I gave the children a bath and, if the weather is good, in a few days I'll start taking walks with them. It will make them happier. One thing that really bothers me is that [little] Tanja's appetite has all but disappeared. She eats nothing except milk all day long. How's Papà? Big Tanja? How all that alarms me, and how hard it is! As I write, I can hear our Hannah having a hearty laugh with her sister Jenny. Isn't it difficult and frightening for her, after all? Jenny's still insisting that I feed her sister, especially meat, five times a day. That's what she's accustomed to. And all that's something I need to sort out. Write me a letter which is *encourageant*. Perhaps it will even arrive with you. Farewell, darling, how I would love to talk with you so we could sort out everything together!

Hugs and kisses from me to all my dear ones in the Kremlin — Papà, Mamà, [my sister] Tanja, and all the [Behrs] children. Tell them to pity me. It isn't easy for me, not knowing the [English] language, to hand over [my] children to her and [have her] twist their tongues. But I'm still glad this step has been taken.

Hugs and kisses to you, as strong as can be. God be with you. Stay healthy and remember me and love me. One day my emotional imprisonment — i.e. life without you — will come to an end.

Sonja.

Nº 30 – LEV NIKOLAEVICH TOLSTOY ❧ SOFIA ANDREEVNA TOLSTAYA
[PSS 83/58]
14–15 November 1866. Moscow. [Preceded by SAT's Nº 3U, 13 November 1866]

Even though it's late, I'm glad that finally nothing is stopping me from writing to you, my darling. The morning is exactly the same as in recent days. But lately I've been feeling as though I'm seventy years old. I went to the Rumjantsev Museum, but it was closed in honour of Dagmar's birthday.[178] From there, in order to save Tanja an errand, I drove over to the English store to buy her a dress and a nightgown for you. Everybody liked the nightgown, but did not approve of the dress, but it was because Tanja said to get one for ten roubles.

From there I went to [Katkov's] printing-house. They've agreed to my conditions, but tomorrow they'll be sending a gentleman over for final negotiations. Before dinner I waited at home for Varvarinskij,[179] who never came. He is ill and tomorrow Tanja and Papà are going to see him. Stupid [Sergej Mikhajlovich] Sukhotin came by. After dinner we went to see [Gounod's opera] *Faust* — Auntie Nadja,[180] Liza, Mamà, Tanja and I. Andrej Evstaf'evich arrived later. The theatre there was holding a gala in honour of [Grand Duchess] Dagmar's birthday. *Faust* is silly, and you may not believe it but I do not like the theatre, and always feel like

178 Grand Duchess Marija Fëdorovna (*née* Princess Marija Sofija Frederika Dagmara; 1847–1928) — wife of Tsarevich Aleksandr Aleksandrovich, the future Emperor Alexander III, who reigned from 1881 until his death in 1894.
179 Iosif Vasil'evich Varvarinskij (1811–1878) — a professor at the hospital therapeutic clinic of Moscow University.
180 Nadezhda (Nadja) Kajutova (*née* Stender).

criticising. There was nobody I knew there except for Severtsev,[181] who came into our loge. He's got uncommonly good-looking and mature. Yes, I forgot. This morning Vasilij Islen'ev[182] dropped by. He was repulsive as usual, but now he's even more obnoxious: he's been promoted to court bailiff — something like a private bailiff. I discovered why he made such an impression on me, and Tanja confirmed it. It's awkward and *shameful* to look at him, as though he had unwittingly lost his trousers. Then there were the Zajkovskijs: Dmitrij Dmitrievich and Èmilija.[183] I retract my first impression of Dmitrij Zajkovskij. You're right, he is an exceptionally dear and clever young man *comme il faut*. And he ought to be good. I was especially nice to him, again remembering you. After dinner I also received your first letter.[184] And Mamà and I got so caught up in praising you that we actually felt embarrassed. How sad about Masha! As for little Tanja, I can just picture her and the thought of her makes me feel radiant. Read this to them: *Serëzha dear, and Tanja dear, and Iljusha dear — I love them. Serëzha is now big, he will write to Papasha.* And have him and Tanja write something — i.e. draw something for me. — I left the theatre in the middle of an act, and went to see the Sushkovs.[185] Everything was just as it was fifteen years ago, even the guests — including Princess Meshcherskaja,[186] *née* Countess Panina — a huge woman with masculine features, very kind and intelligent. I knew her as a young lady, and now she has 4 children, while I have 3. She's invited me over on Wednesday. I don't know whether I'll go. And then there was Princess Liven,[187] a rather silly and primitive young lady. I returned home with our [family] and we really enjoyed our supper together. Tanja is cheerful, but as she came out of the theatre she was [coughing] blood. Oh, this poor, dear Tanja! I can't tell you how sorry I feel for her and how dear she is to me. Your letter so touched her that she couldn't hold back her tears, neither could I. It is very sad that it wasn't we who were to give her this money, but some kind of 'mixed-up fairy godmother'.[188] [Ekaterina Fëdorovna] Tjutcheva, it seemed to me, was truly moved by the part of *The Year 1805* that was published last year and said that she liked the second part better than the first, and the third better than the second. I treasure her opinion just as I treasure Sukhotin's; it, too, is a grass-roots expression, though on a slightly higher level than Sukhotin's. They insisted I read them something, but I said, first of all, that I would be leaving soon and didn't have much time, and that I needed to have someone I wanted there at the same time. They promised to invite anybody I wanted, but I didn't make any

---

181 Pëtr Alekseevich Severtsev (also spelt: Severtsov; 1844–1884) — later married to SAT's cousin Ol'ga Vjacheslavovna Shidlovskaja (1849–1909).

182 Vasilij Vladimirovich Islen'ev (1824–1872) — a staff-captain, second cousin to SAT.

183 Dmitrij Dmitrievich Zajkovskij (1838–1867) — a medical doctor and docent of Moscow University and his sister Èmilija Dmitrievna Zajkovskaja (1846–1922). Their sister Ol'ga Dmitrievna Zajkovskaja (1844–1919) was a childhood friend of SAT's.

184 Letter Nᵒ 28 of 11 November 1866.

185 Nikolaj Vasil'evich Sushkov (1796–1871) — a writer, and his wife Dar'ja Ivanovna Sushkova (*née* Tjutcheva; 1806–1879) — sister to the poet Fëdor Ivanovich Tjutchev, along with her niece Ekaterina Fëdorovna Tjutcheva. LNT was often a guest at the Sushkovs' literary salons in the 1850s.

186 Princess Marija Aleksandrovna Meshcherskaja (*née* Countess Panina; 1830–1903) — wife of the Moscow school-district trustee Nikolaj Petrovich Meshcherskij, grandson to prominent historian Nikolaj Mikhajlovich Karamzin.

187 Probably one of the daughters of Senator Prince Aleksandr Karlovich Liven (1801–1880) and Ekaterina Nikitichna (*née* Pankratova; 1818–1867): either Anna Aleksandrovna (1840–1871), wife of the Tolstoys' future Moscow neighbour Vasilij Aleksandrovich Olsuf'ev, or Elena Aleksandrovna (1842–1915), a Lady-in-waiting, who served as Headmistress of the Elizabeth Institute for Girls from the Nobility in Moscow in the 1880s and 1890s.

188 *mixed-up fairy godmother* — an approximation of LNT's pet name [*krëstnaja putanitsa*] for his sister-in-law Tanja's wealthy godmother, who gave Tanja money to go abroad for treatment.

firm promises myself. Vjazemskij[189] is not in Moscow. — Tomorrow I shall be already expecting your letter in answer to my [previous one], but as of now we won't have to be writing one another for much longer. I'll be home soon. Nothing more to do [here]. And it's very sad being without you. If I'm still not ready to [depart], it's because I keep having the feeling that I might have left some unfinished business behind in Moscow which I shall afterwards regret. Farewell, my precious dove, kisses on your eyes, your neck and your arms. Give a kiss [from me] to Auntie's hand. Tell Natasha that [the dog] Joy is [now] indoors. And take note what good care means — that [it] doesn't make a mess. Keep Dolly indoors as well.

Nº 31 – SOFIA ANDREEVNA TOLSTAYA ❧ LEV NIKOLAEVICH TOLSTOY
[LSA 19]
14 November [1866]. Monday. [Yasnaya Polyana]

We've just come back from a ride [in the sleigh], dear Lëva; they are putting the children to bed, while [now] I am extending my pleasure of writing you the whole day long — morning and evening.

It was warm during our outing, the children are quite healthy, and the [outdoor] air refreshed me. Hannah was so happy she jumped up in the sleigh and kept saying "so nice" [in English] — I'm sure that meant she was having a good time. And right there in the sleigh she explained to me that she loved me and the children very much, that the "country" is good and that she is "very happy". I understand her well enough, but it takes some effort and is quite a challenge. [Right now] she is sitting and sewing little pantaloons for the children, while the elderly nanny is putting them to bed. When [Hannah] takes full charge of them, it'll be a lot better; at the moment her duties are less by half. Still, she's a help to me; I'll soon learn [English], I'm certain, and that would be very nice. For the time being she takes her meals and drinks tea with us. I shan't change anything until you [come home], we'll have time for that [later]. But she's looking forward to — and seems to understand — her future responsibilities. She's no nanny, she behaves quite like an equal, but doesn't see any task as a burden, and seems to be very kind-hearted. The complete opposite of her sister, whom I find [rather] unpleasant. Lëvochka, there's nothing more I can write to you about, since at the moment my whole life is [wrapped up] with the Englishwoman and all my efforts are directed at accustoming the children to her as soon as possible. They spend their whole day upstairs. We both keep looking at our dictionaries and pointing to words in books that we don't understand.

Right now the whole house is being washed — a big bother. As for the estate, I know that they've hired [people] to bring in the wheat, only don't think I was in charge of that — I don't get involved in anything. I've also heard that a Pirogovo peasant said that he hired thirty-five workers and that they'll all be coming in a couple of days.

At the moment I'm just dying to receive mail. Probably it will come today. It's so hard to go so long without news. I keep thinking: if only we had a railway![190] How are you doing in Moscow? What have you decided as regards our 'shrine' — your novel? I've now started to think of it as your (meaning mine, too) baby, and releasing these sheets of paper comprising your novel to Moscow is literally letting go of a child, and I'm fearful lest it come to any harm. I've really fallen in love with your creation. It's doubtful I'll love anything as much as this novel.

189 Prince Pëtr Andreevich Vjazemskij (1792–1878) — a soldier in the War of 1812 (against Napoleon's invading troops), one of the prototypes for Pierre Bezukhov in *War and Peace*.
190 Passenger rail service between Moscow and Tula commenced in the mid-1860's.

If only you knew how much our elderly nanny is grieving;[191] I feel so touched by her and so sorry that the children have been taken from her. And when they take the children out of the nursery for the night, she says she practically dies of longing. She says, "It's like I've suffered a loss, I'm so lonely." I'm so grateful to her, and it moves me to tears that she loves them so much. Even if I stopped having children, I would not part with her. I'd find something for her to do around the house.

Evening.

They've just come back from Tula, but there aren't any letters. I'm simply afraid of myself, how upset I am — how sad and fearful. Tomorrow's the last day: if there aren't any letters [tomorrow] I'll send a telegram, otherwise I may simply go out of my mind. I'll say just one thing: never ever again will I stay alone for a whole week. Why should I suffer so much torment — is it because I love you too much? I can't count all the horrors I imagine might have happened to you once I merely start thinking about it. I've got a lot of things to take care of here — coping with the dear sweet children and the Englishwoman, but my heart shrinks all day long and at any moment I might burst out in desperation with some downright stupid remark. I imagine, too, some sort of terrible thing happening in the Kremlin with Tanja and all of you, whom I love so very much. Lëvochka, farewell. I do want to write to you, but I'm only getting more and more upset. Lord! What has happened with all of you?

Nº 32 – LEV NIKOLAEVICH TOLSTOY ❧ SOFIA ANDREEVNA TOLSTAYA
[PSS 83/59]
15 November 1866. Moscow.

I seem to be very tired for no apparent reason, my sweet darling, and I'll just write you a brief [note].

After coffee I went to the Rumjantsev Museum[192] and stayed there until 3 o'clock reading Masonic manuscripts — very interesting. And I can't tell you why, but the reading brought on a [state of] melancholy, from which I haven't been able to free myself the whole day. It's sad, but all those Masons were fools. —

From there I went to the *gymnasium*.[193] I felt stronger than the last time. And [then] to dinner. Anke was having dinner and Sukhotin devoured everything in large quantities and kept on chattering without stopping. Varin'ka Perfil'eva[194] was there, too, whom I hadn't seen since Sukhotin's. In the evening the Zajkovskijs came by, along with Bashilov and someone from the printers'. The noise, the Zajkovskijs' shouts, the haste, the awkwardness... well, you know the feeling. I was very glad when Princess Èlena[195] called me — I went to see her, and now I've just come from her place — I spent an hour and a half with her there *en tête-à-tête* and wasn't bored at all. Occasionally she can be most pleasant, though I still felt sleepy. — Varvarinskij showed

---

191 Nanny Tat'jana Filippovna had come down with cancer and could no longer take care of children; she lived at the Pirogovo estate.
192 *Rumjantsev Museum* — associated with the Rumjantsev Library (see Letter Nº 20, Note 137).
193 Throughout the book this term (when italicised) is used the European sense of a secondary school aimed at preparing pupils for university entrance, much like a secondary-level 'college' in Britain or Canada.
194 Varvara Stepanovna (Varin'ka) Perfil'eva (?–1890) — see Letter Nº 16, Note 94.
195 Princess Elena Sergeevna Gorchakova (1824–1897) — third cousin to LNT, a writer and headmistress of a Moscow *gymnasium*.

up while I was gone, and confirmed what Rastsvetov[196] had said, though, according to Andrej Evstaf'evich and Ljubov' Aleksandrovna, he said there weren't any tubercles yet, but they might develop. — While listening to Sukhotin's[197] chatter and the Zajkovskijs' squeals, I waited for any letters from you, but the blasted post-office will probably bring two of them tomorrow [instead]. Still haven't finished at the printers'. And now once again there's the possibility of putting in illustrations. I'll probably resolve everything tomorrow. In the morning I'll try to finish up the copying and reading I need to do at the museum. Farewell, sweet dove. Until tomorrow.

Nº 33 – SOFIA ANDREEVNA TOLSTAYA ❧ LEV NIKOLAEVICH TOLSTOY
[LSA 21]
Saturday, 17 June 1867. Evening. [Yasnaya Polyana]

My sweet Lëvochka, I have endured a whole day and night without you around, and it's with such a joyful heart that I am sitting down to write to you. Writing to you — even about the most trifling things — is really my greatest comfort. As soon as you left yesterday[198] I lay down, but awoke after about two hours and wasn't able to fall asleep again almost the whole night from a terribly strong toothache, which was gone in the morning without leaving the slightest trace. It's now almost eleven p.m., and my teeth don't ache a bit. I'm so happy to be freed from that. The children, too, are all healthy and likewise the Behrs family. This morning I kept pacing from corner to corner, feeling so lonely and unhappy. I took tea all alone. Then Aleksandr Grigor'evich[199] came and was very annoyed not to find you here. I entertained him, then let Hannah go bathing with Mamà and [big] Tanja (I didn't go bathing myself), while I myself took the children for a walk in the garden, which is always a delight for me. I told them a story. We looked to see how the wild strawberries were doing, and were very happy. I told them you had gone to Moscow. [Little] Tanja all at once perked up and said: "Yes, he's gone, yes, he's gone." But Serëzha asked: "Will he come today?" Before dinner I was in the nursery and heard Petja's[200] cheerful voice (he was to have gone with the Kuzminskijs[201] to Tula in the morning), and I see Petja with Misha Bibikov[202] standing in the dining room. I told Bibikov I was very happy to see him here, and they left. While travelling along the highway with Kuzminskij, this Petja had met up with a whole convoy of members of the Bibikov family, and brought Misha back on the return coach from Jasenkov and now Misha will stay with us — i.e. with Petja — until next Saturday. Petja is so happy that he laughs all day long and is terribly animated. — After dinner I was busy around the estate — I checked to see whether the horses had been fed, and discovered they hadn't been given bread. I called the village elder, and told him to include bread. Anyway, they saw that I was keeping an eye out, and that's the main thing, isn't it? Then I visited the cattle

196 Aleksandr Pavlovich Rastsvetov (1823–1902) — an assistant at the medical faculty clinic at Moscow University; from 1868 he served as a professor of operative surgery.
197 Sergej Mikhajlovich Sukhotin — see Letter Nº 13, Note 81.
198 LNT was off to Moscow to see about printing his novel *War and Peace*.
199 Aleksandr Grigor'evich Michurin — son of a serf musician and music teacher to the Tolstoys.
200 Pëtr Andreevich Behrs (1849–1910) — younger brother to SAT; later he would serve as special commissioner for the governor of Moscow and superintendent of police at Klin (the home town of the composer Tchaikovsky).
201 Aleksandr Mikhajlovich (Sasha) Kuzminskij (1845–1917) — SAT's second cousin; in 1867 he married her younger sister Tat'jana Andreevna (Tanja) Behrs.
202 Mikhail Mikhajlovich Bibikov (1848–1918) — son of Mikhail Illarionovich Bibikov (1818–1881) and Sof'ja Nikitichna Bibikova (*née* Muravëva; 1828–1892), the daughter of Decembrist rebellion organiser Nikita Mikhajlovich Muravëv (1795–1843).

stalls, and now, after [receiving] your note,[203] I shall take a look at the beehives as well. I'll even try to go there at least twice. This evening a carriage arrived [with Mamà's luggage]; everything's safe and sound. Mamà looked after it and did some unpacking while I sewed and talked a bit with *les gamins*. Aleksandr Grigor'evich left after dinner. Kuzminskij's not here today, he'll come tomorrow. I, too, am not comfortable with either of them, and I'm afraid (and probably know for certain), that there won't be any happiness, because, most importantly, there's no love — or, if there is, it's very little. But he's not a bad sort, and I like him, despite your impression of him. The only thing bad is that there's no love there. Now Tanja's argued with me hotly and excitedly that there can't be any *fervent* love, since they've known each other so long, and they've already loved each other in the past. What's the point of their marriage? Why? So all that's unclear and unhappy. How different it is with you and me, how clear and good everything is; there is so much love [between us] that it's very hard to part from each other, and I'm constantly afraid for you. Maybe Tanja will be able to content herself with Sasha's little and youthful love, but I can't understand it. You see, I know that you love me, and still I often think: "More, more", and I start doubting, and I need proof, and I look within you for some sort of irritation towards me, so that you will keep on saying that you love me, love me, love me. — Lëvochka, I've been feeling very silly all day because I didn't sleep all night, and my letter's silly, and I can't express my thoughts clearly, but that's the way it is. I imagine you're really getting down to your projects, but how will you finish them? For God's sake, be calmer, cheerier, don't quarrel with anyone, preserve your health, think of me a bit more and don't worry about us; I'll take care of everyone, and won't make any stupid blunders myself. And if you should come earlier [than planned], you know how happy that will make me. I'm afraid to ask you about this, but I can't [help it], as this is my most cherished innermost thought. — Tomorrow I'll be going to the church to offer communion to the children and Mamà. While you're not here I will be altogether active and agile, and especially give myself to the children more [than usual]. Today I was so nasty, particularly with Tanja; she put on some kind of hostile and also commanding tone, and I got upset. But we didn't quarrel, it's just that I muttered in the presence of Mamà. Now poor Tanja's come down with a fever, and once again I'm frightened for her, and once again I've felt so much love for her. It's true she's unlucky — she'll never be completely happy — it's something I know and foresee. Lëvochka, write me more regularly, every day, otherwise I'll actually go out of my mind if I don't receive a single letter from you. If you see Papà again, give him and Liza a kiss from me. Lëva, I'll be expecting you Saturday *au plus tard*. That's what I say in words, but in my soul I shall be expecting you on Wednesday, Thursday, Friday and so forth. Farewell, my sweet dove, with tight, tender and passionate kisses.

If you should go bathing in Moscow, don't do anything foolish, don't swim where it's deep. Farewell, I'm going to bed. Where are you this evening? You're probably home by now.

Sonja.

203 On 16 June 1867 LNT wrote his wife while en route: "I forgot to tell you something very important: send Nikolka every day to keep watch at the beehive, and tell him to report how much swarming there has been and when, and tell the elder to watch, too" (PSS, 83: 138).

N° 34 – LEV NIKOLAEVICH TOLSTOY ❧ SOFIA ANDREEVNA TOLSTAYA
[PSS 83/65]
18 June 1867. Moscow.

I am ashamed that I didn't write to you yesterday, dear friend, but it's evidently for the better, as yesterday I would have written nasty things, my letter would not have been in [the right] spirit. — We had an excellent trip, even a particularly lucky one (at the highway toll-gate they asked me for 64 kopeks. I thrust my hand into my pocket and pulled out a fistful of change: exactly 64 kopeks). Then on the train I got to know a sheepherder who has his own company; he gave me a whole course in practical sheepherding — nothing like you'd find anywhere else. I wasn't actually tired, but my liver started to hurt and I felt sick to my stomach. After we arrived in Moscow, despite having a bath, I felt quite out of sorts. Something like the bilious fever I had during Holy Week, but much weaker. They put us downstairs. I'm [staying] in the girls' wing,[204] while Bibikov[205] is in Petja's. This morning I sent for Bashilov[206] and Bartenev.[207] Bartenev will come tomorrow from Petersburg; Bashilov came (his wife hasn't given birth yet) and said that Bartenev has decided to undertake publishing my edition himself. I'll be seeing him tomorrow, and I shall be very glad if I can get by without Katkov and work with him [instead]. There can be no possibility of illustrations in the first edition, Bashilov said. After that I went to the exhibit,[208] which is open for the last time today. I found a lot there that was unsightly and mindless and little that was interesting. Then I drove over to [Petrovsky] Park, where [last night] I had sent Ljubov' Aleksandrovna's letter with my postscript, and arrived at 4 [p.m.].

Your Papà is healthy and cheerful, and kind, and nice to me, as always. — Liza is very nice, too. They were telling me about Gedrojts[209] and his cynicism — that's terrible, unbelievable, and I shall tell you about it with a groan. Then I drove over to see Zakhar'in;[210] he wasn't at home, but he is in Moscow, and I left him a note, asking him to set up an appointment for me. If he sends me a message back to say when, that means he is ready to pay attention to me, and then I'll go see him; otherwise, the day after tomorrow I'll buy [a bottle of] *Kissingen* [mineral water] and on Andrej Evstaf'evich's advice I shall start drinking it [regularly] and send [a supply] to Yasnaya. Then I went to see Samarin,[211] who was out as well (though still in Moscow) and left him my address. —

Yesterday as we were approaching Moscow, when I caught sight of this dust and the crowd and could sense the heat and the noise, I felt so frightened and miserable that I wanted to run as fast as I could and [hide] under your wing. I always love you all the more when I am away from you. The other day, as soon as I drove out past Zaseka,[212] doing quite a bit of thinking

---

204 SAT's sisters Elizaveta (Liza) and Tat'jana (Tanja) were not at home at the time; Tat'jana was at Yasnaya Polyana, while Elizaveta was with her father at the palace at Petrovsky Park.
205 Aleksandr Nikolaevich Bibikov (1827–1886) — the Tolstoys' neighbour, owner of the Teljatinki estate located 3 versts from Yasnaya Polyana.
206 Mikhail Sergeevich Bashilov — see Letter N° 27, Note 170.
207 Pëtr Ivanovich Bartenev (1829–1912) — historian, bibliographer, editor of *Russkij arkhiv*. He was doing the proof-reading for the edition of *War and Peace* that was being prepared for printing at Ris' printshop.
208 *the exhibit* — an ethnographic exhibit organised by the Imperial Society of Lovers of Natural Science.
209 Prince Romual'd Konstantinovich Gedrojts (1842–1899) — a Polish noble, married (as of 1867) to Varvara Fëdorovna Brevern, a friend of the Tolstoys.
210 Dr. Grigorij Antonovich Zakhar'in (1829–1895) — a doctor at the therapeutic clinic of Moscow University.
211 Jurij Fëdorovich Samarin (1819–1876) — a Slavophile writer and social activist.
212 *Zaseka* — a forest preserve.

about the situations of our lovers,[213] I had such [negative] thoughts come to me that I almost asked Bibikov to turn [the carriage] around so that I could go back and say something to them, but I remembered Ljubov' Aleksandrovna's words that everything is God's will, and remembered that she was there, and I calmed down. Oh, if only they could become as happy as I am as quickly as possible, and not remain in the state of alarm and uncertainty that I left them in. —

This evening I feel better, and by tomorrow I hope to be completely well. This attack is also a stroke of luck. If it weren't for it, I would not have thought about Zakhar'in and would not drink the water which he will probably prescribe and which is always healthful. How are your teeth? Have you really been bathing? How precious you are to me — how better, purer, more honest, dearer and more precious than anyone else in the world! I look at your childhood portraits and am filled with delight.

I shall probably leave soon — both because luck is going my way (64 kopeks) and because without you I am devoid of expression.

Hugs and kisses to the children, to Auntie, and to all and sundry. Farewell, my dove.
Sunday evening.

Nº 35 – LEV NIKOLAEVICH TOLSTOY ❧ SOFIA ANDREEVNA TOLSTAYA
[PSS 83/71]
25 September 1867. Moscow.

It's now 5 o'clock in the afternoon on the 25th. I'm on my way to Borodino[214] with Stëpa,[215] whom they allowed to accompany me at my request. I'm carrying a letter with me to the manager of Anikeeva's[216] estate, located ten versts from Borodino, along with a letter to the Mother Superior of the convent[217] there. I shall probably not stop anywhere until I reach Borodino. I'm travelling by post-horse. For a full day and a half I've been rushing about various trifling tasks. The printing is going slowly, and that's not because of me, but because of an interruption in the postal system (this last time the manuscript [I] sent still hasn't been received — send me a receipt) and because of [the printer] Ris's[218] sluggishness — he needs a nudge. I'm so healthy, as I always am in the city.[219]

Our whole family is so precious and kind, as always. Petja is a *good* student, and everyone's immersed in their studies. Hugs and kisses to all our people — you and the children especially.

213 *our lovers* — referring to SAT's sister Tat'jana and her fiancé Aleksandr Mikhajlovich Kuzminskij.
214 *Borodino* (stress on last syllable) — a village in Mozhajsk Uezd, Moscow Gubernia, near the scene of a famous battle between the Russians and the French which took place on 26 August 1812. LNT wanted to view the battlefield for his description of this event in *War and Peace*.
215 Stepan Andreevich (Stëpa) Behrs (1855–1910) — SAT's brother (the sixth of eight children in the family).
216 Ol'ga Dmitrievna Anikeeva (*née* Princess Gorchakova; 1834–1869) — LNT's second cousin, once removed; a land-owner in the settlement of Krasnovidovo, Mozhajsk Uezd, Moscow Gubernia.
217 LNT was carrying a letter to Princess Sof'ja Vasil'evna Volkonskaja (*née* Princess Urusova; 1809–1884), Mother Superior Sergija of the Spaso-Borodinskij Convent, founded in 1828 by Margarita Mikhajlovna Tuchkova (*née* Naryshkina), widow of Major–General Aleksandr Alekseevich Tuchkov (1778–1812), who had fallen at the Battle of Borodino.
218 Fëdor Fëdorovich Ris — owner of a printing-house in Moscow, where the first two editions of *War and Peace* were printed, and later *Anna Karenina* and LNT's *Readers [Knigi dlja chtenija]* (1875).
219 SAT described this statement as "irony", saying he was always ill in the city.

If Masha[220] is visiting us, I hope she understands why my trip is essential. Farewell, darling. I'll send you a wire Thursday morning [28 September]. —

On the envelope: To Her Ladyship Countess Sofia Andreevna Tolstaya in Tula.

Nº 36 – LEV NIKOLAEVICH TOLSTOY ✎ SOFIA ANDREEVNA TOLSTAYA
[PSS 83/72]
27 September 1867. Moscow.

I just got back from Borodino. I'm very, *very* satisfied with my trip and even with how I managed to get through it, despite a lack of sleep and decent food. If only God will grant me health and peace, I shall describe the Battle of Borodino as it has never been described before. [You would probably say:] "He keeps boasting about it!" When I was spending the night in a monastery, I saw you in a dream, and what I remember from the dream is just as clear as reality, and I think of you with some fear.

I shan't write about my trip in detail — I'll tell you [about it upon my return]. The first night I rode 100 versts to Mozhajsk and took a nap in the morning at the station. The second night we stayed overnight in the monastery's guest house. I rose with the dawn, rode around the [Borodino] Field once more [and then] we spent the rest of the day travelling [back] to Moscow.

I received two letters from you.[221] I'm sorry to hear about big Tanja and am frightened, terribly frightened for little Tanja. (I know her and love her and can picture her [in my mind], and am fearful for her with her fever.) But, most importantly, your letters have gladdened my heart because [I see] *you* in them. And you keep putting the best of yourself into your letters — and into your thoughts about me. But in life that is often muffled by nausea and a sense of conflict. I know that.

I'm borrowing 1000 roubles from Perfil'ev[222] and so, being rich, I shall buy a cap and boots and anything you request. — I know you're upset that I am borrowing. Don't get angry; I'm borrowing so that I can be free during this first part of the winter, unencumbered and undisturbed by financial concerns, and with this in mind I plan to save this money as much as I can and keep it only to know that there's money there to get rid of an unprofitable and superfluous person etc. [I know] you will understand and help me. Your letters, my darling, are a great delight to me, and don't be so silly as to suggest I might give them [to someone else] to read.

Borodino was a pleasant experience for me. I felt I was doing something worthwhile; but I find [life] in the city unbearable, while you say I like to gad about. I only wish that you loved the countryside and hated the idle vanity of the city even a tenth as much as do I. Tomorrow I'll go to the Perfil'evs and thank them, and I shall see [the printer] Ris and do some shopping, and if I finish everything and D'jakov is ready, I'll leave Friday morning [29 September]. Farewell, darling, hugs and kisses to you and the children.

27 [September].

---

220 Marija Nikolaevna (Masha) Tolstaja, LNT's sister.
221 These letters have not been preserved.
222 Stepan Vasil'evich Perfil'ev — see Letter Nº 16, Note 94.

Nº 37 – LEV NIKOLAEVICH TOLSTOY ❧ SOFIA ANDREEVNA TOLSTAYA
[PSS 83/80]
1 September 1869. Moscow.

To be read when you are alone.

The whole day I spent in enquiries and uncertainty as to which route to travel: through Morshansk or through Nizhnij [Novgorod].[223] Il'ina,[224] who was riding with me to Moscow, assured me that it was better to head towards Morshansk. But from all the enquiries I made here — at the post office and with the brother of the Manager of the Penza Village whom I found here, I deduced that the route to Morshansk was uncertain and I could [easily] get lost, and so I decided to head towards Nizhnij. Hence you should write to me at the post office in Saransk, and to Sobolev's hotel in Nizhnij. The manager's brother is a rich merchant in Moscow, and from my conversations I gather that his brother has a comfy job there (he has been manager for 15 years already), and that he does not look favourably on a [potential] buyer. That cursed Ris has nothing ready; I haven't seen his corrected proofs, and probably shan't be able to take them with me.

I didn't see Golitsyn[225] and probably shan't. Yesterday I had nothing to eat along the road, and so to have supper and enquire about the route, I went to a club, where I didn't find out any specific information. There I met up with Mengden,[226] Sobolevskij[227] and Fonvizin.[228] I left directly after supper. My liver still hurts, but not as much [now], it seems.

Since it's not yet 2 o'clock, and the train leaves at 5, I'd like to go see the Perfil'evs,[229] to see whether they have any details about Penza. I met Sukhotin,[230] of course. Among other things he told me that [Prince Pëtr Andreevich] Vjazemskij had written some humorous verses about [some] people at the court, such as:

Tolstaja[231] makes fun of Trubetskoj.[232]
In her I see a tempering of the Tolstoys,
A seventh part of *War and Peace* —
I thank you — a surprise release!

223 LNT was on his way to Samara for koumiss (fermented mare's milk) treatments.
224 Ljubov' Petrovna Il'ina (*née* Puzyreva; 1811–1885) — a Tula landowner, wife of Major Ivan Ivanovich Il'in (1799–1865), who had served there. The family lived in the Kremlin palace in the same building as the Behrs family.
225 Prince Sergej Vladimirovich Golitsyn (1823–1879) — brother of LNT's Sevastopol' comrade Prince Aleksandr Vladimirovich Golitsyn (1826–1864).
226 Baron Vladimir Mikhajlovich Mengden (1826–1910) — an Imperial government official for Polish affairs, later a member of the State Council.
227 Sergej Aleksandrovich Sobolevskij (1803–1870) — poet, bibliographer.
228 Ivan Sergeevich Fonvizin (1822–1889) — Governor of Moscow (1868–1879), a comrade of LNT's brother Nikolaj at Moscow University.
229 General Stepan Vasil'evich Perfil'ev, his wife Anastasija Sergeevna Perfil'eva (*née* Lanskaja; 1813–1891), their son Vasilij Stepanovich Perfil'ev (see Letter Nº 16, Note 94).
230 Aleksandr Mikhajlovich Sukhotin (1827–1905) — staff cavalry captain, Tula landowner; brother to Sergej Mikhajlovich Sukhotin (see Letter Nº 13, Note 81).
231 Countess Aleksandra Andreevna Tolstaja (1817–1904) — LNT's great aunt and close friend; a lady-in-waiting during the reigns of four Emperors: Nicholas I (1825–55), Alexander II (1855–81), Alexander III (1881–94), Nicholas II (1894–1917). She was also known by the French name *Alexandrine*.
232 Prince Nikolaj Ivanovich Trubetskoj (1797–1874) — Actual Privy Councillor, Ober-Hofmeister, Member of the State Council, Senator, Chairman of the Moscow Board of Trustees.

Solovëv[233] has only 500 roubles. He says things are tight for him both because it's summer and because they're still waiting for Volume 6 [of *War and Peace*].

I am always with you, and especially when we're apart I find myself in a soft and humble mood. This was the mood I was in when I arrived at Tula and had the misfortune to see [Aleksandr Mikhajlovich] Kuzminskij — a cold, shallow and evil egotist. It was painful for me to get angry at him, but I had no other choice. I am sure he did not let Tanja go [anywhere]. He is one of those people who takes pleasure in doing unpleasant things for others. I am sure he enjoys his dinner more if he takes it from someone else. —

I bought some books and bouillon; the wine I shall buy at Nizhnij. At Shilovo I shall find out for certain whether I can go to Morshansk. But should I? In any case I shall go back to receive your letters.

Farewell, darling.

L. T.

I'm leaving the letter unsealed [for now]. I shall add a postscript at the Perfil'evs' on my way back.

I didn't find anyone at the Perfil'evs' except Nastas'ja Sergeevna,[234] and I'm off to Nizhnij [Novgorod] and shall return, too.

N° 38 – SOFIA ANDREEVNA TOLSTAYA ✒ LEV NIKOLAEVICH TOLSTOY
[LSA 26]
4 September [1869]. Evening. [Yasnaya Polyana]

I'm already experiencing moments of utter despair over your absence, and [wondering] what's happening with you, sweet Lëvochka, especially when the day draws to a close and I'm left all alone in the evening with my dark thoughts, conjectures and fears. It is so hard living in this world without you; everything's not as it should be; it seems everything's wrong and it's not worth it. I wasn't going to write to you anything of the sort, but it came out all by itself. And everything's so confined, so trifling, that I need something better, and that 'better' is none other than *you*, and always you alone.

I received a letter for you from *Alexandrine* in Livadija,[235] written on your birthday [28 August]. She writes you a lot of tender [words], which I find annoying. She writes along the lines of your last letter to her and your last mood — preparation for death, and I thought it might be better for you if you had married her back then instead, you would have understood each other better. She is so eloquent, especially in French. One thing she notes with justification is that because of her unhappy love she has come to regard everything from the point of view of death, but she writes that she doesn't understand how you arrived at that; it seems she wonders whether you might have reached this [conclusion] through the same route. She made me wonder, too — whether in your case it wasn't because of an unhappy love, but because love gave you too little, that you adopted this comforting view of life, people and happiness. Now I've more or less retreated into myself, and am looking outward from myself to see where my own

233 Ivan Grigor'evich Solovëv (1819–1881) — bookseller, LNT's book distributor.
234 Anastasija Sergeevna (Nastas'ja) Perfil'eva (see Note 229 above).
235 *Livadija (Livadiya)* — the Tsar's royal estate and summer palace near Yalta in the Crimea. In February 1945 it was the site of the Yalta Conference, bringing together Sir Winston Churchill, Franklin Roosevelt and Joseph Stalin to discuss the ongoing Second World War and especially the post-war development of Europe. The letter in question has been lost.

comforting path may lie. I wanted to somehow escape from the bustle of my routine life which has so utterly swallowed me up, to get out into the light, find some activity that would give me greater satisfaction and delight, but what that is I have no idea.

You should just hear how little Tanja asks and talks so much about you at every opportune moment — you would be delighted if you heard [her]. Serëzha has asked twice, while Il'ja doesn't comprehend at all: poor thing, Serëzha shoved the door right into his nose and made it bleed, and he keeps wheezing and sneezing. Little Tanja is quite healthy; Mamà, Auntie and everybody are all doing fine, but my throat hurts very badly and I've lost my voice. Somehow Dasha[236] frightened all of us. For twenty-four hours the other day she was perilously close to death. They sent a rider to fetch Mamà; she [Dar'ja] had a fever and was vomiting frightfully. The doctors summoned Knertser;[237] now she's quite better, the fever's lessened, and the vomiting's stopped; she had an attack of diarrhœa. The husband and wife [Aleksandr and Tat'jana] are getting on well again; Mamà says that he is very affectionate and tender with her, puts her to bed; pity he has such a changeable mood.

It's not that good for you to go away from me, Lëvochka; I'm left with an angry feeling over the pain caused by your absence. I'm not saying this means you shouldn't go, only that it's harmful, the same as I don't say [one] shouldn't give birth, I'm only saying that it's painful.

Our life is very peaceful here, there's been no one around, — I hardly sleep at all at night, I get up at nine o'clock (our hours are now back to normal), we take tea all together, every day I read with Serëzha, and he writes; I sew, knit, quarrel with Nikolaj[238] sometimes, in the evenings I read [Mrs.] Henry Wood;[239] it's easy to read her novels — they're more understandable than others. When I breast-feed Lëvushka,[240] I always philosophise, dream, think about you, and so these are my favourite moments [of the day]. Yes, it's funny that yesterday the postman brought me two letters — from you and *Alexandrine*, and both of them contained Vjazemskij's quatrain, which greatly flattered *Alexandrine*, and this I found funny.

It's almost incredible that you won't be coming until the 12th. You can't expect me to calmly wait out another eight days, when these five have seemed to me a century. And now, probably, you haven't quite reached your destination. I shan't ask you to do anything more in Moscow. Hurry home quickly from Moscow; it's silly to [think] of saving a few kopeks on [the more expensive] groceries in Tula at the expense of the several hours that I am deprived of your company.

For some reason Mamà wasn't in a good mood yesterday, and overall her mood has completely changed since she visited the Kuzminskijs and saw their dysfunctional *ménage*. There's a whole lot I could write to you. I keep thinking throughout the day how I want to write this to Lëvochka, and now I've forgotten so much and this letter has turned out all muddled; I was telling you that I've got unaccustomed to writing letters; I'd like to just tell you right off everything I want to say, but I can't do it all at once. Here you are forced to read my letter, my rambling, while if you were at home you would say I'd do better talking to the samovar. I just remembered that and it offended me. So farewell, even though I'm annoyed with you, as here I am

---

236 Dar'ja Aleksandrovna (Dasha) Kuzminskaja (1868–1873) — eldest daughter to SAT's sister Tat'jana Andreevna (Tanja).
237 Nikolaj Andreevich Knertser (1833–?) — a Tula physician.
238 Nikolaj Mikhajlovich Rumjantsev (cook) — see Letter N° 5, Note 27.
239 Ellen Wood (published as Mrs. Henry Wood; *née* Price; 1814–1887) — English author, widely known abroad. Three of her works are to be found in the Yasnaya Polyana library: *East Lynne* (1861), *Oswald Cray* (1864), *The Red Court Farm* (1868).
240 Lev L'vovich (Lëva, Lëvushka) Tolstoj (1869–1945) — the Tolstoys' fourth child (after Sergej, Tat'jana and Il'ja).

tormenting myself on account of your absence. Still, big hugs and kisses. I, too, want to say, as do the Aunties,[241] May God preserve you. It will be a long, long time before we see each other again.

Nº 39 – LEV NIKOLAEVICH TOLSTOY ❧ SOFIA ANDREEVNA TOLSTAYA
[PSS 83/87]
11 or 12 June 1871. Steamship on the Volga.

I'm writing to you on board a steamship. The letter will be despatched from our first port of call.

There was so much going on in Moscow that I couldn't get around to it. Especially since my decision as to whether to go to Saratov or Samara was made just an hour before departure.

I shall write it all out to start with.

I went straight to see Vasin'ka.[242] Volodja[243] went directly to Petersburg. Vasin'ka wasn't at home, but he soon arrived. About where to find koumiss they weren't able to tell me anything. The money — 75 roubles instead of the 100 I was expecting — he handed over to me. That evening I sent a wire to Zakhar'in[244] at Bratsovo. In the morning I went to do some shopping, to find a nanny and a doctor, and found all except a doctor. —

There was no [doctor] in the town, and I decided not to go to the dacha to fetch Pikulin[245] or Zakhar'in, who sent me a wire inviting me to dinner, for that would have delayed me a whole day. We know what the doctors would have said: they would have said there was nothing of significance, and that it wouldn't harm me to travel. For a long time I wrestled with the question of where to go. [Pëtr Ivanovich] Bartenev, who had bought an estate at Atkarsk, assured me that there was good koumiss there. Vasin'ka said the same about Saratov. But the Tambov doctor Filipovich,[246] and Leont'ev,[247] whom I met, as well as [Jurij Fëdorovich] Samarin, all declared that undoubtedly and incomparably the best climate and koumiss recognised by all doctors was in the Samara [region]. Along the way I met another doctor, along with [several] knowledgeable people who all confirmed that Samara was the best, and [so] I am going back to my old place.[248] Write to me, please, as soon as you can, at Samara until I send you another address. I'll arrange with the Samara post office as to how to reach me. —

Now about nannys. I'm afraid that [big] Tanja will have trouble [understanding] my telegraphically brief letter. I went to see the German pastor. The pastor himself[249] and especially the elderly widow Dikgof[250] gave me five addresses, of which I have been to two. One of them was not at home. Stëpa[251] located the other — the one whom Mrs. Dikgof recommended the highest, and whose address I sent [to you in a previous letter]; [her name is] Lindgol'm [Lindholm]

241 Tat'jana Andreevna Ergol'skaja and Pelageja Il'inichna Jushkova, who were living at Yasnaya Polyana. See Letter Nº 5, Notes 33 and 39.

242 Vasilij Stepanovich (Vasin'ka) Perfil'ev — see Letter Nº 16, Note 94.

243 Vladimir Andreevich (Volodja) Behrs — see Letter Nº 15, Note 89.

244 Grigorij Antonovich Zakhar'in — see Letter Nº 34, Note 210.

245 Pavel Lukich Pikulin (1822–1885) — a physician-therapist.

246 *Filipovich* — no details are known about him.

247 Pavel Mikhajlovich Leont'ev (1822–1875) — professor of classic philology at Moscow University.

248 The village of Karalyk in Samara Gubernia where LNT went for koumiss treatment in the summer of 1862.

249 Genrikh Genrikhovich Dikgof (1833–1911) — senior pastor at the Church of Saints Peter and Paul in Moscow, later a bishop in the Evangelical Lutheran church.

250 The pastor's mother, Elizaveta Dikgof (*née* von Strahlborn, 1803–1873) — widow to Karl-Genrikh Vil'gel'm Dikgof (1803–1862), Chief Superintendent of the Moscow Evangelical-Lutheran district and Senior Pastor of the Church of Saints Peter and Paul in Moscow.

251 Stepan Andreevich (Stëpa) Behrs (SAT's brother), who was accompanying LNT.

— and she came to see me. She's 25 years old. She served as a nanny for 6 years, it seems, in one place, at Mezentsov's.[252] She is not that nice to look at. But she seems to be an honest girl, healthy and unspoilt. She's agreed [to work] for 12 roubles [a month], with the possibility of a raise in the future. I wrote out her duties: looking after [our] two elder children, maintaining their clothing in order, sleeping with them and sewing [for them]. And teaching them to read and write German. [Her] German is good. She speaks Russian. I would [recommend] hiring her. She asks that her way be paid to Tula, and that after a year she be given a return ticket, if you don't get along. I said nothing. She promised to wait five days for a reply. If [we] don't like her [we shall] send her back to Moscow — never mind the extra 3 roubles. We can send her 3 roubles through Vasin'ka — i.e. write her that she can stop by his place, and write to Vasin'ka to give her [the money].

I haven't received the money from the [vegetable] oil salesman yet — he promised but didn't come, so it'll be up to you to collect what he owes [us].

I bought an excellent dish with enhancements, and it is being shipped along with a [a game of] *pas-de-géant*, which I bought from Puare[253] for 28 roubles. To set up the *pas-de-géant*, call the men together and try to understand and follow [the instructions].[254]

The things will be sent out on Wednesday. My health is not just all right, it seems to me actually quite good. Hugs and kisses to the children, to yourself and to everybody there. Please do write in more detail. I'm very happy to see Stëpa. He's very meek and kind. Ljubov' Aleksandrovna is probably [staying] with us; hugs and kisses to her and Slavochka [i.e. Vjacheslav Andreevich Behrs]. I'm simply delighted that she's with you.

Nº 40 – SOFIA ANDREEVNA TOLSTAYA ✍ LEV NIKOLAEVICH TOLSTOY
[LSA 29]
[17–18 June 1871. Yasnaya Polyana]

It is not in a cheerful mood that I write you [today], sweet friend Lëvochka. My nanny's ill and Lëvushka, too, has a fever and was vomiting. All this has been a great bother, but I'm not letting myself get depressed — I've been getting excellent help from Mamà, and Hannah, and Liza and Varja. When you're not here I take very good care of myself, I take a nap during the day, I go out for walks, and so forth. The other children — indeed, all of us — are healthy. The children enthusiastically devour [wild] strawberries, they're cheerful, and are out right now for a walk with Grandmother,[255] since Hannah is busy helping me. Lëvushka [i.e. their son Lev] is getting along a little better now, and Nanny, too. Probably, by the time you receive this letter, everything here will be just fine once again. I've just received your letter from the steamer[256] and I'm very happy that you're feeling fine. Along with your letter I also received letters from

---

252 Possibly a reference either to Gen. Nikolaj Vladimirovich Mezentsov (?–1878), chief of the *gendarmerie* or to Lt-Gen. Pëtr Ivanovich Mezentsov (1824–1897), who headed the Moscow Cadet Corps.
253 Jakov Viktorovich Puare (1825–1877) — owner of an athletics facility in Moscow.
254 Starting on page 4 of the letter are to be found instructions for setting up the game, written in an unknown hand.
255 A reference to SAT's mother, Ljubov' Aleksandrovna Behrs.
256 Letter Nº 39 of 11 or 12 June 1871.

Fet[257] and Urusov.[258] Urusov wrote me such a precious, intelligent letter that I find myself loving him even more. And Fet, as always, speaks and writes so grandiloquently.

You ask me to write in more detail, but unfortunately I don't really have time for that today. I really love writing to you — it comforts me to send and receive letters. I am sending you my [new] photo. I had it taken the other day, on Tuesday, at Tula, where I went with Liza and Leonid.[259]

Your jury duty has been causing us no end of troubles. We obtained the [medical] certificate from Knertser, sent it with Ivan Kuzmich to Sergievskoe, and now the penalty has been lifted and the certificate accepted. There's been a big fuss about money, too — the 1000 silver roubles which were sent to you in care of [Aleksandr Mikhajlovich] Kuzminskij. Here we made use of the form which you once left for me and on which [your] signature was confirmed by the police with great difficulty.

Tanja [Tolstaya's sister] is grateful for the nanny. Kuzminskij himself will send her the money; he left today for Moscow. Tanja didn't hesitate for a moment. She's overjoyed and has decided to take her at once. Poor Tanja has a very bad toothache and Mamà has started to feel better at our place. It's hot, sweltering and windy here. The children still go bathing and Knertser has said I should take daily bran-baths. He says my rash is the result of fever and was bound to show up sooner or later. He was quite happy to give me the certificate, saying that you did just the right thing by going for koumiss. He kept saying time and again how helpful it would be for you, since apparently you have become much weaker both physically and emotionally.

And your friends Fet and Urusov are both convinced that you are suffering from *your Greek [studies],* and I agree with them that this is one of the main causes. Under separate cover I shall send you their two letters to me; read them and write to them from the *kibitka* [a small carriage]. I shall write them just a brief note, since I have very little time.

Now the walks and rides and games have ceased. All [available] forces, minds and hearts are concentrated on helping me in the nursery without a nanny. It's all fairly easy to take with such precious helpers. Nanny, too, is suffering from fever and vomiting, she's quite turned upside-down and probably won't get well in under a week's time.

I'm most grateful for the dish and the *pas-de-géant.* When everyone gets better, I'll arrange with the Prince [Leonid Dmitrievich Obolenskij] to have it set up. He says we have to hire soldiers from the camp to set it up. For the building they bought wood[260] for 450 silver roubles and took up all the space around the house with the thickest beams and boards. They'll probably start construction soon. I moved Mamà into the study; here [in the nursery] the children didn't let her have any sleep. I want to write everything down for you as quickly as possible, hence I'm not writing that coherently.

Farewell, dear friend, big hugs and kisses. I'll be writing more soon, but right now there's absolutely no more time. Live longer, get well, write more often and don't worry about us.

Sonja.

---

257 In his letter to SAT of 15 June 1871, Afanasij Fet (see Letter N° 7, Note 51) advised her: "You need to use all your power to stop him (Lev Nikolaevich) from overworking himself the way he is doing. He should rest." (S. A. Tolstaya, *Letters to L. N. Tolstoy [Pis'ma k L. N. Tolstomu]*, 1936, p. 96).

258 Sergej Semënovich Urusov (1827–1897) was a close friend of LNT's, who served with him in the Sevastopol' conflict. In his letter to SAT he also expressed concern over LNT's poor health (*ibid.*, p. 96), attributing it at least in part to his intensive study of Ancient Greek, which he undertook during 1870–71.

259 Elizaveta Valer'janovna (Liza) Obolenskaja (see Letter N° 6, Note 43) and her husband Prince Leonid Dmitrievich Obolenskij (1844–1888).

260 In 1871 an addition was made to the house at Yasnaya Polyana.

17 June.

I'll write more another day. Nanny's got up completely, only she's [still] weak, and Lëvushka's a lot better.

Nº 41 – LEV NIKOLAEVICH TOLSTOY ❧ SOFIA ANDREEVNA TOLSTAYA
[PSS 83/91]
23 June 1871. Karalyk.

I'm delighted to write you some good news about myself, dear friend — namely that two days after my last letter to you,[261] where I complained about melancholy and ill health, I started feeling fine, and I feel ashamed for alarming you. I cannot, as usual, [bring myself to] write or say to you what I am not thinking. The only thing that upsets me is that tomorrow it will be two weeks since I left, and I have not received any word from you. I am overcome with horror, as I think about and vividly imagine you and the children and everything that could happen to you all.

As for my not receiving letters, nobody's to blame — it's just the location: 130 versts not covered by the postal service. Tomorrow it will be a week since the Bashkir messenger left; he was supposed to return on Sunday — today's Wednesday, and he isn't here.

Now I've learnt my new address, which I'll append at the end. Write to me alternately: the first time to Samara, the second to the new address. When I receive the letters, I'll write and tell you which address is better. —

The feelings of melancholy and indifference I was complaining about have passed; I feel I've entered a Scythian state of mind, where everything is interesting and new. I feel no dullness whatsoever, but [I do feel] the eternal fear along with your absence, which makes me count the days when my detached, incomplete existence will come to an end. For six weeks I shall endure from day to day, and so by the 5th of August (and I don't dare talk or think [about it]) I think I shall be home. But what will [I find] at home? Will everybody be well, everyone just the same as I left them? You, most importantly. There's a lot that's new and interesting: the Bashkirs, who have a flavour of Herodotus, and Russian peasants, and villages, especially charming in their simplicity and kindness of the people. I bought a horse for 60 roubles and Stëpa and I are riding together. Stëpa's a fine lad. Sometimes very enthusiastic and he keeps cursing Petersburg with a serious face; he can be annoying at times, and I feel sorry for him because in any case he's bored and [I feel] sorry that he's not at Yasnaya. Altogether, I have a great deal to tell you and I shall be annoyed if you listen to how Masha[262] squeals and not to what I say. Is that going to happen? And when? I shoot ducks, and we eat them. Now we were out riding and hunting bustards, as usual, we just scared them off, and we were also hunting wolves and a Baskhkir caught a wolf cub. I am reading Greek, but very little. I don't really feel like it. Nobody has described koumiss better than the peasant who told me the other day that *we are feeding on grass,* — like the horses. We don't wish to harm ourselves in any way — not with intense activity, nor with smoking (Stëpa is weaning me from smoking and gives me now [only] twelve *papirosas* a day, decreasing the amount each day), nor with tea, nor with sitting [and talking] late into the night.

261 In this 'last letter', dated 18 June 1871, LNT complained: "The most painful thing of all about me is that because of my ill health, I feel only 1/10 of what I should. I have no mental, especially poetic, delights. I see everything as dead, for the same reason that I have not liked many people. And I now I myself see only what there is; I can understand, I can imagine; but I cannot penetrate with love, as I used to. If there is any poetic disposition at all, it is acidic and gushy, [it makes me] want to cry" *(PSS,* 83: 179).
262 Marija L'vovna (Masha) Tolstaja (1871–1906) — the Tolstoys' fifth child (after Sergej, Tat'jana, Il'ja and Lev).

I get up at 6, at 7 o'clock I drink koumiss, and go to a winter hut [in the village of Karalyk] where [a number of] koumiss drinkers live. I shall talk with them, then I'll come back and take tea with Stëpa, then read a bit, walk across the steppes wearing only my *roubashka* [long peasant shirt], keep drinking koumiss, eat a piece of fried mutton, and then we'll go hunting either on foot or on horseback, and in the evening go to bed almost as soon as it gets dark.

You asked me to see what kind of comforts there are for life and travel. I've been asking around here about land, and they offered me some land here at 15 roubles per desjatina, which yields 6% [profit] without any trouble at all, and today a priest wrote me a letter about some land — 2500 desjatinas at 7 roubles per desjatina, which seems quite profitable. I'll go have a look tomorrow.

And since it is very possible that I shall buy this piece of land, or another, I would ask you to send me a note issued by the Merchant Bank, which I might need for the down payment (with a money order through the Bank of Samara).

Here it is sleep that brings me the closest to you. These first few nights I dreamt about you, then about [our son] Serëzha. I am showing the children's portrait to the Bashkirs here. How are Tanja and the nanny doing? Sasha has probably left.[263] I regret that I did not speak with him before their separation, and that I didn't tell him that even though we have had our differences, I am very glad that we parted good friends.

How is my standby, Ljubov' Aleksandrovna, doing? I would gladly share my current state of health with her. What about the dear stallmaster[264] and the girls? I remembered Varja yesterday upon seeing the herds of horses in the hills in the twilight. —

I dreamt that Serëzha was being mischievous and that I was angry with him; it's probably just the opposite in reality.

Serëzha.

Write and tell me how you are getting on. Are you riding horseback and do Mamà and Hannah [Tarsey] curse or praise you often, and what [marks] have you gotten for [good] behaviour? Hugs and kisses.

Tanja!

There's a boy here. He is four years old and his name is Azis. He's chubby, round-faced and drinks koumiss, and is always laughing. Stëpa really likes him and gives him candy. This Azis walks around with no clothes. There's a gentleman living with us who is very hungry, as he has nothing to eat except mutton. And this gentleman says it would be good to eat Azis — he's so fatty. Write and tell me what [marks] you've been getting on your behaviour. Hugs and kisses.

Iljusha!

Ask Serëzha to read to you what I write.

Today a Bashkir went riding and saw three wolves. And he wasn't afraid of anything and leapt from his horse right onto the wolves. They started biting him. He let two of them get away,

---

263 On 18 June 1871 Aleksandr Mikhajlovich (Sasha) Kuzminskij (husband to SAT's sister Tat'jana Andreevna) left for his new government posting in Kutais.

264 Prince Leonid Dmitrievich Obolenskij (1844–1888), husband to Marija Nikolaevna Tolstaja's daughter Elizaveta Valer'janovna (Liza); the other "girl" referred to here is Elizaveta's sister Varvara Valer'janovna (Varja).

but caught one of them and brought it to us. Tonight, maybe that wolf's mother will come. And then we'll shoot it. Hugs and kisses. Give kisses from me to both Aunties [Tat'jana Aleksandrovna Ergol'skaja and Pelageja Il'inichna Jushkova] and Lëvochka, and Masha, and my regards to Hannah and Natal'ja Petrovna [Okhotnitskaja], and to your Nanny,[265] and do go for walks to the village [Yasnaya] and tell Ivan's children and his wife that Ivan[266] is healthy and is talking with the Bashkirs in the Tatar language, and does a lot of shouting at them, but they aren't afraid of him and laugh at him. —

Farewell, darling, hugs and kisses.

[My] address is not certain. Write to the old one. —

Nº 42 – LEV NIKOLAEVICH TOLSTOY ❧ SOFIA ANDREEVNA TOLSTAYA
[PSS 83/97]
16–17 July 1871. Karalyk. [Preceded by SAT's Nº 4U, 24-25 June 1871]

It's been a long time since I've written you, dear friend. I'm somewhat to blame, but mostly Fate. I let one opportunity to write slip by, and since then every day I've been promised "[the post] is leaving, it's leaving", and I kept putting it off, five days, but now I can no longer brook [the delay] and am sending [this letter by] special messenger. My last letter to you, it seems, was on the 10th or the 9th before I left. We've actually started our journey: Kostin'ka[267] (as he is called) [and] Baron Bistrom,[268] a [Russian-]German youth who's just finished a course at the *lycée* with honours, Stëpa and I — [we're all] travelling in [something that looks like] a wicker basket (that's how everyone travels here), [pulled] by a pair of horses without a guide or a coachman. We didn't know ourselves where we were going, and we'd ask people we met along the road whether they knew where we were going. We were actually searching for places where there was koumiss, and where we could hunt, with only the foggiest notion of any [rivers named] Irgiz or Kamelik [tributaries of the Volga]. Our trip lasted four days and turned out splendidly. There was such an abundance of game that there was nowhere to store it — even nobody to eat [all those] ducks — and the Bashkirs, and the places we saw, and our companions were splendid.

Thanks to my title of Count and my previous acquaintance with Stolypin,[269] all the Bashkirs know me here and have great respect for me. They received us everywhere with a hospitality that defies description. Wherever we go, the host will cook a plump and juicy mutton, set forth a huge vat of koumiss, roll out rugs and pillows on the floor, seat his guests down on them and not let them go until they have eaten his mutton and drunk his koumiss. [According to a local custom,] he gives his guests drink from his own hands and with his hands (no fork) stuffs pieces of mutton and fat into their mouths, and one cannot insult him [by refusing]. —

A lot that happened was funny. Kostin'ka and I ate and drank with delight, and that was evidently to our advantage, but Stëpa and the Baron were funny and pitiful, especially the Baron. He wanted to keep up with the others, and he drank, but towards the end he vomited on the

---

265 Marija Afanas'evna Arbuzova (1818–post 1900) — nanny to the Tolstoys' older children.
266 Ivan Vasil'evich Suvorov (1824–1912), who went with him to Samara for koumiss.
267 *Kostin'ka* — an acquaintance of LNT's from Murom, who was also taking koumiss treatments.
268 Baron Nikolaj Rodrigovich Bistrom — son of Rodrig Grigor'evich Bistrom (1810–1886), who was a nobleman from Kurljand Gubernia, from whom LNT bought land in Samara Gubernia in 1878.
269 Arkadij Dmitrievich Stolypin (1822–1899) — general; father of the future Russian Prime Minister (1906–11) Pëtr Arkad'evich Stolypin (1862–1911); comrade to LNT during the defence of Sevastopol.

carpets, and later, on the journey home, when we hinted that we might stop in once more to see our hospitable Bashkir, he all but pleaded through tears not to. From this you can see how healthy I am. My side hurt a little during this time, but only slightly, and it's completely better now. The main thing is that there is no trace of the melancholy, and that now I've had my fill of koumiss and am now in a real koumiss state — i.e. from morning to night I'm slightly drunk on koumiss, and sometimes go for whole days without eating or eating very little. The weather here is marvellous. During our trip it rained; but for three days now the heat has been something terrible, but I like it. Stëpa is no longer bored, and it seems he's filled out a bit and matured. I'd like to bring a lot of people here. You, [little] Serëzha, Hannah. I'm really bothered by her illness. God forbid she should break out again like last summer. Ever since you wrote me about [Aleksandr Nikolaevich] Bibikov, I've been keeping an eye out for him on the road. If he came, I would be very happy and treat him to all that he loves, and would probably undertake a trip to Ufa (staying with the Bashkirs en route), 400 versts, and from there I'd come back by steamship along the Bela River to the Kama, and from the Kama to the Volga. At the moment I shall almost certainly not take this trip, even though I dream about it. I'm afraid it would delay my arrival home by a day at least. Each day I am apart from you I think of you with more urgency, alarm and passion, and it is harder and harder for me. It's indescribable. We still have 16 more days. But the trip to Ufa is interesting because the road to Ufa winds through one of the most remote and richest corners of Russia. You can imagine the land — the forests, steppes and rivers; there are streams everywhere, and the land has been [covered with] feather-grass, untouched since the creation of the world, yielding the best wheat. And [this] land — only 100 versts from a steamship route — is being sold by the Bashkirs for 3 roubles a desjatina. If not to buy, I would at least like to take a look at this land. My plans for purchase aren't going anywhere [at the moment]. I wrote Sasha[270] in Petersburg, asking him to deal with Tuchkov,[271] and to Tuchkov's local agent in Samara, but I haven't yet heard from either one. I overheard rumours that they now want to ask upwards of 7 roubles [per desjatina]. If that is the case, I shan't buy. You know that in everything I leave the decision up to Fate. So too in this.

After my last letter, I received two more letters from you. I wanted to write [you], darling, [and ask you to] write more often and [tell me] more, but the only way you'll be able to get a reply to this letter of mine is through Nizhnij [Novgorod]. Still, your letters are probably more dangerous to me than all the Greek [writers] because of the excitement they arouse in me. Especially since I receive them suddenly. I can't read them without [breaking into] tears; I tremble all over, and my heart beats [fast]. And you write whatever comes into your head, while for me *every word* is significant; I read all of them over and over. Two things you write about are very sad: the fact that I shan't see Mamà unless I go to Liza's and bring her to our place again, which I am planning to do, and, more importantly, that my dear friend Tanja is threatening to leave [Yasnaya Polyana] before I get there.[272] That would be sad indeed. Why don't you write about Auntie Tat'jana Aleksandrovna [Ergol'skaja]? I also received a letter each from Urusov and Fet and shall send a reply. As to Offenberg's[273] letter, I haven't any idea yet of how to respond, but there's no point in hurrying, since his address in Warsaw is good only until the 18th. But I want to answer as follows: to offer him the 90,000 [roubles] he is asking for, but only in instalments, without interest, over 2 ½ [or] 3 years, at 30,000 a year.

270 SAT's brother Aleksandr Andreevich (Sasha) Behrs; the letter has not been preserved.
271 Nikolaj Pavlovich Tuchkov (1834–1893) — an aide-de-camp.
272 Tat'jana Andreevna (i.e. SAT's sister Tanja) was planning to join her husband in Kutais.
273 Baron Fëdor Ivanovich Offenberg (1839–1872) — owner of the Aljab'evo estate 4 versts from Nikol'skoe-Vjazemskoe.

Big hugs and kisses to sweet Liza[274] from you and me, and [ask] her not to get angry if in this heat and being constantly drunk [from koumiss], I don't manage to reply to her letter which gave me such tremendous pleasure. — Hugs and kisses to all, even to Dmitrij Alekseevich,[275] if he is there with his family, and regardless of whether he is teasing you or Tanja. Comfort Tanja. If her husband is good, and [I'm certain] he is, the unavoidable separation will result in nothing except that they will have a greater affection and a stronger love [for each other], and along with a slight love-sickness, which the wife ought to find pleasing. There is far less [danger] of unfaithfulness when they are separated than when they are together, since people who are separated cling to the ideal in *their* soul, which nothing can be compared to. This all concerns you, too. [Ask] Varja [Varja Valer'janovna Tolstaja] to write to me. Stëpa and I will have a lot to say in return. I'm glad that the *pas-de-géant* is up, but I have no clear picture how that all works for everyone. I can only picture Il'ja falling.

Oh, if only God would grant that everything goes along fine without me right to the end, the way it has according to your latest letters. Farewell, my precious dove, a big hug from me. And all my nerves are shot. Now I just feel like crying, I love you so much.

16 July.

17 July, evening. P.S. My health is perfect. I'm counting the days. The Bashkir hasn't brought any letters from you. They didn't give him any, because *Jean* [servant Ivan Vasil'evich Suvorov] is too assiduous and wrote a foolish note to the post office. I am hoping [there will be some] tomorrow.

Nᵒ 43 – SOFIA ANDREEVNA TOLSTAYA ✍ LEV NIKOLAEVICH TOLSTOY [LSA 39]

27 July 1871. Evening. [Yasnaya Polyana]

I don't know why you asked me to write [to you] on the 27th and 28th in Moscow.[276] Does that mean you'll be in Moscow by the 1st [of August]? I want to believe and at the same time I don't; I feel happy and at the same time frightened, and don't know myself what I feel when I think about you and our meeting. Lately I haven't been able to think of anything else but your arrival; nothing interests me, and when I think about this and the children come by, I tell them Papà will soon be here, and I kiss them with delight, and they understand, and they themselves say every morning that now there are only twelve (or ten) days left. We are all expecting you on the 5th of August. But it's not very nice when you don't tell us when you set out. Does that mean I shan't meet you at the station? I'd be glad to go to Tula if I could see you a whole hour earlier. Now I've been following your whole trip in [the railway timetable] *Parovoz* and, if you left Samara on the 2nd, you could be home by the 5th. I'm so afraid to expect you any earlier. For that matter, I'm afraid of everything: the steamships, and the state of your health, and your impatience to get home; I'm afraid that you might have drunk too little koumiss, and that I failed to persuade you [to continue your treatment and] not to hurry home. But lately I haven't been strong enough to keep on persuading you not to [hasten] home. I am plagued day and night by my concern for you.

274 Elizaveta Valer'janova (Liza) Obolenskaja, who was living at Yasnaya Polyana at the time.
275 Dmitrij Alekseevich D'jakov was also visiting Yasnaya Polyana.
276 On 8–9 July 1871 LNT wrote to his wife: "Only a week before I leave, i.e. starting on the 24th, stop writing, and write me on the 25th, say, to Nizhnij [Novgorod], General Delivery, and then on the 27th and 28th to Moscow, General Delivery" (*PSS*, 83: 195–96).

Your latest letter[277] I received the day before yesterday. I read it at the Kozlovka station by lamplight while I was seeing off the D'jakovs. I was given this letter by [our cook] Semën, who was completely drunk at the time we were getting into the carriage to drive to Kozlovka, and as the road was dark and bumpy, I was on pins and needles all the way to the station, I was so anxious. This letter made me frightfully happy to know that you missed me so much, and from the anticipation of seeing you. I wrote you[278] about D'jakov's missing belongings; they haven't been found, though some of the workers were suspected [of stealing them].

Everyone's terribly interfering with my getting any [letter-]writing done: [My sister] Tanja is sitting right beside me (we're all in the drawing-room) along with Liza and Varja — they're sewing, reading and writing. Tanja and Varja are talking about the servants travelling [with Tanja] to Kutais. Almost nobody's agreed [to go to Kutais] yet, except for Nanny and Trifovna.[279] Leonid [Obolenskij], too, has come down with cholerine; he's lying in the study, he has a fever, had a bout of vomiting and strong stomach pains. He's better now, and he's taken some bouillon for the first time. This cholerine makes me terribly frightened for you, too. After the koumiss [treatment], you should be on the strictest of diets. For God's sake take care of your health, don't eat any fruit or anything raw. We're all very careful here, and we're all quite healthy, except for Lëlja and Varja,[280] who are both coughing; still they go out walking and run around the *pas-de-géant*. Lëlja does not go out alone, of course, but with me or Hannah, and I hope this, too, will be over by the time you get home. It strikes me funny that you will be reading this letter in Moscow just a few hours before we meet, but right now it seems like it will be an eternity before that happy moment arrives.

Tanja very often receives letters from her husband, and such tender letters I would not have expected from him. He writes that his only comfort is arranging and thinking about [future] conveniences for Tanja and the children, and says that he thinks about and loves her far more than the children.

This past night Tanja was tormented by a toothache and suddenly at 5 o'clock this morning she became very restless [and wanted] to go to Tula. She went with Verochka,[281] stopping over with Marija Ivanovna,[282] [then] went to see Vigand[283] and [got treatment for] a tooth. Now she's revived, but still very weak and sleepy. These days I've been staying pretty much at home — I don't go out for walks, I don't run around the *pas-de-géant*. I sit, work, read, and make little Masha [the Tolstoys' fifth child Marija L'vovna] jump up and down. She doesn't like me because I make her suck on my breast, and she continues to feed unwillingly, as there is not much milk at all. I've been moving about so much to keep from being bored that all my energy has dissipated — I sit and wait for you, and the only thing [I can do] is go over the details [in my mind] about you and your arrival. I can only delight and take comfort in the thought that I shall be seeing you soon. I'm no longer eager or happy to write to you any more, whereas before this was my comfort and joy. I'm so tired of waiting, of worrying, thinking about you and missing you. I keep dreaming that you are wiring me as to when you are coming, and that I'll have the

277 Letter Nº 42, dated 16–17 July 1871.
278 The letter referred to has not been preserved.
279 Stepanida Trifonovna Ivanova (?–1886) — the Behrs' elderly housekeeper, who later cooked for the Kuzminskijs.
280 The reference here is to the Tolstoys' fourth child, Lev L'vovich (Lëva, Lëlja), and to LNT's niece Varvara Valer'janovna (Varja).
281 Vera Aleksandrovna (Verochka) Kuzminskaja (1871–ca1940) — the third child of Tat'jana Andreevna (Tanja) Kuzminskaja and Aleksandr Mikhajlovich Kuzminskij.
282 Marija Ivanovna Abramovich — SAT's midwife, who lived in Tula.
283 Èduard Il'ich Vigand — see Letter Nº 5, Note 41.

opportunity of going out to greet you. Farewell, my sweet. I probably shan't write you any more letters now [as you will be home soon]. Still, if I don't receive any news from you by the evening of the 30th [of July], on the 31st I'll send one more letter to you at Moscow. Hugs and kisses for the last time in written form; soon I'll be embracing you in person, and I shall see and kiss your sweet eyes, which I now picture as smiling and kind and excited.

Your Sonja.

Hugs from Liza, Varja and Tanja and kisses from the first two.

N° 44 – LEV NIKOLAEVICH TOLSTOY ✿ SOFIA ANDREEVNA TOLSTAYA
[PSS 83/102]
14 July 1872. Farmstead at Tananyk.

13th.

I am writing from the [Tananyk] farmstead. I arrived safely, along with Timrot.[284] Rumours of a decent harvest were not justified. Very bad. I haven't yet seen all the fields; but [judging] by what I have seen and heard, I doubt what's lost can be made up for, especially since the same amount will have to be sown again. It has to be sown, since after two bad years one can only expect some good ones, and to stop now would be pointless. Timrot wrote about what he saw in the spring, and then disaster happened on a scale not [even] the old people could remember; both the grass and the wheat were burnt by the heat, the ground was black, and the people started to move away for fear of famine. Today everyone cannot appreciate too much the blessing that there is grass and wheat to some extent. From the financial point of view, this is how our Samara affairs stand: We shall have to give Timrot between 2,000 and 3,000 [roubles] for the harvest and ploughing for next year and we must hope that once he sells his wheat he will send me back between two and three thousand, and, in addition, set up the farmstead on a firm enough footing so that next year we may come and find a wholly self-sufficient estate.

This has been an unfortunate year, but despite this misfortune, one can say that the Samara lands will yield 8% [profit]. One can say 8% since, even though no money will be forthcoming, the management of the farmstead is already costing no less than 2,000 [roubles]. The lease for hay-cutting brings in 670 roubles. Anyway, I can't explain everything in a letter. I'll tell you [now] about the farmstead itself and the house. The place is not at Tananyk [proper], but on the grounds of an old farmstead; it's very good from the management point of view, and a very cheerful place. My first impression — and one you'll probably share — was very pleasant, despite the fact that there is still no water in the pond.

The house is old (not so nice) and greyish-looking; but it seems that it will suit us perfectly well. It doesn't have any partitioning walls yet, just two large rooms, and I've drawn up a partition plan, which I am sending you. Apart from that, there is a huge kitchen all ready for the foreman and the workers, and a kitchen will be built for us besides. Apart from that, [there is] a cellar, a larder and a small storehouse. These are all made of mud brick with an earthen floor. — Apart from that, on one side of the farmstead there is a huge barn. All this is just about ready. —

There are 5 horses and a 'wicker basket',[285] and I am arranging to buy cows, sheep, yokes, chickens, etc.

---

284 Egor Aleksandrovich Timrot (1831–1908) — a lawyer in Samara, LNT's neighbour next door to his Samara farmstead.
285 See Letter N° 42.

Timrot is a very honest fellow, but, it seems, has been rather tight for money (he built a house in the town), and the accounts for my estate have got mixed in with his; he told me so himself. And [he says] that the balance of the accounts is now such that the amount he owes me is not that much. He is no doubt an honest man, but I find him quite repulsive, along with his whole family, and while his involvement in my affairs is very useful, it's [all] quite repulsive. The deed[286] and receiving-order have been ready for some time now, but not put into effect, since the 450 roubles of land taxes have not been paid. — About myself. We arrived at Timrot's Wednesday evening. I stopped overnight with him and left with him yesterday to come here, and the first night I got a good night's sleep. I sent to the Bashkirs for some koumiss, and so my material needs in respect to koumiss are thus taken care of. Today my friend, a peasant named Vasilij Nikitych, arrived from Gavrilovka, which is visible from the farmstead, about 6 versts distant, and brought chickens, milk and eggs. [Right now] the rain is pouring down in a torrent, and I'm waiting out [the storm] so I can ride over to Timrot's. Today he is travelling to Samara, and I'll have a talk with him about everything and send off [this] letter. The main thing is that the wheat which is still [growing in the fields] will not mature soon, and in any case it's not a pretty picture, and so tomorrow I'm just going to look over the fields, select sites for sowing, take a ride over to one [other] plot for sale and have a look. If there's money to buy it, I'll be coming home a lot earlier than I expected. In my next letter I'll tell you specifically when I'll be home, but I can't yet, because this is something I've made up my mind on just now, and I haven't yet seen the fields or talked with Timrot.

As far as my bodily health is concerned, I can tell you that nothing ails me, and that I have borne the journey superbly; as to my mental state — of course it's awkward, incomplete, and I'm virtually asleep. I don't allow myself to think. The farmstead is home to the foreman — a young bachelor lad and a soldier. All around are people hay-cutting and ploughing. Timofej[287] is very useful and dear to me. —

I could easily stay here four weeks if Petja [Tolstaya's brother Pëtr Andreevich Behrs] were with me, as I would comfort myself with the thought that it would useful for him; and truly, the air here — you won't understand if you haven't tried it yourself. But [to stay here] all by myself — while it wouldn't be exactly boring, it would be shameful to waste part of one's happy and useful life on trifles. But to work without you — without knowing you're right here — that's something, it seems, I can't do. Tell Stëpa [Stepan Andreevich Behrs] — what a tragedy! — Vasilij Nikitych's precious little granddaughter Sasha, has died from measles.

Farewell, darling. I'll write you [again] in three days. And I'll wire you when I leave. —

Hugs and kisses to the children and our whole family.

N° 45 – SOFIA ANDREEVNA TOLSTAYA ❧ LEV NIKOLAEVICH TOLSTOY
[LSA 42]
[4 September 1876. Yasnaya Polyana]

My dear sweet Lëvochka, at the moment I'm on my way to see [my sister] Tanja off [to Kutais with her family], and even though everything here is in a terrible bustle, I am still thinking of you and feel for you such tenderness that I wanted at least to write a line or two. The whole morning we've spent packing and running about; not only that but the whole house is being

---

286 The deed is to the land in Samara Gubernia acquired by LNT, validated in Samara on 9 September 1871.
287 Timofej Mikhajlovich Fokanov (1822–1891) — a Yasnaya Polyana peasant who served as foreman of LNT's Samara farmstead.

washed and cleaned up, and Lëlja's cough, too, is making me worry and fuss. It will all work out, things will calm down very soon, and then I'll write you again. Right now my hand is trembling and I'm in a hurry. Last night I did a rough outline of an *ordre du jour,* and it seems fine. Tomorrow I'll clarify further, and on Monday we'll begin our studies. Stëpa's still working on his kite. Last night he and I sat around and chatted until 2 in the morning, Tanja went to bed early. Today you're on the steamer;[288] our weather is warm today, with moments of clear sky.

[Neighbour Aleksandr Nikolaevich] Bibikov[289] himself brought over two series today and had dinner at our place, and at the moment is still sitting with Stëpa. Trifovna [Stepanida Trifonovna Ivanova, the Behrs family's housekeeper, then helping Tolstaya at Yasnaya Polyana] is crying a lot over having to part from Tanja and her children; I comfort her, telling her I'll come and see her in Moscow. My [hand]writing is terrible, but you'll [be able to] read it and understand; you simply can't imagine the noise here and how excited the children are before [Tanja's] departure. I am full of cares and good intentions for my life from now on, but yesterday there were moments of tearful sorrow [when I realised] that I'm all alone, and that it will be difficult to teach [the children] and to live without either you or Tanja. But today I feel healthy and energetic. Take care, precious; don't catch cold, don't get angry, don't worry about us. If it weren't for Lëlja's cough, we would all be healthy.

Stëpa and my Tanja are also going to see [my sister] Tanja off. What kind of spirits are you in, and how are you doing on the steamer? Does Nikolen'ka like the Volga? I think about you every moment and this makes me happy during this time [of separation]. The only thing bothering me is that mice are eating away at the roots of life, and that things won't always be the way they are [now]. For some reason today I keep thinking about [Zhukovsky's] tale of the Wise Man Kerim (1844). But that's what happens when I am sad. Farewell, you'll receive this letter on your return journey. Big hugs and kisses, regards to Nikolen'ka. Really, I've hardly ever written such incoherent letters.

Your Sonja.

N° 46 – LEV NIKOLAEVICH TOLSTOY ❧ SOFIA ANDREEVNA TOLSTAYA
[PSS 83/115]
5 September 1876. Kazan'.

I am writing to you, dear friend, from Kazan', on today, the 5th, at 11 o'clock at night, and not from the steamer, but from the city of Kazan' itself, where we have come to stay overnight, since we lost a whole twenty-four hours because of the chaos aboard a *Samolët* steamer[290] we had the misfortune to travel on — it got stuck in the shallows and broke down. You can't imagine how annoying this has been, when one is counting every minute, as I [am doing] now for you and even more for myself. The trip down the Volga was unpleasant enough up until now — the stuffiness and the [mainly] tradesmen passengers. Anyway, I did find several interesting and even extremely interesting people, including the merchant Deev,[291] who owns 100,000 desjatinas of land; I am sitting with him at the moment in a hotel room, while Nikolen'ka has gone with a man from [the Khanate of] Khiva to a Kazan' theatre. There was also a Tatar [who was] a priest. —

288 LNT had left for Orenburg with his nephew Nikolaj Valer'janovich Tolstoj (1850–1879), eldest son of Marija Nikolaevna, to buy some horses. They took the train from Moscow to Nizhnij Novgorod, then went by steamer down the Volga.
289 Aleksandr Nikolaevich Bibikov — see Letter N° 34, Note 205.
290 LNT was travelling down the Volga on a steamer of the *Samolët* shipping line.
291 One of the sons of the wealthy Orenburg merchant Mikhail Stepanovich Deev (1792–1856).

The weather here is magnificent, and my health is good. You are probably riding out to collect mushrooms. Please, don't ride Sharik.[292]

I'll be writing you from Samara about my plans for Orenburg. I should enjoy visiting Orenburg as that fellow Deev is from there and will help me buy some horses. I'd also like to see Kryzhanovskij[293] there. In any case I shall try not to go beyond my 14-day schedule. —

Kazan' awakens in me memories of unpleasant sorrow.[294] Oh, I only hope you and the children — especially you — are healthy and at peace. Hugs and kisses to you, my darling dove, and to the children and my greetings to both Sofesh,[295] if she is there, and Mr. Rey.[296] —

Yours, L.

It seems I very much feel like writing.[297]
On the envelope: Tula. Her Ladyship Countess Sofia Andreevna Tolstaya.

N° 47 – SOFIA ANDREEVNA TOLSTAYA ❧ LEV NIKOLAEVICH TOLSTOY
[LSA 45]
15 [January 1877]. Saturday evening [St. Petersburg.]

My dearest Lëvochka, here I am writing you from Mamà's and I still haven't quite figured out how I got here so quickly and ended up in Petersburg.[298] On [the train] to Moscow I sat with some elderly woman, the wife of a Saratov landowner, talking all the time with her and her daughter, and reading without getting tired. [At the Kursk Station] in Moscow I was met by Istomin,[299] and he and I, along with Stëpa [Stepan Andreevich Behrs], [stayed] in the railway carriage [as far as the Nikolaevsky Station, where I] transferred to the Nikolaevsky Express.[300] There [at the station] I was met [first] by Serëzha, and later by my Uncle Kostja,[301] — he's so splendid, it's practically a shame; he's off somewhere for the evening.

Serëzha reacted rather strangely to meeting Uncle, and kept staring at him intently, but it all worked out; we sat there for a whole hour, drinking tea over a cheerful chat. Then we spent quite a while looking for a place for me — the whole [train] was full — and finally found a compartment with two benches, where some lady was seated. At this point Uncle Kostja brought

---

292 *Sharik* — a horse which had been shipped to Yasnaya Polyana from the Kirghiz steppes.

293 Nikolaj Andreevich Kryzhanovskij (1818–1888) — an acquaintance of LNT's from the Sevastopol' campaign, who served as Governor-General of Orenburg from 1865 to 1881.

294 From 1841 to 1847 LNT lived in Kazan' with his guardian-aunt Pelageja Il'inichna Jushkova (see Letter N° 5, Note 14). He was a student at Kazan' University, and had a youthful romance with Zinaida Modestovna Molostvova (1828–1897).

295 Sof'ja Robertovna (Sofesh) Vojtkevich (1844–1880) — married (in 1877) to Dmitrij Alekseevich D'jakov.

296 Jules Rey (ca1850–?) — Swiss tutor to the Tolstoys' older sons; lived at Yasnaya Polyana June 1875 to January 1878.

297 At the time LNT was working on Part v of *Anna Karenina*, which was published in *Russkij vestnik*, N° 12 (1876).

298 Concerning her trip to Petersburg in January 1877, SAT wrote in a letter to her husband (not included here): "I went to consult about my health with Dr. S. P. Botkin. I was ill for a long time after giving birth to a stillborn girl Varvara, as a result of my sufferings from whooping-cough and peritonitis" (*Letters to L. N. Tolstoy [Pis'ma k L. N. Tolstomu]*, p. 139). She stayed with her mother, Ljubov' Aleksandrovna Behrs. Dr. Sergej Petrovich Botkin (1832–1889) was a professor of therapeutics at St. Petersburg's Medical-Surgical Academy.

299 Vladimir Konstantinovich Istomin (1848–1914) — a former regimental chum of SAT's brother; a writer and publisher with *Moskovskie vedomosti*.

300 *Nikolaevsky Express* — an overnight train between Moscow and St. Petersburg.

301 The reference is to LNT's brother Sergej Nikolaevich Tolstoj and SAT's uncle Konstantin Aleksandrovich Islavin (1827–1903) — at the time, secretary of the journal *Russkij vestnik*, which printed all but the last instalment of *Anna Karenina* (up to April 1877).

Katkov[302] over to see me. We talked, he was taking the same train to Petersburg for five days. The lady turned out to be very respectable; she was from Orlov, wealthy, a landowner's wife whose maiden name was Obukhova. I talked with her a lot about literature. She was enthusiastic — and quite intelligently so — about your works. In fact, she told me a great deal: she is very well-travelled — both abroad, and to Petersburg, and all over Russia. Later we both lay down on our respective benches and had quite a good sleep, despite the same perspiration, the same melancholy and coughing, though the coughing wasn't as bad [as before].

In the morning Katkov dropped by twice to ask me had I slept well and did I need anything. I thanked him and enquired in return, saying that it was hot [in the carriage] along with some other remark. Then Stëpa and I went to see Mamà. She was still in bed, expressing through tears her joy upon seeing me. She was distressed that [my sister] Tanja wasn't there, but she wasn't as upset as I had expected. Stëpa went to see Strakhov,[303] while Mamà and I chatted away; she is very advanced in years and is constantly in ill health. And she kept repeating: "I'm so happy to see you! So happy!" Strakhov was at Botkin's;[304] he was talking about me, and gave [the doctor] my visiting card, and Botkin wrote on my card:

"If the Countess drives out, I shall be at her service on Monday, Wednesday and Friday from 8 p.m. on. If the Countess wishes me to visit her at her home, please give me the address and then I shall arrange a day and time for an appointment."

Today I wrote Botkin a note saying I had arrived [in Petersburg], and thanking him for his agreeing to come and see me. I asked him to name a time when he was free. He replied that he could come tomorrow between 3 and 5. Mamà and Stëpa, as well as Petja [Tolstaya's brother], had all advised me to invite Botkin to the house, and not go to him myself. Mamà assures me that I might waste 4 or 5 hours at Botkin's, [which would be] indecent and unbearable. And Botkin, it seems, does not do a good job of treating patients who come to him, since he has little time to see 60 people. And Stëpa says that you'll be glad that I invited him over, even though it costs more.

Petja came for lunch with us, along with his wife and daughter.[305] She's really very sweet, his wife, and they are most touching with their dear little daughter and their poverty. Petja would very much like to find some means of getting out of his dismal situation, even if it means taking the first available job so as not to build up further debts. Vjacheslav[306] was dressed in a frock coat. He is extremely well-mannered, but is thin and pale. He is in a class equivalent to Grade 5 at a *gymnasium*.

Liza[307] appeared just before [going to] the opera in a magnificent silk outfit with diamonds on her head and everywhere — some sort of stars like Polina's,[308] and plump — horrors!

While Petja was giving his little daughter a drink of milk, he managed to spill some on her dress. She jumped up, shouting: "Stupid! Fool!" etc. [Her] arrogance is amazing. Yes, I agree with you: [it's better to keep] as far away from her as possible. Tomorrow I'm going to see

---

302 Mikhail Nikiforovich Katkov — see Letter Nº 12, Note 73.

303 Nikolaj Nikolaevich Strakhov (1828–1896) — librarian with the St. Petersburg Public Library, also a philosopher and critic, who became closely acquainted with the Tolstoys (he was often a summer guest at Yasnaya Polyana), and LNT's chief editorial consultant. See my editions *The Tolstoys' correspondence with N. N. Strakhov* (2000) and *Leo Tolstoy & Nikolaj Strakhov: Complete correspondence*, 2 vols. (2003).

304 Sergej Petrovich Botkin (1832–1889) — a famous physician and professor of therapeutics at Moscow's Medical-Surgical Academy, whom SAT consulted.

305 SAT's brother Pëtr Andreevich Behrs with his wife Oľga Dmitrievna Postnikova and daughter Evgenija Petrovna Behrs.

306 Vjacheslav Andreevich (Slava, Slavochka) Behrs, SAT's youngest brother.

307 Elizaveta Andreevna (Liza) Behrs, SAT's elder sister.

308 Praskov'ja Fëdorovna (Polina) Perfil'eva (*née* Tolstaja; 1831–1887) — LNT's second cousin, twice removed.

Alexandrine,[309] and somewhere else besides, if I can do it by three o'clock. I'll be seeing Alexandrine between two and three. In the evening I'll stay once again with Mamà and Petja and Stëpa. I'll drop around to see all my relatives for a minute. All-in-all, nothing yet is clear to me [at the moment]; today I didn't even step outside the house; I stayed the whole day with Mamà and I feel comfortable with her. I keep remembering you all, my dear ones, but I try not to think too much and not to get upset. I'm afraid that at night I shall feel this great longing for you all, and that I'll imagine all sorts of horrors. But in telling Mamà about my family, about you and the children, it's just like I'm coming home again and I like talking about you all. Thank my dear [sister] Tanja — she always cares about everything — for the pears. I ate them with delight along the way when my mouth was dry.

Your *Anna Karenina* (the December [instalment]) was praised to the skies in *Golos* and *Novoe vremja*.[310] I haven't read them yet; I'll bring them along, if I can. Mamà, Stëpa and Slavochka told me [about them]. Lëvochka, my precious dove, take care of yourself and the children. A hundred hugs and kisses to you, and Serëzha, and Tanja, and Iljusha, and Lëlja, and Masha.[311] I'll definitely arrive [home] Wednesday evening.

Yours, Sonja.

№ 48 – LEV NIKOLAEVICH TOLSTOY ❧ SOFIA ANDREEVNA TOLSTAYA
[PSS 83/122]
16 January 1877. Yasnaya Polyana.

As you can see, everything here is going along fine. — Yesterday I taught Lëlja and Tanja, and Tanja got me so angry that I yelled at her, for which I am quite ashamed of myself. I can't get any work done. Last night the children sat with me and did some colouring, and I played chess with Vladimir Ivanovich,[312] and later played the piano until one o'clock [in the morning]. Even then I couldn't get to sleep for a long time and awoke early. Now I'm off to the station. The children went skating, but right now we have a severe frost; overnight it was 19 degrees [below zero], but [today] in the sunshine it's plus 5. —

The most boring part of life for me is taking meals with teachers constantly sniping at each other.[313] Every minute I think of you and try to imagine what you are doing. And it always seems to me that even though I'm depressed (on account of my stomach), that everything will be all right.

Please don't hurry [home]. Besides, even though you said you wouldn't be buying anything, don't think about the money, and if you take it into your head to buy something, borrow the money from [your mother] Ljubov' Aleksandrovna and go shopping, have fun. — After all, we'll pay her back in three days.

309 Countess Aleksandra Andreevna (Alexandrine) Tolstaja — see Letter № 37, Note 231.
310 In the December 1876 issue of *Russkij vestnik* were published Chapters 20–29 (Part v) of *Anna Karenina*. The newspaper *Golos* (№ 13, 1877) ran the following review: "The latest issue of *Russkij vestnik* gives us only 50 pages of text of *Anna Karenina* — but what a literary treasure these page are […] In terms of psychological insight, Count L. Tolstoj has, at the present moment, not a single equal in any foreign literature, and the only writer in ours that could be compared with him is possibly Dostoevsky." The journal *Novoe vremja* (№ 303, 1 January 1877) said that "apart from the new chapters of *Anna Karenina*, one cannot point to anything worthy of being considered an exceptional work [of literature]".
311 The Tolstoys' five children to date: Sergej (Serëzha), Tat'jana (Tanja), Il'ja (Iljusha), Lev (Lëlja) and Marija (Masha).
312 Vladimir Ivanovich Rozhdestvenskij — a seminarian, tutor to the Tolstoys' older children.
313 Besides Rozhdestvenskij, three tutors were present at Yasnaya Polyana: M. Jules Rey, Mlle Gachet (a Swiss governess who joined the Tolstoy household in 1876) and Miss Annie Phillips (who had a brief romance with Mr. Rey).

Farewell, darling. I still haven't received any letters from you. I try not to think of you while you're away. Yesterday I went over to your desk and jumped back as though I had burnt my fingers, so as to avoid picturing you so vividly. Same thing at night-time — I don't look at your side [of the bed]. As long as you are in a strong, vigorous spirit for the duration of your stay, then everything will be fine.

Please give my greetings to everyone, especially Ljubov' Aleksandrovna.

On the envelope: Petersburg. Èrtelev Lane, House N° 7, Apt N° 1. Countess S. A. Tolstaya, c/o Her Ladyship Ljubov' Aleksandrovna Behrs.

N° 49 – LEV NIKOLAEVICH TOLSTOY ❧ SOFIA ANDREEVNA TOLSTAYA
[PSS 83/125]
28 or 29 May 1877. Moscow. [Preceded by SAT's N° 5U, 28 May 1877]

I am writing to you from Ris's,[314] from his magnificent apartment and under the influence of his reassuring geniality. — Kostin'ka[315] sent me [back] the original, and he himself came. Kostin'ka's acid nature is unimaginably disturbing. He's to blame for everything. I poured out all my anger to Ljubimov,[316] whom I met in the railway carriage as we were coming into Moscow. But I didn't get overly wrathful. I remembered 'the spirit of patience and love'.[317]

I am publishing [*Anna Karenina*] as a separate book with Ris, without censorship, adding from previous [editions] whatever is needed to make up 10 printer's sheets.[318]

Now it's 2 o'clock, and I shan't manage to leave today, but I'll go at 4 o'clock tomorrow.

Stay completely calm, and, most importantly, healthy.

If I was annoyed, that's all passed now.

Strakhov recommends publishing as a separate book.

Hugs and kisses, my darling.

Yours, L. Tolstoy.

I would desperately like to leave today.

---

314 Fëdor Fëdorovich Ris — print-shop owner (see Letter N° 35, Note 218).
315 Konstantin Aleksandrovich (Kostin'ka) Islavin — see Letter N° 47, Note 4.
316 Nikolaj Alekseevich Ljubimov — see Letter N° 15, Note 87. The editor of *Russkij vestnik*, Mikhail Katkov, did not want to publish Part VIII of *Anna Karenina* in the form envisaged by LNT because of the author's disapproval (as expressed in this part) of the movement of Russian volunteers aiding the Serbs. LNT refused to compromise by changing the text and decided not to publish the last part of *Anna Karenina* in *Russkij vestnik*.
317 An excerpt from the prayer of Saint Ephrem the Syrian: "Grant unto me, Thy servant, a spirit of chastity (integrity), humility, patience and love".
318 On the advice of Nikolaj Nikolaevich Strakhov, LNT printed Part VIII of *Anna Karenina* as a separate booklet, which in printing terms could only take place if the manuscript were at least 10 printer's sheets in length.

Nº 50 – LEV NIKOLAEVICH TOLSTOY ❧ SOFIA ANDREEVNA TOLSTAYA
[PSS 83/127]
26 July 1877. Optina Pustyn'.

26th, evening.

I am writing to you, dear friend, from the Optina[319] [Pustyn' Monastery] hotel after a four-hour vigil.

We had a safe arrival thanks to Obolenskij.[320] A magnificent four-seater carriage was waiting for us at the train. We were exhausted, but still arrived at 3 o'clock in the morning. This morning Dmitrij Obolenskij came and spent the whole morning with us, partially interfering. I barely managed to excuse myself, to avoid going to his place today, but tomorrow I shall go at 5 o'clock, spend the night there, and leave at dawn, to make it to Kaluga by 12 and to Tula by 5. I would ask you to send horses there for 5 o'clock on the 28th.

If I don't arrive [then], have them come [later] the same day, for 11 [p.m.].

I might oversleep and be late. I am healthy, and in very good spirits.

I'm terribly disappointed that Sasha[321] didn't come with us. Only God grant that you're healthy and not troubled by anything. Good-bye, darling. —

Nº 51 – LEV NIKOLAEVICH TOLSTOY ❧ SOFIA ANDREEVNA TOLSTAYA
[PSS 83/130]
9 February 1878. Moscow.

I was tormented the whole journey by the thought that I didn't say good-bye to you properly and didn't ask you to write to me.

My only [concern] is that you're in good health. — Take care, be healthy and don't worry. I arrived safely, talked with the old fellow Levashev[322] the whole way. I spent the evening in our 'nest'[323] with Kostin'ka [i.e. Konstantin Aleksandrovich Islavin] and [Vladimir Konstantinovich] Istomin talking business — i.e. about books.[324] He gave me a lot [of information]. Today I went to see two Decembrists,[325] had dinner at the [English] club and in the evening I was at Bibikov's,[326] where Sof'ja Nikitichna[327] told me and showed me a great deal.

Now I've been spending the rest of the evening at the [Dmitrij Alekseevich] D'jakovs' with Mashen'ka [Marija Nikolaevna Tolstaja], Lizan'ka [Elizaveta Valer'janovna Obolenskaja] and

---

319 The Optina Pustyn' Monastery, located in Kozel' Uezd, Kaluga Gubernia, has been visited by many Russian writers, including Nikolaj Gogol', Fëdor Dostoevsky, Vladimir Solovëv and Lev Tolstoy. Concerning LNT's trips to Optina Pustyn', see *My Life*, III.21, III.80, V.39, VII.18; also S. A. Tolstaya, *"Chetyre poseshchenija L. N. Tolstogo monastyrja Optina Pustyn'"* [Four visits by L. N. Tolstoy to the Optina Pustyn' Monastery] (1913).

320 Prince Dmitrij Aleksandrovich Obolenskij (1822–1881) — Actual Privy Councillor, Member of the State Council.

321 Aleksandr Mikhajlovich (Sasha) Kuzminskij, husband to SAT's younger sister Tat'jana Andreevna.

322 Aleksandr Ivanovich Levashev (1807–1893), a wealthy landowner in Krapivna Uezd, Tula Gubernia.

323 'nest' — referring to a room at the Hotel Viktoria, where L. N.'s sister Marija Nikolaevna often stayed with her children.

324 In connection with his historical investigation into the period of the Decembrist rebellion in 1825, LNT borrowed two books from Istomin: *Russkaja starina [Russian antiquity]* and *Russkij arkhiv [The Russian archive]*.

325 Pëtr Nikolaevich Svistunov (1803–1889) and Aleksandr Petrovich Beljaev (1803–1885).

326 Mikhail Illarionovich Bibikov (1818–1881), son of First Lieutenant Illarion Mikhajlovich Bibikov (1793–1860), who on the day of the Decembrists' uprising (14 December 1825) was in the company of the Emperor; he tried to persuade the rebellious troops of the Marine Guard to disperse, but was wounded by the soldiers.

327 Sof'ja Nikitichna Bibikova (*née* Muravëva; 1829–1892) — daughter to Decembrist Nikita Mikhajlovich Muravëv (1795–1843), born in exile in Siberia. She eventually married Mikhail Illarionovich Bibikov.

Kolokol'tsova,[328] and that's where I'm writing from. Tomorrow I'll go see the Decembrist Svistunov, have dinner at Istomin's, and spend the evening with Vladimir.[329]

Hugs and kisses to you and the children. The time is passing terribly quickly — nothing gets done and one gets horribly tired.

This morning I was at a funeral service for the old man Perfil'ev.[330]

Tolstoy.

On the envelope: Tula. Her Ladyship Countess Sofia Andreevna Tolstaya.

N° 52 – SOFIA ANDREEVNA TOLSTAYA ❧ LEV NIKOLAEVICH TOLSTOY
[LSA 47]
[5 March 1878. Yasnaya Polyana].

I am very grateful to you, dear Lëvochka, for sending me the note from Tula,[331] but to my concern over you was added another even stronger worry; you shouldn't have gone; of course, it's all finished now, and you are probably either in Petersburg or on your way there, but how did your journey end? Yesterday and today my little one[332] was extremely restless on account of the snowstorm, and as I paced the children's room in quiet, measured steps with the baby in my arms, I paid heart-stopping heed to the howling of the wind. This snowstorm has been blowing for three days now, and I imagine that the trains are delayed everywhere, and that you with your weak nerves and from the unfamiliarity [of the situation] are exhausted from your lengthy journey. And what made you feel you had to go? After all, you didn't make it to Solovëv's[333] lecture, and you probably had a difficult journey. I shall wait impatiently for a letter from you from Moscow on Tuesday. And now you won't be returning from Petersburg until Saturday at the earliest, otherwise you will have precious little time.

Everything here is always worse when you're away. The children are acting up; Serëzha and Tanja ran out into this fearful storm wearing nothing but light frocks; I punished both of them and shut Serëzha up in your study and Tanja in Auntie's room. Then they got into a fight; Il'ja and Lëlja threw paper darts at Serëzha; he got angry and struck them, and they struck back, — [then] they came to me in the nursery to complain. I naturally got very upset with them. After dinner Serëzha bashfully took my hand and said: "Don't be upset, Mamà!" I told him: "Children, after dinner let's all get along together — otherwise, what kind of Sunday is this?" Serëzha [then] went off to write his diary. Tanja, too, calmed down, but Il'ja, Lëlja and Masha

---

328 Marija Dmitrievna Kolokol'tsova (*née* D'jakova; 1850–1903) — daughter to LNT's friend, Dmitrij Alekseevich D'jakov.
329 Vladimir Aleksandrovich Islavin — SAT's uncle (see Letter N° 5, Note 31).
330 Stepan Vasil'evich Perfil'ev — see Letter N° 16, Note 94.
331 LNT was on his way to Petersburg through Moscow to draw up the deed to the Samarian plots of land which he had acquired from Baron Nikolaj Rodrigovich Bistrom (see Letter N° 42, Note 268), as well as to gather materials from the Decembrists era for a novel he had in mind. In a note sent to his wife from Tula on 3 or 4 March 1878 he informed her that the train to Moscow would be delayed several hours.
332 *my little one* — Andrej L'vovich (Andrjusha) Tolstoj (1877–1916), the Tolstoys' sixth surviving child, after Sergej (Serëzha), Tat'jana (Tanja), Il'ja (Iljusha), Lev (Lëva, Lëlja) and Marija (Masha) — plus three that did not survive: Pëtr (Petja; 1873–1873), Nikolaj (Kolja; 1874–1875), and (Varja; 1875-1875).
333 Vladimir Sergeevich Solovëv (1853–1900) — a prominent Russian philosopher, poet and translator, son of a famous historian, Sergej Mikhajlovich Solovëv (1820–1879). Tolstoy was hoping to attend his public lectures in Petersburg in early 1878.

were unrestrainable, they would hide under the bed, and would call out "Fool!", and Mr. Nief[334] even got depressed.

Before bedtime Il'ja and Lëlja came to see me in the nursery to apologise; they lay down on the sofa and kept repeating "What a boring day it's been!", to which I responded by giving them a lesson about conscience and pangs of conscience and said that unfortunately I would have to write Papà about their conduct. Lëlja said: "Also say that starting Monday we'll behave ourselves all week long."

I still have a fever condition; I've stopped following my Lenten fasting.[335] Yesterday the German woman[336] came by, saying that you sent her a fur coat, and Kurdjumov[337] didn't go on account of the snowstorm and a sore throat. Today Vasilij Ivanovich[338] took a trip to Tula. Yesterday he and I talked a lot about spiritualism and all the children gathered around in a circle to listen.

I am very interested in your acquaintanceship and conversation with Pushchina.[339] You will have a lot of interesting things to tell me. Farewell, dear friend, hugs and kisses to you and Mamà; I can't wait to hear your news.

Sonja.

Nº 53 – LEV NIKOLAEVICH TOLSTOY ❧ SOFIA ANDREEVNA TOLSTAYA
[PSS 83/134]
7–8 March 1878. Petersburg.

I am writing to you once more in the evening time, dear friend, from Mamà's. This morning I went to visit Aleksandra Andreevna,[340] and stayed with her until 3 [o'clock]. From her place I went to see Bistrom.[341] The terms [of his sale of land to me] are splendid. I pay 20,000 [roubles] now, the rest over two years at 6% [interest]. He's very kind and accomodating. From there I went to have dinner with Vladimir [Aleksandrovich Islavin]. I played cards there until 8 [o'clock]. Then I went to see Praskov'ja Vasil'evna;[342] I [stayed] there until nightfall, and [then] went home.

Yesterday I fell ill, but today I'm quite healthy. Tomorrow I'll find out from the notary how and when I can draw up a bill of sale, and I'll write [you about it].

I received your telegram [sent 7 March] last night and am not replying, since you will probably receive my letter faster than a telegram. I also received your letter.[343] [344] Pity that the children acted up so badly. If you don't receive a telegram, don't get upset, darling. —

334 Jules Nief (real name: Vicomte de Montels; ca1843–?) — French tutor to the older Tolstoy boys, replacing Jules Rey; he lived at Yasnaya Polyana from January 1878 to October 1879.
335 Lent in 1878 lasted from 27 February to 15 April according to the Russian Orthodox (Julian) calendar.
336 Amalija Fëdorovna Funk — German language tutor to the Tolstoy children, who came to Yasnaya Polyana from Tula.
337 Evgenij Kurdjumov — a *gymnasium* pupil from Tula, who came to tutor the Tolstoys' sons.
338 Vasilij Ivanovich Alekseev (1848–1919) — maths teacher for the Tolstoy children.
339 Evgenija Ivanovna Pushchina (1838–1900) — a lady LNT stopped to see in Tula. There he met with her sister-in-law (husband's brother's wife), Anastasija Kondrat'evna Pushchina (*née* Ryleeva; 1820–1890), daughter to a Decembrist named Kondratij Fëdorovich Ryleev (1795–1826).
340 Countess Aleksandra Andreevna (Alexandrine) Tolstaja — see Letter Nº 37, Note 231.
341 Baron Nikolaj Rodrigovich Bistrom — see Letter Nº 42, Note 268.
342 Countess Praskov'ja Vasil'evna Tolstaja (*née* Barykova; 1796–1879) — mother to Aleksandra Andreevna Tolstaja, wife to Andrej Andreevich Tolstoj (1771–1844), whose brother was LNT's grandfather Il'ja Andreevich Tolstoj (1757–1820).
343 Letter Nº 52 of 5 March 1878.
344 *Her Ladyship* — an approximate English equivalent of *Eë Sijatel'stvo*.

All the Tolstoys have a sincere love for you and praise you, and I'm delighted. I shan't stay even an extra hour beyond what is needed. It is boring and alarming here, though I feel very calm and settled.

Hugs and kisses to you and the children. Tell Andrjusha not to worry.

L.

On the envelope: Tula. Her Ladyship Countess Sofia Andreevna Tolstaya.

Nº 54 – LEV NIKOLAEVICH TOLSTOY ❧ SOFIA ANDREEVNA TOLSTAYA
[PSS 83/143]
14 June 1878. A steamer on the Volga.

14 June.

Dear Friend,

I'm writing from the steamship[345] in the evening so that I can send [this letter] off early tomorrow morning in Kazan'. The children are sleeping soundly beside me and the whole day our trip has been calm, safe and, as always, not boring. [I have seen] some new and interesting faces, especially a professor from Helsinki on his way to study the idol-worshipping religion of the Mari — the only representatives of the Finnish peoples who have not converted to Christianity. Then there is a young man named Ermolov[346] — he used to travel with us as a *lycée* student, but now as a soldier of the Chevalier Guard. Having heard my story,[347] he offered [to lend] me some money, and I borrowed 50 roubles from him. With the same post I am writing to Moscow, asking Nagornov[348] to send him and to the *Samolët* [steamship] office 50 and 60 roubles [respectively]. My chagrin and shame over losing the money has still not passed.

The children are very good, they converse with the ladies, as well as [other] boys their own age, and are not giving Mr. Nief and me too much trouble. Besides, Nief is assiduous as usual, kind-hearted and cheerful. We bought [walking-]sticks at Kuzmodem'jansk and have been buying berries through Sergej [Petrovich Arbuzov].

All the bustle and crowds of people are tedious and difficult to endure, and it's as though I am unable to breathe spiritually. I shall breathe freely when we get to our destination, and then the usual pattern of feelings and thoughts will ensue.

Are you bored without me? Please don't let yourself [be bored]. — I can just picture you — if, God forbid, you're not in good spirits, — saying: "How can I help it? [How could you] go away, abandon me, etc.?" Or, better still, I picture you smiling as you read this. Please, do smile. —

Today is Serëzha's exam. Please write and tell me what the headmaster[349] says. I hope Serëzha, even if he doesn't distinguish himself all that much, at least won't fall flat on his face. Hugs and kisses to Tanja — I'm asking her not to walk bow-legged, not to forget to brush her teeth, and not to get thrown by hooks and buttons. Here on the ship the little girls are all very

345 On 12 June 1878 LNT, accompanied by his sons Il'ja and Lev, their tutor Jules Nief and servant Sergej Petrovich Arbuzov (see Letter Nº 4, Note 4), set off from Yasnaya Polyana for his Samara farmstead.

346 Dmitrij Fëdorovich Ermolov — chamberlain from Simbirsk; graduated from *Tsarskoe Selo Lycée* in 1874.

347 While stopped at a way-station, LNT lost his wallet with all the money (around 300 roubles) he had taken for the trip.

348 Nikolaj Mikhajlovich Nagornov (1845–1896) — husband to LNT's niece Varvara Valer'janovna (Varja) Tolstaja. He was responsible for keeping track of LNT's accounts, including book sales. For LNT's letter to him dated 14 June 1878, see *PSS*, 62: 433.

349 Aleksandr Grigor'evich Novoselov (1834–1887) — headmaster of the Tula *gymnasium* where on 14 June 1878 the Tolstoys' eldest son Sergej L'vovich (Serëzha) sat his Latin examination.

good about this. Hugs and kisses to the dear *Geschwister* Auntie Tanja and Stëpa[350] and I am grateful to them for looking after you. I know.

Farewell, darling, hugs and kisses to you and Andrjusha. I have not forgotten — and am not forgetting — Masha.[351] Love and kisses to her.

Yours, L. T.

On the envelope: Tula. Her Ladyship Countess Sofia Andreevna Tolstaya.

N° 55 – SOFIA ANDREEVNA TOLSTAYA ❧ LEV NIKOLAEVICH TOLSTOY
[LSA 53]
18 June 1878. 12 o'clock a.m. [Yasnaya Polyana].

It seems this is already the fifth letter that I'm writing to you, my dear Lëvochka, and every day I receive letters from you, to my great delight. Today I received the one you wrote on the steamship and despatched at Kazan'.[352] Why are you still bothered about [the] money [you lost]? It's neither here nor there, it's time to forget about it, we'll just earn more money and shan't notice those 300 roubles.

I'm writing you this letter against a background of a loud argument between Stëpa and Tanja about the feeding and raising of children, and so I fear it will be an incoherent letter; still, I want to write in a little more detail.

Our *grande nouvelle* is that Nikolaj Nikolaevich Strakhov is with us. He arrived yesterday on the night train and was very surprised not to find you here. But, it seems, he is very happy that he came. Last night we talked about Samara, and somehow our conversation led to my giving him an invitation, and he will be coming to see us at the end of July at our farmstead,[353] and [then] we'll [all] come back together. Now he is on his way to see Fet.[354] I still haven't made up my mind whether I shall come [to see you] or not. These past three days my little one [Andrjusha] has not been well, but today, especially this evening, he has shown improvement; the weather has again been warm and delightful, and I am getting ready [to go] again. But, faithful to your rule — and mine, too — I keep repeating: "If God be willing!" I want to go see you as soon as I can, but then I look at Andrjusha's thin little neck and sunken eyes of these past three days and think: "No, I shan't go for anything!"

I'll decide everything after I receive your telegram. The other day my little boy experienced a bad bout of vomiting and I became alarmed to the point of desperation, thinking this was another attack of brain disease. Then yesterday he had diarrhœa and, now that the warm weather has returned, he's a lot better. I haven't written you about his disease so as not to scare you, [being] so far away, and still not knowing the specific nature of his illness. Now, apparently, it's because of his teeth, which are going to be coming out very soon; in the meantime God has shown mercy. Nikolaj Nikolaevich is delighting in Nature, he went swimming with

---

350 *Geschwister* — the German word for 'siblings'. The reference is to SAT's sister Tat'jana (Tanja) and brother Stepan (Stëpa), who were visiting Yasnaya Polyana at the time.

351 *Andrjusha, Masha* — the Tolstoys' sixth and fifth (surviving) children Andrej and Marija, respectively.

352 Letter N° 54 of 14 June 1878.

353 Strakhov kept his promise and visited LNT at his Samara farmstead.

354 Strakhov was on his way to see poet Afanasij Afanas'evich Fet (see Letter N° 7, Note 51) at his Vorob'ëvka estate in Kursk Gubernia.

Stëpa, Serëzha and Antosha,[355] laughed with [my sister] Tanja, played croquet — he and Tanja against me and Vasilij Ivanovich [Alekseev], and we won, much to Tanja's disappointment. The older children are behaving themselves well, pretending to be grown-ups. Serëzha sometimes even makes bold, but is quick to shy away if I shame him for that. The headmaster has told me nothing about his marks; rumour has it that he passed his exams, only with a '3 minus' in Latin. — Today they did some horseback riding: Stëpa, Serëzha and Antosha went to see Aleksandr Grigor'evich,[356] and gave him 66 roubles for lessons. Now I have 300 roubles and am waiting for a similar amount from Aleksej,[357] [also] from Nagornov, but I hesitate to take and carry with me the 3500 roubles from Solovëv.[358] How come you asked me: "Are you bored without me?" Do you actually have your doubts about that? But it's not so much that I'm bored (there's no time for boredom), as much as I worry terribly about you and the children [Il'ja and Lev], and, believe me, it takes every bit of my soul's powers to keep from sometimes falling into a state of gloom and alarm. You can't imagine what goes through my head! And we shan't be seeing each other again all that soon. [I'm concerned about] how you're settling in on the farmstead, whether you might have forgotten to buy supplies, having lost my note (a list of provisions for you) in your wallet?

Strakhov says to tell Iljusha that the things for collecting insects have been in Tula for some time, but he forgot to send the receipt and now they will be sending it. [The dogs] Dybochka and Korka are very happy, they were running and playing around the croquet pitch. I'm very glad that Lëlja was so easy to travel with; hugs and kisses to my precious boys, I think quite a lot about them. When I come to the farmstead, I hope they will have lots of interesting things to tell me. My regards to Mr. Nief. God grant we shall meet very soon, and that it will be possible for us to travel. Farewell, my dove; I am going to feed my boy who is calling out, and then to bed.

Sonja.

Tanja and Stëpa are very nice with me, and, of course, a great joy to me.

N° 56 – LEV NIKOLAEVICH TOLSTOY ✍ SOFIA ANDREEVNA TOLSTAYA
[PSS 83/145]
18 June 1878. Farmstead on the Mocha.

I am sending you two good letters from the boys.[359] They wrote them cheerfully and enthusiastically. They were acting up because they were tired, but now they're calm, cheerful and precious. I shall begin at the beginning — at the time I wrote my last letter, from the steamer, as we approached Samara. We disembarked before 8 [a.m.], hired drivers and went to buy groceries. We got everything done and made it to the train without hurrying. It leaves at ten minutes to ten.

We boarded a 3rd-class [carriage]. We had plenty of room on board and at 2 o'clock arrived safely at the Bogatovo station. Here we were met by [the Bashkir coachman] Lutaj with a coach. The coach really shows its age, but it is nevertheless solid and comfortable. We left at 3. We took turns sitting in the best seat, beside the coachman, and easily arrived at Zemljanki by 9 o'clock

---

355 Baron Anton Aleksandrovich (Antosha) Del'vig (1861–1919) — son of Tula landowners (friends of the Tolstoys); a future regional politician.
356 Aleksandr Grigor'evich Michurin (music teacher) — see Letter 33, Note 199.
357 Aleksej Stepanovich Orekhov (foreman) — see Letter 5, Note 38.
358 Ivan Grigor'evich Solovëv (1819–1881) — Moscow bookseller, commissioned by the Tolstoys in connection with the sale of *War and Peace*.
359 The boys Il'ja (Iljushka) and Lev (Lëlja) also wrote letters to their mother on the same sheet of paper.

— it was still light. If there had been a moon out, we might have got to the farmstead before midnight. But since we didn't know what condition [the estate] was in, and because it was dark out, we decided to spend the night at Truskov's — a hospitable fellow. We all slept next door in the barn, but Mr. Nief and Lëlja suffered from fleas, and in his sleep Lëlja kept scratching himself and kicking me. We arrived [at the estate] in the morning, and I went straight to see Mukhamedsha,[360] who had made his home here, too, a little distance away. They wanted to marry him off, and yesterday he asked my advice about that. Then I went to the house and, in planning out the rooms, I discovered that there will even be extra rooms [available]. Though, if you decide to come on the basis of the telegram I am sending you today, you won't get this letter, but I'm sending you the plan and description in any case.

Here is the plan of the house, and my idea for the apportionment of the rooms. I've given a lot of thought to it, and this seems to be the best [choice]. And this is how I'll set it up if I receive a telegram from you that you are coming. It's quite clean and pretty warm; the floor has just a few holes here and there — I'll have it taken care of — and there are even stoves. One is in the office part, one in [the main part of] the house. There are willow-bushes around the house itself and rather pitiful-looking gooseberry bushes, and there's water right in front of the house. Just one drawback: the farmstead also includes a pit full of dung with flies, which won't allow us to have dinner, or drink tea, or work [outside] except in the evenings.

I am drinking koumiss — I can't say with any special pleasure, rather from habit; and I don't have any particular desire to stay here over the summer. Mr. Nief is discouraged; evidently he doesn't like it [here]. It's good that there are lots of horses, and Bibikov[361] has made us a fine carriage: it easily seats 9 people; it is low and safe. And if you should come, then every day after dinner I imagine we shall [all] take an excursion, some of us on horseback and some in the carriage.

Bibikov is splendid at looking after things. He won't need money for the harvest. There are melon fields. The horses are very good. The wheat is very good, too. Much better than I had expected. I don't do anything, I almost don't do any *thinking* and I feel I'm in [some kind of] transitional state. I'm concerned about you, and think [about you] whenever I'm alone. Only God grant that everything may be safe during our time apart, and I love this feeling of special love, the very highest spiritual love toward you which I feel all the stronger when we're apart. Now here's the main question: should you come or not? Probably not, and this is the reason. I know that I am the principal [focus] in your life. I'd rather return [home] than stay here. I don't believe in the benefits of koumiss for me. And since there is a drought here and [rumours about] diarrhœa are heard, [I am concerned] about the harmful effects it might have on you and [our youngest son] Andrej. As for major comforts, it's hardly any better than before. — But don't forget one thing: whether you decide to come or stay, and whether something happens outside our control, I shall never blame either one of us, even in my thoughts. It shall be God's will in everything, except our foolish or good behaviour. Don't get angry — the way you sometimes get upset when I mention God.[362] I can't stop myself from saying this, as it is the very basis of my thought. Hugs and kisses, my precious.

Hugs and kisses to the children and all our family.

If you do come, I'll drive out and meet you at Zemljanki.

I forgot the most important thing: if you don't come, we'll be leaving on the 1st of July.

360 Mukhamet Romanych Rakhmetullin — a Bashkir who traditionally made koumiss for LNT.
361 Aleksej Alekseevich Bibikov (1837–1914) — manager of LNT's Samara farmstead.
362 SAT commented on this statement: "I got upset at his mention of God, since it completely shut out all earthly concerns" (PSS, 83: 263).

I-1. Sofia 1863

1-2. Lev Nikolaevich Tolstoy and his brother Nikolaj Nikolaevich Tolstoj, 1851.
Daguerreotype by Karl Peter Mazer

i-3. Lev Nikolaevich Tolstoy (far right) and his three brothers (left to right) Sergej, Nikolaj and Dmitrij. Daguerreotype, 1854

1-4. Letters from Sofia Andreevna Behrs and her siblings congratulating Lev Nikolaevich Tolstoy on his 34th birthday, 28 August 1862, signed (in order): El[izaveta] Behrs, Sonja, A[leksandr] Behrs, Mlle Tatiana Behrs [note written in French]. The note from Sofia Andreevna (Sonja) appears as Letter № 1 in the current volume.

I-5. Congratulatory letter to Lev Nikolaevich Tolstoy on his birthday (28 August 1862) from Sofia Behrs' father, Andrej Evstaf'evich Behrs, inviting Tolstoy to take dinner with him and his family and to stay overnight. Signed "your sincerely loving Behrs".

1-6. Sofia Andreevna Tolstaya, Tula, 1866.
Photo by Felitsian Ivanovich Khodasevich

1-7. Lev Nikolaevich Tolstoy as a warrant officer in the Imperial Russian army. Daguerreotype, 1854

1-8. Sofia Andreevna Tolstaya with her two eldest children: Sergej L'vovich [Serëzha] (b. 1863) (right) and Tat'jana L'vovna [Tanja] (b. 1865) (left).
Photo: Tula, 1866

1-9. Lev Nikolaevich Tolstoy's letter to his wife written on the day of his final departure from Yasnaya Polyana, 28 October 1910. (The two words at the top read "To Sofia Andreevna".) It appears as Letter № 234 in the present volume.

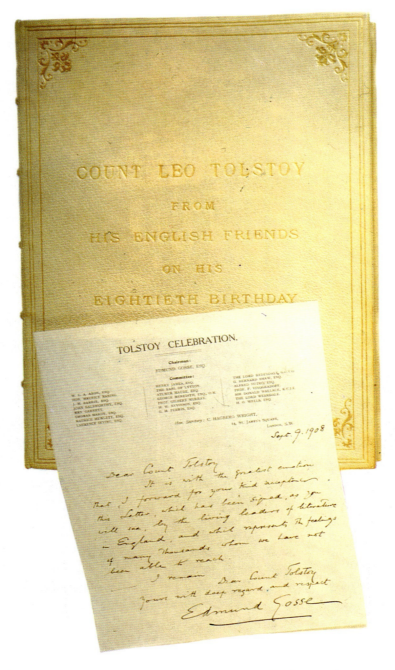

I-10. A booklet of congratulatory messages to Count Lev Nikolaevich Tolstoy on his 80th birthday, 28 August 1908 O. S. (9 September N. S.), with an accompanying letter signed by English author Edmund Gosse.

I-11. Lev Nikolaevich Tolstoy, 1878 or 1879.
Photo by Mikhail Mikhajlovich Panov

1-12. Sofia Andreevna Tolstaya with two of her grandchildren (Sonja and Lev), along with her daughter-in-law (Andrej L'vovich's wife) Ol'ga Konstantinovna Tolstaja (née Diterikhs).
Photo by Sofia Andreevna Tolstaya, October 1900

1-13. Lev Nikolaevich Tolstoy with writer Maksim Gorky, Yasnaya Polyana, 1900.
Photo by Sofia Andreevna Tolstaya

1-14. Lev Nikolaevich Tolstoy on horseback near Yasnaya Polyana, 1908.
Photo by Karl Karlovich Bulla

1-15. Ivan L'vovich Tolstoj (Vanja, Vanechka), the Tolstoys' youngest son (1888–1895).
Photo by Sherer, Nabgol'ts & Cᵒ, 1893 or 1894

1-16. Lev Nikolaevich Tolstoy telling a story to his grandchildren Iljusha (centre) and Sonja (right), children of Andrej L'vovich Tolstoj, September 1909.

Photo taken at Krekshino by Vladimir Grigor'evich Chertkov

1-17. Lev Nikolaevich Tolstoy in St. Petersburg, 1897.
Photo by Vladimir Ivanovich Krivosh-Nemanich

PART II

LETTERS 1880–1888

INTRODUCTION TO LETTERS, PART II

The 1880s were marked by two major events — one personal, the other national — and their consequences: for Tolstoy and the family, it was his 'spiritual crisis' and the resulting evolution of his idealistic world view; for the nation, it was the assassination of Emperor Alexander II in 1881 by revolutionary terrorists and the conservative backlash (with moderates and extremists on both sides) that began dominating the political and official social landscape immediately thereafter.

The moral principles Lev Nikolaevich adhered to — through which he was hoping to come to terms with the philosophical problems that he had not been able to resolve analytically — came under additional stress when the family had to abandon its long-lasting country lifestyle and move to Moscow, primarily to provide a better formal education for the eldest children (1881).

Lev Nikolaevich had significant difficulties in adapting to these new conditions. It required a noticeable change in his personal habits; it brought new (fresh and vivid) but mostly negative impressions of nineteenth-century urban life, which by and by translated themselves into his need to express them in socially charged articles. On the other hand, it failed to inspire a single significant belletristic work and so prevented him from either returning to his innate talent for fiction or finding his lost moral equilibrium — both of these losses much to the chagrin of Sofia Andreevna. In the meantime, Lev Nikolaevich continued to spend his winters apart from the family at Yasnaya Polyana, offering the couple yet another opportunity to renew their communication through letters.

In 1883 Tolstoy met Vladimir Chertkov, in whom he saw a kindred soul and who would become his close friend for the rest of his life. At the same time, he and Sofia Andreevna were drifting more and more apart. Tolstoy could not forgive his wife for being unable and largely unwilling to follow him in what he perceived as his most serious and important moral and intellectual pursuit. For her part, Tolstaya, now exhausted with frequent pregnancies and never-ending wifely and motherly household duties, began experiencing nervous breakdowns and had neither the energy nor, indeed, the inclination to share her husband's new ideas. She kept bemoaning his apparent unwillingness to fulfil a practical role as her attentive husband and the father of her children. Instead she found herself besieged by the complaints of a tormented genius and compelled to taking on additional duties of caring for his physical and spiritual well- being.

In 1883 Tolstoy, in accordance with his new principles, renounced the publication of his literary works for his personal profit and, along with a power-of-attorney, transferred to his wife the right to publish his works written before the end of 1881.

In 1884 Tolstoy, in collaboration with Chertkov, founded his own publishing house he named *Posrednik* [*The Intermediary*], to publish his new stories 'for the people'. In 1885, Tolstaya visited St. Petersburg, where she unsuccessfully petitioned the Empress Marija Fëdorovna for permission to publish her husband's banned works.

On the broader scale, Russian culture continued to flourish in a number of spheres. In music, the 1880s marked the flourishing of Peter Tchaikovsky and the rise of composers like Anton Arensky, Alexander Glazunov and Mikhail Ippolitov-Ivanov. Prominent painters coming to the fore in this period included Konstantin Korovin, Mikhail Nesterov and Valentin Serov. Among new novelists and poets on the literary scene were Vladimir Korolenko, Dmitry Merezhkovsky and Fyodor Sologub. Tolstoy, in the meantime, was transforming himself from one of the world's greatest novelists into a moralist writer of religious and philosophical treatises.

N° 57 – SOFIA ANDREEVNA TOLSTAYA ❧ LEV NIKOLAEVICH TOLSTOY
[LSA 55]
[28 August 1880. Yasnaya Polyana].

Dear Lëvochka, I am sending you Urusov's[1] letter, which you have been expecting; the letter is one I could have predicted, i.e. nothing new. Today everyone celebrated your birthday. Maybe it was because you weren't here or on account of your ill health, but our souls were very sad. Yesterday I started moving about — that was a mistake, it appears, as it had a bad effect on my health. Somehow you with your head condition must have slept poorly, too, with the wind, rain and cold all night long. Yesterday I decided I had better stay in Tula a little longer, but to go visiting, and I was at the Bestuzhevs,[2] as well as at the Kislinskijs.[3] I found them all in, and everybody was very nice; of course, wherever I went, I only stayed for a few minutes, then excused myself and left. At the Bestuzhevs, Vasilij Nikolaevich told me that a teacher of ancient languages had come to the Tula seminary the night before from the Philological Institute,[4] and that all this [year's] graduates decided to become teachers, that they would work for 150 silver roubles a month, and that it might be very easy to get one. If I had known ahead of time, I could have asked whether this teacher had a colleague and see if we could hire him by mail. At home I found everything safe and sound. Iljusha brought [home] two snipes, and today Serëzha, too, went hunting. And Lëlja went off to collect mushrooms with Sasha [i.e. Aleksandr Mikhajlovich Kuzminskij], who is extremely kind to him for some reason and constantly enquires: "Well, you're the paper — what's the news?" He invites him for coffee and hardly ever lets him out of his sight.

Today everyone's having dinner here with us, including Vasilij Ivanovich [Alekseev] and his family.

Yesterday as [our daughter] Tanja and I were driving home, we had a very good chat. I used to hurry to share all my good thoughts and conversations with you, but now this need has passed. However, one shouldn't neglect to share with the children what are undoubtedly good [ideas]. Some of it must sink in, otherwise there is confusion in their soul, as [I discovered] when I listened yesterday to Tanja.

Farewell, dear friend, tomorrow I'll send [to see if] there is a letter from you. Yesterday I kept thinking about you while I was riding, about what I would give to know what was in your heart, what you were thinking about, and I'm very sorry that you share so little of your thoughts with me; it would give me needed moral support and would be very good. You're probably thinking about me that I am persistent and stubborn, but I feel that a lot of the good you possess quietly slips into me, and this makes it easier for me to live in the world.

Now, it's really farewell.

Sonja.

---

1   Leonid Dmitrievich Urusov (1837–1885) — Deputy Governor of Tula Gubernia (1876–85) and family friend of the Tolstoys, with whom he became acquainted in early 1878. He took special pleasure in introducing SAT to the study of philosophy (see Editor's Introduction, "Philosophy and Leonid Dimitrievich Urusov"). The letter referred to has not been preserved.
2   Vasilij Nikolaevich Bestuzhev-Rjumin (1835–1910) — Lt-General; from 1876 to 1889 he headed the Tula Arms Factory.
3   The family of Andrej Nikolaevich Kislinskij (1831–1888) — Chairman of the Regional Government of Tula Gubernia.
4   The reference is to the St. Petersburg Historical-Philological Institute, founded in 1867, which prepared teachers of various subjects for *gymnasiums* and regular secondary schools.

Nº 58 – LEV NIKOLAEVICH TOLSTOY ✎ SOFIA ANDREEVNA TOLSTAYA
[PSS 83/165]
28 August 1880. Moscow.

Yesterday I rode over to Mejer's [employment agency] and put in a request for tutors and governesses. This morning two showed up: [The first was a] Mlle Velti — her French is very good and she [can teach] music; — [she charges] 600 roubles [a year], and is very well-mannered; she lived a year at [Dr. Grigorij Antonovich] Zakhar'in's; but I don't like [the attention she pays to] her appearance. It's not that I don't like her, but I wish she could be less self-absorbed. She [looks] about 25.

The second one is a Mlle Bossoney, the one that wrote to you: [she can teach] French and English — she is elderly, dry, and very proper. Her French is worse than the first woman's, but she is very dignified, even too much so. She would very much like to have the position. She was asking 800 [roubles], but will go with 600.

If I were to choose just between these two, I would still take [Mlle] Velti. They promised teachers at the agency, but none have appeared yet. Now it is almost two o'clock, and I'm going around to the universities and *gymnasiums.*

I have taken a room at Sokolov's, but the Perfil'evs have invited me to stay with them, and I shall move to their place. My health is good. Hugs and kisses to you and the children.

L.

On the envelope: Tula. Her Ladyship Countess Sofia Andreevna Tolstaya.

Nº 59 – LEV NIKOLOAEVICH TOLSTOY ✎ SOFIA ANDREEVNA TOLSTAYA
[PSS 83/168]
8 October 1880. Moscow.

Once more I'm writing in the morning, around people — [your brother] Petja, Golokhvastov,[5] Obolenskij[6] — but, alas, not around any governesses. Today there was one from the Governesses' Society, but she won't travel. She came by mistake, and I see there is absolutely no one who meets our needs — namely, *a Frenchwoman with music.* There simply isn't even a good Frenchwoman without music. There's just one, and without music — [she can teach] German, English and French — [her name is] Mlle Guillod.[7] She came to see me yesterday, and Varin'ka[8] was with me and we liked her. If today I don't find anybody else, I'll take her. I really like her, though she [can't teach] music. Then at least we can have Aleksandr Grigor'evich[9] for a second time each week. It's the same story at all the agencies, [i.e.] Frenchwomen with music are very rare and currently non-existent. Yesterday I was with Varin'ka [Varvara Valer'janovna] at Botkin's.[10] I looked at the pictures, [then] took dinner at [Varin'ka's] place. In the evening

---

5 Pavel Dmitrievich Golokhvastov (1838–1892) — writer, historian, folk musicologist.
6 Leonid Dmitrievich Obolenskij — see Letter Nº 41, Note 264.
7 *Mlle Guillod* — served as tutor in the Tolstoy household from October 1880 to October 1881.
8 Varvara Valer'janovna (Varin'ka) Tolstaja (LNT's niece) — see Letter Nº 6, Note 43.
9 Aleksandr Grigor'evich Michurin — see Letter Nº 33, Note 199.
10 Dmitrij Petrovich Botkin (1829–1889) — owner of a gallery in Moscow and Chairman of the Moscow Society of Art Lovers; elder brother to Dr. Sergej Petrovich Botkin (see Letter Nº 47, Note 7).

I was with Repin,[11] Perfil'ev[12] and Istomin.[13] There I found Petja with his wife.[14] I didn't get a good sleep, and my nerves are frayed. Farewell, darling, hugs and kisses to the children, I'll be home tomorrow.

L. T.

On the envelope: Tula. Her Ladyship Countess Sofia Andreevna Tolstaya.

N° 60 – LEV NIKOLAEVICH TOLSTOY ❧ SOFIA ANDREEVNA TOLSTAYA
[PSS 83/170]
11 June 1881. Krapivna.

Between 1 and 2 o'clock in the afternoon. Krapivna.[15] The walk was worse than I had expected. My calluses chafe, but I slept, and I feel my health is better than I had anticipated. Here I bought hemp workboots, and it will be easier to walk in them. — [This experience has been] pleasant, useful and very instructive. Only God grant our whole family will see each other in good health, and that nothing bad will happen with either you or me, so that I shan't have any reason to regret that I went. — You can't imagine how new, important and useful to the soul it is (for one's outlook on life) to see how God's world lives — the world which is big and real, and not the one we have constructed for ourselves and which we never leave, even though we have travelled around the globe.

Dmitrij Fëdorovich[16] is walking with me to Optina. He is a quiet and obliging chap. — We spent the night at Selivanovo at the home of a rich *muzhik,* a former elder and tenant farmer. I shall be writing from Odoev and again from Belev. I am taking very good care of myself and today I bought some dried figs for my stomach.

Farewell, darling. Hugs and kisses to you and everyone.

If you could have seen the baby girl about Misha's[17] age at the place we stopped last night, you would have fallen in love with her — she doesn't say anything but understands everything, and smiles at everything, and nobody's looking after her.

The most important new impression here is to see myself (in my own eyes and in the eyes of others) as just what I am, and not what I am in the context of my surroundings. — Today a *muzhik* in a wagon caught up to me [and called out]: "Grandpa! Where is God taking you?" — "To Optina." — "Well, are you going to be living there?" And a conversation ensued.

Only [I hope] that you aren't letting yourself get distracted by either the older or younger children, that there aren't any unpleasant visitors, that you yourself are healthy, that nothing

---

11   Il'ja Efimovich Repin (1844–1930) — celebrated Russian artist, who became acquainted with LNT in 1880 and painted a number of portraits of him; he also illustrated some of his works (such as *The death of Ivan Ilyich* [*Smert' Ivana Il'icha*], *The power of darkness* [*Vlast' t'my*]).

12   Vasilij Stepanovich Perfil'ev — see Letter N° 16, Note 94.

13   Vladimir Konstantinovich Istomin — see Letter N° 47, Note 299.

14   SAT's brother Pëtr Andreevich (Petja) Behrs with his wife Ol'ga Dmitrievna Behrs (née Postnikova).

15   LNT was walking through the regional centre Krapivna on his way to the Optina Pustyn' Monastery in Kaluga Gubernia.

16   Dmitrij Fëdorovich Vinogradov, a teacher at LNT's school at Yasnaya Polyana, who would later transcribe for LNT.

17   Mikhail L'vovich (Misha) Tolstoj (1879–1944) — the Tolstoys' seventh (surviving) child after Sergej (Serëzha), Tat'jana (Tanja), Il'ja (Iljusha), Lev (Lëlja), Marija (Masha) and Andrej (Andrjusha).

[bad] is happening, that… I shall do my best in everything, and you, too, and then everything will be splendid.

On the envelope: Yasenki, Yasnaya Polyana. Her Ladyship Countess Sofia Andreevna Tolstaya.

Nº 61 – SOFIA ANDREEVNA TOLSTAYA ❧ LEV NIKOLAEVICH TOLSTOY
[LSA 56]
[12 June 1881. Yasnaya Polyana]

My dear Lëvochka, I don't know where to begin this letter. There have been various things happening these past two days, and it seems to me it's been such a long time ago that you left. In the first place my [baby] Misha has taken ill like never before in his life. He has extreme fever, keeps groaning, won't eat, won't play. Today he was much better, but for two nights now I have not slept because of him.

Yesterday Khomjakova[18] came for dinner, together with Urusov.[19] Khomjakova was very nice and I am continuing to find her very friendly, but Urusov was first set upon by your brother Serëzha,[20] who got off the express train the same day at Kozlovka [Station], and then by [my sister] Tanja for inconsistencies in his Christianity. They played croquet (without me), chatted and left around ten [p.m.]. Serëzha talked about the reception for the Tsar,[21] though nothing of significance. The Empress[22] began the conversation by saying "What a terrible time!" Then the Tsar enquired as to who was serving where; he thanked and ordered thanks be accorded to the "comrades", as he put it. Serëzha was to give the first speech, and carried it off very well, as he told me.

He is very pleased and interested that this was mentioned in all the papers. Today after dinner he is leaving in a carriage for Pirogovo and asked me to let [our daughter] Tanja accompany him, to which I agreed. There's nobody there except for his household; I cannot leave my house, or else I would have gone [with them]. Serëzha himself will bring her back.

Il'ja isn't doing anything; today he went by train to Tula; but to refuse him — that would only repeat the scene that happened in your presence, as the watch is ready and needs to be picked up. He'll come back by train, too. [Our son] Serëzha went to Borolomka, where they let [some water from the pond] flow through the mill dam — for some fishing. The other day he came back from Tula and brought with him — who do you think? — Bogojavlenskij.[23]

[Our son] Serëzha and I had words between us; I expressed my displeasure with him and said that you disapproved even of his going to see him [i.e. Bogojavlenskij] himself. Serëzha was submissive and said that he would be more careful in future. Bogojavlenskij was repulsive; he ranted on about the uselessness of good manners and quarrelled with Auntie Tanja.[24] I don't do too much quarrelling these days, mostly keep silent. Tanja's children are healthy. Right now I have asked that my [little] Misha be taken out for a walk. We are [all] going bathing, the berries are ripening; it's very hot, and boring without you. I think it would be torture for you to go out into this heat carrying a bag, and I'm very much afraid for your head condition. I hope that you

---

18 Anna Sergeevna Khomjakova (1856–?) — daughter to Tula governor Sergej Petrovich Ushakov (1828–1894).
19 Leonid Dmitrievich Urusov — see Letter Nº 57, Note 1.
20 Sergej Nikolaevich Tolstoj — see Letter Nº 4, Note 12.
21 The reference is to the Tula nobility in Moscow attending a reception for the recently installed Emperor Alexander III.
22 Empress Marija Fëdorovna — see Letter Nº 30, Note 178.
23 Nikolaj Efimovich Bogojavlenskij (1867–?) — a *gymnasium* pupil from Tula, who tutored the Tolstoy boys.
24 Tat'jana Andreevna Kuzminskaja, SAT's younger sister, 'Auntie' to SAT's children.

are sitting out this heatwave in the shade or sleeping, and that you won't drink [too much when you are] sweating, or go bathing, which would be terribly harmful — you might suffer a stroke.

While you were away I received two letters addressed to you: one from Samarin,[25] full of repentance and even emotion; the other from Stasov,[26] regarding your manuscript. It's complicated — you can read it yourself. Pity you're not home at this time. Professor Solovëv[27] was going to come and see us; Samarin (a minor consideration) wanted to come after the *Zemstvo* [district council] meeting, then [the writer] Turgenev and Bestuzhev[28] on Sunday, who said that he would bring his brother. These would all have been interesting for me, but what to do? Maybe (or even probably) you're glad [that you weren't here].

I hope you are healthy, not too exhausted, and that you'll arrive home earlier than you promised — ten days.

Bogojavlenskij brought a lithograph of Solovëv's lecture;[29] it was most interesting to read; I've left it for you.

Farewell, dear friend. It's seems I've written everything [I wanted to], but I don't know whether I should write to you again or not, and whereto?

Hugs and kisses and, again and again, I ask you to watch and take good care of yourself.

Sonja.

N° 62 – SOFIA ANDREEVNA TOLSTAYA ⚬ LEV NIKOLAEVICH TOLSTOY
[LSA 58]
[3 July 1881. Evening. Moscow]

I wanted to wire you, dear Lëvochka, to ask your advice, otherwise I shall simply go mad with dithering. Today in [the neighbourhood of] Prechistenka, in Denezhnyj Lane, I came across a house belonging to Princess Volkonskaja,[30] which strikes me as being very comfortable and splendid both in its location and in its arrangement [of rooms]. But Dmitrij Alekseevich [D'jakov] says one thing, [my sister] Tanja another, [Leonid Dmitrievich] Obolenskij something else, besides my own doubts — and I don't know what to do. This house is selling for 36 thousand [roubles], and is to let for 1,550 silver roubles [a year] unfurnished. It is impossible to find less expensive apartments, and everyone is [already] surprised [at this offer]. There are a lot of houses for sale, but I'm still hesitant about [making a decision like] this. All of them without exception don't seem to fit the bill. Tomorrow morning [my brother] Petja and a contractor will inspect Volkonskaja's house along with the previous house, Kalachëv's. Apart from these I shall take a look at two other houses in the area of Novinskij [Boulevard], along with one furnished apartment for 1800 silver roubles [a year]. I want to get everything finished tomorrow and leave the city tomorrow night; I am tired and afraid for my pregnancy,[31] but in any case my chances of finding something either bad or good would be the same now as a month from now.

25 Pëtr Fëdorovich Samarin (1830–1901) — a landowner from Epifan Uezd.

26 Vladimir Vasil'evich Stasov (1824–1906) — art historian, a librarian at the St. Petersburg Public Library, whom LNT got to know in 1878 while he was collecting materials for his novel set in the time of Peter the Great.

27 Vladimir Sergeevich Solovëv — see Letter N° 52, Note 333.

28 Vasilij Nikolaevich Bestuzhev-Rjumin — see Letter N° 57, Note 2. The brother mentioned is Konstantin Nikolaevich Bestuzhev-Rjumin (1829–1897), a professor of history at St. Petersburg University.

29 Vladimir Solovëv's final public lecture, given 28 March 1881, which ended by calling upon Tsar Alexander III to refrain from executing his father's assassins.

30 Sof'ja Vasil'evna Volkonskaja (*née* Urusova; 1809–1884). The Tolstoys lived here over the winter of 1881–82.

31 On 31 October 1881 SAT gave birth to a son Aleksej (Alësha), who would die aged only 5 in January 1886.

Today we all had dinner together at the Slavjanskij Bazaar,[32] and then all spent the evening at Petja's. I didn't go to the Perfil'evs' — I was busy in the morning, and too tired in the evening. We shouldn't have brought Lëlja along, one of his baby teeth [is coming out]; but I am just as glad not to be alone; we travel together and shall go home together, and we sleep in the same room.

I am writing just in case I stay any longer than tomorrow. If I get everything done, I shall leave tomorrow night and arrive before this letter [can reach you].

Tanja[33] and her little girls are healthy, but because of their teeth they need to stay another four days, which is upsetting to Tanja, but there's nothing that can be done — their teeth have turned out very badly.

I hope that you are all healthy, that [our daughter] Tanja is looking after the household and not neglecting the young boys — after all, she, too, is *Mummy* Tanja. What are you, the older boys and Masha doing? No letter from you — [I realise] there couldn't be any.

I'm still thinking of how to make a little better accommodations for all of you, but it's hard to please everyone — some will still be disappointed; but large houses and apartments are not within our means.

Farewell, dear friend. Hugs and kisses to all of you.

Sonja.

Nº 63 – LEV NIKOLAEVICH TOLSTOY ❧ SOFIA ANDREEVNA TOLSTAYA
[PSS 83/174]
4 July 1881. Yasnaya Polyana.

Saturday noon.

Everything is going very well with us here: no unpleasant incidents, no quarrels, no tricks — the main thing is, everyone's in good health. The little ones [Andrej and Mikhail] are precious and touching in that, as I say to [our daughter] Tanja, they are conveying to her and me what they [usually] give to you, at least in part — Andrjusha just now came up to me (it's morning now and the children are having their breakfast) to tell me how he will eat his eggs; I asked him: What should I write to Mamà? He thought for a moment, then looked at me intently and broke out into a smile: This [i.e. my smile] is what I would like to 'write' to you. Iljusha sometimes goes to Yasenki, sometimes to Tula, but he puts in his hours of study. [Our son] Serëzha and Ivan Mikhajlovich[34] are looking through books in the annexe. Mlle Guillod keeps going for rides with *Mania*.[35] Tanja is conscientiously and cheerfully occupied in household tasks. Today she ran off to see Kostjushka.[36] And Iljusha is going to Tula to buy bandages for Kostjusha's wife. The Kuzminskijs[37] are coming to dinner; our conversation is pleasant enough, but he seems to fear being a burden on me and is quick to leave, and last night he didn't come at all. I'm lazy. —

You must have finished with your business dealings by now. I calculated that a selection could be [easily] made if you looked at 20 houses, and 20 houses could be looked at in 3 days.

---

32 *Slavjanskij Bazaar* — a popular restaurant and hotel in Nikol'skaja Street in Moscow, built in 1873. It was frequented by a number of prominent musicians and writers.

33 SAT's sister Tat'jana Andreevna Kuzminskaja with her daughters Marija and Vera.

34 Ivan Mikhajlovich Ivakin (1855–1910) — a student in the History/Philological Faculty of Moscow University who was tutoring at Yasnaya Polyana. He would later serve as a librarian in the Rumjantsev Museum (see Letter Nº 20, Note 137).

35 *Mania* — a French-derived variant of the Tolstoys' daughter's name *Marija (Masha)*.

36 Konstantin Nikolajevich (Kostjushka) Zjabrev — a poor Yasnaya Polyana peasant.

37 *The Kuzminskijs* — in this case referring to Tat'jana's husband Aleksandr Mikhajlovich and their sons Mikhail and Aleksandr. Tat'jana Kuzminskaja and their daughters were in Moscow at this time.

— Please do count on me. I'll come and take a look and finish up what you haven't got done. Hugs and kisses to [your sister] Tanja and the children, and to you.

On the envelope: Moscow. Arbat, Karinskij's house. Obolenskij's apartment. Her Ladyship Countess Sofia Andreevna Tolstaya.

Nº 64 – LEV NIKOLAEVICH TOLSTOY ✍ SOFIA ANDREEVNA TOLSTAYA
[PSS 83/179]
19 July 1881. Farmstead on the Mocha.

Tomorrow it will be a week, dear friend, since I left,[38] and already five days since I last wrote to you, and I am feeling terribly weighed down by our separation, even though I am getting along very well here. When I receive your letters and know that you have received mine, then I am able to calm down. This year has been marvellous here in every respect. — The weather is hot, clear, and we haven't had any dryness to date; the steppes are green, fresh, and the feather-grass is green everywhere, flourishing for the second time. The harvests are good, though not everywhere, but ours are very good. The house is clean and spacious, no flies at all — just like at Yasnaya. There are lots of horses to ride, and splendid koumiss. Vasilij Ivanovich,[39] and especially Lizaveta Aleksandrovna[40] take care of us so well, it's [almost] shameful! Aleksej Alekseevich[41] [Bibikov, manager of the Tolstoys' Samara estate] lives half a verst downriver on the Mocha [a tributary of the Volga], in an earthen cottage. I went to see him yesterday. His cottage is papered with wallpaper: it's clean and cheerful. His wife is a taciturn, timid woman. [Their] koumiss is superb. Mukhamedsha is even chubbier than he was before. Behind the curtain [I can hear] his wife and a squealing baby [also named] Mukhamedsha. Through laughter and embarrassment, he says: "I obliged the young'un."

Horses, stallions, more than 10 head, are very good, beyond what I expected. I ought to bring them [home] in the autumn for sale and for myself. The horses have prospered remarkably, despite the lean years when they went hungry, and so much was lost. — There are horses, I believe, selling for no less than 300 [roubles].

[Our son] Serëzha was fine during our first days here, but on account of his stubbornness and negligence he went bathing more than once during the hottest time of the day, and now, just since yesterday, he has come down with the Samaran disease [i.e. dysentery] which you hate so much. Kostja[42] had it too, as well as Bibikov, and everybody else after bathing. I am drinking koumiss with great delight, and feel my thoughts slowing down, and am becoming more drowsy, quiet and dim-witted. —

Prospects for income of more than 10,000 [roubles] seem likely, but I have been mistaken so many times that I'm afraid to believe it. Today Vasilij Ivanovich and I spent the whole day at Patrovka, at a Molokan [prayer] meeting, had dinner and [attended a session of] the district court, and [then] went back to the Molokan meeting. At Patrovka we found Prugavin[43]

---

38 On 13 July 1881 LNT left for his Samara farmstead, accompanied by his son Sergej (Serëzha).
39 In 1881 maths tutor Vasilij Ivanovich Alekseev (see Letter Nº 52, Note 338) leased some land from LNT and settled in Samara Gubernia.
40 Elizaveta Aleksandrovna Malikova (1861–?) — common-law wife to Vasilij Ivanovich Alekseev.
41 Aleksej Alekseevich Bibikov (farmstead manager) — see Letter Nº 56, Note 361.
42 Konstantin Ignatovich (Kostja) — grandson to SAT's midwife Marija Ivanovna Abramovich.
43 Aleksandr Stepanovich Prugavin (1850–1920) — political commentator.

(he writes about the schism [in the Russian Orthodox Church]) — a very interesting, moderate fellow. It was a very interesting day all told. At the meeting there was a discussion about the Gospels. There are interesting people there, remarkable in their boldness. —

The work here is coming along — harvesting rye with a threshing machine right in front of the house. Everything's proceeding quickly, fine. Bibikov's workers and all his management tasks are being settled very nicely. Our first night here I wakened Serëzha by yelling "Sonja!" at the top of my lungs. It was a nightmare — something was choking [me]. Since then I have been sleeping well at night — I in the last room, Emily[44] in the same room as before, while Serëzha is in our bedroom. Serëzha takes breakfast at 12 [noon] and supper after 9 [p.m.], along with Vasilij Ivanovich's family. The only time I eat is at supper. — How are you personally? How are the children doing? All of you? Many times a day I reminisce [about all of you] and look out into the darkness, and don't see anything. Hugs and kisses to everyone, [including] the boys,[45] such dears, and the Kuzminskijs.[46] It [must be] very hard and boring for you. God grant that [when] I come, I will devote myself to taking care of your business in Moscow; just tell me what to do. The next letter you send should be addressed not to Samara, but to Bogatoe. It'll have [a better] chance [if sent] there. I still want to start working, and I have tried, but without success. There's just one thing I want — to take care of my hæmhorroids, otherwise they adversely affect my mental state. Watch that you do a good job of loving me.

On the envelope: To Tula. Her Ladyship Countess Sofia Andreevna Tolstaya.

Nº 65 – SOFIA ANDREEVNA TOLSTAYA ❧ LEV NIKOLAEVICH TOLSTOY
[LSA 59]
27 July 1881. 12 a.m. [Yasnaya Polyana]

Dear Lëvochka, you aren't [exactly] spoiling me with letters. I thought you would be kinder in that respect. It's been two weeks now since you and Serëzha left, and I've only received a single letter from our farmstead.[47] It wouldn't bankrupt you if you sent a courier with a letter more often; and there was still mail pick-up during that time twice a week from Zemljanki.

Everything's going along here little by little: we live from day to day; the weather is terrible: you go out [even just] for a half-hour, and again there's wind and rain, so we still stay home, working, or studying, or reading. The other day Lëlja, Masha, [along with my nieces] Masha and Vera wrote compositions under my guidance, and everybody wrote quite well. Yesterday Il'ja (who left the day before yesterday on the night train to Zhitovo) spent the whole day hunting, and came through the bog, to everyone's surprise, at Pirogovo — cold, hungry, dirty and tired. He was clothed and fed, and Serëzha[48] himself came with him [on the train] to Kozlovka.

I spent the whole day worrying and regretting my decision to let him go; last night they both arrived and we sat down for supper and talked until half-past two in the morning. Serëzha came to ask me for the sum of 1500 silver roubles for the harvest. I have 1000 roubles, but I

---

44 Emily Tabor — an English tutor to the Tolstoys' children.
45 *the boys* — Il'ja, Lev, Andrej and Mikhail.
46 *the Kuzminskijs* — Aleksandr Mikhajlovich and his sons, who were spending the summer at Yasnaya Polyana.
47 Letter Nº 64 of 19 July 1881.
48 Sergej Nikolaevich (Serëzha) Tolstoj, joint-owner with his sister Marija Nikolaevna of the Pirogovo estate (see Letter Nº 4, Note 1).

couldn't give them [to him], since on the night of 2 August I am travelling to Moscow, and even though it is not a large sum, I shall be able to begin the renovation of the [Volkonskaja] house [in Denezhnyj Lane], and choose a few things without paying [right away], but the main thing is to choose the wallpaper and have it installed. They are waiting for me on this. Serëzha was so persistent with his pleading that I gave [him] a little, i.e. 133 silver roubles. He gave me a promissory note for the 600 silver roubles which he owes me, and when he handed me the paper, his hand was trembling like an old man's, and I felt so sorry for him. Il'ja killed only one snipe, and was so tired that he's been just lazing around all day.

Today all of them — [my sister] "Auntie Tanja", [our daughter] Tanja, all the Kuzminskij children, Iljusha, Lëlja, Masha and Uncle Serëzha headed off to Tula on the suburban train. Everybody had some business [there] — while for me, the mail was the major concern, but there was no letter. They took care of everything just fine, while I stayed [here] with the little boys and walked around a bit, and sewed little shirts for our present boys as well as the one to come.[49] Tomorrow morning I'm going with [our daughter] Tanja for a full day to the Mengdens.[50] I really don't feel like it, as everything has become difficult for me, and my health has not been good these days; I have some kind of hæmorrhoidal condition unlike anything I have ever seen.

Some Cossack is staying with us, an eccentric, who has come from the Starogladovskoe village — Feodor, Epishka's[51] nephew, of the same age as you. He rode here on horseback from the Caucasus on a chestnut-coloured horse, wearing a red capote and a fur cap, with medals and orders, a grey-haired, dry and frightening chatterbox; a clown, a show-off — not a nice fellow at all. He says he is on his way to the Tsar to ask to serve as a convoy guard, "where one of our people has been slain", as he puts it. "I want to serve a 3rd tsar, I've served two [already]." He went to see Aleksej Stepanovich [Orekhov], and the two of them had a lively conversation about various reminiscences and mutual acquaintances from the Caucasus. Yesterday we all went riding — the two Tanjas on [their] horses, and the Cossack in the red capote as their gallant escort, on his horse. It was a strange *coup d'œil*. [His] horse was meek and hand-reared, like a dog, and he gave all the children a ride on her by turns.

Today Tanja was asking Andrjusha: "What shall I bring you from Tula?" And he said: "Bring Papà back." He really surprised everyone. Farewell, dear Lëvochka, I'm sad that there's no news [from you].

Nº 66 – LEV NIKOLAEVICH TOLSTOY ❧ SOFIA ANDREEVNA TOLSTAYA
[PSS 83/182]
31 July 1881. Farmstead on the Mocha.

31 July.

On the 28th I received three letters[52] from you, dear, dear friend. And I was carried away by that Yasnaya Polyana spirit which we don't appreciate when we live in it. — One thing makes

---

49 *the one to come* — see Letter Nº 62, Note 31.

50 Baron Vladimir Mikhjlovich Mengden (see Letter Nº 37, Note 226) and his wife Elizaveta Ivanovna Mengden (née Bibikova; 1822–1902) — a writer who had briefly attracted LNT's attentions in 1857; she maintained her friendship with the Tolstoys throughout the rest of her life.

51 Epishka — an elderly retired Cossack, whom LNT used as a prototype for Uncle Eroshka in his story *The Cossacks* [*Kazaki*].

52 These letters have not been preserved.

me sad, namely how difficult [life] is for you — very difficult. As I see it, you are tormented by three things: Lëlja's exam,[53] Iljusha's naughtiness and cold floors. Of these, I consider cold floors the most serious. This letter will probably not reach you [at Yasnaya Polyana], and you'll be going through hell in Moscow[54] — to fix all this: have the floors redone, cover them with lime, spread a felt cloth over them — or even find another place to live — that's how I see it. Of course, it's late now, and you've taken upon yourself all these torments, but living here far away from you, I've come to have a different view of our life in Moscow. It sounds funny to say this — I've begun to accept it. In particular, I understood how difficult it is for you to work alone. When I return, I shall work along with you, and not merely to relieve the burden on you, but [it's something I'll do] with pleasure. I feel very sorry for you, and I'm weighed down without you. This is the third week already. And probably we'll come shortly after this letter. The second matter in importance is Iljusha's naughtiness. It's not a serious calamity; but, again, your efforts to watch over him and guide him [are very much needed]. The third problem is poor Lëlja; I would suggest we forget about his entering school this year. This year there is so much to think of, and he can study up at home and get into Grade 4. He's the kind of boy that learns quickly and forgets quickly.

I was really pleased with Strakhov's letter.[55] Our letters crossed in the mail. I wrote him before I left. — What you tell me about Sasha [Aleksandr Mikhajlovich] Kuzminskij made me very, very happy. There's no room for vainglory here. Only joy and concern over there being no falsehood or mistake in my interpretation. Of course you can let Dmitrij Fëdorovich[56] copy [my treatise *The Gospel in brief,* a.k.a. *A short exposition of the Gospel*]. I didn't let the Molokans copy it here for fear that it might be distorted by semi-literate people. But copying is the truest and most legitimate form of distribution. They say that *Woe from wit*[57] went through tens of thousands of copyings. If it is needed, it will find a way.

Now about us. [Our son] Serëzha is quite healthy and has become cheerful, he shoots ducks and rides horseback and goes for walks. The melons aren't ripe yet. — This is how we live: we rise at 7, take tea all together, i.e. me, Serëzha, Vasilij Ivanovich,[58] Kostja [Ignatovich], Mitja, Liza[59] and Aleksej Alekseevich [Bibikov], for the most part. Elizaveta Aleksandrovna keeps busy with dinner, the laundry, and [making] butter, as well as with Masha, and rarely joins us at the table. I go walking for three versts, drinking koumiss, and I try writing (true, it doesn't work out), then I go, either walking or riding, to [check on] the herd at that farmstead, [or] the crops, [or] to Ivan Dmitrievich's[60] farmstead, or somewhere else. It's not very pleasant walking or riding in the village. And I am [often] late for dinner — at 12 o'clock, and often don't eat anything until evening. In the evening I go for another horseback ride either alone or with Serëzha or

<hr />

53 The Tolstoys' son Lev was sitting his entrance examination for admission to Polivanov's *gymnasium* in Moscow.
54 SAT left for Moscow on 2 August to fix up the Volkonskaja house they had rented for the winter.
55 Strakhov announced his intended summer visit to Yasnaya Polyana in his letter of 22 July 1881 — see: Leo Tolstoy & Nikolaj Strakhov: Complete correspondence (2003), Vol. II, p. 616. For LNT's letter to Strakhov, see ibid., p. 615.
56 Dmitrij Fëdorovich Vinogradov (teacher) — see Letter Nº 60, Note 16.
57 *Woe from wit [Gore ot uma]* — a comedic play by Aleksandr Sergeevich Griboedov (1795–1829).
58 Vasilij Ivanovich Alekseev (maths tutor) — see Letter Nº 52, Note 338. His daughter Marija Vasil'evna (Masha) Alekseeva is mentioned in the following sentence.
59 Dmitrij Aleksandrovich (Mitja) Malikov and Elizaveta Aleksandrovna (Liza) Malikova [Jr] — son and daughter (respectively) to Elizaveta Aleksandrovna Malikova [Sr] (see Letter Nº 64, Note 40).
60 Ivan Dmitrievich Kudrin — a Molokan peasant.

Kostja, and again we take supper all together around 9. Sometimes we have tea in the middle of the day or after supper. Everybody likes it except me. Serëzha doesn't drink koumiss at all. I drink koumiss with pleasure, and a lot of it (as many as 12 cups), but today I haven't had a drop all morning. It makes me very excited and irritated. But as to what concerns you — the benefits for my health — I can say that the koumiss is and has been very beneficial, it invigorates me physically. The question is: is this necessary or not. Our *repas* are not at all varied — they are filling, but not stylish. Mutton (fried or boiled), cutlets, even with peas, splendid carp, cottage cheese, kasha, cottage cheese fritters.

I did sleep well at first, but now the nights are worse, probably on account of too much koumiss. Since Monday they've had as many as 300 reapers at work. [There have been] concerns over flour, bread and kasha [for all the workers]. Each [worker] is asking 12 roubles. Tomorrow is the Festival of the Saviour[61] and today they've stopped working. They have [already] harvested 2/3, and my hopes for a [good] income are not disappointing. I'm also happy about the horses. At first I wanted to bring 15 stallions to Tula to sell. But I've had second thoughts. I was offered 120 roubles each for the two weakest stallions. So I can sell them here for 200 or 150 roubles each. I've also earmarked 16 of the poor and superfluous mares for sale and I can sell them for 50 or [maybe] 40 roubles. — Only I would like to bring four or so stallions [home] with me for myself or for show. Yesterday I was admiring a pair of suckling colts, dun-coloured — like two peas in pod. So, if we're still alive, you will have a pair your favourite colour. — I don't know about you, but the further I am away from you, the more I think about you and miss you. Yesterday an old hermit was here. He lives in the woods along the Buzuluk road. He himself is hardly interesting or pleasant. But he is interesting in that he was one of six *muzhiks* who 40 years ago settled in Buzuluk, on the hillside, and established that huge monastery[62] which we saw. I jotted down his story. You haven't sent me Urusov's[63] letters, and I've been somewhat disappointed not to have them. Please give him my best wishes. I haven't received the book of Marcus Aurelius[64] either, despite my writing a request to the postmaster that he send it to me without delay. And I haven't received any notice. Perhaps it went through the district post office?

I am sending you a telegram along with this letter.

Hugs and kisses to big Tanja and little Tanja. Did she have a good time at the Mengdens? If only she could see how Liza [Malikova] helps her mother [here], smooths and churns the butter and crawls over the rooftops after baby chicks.

I'm not saying anything about Il'ja, as I am certain he was ashamed and hurt, and that he is working and looks upon hunting as a holiday and a treat, and not as a routine activity. Let Lëlja keep on working. And, may Ivan Mikhajlovich [Ivakin] forgive me, he knows his arithmetic. He needs to be probed from all sides. And he is [too] dull-witted to guess the meaning of a question and answer it when it is presented to him in a different form. — Hugs and kisses to your Masha and [Masha] Kuzminskaja, as well as Verochka [Kuzminskaja], and Andrjusha for refreshing himself, and chubby little Misha, and to Misha Kuzminskij. How many there are! How could they not be a challenge to care for?

---

61 *Festival of the Saviour [Medovyj Spas]* — an annual festival celebrated with honey-gathering, beginning 1 August.
62 The reference is to the Buzuluk Spas-Preobrazhensk Monastery, founded in 1853.
63 Leonid Dmitrievich Urusov — see Letter N° 57, Note 1.
64 Marcus Aurelius Antoninus Augustus (121–180 C. E.) — Roman emperor (161–80). The book referred to is his *Meditations*, translated by Leonid Dmitrievich Urusov and published in Tula in 1882.

A smallpox specialist came here and gave Masha [Alekseeva] a smallpox injection. As soon as [her brother] Kolja saw him cut Masha['s skin] with a scalpel, he flung a hook and line at the doctor and angrily cried out in all seriousness that he would put him in the stable.

Farewell, my dove. It won't be long now.

On the envelope: Tula. Countess Sofia Andreevna Tolstaya.

N° 67 – SOFIA ANDREEVNA TOLSTAYA ❧ LEV NIKOLAEVICH TOLSTOY
[LSA 61]
26 August [1881. Moscow]

Dear Lëvochka, I didn't manage to write this morning and am writing at 6 o'clock in the evening. I arrived quite safely, as I slept the whole way to Moscow and the conductor woke me up as we were approaching [the city]. Sleeping on the opposite bench in my compartment was a stranger who boarded the train in Tula — a very respectable lady, who was with me the whole way to Moscow. Ivan [Tolstaya's coachman] and I went to [my brother] Petja's [Pëtr Andreevich Behrs] and found everybody well, but they didn't come to the play, as Jenny[65] was ill; Natusja[66] was also in bed today with fever and nausea.

After I washed up and took some tea, I went to my [new] place. It's very nice there, everything at the ready, only the blue bedroom wallpaper was much too bright. Either I made a mistake, or they sent me the wrong [colour] — I don't know.

The little garden has not been well kept up, but I can live with it; it is 40 sazhens [about 85 metres] long. There's no paint odour; it's clean and bright. Yesterday I took a drive with Ol'ga[67] for a little shopping, and spent the evening with Polin'ka,[68] who offered some suggestions, but very few. The Istomins[69] were there, along with Petja and his wife. By evening I was exhausted and left after 11 o'clock. My health was excellent all day long. Both the Perfil'evs are very kind and dear.

This morning I headed out with Petja; earlier I had congratulated him and [his daughter] Natasha [a.k.a. Natusja] on [her] birthday and name-day;[70] I gave him a small rug, and toys to Natusja, and then drove him all over Moscow. This morning I had pain in both my stomach and my lower back. The morning workers gave me no rest, but now, despite driving about all day long, I feel quite myself again. Today we bought a whole lot of furniture — for practically the entire house, except for the drawing room. But I found a store where I shall almost certainly buy drawing-room [furniture]; the store owner is a very reliable elderly gentleman. A few things I returned, and there were a few things that were cheaper [elsewhere], but I can't say that I was unhappy with my purchases.

Tomorrow I'll look into dishes, lamps, and so forth. But there's still terribly much to be done: the upholsterers still haven't started on their work, there's a lot still to buy, and nothing has been settled. I can't come earlier than Sunday evening, that's clear to me. On Sunday morning I have

---

65 Jenny Tarsey (governess) — see Letter N° 29, Note 177.
66 Natal'ja Petrovna (Natusja) Behrs — daughter to SAT's brother Pëtr Andreevich (Petja) Behrs.
67 Ol'ga Dmitrievna Behrs (*née* Postnikova) — wife to SAT's brother Petja.
68 Praskov'ja Fëdorovna (Polin'ka) Perfil'eva — see Letter N° 47, Note 308.
69 Vladimir Konstantinovich Istomin (see Letter N° 47, Note 299) and his wife Natal'ja Aleksandrovna Istomina (*née* Remi; 1851–1927).
70 *name-day* — 26 August is celebrated as St-Natal'ja's Day.

to go with Petja to Sukhareva Square, where there is a market only on Sundays, and there's still a lot of little things to buy, which can't be bought without me — things we're in great need of. Write to me and send me another wire on Saturday.

If I can't stand the boredom and loneliness and worry over you, I shall return, as I said, at 4 o'clock in the morning on Saturday; in any case, send horses to Kozlovka. Once I finish this letter, I'll go over to Denezhnyj Lane to receive the furniture and pay for everything on the spot. I have one comfort: that I am buying everything for my family, so they may all be fine and happy.

Hugs and kisses to you all. How's Sasha[71] doing? How are you, [our daughter] Masha and everyone? I am enduring my labours splendidly. Farewell, my dears.

Sonja.

№ 68 – LEV NIKOLAEVICH TOLSTOY ❧ SOFIA ANDREEVNA TOLSTAYA
[PSS 83/186]
26 August 1881. Yasnaya Polyana.

Right now it's Wednesday evening. I am writing to you in the drawing room, and all around me in the room our children and the Kuzminskijs' [Marija, Vera and Mikhail] are singing couplets. Everyone's healthy and cheerful. All Sasha [Kuzminskij] had was a cough. I let Masha leave her room today. There's nothing wrong with her. The little ones are altogether well and precious, especially Misha. Just as soon as you're not around, he clings to me, [crying]: "Papà!". He climbs into my arms and then makes me run around with him.

This morning Mlle Guillod took everyone to Sudakovo to buy honey. They wanted to take Andrjusha, too, and though I felt sorry to disappoint Nanny, I didn't permit it, fearing that the morning air would be too fresh [for him]; besides, it was quite a distance.

This morning I heard a rumour through some woman that Vasilij Ivanovich,[72] the priest, died. I went to the church, but the rumour was not confirmed. Mar'ja Dmitrievna [his wife] was with him yesterday. He is at his son-in-law's in Obidimo on the Kaluga road, and she hasn't heard any news. If the rumour is not confirmed, I'll go see him tomorrow. I asked [your sister] Tanja to look after the house while I'm gone. Iljusha returned yesterday. He killed six birds. People are complaining that there is no wild game. Today Serëzha rode over to Malakhovo and he, too, killed only one duck. Today Iljusha headed out with the Bibikovs[73] to hunt wolves, but they didn't find any.

All yesterday morning I was writing Petja's story,[74] and still can't finish it. —

I felt very sad the night of your departure, but now I'm getting over it. —

Please don't imagine that it is absolutely necessary for you to finish everything. Do what you can get done by Saturday without haste — the rest I'll finish off [when I come]. Today's the coronation;[75] didn't that interfere with your activities? These past couple of days I haven't been quite myself — my liver hurts, but I am not downhearted, as I know that it will soon pass. — I feel very sorry for the priest and his family, and I would like to see him before his death.

---

71 SAT's brother-in-law Aleksandr Mikhajlovich (Sasha) Kuzminskij.

72 Vasilij Ivanovich Karnitskij (1831–1881) — priest at the Kochaki church close to Yasnaya Polyana; religious teacher for all the Tolstoys' children up to his death.

73 Vladimir Aleksandrovich Bibikov (1874–1938) — son of the Teljatinki estate owner Aleksandr Nikolaevich Bibikov (see Letter № 34, Note 205) — along with Aleksandr Nikolaevich's second wife, Ol'ga Adol'fovna Firekel'.

74 The reference here is to LNT's story *What men live by* [*Chem ljudi zhivy*], intended for the magazine *Detskij otdykh*, put out between 1881 and 1907 by Pëtr Aleksandrovich Behrs.

75 26 August 1881 was the 25th anniversary of the coronation of Emperor Alexander II in 1856.

Tomorrow I'll go [there] around noon and if there is no train coming back early, I'll take the horses. — Tomorrow I'll send a wire. Hugs and kisses to you, darling. 'Til Saturday — morning. —

On the envelope: Moscow. Kamennyj Bridge, Sofia Embankment. *[Fragment torn off.]* [...] Academy. Supervisor's apartment. *[Torn off.]* Sofia Andreevna Tolstaya.

Nº 69 – LEV NIKOLAEVICH TOLSTOY ❧ SOFIA ANDREEVNA TOLSTAYA
[PSS 83/188]
3 February 1882. Yasnaya Polyana.

I am writing to you, my darling, from Yasnaya [Polyana], from Aleksej Stepanovich [Orekhov]'s room, where I feel very comfortable. I have arrived in Tula. [Leonid Dmitrievich] Urusov met me, gave me food and drink, — we had a chat, he did most of the talking, — and I went to bed. I was going to take the morning train at 8:30, but didn't realise it would go only as far as Uzlovaja. So I got up at 7 and went. At 11 o'clock I reached Uzlovaja, tired and sluggish; I looked — it was snowing on the fields, [I would have] to wait five hours at the station, but a train heading back to Tula was leaving right away. I wired Raevskij[76] and set out for Yasnaya [Polyana]. I spent the night in Aleksej Stepanovich [Orekhov]'s [room]. He's very nice, but because of his snoring I made him move into the servants' quarters, and that's not good. I slept on the stove[77] with Pëtr Shentjakov.[78] Mar'ja Afanas'evna[79] and Agaf'ja Mikhajlovna[80] drank tea and chatted [with me] yesterday, and today I went riding, had my fill of coffee and began to write, but couldn't get much done — my head was suffering from migraines, and I feel weak. I am not overexerting myself and am reading old *Revues*[81] and thinking — enjoying the silence; avoiding solicitors. — I really feel like writing something I had in mind.[82]

In the house [at Yasnaya Polyana] they are stoking [the stove] in Auntie's [old] room.[83] I shall move [there] only if it is quite warm and the air is fresh. I shall stay here as God dictates to my heart and as you command. Communication is fast these days. [Send] telegrams to Kozlovka and letters to Tula.

How are your lungs and your health in general, and how are the children — both the older and the younger ones? If it would give you some respite, and if Iljusha would really like it, send him here for a few days. I just want to make things right for you. Please tell me the whole truth. Don't worry about alarming *me*. — If you would feel better if I were with you, if you need to talk with me — just wire me, and in twelve hours I can be in Moscow. —

Farewell, darling, hugs to you and the children.

---

76 Ivan Ivanovich Raevskij (1835–1891) — a landowner in Tula and Rjazan' Gubernias; a friend of LNT's.

77 Russian masonry stoves (or ovens) are large structures designed to maintain heat for a long period of time. Especially in rural dwellings, they have a flat top which provides the warmest place to sleep on cold winter nights.

78 Pëtr Pavlovich Shentjakov (1858–?) — a Yasnaya Polyana peasant, son to harness-maker Pavel Fëdorovich Shentjakov (1826–1899).

79 Marija Afanas'evna Arbuzova (nanny) — see Letter Nº 41, Note 265.

80 Agaf'ja Mikhajlovna (maid) — see Letter Nº 21, Note 141.

81 *Revues* — issues of the French journal *Revue des deux mondes*.

82 The reference here is to LNT's article *What then must be done?* [*Tak chto zhe nam delat'?*].

83 The room where LNT's aunt, Tat'jana Aleksandrovna Ergol'skaja (see Letter Nº 5, Note 33) used to sleep when she lived at Yasnaya Polyana (she passed on in 1874).

[Our daughter] Tanja worries me the most, when I think about [the children]. Tanja, don't be alarmed; be like Varen'ka[84] or like almond oil. —

After all, all stupidities and distractions, whether real or not, will pass without leaving the slightest trace, but making someone miserable — that will not pass.

Sjutaev's[85] portrait, of course, has been [temporarily] abandoned, but it could be finished in time for *Maslenitsa*.[86]

On the envelope: Moscow Prechistenka, Denezhnyj Lane, Volkonskaja house. Countess Sofia Andreevna Tolstaya.

N° 70 – SOFIA ANDREEVNA TOLSTAYA ❧ LEV NIKOLAEVICH TOLSTOY
[LSA 63]
[4 February 1882. Thursday. Moscow.]

Today, dear Lëvochka, I received your letter,[87] which was calm and humble, though apparently happy, judging by your frame of mind. No, I am not summoning you to Moscow, stay [at Yasnaya Polyana] as long as you like. Let me be the one to burn out, why both of us? You are more needed than I am by all and sundry. If I fall ill again, I'll send a wire, in that case there's nothing to be done. Enjoy the silence, write and don't get alarmed; really, it's all the same whether you are here or absent, only with fewer visitors. Even in Moscow I don't see you all that often — our lives have taken different directions. What kind of life do we have anyway? — it's some kind of chaos, labour, bustle, lack of thought, time and health and everything *that people live by*.[88]

Today the boys, Il'ja and Lëlja, were at the opera, along with Kolja Obolenskij,[89] Ivan Mikhajlovich[90] and Serëzha. Lëlja shed a few tears, they said, when in *Faust* one man killed another in a duel. In the evening they were at the circus with the Këllers,[91] the Ljarskijs,[92] the Obolenskijs[93] and the Olsuf'evs.[94] They took up five loges. Tomorrow morning I shall take the girls and Andrjusha to the circus, and in the evening to a party at the Obolenskijs. On Saturday [we're going] to the Ljarskijs' party. The Olsuf'evs have cancelled their party, as their Grisha is ill and Anna[95] has swollen cheeks.

It's very boring going to the Ljarskijs, in fact, it's boring everywhere. Today I kept working on Masha's dress for tomorrow. I'm very tired, and Fet[96] chattered away the whole evening, while

---

84 LNT's niece Varvara Valer'janova (Varen'ka) Nagornova (née Tolstaja) — see Letter N° 6, Note 43.

85 Vasilij Kirillovich Sjutaev (1819–1892) — a peasant sectarian in Tver' Gubernia, whom LNT got to know in 1881, and whose ideas made a considerable impression on LNT.

86 The Tolstoys' daughter Tanja was painting a portrait of Sjutaev at the same time as the professional artist Il'ja Efimovich Repin (see Letter N° 59, Note 11). *Maslenitsa* (Shrovetide) is an annual Russian winter festival just prior to the Orthodox Lent.

87 Letter N° 69 of 3 February 1882.

88 LNT's story *What men live by* [*Chem ljudi zhivy*], published in the magazine Detskij otdykh (1881, N° 12, pp. 407–34).

89 Nikolaj Leonidovich (Kolja) Obolenskij (1872–1934) — grandson to LNT's sister Marija Nikolaevna Tolstaja.

90 Ivan Mikhajlovich Ivakin (tutor) — see Letter N° 63, Note 34.

91 *the Këllers* — the family of Major-General Count Viktor Fëdorovich Këller (1834–1906), married to Countess Sof'ja Vasil'evna Bobrinskaja (1837–1891).

92 *the Ljarskijs* — the family of Mikhail Alekseevich Vonljarljarskij (1830–?), a justice of the peace in Moscow.

93 *the Obolenskijs* — the family of LNT's niece Elizaveta Valer'janovna Obolenskaja (see Letter N° 6, Note 43).

94 *the Olsuf'evs* — the family of the Tolstoys' Moscow neighbour Vasilij Aleksandrovich Olsuf'ev (1831–1883).

95 Grigorij Vasil'evich (Grisha) Olsuf'ev, their son, and Anna Vasil'evna Olsuf'eva (married name: Levitskaja), their daughter.

96 Afanasij Afanas'evich Fet (poet) — see Letter N° 7, Note 51.

I kept on sewing and sewing. This morning I went out shopping for the parties; the roads and weather are terrible; the ride was very bumpy and I even began to feel sick. Uncle Kostja is still with us, and today he helped together with Fet, and it wasn't so lonely. Farewell, dear Lëvoch-ka, stay healthy. Where are you? That is: [where is] the person you used to be in your feelings towards me? You haven't been that kind of person for a long time.

Farewell. It's already two in the morning, and I still have a lot to do.

Sonja.

N° 71 – LEV NIKOLAEVICH TOLSTAY ✎ SOFIA ANDREEVNA TOLSTAYA
[PSS 83/189]
4 February 1882. Yasnaya Polyana.

3 p.m., Thursday

I just received your letter,[97] dear friend, and am so happy that you have been keeping well to date. Don't worry about me. I'm doing quite well in Aleksej's[98] room, and I probably shan't move into the [main] house. I dropped in there today — [the house] can hardly be made warm enough without feeling the fumes. I'm afraid of that myself. I didn't feel well, rather weak, in fact — my spine hurts a little, as well as my head. And on account of that I didn't go see the Raevs-kijs[99] — I simply didn't have the energy. Yesterday my head was still hurting. Today, despite a terrible snowstorm in warmish weather, my head actually feels better, and I just feel lazy. I'm having a bad time working. Still, my nerves are relaxing and I'm getting stronger. I told Aleksej I couldn't see any *muzhiks,* and nobody showed up except some beggars, whom I didn't see.

Yesterday I slept all by myself, and very well. Last night Agaf'ja Mikhajlovna's muttering was quite soporific.

I think there's no place I could feel better or calmer. You with your [focus] on the household and all your cares for the family, are unable to sense the difference I feel between the city and the country. In any event there is no need to speak or write about it in a letter; I'm writing about this now, and you'll read it more clearly if I manage to get it written down.[100]

The chief trouble with the city for me and for all thinking people (which I am not going to write about) is that one is constantly called upon to argue and refute false opinions, or agree with them without questioning, which is even worse. But arguing and refuting trifles and lies is the most pointless activity, and it has no end, since the number of possible lies has no limit. And you get involved in it and start to imagine that it is a *useful activity,* while it is actually the most *useless activity.* — If you don't argue, you end up clarifying something for yourself in a way that excludes the possibility of argument. And this is all done in silence and solitude. — I know that interaction with like-minded thinkers is necessary, and my three months in Moscow were very necessary — for one thing, they gave me a great deal, not to mention Orlov,[101] Nikolaj

---

97 The letter referred to was written on 2 February 1882 (not included in the present volume).
98 Aleksej Stepanovich Orekhov — see Letter N° 5, Note 37.
99 Ivan Ivanovich Raevskij and his family — see Letter N° 69, Note 76.
100 The reference here is to LNT's treatise *What then must be done?* [*Tak chto zhe nam delat'?*].
101 Vladimir Fëdorovich Orlov (1843–1898) — son of a priest of Vladimir Gubernia, a teacher who got involved in a revolutionary movement; he became acquainted with LNT in 1881.

Fëdorovich,[102] [Vasilij Kirillovich] Sjutaev, — and getting to know people better, society, too, which I used to judge coldly from afar, gave me a whole lot. And I am [gradually] sorting out all this material. — The census[103] and Sjutaev clarified quite a lot of things for me.

So don't worry about me. Anything may happen and in any place, but I am here in the best and safest conditions. God grant everything is well with you. Hugs and kisses to the children. Everything has settled down, but I'm afraid that *Maslenitsa* will take its toll, and [the children] will be bothering you [more and more]. [Our daughter] Tanja has probably thought up some sort of pleasurable activity for herself, and probably more than one. And if not, that can only be better both for her and for us. Why does she hold out her hand to young men with some kind of beastly expression and without even turning to face them? —

Tanja, you must understand that I am writing this because I see you as though you were right before mine eyes, and it is only people that I love very much that I see this way.

Farewell, darling, there's nothing [more] to write. Talking — [well,] I could stay talking until Andrjusha and Misha come running up and interrupting, but there's nothing to write. Nanny is boiling me some chicken soup in a pot, she brings it [to me] herself and [then] stands stock still, the way people do at mass. Yesterday it was *kasha* and corned beef. In Tula I bought myself some white wine and buns. Today they brought some fresh ones. The eggs are fresh, [too]. I sleep on a wooden sofa with a mattress, there are no bedbugs. Today Mitrofan[104] sold [the horse] Balabënok for 65 roubles. For Gnedoj [they are offering] 110 roubles. If the weather is nice and I get a little work done, I'll take a trip to Tula. [Leonid Dmitrievich] Urusov isn't even aware that I'm at Yasnaya. If there are any interesting letters, let me know.

Farewell, precious, write every day, and I shall, too.

T.

On the envelope: Moscow. Prechistenka. Denezhnyj Lane. Countess Sofia Andreevna Tolstaya.

N° 72 – SOFIA ANDREEVNA TOLSTAYA ❧ LEV NIKOLAEVICH TOLSTOY
[LSA 64]
6 [February 1882]. Friday night. [Moscow]

We just got back from the Obolenskijs, dear Lëvochka, weary, and it seems the children had a good time. [Our daughter] Tanja, too, did some dancing, and Tanja Olsuf'eva[105] was there, along with the two Ljarskis, and the Këllers — about 15 couples, I think. Even the elderly [Vasilij Aleksandrovich] Olsuf'ev came and kept repeating: "I'm having such a good time!" It's now half-past one, thank God everybody's now in bed; we're all healthy and not too alarmed. I have a hurt in the pit of my stomach, and I am afraid of my hurts. We were at the circus this afternoon: a splendid circus, and I had fun watching Andrjusha, even though I know that such

102 Nikolaj Fëdorovich Fëdorov (1829–1903) — Russian religious thinker and philosopher, sometimes dubbed the "Moscow Socrates", founder of a movement known as *Russian cosmism*, whose later adherents included the rocket scientist Konstantin Èduardovich Tsiolkovskij (Tsiolkovsky; 1857–1935) and the naturalist Vladimir Ivanovich Vernadskij (1863–1945). As a librarian at the Rumjantsev Museum (see Letter N° 20, Note 137), Fëdorov initiated a series of intellectual discussion forums, which were attended by many prominent contemporary thinkers; he also introduced a number of reforms in library science, including the setting up of a systematic book catalogue.
103 LNT took part in the Moscow census of 23–25 January 1882. He chose to collect data in the Khitrov Market district that had the very poorest population. He wrote about his impressions in an article *On the Moscow census* [*O perepisi v Moskve*].
104 Mitrofan Nikolaevich Bannikov — son to a former tutor of LNT's and his brothers'; a Yasnaya Polyana foreman.
105 Tat'jana Vasil'evna Olsuf'eva — daughter to Vasilij Aleksandrovich Olsuf'ev.

amusements are harmful for children. But he was expressing himself out loud, laughing, and even clapping for a boy and a pony.

I had to interrupt my letter: I've been feeding [Aleksej],[106] getting undressed, finishing up all my tasks and now it's almost three o'clock in the morning — this is when I go to bed every day.

I just re-read your letter which I received today. Do get better, stay at Yasnaya as long as you want, do some writing and enjoy yourself. If our lives have diverged, then each of us must work things out as best we can, which I try to do for us — i.e. myself and the children. It is still very challenging and unfamiliar to me, but people get accustomed to everything. Why city life should spawn *arguments* — that I don't understand; why on earth would anyone want to preach and proselytise? It is merely inexperience and stupidity to do things like that, and this should be left to the naïve and inexperienced Sjutaev.

Masha[107] was here today, [and] Uncle Kostja's utterly moved in with us. What a bitter mockery of fate — Kosten'ka in place of you! I am still carrying a cross for my move to Moscow. But you won't catch me out on this in future — I shall not move to Moscow again — that is, if I'm still alive.

The clock just struck three. Farewell. When I write, I'm always so tired that my letters come out spiteful. I myself have become spiteful, probably from some bilious disease. Don't come to see me for the time being; you do much better without me. My little one [Aleksej] is still in poor health. But that's not interesting for you. These little children are exclusively *mine,* and I shouldn't — and shan't — have any more. Superfluous sufferings and for what — our lives have gone their separate ways, and let's keep them *completely* separate.

How I want to hurt your feelings, but [you would understand] if only you knew how I weep every day when, after a day of torment *for the life of the flesh,* as you call it, at night-time I'm all alone with my thoughts and longings. My one joy is when Andrjusha says to me, as he did today: "Mamà, who loves you?" — I tell him: "Nobody, Andrjusha, nobody loves me, Papà has gone." And he says: "I love you, Mamà!" And how did that get into his head? I was undressing him quietly upstairs, and he stared at me intently; probably I looked unhappy.

I just wanted to put down facts: I was there, I did that … simply without emotion, and once again I've distressed you and felt sorry for myself. Don't pay any attention. Tomorrow I'll give Tanja your instructions.[108] What a terrible dustup they had with [our son] Serëzha today! He yelled, and I even got frightened.

Sonja.

Nº 73 – LEV NIKOLAEVICH TOLSTOY ❧ SOFIA ANDREEVNA TOLSTAYA
[PSS 83/190]
6 February 1882. Yasnaya Polyana.

Saturday, 11 a.m., before coffee.

Yesterday I felt the best ever — my spine ceased hurting, and no sooner had I got down to work than [Leonid Dmitrievich] Urusov came by. And I had just written him a letter[109] with

---

106 Aleksej L'vovich Tolstoj — see Letter Nº 62, Note 31.
107 Marija Nikolaevna (Masha) Tolstaja (LNT's sister) — see Letter Nº 4, Note 12.
108 Concerning LNT's instructions to their daughter Tanja, see the last few paragraphs of Letter Nº 69 (3 February 1882), as well as the fifth and sixth paragraphs of Letter Nº 71 (4 February).
109 Letter unknown.

the delicate hint that he not come. He had met Filip[110] at the gate and came in, and I was extremely upset.

I did do some work in the morning, but everything turned out wrong, and in the evening I was terribly exhausted from conversation. — These days, there is nothing more terrible for me than conversation. He isn't to blame and he's very nice, but I've already had enough conversation to last me a lifetime — I don't want [any more].

He spent the night in the house, in Auntie's room, and Nanny stayed in the servant girls' room, and while neither of them died from gas poisoning, it is very warm there, and today I'm moving there, at least for a couple of days. If I live, I'll head out on Monday or Tuesday — depending on how my work is going and also on [what] news [I get] from you. —

The pancakes the other day were superb. Arina[111] cooked them. But I don't have an appetite. I've been feeling the whole time out of sorts. It's better now. —

Yesterday Urusov threw me off, and I didn't write you a letter. In place of that I am sending you a wire.[112] And I haven't received any letter from you except the first. Now two will probably come. Farewell, darling. Don't worry about me. I'm fine. And I still love you the same whether we're together or apart. — How are you celebrating *Maslenitsa* [Shrove Tuesday]? Do the children help you?

T.

On the envelope: Moscow. Denezhnyj Lane. Volkonskaja House. Countess Sofia Andreevna Tolstaya.

Nº 74 – SOFIA ANDREEVNA TOLSTAYA ❧ LEV NIKOLAEVICH TOLSTOY
[LSA 67]
[7 February 1882. Moscow]

For the first time in my life, dear Lëvochka, today I was not happy that you are coming back so soon. You write that you'll be leaving on Monday or Tuesday: that means maybe you'll arrive tomorrow and once again start to suffer and be bored; you'll be a living but silent reproach to my life in Moscow. Lord, how much pain that has given me and how it has tormented my soul!

This letter may not reach you; if it does, don't get the idea that I am greatly desiring your return; on the contrary, if you are healthy and busy and, especially, if you're feeling well, why come back? It's undoubtedly true that I don't *need* you for any of life's tasks. I am managing to keep everything in order and balance for now: the children are obedient and trusting, my health is better, and everything in the house is going along as it should be. As for my spiritual life, it's buried so deep it'll take you a long time to dig down to it.

And let it stay that way for now; it's frightening for me to dig it up and bring it to the light of day, and then what shall I do? This inner spiritual side of life is so incompatible with my external life.

---

110 Filip Rodionovich Egorov (1839–1895) — coachman at Yasnaya Polyana.
111 Arina Fëdorovna Frolkova (a.k.a. Irina Fëdorovna Khrolkova; *née* Shentjakova; 1831–after 1906) — cook at Yasnaya Polyana.
112 The wire was sent the same day: "Didn't manage to write yesterday; distracted. Healthy. Working" (PSS 83: 317).

This morning we were at the Manège[113] with all the children, [as well as] Mashen'ka and Hélène.[114] But there was a huge crowd, we saw some sort of unappealing mechanical puppet theatre and weren't able to get to anything else. We [managed to] take Misha and Andrjusha for rides on the circular swings, [but] were terribly bothered by the crowd and it didn't work out well. [Dmitrij Alekseevich] D'jakov and Mashen'ka and Uncle Kostja[115] had dinner at our place. D'jakov and Mashen'ka took Tanja to a gipsy concert, and in the evening Lizaveta Petrovna Obolenskaja came to see us with Lili,[116] along with two of the Olsuf'ev children and our own Liza Obolenskaja[117] with her children. They played *petits jeux,* ate sweets and had a very good time.

All our children enjoyed themselves so much on *Maslenitsa* that they are now even getting down to their studies with pleasure. We have very few guests and it's terribly quiet here without you. And you don't know how to shield yourself from the crowds that press in on you; they've even imposed on you at Yasnaya.

Farewell, dear friend; if you come back, I shall despotically keep any *conversation-loving wiseacres* away from you. Then you will see how good and peaceful your life here can be.

Today I am going to bed early, I hope it will make me feel better and give me some rest. Pity you are not in complete health, weak and with no appetite. How could the country air not give you an appetite? Have you been out hunting?

Farewell. If you don't come, do please write.

Sonja.

Sunday, 7 February [1882].[118]

N° 75 – LEV NIKOLAEVICH TOLSTOY ❧ SOFIA ANDREEVNA TOLSTAYA
[PSS 83/195]
2 March 1882. Yasnaya Polyana.

Iljusha will tell you about me. I tried to write [earlier] today, but didn't get very far. It's all because of some feeling of tiredness, although today I feel more lively. — I haven't received any letters from you yet and I am concerned about you. Today I hardly went out at all — the weather is poor. I'm playing *patience,* reading and thinking. — I'd very much like to finish that article I began, but even if I don't get it written this week, I shan't be upset. In any case it would do me a lot of good to get away from this confrontational city life and concentrate on my inner self — to read others' thoughts about religion, listen to Agaf'ja Mikhajlovna's chatter and think not about people, but about God.

---

113 *Manège* — a large exhibition hall located just near the Kremlin in Moscow.
114 LNT's sister Marija Nikolaevna (Mashen'ka) Tolstaja and her daughter Elena Sergeevna (Hélène) Denisenko (see Letter N° 24, Note 160).
115 Konstantin Aleksandrovich Islavin — see Letter N° 47, Note 301.
116 Princess Elizaveta Petrovna Obolenskaja (*née* Vyrubova; 1843–1931) — wife to Dmitrij Dmitrievich Obolenskij (see Letter N° 13, Note 79), with her daughter Elizaveta Dmitrievna Obolenskaja (1871–1894; married name: Kazem-Bek).
117 Elizaveta Valer'janovna (Liza) Obolenskaja (LNT's niece) — see Letter N° 40, Note 259.
118 Misprinted in the published Russian version as 1881.

Now Agaf'ja Mikhajlovna has been entertaining me with stories about you, about what kind of man I would have been if I had married Arsen'eva.[119] [And Agaf'ja says to me:] "And now [you've] gone off, abandoned her there with her children, — [you tell your wife:] 'Manage as best you can', but then you just sit there, stroking your beard." —

That was good. Her stories about dogs and cats are funny, but as soon as she starts talking about people, they turn sad. Someone's either begging, epileptic, consumptive, crippled, beating his wife or abandoning his children. And everywhere there's suffering and evil, and people have come to accept that that's the way it ought to be. — If I were writing in the morning, my letter would be more cheerful, but at the moment I feel depressed again. —

Right now it's past 11, and I'm on way to take Iljusha to Kozlovka [Station]. —

Farewell, darling, hugs and kisses to you and the children.

The greenhouses are now ready for planting; send some seeds.

If nothing [unexpected] happens, I'll be there on Sunday.

On the fourth page: Moscow. Denezhnyj Lane. Volkonskaja House. Her Ladyship Countess Sofia Andreevna Tolstaya.

Nº 76 – Lev Nikolaevich Tolstoy ✉ Sofia Andreevna Tolstaya
[PSS 83/196]
3 March 1882. Yasnaya Polyana.

3rd [March], 10 p.m.

How painful it is for me, my precious darling, that I am upsetting you with my letters. — [The reason is:] I had a bout of colic: my mouth feels bitter, my liver aches and I feel all gloomy and depressed. — There's no better place for me to be than here, completely alone in wordless silence. — Today I can't say that my sleep was bad, but it wasn't enough and I didn't even sit down to work, just reading. —

I haven't received any letters from you yet, apart from the nonsensical letter from Aleksandr[120] and the less than sincere letter from Aleksandra[121] — on which you jotted a few words of your own. This letter of Aleksandra's upset me — irritated me — and I wrote a very harsh reply, which I took to Yasenki on horseback myself, where I bought envelopes. But on the way home I

---

119 Valerija Vladimirovna Arsen'eva (1836–1909) — daughter to neighbouring landowner Vladimir Mikhajlovich Arsen'ev (1810–1853) and his wife Evgenija L'vovna Arsen'eva (née Shcherbachëva). After Vladimir Mikhajlovich's untimely death, LNT became guardian of his children and often visited their Sudakovo estate. In 1856–57 LNT was romantically attracted to Valerija Vladimirovna and thought about marrying her, but considered her of too frivolous character. A year or so later she married Anatolij Aleksandrovich Talyzin (1820–1894), but then divorced him and married Nikolaj Nikolaevich Volkov (?–1901). His attraction to Arsen'eva inspired him to write *Family happiness* in 1858, which was first published in the journal *Russkij vestnik* (1859, Nº 7–8).

120 Aleksandr Andreevich (Sasha) Behrs (SAT's brother) — see Letter Nº 4, Note 13.

121 The reference is to a letter from LNT's great aunt Aleksandra Andreevna Tolstaja (see Letter Nº 37, Note 231) which has been preserved only in part. For ten days in February 1882 Aleksandra Andreevna was in Moscow, where she met with LNT, arguing with him on religious topics. While she strongly defended traditional Orthodoxy, he attacked the Church and accused its followers of hypocrisy. This dispute affected their subsequent relationship. Aleksandra Andreevna described their further irregular correspondence as "lame".

remembered that you would not have approved of this letter and I myself began to have regrets, and so I sent [someone] to bring the letter back, hence it wasn't sent.[122] —

This morning was sunny and warm, and you could hear the larks warbling all over the place, and the ride was pleasant. And now it's windy, warm and dark, but I shall be going to Kozlovka [Station] by sleigh; I'll post this letter and enquire [as to whether there are any letters] from you. Nanny[123] went to Tula, carrying money from Avdot'ja Vasil'evna;[124] she was at the post office, but didn't bring any letter back. A letter from you will bring a great deal of cheer to my life. —

Kostjushka[125] was here — his wife is very ill — still the same [illness], in her breast. They say she got through it because of your medicine, but then her child died, and the same thing happened again, [this time] in both her breasts. She's asking for that bandage or ointment which you gave her [before]. Send it if you can.

People are coming by asking [for money], but I refuse, — [I have] no money; albeit [refusing] is somewhat easier this year [than last], and I've thought a lot about this, and I don't feel so bad about refusing.

Did Iljusha arrive safely? Is everything all right with you? Your health? And are the children fine? That's the main thing.

Farewell, darling. Don't think I'm not sad being apart from you; I am sad, but I feel that I am resting, and despite my ill health I am gaining strength, and thinking things through a lot better, more clearly and simply. Perhaps it's simply the dreams and fancies of a decaying man, but thoughts of doing some creative writing keep coming to mind.

That kind of work would really rest me.

Thinking about it is just like thinking about going bathing in the summertime.

But please don't tell this even to the children. — With you, I am [simply] thinking aloud.

Just now I received the letter[126] you sent to Kozlovka, and it has brought me a great deal of cheer.

On the envelope: Moscow. Denezhnyj Lane, Volkonskij house. Her Ladyship Countess Sofia Andreevna Tolstaya.

Nº 77– SOFIA ANDREEVNA TOLSTAYA ❧ LEV NIKOLAEVICH TOLSTOY
[LSA 70]
3 March 1882. Wednesday evening. [Moscow.]

Today did not go so peacefully and successfully for me as those days [of the past]. Perhaps it seems to me that way because Agaf'ja Mikhajlovna made me feel sorry for myself,[127] and it started to even feel funny to me that at the same time as I was reading the letter you sent with

---

122 In the unsent letter of 3 March 1882 LNT wrote: "There can be no common ground between you and me, since that spiritually sacred faith which you profess, I professed with all my soul and studied with all my strength of mind and became convinced that it was not faith, but a bitter deception" (*L. N. Tolstoy and A. A. Tolstaja: Correspondence 1857– 1903* [*L. N. Tolstoj i A. A. Tolstaja: Perepiska*], pp. 402–03). The following day he wrote another letter (ibid., pp. 404–05), but did not send it either.

123 *Nanny* — Marija Afanas'evna Arbuzova — see Letter Nº 41, Note 265.

124 Avdot'ja Vasil'evna Popova — housekeeper for the Tolstoys at Yasnaya Polyana.

125 Konstantin Nikolaevich (Kostjushka) Zjabrev — a poor peasant at Yasnaya Polyana.

126 This letter is dated 1 March 1882 (not included in the present volume).

127 See Letter Nº 75 of 2 March 1882.

Iljusha, your brother Serëzha was telling Vasilij Ivanovich,[128] who had arrived [earlier this] morning, that it was all very well for Lev Nikolaevich, spoiled as he was by Fate and his wife, to complain — he has somebody to complain to, somebody who will pity him. [And Serëzha continued:] "And if I say 'I've become weak', my wife says: 'It's already high time you died.' Or I'll say: 'I'm not well', and she says: 'May you come down with convulsions!'"

But here is my day: the first thing, the most sad and depressing when I awoke, was your letter. It keeps getting worse and worse. I start thinking that if a happy person suddenly could see *only* the terrible things, and closed his eyes to the good, then that is what should come from ill health. You would just need to have treatment. I say this without any ulterior motive; it seems quite clear to me; I feel terribly sorry for you, and if you calmly considered my words and your situation — you would possibly find a solution.

You had this melancholy condition already — a long time ago. You used to say: "From lack of faith", you wanted to hang yourself.[129] And now? After all, you do live by faith, why then are you unhappy? And weren't you aware before that there are starving, sick, miserable and evil people out there? Take a closer look: there are cheerful, healthy, happy and kind people, too. If only God could help you — what can I do?

Anyway, later Il'ja came to see me this morning, his lips and voice trembling. Malysh[130] has gone missing. We've done all we could to look for him — I myself feel very sorry for him. He's been missing since yesterday evening, and I wasn't aware. Thank God they found him — some servant in Denezhnyj Lane caught him and brought him back. Then I went to make two boring calls — on Sverbeeva[131] and Bojanus,[132] but I didn't find either of them [at home].

Vasilij Ivanovich is coming to see you himself, and so I'm not writing anything about him. He's sad: he brought two thousand [roubles], he was looking to buy a threshing machine — in Rjazn' Gubernia, it seems.

When I got home, Misha was experiencing severe vomiting. I got frightened, but by evening he had cheered up, and was apparently healthy. But then there was one bad thing after another. Now Fet and both Serëzhas — your brother and our son — are in the study, along with Vasilij Ivanovich. Here I am writing this letter in haste. I've given Masha her lesson, fed Alësha [baby Aleksej], talked with horse sellers and coachmen, and the samovar is boiling; I'm being called, and I'm hurrying.

Concerning the horses: [the horse dealer] Konëk brought a horse and I paid 160 silver roubles [for it]. Tomorrow at 10 a.m. they'll be bringing that other horse, and tomorrow, too, I'll send the horses to Tula. The difference in the asking price according to my sources turned out

---

128 Vasilij Ivanovich Alekseev (tenant in Samara) — see Letter N° 52, Note 338.

129 LNT described this condition of his in *A confession* [*Ispoved'*]: "The truth is that life is meaningless. I seemed to live a bit, move a bit, came to the edge of an abyss and saw that there was nothing ahead of me but doom… And so then I, a happy man, removed [all] ropes from my room where I was alone, undressing, every night, so as not to hang myself on the crossbar between the closets, and I ceased hunting with a rifle, so as not to be tempted by an all-too-easy method of saving myself from life… And this was happening with me at a time when I was surrounded on all sides by what might be considered complete happiness: this was before I turned fifty. I had a kind, loving and beloved wife, good children, a large estate which was growing and increasing without any labour on my part. I was respected by family and acquaintances; praised by others more than ever before, and could say that I enjoyed popularity without any exaggerated delusions of grandeur" (PSS 23:12).

130 *Malysh* — Il'ja L'vovich's beloved pointer.

131 Ekaterina Aleksandrovna Sverbeeva (*née* Princess Shcherbatova; 1802–1892) — widow of historian and diplomat Dmitrij Nikolaevich Sverbeev (1799–1874).

132 Ol'ga Semënovna Bojanus (*née* Khljustina; 1st married name: Davydova; 1837–1910 — mother to friends of Il'ja's, wife to homœopath Karl Karlovich Bojanus (1818–1897).

be something around 5 silver roubles. And I know how much you want to see [these] horses [for yourself], and so I am sending them. Vasilij Ivanovich will tell you when to send a horse and a man to Tula for them. Tomorrow I'll hand over the money for the other horse. Have I taken care of everything, and are you satisfied with me?

I just gave everyone some tea before finishing this letter. Now Fet's gone, after a long conversation with your brother Serëzha. I stayed talking by the samovar, chatting with Vasilij Ivanovich. Iljusha had a good nap and then took tea with us, too. He didn't go to the *gymnasium* [today], his [missing] Malysh was driving him crazy. I had so many thoughts that my pen could hardly keep up with what I was thinking and wanting to write; now I've interrupted my train of thought and forgotten everything.

Now with this interruption I need to think about what might interest you [concerning our children]. Tanja went to school; Serëzha was at the university;[133] Lëlja has had a bad cold all day; the little ones are healthy. Farewell, my dear friend. As to how to comfort you, my dove, there's only one thing I can do: love and feel sorry for you, but you don't need that any more. What *do* you need? [I'd like] at least to know. Hugs and kisses to you, and I am hastening to send off this letter.

Sonja.

Nº 78 – SOFIA ANDREEVNA TOLSTAYA ❧ LEV NIKOLAEVICH TOLSTOY
[LSA 73]
8 April 1882. 11 p.m. Thursday. [Moscow]

My dear Lëvochka, I've just got back from carrying out your wishes [expressed in] your letter about helping a poor student. I started by going to Sukhotin;[134] there I was told that everyone was at Fokht's,[135] who is on the verge of death. I then asked to be taken to L'vova's,[136] but changed my mind and went to Konjushkovskij Lane [where the D'jakovs live]. I went into D'jakov's house; all the Sukhotins were there, down to the last one: the husband Sergej Mikhajlovich, his wife, and their son with his [first] wife.[137] So strange to see them all together. Fokht's agony ended and he didn't die; hope appeared once more. Liza Obolenskaja[138] was also there. Somehow I managed to get hold of that letter and read it aloud. I saw that everyone took it to heart, and I'm certain that D'jakov will also help, though he did not say anything. Misha Sukhotin has undertaken to deliver this letter tomorrow to the spiritualist L'vov; everyone says he will do what he can, and I left your 20 silver roubles in an envelope [for the poor student].

133 Tat'jana L'vovna was studying at the Academy of Painting, Sculpture and Architecture; Sergej L'vovich was in his first year in the Natural Sciences department of Moscow University.

134 Sergej Mikhajlovich Sukhotin (1818–1886) — chamberlain, a Tula landowner, since 1851 a councillor with the Moscow Court Office. He helped LNT secure archival materials for work on his novel *War and Peace*.

135 Nikolaj Bogdanovich Fokht (?–1882) — Russian language teacher at the First Moscow *Gymnasium*, married to Sergej Sukhotin's daughter Elizaveta Sergeevna (1851–1902).

136 Marija Mikhajlovna L'vova (née Chelishcheva; 1843–1915) — wife to amateur spiritualist Nikolaj Aleksandrovich L'vov (1834–1887). LNT's impressions of his séance were embodied in his comedy *The fruits of enlightenment* [*Plody prosveshchenija*], particularly in the character of Zvezdintsev.

137 Sergej Sukhotin's son was Mikhail Sergeevich (Misha) Sukhotin (1850–1914), whose first wife was also named Marija Mikhajlovna (née Baroness Bode; 1856–1897). Later, in 1899, he married the Tolstoys' daughter Tat'jana L'vovna (Tanja; 1864–1950).

138 Elizaveta Valer'janovna (Liza) Obolenskaja (LNT's niece) — see Letter Nº 6, Note 43.

Now to your other matter — the proofs.[139] They brought them at 8 o'clock this evening; the envelope was so big and thick that they couldn't get it into the postbox, and I shall send it tomorrow by post to Yasenki, where you will receive it as a package. I also included some tape for the furniture; give it to Ivan.[140]

We're all in good health here, and for the moment it's pretty quiet. Yesterday they got our Tanja all flustered regarding the party at the Khomjakovs.[141] Vsevolod[142] came and said that this would be the last Wednesday and there would be so many good guests, etc., etc. Then Valentina[143] arrived, and started to ask and plead for [our daughter] Tanja to be allowed to go [with them]. They both [Valentina and Tanja] kept insisting so much that I hesitated a moment and said, maybe for an hour or two. By this I managed to spoil the whole situation: I gave Tanja a faint hope, and in the evening she began to insist: "Let's go, let's go!" It was very hard not to give in. But all at once I had second thoughts: I remembered that you did not want this, that it was completely contrary to my views, and so I didn't go. Tanja started crying and got angry, but things were resolved almost peacefully.

Today I was with my namesake [Countess Sof'ja Andreevna] Tolstaja.[144] These two mysterious ladies played a game of simplicity with me, but I didn't like them. We're simply not compatible! Let's forget about them — I have no desire to continue our acquaintance, and I hope they feel the same way about me. But they will be living in Moscow all spring and [all] next winter. Whoever meets up with them is in for a rough time!

Tanja and Il'ja are at Deviche Field at the Olsuf'evs'.[145] Serëzha passed his first exam with *high marks,* and he's happy, and satisfied. Lëlja and Masha are pale, nervous and pitiful. The boys are noisy; Alësha's a dear and he smiles as he shakes his head on his delicate little neck.

Farewell, Lëvochka, write and tell me about your health and your nerves, ask me to do something, and don't ever be *a stranger* [to me].

Sonja.

Nº 79 – LEV NIKOLAEVICH TOLSTOY ❧ SOFIA ANDREEVNA TOLSTAYA
[PSS 83/200]
9 April 1882. Yasnaya Polyana.

Friday 9:30 p.m.

I've just come back from [hunting near] the apiary, took three shots, didn't kill anything. — A marvellous evening, warm, quiet, there's a crescent moon shining. A lot of good thoughts, which I would write [to you], only I have a feeling you may read [this letter] to others, and I shall prepare myself. — Don't take the plan [I outlined] yesterday (I [am prepared to] remain in Moscow to the end of [the children's] exams) for a *combat de générosité.* I shall be quite happy

---

139 the proofs — of LNT's article *Introduction to an unpublished treatise* (*A confession*) [*Vstuplenie k nenapechatannomu sochineniju (Ispoved')*], which was to have been published in *Russkaja mysl'*, but was blocked by the censors.
140 Ivan Alekseevich — a harness-maker.
141 Dmitrij Alekseevich Khomjakov and Anna Sergeevna Khomjakova (*née* Ushakova; see Letter Nº 61, Note 18).
142 Vsevolod Vsevolodovich Shidlovskij (1854–1912) — first cousin to SAT.
143 Valentina Sergeevna Ushakova (married name: Gordeeva; 1863–1931) — lady-in-waiting; sister to Anna Sergeevna Khomjakova.
144 Countess Sof'ja Andreevna Tolstaja (*née* Bakhmeteva; 1827–1895) — widow of the poet Count Aleksej Konstantinovich Tolstoj (1817–1875). The other 'mysterious lady' referred to is her namesake's extra-marital daughter, Sof'ja Petrovna Khitrovo (*née* Bakhmetova; 1848–1910).
145 *the Olsuf'evs'* — see Letter Nº 70, Note 94.

to stay [there], knowing that you are at Yasnaya with the children. And I shall take care of all our Moscow affairs to a T. Do allow me, too, that pleasure. And I shall find some things to do in Moscow — possibly there will be some proofs [to check]. —

Yesterday Agaf'ja Mikhajlovna sat and cried and grieved for a long time — strange, as always, but sincerely: "Lev Nikolaevich, *Batjushka*,[146] tell me what I should do. I'm afraid I'm going out of my mind. I go to [my dog] Shumikha, give her a hug, and start to cry: 'No, Shumikha, our dear one is not here'", and so forth. And she herself starts weeping. And today I was on my way back from Yasenki, where I went to get percussion caps, cartridges and envelopes, and happened to meet a troika of fine peasant horses moving along at a slow trot. It was being driven by two young men and carrying something rather strange — as it seemed to me — flowers in pots, all in pink and white. As I caught up to them, [I saw] a black coffin all decked out with wreaths of fresh, living flowers. "What are you carrying," [I asked]. "A gentleman." "What kind of [gentleman]?" "A dead gentleman." "Who is he?" "Glazkov."[147] They were taking him to the estate. How strange!

Yesterday after [my talk with] Agaf'ja Mikhajlovna I went and ate some sauerkraut for the night. And there is no sauerkraut like Marija Afanasevna's anywhere in the world! And while I couldn't get to sleep for a long time, I did sleep well. And today I got down to work with pleasure. Just a bit, but meaningfully, so that I am experiencing something I haven't felt in a long time — a sense that I have "earned my bread". And the "bread" is excellent — green cabbage soup, corned beef, and sauerkraut again with *kvass*.

This morning before coffee I walked to the village to see the village elder, and there, together with three old men: Matvej Egorov,[148] Tit[149] and Pëtr Osipov[150] — discussed how to divide Aleksej's[151] inheritance fairly. Varvara[152] is the only one who is terribly greedy. How could the curse of money not be an evil?! She's crying out of envy, and [I] pity her. We have to try to undo sin, like you did with Lokhmacheva.[153]

Another pitiful woman from Vorobëvka[154] came for some quinine. And another, who was left alone after her husband was imprisoned in a dungeon — really pitiful; I know both the husband and the wife. And then there was the widow Kurnasenkova,[155] who couldn't end her dispute with Grigorij Bolkhin[156] over a plot of land. And I hope to reconcile these two. — Osip Naumych[157] was here this morning. He brought honey. And he keeps complaining about his son. He [the son] sends him [the father] to spend the night in a fenced-in paddock. It's cold under just an old fur coat. He chases him out, or else, he says, 'I shan't give [you] any bread.' — This is an episode from actual peasant poverty, which we know little about.

---

146 *Batjushka* — a term of endearment derived from the word for "Father", akin (in this particular instance) to "Precious one" (used by Russians in addressing an Orthodox priest and by peasants in addressing their masters).

147 Ivan Ivanovich Glazkov (1823–1882) — a landowner in the settlement of Pokrovskoe-Ushakovo, Krapivna Uezd, Tula Gubernia; he passed on 6 April 1882.

148 Matvej Egorovich Egorov (1816–1892).

149 Tit Ermilovich Zjabrev (1829–1894).

150 Pëtr Osipovich Zjabrev (1843–1906).

151 Aleksej Stepanovich Orekhov — see Letter N° 5, Note 38.

152 Varvara Nikolaevna Bannikova — second daughter to LNT's servant Nikolaj; her sister Evdokija (see Letter N° 5, Note 12) was married to Aleksej Stepanovich Orekhov.

153 Tat'jana Ivanovna Lokhmacheva (1832–?) — a Yasnaya Polyana peasant.

154 Probably a reference to the peasant Anna Alekseevna Gasteva (?–ca1927).

155 Tat'jana Ivanovna Kurnasenkova (or possibly Kurnosova; 1842–?) — a Yasnaya Polyana peasant.

156 Grigorij Il'ich Bolkhin (1836–?) — father to coachman Adrian Grigor'evich Bolkhin (1865–1936).

157 Osip Naumovich Zjabrev (1802–1884) — husband to LNT's wet-nurse. His son was Pëtr Osipovich Zjabrev.

I haven't been receiving any letters from you and now I shall take this letter unsealed to Kozlovka, where I'll add a reply [if I receive a letter from you there]. The night is marvellous — no policemen, no lamps burning, but it's bright and calm out. Regarding our household situations, there was one that almost got me angry — the fact that mice have eaten away at about 300 beautiful apple-trees on the other side of the orchard. — Another thing: we owed Aleksej Stepanovich — and now his heir — a salary of 260 roubles. This is correct according to the [record-]books and his [note]book — still, it was an unpleasant [shock] to me. —

I took with me a [book by] Balzac[158] and am reading it with delight when I have [a few] moments free. — You see, I am carrying out your plan of letter-writing — I never write *I hope*,[159] but only about myself. However, I very much wanted to say *I hope* a number of times concerning both you and the little ones, and about Masha's health, and about Iljusha's studies, and about Tanja's passion for fun and reluctance to study. Anyway, hugs to you and the children.

[P.S.] I've just received your fine letter.[160] You did just the right thing, not letting Tanja go,[161] and for now everything's going well with you, as it is with me. [We'll see] what God gives [us] tomorrow. Hugs and kisses, precious.

On the envelope: Moscow. Denezhnyj Lane, Prechistenka. Princess Volkonskaja house. Her Ladyship Countess Sofia Andreevna Tolstaya.

N° 80 – LEV NIKOLAEVICH TOLSTOY ✒ SOFIA ANDREEVNA TOLSTAYA
[PSS 83/205]
17 May 1882. Yasnaya Polyana.

I'm feeling unbearably happy here. I had a splendid sleep, got up at 10, had my fill of coffee with Tanja,[162] played with the children (they are very happy and healthy), and went for a walk along the perimeter [of our estate], through yellow flowers and the *Zaseka*, along the road to Krapivna, to the apiary, to the circular birch grove, the swimming-hole, all around the *Zakaz*,[163] and returned home at 3 o'clock. [I say] "unbearably", because I can't feel my joy for a moment without thinking of you and your ordeals in Moscow. I'm so revived and refreshed in just one day that I feel I could go to Moscow and take over your [duties]. Please, darling, if you want to truly please me, summon me as soon as you can. But only if Lëlja's health improves[164] and if it is decided that it would be better for him to go [to Yasnaya Polyana]. News that you are calling upon me to relieve you tomorrow would give me joy. I shall go with pleasure, and I hope that after my recovery here and the whole experience of surviving my illness, I shall be able to have a splendid time in Moscow for ten days. —

After returning home, I gathered the three girls together and went for a walk with them to meet [Leonid Dmitrievich] Urusov. We saw him yesterday. He was supposed to meet Nikolaj

158 Possibly a reference to the 1833 novel *Eugénie Grandet* by Honoré de Balzac (1799–1850), published in the 1884 issue of *Revue étrangère*, which LNT was reading at the time (see his letter to SAT dated 4 March 1882, PSS 83: 325).
159 The words *I hope* are given in English (not Russian).
160 Letter N° 78 of 8 April 1882.
161 Tanja wanted to go to a ball at the Khomjakovs'.
162 SAT's sister Tat'jana Andreevna (Tanja) Kuzminskaja was spending the summer in the annexe at Yasnaya Polyana.
163 The *Zakaz* was the Tolstoys' private forest preserve on the Yasnaya Polyana estate (where LNT's grave is located today), while the *Zaseka* was another designated conservation area outside the perimeter of the estate.
164 The Tolstoys' son Lev L'vovich (Lëlja) was ill with a fever, and so SAT decided to delay her departure to Yasnaya Polyana (where she was planning to spend the summer) until such time as the doctors deemed it safe for Lev to go there.

Nikolaevich the Younger,[165] who always travels on the same train as I do. We didn't meet him and got back at 6, in time for the dinner Auntie Tanja had arranged. Yesterday, it turns out, I made a tragic mistake — inadvertently. In Moscow I was buying a ticket for myself and when I asked a porter to buy tickets for the servants, I [mistakenly] blurted out "To Tula" [instead of "To Kozlovka"]. Yesterday they sent [horses] to Kozlovka but there were no servants there. This morning Garasim [the Tolstoys' butler] came to see about despatching the horses [to collect the servants at Tula]. —

They played some kind of [card] game [while they were waiting]. But everybody arrived back safe and sound.

I'm keeping my eye on the little ones, and, most importantly, having them spend as much time as they can in the garden. Inside is more dangerous and unhealthy.

These days the heat has been terrible, even here. How have you been surviving? Here we're having a drought — it seems both the grass and the rye are doing poorly. —

Neither I nor Tanja have heard Andrjusha coughing, but now I'll ask the nanny and report: — the nanny says that the cough is much better. — *Two or three times a day.*

This evening at 8 Urusov came, — he brought a pie for [our] tea — a token of hospitality, which was intended for you, but which we shall eat at [your sister] Auntie Tanja's [in the annexe]. —

So do me a favour and summon me as soon as you can. I shall keep gloriously busy in Moscow finishing up my writing projects, going shopping, and renovating the house,[166] and the main thing, it will be delightful to know that you are in the fresh air [here at Yasnaya Polyana] with the little ones. —

Farewell, darling, hugs to you and kisses to my four boys. [Your sister] Tanja is writing, too.

Yours, *L.*

Nº 81 – SOFIA ANDREEVNA TOLSTAYA ❧ LEV NIKOLAEVICH TOLSTOY
[LSA 75]
Tuesday 18 May [1882. Moscow]

Today things are going very much better, dear friend Lëvochka. Lëlja's health has evidently improved. Today he didn't take any quinine, there is no fever, and his convulsions have eased. But he gave me a terrible fright during the night. Here I am asleep, and all at once I hear a cracking noise on the other side of the partition. I thought he might have fallen off the sofa — I rushed to his bed, but found it empty. I see him already running into the drawing room in just his nightshirt. I approach him and say, "What is it, Lëlja, where [are you going]?" I see the idiotic [grin on] his face and he tearfully answers: "Yes, over there, to sit, let me go, I'll go." Then I realise he's sleep-walking and I lead him quietly to his bed. For a long time I couldn't get to sleep; this really shook me. The little one is better, too, he's not coughing as much and had a very good sleep. Today I wasn't tired and experienced no melancholy… I did drive out to finish a few errands, but I shan't be going out again, I got everything done. Yesterday at dinnertime

---

165 Grand Prince Nikolaj Nikolaevich the Younger (1856–1929) — grandson to Tsar Nicholas I, eldest son to Grand Prince Nikolaj Nikolaevich the Elder (1831–1891); commander-in-chief of the Russian Imperial army and navy at the start of World War I.

166 In the summer of 1882 the Tolstoys purchased a house from Ivan Aleksandrovich Arnautov at 15, Dolgokhamovniki Lane in Moscow, where after repairs and renovations they lived nineteen winters (up to 1901), spending their summers at Yasnaya Polyana. LNT would often stay at Yasnaya Polyana even during the winter.

Urusov[167] came by together with his niece Bogdanova to look at the house. It seems she doesn't want to buy it — she's afraid of the mould. [Ivan Aleksandrovich] Arnautov was here today, perfumed and pleasant. He says that there are other [potential] buyers, and he can't reduce the price [for us]. [Our son] Serëzha went to see Shchepkin,[168] didn't find him in, but left a message [enquiring] about an architect.[169] Il'ja got a '3' [out of 5] today on his Latin and is very happy. Last night I had an [unpleasant] situation with him. He spent the whole evening in the company of drunken housepainters. I chased him out of there and swore at him. He retorted, and I told him that I considered it my duty to protect and watch over him, and for that he could even strike me if he wanted, but I would still keep on protecting him to my last breath from what I thought might harm him. He mellowed considerably, and we parted friends. We took tea *en famille*: [my brother] Sasha, Masha Sverbeeva with her husband,[170] Uncle Kostja and I with the children. We had a very good time. Today Sasha and Uncle [Kostja] went to Neskuchnyj Gardens,[171] while Serëzha and Il'ja went with Adam[172] to go bathing. I am clearing things away and packing them little by little. Liza[173] has started to get accustomed to the baby and I've found a bit of relief [from looking after him].

Oh, what smudges! I hadn't noticed them [until just now]!

How are all of you doing? Happy! And I shall be happy soon. [My brother] Sasha went to see the Arnautov house and garden and was ecstatic over the garden. They brought me a huge bouquet of flowers. Farewell, my dears, hugs and kisses to all. I hope you are all healthy, that [our daughter] Tanja is taking good care of the household and *qu'elle fait la maman*. I bought her some pale blue and pink ribbons today. Don't you need something to go with your *foulard* dress, Tanja — the dress you will be sewing from two [older ones]? Today Il'ja will pick up your canvas and portfolio from the Tret'jakov Gallery. Sasha praised your first piece[174] a lot. We get along very well together. Tomorrow we'll send my sister Tanja a telegram to Kozlovka. Farewell once more, love me and don't be [too] strict [with me].

Sonja.

N° 82 – LEV NIKOLAEVICH TOLSTOY ❧ SOFIA ANDREEVNA TOLSTAYA
[PSS 83/213]
11 September 1882. Moscow.

We arrived safely and on time. [Our son] Serëzha met us, we said good-bye to Tanja[175] and went to the Volkonskaja house, and from there to the Arnautov [house]. The renovation is coming along, but there is still a lot to be done. Serëzha's report was accurate. We shall be able to move into the lower rooms in about two or three days — namely, the boys' room, the dining

---

167 Sergej Semënovich Urusov (see Letter N° 40, Note 258) with his niece, surnamed Bogdanova.
168 Mitrofan Pavlovich Shchepkin (1832–1908) — owner of a printshop where individual works of LNT's were printed.
169 The Tolstoys needed an architect to renovate their house in Khamovniki Lane, newly purchased from Ivan Aleksandrovich Arnautov (see Letter N° 80, Note 166). The architect selected was Mikhail Illarionovich Nikiforov (1837–after 1897).
170 Marija Vjacheslavovna Sverbeeva (née Shidlovskaja; 1853–1912) — a cousin of SAT's, married to Mikhail Dmitrievich Sverbeev (1843–1903).
171 *Neskuchnyj Gardens* — a popular recreational park on the banks of the Moskva River.
172 Adam Vasil'evich Olsuf'ev (1833–1901) — a major-general; a neighbour of the Tolstoys' in Moscow.
173 *Liza* — in this case a reference to the nanny hired to look after the Tolstoys' baby Aleksej (see Letter N° 62, Note 31).
174 *your first piece* — probably a reference to a drawing by the Tolstoys' daughter Tat'jana L'vovna (Tanja).
175 SAT's sister Tat'jana Andreevna (Tanja) Kuzminskaja accompanied LNT to Moscow.

room, Tanja's room and [our] bedroom. They are already wallpapered. The dining room has that yellow paper with the appearance of wood, which you picked out. I think it looks fine. The corner room won't be ready yet, since they are painting the floor. That's too bad. If I had managed to catch them in time, I would have left it unpainted. — I am thinking of moving furniture into these rooms — the ones that are ready — and [start] clearing out the Volkonskij house in about three days. I think you will be able to move when the whole of the ground floor and the old upper floor are ready. Let them finish the drawing room and dining-rooms [of the old house] while we are still there. How do you feel?

I haven't seen the architect yet. I shall go see him today and write you in more detail after talking with him. — I'm staying at the Volkonskij house. We've been sleeping in the children's room. Today we want to move to the annexe of the Arnautov [house]. —

Yesterday I dropped in with Lëlja to see Polivanov.[176] He's more doubtful about Lëlja than Iljusha — [afraid] that he will lag behind. Il'ja can go into Grade 6 for classes and at the same time sit the exam. — The Tsar [Alexander III] lives a kind of a mysterious life; nobody knows in which palace he resides, but crowds gather here and there and nobody knows. Kosten'ka is still the same. He has everything, and he's still pitiful, and is still waiting for [some kind of] position. —

I'm hurrying off to the post office. Farewell, my dear. Please don't feel bored. I'll probably be back some time [soon]. I'll get Lëlja established in the *gymnasium,* and with the help of Serëzha and Sergej [Petrovich Arbuzov] I'll move the furniture and then come for you. We want to hire a cook and eat at home. And that will be better for Serëzha as well. Lëlja will stay either with Serëzha or [our neighbours] the Olsuf'evs[177] when I'm not here.

Hugs and kisses to all. —

On the envelope: Tula. Her Ladyship Countess Sofia Andreevna Tolstaya.

Nº 83 – SOFIA ANDREEVNA TOLSTAYA ❧ LEV NIKOLAEVICH TOLSTOY
[LSA 78]
[12 September 1882.] Sunday evening [Yasnaya Polyana]

Today I received your letter,[178] dear Lëvochka, and it perplexed me. The tone of it suggests that the house is not ready at all, and God knows when we shall be able to move. I can't make out any details from the contents [of your letter]. *What* exactly is not ready on the upper floor? Are the two rooms off the hallway — and the [servant] girls' room and the kitchen — ready? You somehow always [manage to] forget the servants.[179] Then, if the downstairs is taken up with furniture, where shall we live? After all, we have a lot of furniture; it's bulky and it could all be broken in the tight space, if [we are going to] be living there. Anyway, I can't tell you anything about what I am thinking or when I shall move; I would need to know everything in detail [in advance]. One thing is clear to me: it is a thousand times more dangerous for Iljusha to live here than in Moscow; and to walk through the snow and frost for five hours straight,

---

176 Lev Ivanovich Polivanov (1838–1899) — founding headmaster of a private boys' *gymnasium*, where the Tolstoys' sons Il'ja (Iljusha) and Lev (Lëlja) were enrolled.
177 In this case the family of Vasilij Aleksandrovich Olsuf'ev, neighbours to the Tolstoys in Moscow.
178 Letter Nº 82 of 11 September 1882.
179 The Tolstoys' had about ten servants in all — nannies, maids, cooks, yardkeepers, stable-men and so forth. They all needed accommodation: some were lodged in the gate-house, others in the kitchen, the annexe and the main house.

God knows how far, is much worse than going to the *gymnasium*. He studies two hours a day or less. I tremble every moment for fear [that he might come down with] inflammation of the lungs, and my one thought is to get him to Moscow as soon as possible. He is recovering slowly [from typhoid fever], and how can he recover if he spends so much time walking [12 km to Tula, either to the *gymnasium* or to see his tutor]? The ground everywhere is covered with snow; the temperature here, out of the wind, is only three degrees during the day, the wind is from the north and [stoves] are burning everywhere.

Please don't forget two things [in particular]: [*the stoves*] should *be kept burning everywhere,* and that *the ventilation windows* and *the winter window-frames* should be installed. Pity that you were so unclear about the cook. If you had written *positively,* I would have sent Alëna[180] — a week earlier or later wouldn't have made much of a difference, would it? — while any woman could have replaced her here. If you are really determined to have meals at home, just wire me and I'll send Alëna at once. They can take food from the larder, and there are dishes [already] there. I could send some casserole dishes with her.

Bored? — I'm not bored at all. It feels so good to be in a quiet [home] and concentrate on my thoughts, [to be] with innocent little ones and the girls who are very nice to me and even cheerful.

But they have to start school, [they] all need to live a proper life, [we] all need to be together. The weather is repulsive, so in any case we can't go [yet]. Today I actually had them saddle up Sharik, and put Gnedoj in a harness for the carriage — we wanted to go for a ride. But no sooner had I started off on Sharik on the road to Tula than a north wind blew so piercingly that I came back and [decided to] keep everyone at home. The children went out for a walk. Iljusha killed a woodcock and a drake.

I am sending you Turgenev's letter.[181]

What a stupid move on the architect's part to have the floor painted in the autumn! Anything would be better than a now damp floor which everything will stick to, and [we'll be] tormented by the smell of paint.

Well, enough talk! God willing, everything will work out; only stay healthy and cheerful, and love me. An elderly woman from Gorodnja has come; I gave her a head-scarf. She is very happy, sits with me and chatters on. Alësha is petting [the hunting dog] Bul'ka at the same time. The sky has cleared somewhat. When will you finally come? I would be so happy. Farewell, dear! I've run out of paper.

Sonja.

Did you get the receipt for the apples and your books and the inventory?

---

180 Elena Ivanovna (Alëna) Prasekina — a cook at Yasnaya Polyana.
181 A letter from the writer Turgenev in Bougival (France), dated 4 September 1882, asking for a copy of *A confession,* which had been blocked by the censors.

Nº 84 – LEV NIKOLAEVHICH TOLSTOY ❧ SOFIA ANDREEVNA TOLSTAYA
[PSS 83, p. 578]
POWER OF ATTORNEY[182]
21 May 1883. Tula.

> Your Ladyship
> Most kind Countess and
> dearest wife
> Sofia Andreevna.

I hereby grant you the authority to manage all my affairs and also authorise you to represent me in all legal, out-of-court, public-office and administrative places and institutions and with official persons of any and all agencies in [matters] concerning all my affairs: civil — in the capacity of claimant or respondent and criminal — in the capacity of counsel for the prosecution or defence or of civil plaintiff, to file any last wills and testaments drawn up at my request for probate and in confirmation of my rights of inheritance regarding estates which have come into my possession by legal inheritance, regarding my taking possession of real estate and securing my rights to real estate by all legal means. To carry out all this you are authorised: to submit any petitions, declarations, explanations, comments, replies, objections, refutations and other business documents; to present in court verbal and written explanations; to file recusal motions, to commence third party claims and to act on my behalf as a third party in proceedings, to counterclaim against a plaintiff, to deliver a defence to counterclaims against me; to raise doubts concerning the authenticity [of statements or claims] and suspicions of forgery of instruments and documents and to respond to such suspicions [on the part of others], to claim damages and legal costs for court proceedings; to bring motions to quash enforceable court orders, to bring appellate and cassation complaints in all forums, not excluding the Directing Senate; to receive from any source any kinds of copies, testimonies, memoranda, certificates, original documents and instruments, extracts from and copies of instruments, writs of execution, deeds and other business documents, to request the enforcement of decisions currently in legal force; to direct how all my real estate shall be managed; I authorise [you] to fully act on my behalf, to hire and discharge officials and servants, to lease lands, various [agricultural and hunting] grounds and government estates in operating lease on terms according to your discretion, through oral or written agreements with or without penalty. Any [of my] real estate in whole or in part I authorise you to sell at a price and under terms according to your discretion, to draw up deeds of purchase, purchase and sale agreements with or without penalty, to receive deposits and to issue receipts of deposit. Also to mortgage my real estate through private hands, Banks and societies, to draw up mortgages, to receive mortgage deeds, to issue obligations on credit terms in respect to sale and securities, to receive all receivable sums and loans, and also out of my Eastern loan bonds deposited in the State Bank to take from the Bank all or as many

---

182 In the 1880s LNT came to believe in the simplification of his life-style and the rejection of private property. He expressed these views in his writings of the time (*A confession* [*Ispoved'*] and *What I believe in* [*V chëm moja vera?*], and endeavoured to express them in his life. However, so as not to leave his large family in poverty, his first step was to transfer to SAT all rights to manage all his affairs (hence this power of attorney). Later, in 1890, he divided his property between his wife and his children, transferring to them all his property along with the rights of publication of all his works written up to 1881 — i.e. to his spiritual crisis — including his fiction works, which realised a basic income. Any works written by him after 1881 he declared to be in the public domain — i.e. anyone wishing to could publish them without paying royalties. In his 1910 will, drawn up without SAT's knowledge, he bequeathed his whole literary legacy to the public domain through his executor — i.e. his youngest daughter Aleksandra L'vovna Tolstaja.

as are deemed necessary and sign the Bank records in my stead. In general, to receive any sums owing to me from any source, as well as postal shipments, moneys and interest notes, registered letters. This authorisation may be assigned by you in whole or in part to other parties and in everything you and your fiduciaries do legally, I trust [you] and shall not argue or dispute. This power of attorney is given to Countess Sofia Andreevna Tolstaya. Lieutenant [ret.] Count Lev Tolstoy. The year one thousand eight hundred and eighty three. The twenty-first day of May. This power of attorney was executed before me, Jakov Fëdorovich Beloborodov, a Notary in and for the city of Tula, at my office, located in the First City District in Kiev Street in my own house by Lieutenant [ret.] Count Lev Nikolaevich Tolstoy living in the village of Yasnaya Polyana, Krapivna Uezd, who is personally known to me and possesses the legal capacity to draw up legal acts. Whereby I, a Notary, certify that this power of attorney was signed by Count Tolstoy in his own hand. Register № 562. Notary Beloborodov.

Nº 85 – LEV NIKOLAEVICH TOLSTOY ✒ SOFIA ANDREEVNA TOLSTAYA
[PSS 83/234]
25 May 1883. Samara farmstead.

[25th]. Wednesday.

Second morning at the farmstead.[183] —

I am not at all happy or feeling pleasant. [I would say, I am] even depressed and sad. I saw you in a dream, and I think unceasingly of you all, but I do not regret coming. I have to clear up the mess I started here. Half of last year's foals have died, and now from 80 mares [we have only] 24. I'm ashamed to say I was extremely upset, but later I rejoiced, and now I'm very glad that this silly desire has left me, and I decided to get rid of everything and sell it off. This is like the fire in the greenhouse,[184] which freed me from many vexations. It's high time I did this. We shall [still] get between 4 and 6 thousand [roubles] — of that there can be no doubt. — The leasing will take place only for mowing and ploughing, with payment in advance. At the moment we are owed 10,000 [roubles], 5,000 of which should be written off. — Please don't let this upset you, but rather let it make you happy. In any case we have a lot of extra [assets]. The sale of all our cattle, horses, buildings and sown wheat should bring us in more than 10,000 (I am deliberately underestimating the figures), so your desire to pay off the mortgage on the [Arnautov] house may come true. —

I am in a serious mood — not a joyful mood, but a calm one, and I cannot live without work. Yesterday I spent the [whole] day messing about, and I felt rotten and ashamed, and now I'm busy. I'm not interested in the lifestyles of Bibikov and Vasilij Ivanovich — they're neither fish nor fowl nor good red herring. No physical labour and no want. Nor any intellectual labour. And their relations to the *muzhiks,* the leasing of lands, bargaining, tea-drinking — these are all terribly dull, stupefying and repulsive activities. — This whole morning Pëtr Andreevich[185] (the new farmstead manager) spent in the large room, leasing out pasturelands and haggling [over the price], and I couldn't help overhearing. I'm in the end room — the children's room. I don't know how it will be later on, but right now I am uncomfortable with my unavoidable communication with Bibikov [and] Vasilij Ivanovich, and my position as a landlord, as well as

---

183 LNT left for his Samara farmstead shortly after signing the Power of Attorney on 21 May 1883.

184 The greenhouse at Yasnaya Polyana, where they grew peaches for sale, burned to the ground on 14 March 1867.

185 Pëtr Andreevich Arkhangel'skij, who took over from Aleksej Alekseevich Bibikov (see Letter Nº 56, Note 361) as manager of the Samara farmstead.

the petitions from the poor which I cannot fulfil. — Even though I'm ashamed and find it repulsive to think about my foul body, the koumiss, I know, will be helpful, especially in improving [the condition of] my stomach and, consequently, my nerves and mental state, and I will be able to do more while I am still alive, and hence I feel I should stay drinking longer, but I'm afraid I shan't hold out. Perhaps I shall move to the Karalyk. There I shall be more independent.

How is [our son] Serëzha doing? The longer I wait for him here, the more I worry about him. I shall wire you directly he arrives. —

It was interesting for me to measure myself against the life here. It seems I haven't been here that long, but I've changed enormously, — and even though you may find that it's for the worse, I know that it's for the better — I feel more at peace, and find myself more at ease with the person I am now than with what I used to be.

On my way here I saw many migrants — quite a touching and majestic sight.

Even when I am with you I worry about you all, but when I'm at a distance I try either not to think at all or think more seriously — otherwise, if I think about what could happen, I could go out of my mind with worry.

Please write me honestly, and not in a moment of concern, but in a moment of calm, how you feel about my absence; I need to know this to make a decision as to when to return. The koumiss, after all, is just a fantasy. I am ready to come home now and my heart wants to come home now, and I shall be very happy. In any case, my trip has already had a result, a very important result, namely the simplifying of household management. Farewell, darling, hugs and kisses to you, the children, Tanja and her children.[186] And to the whole family.

On the envelope: Tula. Countess Sofia Andreevna Tolstaya.

Nº 86 – SOFIA ANDREEVNA TOLSTAYA ❧ LEV NIKOLAEVICH TOLSTOY
[LSA 85]
29 May [1883. Yasnaya Polyana]

Dear Lëvochka, I already sent you a letter to Samara, General Delivery, and that's how I shall write from now on, but just this one letter I am sending through the local Patrovka administration — hopefully it will reach you. My home situation is not entirely peaceful, since Alësha[187] and Andrjusha are coughing terribly — very much like whooping-cough. Alësha vomited several times yesterday from the coughing; Andrjusha hasn't done any vomiting yet, but he chokes and coughs in fits. Misha, on the other hand, is just about healthy. My sister Tanja has also had a terrible cough. Nighttimes are horrid because of the children's coughing, but in the morning they get up and seem much better, they play and eat — and I tend to calm down. We're having marvellous weather. Not hot, but clear, calm and beautiful. The evening and night [air] is fresh, there's a new moon out; the greenery, grass and foliage — it's all so fresh, strong and thick, and is growing fantastically this year. Il'ja, Alcide[188] and Lëlja go hunting with dogs in the company of Golovin and his wife;[189] Il'ja killed two hares. They apparently have quite a fun time: they have tea and bread; yesterday they asked me for a pie with jam — and off they go to the woods.

---

186 SAT's sister Tanja and her children Marija, Vera, Mikhail, Aleksandr and Vasilij.
187 Aleksej L'vovich (Alësha) Tolstoj — see Letter Nº 62, Note 31.
188 Alcide Seuron (1869–1891) — son to Mme Anna Seuron (*née* Weber; 1845–1922), French/German governess to the Tolstoys' children, author of the reminiscences *Graf Leo Tolstoi von Anna Seuron.*
189 Jakov Ivanovich Golovin (1852–?) — landowner, hunter, and his wife Ol'ga Sergeevna Golovina (*née* Fëdorova).

[Our daughter] Tanja works on a portrait of Mme Seuron in the mornings, sometimes she also takes a pencil and does some drawing. Then she reads. Sometimes they go for a ride or play croquet. I write all day long now — transcribing this French article.[190] In the evenings I play croquet with Tanja. Today [Leonid Dmitrievich] Urusov is here, as was Ivan Ivanovich Raevskij — he had dinner and spent the evening with us. I went to see Marfa Evdokimovna,[191] who is ill. I think she has typhoid fever; I gave her a little advice, and want to look after her properly. The one thing that gives me real pleasure is treating the sick, especially when the treatment is successful. There are an awful lot of sick people; [many] come from far away. Today they brought in such an unfortunate *muzhik,* who was simply a fright with his fever. [When] I gave him some wine, he trembled all over, [then] I gave him tea and quinine. I have no idea what will become of him, but I would like to know if he will recover.

We all live calmly and on good terms; the children study and behave themselves well.

There are times when I feel unbearably lonely and melancholy without you, but these last but moments, and in my mind I want you to go on drinking koumiss [at least] a little longer and take a little rest from us and our life that you do not much care for. Just so that some 'M-a'[192] doesn't come skipping up [to you] and that people claiming moral possession over you don't distract your soul. — [Our son] Serëzha is probably with you by now; I am grateful to him for selling the boat, and for being rational, and for writing me — I received all his letters. But from you I've received only one letter;[193] I'd like there to be another one as soon as possible; when you're away, your letters help me live, just like your voice when you're around; but your voice helps me [only] when you love me along with it, — but now that's changed a great deal.

Farewell, hugs and kisses to you and Serëzha.

Sonja.

Nº 87 – LEV NIKOLAEVICH TOLSTOY ✷ SOFIA ANDREEVNA TOLSTAYA
[PSS 83/244]
29 September 1883. Yasnaya Polyana.

Thursday.

Today I arrived from Krapivna. I went there on a summons to jury duty. I arrived between 2 and 3 in the afternoon. The proceedings had already begun, and I was fined 100 roubles. When I received the summons, I said I could not be a juror. They asked: Why? I replied: On account of my religious convictions. Then they asked a second time whether I was refusing categorically. I said there was no way I could [accept]. And I left. The whole conversation was very polite. Now they will probably impose an additional 200-rouble fine, and I don't know whether it will end there. I think it will.

As to whether I was absolutely *unable* to act otherwise, I'm sure you will have no doubt. But please don't be angry at me for not telling you that I was appointed a juror. I would have told you if you'd asked or I had the occasion to; but I didn't feel like telling you outright. You would

---

190 this French article — a French version of *A confession [Ispoved']* which LNT was preparing for *La Nouvelle revue*; in this journal Nº 23 (1883), was published his *Foreword to The Gospel in brief [Krakoe izlozhenie Evangelija]* under the heading *Pages inédites de Léon Tolstoi [Unpublished pages by Leo Tolstoy].*

191 Marfa Evdokimovna Fokanova — a Yasnaya Polyana peasant.

192 *M-a* — an abbreviated reference to a landowner named Pelageja Nikolaevna Metelitsyna, who spent a year doing farm labour and wrote an article entitled *God v batrachkakh [A year as a farm labourer],* published in *Otechestvennye zapiski.* In 1883 the Tolstoys' Samara farmstead began to be worked by women farm labourers.

193 A letter written 23 May 1883, not included in the present volume (see PSS 83: 375–76).

have worried, and you would have alarmed me; I was alarmed as it was and was trying with all my might to calm myself down. I did want to stay [in Moscow] or go back to Yasnaya, but then there was this [summons]. And so please don't be angry with me. I could have simply not gone at all. In that case there would have been the same fines, and they would have summoned me again the next time. But now I've told them once and for all that I cannot be [a juror]. I told them in as soft a manner [as I could], and even with that kind of expression nobody — [they were all] *muzhiks* — understood. — I didn't see any of the court officials. I spent the night at Krapivna. I kept reading Turgenev.[194] And today at 9 o'clock I headed out. The day is clear and hot — miraculously fine! I arrived at 12, and since nothing was ready [to eat], I went out after some woodcocks, and ended up walking around until 5 o'clock; now I've come back and am writing to you. —

I still have not received my proofs[195] yet. I've been working just one day and haven't finished the conclusion. But it seems very important to me, and I'm constantly thinking about it. — Tomorrow I'll get down to it, if the spirit moves; if not, I'll go [hunting] with my dogs. I haven't yet decided when I'll go. I want to get [this] finished; if only I could put in a day or two of solid work, I'd come [to see you] right away, since I miss you all and am worried about you. Pity that I write and think not just about you alone, but about you and the children, imagining that they will be reading this letter, and so I don't write the way I want to. In any case I am writing it all on the same page.

I especially want to see you. During this past while (I can't say exactly how long — it's been continuing to grow) you've become especially dear and interesting to me, and *dear* in all respects. It seems a new bond is being forged between us, and I worry terribly that it might break. —

Despite the beauty here, I shall soon come [to see you]. I haven't been receiving any letters, as I have not sent [anyone] to Tula [to check the post]. I'll do that tomorrow.

Farewell, darling. Hugs and kisses to you and the children. Regards to Mme Seuron.

Right now I'm very tired and I'm famished. I'm writing before dinner. And I'll write you [another] letter. —

On the envelope: Moscow. Khamovniki Lane. Countess Sofia Andreevna Tolstaya. Private house.

N° 88 – LEV NIKOLAEVICH TOLSTOY ❧ SOFIA ANDREEVNA TOLSTAYA
[PSS 83/245]
30 September1883. Yasnaya Polyana.

Friday evening.

I have now received from Kozlovka your two letters and a telegram, — two splendid letters.[196] Both of them indicate to me that you are in that same lovely good spirit which I left you in, and which you've been in, with minor interruptions, for a long time. — Read this letter

194 Turgenev passed away in Bougival (France) on 22 August 1883. LNT was reading Turgenev's works in preparation for speaking on Turgenev (by invitation) to the Society of Lovers of Russian Language & Literature [Obshchestvo ljubitelej rossijskoj slovesnosti] in Moscow.

195 A reference to the proofs of his treatise *What I believe* [*V chëm moja vera?*], originally scheduled to be published in the journal *Russkaja mysl'*. LNT was currently working on the conclusion to this treatise. He later decided to have it published as a separate edition rather than in the journal.

196 These letters were written on 28 and 29 September 1883 (not included in the present volume) — see *Letters of S. A. Tolstaya to L. N. Tolstoy [Pis'ma k L. N. Tolstomu]*, pp. 230–32.

alone to yourself. — Never have I thought about you so much, never have my thoughts about you been so good and absolutely pure as now. — You are precious to me in every respect. —

I keep thinking about Turgenev and I love him terribly; I feel sorry for him and can't stop reading him. I am constantly living with him. I shall for certain be either reading him, or I shall write something about him and share it with others.

Tell Jur'ev[197] that I will [speak], but that the 15th [of October] is better.

As to the proofs, I asked the printshop technical manager and Lavrov[198] to send them to me at Yasenki. I think they sent a second copy to Yasenki. In any case send them to me at Yasenki. I am getting along here very well indeed. I haven't got anything written down on paper, but have been doing a lot of good thinking and am waiting for the first good working day. My health is not perfect — my stomach is still disordered. Today I did a little work — [but] I saw it wasn't going well and [instead] I went [hunting] with Tit[199] and the dogs — we caught a splendid fox and a brown hare.

I feel very ashamed, knowing that you are miserable, troubled and burdened, while I am doing so splendidly; but I comfort myself with the thought that this is necessary for my work. What seemed fine to me in Moscow with my frazzled nerves is here being transformed and becoming so clear that I actually find joy in it. On the scale of life I feel perfect here. Of course I sense the absence — and very much so — of you and the children, but the quiet and the solitude are like a bath to me.

Whether I stay here another week I shall decide on the basis of your letters. Only don't think that I very much want to stay. I feel good with all of you, and good here, too, and neither one nor the other predominates, so that even if one move of the finger should tip the scale to either side, I shall be satisfied in every way. Despite my stomach disorder, I am in good spirits, and I love everyone — you most of all. — I've been reading Turgenev's [1864 story] "Enough" [*Dovol'no*]. Read it, what a charming piece! — Hugs and kisses to you and the children. Regards to Mme Seuron. I feel sorry for you most of all regarding Kostin'ka.[200] Don't spend [a lot of time] with him. —

On the envelope: Moscow. Khamovniki Lane. Tolstoy house. Countess Sofia Andreevna Tolstaya.

Nº 89 – SOFIA ANDREEVNA TOLSTAYA ❧ LEV NIKOLAEVICH TOLSTOY
[LSA 98]
1 October [1883. Moscow]

It's now the third day that I've received your letters on time,[201] dear Lëvochka. Pity that [in your letters] to me you write mostly about me, since that prevents me from being completely

---

197 Sergej Andreevich Jur'ev (1821–1888) — literary critic, appointed in 1878 as the Chairman of the Society of Lovers of Russian Language & Literature, who was in charge of setting up the memorial service for Turgenev. Jur'ev had visited SAT in Moscow to ask what day LNT could give his speech on Turgenev — the 8th or the 15th of October.

198 Vukol Mikhajlovich Lavrov (1852–1912) — writer, editor (from 1880) of the journal *Russkaja mysl'*, which proposed to publish LNT's treatise *What I believe* [*V chëm moja vera?*].

199 Tit Ivanovich Polin (Pelagejushkin; 1867–1932) — one of the Tolstoys' servants.

200 SAT wrote on 29 September 1883: "Uncle Kostja is here again; last night he spent up to 2 a.m. pouring out all the bitterness of his situation to me and his reproaches to everybody in the world" — *Letters of S. A. Tolstaya to L. N. Tolstoy* [*Pis'ma k L. N. Tolstomu*], p. 232.

201 In response to Letter Nº 88 of 30 September 1883.

natural, and instinctively I shall be trying either to write what pleases you or to make a deliberate effort to be natural and genuine — which often leads to harshness.

I'm afraid that in my letter of yesterday I was not sufficiently soft in responding to your refusal to be a juror. The old selfish feeling arose in me that you don't care about your family and are making us alarmed about you and your safety. Of course you acted according to your convictions, but if you had not gone at all nor said anything, and [simply] paid the fine, you would also have been acting on your convictions, only without taking any risks and without upsetting anybody. You hid this from me because you knew that this is what I would have wanted and insisted upon. But you inadvertently took pleasure in saying it publicly and taking some kind of risk.

I am not moving my finger to tip the scale in my favour. I well understand that quiet is something extremely necessary for a man who works with his mind. Stay [at Yasnaya] as long as you need to and as long as you like. It seems to me that when you feel good, peaceful and calm, I feel [at least] half better on account of that. Our times here are very troubling and sometimes extremely difficult. I am quite calm, even overly so, but my back hurts and I have a gnawing feeling in my soul. *Nothing,* positively *nothing,* brings me joy.

Can I be better for having lost my capacity for joy?

I bought [a picture of] Turgenev lying in his coffin; the photo is marvellous. I've been looking into his calm visage and thinking so clearly, so sincerely: "If only I could go where he is… how good it would be!"

Today I went with [my children] Tanja, Masha, Andrjusha and Misha to vespers at the Cathedral of the Saviour.[202] My little ones have been tormenting me, they kept asking to go there as Liza and Varja had been there and told [them about it]. It made no [particular] impression [on me] — it was majestic, bright, crowded, nothing more. But the little ones were happy about both the [carriage] ride and the church.

Tanja all this time has been very precious and friendly. Il'ja, Masha and Lëlja very well behaved, while Serëzha is very often rude and unpleasant. That's so sad! We hired a teacher for Lëlja today, a student, on Serëzha's recommendation. I liked his looks and his modesty.

Liza Obolenskaja[203] was here with her two daughters, who played croquet with Masha and Andrjusha and really had a good time.

You know, Lëvochka, that Kosten'ka[204] has practically made himself a home here! He sleeps in your study, and from morning 'til night he keeps after me — confidently and boldly — he either demands all sorts of improvements in my household, or snacks, or wine, or he starts making fun of me for writing you every day, or he [tries to] teach me how to live… Sometimes I just feel like crying, I've run out of patience! Everything my frail soul can muster to combat this troublesome everyday life and clamber out of it into the light — all that is suddenly, I feel, perishing. I am getting weaker, I listen patiently to [stories] about gilded picture-frames or his social successes, while all along just as patiently a book lies before me, waiting for me [to read]. — Our daughter Tanja is beginning to experience the same thing. Today she, [too,] kept running around the house with a book [in her hand], just [trying] to get away from him.

202 Cathedral of Christ the Saviour in central Moscow. The foundation was laid on 23 September 1839 — an event witnessed by LNT as a child — and the cathedral was consecrated on 26 May 1883. It was destroyed by Stalin's order in 1931, and from 1960 to 1994 the site was used for a huge swimming-pool. After the collapse of the Soviet system, the original church was reconstructed (1994–97).
203 Elizaveta Valer'janovna (Liza) Obolenskaja (see Letter Nº 40, Note 259) with her daughters Marija and Aleksandra.
204 Konstantin Aleksandrovich (Kostja, Kosten'ka) Islavin — SAT's uncle (see Letter Nº 47, Note 301).

But it seems that I complain too much. He's [actually] quite pitiful. Madame [Seuron] thanks you for remembering her. They didn't manage to get the proofs to the post office today. According to their new procedures they are only open 'til noon on major holidays, and I got the telegram[205] right at 12, and it was frightfully mixed up. I'll send [the proofs] off tomorrow; pity that they will [arrive] a whole day later.

I'm glad that you're doing fine at Yasnaya, but [try to] be more careful with your stomach. Farewell for now. My letters are too long and empty. Tell Mitrofan[206] to prepare your fox fur, give it back [to you] and send it to me along with Tanja's [furs]. Go to Chepyzh[207] and dig up three or four young oaks and bring them to me to plant in the garden here (for sentiment's sake). There are no oak trees here. Well, now I've run out of paper. Hugs and kisses.

S.

N° 90 – LEV NIKOLAEVICH TOLSTOY ❧ SOFIA ANDREEVNA TOLSTAYA
[PSS 83/251]
10 November 1883. Yasnaya Polyana.

Thursday, 10 p.m.

I had a bad sleep. It was cold and I didn't feel well. But everything's fine now. I stoked [the stove] in my study, greased the windows, and the evening is good and warm now, I feel marvellous. — Today I received letters from Yasenki — some interesting ones from Sandoz[208] and another one from a Frenchman [unknown]. I went to look at the horses. Very good ones, but I'm afraid there will be some worries and troubles on account of them, and I shall try to sell them. — They will eat hay, but it'll be a while before they fetch an income. Filipp[209] was not at home. He was taking [his son] Mikhail to the conscription office. Thank God they didn't take him; he remains exempt. Nikolaj Mikhajlovich[210] brought [his son as well], but they didn't take him either. At the stable [I] met a *muzhik* with a woman. The *muzhik* came to see you from some distance, from the other side of the *Zaseka*, for treatment; he was terribly disappointed that you weren't here. He said he knows one *muzhik* whom everybody treated and nobody could cure him, but you cured him.[211] I even felt flattered. Then a woman in her late pregnancy who had four little children — along with her elderly mother-in-law and a young relative who is the daughter-in-law of her husband's brother. There were two *muzhiks* [in the family], and in a single week her husband was put in prison for a fight which resulted in someone's death, and her brother-in-law was forcibly conscripted. And she was left all alone. I wrote a letter to Davydov,[212] asking whether [her husband] couldn't be released on bail. After that I sat down to work, but got very little done. Mitrofan [Nikolaevich Bannikov] told me that [my brother] Serëzha will be having dinner at Bibikov's.[213] I walked over to Teljatinki, but Serëzha had left for Moscow. I returned and had dinner. Agaf'ja Mikhajlovna is sitting [here] and Dmitrij

---

205 A telegram from the print-shop demanding that the proofs be sent at once.
206 Mitrofan Nikolaevich Bannikov (foreman) — see Letter N° 71, Note 104.
207 *Chepyzh* — the name of a grove on the Yasnaya Polyana estate.
208 *Sandoz* — a Tolstoyan from Switzerland (no further details known).
209 Filipp Rodrigovich Egorov (coachman) — see Letter N° 73, Note 110. His eldest son was Mikhail Filippovich Egorov.
210 Nikolaj Mikhajlovich Rumjantsev (cook) — see Letter N° 5, Note 27.
211 The reference here is to a peasant from the village of Rvy (see SAT's Letter N° 92 of 12 November 1883).
212 Nikolaj Vasil'evich Davydov (1848–1920) — prosecutor of the Tula District Court, whom LNT became acquainted with in 1878. LNT's letter to him is dated 10 November 1883 (PSS 63: 140).
213 Aleksandr Nikolaevich Bibikov (neighbour) — see Letter N° 34, Note 205.

Fëdorovich[214] is transcribing. The room has warmed up. I'm also stoking [the stove in] the boys' room with the vaulted ceiling. If it warms up, I'll move in there tomorrow. I forgot [my copy of] *Une Vie*[215] at home. In the meantime read it and keep it in a safe place.

Your portrait in pencil[216] seems poor, but whenever I look at it, I have terribly vivid memories, and there's something sorrowful in it, something like the feeling I had when we last said good-bye to each other. And that moves me deeply. Darling, why are you unhappy? It is so evident to me how you can and should be happy, and how you torment yourself with your *révolte* against everything. Is self-resignation truly impossible? How good everything would be for you and everybody around you! As I write this I can just imagine how it might make you angry. Don't be angry, my dove; just looking at this portrait makes me realise how much I love you and need you. —

Hugs and kisses to you and the children, and regards to Mme Seuron.

On the envelope: Moscow. Khamovniki Lane in her private house. Countess Sofia Andreevna Tolstaya.

Nº 91 – LEV NIKOLAEVICH TOLSTOY ❧ SOFIA ANDREEVNA TOLSTAYA
[PSS 83/252]
11 November1883. Yasnaya Polyana.

It is my fate [for the time being] to be here at Yasnaya in a bad mental state and incapable of working. It's that way right now, too. I can't finish what I started. I feel warm, good, comfortable, and have my customary food. I received your letter[217] today and hope to receive another one tomorrow.

Just imagine, the Lieutenant's wife died. I was out for a walk today and dropped in to see Frants Ivanovich,[218] and he told me. She went to Tula. An acquaintance was staying in the room next door. He spent the evening with her. She didn't come out of her [hotel] room all the next day. They broke down the door. She was lying in bed, in the most restful pose — dead — from a heart rupture. I am reading both Stendhal[219] and Engelhardt.[220] Engelhardt is a charm. I can't read him or praise him enough; — a real contrast between our life and the actual life of the *muzhiks,* which we try so hard to forget. For me, it's one of those books that free me, in part, from what I feel obligated to do. But he did it, and nobody reads it. Or they read and say: "Well, he's a socialist." But he's by no means a socialist, he just tells it like it is. — Today I received a reply from [Nikolaj Vasil'evich] Davydov regarding the woman I was asking him about. He promises to do whatever he can and asks if he can come see me Sunday; he says he needs to

214 Dmitrij Fëdorovich Vinogradov (teacher) — see Letter Nº 60, Note 16.
215 *Une Vie* — an 1883 novel by Guy de Maupassant. LNT was quite enamoured of this work. In a preface to a Russian translation of de Maupassant's works (1894) he wrote: "*Une Vie* is a superb novel, not only de Maupassant's best novel without compare, but possibly the best French novel [ever], after Hugo's *Les Misérables*" (PSS 30: 7).
216 A pencil portrait of SAT, executed (in her words) "by a student at the Sokolovskij Institute".
217 Most probably, a letter written 10 November 1883 (*Letters to L. N. Tolstoy,* p. 240).
218 Lieutenant Frants Ivanovich Baratynskij — a state forester in the Zaseka, whose wife had just passed on.
219 LNT was reading the novel *Le Rouge et le Noir* by Stendhal (real name: Henri Beyle), whom he considered a writer that had greatly influenced him. In November 1883 LNT wrote: "I read this about 40 years ago, but don't remember anything except my feeling towards the author — an affinity with [his boldness], a kinship, but also a dissatisfaction. And it's strange: I have the same feelings now, but with a clear awareness of why and wherefore" (PSS 83: 410).
220 LNT was also reading *Pis'ma iz derevni* [*Letters from the country*] by political commentator and agricultural scientist Aleksandr Nikolaevich Engel'gardt (Engelhardt; 1832–1893).

see me regarding something *for himself*. If I have an opportunity, I shall invite him. — Today another woman came by, also in her late pregnancy, who has also been left all alone with four children. This is the widow of the one who was killed in the fight. She came to ask me not to request her husband's murderer to be released on bail. — Amazing!

How are you and all our people doing? *I hope*,[221] they're doing fine. I'll know tomorrow. Hugs and kisses to you, darling. Today your portrait doesn't seem so bad.

Hugs and kisses to the children.

Friday, 11 o'clock.

I'm alone at the moment. Only Dmitrij Fëdorovich [Vinogradov] was here; we talked about how he gets by (himself and his family) on 11 roubles 40 kopeks a month. He gets by.

On the envelope: Moscow. Khamovniki Lane. Countess Sofia Andreevna Tolstaya. (Private house.)

Nº 92 – SOFIA ANDREEVNA TOLSTAYA ❧ LEV NIKOLAEVICH TOLSTOY
[LSA 102]
12 November [1883]. Saturday. [Moscow]

I'm terribly sorry you are not feeling yourself, dear Lëvochka. It's as though you simply wasted your time going and living at Yasnaya. Maybe someone will need you there, and that's fine. I myself would be only too glad to treat anyone — but there's nothing to do here in Moscow [along that line]. I'm happy that the *muzhik* with wounds on his legs recovered — for three years he hadn't walked (probably [the man] from Rvy)[222] — I tried my best with him; sometimes you're just not in the mood, and you barely care about your patient, while at other times everything becomes clear and you're eager to get involved, and things come out right. Today I'm not myself either: my back aches terribly, I spent an alarming, feverish night, and woke up all in a sweat. Thinking of how hot I felt, I looked at the thermometer and it was only 13. I dreamt that two teeth had fallen out[223] and you see — I learnt the news, and so I was profoundly shocked by the Lieutenant's wife's death; and now Sasha Perfil'ev,[224] a cadet, comes and tells me Koshelev[225] died. Which Koshelev, I don't know, the father or the son, it's not in the papers yet, but it is known that the Beklemishevs (Aleksandr Ivanovich's daughter) are very distressed.

Today I received a letter from Arkhangel'skij[226] — he sold 57 bulls for 59 roubles each, and is sending 4,000 silver roubles to my name through the State Bank. Now I shall send the money to Tula and purchase a grand piano, as the children are really after me about that.

Today was a marvellous frosty day; on days like these we've usually gone skating around the whole pond. And since I am especially skilled at grieving, I was once again brought to tears by my past experiences — what used to weigh me down but has now become dear and precious [to

221 *I hope* — phrase given in English.
222 See the first paragraph of Letter Nº 90 (of 10 November 1883) and Note 211 therein.
223 In Russian tradition, two teeth falling out with no blood can be seen as a premonition of ill health or a personal loss.
224 Aleksandr Sergeevich (Sasha) Perfil'ev — grandson to Stepan Vasil'evich Perfil'ev (see Letter Nº 16, Note 94).
225 Aleksandr Ivanovich Koshelev (1806–1883) — Slavophile political commentator and activist. His son Ivan Aleksandrovich Koshelev (1836–?) had the rank of Court Councillor. His daughter, Dar'ja Aleksandrovna (1844–?) was married to Fëdor Andreevich Beklemishev (1830–1906), a chamberlain and governor of Khar'kov. They were acquaintances of the Tolstoys' in Moscow.
226 Pëtr Andreevich Arkhangel'skij (farmstead manager) — see Letter Nº 85, Note 185.

me]. And I was thinking about myself — that if *I* wasn't good before, what kind of a meanie am I now?! And if *you* were good before, how much better you are now!

[Our daughter] Tanja is asking me to write something about her — but I haven't anything good to write about her. She doesn't do anything, hasn't been going to school. She's enthusiastically preparing for the student concert tomorrow — she's getting flowers and gloves ready, and is asking me to go, which I find extremely difficult. Her health is not good either. Her time of the month lasted just one day, and this after almost seven weeks. Andrjusha is also getting frail, pale and weak, and still has diarrhœa. The others are fine: Alësha is so cheerful he amuses the whole house.

[Since] Mme Seuron is reading *Une Vie*, I am still reading Alexandre Dumas *fils*,[227] but I don't really care for his reflections on Faust; you can't make sense of *his* point of view.

Tanja and Anna Olsuf'eva[228] were here, along with Madame Bojanus,[229] whom I didn't see.

Sergej [Petrovich Arbuzov] drinks without stopping. He keeps asking to go to Yasnaya, but I'm afraid to let him go; they'll put him off [the train] at the first station. If I didn't think that Arisha[230] was coming, I would have sent him [to Yasnaya], and I don't know what to do! New instances of his wretched behaviour have come to light; I'll have to send him off, even though I've grown accustomed to him.

I write every day on time, and every day I receive a letter from you. When are you thinking of coming back? And now farewell. What long letters we write to each other, even if it's [as often as] every day!

S.

I just read over [my] letter — it is indeed pretty empty, with no real content.

Nº 93 – LEV NIKOLAEVICH TOLSTOY ❧ SOFIA ANDREEVNA TOLSTAYA
[PSS 83/258]
28 January 1884. Yasnaya Polyana.

Saturday evening.

Yesterday I was up late reading Droz's book.[231] Tell [my brother] Serëzha that the book is very good. The overall view is not good — [the author] is young and still green behind the ears, but there's a lot [in him] that is good and clever. Today I've been reading Shakespeare's *Coriolanus* — in an excellent German translation — it reads very easily, but — [the story is] undoubtedly nonsense, which can please only the actors.

I'm not feeling well today and don't want [to go outdoors] into the frost. Must be that I got overly tired yesterday. I have guests here at the moment: Agaf'ja Mikhajlovna, Dmitrij Fëdorovich[232] and Mitrofan [Bannikov], and they are keeping me from writing [this letter] — in any case, there's nothing to write about. — It's warm in the house, and I'll move [there] tomorrow, if

227 This is probably a reference to Alexandre Dumas-fils' Preface to the French translation of Gœthe's *Faust*, published in 1873.
228 Tat'jana Aleksandrovna Olsuf'eva (a friend of the Tolstoys' daughter Tanja) and her sister Anna Aleksandrovna Levitskaja (*née* Olsuf'eva) — daughters to the Tolstoys' Moscow neighbour Vasilij Aleksandrovich Olsuf'ev.
229 Ol'ga Semënovna Bojanus (acquaintance) — see Letter Nº 77, Note 132.
230 Arina Grigor'evna (Arisha) Arbuzova — wife to Sergej Petrovich Arbuzov (see Letter Nº 4, Note 15).
231 The reference is probably to the book *Tristesses et sourires* (35th ed., Paris, 1884) by French author Gustave Droz (1832–1895), a copy of which is to be found in the Yasnaya Polyana library.
232 Dmitrij Fëdorovich Vinogradov (teacher) — see Letter Nº 60, Note 10.

it's not too cold and there's no carbon monoxide. — Don't worry [about me], as I approach my old age I involuntarily watch out for myself, so much so that it's even repulsive. How are you all doing? There are quite a lot of you now, and each of you has many temptations [to deal with]. Hugs and kisses to you and the children.

L. T.

On the envelope: Moscow. Khamovniki. Count Tolstoy's house. Countess Sofia Andreevna Tolstaya.

Nº 94 – SOFIA ANDREEVNA TOLSTAYA ✍ LEV NIKOLAEVICH TOLSTOY
[LSA 104]
29 January. Sunday evening. 1884. [Moscow]

I've just received your letter,[233] dear Lëvochka, and I'm very sorry [to hear] you're not well. If this continues, it's better you come back; otherwise with a below-normal room temperature and unhealthy food you'll really get ill. And the weather [here] is magnificent, healthy and exhilarating — today I drove out, took a book to Princess Urusova,[234] and from there I went to see Kushnerëv[235] and Marakuev for copies. I really liked Princess Varvara Dmitrievna, too; she and I talked a lot — I stayed there for over an hour. She is both intelligent and understanding about everything, and must be a kind [person]. She has a very pleasant and lively face; I shall visit them on occasion. Another of his sisters, Ivanova,[236] is also quite likeable, but I didn't talk as much with her. — I found Kushnerev ill, in a dressing-gown. He was greatly apologetic, but I needed to obtain some copies, and I asked him [for them]. He said: "Here's my card, but ask Marakuev." However, the night before I had sent Serëzha to see Marakuev, but Marakuev very simply declared that since everyone was really interested in this work, he'd given all [the copies] out for reading and transcribing. I got so angry that today I went myself and told him: "The copies are not yours, but the Count's, and he did not ask you, nor did he authorise you to give them out. And you must agree that the Count's close relations, too, at the very least are equally entitled to their interest in his works, if not more." He promised to bring two [copies] tomorrow. But don't get upset with me: it simply confirmed to me that he is an extremely arrogant man, and we must be careful with him. (There were no unpleasantries between us.)

[Our daughter] Masha is still in the same condition: she has a temperature of 39.3 and her throat is very red and bloated. But there is no gathering and no abscess. She stays lying [in bed] and will not eat anything. Tanja has a stomach ache; she didn't eat dinner, it's just *the time* [of the month]. I'm trying to persuade her not to go to the ball today, but she is determined; it would grieve me to go today and leave Masha and get all tired myself, and pull Tanja away on the first day of her time.

---

233 Letter Nº 93 of 28 January 1884.
234 Princess Varvara Dmitrievna Urusova — sister to Prince Leonid Dmitrievich Urusov (see Letter Nº 57, Note 1).
235 Ivan Nikolaevich Kushnerëv (1827–1896) — print-shop owner; also a writer and publisher of the journal *Russkaja mysl'*. Here, too, Tolstoy's censored *What I believe* [*V chëm moja vera?*] was printed as a separate edition in 50 copies, which were mainly distributed by Vladimir Nikolaevich Marakuev (?–1921), a journalist, publisher of books for the common people, to whom LNT turned to for copies.
236 Adelaida Dmitrievna Ivanova (*née* Urusova) — another sister to Leonid Dmitrievich Urusov.

Marakuev said that the secular censorship board passed your new book along to the religious censors; and that the archimandrite,[237] the head of the censorship committee, read it and said that this book contains so many exalted truths that one cannot help but admit them, and that he from his point of view saw no reason not to let it through. — But I think that Pobedonostsev,[238] tactless and pedantic as he is, will once again reject it. For the moment it is locked away at Kushnerëv's and there is no [final] decision.

Il'ja and Lëlja had dinner at Uncle Serëzha's. [Our son] Serëzha [dined] at home, but now he's off to Petrovskoe-Razumovskoe with the Counts Olsuf'ev, while Il'ja and Lëlja will stay at home.

For a black [steed] they're offering 250 silver roubles, the purchaser is *serious*; I saw him today. Wire me as soon as you can whether I should sell, and include [a word about] your health in the telegram. Don't worry about us; while you're gone I have [enough] energy for the two [of us], and if it gets bad, I'll wire you.

Hugs and kisses.

S.

N° 95 – LEV NIKOLAEVICH TOLSTOY ❧ SOFIA ANDREEVNA TOLSTAYA
[PSS 83/260]
30 January 1884. Yasnaya Polyana.

At Bibikov's I ran into Borisevich.[239] He's 89 years old, and he's strong, fresh and agile as a young man. He talked incessantly and told me a lot of interesting things. Close to 12, Filip[240] came for me and I went home. I read *Kaliki perekhozhie*[241] [Wandering minstrels], poems. I was led to read these by my ideas for a folk drama.[242] I'm contemplating this with great pleasure. And, as always, it is continuing to grow and, most importantly, deepen, and is starting to become a very serious [project] for me. I spent all afternoon at home from 12 to 10 [p.m.], except for taking a two-hour walk, and even though I didn't have gas poisoning, I'm still afraid of carbon monoxide, and now I've opened the pipe and I myself will take a ride over to Kozlovka. At the moment you're probably getting ready to go to the ball. I feel very sorry for both you and Tanja.

Today Vlas[243] was saying that a boy came to the door begging. I said: "Tell him to come here." A lad came in a little taller than Andrjusha, with a bag over his shoulder. "Where are you from?" [I asked.] "From the other side of the *Zaseka*" [he replied]. — "Who sent you?" — "No one. I'm alone." — "What does your father do?" — "He's abandoned us. When Mama died, he left and never came back." And the boy started to cry. He has three others left, younger than he. A landlady took the children. "She feeds the poor," he said. — I offered the boy some tea. He

---

237 Archimandrite Amfilokhij (secular name: Pavel Ivanovich Sergievskij-Kazantsev; 1818–1893) — Prior of the Svjato-Danilov Monastery; chairman of the censorship committee.
238 Konstantin Petrovich Pobedonostsev (1827–1906) — Senior Procurator of the Holy Synod (1880–1905).
239 Possibly a reference to Ivan Ignat'evich Borisevich (Borysiewicz?; 1792–1888) — a Polish nobleman living in Chern' (Tula Gubernia).
240 Filip Rodionovich Egorov (coachman) — see Letter N° 73, Note 110.
241 *Kaliki perekhozhie* [*Wandering minstrels*] — a collection of spiritual verse by Slavic philologist Pëtr Alekseevich Bessnov (1828–1898) published in Moscow in two parts (6 editions) between 1861 and 1864.
242 In early 1884 LNT sketched out a plan for a folk drama *Peter the Publican* [*Pëtr khlebnik*]. In his introduction to Act I he mentions Bessonov's collection "Kaliki perekhozhie, Part II, 5th ed., p. 26". A rough draft was completed in 1894, but the play was not published during LNT's lifetime.
243 Vlas Anisimovich Vorobëv (1853–1929) — a Yasnaya Polyana peasant, who did yard-keeping for the Tolstoys.

drank it up, turned the glass over, put a tiny bit of sugar on top and thanked me.[244] He didn't want anything more to drink. I was going to give him something more to eat, but Vlas said they had given him something to eat in the office. But then he started to cry and didn't eat anything more. — His voice was hoarse, and he smelt like a *muzhik*. — Everything he told me about his father, his uncles and those he came in contact with — all that is a tale of poor, drunken and cruel people. Only the landlady was kind. There are so many boys, women, old men and women like him that I see here, and I love to see them. — Agaf'ja Mikhajlovna is very grateful to Mme Seuron, to whom she sends her respects. Mar'ja Afanas'evna [a retired nanny] was here. She seems to be kinder to us, and sends her regards to everyone, especially Masha. I hope that [Masha's] throat condition has passed. I am talking with Vlas about books [aimed at common people]. We'll have to start a library for *muzhiks*.

On the envelope: Moscow. Khamovniki. Countess Sofia Andreevna Tolstaya. Private house.

N° 96 – SOFIA ANDREEVNA TOLSTAYA ✍ LEV NIKOLAEVICH TOLSTOY
[LSA 106]
31 [January 1884]. Tuesday. [Moscow]

Your letter today[245] is a whole story — idealised, as always, but still interesting and touching. I feel a bit as though you're rebuking me and drawing a deliberate contrast between the poverty of the people and the mindless luxury of the balls we've been attending.

And these balls have left my head so empty; I'm so tired that I've been cranky the whole day.

In any event, I got up and gave Andrjusha a lesson; I am constantly trying to develop him, and he is very compliant in this. Then I did some sewing. I kept my eye on Lëlja the whole day and followed his lessons, since Madame [Seuron] has been off somewhere since this morning. Il'ja entered Malysh in a dog-show and is terribly cheerful; Serëzha's gone to the [university] canteen today where there's a big gathering of students. They have a story: they planned to organise a student ball at the Bolshoi Theatre. The authorities were willing to permit it if the rector vouched for the students. The rector did so. But a couple of second-year medical students went to the rector on their own, without the knowledge of students from other courses and departments, [telling him] they, the students, didn't want any authorities attending the ball. The rector[246] said: "In that case I cannot allow the ball, since I can't take on the responsibility." The students attacked the 'medics', and today they were summoned to the canteen to explain themselves. If only this doesn't result in a fight or any unpleasantries; I'm anxious about Serëzha, he hasn't come home yet.

Marakuev finally brought two copies[247] and Serëzha, Tanja and Uncle Kostja have started reading. I haven't yet heard anything about censorship, beyond what I wrote you [earlier].

The Samara estate manager sent me 2,500 silver roubles, but there's no indication what sale they're from; he doesn't write anything [about it], but he does promise to find out about the Gavrilovka payment.[248] Now we could pay off [the mortgage] on the [Arnautov] house,[249]

---

244 A peasant custom.
245 Letter N° 95 of 30 January 1884.
246 Nikolaj Savvich Tikhonravov (1832–1893) — a philologist; rector of Moscow University from 1877 to 1884.
247 two copies — of LNT's treatise *What I believe* [*V chëm moja vera?*].
248 The reference is to the payment of rent for use of LNT's Samara lands by the peasants of the village of Gavrilovka.
249 See Letter N° 85.

but I forgot all about what you explained to me. Besides, driving foolishly in the morning over bumpy roads has become unbearably painful [for me, on account of my pregnancy];[250] I get a new pain on the right side of my stomach with every trip in the sleigh.

Masha got up this morning, she's healthy. The little ones are well, too. I'm waiting word from you on the sale of the horse. The purchaser hasn't been around since Sunday.

At the ball yesterday Dolgorukov[251] was more courteous than ever. He asked for a chair and sat down beside me, talked for a whole hour, as though he'd deliberately planned on showing me special attention, which even gave me cause for some embarrassment. He kept showing Tanja, too, a plethora of kindnesses. — But for some reason we didn't enjoy last night all that much; we were probably too tired.

It looks as though you will be staying at Yasnaya for quite a while. My only worry is that your diet and the [room] temperature are not being watched sufficiently, and you are not able to [properly] care for yourself. But you should realise that if you get sick, you will cause others much more trouble and grief than if you [simply] bought yourself white bread, chicken and some good bouillon.

Life here will be quieter from now on; there's nothing happening until the play at the Obolenskijs' on the 12th.[252] Tanja's getting ready to attend school, and I'm going to be working some more with the children. That rascal Lëlja is the most difficult. At this age the boys should be in the care of their father or school. It's torture [working] with them for us women, and we still don't [see] any results from our efforts. He's becoming lazier and lazier and extremely impudent; he doesn't obey anyone and has no fear.

Yesterday at the ball Sollogub[253] said that he had finished decorating the first set for the play, for the first act; he asked after you, and about your attitude [towards staging the play], whether you're serious or not.

Farewell for now; I am writing — and receiving — letters every day and have got so carried away with this that I'd be very distressed if I didn't receive [at least] one.

S.

N° 97 – LEV NIKOLAEVICH TOLSTOY ❧ SOFIA ANDREEVNA TOLSTAYA
[PSS 83/266]
5 February 1884. Yasnaya Polyana.

Sunday evening.

I didn't receive any letter today, and that was not pleasant. Besides, I got up this morning with a bad headache. After coffee I went for a walk and got very tired, but that hasn't passed completely. While out walking I dropped in to see Osip Naumovich.[254] The old fellow is in a pitiful situation, not on account of old age or poverty, but because he doesn't get along with his son. Pëtr Osipovich [his son] is very interesting in connection with the reading [habits] of everyday people. Almost the whole winter long literate *muzhiks* gather at his place and read.

---

250 SAT was pregnant with her youngest daughter Aleksandra L'vovna (Sasha) Tolstaja (1884–1979), who was born on 26 September 1884.

251 Prince Vladimir Andreevich Dolgorukov (1810–1891) — Governor-General of Moscow from 1865 to 1891.

252 On 12 February 1884 Princess Agrafena Aleksandrovna Obolenskaja (1823–1891) put on an amateur performance of the 1840 play *Novichki v ljubvi* [*Novices in love*] by Nikolaj Arsen'evich Korovkin (1816–1876).

253 Count Fëdor L'vovich Sollogub (1848–1890) — set decorator, amateur actor; nephew to the writer Vladimir Aleksandrovich Sollogub (1813–1882).

254 Osip Naumovich Zjabrev — see Letter N° 79, Note 157.

He brought me his library — a [whole] box of books — including Lives of saints, catechisms, [copies of] *Rodnoe slovo*,[255] history and geography books, *Russkij vestnik,* and Galakhov's[256] anthology, not to mention novels. He gave me his opinion about every sort of book. And this was of tremendous interest to me and made me give a lot of thought once more to [establishing a publishing house] for literature for the common people.[257] I found Urusov at home. We had dinner, and since we were reading Montaigne aloud, we had little [time for] idle chat. In the evening Agaf'ja Mikhajlovna[258] came and a [congratulatory] telegram for her arrived. She's very happy. Urusov's gone now, and I shall go to bed. Tomorrow I'll pull myself together — that is, I shall remember and do what's needed, and the day after tomorrow I shall come on the express train. If there were any doubt [as to the depth of my feeling for you, my sadness at] not receiving a letter [from you] today has dissolved it. I hope to find you all safe and sound and look forward to our getting together. Hold off on the business with the bank[259] and the coachman until I come.

Hugs and kisses to you and the children.

L.

On the envelope: Moscow. Khamovniki. Countess Sofia Andreevna Tolstaya. Private house.

N° 98 – SOFIA ANDREEVNA TOLSTAYA ✍ LEV NIKOLAEVICH TOLSTOY
[LSA 109]
5 February [1884]. Sunday. [Moscow]

I've written three letters to you, dear Lëvochka, but I'll probably send only the third one. Just now I received your letter,[260] a little longer than the preceding ones. What's this with your thumb? If you make a movement, that doesn't mean a dislocation, but that a tendon is stretched out of shape. My back pain is almost gone — it's only just a little painful when I move or touch [my back]. Of course I'm glad that you want to return on Tuesday, only I'm afraid that the *Maslenitsa* holiday[261] will make your head spin more than a whole month of ordinary days. Stay [a little longer] if you like; maybe I won't be entirely run off my feet without you; it will be better than seeing you depressed, discontent and still inactive. I can't boast about my own

255 *Rodnoe slovo* — an anthology for younger children, compiled by the 'father' of scientific pedagogy in Russia Konstantin Dmitrievich Ushinskij (1823–1870).

256 Aleksej Dmitrievich Galakhov (1807–1892) — historian of Russian literature, compiler of the popular *Russkaja khrestomatija* [*Russian anthology*] (1842).

257 This idea came to fruition in 1884 when LNT, in collaboration with his friend and kindred thinker Vladimir Grigor'evich Chertkov (1854–1936), founded the Posrednik publishing house with the aim of providing inexpensive literature for the common people.

258 On 5 February Agaf'ja Mikhajlovna (see Letter N° 21, Note 141) came to LNT's home to celebrate her name-day, where she received a congratulatory telegram from Mikhail Aleksandrovich Stakhovich (1861–1923), a poet and writer from Orël Gubernia, who switched from his liberal views to being an arch-conservative and served as a right-wing deputy in the First and Second State Duma (Russian parliament).

259 In a letter dated 3 February 1884 (not included here) SAT said that she had gone to the State Bank where she had received 2,500 roubles to transfer to the publisher Ivan Nikolaevich Kushnerëv (see Letter N° 94, Note 235) to cover the printing costs for the booklet *What I believe* [*V chëm moja vera?*].

260 A letter dated 4 February 1884 (not included here), in which LNT described dislocating the thumb on his right hand (PSS 83: 423).

261 *Maslenitsa* — see Letter N° 69, Note 86.

spirits. Nothing is easy, nothing's cheerful, nothing's [turning out] the way I expected it to; and physically I feel weak, my heart beats fearfully at the slightest movement, and I'm sleepy and frightfully lazy.

Today I finished La Boétie[262] and read with interest about his death. You know, this is the way I would like to die, i e. in a state of mind like this, and it always seems to me that I would die well, peacefully. — I do not like life and do not value it. I shall never attain moral perfection — that much is clear to me. I am incapable of enjoying material pleasures, as the rational critic [in me] always appears much too severely and immediately drives me to despair. — That is why I do not like life.

Everybody's healthy and of sound mind; Tanja keeps going off to rehearsals; Il'ja received a Certificate of Distinction for Malysh. Boris married Countess Miloradovich.[263] I can just imagine how happy he is! Varja[264] is feeling much better. Your brother Serëzha greatly disturbed me with his stories about you, [saying] you'll never want to come back to us. Why [would you not want to return]? Farewell. This, I take it, will be my last letter. Hugs and kisses.

Sonja.

Nº 99 – LEV NIKOLAEVICH TOLSTOY ❧ SOFIA ANDREEVNA TOLSTAYA
[PSS 83/271]
21 October 1884. Yasnaya Polyana.

After seeing you all off, I went home on foot, since [the coachman] Filip was otherwise occupied. He caught up with me at Rudakovo Hill. When I got back, I moved into the boys' room and made myself at home. My health is good. Avdot'ja Vasil'evna[265] set me up according to your instructions and made me feel really comfortable. Dmitrij Fëdorovich [Vinogradov] sat in the next room and transcribed, while I did some reading.

Today I awoke and got up close to 8 [o'clock]. The day is even better and warmer than a few days ago. I dismissed Adrian,[266] did some cleaning myself and then chopped wood, which gave me great pleasure. At 10 [o'clock] I had some coffee and offered tea to Marija Afanas'evna[267] and Dmitrij Fëdorovich, and had a successful time reviewing and correcting *Theology*.[268] I wanted to take up some other work, but I don't feel up to that [at the moment]. I had dinner at 3 and went out to enjoy the beauty of the day. I walked through the *Zakaz* to the pine forest beyond the Kochak [a stream], past Bibikov's garden in the direction of the church. There I dropped in to see Ivan Nikanorovich.[269] A *muzhik* had asked me to put in a word so that the priest might reduce the 7-rouble fee he is charging for the wedding. The priest has [a family of] nine children, and he can't ask any less. We had a friendly chat, and I made my way home in

262 SAT was reading a work at the time by French writer and philosopher Étienne de la Boétie (1530–1563) entitled *Le Discours de la servitude volontaire ou le Contr'un*.

263 SAT's cousin Boris Vjacheslavovich Shidlovskij (1859–1922) was marrying Countess Vera Nikolaevna Miloradovich (née Shabel'skaja; 1861–1916), who had just divorced Count Grigorij Aleksandrovich Miloradovich (1839–1905). In 1896 the marriage was declared illegitimate and three years later Vera Nikolaevna entered a convent.

264 Varvara Valer'janovna (Varja) Nagornova, niece to LNT (see Letter Nº 6, Note 43).

265 Avdot'ja Vasil'evna Popova — housekeeper at Yasnaya Polyana.

266 Adrian Grigor'evich Bolkhin (1865–1936) — a Yasnaya Polyana peasant, who served as a coachman for the Tolstoys.

267 Marija Afanas'evna Arbuzova (nanny) — see Letter Nº 41, Note 265.

268 LNT was working at the time on *A criticism of dogmatic theology* [*Issledovanie dogmaticheskogo bogoslovija*] (1884).

269 Ivan Nikanorovich Mukhalevskij (1852–1884) — priest at the Kochaki church, whose parish included Yasnaya Polyana.

the moonlight. When I got home [I found] Anna Ivanovna[270] (who had been bitten by a wolf), with a boy [i.e. her son]. She had come to find out whether there were any news [about her petition]. I put on the samovar, and we had a chat. She told me a lot of interesting things about the detainees who are staying with her, including Rybin[271] who had been caught, and had passed by their place, and who was a hero in her eyes, and especially her son's. Now I'm going to bed. I'll just take this letter down. Yesterday's news about the death of Pisarev[272] (is it true?) had a strong impression on me. I became terribly sad and depressed. The whole thickness of the wall separating people from truth became so clear to me.

While still under this impression I read reminiscences and descriptions of wars in *Russkaja starina*. How thickly people are blanketed by deception! You don't see any possibility of destroying it. But I know that it's a weakness. If it weren't for this deception, there would be nothing to do in the world — at least for me. But it is always frightful when you see its whole thickness. One must not think about this, but destroy it insofar as one is able. And then comes joy. —

How was your trip? Have those cruel ladies softened and have you calmed down? And haven't there been unpleasant impressions in Moscow, and if so, have you given into them? How are the boys? How is Ol'ga Zajkovskaja?[273] Have you seen her again? I still feel guilty that in my haste I greeted her rather coldly. She has such a tortured face and I pity her.

Write me a few more details, more specifically, and don't hurry. Hugs to you and all the children.

On the envelope: Moscow. Khamovniki. Count Tolstoy's house. Countess S. A. Tolstaya.

Nº 100 – SOFIA ANDREEVNA TOLSTAYA ✇ LEV NIKOLAEVICH TOLSTOY
[LSA 111]
23 October 1884 [Moscow] [Preceded by SAT's Nº 6U, October 1884]

Yesterday I received your *first* letter,[274] and it saddened me. I see that you have been staying at Yasnaya not for the sake of your intellectual work which I prize above everything else in life, but for some sort of 'Robinson Crusoe' game. You dismissed Adrian, who longed to stay to the end of the month; you dismissed the cook, who would have been happy to do some work in exchange for a stipend, and from morning to night you engage in inappropriate physical labour which in ordinary life is done by young [peasant] men and women. Really, it would be better and more productive [for you] to live with the children. Of course you will say that this kind of life is in accord with your convictions, and that you are feeling so good [about it]. Well, that's another matter, and I can only say '"Enjoy!" — and still be upset that such intellectual forces are wasted in chopping wood, putting on the samovar and sewing boots — which are all very fine

270 Anna Ivanovna — a widowed smallholder, who ran a post-station. Tat'jana Andreevna Kuzminskaja based her story "Beshenyj volk" [*The mad wolf*] on Anna Ivanovna's words; it was published in *Vestnik Evropy* (1886, Nº 6).
271 *Rybin* — nickname of a bandit named Nikolaj Kurnosenkov, who would steal fish from railway carriages (*ryba* is the Russian word for 'fish').
272 Sergej Alekseevich Pisarev (ca1855–1909) — retired cavalry captain, a Tula landowner. In October 1884 he fought a duel with SAT's brother Aleksandr Andreevich (Sasha) Behrs over Behrs' wife Matrona Dmitrievna (Patti; née Èristova). The duel took place in the *Zaseka* near Yasnaya Polyana; Pisarev was wounded but not killed. He married Patti Behrs, but their married life was less than successful.
273 Ol'ga Dmitrievna Zajkovskaja (1844–1919) — SAT's childhood friend.
274 Letter Nº 99 of 21 October 1884.

as a relaxation and a change of pace, but not [at least for you] as professional activities in themselves. — Well, enough of that. If I hadn't written it down, I would continue to feel vexed, but now that's passed: I even find it funny, and I find peace in the thought: "[Give] the child what he likes, just so long as he doesn't cry!"

Yesterday I was at the Obolenskijs,[275] it was Liza's name-day. There were guests and relatives; everything went as usual; [we had] a late supper. I was tired, but upon my return I found a note to me from Lëlja, asking [me] to correct his Russian essay; I was glad to do it, but that meant I didn't get to bed until 3 o'clock. After 8 in the morning the children don't let me sleep, but I'm used to it, and only feel [somewhat] distracted. — Our belongings arrived, we unpacked them, then Masha and I walked over to the Smolenskij market and bought a table, a commode for Masha and a few other necessities. Tomorrow I'll go see Chizh,[276] [as] my health is still not completely good. I don't have any life yet, there's still far too much disorder, and since I'm not feeling well, I don't hurry and I'm very slow at clearing away clutter.

Yesterday I had a minor confrontation with Lëlja. On the morning of our arrival he didn't go to the *gymnasium,* telling Vlas[277] the night before that he might not go. Then he told Madame [Seuron] that his stomach hurt. She didn't believe him and didn't sign his [student record] book. Then he asked me, and I told him that I couldn't lie [either] — I didn't know whether his stomach had been hurting while I was at Yasnaya. Lëlja began to insist, trying to persuade me, but I didn't give in. That's how it ended. For the second day in a row Serëzha simply disappeared from the morning on; he said he was in the laboratory. Il'ja has been very dear and has a fresh look. Masha has become quite conscientious and is getting ready to approach her studies in earnest. All her previous teachers have come and [said how] shocked they were at how much she forgets [of what she learns]. The little ones are noisy and bothersome, since we have not yet got our lives together; only Sasha[278] smiles meekly and cheerfully and you never hear a peep out of her; and when you do, you only feel pity [for her]. She hasn't been out for a walk today; they let her catch cold and she has the sniffles really bad.

Just now I received your second letter,[279] and it's a good one. I blamed you for being too caught up in *physical* labour, and now you've done just the opposite — you're too busy *intellectually.* The main thing, my dear friend, is to take care of yourself in every respect. There's only one way to make me happy, and that's for you to be happy, healthy and without a sense of pressure. With that in mind, I am constantly racking my brains as to how to arrange our lives so that you can bear living in Moscow as easily as possible. I probably shan't succeed, but how I desire that!

As far as [household] affairs go, what can I say? — you know all about that [already]. We have 3,300 silver roubles in the bank; I have 700, which are diminishing not by the day, but by the hour in Moscow. Apples here fetch 250 silver roubles. As I see it, until all the Samara debts owed to us are paid — Bibikov, the peasants and Uncle Serëzha — until then, we shouldn't take on any new ventures, or we risk being left without any money at all. If Bibikov pays us the money [he owes], we should spend it on the factory[280] — that's not income, but capital [in the

275 Leonid Dmitrievich Obolenskij and Elizaveta Valer'janovna (Liza) Obolenskaja (LNT's niece). 22 October (Liza's name-day) honours St. Elisabeth of Adrianopolis [Elisaveta Adrianopol'skaja] who was martyred in the third century C. E. for professing her Christian faith.

276 Dr. Mikhail Il'ich Chizh (?–1895) — obstetrician and gynæcologist.

277 Vlas Anisimovich Vorobëv (yard-keeper) — see Letter Nº 95, Note 243.

278 Aleksandra L'vovna (Sasha) Tolstaja (daughter) — see Letter Nº 96, Note 250.

279 A letter dated 22 October 1884 (not included here) — see PSS 83: 431–32.

280 Nikol'skoe-Vjazemskoe estate foreman Ivan Ivanovich Orlov (see Letter Nº 5, Note 34) proposed constructing a potato factory there.

form of] buildings, hence let it be invested again in construction. I have just one piece of advice, namely, to be sure to send Ivan Ivanovich [Orlov] to Samara and he will either demand the money [on our behalf] or re-sell the land and find out what we can expect in January. Or what guarantee is there of receiving the money in January if it hasn't been received up to now?

As to Mitrofan,[281] I don't think that's our problem. If you hire someone else, what makes you think that he won't seduce ten other men's wives? The question is whether he does his job well and not who lives with whom; nobody can vouch for anyone in the world in that regard. You shouldn't change foremen on the basis of their relationships with women.

You asked me to write everything in more detail; but as I am writing you this letter I'm being interrupted a dozen times, and not only can I not concentrate, but I simply can't finish [the letter] — not because of my own bustling, but on account of all the bustle around me.

As to [Uncle] Kosten'ka, I haven't heard anything. Mashen'ka's[282] in very good spirits. Serëzha[283] arrived yesterday at dinner time; then came Sergej Semënovich Urusov and Uncle Serëzha was very unpleasant; again [it was about] Katkov.[284] [Uncle Serëzha] kept cursing our Serëzha terribly on account of the student protest simply because Serëzha is a student. [Uncle Serëzha] wouldn't listen to anybody telling him that Serëzha himself knew nothing about the protest. *You've* come in for your share of the blame, too.

We also talked with Urusov concerning your question about astronomy. But he just gave a hearty guffaw and looked at Tanja with oily eyes. But he is a kind-hearted soul and gentle with everyone, and pleasant in this matter, too.

Farewell, dear friend, hugs and kisses to you; I've just had a clear picture of you in my mind and suddenly I'm full of tenderness towards you. There's something in you that is so intelligent, kind, naïve and persistent, and everything is illumined by your unique tender compassion for everyone and your penetrating insight into people's souls.

Sonja.

Nº 101 – LEV NIKOLAEVICH TOLSTOY ❧ SOFIA ANDREEVNA TOLSTAYA
[PSS 83/273]
23 October 1884. Yasnaya Polyana.

Last night I went to bed quite late; but this morning I got up at 8 and again took tea with Dmitrij Fëdorovich.[285] I am continuing to correct the transcription. Today I didn't want to tire myself out and finished at 3, and went to Yasenki to buy post-office envelopes. The weather's turning bad — a haze and fog. But I had a glorious walk and did a great deal of thinking on the way back about how I should manage the household while we are alive, and [given] the way we live. I should start with Yasnaya. I have a plan as to how to manage things [here] in accordance with my convictions. Maybe it's hard, but it has to be done. — My general reasoning is this: even if we manage our household on the (false) basis of property, we still have to manage it as best we can in terms of justice, inoffensiveness and, if possible, kindness. Even disregarding that, it's

---

281 LNT wanted to dismiss his Yasnaya Polyana foreman Mitrofan Nikolaevich Bannikov (see Letter Nº 71, Note 104) for seducing the wife of peasant Fëdor Sergeevich Rezunov (1858–1920).

282 Marija Nikolaevna (Mashen'ka) Tolstaja (LNT's sister) — see Letter Nº 4, Note 12.

283 Sergej Nikolaevich (Serëzha) Tolstoj (LNT's brother) — see Letter Nº 4, Note 12.

284 Mikhail Nikiforovich Katkov (editor of *Russkij vestnik*) — see Letter Nº 12, Note 73. Sergej Nikolaevich was angered that students had vandalised the Moscow University print-shop rented by Katkov.

285 Dmitrij Fëdorovich Vinogradov (teacher) — see Letter Nº 60, Note 16.

now clear to me that if what I consider to be the truth and the law of the people must become that law applied in actual life, this will only happen if we, who are the wealthy and oppressing, voluntarily renounce wealth and oppression; and this will happen not suddenly, but by a gradual process which will lead to this [goal]. This process can be set in motion only when we ourselves control our own affairs and, most importantly, when we ourselves enter into communication with the people who are working for our benefit. I want to try to do this. I want to try, completely openly, with no force but with kindness, to deal directly with the people at Yasnaya. I believe this can be done without mistakes or great loss, even without any loss at all. It could actually be a good project. At the right moment when you are listening, I would like to tell you [all about it], but it's all so difficult to describe. — I think I'll start [this project] right away. I [plan] to take over all [responsibility] from Mitrofan and take charge of things myself, and come occasionally [to Yasnaya] during the winter, and then work [here] consistently, beginning in the spring. — Maybe I'm being inadvertently corrupted by the desire to spend more time in the country, but I feel that my life has taken a wrong turn as a result of my neglect, my disregard for what has been done, and done for my benefit, completely contrary to all my convictions. — This disregard has also included the fact that I, with my public disavowals of private property, out of *fausse honte* was unwilling to get involved with private property lest I be accused of inconsistency. Now it seems to me that I have grown out of that. I know in my own conscience how consistent I am. But, my dearest, please bear in mind that this is a matter very precious to me, and don't react with unthinking fervency and don't spoil my mood. I am confident that no harm will come from this, and that something both good and important may come of it. — I fear that you will not understand me. And how could you from this muddled expression?

This morning I received your brief but pleasant letter[286] — I see that everything's fine for the time being. How is your health? Write to me with more details — if you have the time and desire [to do so]. — I am quite healthy [myself]. Today I had some black radishes with *kvass,* country soup and baked turnip.

I received nothing from Tula; only a registered letter for you, which I shall try to col-lect tomorrow. Tomorrow I'll ride over to buy materials for the boots [I'm sewing] for Stakhovich.[287] I'm so happy that [the writer Sergej Alekseevich] Pisarev isn't dead![288]

Put the following advertisement in the papers — which ones, I don't know, whichever [your] Muscovite [acquaintances] recommend: "For sale, 15 versts from Tula on the Kiev Highway in the village of Yasnaya Polyana: 10 young stallions from Kirghiz mares, as well as factory-farm stallions, ready for the harness and riding. Mares of the same breed are also for sale here. Ask the foreman."

Hugs and kisses to you and the children.

Regards to Mme Seuron and M[iss] Lake.[289]

286 A letter written by SAT from Moscow on 21 October 1884 (Letters to L. N. Tolstoy, pp. 255–56).

287 LNT was sewing boots for Mikhail Aleksandrovich Stakhovich (1861–1923) — poet and writer from Orël Gubernia, who switched from his liberal leanings to arch-conservative views and took part in the first two State Dumas (parliaments) as a right-wing deputy. After the February 1917 revolution he served the Provisional Government as Governor-General of Finland (at the time a Russian province). Tolstoy had studied boot-making as part of his conviction (outlined in *What then must be done?* [*Tak chto zhe nam delat'?*] that one's day should comprise four basic activities: intellectual labour, physical labour, work with handicrafts and interaction with people (PSS 25: 388). The boots he made for Stakhovich are on display at the Tolstoy Museum in Moscow.

288 In her letter of 21 October SAT told her husband that Sergej Alekseevich Pisarev was still alive after his duel with her brother Aleksandr Andreevich (Sasha) Behrs (see Letter N° 99, Note 272).

289 *Mme Seuron and M[iss] Lake* — governesses to the Tolstoys' children.

Sharik[290] *présente ses respects à Mme Seuron. Il me fait l'honneur de m'accompagner dans mes promenades.*

On the envelope: Moscow. Khamovniki Lane. Countess S. A. Tolstaya. Private house.

Nº 102 – SOFIA ANDREEVNA TOLSTAYA ❦ LEV NIKOLAEVICH TOLSTOY
[LSA 112]
[25 October 1884. Moscow]

I had just sent off my letter [to you] yesterday, dear Lëvochka, when I received yours[291] [dated 23 October 1884]. By some strange co-incidence, everything you say to me I not only do not object to, but I myself have been thinking exactly the same thing — i.e., on the estate where we live at least half the year, it is unconscionable not to manage it ourselves when it comes to dealing with the [local] people. We can draw the same benefit — if not an even greater benefit, I think — while anything that is [as of now] disappearing, or being stolen, or being treated wastefully, can thoughtfully be given away, or [used to] help or share with the peasants. Our relations [with them] will be the most favourable — our profit from Yasnaya has been so insignificant that it is not worth talking about; but with your skill and cleverness (once you have the desire) you can carry out any task superbly. So what if it *were* an excuse to take a trip to the country — so much the better — you won't feel ashamed or listless by leaving us to take care of the business which feeds, educates and maintains us. — I don't know whether I've understood you [correctly], but I am responding *according to* my understanding.

If you are settling with Mitrofan, ask him for the housekeeping records [for the purchase of] provisions. I gave him 100 silver roubles to give to Popov's butcher shop [in Tula]. It will also be necessary to take the keys from him for the larder and the annexe. He himself might be honest, but the females around him are fearsome swindlers. Make sure you dismiss Arina[292] — there's been a whole history attached to her; she was caught stealing half the milk. Judging from [the way she handed] the bottle of milk to the unfortunate Fedot,[293] I saw how reluctant and frustrated she felt — [an attitude] simply out of spite. She's such a despicable evil woman, a gossip and a schemer. But we shall not retain [such] evil people on our new estate. Take me on as your assistant — I'll gladly do all sorts of jobs, if only my health gets a little better, but in spirit I am so cheerful and at peace, and ready for anything.

Today I am feeling somewhat better, though yesterday I was up until 3 in the morning with a fever, shaking all over with pain, and even my teeth were chattering. I need *physical peace,* of the strictest kind, and I know that myself, and will strive for it, so that I can all the sooner be *more fit* for any task.

I interrupted my letter as I just received your letter and that of Vasilij Ivanovich.[294] My whole good and peaceful mental state has been shattered. As much as you try to comfort me with assurances that the money will be there, I simply can't imagine where it's going to come from.

---

290 *Sharik* — the name of a mongrel dog trained by Anna Seuron (the Russian name literally signifies *balloon,* but is a common name for a pet dog).

291 Letter Nº 101 of 23 October 1884.

292 Arina Fëdorovna Frolkova (née Shentjakova; cook) — see Letter Nº 73, Note 111

293 Fedot Terent'evich Orekhov (1846–1884) — a Yasnaya Polyana peasant on the verge of death.

294 SAT's letter to LNT dated 24 October 1884 (PSS 83: 436–37, not included here) and a letter from Vasilij Ivanovich Alekseev (see Letter Nº 64, Note 39) from Samara, dated 15 October 1884.

And our expenses in Moscow, even with the strictest economising, are so great that it's a sheer disaster, becoming more terrible every day. — Of course it would be easy if you were with me and could help, and were kindly able to assist me in all my activities. When we get together, we'll have a talk. We need to clarify what should be done in Samara, and it would be good if you or Ivan Ivanovich could do this. Don't you see how hard it is on the peasants themselves without papers and specific conditions? You are ruining yourself and them, too.

You say that the children won't write to you? I remind them every day, but they're pretty lazy. I give them all sorts of encouragement, but it still doesn't make any difference. Today Lëlja was contrary. Kashevskaja[295] was supposed to give him a lesson, but he complained he was tired. "I don't want to," [he screamed,] "I just got home from the *gymnasium*." (Today [on Thursdays] he arrives home at 3, and so his music lesson is from 3:30 to 4:30.) Then Masha studied in his room — there was nowhere else she could do it — he complained loudly again that there was nowhere else for *him* to go, that he wanted to do some wood carving right at that very moment. When I tried to tell him we have to live as a family and make concessions to each other and get along, so that everyone feels comfortable, he snorted and said that he would lock the door to his room. Yesterday, however, all the older kids went to the Tolstojs,[296] and he and I played four-handed [piano], and we had such a happy and friendly time! — Serëzha's very good; yesterday he kept criticising Tanja and meekly offered her good, serious advice not to let herself go but get involved in some serious activity, and she listened and said: "Yes, I have to, absolutely." Il'ja's rather taciturn, but at the same time meek and nice to me. Masha today got down to all her lessons right away.

Before you come, write me, otherwise your stove is not yet stoked and it will be cold. — Regarding the cow mentioned by Ivan Ivanych, you still haven't given me your answer.

I haven't gone out visiting, and shan't go out, for 12 days now. That's what the doctor ordered — to move as little as possible, and so I am not seeing anybody, which is very pleasant — [it means] I can do [more] things with the children. [Visitors] can come and see me, if they like, in the evening, when the children are asleep.

You didn't write anything today about your activities, your health and your mental state. Probably because you were in Tula; in any case, I looked [at your letter] just now and [I can] see you're not that well, not as well as I had hoped.

You keep asking me to write in more detail. Well, this is how our day went: I got up late, went to [check on] the little ones; Sasha ran a fever all night long, now it's just the sniffles; the boys were at the *gymnasium,* Serëzha spent the whole morning at home, playing the piano, and then after a hearty breakfast, spent the whole rest of the day without dinner at the laboratory. Kashevskaja gave lessons to Masha and began [to hold classes] with Andrjusha, which made the boys terribly excited, even ecstatic. Lëlja began to feel out of sorts, as I already wrote you. Tanja and Vera[297] went to Kuznetskij Most [Street]. Tanja needs a dress. She didn't buy one, she doesn't want a cheap one, nothing appealed to her, and she wasn't prepared [to buy] an expensive [dress].

Masha's Russian teacher took dinner with us; she's very simple and nice. After dinner everyone went upstairs to play, or work under the lamp in the drawing-room, while I sat down to

---

295 Ekaterina Nikolaevna Kashevskaja (married name: Fridman; 1862–1939) — teacher of music and French to the Tolstoys' children.

296 the Tolstojs — in this case referring to LNT's brother Sergej Nikolaevich Tolstoj and his family.

297 The Tolstoys' daughter Tat'jana L'vovna Tolstaja and her first cousin Vera Sergeevna (Verochka) Tolstaja (1865–1923) — daughter to LNT's brother Sergej Nikolaevich Tolstoj.

write you. In the morning I taught Andrjusha. I put together and assembled a whole [sewing] machine, quietly tidying up. But no matter what I do, it keeps hurting more and more inside, especially now, towards evening.

Tanja asked at Gauthier's[298] whether they could order the works of Chinese [philosophers].[299] They said they could, but it would cost about 80 shillings. We declined [to order] from Wolff's[300] [a similar shop nearby], since he said he hadn't received [any copies], and that probably the whole edition was sold out.

As for astronomy, I haven't yet found anyone to ask; twice now [our son] Serëzha has not found Ivakin[301] at home. That's all for your requests. There have been no letters that have come [here] for you lately.

They haven't finished renovating the upstairs yet here, and today I felt rather upset on looking back at all the projects I initiated, and now I have started to feel such hatred toward all this construction going on in the drawing room, which the wallpaperers are putting in order. Farewell, dear Lëvochka. Today I wrote something longer, but I fear it's pretty much an empty letter again. My nerves are frightfully weak, and I shall take some potassium bromide — [Dr.] Chizh prescribed it for my back pain and because my nerves are currently so weak that the disease is not yielding to treatment. I received an unpleasant letter from Tanja: she approves of the duel,[302] and chides Mamà for reading her letter to her [family]. Hugs and kisses. I love you.

Sonja.

N° 103 – LEV NIKOLAEVICH TOLSTOY ❧ SOFIA ANDREEVNA TOLSTAYA
[PSS 83/278]
28 October 1884. Yasnaya Polyana.

Your letter yesterday[303] greatly upset me — greatly. If it weren't for our projected change in management, I would come right away, which I shall now do very soon. I've been feeling very gloomy these days. I don't know whether it's something physical going on here, and some sort of upheaval going on in me, or my loneliness, but your condition seems to me to be the main [culprit]. What will [your] letter tomorrow say? —

Today I remembered that I'm 56 years old, and I've heard, and noticed, that [in each] seven-year period a person undergoes a change. The main upheaval in me was: $7 \times 7 = 49$, precisely when I entered the period in which I now find myself. These seven years have been frightfully fraught with inner life, clarification, fervour and breakdown. Now, it seems to me, that has

298 *Gauthier's* — a shop specialising in foreign books in Kuznetsky Most Street (a major thoroughfare in central Moscow) operated by Vladimir Ivanovich Gauthier-Dufayer (1815–1887), who inherited the business from his father and grandfather; the latter had emigrated to Russia from Picardy (France) in 1764, thanks to a promotional campaign sponsored by Empress Catherine the Great to attract entrepreneurs to Russia from Western Europe.

299 In 1884 LNT was doing a lot of reading in Confucius and Lao-Tse (Laozi). SAT wrote her sister Tat'jana Andreevna that her husband was "reading Confucius enthusiastically, along with anything written about the Chinese, their life, religion and so forth" (Tolstoy Museum archives). At this time LNT was working on a series of articles which he grouped together under the general title *Chinese wisdom* [*Kitajskaja mudrost'*].

300 Maurycy Bolesław Wolff (Russian name: Mavrikij Osipovich Vol'f; 1825–1883) — a publisher and bookseller originally from Poland who opened a chain of bookshops in Russia, including the one on Kuznetsky Most in Moscow.

301 Ivan Mikhajlovich Ivakin (tutor) — see Letter N° 63, Note 34.

302 See Letter N° 99, Note 272.

303 In her letter of 26 October 1884 (not included here) SAT complained: "I've been missing you something terrible; I've held my chin up so far, but today I literally let myself go, just longing for you, it's simply a fright! If I were healthy, I guess I would hop on the next train and come to Yasnaya. But my health is really bad…" (Letters to Tolstoy, p. 265).

passed, it has gone into flesh and blood, and I am searching for activity on this path. And either I shall die, or I shall be most unhappy, or I shall find [some] activity that will completely absorb me on my path. Writing activity, it stands to reason — the one I can most relate to and am attracted to. — Oh, if only you weren't unhappy — the way you describe it to me in your latest letter.

I went around the whole estate today — found out everything [I need to know] and tomorrow I'll get the keys. There's no special complication, but there's no one to put in charge when you leave. Especially the house and everything pertinent to our lives. If I leave now, I'll put Filip in charge for the time being. At least he won't get drunk, he won't lose the money, and won't allow [the place] to be ransacked.

[Our] poultry must be liquidated. They cost around 80 roubles to feed. Of course, it's frustrating. By the way, I don't really feel like writing [this letter]. I probably shan't get any reply. I am missing you terribly. The letter [you're writing] today, [which I'll get] tomorrow, will be decisive. Please don't think that I'm unhappy with my mental state. I'm unhappy with myself and I worry about you. As for me, my mental state I find useful.

Today I walked around the estate, then rode horseback, and the dogs followed me. Agaf'ja Mikhajlovna said that without a leash they would attack the cattle, and she sent Vas'ka[304] along with me. I wanted to test out my hunting sense. To ride and hunt after 40 years of experience is very pleasant. But a hare jumped out [onto my path], and I wished him luck. Mainly, I feel shame [for having been a hunter]. —

I returned home, took dinner and sat down with the old women and Dmitrij Fëdorovich [Vinogradov]. Your account statement[305] [of necessary monthly expenses] doesn't frighten me. In the first place, the money will be there, in all probability. Secondly, if it isn't, the seemingly irreducible expenses will turn out to be quite reducible. — Don't get upset, my darling, but I cannot attribute the slightest importance to these monetary expenses. None of this constitutes an event — as does, for example, disease, marriage, birth, death, acquired knowledge, good or bad behaviour, the good or bad habits of people near and dear to us — but this is our own life-style which we ourselves have constructed in this manner and are free to reconstruct some other way or in a hundred different ways. — I know that this is often unbearably tiresome for you — and always for the children ([you all] think you are aware of all this) — to hear me say this, but I can't help repeating that the happiness or unhappiness of all of us cannot depend even a whit on whether we lose everything or become rich, but only on what we ourselves are. So, if Kosten'ka[306] is left a million, will that make him any happier? — To avoid that sounding like a banality, we need to look at life more broadly, more extensively. — Whatever form our life together (yours and mine) takes, along with our joys and sorrows, that will also shape the actual lives of our nine children.[307] And so it is essential to help them obtain what has given us happiness, and help spare them what has brought us unhappiness; but neither [foreign] languages, nor academic degrees, nor society, nor less money, has played any part in our happiness

---

304 Vasilij Sevast'janovich (Vas'ka) Makarychev (Makarov; 1846–?) — a Yasnaya Polyana peasant.

305 To her letter of 26 October SAT attached a statement of their household accounts, calculating their monthly household expenses to be just over 900 roubles.

306 Konstantin Aleksandrovich (Kosten'ka) Islavin — see Letter N° 47, Note 301.

307 The nine surviving children to date were: Sergej (Serëzha, born 1863), Tat'jana (Tanja, 1864), Il'ja (Iljusha, 1866), Lev (Lëlja, 1869), Marija (Masha, 1871), Andrej (Andrjusha, 1877), Mikhail (Misha, 1879), Aleksej (Alësha, 1881) and Aleksandra (Sasha, 1884).

or unhappiness. And so I can't [let] the question of how much we spend occupy my [thought]. If I attach importance thereto, it will overshadow what is really important.

On the envelope: Moscow. Khamovniki. Countess S. A. Tolstaya. Private house.

Nº 104 – LEV NIKOLAEVICH TOLSTOY ❧ SOFIA ANDREEVNA TOLSTAYA
[PSS 83/287]
12 December 1884. Yasnaya Polyana.

I haven't had much sleep — my liver hurts, but [I'm] in a good, cheerful and writing mood. I did a lot of writing[308] and, as usual, the deeper into the woods, the thicker it gets. Everything grows and develops, and becomes more interesting (for me). — I did start out for a walk, but [because of] the rain and wind I turned back. I was going to take a nap, but I couldn't sleep and read 'til the evening. At Bibikov's, a while back, I had met a young doctor[309] in place of Kholevinskaja,[310] who told me about a book[311] on prostitution and syphilis in Russia, and now he's sent it to me. The [arguments in the] book [are] quite rational. It's frightening, wretched, pitiful and upsetting. It's so easy and simple to live a good life and avoid all those horrors whereby we ruin [not only] ourselves (it wouldn't be so bad to ruin only one's self, if one wanted it) but others as well.

Around 5 o'clock I went to the village to see Pëtr Osipovich,[312] [as well as] the new teacher[313] — to ask him to do some transcribing — along with Sergej Rezunov.[314] [When I'm] with the *muzhiks* and in conversation with them I feel rather lonely; I feel they are incapable of understanding me, but not to the same degree as with Professor Kovalevskij[315] and many others. Pëtr Osipovich greatly surprised me. Without any prompting on my part he began to tell me he doesn't go to daytime mass, since the deacon keeps referring to the tsars and [the Empress] Marija Fëdorovna. [In the church they pray] for the health [of the Imperial Family]. They already look pretty well-fed, yet you're supposed to pray for their health to make them look even more well-fed — and [he says] the same thing about the Tsar [himself]. [The Tsar] has so much on his plate, they say, and just look how fat he's got 'cuz of this 'plate'! And so I changed the subject.

By your letters[316] I see that you're not in the best of spirits — not that you're angry or sad, but in a lackadaisical and superficial mood. And you yourself are feeling discontented, and that's a shame. However, you change so often that perhaps tomorrow's letter will be quite different. — As to my return, I wrote to you saying that if [Leonid Dmitrievich] Urusov comes on the 16th, I shall spend a day with him and [then] come. Whether it's good or bad, my situation is different from others' in that interaction with certain kindred spirits — and Urusov is one of them — is especially dear to me. — Are there any letters addressed to me which need answering?

---

308 LNT was working on his article *What then must be done?* [*Tak chto zhe nam delat'?*].

309 *a young doctor* — identity unknown.

310 Marija Mikhajlovna Kholevinskaja (1858–1920) — a physician in Krapivna Uezd, who shared LNT's views.

311 Mikhail Ivanovich Kuznetsov, *Prostitutsija i sifilis v Rossii: istoriko–statisticheskie issledovanija* [*Prostitution and syphilis in Russia: historical-statistical research*] (St. Petersburg, 1871).

312 Pëtr Osipovich Zjabrev — see Letter Nº 79, Note 149.

313 *the new teacher* — identity unknown.

314 Sergej Semënovich Rezunov — a Yasnaya Polyana peasant carpenter.

315 Maksim Maksimovich Kovalevskij (1851–1916) — a professor at Moscow University; author of reminiscences on LNT.

316 Letters written 9, 10 and 11 December 1884.

Farewell, darling. I'm going to have some tea and go to bed. Hugs and kisses to you and the children. Today I sold the hinny.[317] I hope that none of the children will feel disappointed. Otherwise it would keep on eating as much food as a cow.

The trunk is safe[318] — Marija Afanas'evna and I are keeping watch, along with [the dog] Bul'ka. Regards to Mme Seuron. I would say she's exerting a harmful influence on you, and today the thought crossed my mind that she might be doing this deliberately because she doesn't like you. All that flattery of outward appearance can be frightfully contaminating. I liken this to flattery of [my] writing; when you give into it, it seems as though you're getting weaker and dumber. Write something good. I don't mean write lies, — but I mean I very much want you to be in good spirits. I would advise you to get treatment and follow it strictly for at least a month, and then you can decide. The worst thing would be no decision at all.

Pity that Tanja doesn't write [to me]. Even if she could just describe her ball gown,[319] I could at least deduce a little about her mental state. — Oh, how wretched! How come Iljusha sleeps all the time? He was doing that even when I was there. That's not good. — If this letter seems disjointed or gloomy, chalk it up to my liver complaint and be forgiving.

My liver complaint has now become better towards evening.

On the envelope: Moscow. Dolgokhamovniki Lane. Count Tolstoy's house. Countess Sofia Andreevna Tolstaya.

Nº 105 – SOFIA ANDREEVNA TOLSTAYA ❧ LEV NIKOLAEVICH TOLSTOY
[LSA 125]
13 December 1884. [Moscow]

You make excuses at the end of your letter[320] as to why it is gloomy and not good. No, it is very good. There's something in there that makes me look back at myself and regret that [my life] has been going downhill as I approach old age. Indeed, it's strange. Everyone regards me as the pillar of the family, as firm, as *"une femme vertueuse"*,[321] but I myself feel weak, frivolous, half-crazy and ready for any — even the most senseless — extremes.

I am not affected by Madame [Seuron]'s flattery. I know her, and now at times it seems that she flatters me on the one hand so that she can flirt with you on the other. If this latter can be confirmed, then *elle aura affaire à moi,* and I pity her in advance, for in my half-crazed state I can't guarantee anything [as to my actions]. But again, that's one of those senseless things; I still like Madame; she is kind and intelligent, but life has spoilt her. — I'm sorry to hear about your liver complaint, but I'm really happy about your mood, and I'm afraid of destroying it with this crazy time of holidays, which always have a worldly and melancholy effect upon us oldsters.

Do whatever is best for you and take care of your soul and your health. You are needed and cherished by everyone in the world, and don't pay any attention to me, I am not worthy of it — insignificant, stupid and feeble-minded creature that I am.

317 *hinny* — a cross between a stallion and a donkey.
318 In her letter of 10 December SAT asked: "Have you been in the storeroom, and is Dunja's trunk safe, and all our [things]?" (*Letters to L. N. Tolstoy*, p. 285).
319 See *My Life*, IV.26. In her letter of 10 December SAT wrote about her daughter: "Tanja, who you send special hugs and kisses to, is up to her ears in making her gown.... I told her 'Be sure to write Papà', and she said: 'All I can do is describe my outfit to him!'" (ibid., p. 285).
320 Letter Nº 104 dated 12 December 1884.
321 See Proverbs 31: 10.

Today Alësha took ill with something, ran a fever night and day, won't eat anything and is quite listless. It may be just the flu, as with everyone else. Today I had visitors: Dmitrij Fëdorovich Samarin, Count Kapnist,[322] and the Obolenskijs[323] (from Krivo-Nikol'skij Lane); they interrupted Lëlja's music lesson, which was very sad. Still, he [was able to use the time] practising skating in the garden. Andrjusha and Masha have also learnt to skate; they can now stand and move on skates and are very brave, and Lëlja is cheering them on. This past while Lëlja's become very good and easy [to get along with] and does his lessons on time. Il'ja hasn't been sleeping for two days now and instead, sharpens cigarette-holders and match-holders on a lathe.

Serëzha comes home from university and promptly sits down at the piano. Tanja has again been copying [a painting], and tomorrow goes to the Beklemishevs for her first [art] lesson.[324] I'll be dropping by to pick her up after one o'clock. Since my visit to the doctor I haven't gone out anywhere; it's been very painful; today it's a little better. I've been writing and writing without a break and now I don't know what else to say. You ask me to write *good things,* but I can't really — my head, heart and soul are empty! Wouldn't such a condition result from potassium bromide? — Last night I couldn't get any sleep until past three — there was a ringing and cracking [in my head], along with horror and fear. Finally the sounds took on a specific character of furniture being moved in your room. Then I leapt up, I experienced some kind of frightening panic attack; I awoke Dunjasha[325] and said "We'd better go see if there's an intruder!" Dunjasha crossed herself, groaned and sighed, but went ahead of me with a candle. We took a look around — there was nobody there, of course.

I was ashamed and sorry to have woken Dunjasha, but I was still fearful after that. Still, I continue to sleep alone, upstairs, to overcome my [frightened] self. Yes, I need to overcome and keep overcoming myself to be better and stronger.

Farewell, dear Lëvochka. Tanja and Masha have gone to Uncle Serëzha's, and nobody's written to you today. I'm sending along Chertkov's[326] letter, the only one that has come while you've been away. Hugs and kisses.

Sonja.

Nº 106 – LEV NIKOLAEVICH TOLSTOY ❧ SOFIA ANDREEVNA TOLSTAYA
[PSS 83/289]
13 December 1884. Yasnaya Polyana.

I've just written a letter on a postcard[327] — I started well but ended poorly, so I'm not sending it, and am now writing on paper so that this doesn't happen again. It happened in connection with Lëlja's letter,[328] which I was really happy about. I can just imagine that everyone's after him for this — i.e. that he has something to say to me and he knows just how to say it, and he knows how to say it in such a way that I feel he's close to me, that he knows that all his

---

322 Count Pavel Alekseevich Kapnist (1842–1904) — a Moscow school trustee from 1880 to 1895.

323 Princess Agrafena Aleksandrovna Obolenskaja and three nieces.

324 At the home of Fëdor Andreevich Beklemishev and his wife Dar'ja Aleksandrovna Beklemisheva (see Letter Nº 92, Note 4) Tat'jana L'vovna was taking art lessons along with their daughters.

325 Avdot'ja (Evdokija) Nikolaevna (Dunjasha) Bannikova (see Letter Nº 5, Note 37).

326 Vladimir Grigor'evich Chertkov (neighbour) — see Letter Nº 97, Note 257.

327 LNT's postcard note of 13 December 1884 was never sent. It ends with the words: "If nothing [unforseen] happens, I shall arrive on Sunday. It will be a sad trip" (PSS 83: 465).

328 Lev L'vovich's letter has not been preserved. LNT's correspondence with his son Lev (Lëlja) was published in 2014 under the editorship of Liudmila Gladkova (see Bibliography under Tolstoj, Lev L'vovich for details).

interests are close to mine, and that he knows or wants to know what my interests are. — I shan't say more, so that I don't have to tear up this letter, too.

I got up early this morning and got down to work early, and have been working now for five hours straight, and did a lot of crossing-out, but whether there's any sense in this crossing-out or not — I don't know. But that's not true: I know there is, and so my soul feels light. How different all other people's lives might have turned out, and how much happier they themselves would have been, if only they had set as their goal the *creation* of something that wasn't there [before] — something good and needful, rather than [mere] pleasure. In fact there is no other real pleasure than that which results from creation. You can create pencils, and boots, and bread, and children — i.e. human beings, and thoughts which feed these human beings. Without some kind of creation there is no real pleasure — i.e. [no real] pleasure unmixed with fear, suffering, pangs of conscience or shame; and the more important the creation, the greater the pleasure. Thus it is with us, adults and oldsters; for children and young people creation is replaced for the most part by the acquisition of knowledge or skills. This is true of oldsters as well. But the oldsters have a large proportion of creations, and a small [proportion] of acquisition of knowledge and skills, while with the young it's the other way round. However, when this is replaced by seeking pleasure and the taste for creating things and the acquisition of knowledge and skills is lost, then this is not a joke, but perdition.

I remember my youth and remember that I went through periods like that, but they were short periods, exceptions, times that have been completely erased from my memory, of which any memory I have is accompanied by [a sense of] loathing. I later remembered the words of Ermolova,[329] an erstwhile beauty with a small patch on her nose — how she assured me that I would dance with her right through my youth (which I don't remember), but mainly her words: *il faut que [la] jeunesse se passe.* People who in their *vieillesse* have not outlived their *jeunesse* love to repeat these words. These words are probably said by Grushen'ka Obolenskaja,[330] Uncle Serëzha and Uncle Kostja. *[La] jeunesse se passe* safely when there is *vieillesse* — I don't know how to put it — which is doing its job; but when oldsters themselves 'turn up their toes' — i.e. when they give themselves over to vanity, idleness and luxury, then where is *jeunesse* going to end up? That is not good, and, most importantly, it is not true. And the oldster who tells young people what he sees with his elderly mind and talks seriously to young people, no matter how unpleasant it may be for the young people, that oldster probably has a far greater love for and understanding of young people than [all] the Grushen'kas, Ermolovas, uncles and [Sergej Semënovich] Urusovs, as though out of some common interests with young people they were frolicking with them.

I received your letter[331] this morning. I hope that you will receive [this one] in just as timely [a fashion], and that it will be just as important for you as it is for me. Each time I have noticed that I hold your letter in abeyance for a period of time and choose a [specific] time for reading it. This is more important for me than for you. Your letters reflect not only your mental state, but that of the children, too — [the ones] at home. Of course I may be mistaken, but I use your letter[s] (as though they were a thermometer) to follow the moral temperature of the family — has it gone up or down? — Your letter today was good, but the temperature, I see, has fallen somewhat and continues to stay at a low level. — After work I rode over to Yasenki. The

329 Ekaterina Petrovna Ermolova (1829–1910) — elderly, unmarried lady-in-waiting (from 1847) to the Imperial Court. It is said that Nicholas I offered her a tempting position if she would move to his St. Petersburg palace, but she refused.
330 Princess Agrafena Aleksandrovna (Grushen'ka) Obolenskaja — see Letter N° 96, Note 252.
331 A letter dated 11 December 1884 (*Letters to L. N. Tolstoy*, pp. 285–86).

weather's pleasant: calm, [snow] melting, fog. I came back, spent time in the bathhouse and am now reading the Gospel in Hebrew,[332] and I want to go to bed earlier [than normal]. —

Farewell, dear friend, hugs and kisses to you and the children. — I shall come Sunday, if nothing happens [in the meantime]. — Why did my railway carriage so displease you? This carriage is a reflection of Moscow [itself] — here all in a compact form.[333]

I'm afraid that this letter, too, is not good and will have an unpleasant influence on you. If so, please forgive me. Give Lëlja a big kiss from me. How are the four little ones[334] getting on?

On the envelope: Moscow. Dolgokhamovniki Lane. Count Tolstoy's house. Countess Sofia Andreevna Tolstaya.

Nº 107 – LEV NIKOLAEVICH TOLSTOY ❧ SOFIA ANDREEVNA TOLSTAYA
[PSS 83/297]
2 February 1885. Yasnaya Polyana.

This morning, Friday, I received your latest letter.[335] It's a little better, perhaps, and I'm a little better; but it has lessened my longing for you. — I spent the whole day at home — writing, reading, and quietly sitting and thinking. In the evening I walked to the village to see Nikolaj Ermilovich[336] to shame him on account of the debt he refuses to pay, and to Kostjushka,[337] and to Ganja the thief.[338] *There's* a miserable creature for you, hunted down by people and so turned nasty — alone with three children.

I have been having a lot more impressions of poverty and suffering. I see them always and everywhere, but it's easier to spot them in the countryside. Here you see *everything* down to the last detail. And you see both the cause and the means. And I love it — not actually love it, but feel good — when I can clearly see my own situation amidst other people's.

Judging by what you wrote about Garshin,[339] I don't regret not having seeing him. On the whole, I'm obliged to see so many people in Moscow that the fewer I see the easier it is on me. It always seems that they don't need me at all. —

I am reading [George] Eliot's[340] *Felix Holt*. A first-class work. I had read it [before], but back when I was very stupid, and I'd completely forgotten. Here's something that needs to be translated, if it hasn't been already. A job for Tanja. I haven't finished it yet, and I'm afraid the ending will be disappointing. It was given to me by my brother Serëzha. Tell him it's all true what he

---

332 SAT added the following comment to this passage: "Lev Nikolaevich was meticulously studying the Hebrew language. He was receiving lessons in Moscow by the Rabbi Minor, an outgoing and clever fellow" (PSS 83: 468). The rabbi in question was Rabbi Solomon Alekseevich Minor (1826–1900), head of the Jewish religious community in Moscow from 1869 to 1892. He ran a Talmud-Torah school for children from poor families.

333 In a letter dated 8 December (not included here), LNT describes what he saw as the unsavoury characteristics of his fellow-passengers on the Moscow–Tula train (PSS 83: 454).

334 *the four little ones:* Andrej (Andrjusha), Mikhail (Misha), Aleksej (Alësha) and Aleksandra (Sasha).

335 This letter has not been preserved.

336 Nikolaj Ermilovich Zjabrev — a Yasnaya Polyana peasant.

337 Konstantin Nikolaevich (Kostjushka) Zjabrev (peasant) — see Letter Nº 63, Note 36.

338 *Ganja* — wife to the Tolstoys' employee Grigorij Ivanovich.

339 Vsevolod Mikhajlovich Garshin (1855–1888) — writer, highly appreciated by LNT, who published several of his stories through Posrednik (see Letter Nº 97, Note 4).

340 George Eliot — pseudonym of Mary Ann Evans (1819–1880), English writer. In the Yasnaya Polyana library there is a copy of Felix Holt, the Radical with LNT's marginal notations.

told me about this book — it's all there. This is the second time I'm praising from the country a book he recommended.[341] —

In front of me lies a note from a widow who was here today. She has no home, no land — her husband was a soldier at the Grumont barracks. She was left a widow at age 32 with 8 children — the eldest was 11. — When I began to write [about her], for a long time I couldn't understand — it turns out [these included] one set of twins. The lieutenant[342] has offered her a corner of a room for the winter.

Tomorrow I shall go to Tula and try to see what can possibly be done for her.

I'm taking this letter to Kozlovka — and shall tremble as I open the [next] one from you. How is your health? Judging by your letters, you're not doing very well. How is Misha[343] and the whole house?

Yesterday I was regretting our temporary absence of love. A consequence of this is a lack of clarity in our mutual aspirations. I told you that if you want me to come back, write to me and I'll come at once — and not through pressure, but with genuine joy that I can fulfil your desires. But you haven't written anything, or [at least] nothing definite.

Farewell, my darling. Hugs and kisses to you and the children.

L.

Urusov is much better than in Moscow. He has to take care of himself, and he is taking care of himself, but I see that in taking care of himself in this way he might live a long time.

Just now at Kozlovka I received your thoroughly kind letter[344] and I am heading home calm and happy. You have called me, and so I shall come on Monday [4 February]. —

On the envelope: Moscow. Khamovniki, Count Tolstoy's house. Countess Sofia Andreevna Tolstaya.

Nº 108 – SOFIA ANDREEVNA TOLSTAYA ❧ LEV NIKOLAEVICH TOLSTOY
[LSA 127]
[21 February 1885. St. Petersburg]

I'm very sad [to hear] that you're not healthy, dear Lëvochka. If I'd known that you were getting worse, I wouldn't have gone.[345] Please, take care of yourself, don't go outdoors and don't catch cold.

As for Madame Seuron, I can only say I feel genuinely sorry for her, but I'd stake my life on the [diagnosis] that she has intermittent fever, and that I could cure her in three days. Ask her or you yourself write to [Dr.] Chirkov,[346] asking him to give her quinine. It is pitiful to see people perishing on account of stubbornness and moral weakness. After all, she might end up God knows where. When Misha had typhoid fever, his temperature did not fall below 39° the whole time without exception, and here this morning she was [only] 37.2.

341 The other book was Gustave Droz's *Tristesses et sourires* (see Letter Nº 93, Note 231).
342 Lieutenant Frants Ivanovich Baratynskij (forester) — see Letter Nº 91, Note 218.
343 Mikhail L'vovich (Misha) Tolstoj was ill with typhoid fever.
344 This letter has not been preserved.
345 SAT and her daughter Tanja had gone to St. Petersburg, where they stayed with SAT's sister and brother-in-law (the Kuzminskijs).
346 Vasilij Vasil'evich Chirkov (also spelt: Cherkov; 1846–1907) — therapist-assistant to Dr. Grigorij Antonovich Zakhar'in (see Letter Nº 34, Note 210).

Anyway, this morning I got up at 10 o'clock, my sleep was bad and very fitful. I received a letter from Urusov,[347] his [chest condition] is worse again, and he is leaving on the 26th. Then Lukovnikov[348] came; he brought all the money [he owed] and ordered 500 more *Primers [Azbuki]*, for which he paid as well. Altogether today he behaved himself in a very polite and gentleman-like manner. According to [your] letters, I ordered samples of paper and type, made a variety of appointments, and starting tomorrow I shall receive [visitors] between 11 and 1 o'clock. Then I went with Tanja to see relatives. I found Polivanova[349] at home — she is sending something in a letter to Uncle Kostja — either money or tender words on paper — I don't know, it's sealed. I also found Kiriakova[350] along with Madame Shostak[351] at home, but not *Alexandrine;*[352] I shall try again on Saturday; she's fasting. Contrary to my expectation, I really liked Mme Shostak.

Here I am sitting and chatting with her, and suddenly someone calls out "The Empress!"[353] I say: "Find a spot where I can see her." Ekaterina Nikolaevna jumps up like an arrow and cries "My stick, quickly!" (she has a game leg and walks with a stick), then turns to me [and says]: "*Sofie, restez,*" and off she runs. I wait; my daughter Tanja is here, along with Vera Shidlovskaja,[354] and Sofa Islen'eva.[355] We waited and waited, all at once there was a hum, some noise, and people crying out: "She's coming!". A lady sweeps by carrying a musical notebook, and says in passing: "*L'impératrice fera une visite à Madame Schostak.*" We were taken aback at first, but before long a whole procession passed in front of us. I thought that this was the end of it, but Ekaterina Nikolaevna called out to me: "*Sofie, venez et* Tanja". I went over to her, and she presented me to the Empress, then she called Tanja and at this point I said "*ma fille*". I can say in all honesty that I was greatly excited, but did not lose my composure. She, i. e., the Empress asked [me]: "*Il y a longtemps que vous êtes arrivée?*" I say: "*Non, Madame, depuis hier seulement.*" Then we went into the grand hall. The Empress again turned to me [and said]: "*Votre mari se porte bien?*" I say: "*Votre Majesté est bien bonne, il se porte bien.*" "*J'espère qu'il écrit quelque chose.*" I say: "*Non, Madame, pas en ce moment, mais je crois qu'il se propose d'écrire quelque chose pour les écoles, dans le genre de* 'What men live by' [Chem ljudi zhivy]". Ekaterina Nikolaevna interrupted, saying: "*Il n'écrira jamais des romans, il l'a dit à la comtesse Alexandrine Tolstoy.*" The Empress says: "*Est-ce que vous ne le désirez point, cela m'étonne.*" And she turned to me. I say to her: "*J'espère que les enfants de sa Majesté ont lu les livres de mon mari.*" She nodded her head, saying: "*Oh, je crois bien.*" Then she sat down, the singing began, and soon she left. — I can see you all saying: "Well, *Mamasha's* had quite an adventure." But truly, it's the last

---

347 This letter was written by Prince Leonid Dmitrievich Urusov on 18 February 1885. The seriously ill Urusov was about to head off for treatment in the Crimea with a stop at his wife's Djat'kovo estate in Brjansk Uezd, Orël Gubernia.

348 Pëtr Vasil'evich Lukovnikov (1847–?) — owner of a bookshop in St. Petersburg.

349 Probably a reference to Anna Mikhajlovna Polivanova (*née* Parmont) — wife of Major-General Mitrofan Andreevich Polivanov (1842–1913).

350 Ol'ga Aleksandrovna Kiriakova (née Islen'eva; 1845–1909) — aunt to SAT.

351 Ekaterina Nikolaevna Shostak (née Islen'eva; ?–1904) — first cousin to SAT's mother; director (1863–92) of the Nicholas Institute, founded in 1837 in St. Petersburg for daughters of slain military personnel.

352 Countess Aleksandra Andreevna Tolstaja (LNT's great aunt) — see Letter Nº 37, Note 231.

353 On SAT's meeting with Empress Marija Fëdorovna at the Nicholas Institute, see *My Life*, iv.32.

354 Vera Vjacheslavovna Shidlovskaja (married name: Meshcherinova; 1866–?) — SAT's first cousin.

355 Sof'ja Leonidovna (Sofa) Islen'eva (married name: Islavina; 1866–1931) — SAT's second cousin.

thing I expected in Petersburg. Now I'm going with Tanja to a concert, and from there in the evening to Shostak's — a reception she's having. I didn't find Orzhevskaja[356] at home.

The Empress was precious, tired-looking [face], but[–][357]

Nº 109 – LEV NIKOLAEVICH TOLSTOY ❧ SOFIA ANDREEVNA TOLSTAYA
[PSS 83/300]
22 February 1885. Moscow.

This morning I received your note.[358] Everything here is quite fine, in spite of your dream. The little ones are doing splendidly, both physically and morally. And the older ones are good, too. — Iljusha has now reconciled with his teacher.[359] I slept well, but I still have the flu; I am reading my *George*.[360] Tell Sasha[361] that he should read it if he has the time. It's an important book. In the path of community life it is a step equal in importance to the liberation of the peasants — [i.e.] the liberation from owning land as private property. One's views on this subject constitute a test for human beings. And one must read *George*, who has put this question clearly and definitively. After reading him one cannot [simply] shilly-shally, one has to declare for one side or the other. My demands are much more far-reaching than his; but it is the first step on the ladder I'm climbing.

In the evening I sewed boots — it didn't go well, the children were with me.

In the morning they went for a walk, in spite of their stomachs, and came back happy and healthy. Then Marakuev[362] came. Masha asked [me for my permission to go] to Uncle Serëzha's to listen to Lopatin[363] [performing live]. I had a cup of tea, fetched my big fur coat and went with Ma-ra-ku-ev — first to the Olsuf'evs,[364] to get from her [Anna Mikhajlovna] the manuscript of *The teachings of the Twelve Apostles [Uchenie dvenadtsati apostolov]*,[365] and give it to Marakuev. He hopes to get it through the censors and publish it. Then I stopped by [Uncle] Serëzha's for Masha. The singing had just begun and [so] I brought her and Lëlja home at one o'clock. I didn't catch cold and tomorrow I should be quite recovered. There was a letter for you from Varvara Dmitrievna Urusova.[366] Hugs and kisses to you and [our daughter] Tanja, as well

---

356 Natal'ja Ivanovna Orzhevskaja (*née* Princess Shakhovskaja; 1859–1939) — wife of Senator and Deputy Minister of Internal Affairs Pëtr Vasil'evich Orzhevskij (1839–1897); granddaughter of Decembrist Prince Fëdor Petrovich Shakhovskoj (1796–1829).

357 The ending of this letter has been lost.

358 This note has not been preserved.

359 In a letter of 20 February 1885 (not included here), LNT wrote to his wife: "Iljusha has somehow angered his teacher, Janchin, who wrote me a letter, but tomorrow Il'ja has promised to make everything right" (PSS 83: 479). Ivan Vasil'evich Janchin (1818–1889) was a teacher of geography and a class mentor at Polivanov's *gymnasium* (see Letter Nº 82, Note 176); he authored *Kratkij uchebnik geografii [A brief guide to geography]*, which ran through more than 30 editions.

360 A book (1879) by American political economist Henry George (1839–1897) entitled *Progress and poverty*. LNT liked George's ideas about a 'single tax' and the nationalisation of land.

361 Aleksandr Mikhajlovich (Sasha) Kuzminskij (SAT's brother-in-law).

362 Vladimir Nikolaevich Marakuev (journalist) — see Letter Nº 94, Note 235.

363 Nikolaj Mikhajlovich Lopatin (1854–1897) — singer, collector of folk songs.

364 Count Adam Vasil'evich Olsuf'ev (see Letter Nº 81, Note 172) and Countess Anna Mikhajlovna Olsuf'eva (*née* Obol'janinova; 1835–1899).

365 A work LNT translated from the Greek — a manuscript discovered in 1873 in Constantinople, which fascinated LNT.

366 Varvara Dmitrievna Urusova (sister to Leonid Dmitrievich Urusov — see Letter Nº 94, Note 234.

as the dear Kuzminskijs. I trust them more now that you are with them; otherwise they might as well be in New Zealand.

On the envelope: St. Petersburg. 75. Nevskij [Prospekt]. For S. A. Tolstaya c/o A. M. Kuzminskij.

Nº 110 – LEV NIKOLAEVICH TOLSTOY ❧ SOFIA ANDREEVNA TOLSTAYA
[PSS 83/301]
22 February 1885. Moscow.

Today, Friday, I received your letter about your meeting with the Empress.[367] Your luck is truly amazing. This is something you really wanted, after all. For me it was flattering for my vanity, but actually rather disturbing. No good will come of it. I remember that in Pavlovsk there was a man who always sat in the bushes and warbled like a nightingale. I once struck up a conversation with him and right away from the unpleasant tone of his voice I could tell that someone of the royal family had been talking with him. Be careful the same doesn't happen to you. Yesterday I was ill, but today I feel much better, although still by no means normal. I can't write. I keep reading *George* and have grown a lot wiser. The children are all healthy and good — Masha will write about them [in a postscript]. Orlov[368] came to see me in the evening, then Shirkov,[369] and we sat [talking] until 2 o'clock [in the morning]. [Uncle] Kostja was here in the morning; Lëlja had just read your letter and said right away upon meeting him: "'Mama talked with the Empress." Without a moment's hesitation, Kostin'ka said: "Now I can die. 'Now lettest Thou Thy servant depart in peace."[370] Hugs and kisses to you and the dear Kuzminskijs. Why did you not tell [the Empress] what I am writing, but [instead you said] that I'm not writing? You got shy. Well, farewell. I am starting to count the days until you return.

Nº 111 – SOFIA ANDREEVNA TOLSTAYA ❧ LEV NIKOLAEVICH TOLSTOY
[LSA 128]
[22 February 1885.] Friday evening [St. Petersburg]

Dear Lëvochka, perhaps God sent you the flu so that you could be with your children. Thank you for taking care of yourself and not venturing outdoors. But these constantly repeating bouts of flu you suffer have come from your gathering wood for the stove. You go out in the cold, then you sit by the fire and then again you go outdoors — that's very harmful. I hope you don't do this when you are ill, or else you could also get pneumonia. You worry me most of all, and I am constantly thinking about you. Iljusha's behaviour with his teacher upset me; he can exhibit incredible rudeness once he gets a mind to — I experienced this in his relations with me. Why aren't any of you writing me about Lëlja? I hope everything's fine with him.

Today I saw Chertkov;[371] he'll be coming again tomorrow evening. I really liked him — so simple, friendly and, I would say, cheerful! I gave him the notebook. I haven't seen

---

367 Letter Nº 108 of 21 February 1885.
368 Vladimir Fëdorovich Orlov (teacher) — see Letter Nº 71, Note 101.
369 Valerian Valerianovich Shirkov (1843–1912) — amateur composer; son of artist-poet Valerian Fëdorovich Shirkov (1805–1856), a landowner in Kursk.
370 The beginning of a canticle known in the Bible as the *Nunc dimittis* in the words of St. Simeon (see Luke 2: 29–32).
371 Vladimir Grigor'evich Chertkov's mother — Elizaveta Ivanovna Chertkova (née Chernysheva-Kruglikova; 1832–1922) — lived in St. Petersburg. The Posrednik publishing house, co-founded by LNT and Chertkov, was also located there.

Shakhovskoj[372] yet; his arm was once again out of joint and they had to break it and set it again, as they did with yours.[373] Alexandrine[374] wrote me that she would not be seeing me until Saturday, as she is fasting and today she is going to confession, which is very important to her. I shall go see her tomorrow. I still haven't been able to do anything for the medical student. As to the books, there is clarification and progress taking place. I shan't print them here, I'll explain when I get home, but I'll bring Stasjulevich's[375] estimate and paper samples with me for our consideration. I'm very comfortable with the Kuzminskijs; it seems I'm not much of a bother to them, and it's easier and more joyful for Tanja when I am here to bear [the burden of] Misha's illness along with her. I feel quite good and peaceful here, quite at home; only I miss you very much. Our daughter Tanja is spending the whole day today at the Shidlovskijs, going skating with Vera;[376] she was at the Olsuf'evs';[377] they're coming to see us tomorrow. Tanja (our daughter) is very cheerful and lively. I don't know what [her] overall impression will be. Tomorrow we go to the Hermitage, and on Sunday to the Academy [of Arts] to see paintings. If you find it boring correcting the proofs,[378] leave them for me. Farewell, my dove; everything's in a mad rush here. Hugs and kisses.

Sonja.

N° 112 – SOFIA ANDREEVNA TOLSTAYA ❧ LEV NIKOLAEVICH TOLSTOY
[LSA 133]
11 March [1885. Moscow]

I write to you every day, yet from you I've only received a postcard to date. Why aren't you writing? I don't know… as of now, have you left for the Crimea?[379] Today I received the kindest letter[380] from Chertkov. He asks me to send him the printer's sheets of your article[381] which he brought me and says, for example: "I constantly think of you and your family as my relations, and close relations at that. Whether that's good or bad, I don't know. It seems to me that it's good."

How like him that is!

My Misha is still not well, though today he was on his feet. Last night and this morning he had no temperature, but now, as of 4 o'clock this afternoon, he has a temperature again: 38.7. Apparently, a fever. I gave him quinine twice, but it didn't help. Now I'm not giving him anything; I'll wait a couple more days. Tanja and Madame [Seuron] are slowly recovering, but they go out [just] a bit for walks and are eating a little more [than before].

I've just received your first letter from Djat'kovo.[382] Why did you all postpone your trip?

<hr>

372 Prince Dmitrij Ivanovich Shakhovskoj (1861–1939) — a political activist, one of the founders of the so-called Cadet Party; a graduate of St. Petersburg University who was then active in establishing state schools in the countryside.

373 See Letter N° 10, Note 60.

374 Countess Aleksandra Andreevna (Alexandrine) Tolstaja — see Letter N° 37, Note 231.

375 Mikhail Matveevich Stasjulevich (1826–1911) — editor and publisher of the journal *Vestnik Evropy*.

376 Vera Aleksandrovna Kuzminskaja (SAT's niece) — see Letter N° 43, Note 281.

377 Aleksandr Vasil'evich Olsuf'ev (1843–1907), brother to Adam Vasil'evich Olsuf'ev, and his wife Ekaterina L'vovna Olsuf'eva (*née* Sollogub; 1847–1902).

378 The reference is to the proofreading of the new fifth edition of LNT's collected works. At the moment they were working on the proofs of *What men live by* [Chem ljudi zhivy] and *Childhood* [Detstvo].

379 On 7 March 1885 LNT left for the Mal'tsovs' Djat'kovo estate in Orël Gubernia where the ailing Prince Leonid Dmitrievich Urusov was staying. On 10 March, on the advice of his doctors, he left for the Crimea, accompanied by LNT.

380 The letter was dated 10 March 1885.

381 A reference to LNT's article *What then must be done?* [Tak chto zhe nam delat'?].

382 This letter was written on 8 March.

That was not so nice for me; it prolongs your absence. Already now the days leading us to death are passing slowly, and what are they filled with? Emptiness and vanity. You probably left today. The day here has been fantastic; spring is coming with a great hurry; people have already [replaced the sleigh-runners] on their carriages with wheels, and water is pouring out from everywhere. Today I went out for a drive and happened to look at carriages for sale, but decided to put mine in for new wheels. Spring without a carriage is boring; without a carriage it's not even worth keeping horses with such a large family. Then I went to see Liza Obolenskaja, but didn't find her in; then I went to check on Khovrina's [family][383] — [her daughter], the young Liza, is dangerously ill. Back at home I gave Andrjusha a lesson, and received the proofs of *Childhood*. Pity I don't have the first edition here[384] — it's at Yasnaya. Proofreading your complete collected works, I feel, will turn my whole soul inside out. Your old writings have a fearsome effect on me, and I shall shed many tears as I correct the proofs. But I think this will be good [for my mental state].

Yesterday (Sunday) Uncle Serëzha came; he is kind and feels guilty in respect to his debt and to the gipsies. He was so dear and cheerful that I took to loving him again even more. We played Russian whist, two tables: Serëzha, Leonid,[385] myself and Liza[386] Olsuf'eva, and our own Serëzha made a fifth. And then the young ones played their own table. Just imagine, only Zolotarëv[387] remained to sit and look on with interest. What a creature! Why is he in the world? Liza, Varja, Fet — none [of these] were there. Vasnetsov[388] left early. Lopatin was planning to come and sing [for us], but he was ill. Still, we had a pleasant, fun time *en famille*. We didn't do all that much playing, but over supper we had a good and fun chat.

Farewell for now, there's nothing more to write. I have to finish the proofreading by morning, and there's so much to do. Hugs and kisses to you, dear friend. It is strange to be writing to the Crimea and knowing that you have just left, — quite mind-boggling.

Take care, Lëvochka, in everything. Don't take any risks at all, try to stay healthy and cheerful, also so you will have some good memories of your trip. My regards to the prince.[389] How sorry I am for him! Why don't you write and tell me what kind of mood he's in.

Sonja.

Are you going to be back by the [Easter] holidays? Also, please do send me one telegram from the Crimea.

I'm very lonely without you; nobody's around to love me. It's so sad. I'd really like to be with you right now. This is the third letter [I've sent] to the Crimea.

---

383 Most probably a reference to Evdokija Ljubimovna Khovrina (*née* Princess Engalycheva; 1833–1895) and her daughter Elizaveta Leonidovna [Liza] Khovrina, a friend of the Tolstoys' daughter Tanja.

384 *Childhood [Detstvo]* was first published in the journal *Sovremennik* (1852, N° 9, pp. 6–104), attributed to "L. N.". The first book edition was published in 1856 jointly with *Boyhood [Otrochestvo]*.

385 Leonid Dmitrievich Obolenskij — see Letter N° 40, Note 259.

386 Countess Elizaveta Adamovna (Liza) Olsuf'eva (1857–1898) — daughter to Count Adam Vasil'evich Olsuf'ev and Anna Mikhajlovna Olsuf'eva (see Letter N° 109, Note 7).

387 Aleksandr Ignat'evich Zolotarëv (1848–?) — a Tula landowner.

388 Viktor Mikhajlovich Vasnetsov (1848–1926) — an artist.

389 Prince Leonid Dmitrievich Urusov.

Nº 113 – LEV NIKOLAEVICH TOLSTOY ❧ SOFIA ANDREEVNA TOLSTAYA
[PSS 83/314]
14 March 1885. Bajdary.

I am writing you another letter today, the 14th [of March]. One from Sevastopol' — a post-card[390] — I sent in the morning, and now [this one] is from Bajdary (it's half-way to Simeiz). — We are feeding [our horses] here, and have run into a gentleman who is on his way to Moscow, who is feeding [his horse], too. It turned out to be Mr. Abrikosov the younger.[391] He recognised me and has read [my books], and his wife, too, whom he took to the Crimea, and I'm taking advantage of the fact that he will arrive before the post. The weather is marvellous — hot in the mountains through which we rode. Urusov hired a landau, but they put one over on him: it turned out the landau's [roof] did not open, it was worse than a carriage, and I climbed up onto a trunk where the coachman's seat was. As I rode, I can't say that I was actually thinking, but a new order of thoughts, good thoughts, flowed in [to my head]. —

Here's one of them: See! I'm alive, and can go on living! Still! How I would like to live out at least this last [part of my life] in God's [way] — i.e. in a good way! It's very silly, but it's joyful to me. The flowers are blooming, and it's hot even in just a shirt. The trees are bare, but fragrances blend together in the crisp spring air: limp leaves, human excrement, violets, and they all merge together. We rode through places that [during the war] seemed inaccessible, where there were enemy batteries, and, strange as it may seem, memories of the war actually join together with feelings of vigour and youth.[392] What if it were a memory of some folk celebration — a common cause — could there be such things? Right there on the coachman's seat I thought [a story about] an English lord.[393] And that's good. And I also thought — while Urusov was sitting in the carriage and kept urging on the coachman and horses, and while I, sitting next to the coachman, felt love for both the coachman and the horses — how unhappy rich people are who don't know either what they are riding on or what they live in (i.e. how their house is constructed), nor what they are wearing or eating. The *muzhiks* and the poor know all this, they appreciate it and take even greater delight in it. You can see that I am in a good, sprightly mood. If only I had some news about you and the children! Kisses to them all and a hug to you. Abrikosov's been given [fresh] horses. He's on his way.

L. T.

On the envelope: Moscow. Khamovniki, Count Tolstoy's house. Countess S. A. Tolstaya.

---

390 LNT's postcard from Sevastopol' dated 14 March, 9 a.m., reads: "We are departing Sevastopol' in a landau (at the request of the Prince [Urusov])… We'll be at our destination by 5. I'm weary from idleness and miss having news from you. My health is good" (PSS 83: 494).

391 Vladimir Alekseevich Abrikosov (1858–1922) — son of the merchant Aleksej Ivanovich Abrikosov (1824–1904); later director of the Moscow branch of the Imperial Russian Musical Society; author of memoirs concerning LNT. His wife was Marija Filippovna Abrikosova (née Chemjakina; 1866–1948).

392 LNT had participated in the Crimean War of 1854–1855 in the defence of Sevastopol', to which he devoted his *Sevastopol' stories* [*Sevastopol'skie rasskazy*].

393 A reference to the pulp-fiction *Povest' o prikljuchenijakh anglijskogo milorda Georga i brandenburgskoj marktgrafini Frederiki-Luizy* [*The story of the adventures of the English Milord George and the Brandenburg margravine Frederika-Louisa*] written in 1782 by Matvej Komarov (1730s–1812). See *My Life*, IV.12.

Nº 114 – SOFIA ANDREEVNA TOLSTAYA ✍ LEV NIKOLAEVICH TOLSTOY
[LSA 140]
[18 August 1885. Moscow]

Another day has gone by, useless and wasted. Up to now the boys would just loaf about, but today, instead of studying on the eve of exams, they just staggered from corner to corner, as if deliberately intending to do absolutely nothing, and this only drove me to despair.

This morning I went to buy something to eat (everything's closed on Sunday); I arrived to find two schoolmistresses; they had brought me two articles about you, Lëvochka. One was torn from *Vestnik Evropy*, the other copied from somewhere. In the latter it said that *Ma Religion*[394] was having great success in Paris, and a whole sect of *Tolstoïstes* had been formed which was promulgating your teachings. Pity that two more [of your philosophical-religious] articles have not been translated [into French] — then there would have been more of a complete impression and understanding. I'll now read these articles myself and bring them with me. The schoolmistresses also brought what they copied [i.e. the second one] from: *Zakon i Gosudarstvo [Law and State]*,[395] and asked for any more,[396] which I have no idea where to find. — Then I went to see Ivantsov-Platonov.[397] I was received by his daughter, 19 years old, a pupil of Fisher's[398] classical *gymnasium* — such a fine, clever girl. Then her father came. Apparently he had done practically nothing; he kept making excuses that there wasn't time, but persevered in his opinion that [the work] must definitely be published. I asked him to hurry to make his remarks, and he promised. He also talked about the big work, saying it would be good to [publish] excerpts from it. I took— *je l'ai pris au mot*, but he vigorously began to make excuses that now was not the time, and there was no way he could do it, he was so busy.

He said that Pobedonostsev[399] had ordered the papers to print articles by various people denouncing you and your teachings. But Solovëv,[400] a teacher of law at the Katkov *lycée*, wrote such a silly article; you can't help feeling pity for him as he only brought shame upon himself with his lack of understanding.

He talked to me a lot about what needs changing in your articles to make them fit to print; about your foreword, which he claims is necessary; about what to delete and how to change the titles and so forth.[401] He recommends publishing without going through the censorship board, but getting Feoktistov's[402] promise in advance not to block it. He recommends, once the article

---

394 In Russia LNT's article *What I believe* [*V chëm moja vera?*] was banned by the religious censorship committee and was first published in Paris in 1885 under the title *Ma Religion*, translated from the Russian by Prince Leonid Dmitrievich Urusov.

395 The reference is apparently to LNT's *Church and State* [*Tserkov' i gosudarstvo*], distributed in Russia in hand-made and lithographed copies. It was first published in Berlin by Cassirer & Danziger in 1891; in Russia its first appearance was in the St. Petersburg journal *Obnovlenie* (1906, Nº 8).

396 A reference to LNT's collection *A criticism of dogmatic theology* [*Kritika dogmaticheskogo bogoslovija*], from which *Church and State* was taken.

397 Aleksandr Mikhajlovich Ivantsov-Platonov (1835–1894) — archpriest and theologian, appointed Professor of Church History at Moscow University, author of *Ocherk istorii khristianstva u slavjan* [*Outline of the History of Christianity among the Slavs*]. At LNT's request he read his article *What I believe* and other religious writings and gave LNT his comments in writing.

398 Sof'ja Nikolaevna Fisher (*née* Bogdanova; 1836–1913) — founding headmistress of a private *gymnasium* in Moscow.

399 Konstantin Petrovich Pobedonostsev (Synod procurator) — see Letter Nº 94, Note 238.

400 Ivan Il'ich Solovëv (1854–1918) — a theologian, Master of Divinity; a clerical writer.

401 On the advice of Ivantsov-Platonov, in the 1886 edition the title *What I believe* [*V chëm moja vera?*] was changed to *How I have understood the teachings of Christ* [*Kak ja ponjal uchenie Khrista*].

402 Evgenij Mikhajlovich Feoktistov (1828–1898) — government press supervisor (1883–1896).

is typeset and published in its final form, to definitely send a copy to Feoktistov and definitely go to Petersburg myself and personally make intervention. He recommends including your latest stories as a literary expression of your teachings. We'll talk about all that in person; there's no room to write it all out. But it's good that I went to see him, or God knows how long this might be drawn out.

From Ivantsov's I went to Mjasnitskaja Street, to see Alcide [Seuron].[403] Unfortunately, he wasn't at home. He had gone off somewhere, and nobody knew when he might be back, since Grade 7 and 8 students have the right to walk out without permission. The porter said that Alcide was quite healthy and wasn't coughing. I asked for the headmaster — he is still at his dacha, and hasn't come into the city. I went to see the inspector, but he had just gone down the front steps with his wife. What a pity! I wanted to do something about Mme Seuron's request, but didn't have the opportunity. Please pass all this along to her — *avec mes saluts.*

I came home; the three of us took dinner, and I went into the kitchen, boiled some vinegar, poured vinegar on the plums and Chinese apples, made some jam, and in general carried on [the tradition of] *Ankovsky pie.*[404] Varvara Petrovna and Faddeevna[405] and I still had a pleasant time together. [Then] the ever-beloved Kolichka Ge[406] came into the kitchen and took a real interest in our [conversation]; my boys came, and despite my intensive urgings to them to get busy, they with equal intensity helped eat the plums. Then they went into the house and made Kolichka laugh so hard that he went completely bonkers and left. Then Uncle Kostja appeared in the kitchen window — he had come in today from Pirogovo. Everyone chatted together in the kitchen; eventually they took tea and dispersed… Il'ja and Lëlja went to finally go over their lessons, and I've now sat down to write.

Tomorrow morning I'll go around the print-shops, examine the accounts as to the inventory and use of paper; I shall go to Salaev's[407] and find out whether a subscription could be announced; I shall go and collect some money from the books [already sold]. After that I shall concern myself with [our children's] exams. Alësha's sniffles are not a disaster, but he needs to take care of his throat, and colds in general can be dangerous for anybody. Why have we been invaded by so many guests?! It was never like this before. I still don't know when I'll come. Lëlja still cuddles up to me; I feel sorry about leaving him, even though he's very unpleasant, fussy and lazy. How is everybody doing — the Kuzminskijs, Auntie Tanja, Uncle Sasha? How is my Tanja performing the role of mother and head of the household? It was very nice to receive [your] letter, and I am really looking forward to tomorrow's. Hugs and kisses to all.

Sonja.

403 Alcide Seuron (son of the Tolstoys' governess Anna Seuron) was studying at the Lazarev Institute of Oriental Languages.

404 *Ankovsky pie* — a traditional symbol of hospitality in the Behrs family, named after their doctor, Nikolaj Bogdanovich Anke (1803–1872)

405 These are two of the Tolstoys' servants in Moscow.

406 Nikolaj Nikolaevich (Kolichka) Ge Jr (1857–1940) — son of prominent Russian artist Nikolaj Nikolaevich Ge (Gay) Sr.

407 The reference is to the Salaev Brothers' publishing house, which had printed the preceding, fourth, edition of LNT's works in 1880.

N° 115 – LN ❧ SA
[PSS 83/327]
12 October 1885. Yasnaya Polyana.

I am writing a letter[408] to Masha, along with an order for books brought from Tula. I did a little work — almost nothing, and then I went out to saw [some wood] with Frey.[409] And we did some wonderful work. Then we took dinner. Now I've just written a letter to Chertkov[410] and now I'm writing you. Fejnerman[411] is engaged in a dispute with Frey; I'm listening with one ear and can tell that Fejnerman is winning, but I keep silent. Frey is such a precious, such a good person, that I feel bad about embarrassing him. In a couple of hours from now I'll see him off, and take myself to the vault room, where I shall be sleeping [tonight]. I shall try to behave myself well in every respect — food, sleep and work — in the wisest possible way, so that I can work a little more, and I specifically want to finish my *Ivan Ilyich*.[412] But in these affairs I know that it is least of all possible to expect everything to turn out the way I want it to.

Hugs and kisses to you and all the children. I forgot to affirm to Tanja and Masha that it would be pitiful if they abandoned what they started — namely, cleaning their rooms and vegetarianism[413] — in the sense of restraint. — Farewell, darling, until the next letter.

L. T.

N° 116 – SOFIA ANDREEVNA TOLSTAYA ❧ LEV NIKOLAEVICH TOLSTOY
[LSA 143]
13 October 1885. [Moscow]

The letter I wrote you yesterday,[414] dear Lëvochka, has tormented me the whole day as though [I had committed] a crime. But it is so lonely here in Moscow without you, and I miss you so much that I was overcome by some kind of malicious despair. And I thought: I came to see my beloved sons and live with them and for them, and here they are spiteful, asking for money, and with hardly any love.

I came to do things. I thought that money was needed for them, for the children — they don't want to know this; it's as though my edition[415] and everything else is just a caprice, or fantasy of mine [...]. But this is difficult and hurtful for me.

---

408 This letter has not been preserved.

409 William Frey [in transliteration from the Cyrillic: Vil'jam Frej] (real name: Vladimir Konstantinovich Gejns; 1839–1888) — a Russian intellectual of noble birth who embraced revolutionary ideals and in 1868 emigrated with his wife (who shared his views) to America, where he adopted the pseudonym Frey, from the English word free. Here he became a lifelong vegetarian and joined a Kansas commune, following French philosopher Auguste Conte's (1798–1857) doctrine of 'positive religion'. See also *My Life*, IV.52.

410 This letter was dated 11 October 1885 (PSS 85: 260–61).

411 Isaak Borisovich Fejnerman (pseudonym: Teneromo; 1863–1925) — a Tolstoyan. For further information, see *My Life*, IV.41 and IV.50.

412 A reference to LNT's work *The death of Ivan Ilyich* [*Smert' Ivana Il'icha*], first published in 1886.

413 LNT's daughters Tat'jana (Tanja) and Marija (Masha) both became vegetarians, much to SAT's disapproval (see Letter N° 116 below).

414 This letter has not been preserved. On 16 October 1885 LNT wrote: "How fortunate that the letter you were unhappy with did not arrive; if it does still arrive, I shan't read it. But I'd still like to know the reason" (PSS 83: 513).

415 The reference is to the 5th edition of LNT's collected writings which SAT was preparing for publication.

But my whole mistake is always the same: I want to be *appreciated*. And that is silly and bad. I get frustrated when they do not *understand* me and do not *appreciate* me, and with this attitude I am spoiling everything to such an extent that the scales are tipping to the side of *evil*. Now I've come to my senses somewhat. I shall do everything *according to my conscience,* and shall not think that I have the right to expect gratitude or silly *appreciation* from anyone. It will be calmer and better this way. And I ask you to please be calm, love me and support me without condemnation, if you can.

Today I received [another] letter[416] from you, and it was a pleasant one, but I'm annoyed that you are encouraging the girls to be vegetarians. Two [kinds of] soup, special vegetables — all that has to be prepared, and it is hard for a mother not to feed her children. Ever since Tanja sucked on my breast, I can't get away from the desire to feed her better and more substantially. I can't stop them from preparing special dishes, but it is more expensive and more challenging.

[Also] today [I have] six printer's sheets to proofread; I spent the whole day reading [them] by myself. Now Serëzha, along with Nikolaj Nikolaevich Ge [Jr], is reading two sheets for a second time, but all of them: Serëzha, Treskin,[417] Il'ja and Ge are off to the theatre, while Tanja and I will be reading the other four sheets. Ge lives for art; he rented a room for 20 silver roubles a month where his daughter[418] could board [while attending school]. Alcide is here. The boys and the younger ones have been skipping rope and running in the garden. I didn't see much of them during the day, I was busy the whole time with proofreading. [The governess] Miss Gibson has gone off to see relatives or friends. It's very difficult for me these days, especially since I'm tired; last night I got to sleep after two o'clock in the morning, and this morning I was awakened at seven.

I still haven't unpacked anything or put things away — there's simply been no time. The girls have tidied up their room and moved everything around. They, too, are bored here in Moscow and long for their life at Yasnaya Polyana.

I'll be urging Masha to get down to her studies soon. Tanja's now mature enough to choose her own pathway in life for herself. The Beklemisheva lady came to see her, and warmly invited her to visit; she'll be going there tomorrow.

[I] really need to be here to see to [the 5th] edition. I received a letter from Mamontov's[419] printshop that Kuvshinov's[420] has no more paper. This really surprised me. I worry we may have more delays as a result. Starting tomorrow morning I'll go and attend to all these things, I'll find out everything [I can], settle and clarify everything. I shall take *The story of a horse*[421] and the articles with me. Today is Sunday; I wasn't able to do anything today.

I'm glad you've moved into the 'vault room'.[422] It's good in there. But you should have the chimney cleaned, so that [soot] doesn't clog up the chimney; it hasn't been cleaned for a long

416 Letter N° 115 of 12 October 1885.

417 Vladimir Vladimirovich Treskin (1863–1920) — a Tula landowner; a jurist; friend to Il'ja L'vovich Tolstoj.

418 Nikolaj Nikolaevich Ge Jr (see Letter N° 114, Note 406) placed his illegitimately conceived daughter, Praskov'ja Nikolaevna Ge (1878–1959), with a Moscow family — probably with Vera Pavlovna Ziloti (*née* Tret'jakova; 1866–1940), daughter to Tret'jakov Gallery founder Pavel Mikhajlovich Tret'jakov and wife to pianist Aleksandr Il'ich Ziloti (1853–1945).

419 Anatolij Ivanovich Mamontov (1839–1905) — publisher, printshop owner and book distributor.

420 Mikhail Gavrilovich Kuvshinov — paper manufacturer.

421 The reference is to LNT's work Strider [Kholstomer] (written between 1856 and 1863), which SAT included in Part III of the 5th edition of LNT's collected works.

422 the 'vault room' — a room with a vaulted ceiling at Yasnaya Polyana which LNT used as an office.

time. Here in Pljushchikha [Street], on the very day of our arrival, eight people were burned to death [in a chimney fire], including a nanny and a child. .

Well, farewell, dear friend. Now I shan't write any more bad letters. God grant that you stay healthy; I was so glad to hear you're writing *Ivan Ilyich*. God help you. Hugs and kisses.

Sonja.

I ruined your whole day with my letter yesterday! Oh how ashamed and how sorry I am! I am kissing your dear, kind eyes. I can see them right this moment, and I regret that I shan't see them for a long time.

Nº 117 – SOFIA ANDREEVNA TOLSTAYA ❧ LEV NIKOLAEVICH TOLSTOY
[LSA 147]
21 October [1885. Moscow]

Kramskoj[423] was just here and was very sorry not to find you [at home]. People like him are like a light shining amidst the gloom and darkness. He sat with us for about an hour: Serëzha, Masha and Tanja were present and also took part in the conversation, then he left for an artists' meeting. He came from Petersburg specifically to discuss various questions about the exhibit, and to renew and reinforce the old rules of this *society of artists*. A clever fellow, indeed, and he understands everything — what a charm!

Just now I read Serëzha's letter.[424] Very disjointed — he's not delicate. He writes: "Mamà is offended that you are not interested in her publication activities". How can he so misunderstand his own family! How can I be offended if others are not interested in something that does not interest me in my heart at all?! I finish what I have started, and always get *deeply involved* in everything, as in this. — I might be offended if you were not interested at all in the children or in me, in our inner life, our sorrows and joys; I might be saddened by the fact that *when you are living together with the family, you are more distant than when we are not together...* Now all this is sad, and if we can't heal it, then we have to try to live with it. And I am making some headway in this and am getting a bit accustomed to it. We have not left you, but you have left us. [We] can't hold on to [you] by force. — You often forget that you're ahead of Serëzha, for example, in life by 35 years; ahead of Tanja and Lëlja, for example, by 40, and you want them all to race ahead and catch up to you. That's a misunderstanding. I, on the other hand, see how they walk, fall, stagger, stumble, and again cheerfully pursue the path of life, and I try to lend a helping hand here and hold back there, and keep a watchful eye out so that they don't stray off somewhere where they could have an irreversible failure. — How far my skill and ability extend [in this matter], well, that's another question. But as long as I am alive and am still of sound mind, I shall never say that I am distant from my family, and could never accept the thought that I am distant from my children, even though I live with them in the same house. — So this is what has irritated me, and not [your] lack of interest in Kuvshinov's paper.

Farewell. Pity that you are having liver complaint and that you're not working.

Sonja.

423 Ivan Nikolaevich Kramskoj (1837–1887) — artist, co-organiser of exhibitions by the 'Itinerant' Society of Artists, along with Nikolaj Nikolaevich Ge Sr (1831–1894), Grigorij Grigor'evich Mjasoedov (1834–1911) and Vasilij Grigor'evich Perov (1833–1882); painter of a famous 1873 portrait of LNT.
424 The reference is to a letter from the Tolstoys' son Sergej L'vovich to LNT, which has not been preserved.

Nº 118 – SOFIA ANDREEVNA TOLSTAYA ❧ LEV NIKOLAEVICH TOLSTOY
[LSA 148]
[22 October 1885. Moscow]

Today is Liza Obolenskaja's name day and the day of the [icon] *Our Lady of Kazan [Kazanskaja Bogomater']* and we are all spending the evening at the Obolenskijs'. The boys are also enjoying some free time, but Il'ja has been quite busy all day writing some sort of composition; Lëlja's playing the piano, and was reading [earlier]; Alcide [Seuron] is here. The three little ones,[425] too, were at the Obolenskijs' this morning and had some hot chocolate. Tanja's finger is hurting, and she wants to go to the doctor's again. I spent the whole morning before dinner poring over records, accounts and papers. I did some transcribing for *The Decembrists [Dekabristy], A confession [Ispoved']* and also proofread *The story of a horse [Strider / Kholstomer]* and *Two old men [Dva starika]*.

The publication is moving ahead slowly; there's still no paper. I looked over *A confession,* and a fear came over me that I shan't be successful at the Censorship Board, but that they'll send me to the Religious censors, and there's little hope there. Still, it is worth trying, and I'm going to keep trying as long as I can. Today I was sitting in the dining-room when all at once I saw before me Mlle Sof'ja Fominichna Brandt.[426] She frightened us. She, poor thing, is in such a bad way; she says that Golosova,[427] the director of the lunatic asylum, locked her away, and I appeared to her to be this same Golosova; she didn't recognise me. Later she found out from the registry office where the Obolenskijs were, and she went to see them and frightened them. I offered her breakfast, [but] she put on a ferocious face, refused everything and hurried off.

Today I received a letter from Tanja; she's very happy and is still planning on doing some writing, [an activity] she's quite fond of.[428]

I'm losing my eyesight, and that upsets me. I'm writing, but I can't see clearly what I'm writing — this is what it's come to! — Our life is boring, burdensome and unsatisfying. It's never happened to me up to now, but I haven't tidied up and haven't got the drawing room or the other rooms in order. Everything's jumbled together in a heap and [the stoves] are not stoked. You'd better give me notice if you are coming, so we can stoke [the stoves ahead of time]. There's no place upstairs either to sleep or sit anywhere but the salon.

They promise [to deliver fresh] paper on Saturday. Next week they'll print the end of *The Cossacks [Kazaki],* also *The Decembrists* and the beginning of Volume 12, and again, the week after, they'll typeset the articles.[429] So then I'll go to Petersburg — that means, in two weeks. If you need to, and if you are healthy and fine, you can stay on at Yasnaya another ten days, after which I would ask you to come at least for the time I'm away; I'm afraid to leave the children alone without at least one of us. Has your liver complaint passed? Where are you staying and what are you writing? There's been no letter yet [from you] today; perhaps one will still come.

---

425 *The three little ones:* Mikhail (Misha), Aleksej (Alësha), Aleksandra (Sasha).
426 Mlle Sof'ja Fominichna Brandt (married name: Dzhons) — daughter to the Tolstoys' neighbours in the village of Baburino.
427 *Golosova* — no further details available.
428 At the time SAT's sister Tat'jana (Tanja) was working on a story called *Beshenyj volk [The mad wolf].*
429 *the articles* — here referring to *A confession [Ispoved']* and *What I believe [V chëm moja vera?].*

Farewell, dear friend, hugs and kisses to you. Perhaps your time of mental exhaustion has passed, and you are working again — and consequently happy. We here, thank God, are all healthy and getting along well.

S.

22 October.

Today the whole Tolstoj family[430] are moving here.

N° 119 – LEV NIKOLAEVICH TOLSTOY ❧ SOFIA ANDREEVNA TOLSTAYA
[PSS 83/336]
23 October 1885. Yasnaya Polyana.

In both your recent letters, dear friend, I can detect a hint of irritation at me over what I wrote in my letter to Tanja.[431] Why get irritated and accusatory, and say that it is irredeemable? Everything is redeemable, especially one's views on life. As long as we live, we are constantly changing; we *can* change, thank God, and draw closer and closer to the truth. This is the only thing I desire for myself and my family, for you and the children, and not only am I not disheartened in this, but I believe that we shall come together, if not in my lifetime, then afterwards. If I wrote that we live together but at a distance, though it may be true, it is exaggerated, and I shouldn't have written that, as it's equivalent to a reproach. I consider reproaches worse than anything else and I take [my words] back. — I did miss one day[432] of writing to you, and I apologise for that, too. It's hard on me, too, when I don't write, when there's something I should have done but didn't.

Yesterday I wrote a few words and said that my side was hurting. It *was* hurting, but that's all passed now, and I am very cheerful and healthy, and am again doing a lot of work. Now I've almost glimpsed the end of my article.[433] I've decided that, as long as I don't get too worried about all of you, I shall finish it here, which may take [another] three days. — When you write me about your life, I talk it over [with you]; I don't always approve of your impulsiveness; but when you don't write [me] anything, like today, that is annoying and painful for me. Please do write. — Fejnerman has been dismissed,[434] and a new teacher has already arrived. I don't know what he's going to do, but he wants to stay living in the village with Konstantin,[435] and transcribe [Tolstoy's drafts]. If you find any volunteers [to transcribe] *What then must be done?*, give me [their names].

Thanks to Serëzha for his letter.[436] There was no need for him to criticise it as disjointed. As to Lëlja, we all know what kind of a correspondent he is. Hugs and kisses to them all. Here are the events of my day: I get up when it's dark. And it's the same right now. After tidying up, I went to fetch some water [with a barrel on a horse-drawn wagon]. That's a great pleasure. But

---

430 Sergej Nikolaevich Tolstoj (LNT's brother) and his family.
431 In his letter to his daughter Tanja of 18 October 1885, LNT wrote: "…my only dream and possible joy, which I dare not hope for, is to find in my family [true] brothers and sisters, and not what I have seen to date — alienation and deliberate counteraction, which smacks of a cross between disdain (not for me but for the truth) and fear of something" (PSS 63: 292–93).
432 21 October.
433 A reference to LNT's article *What then must be done?* [*Tak chto zhe nam delat'?*].
434 For the background to Isaak Borisovich Fejnerman's dismissal, see *My Life*, IV.50.
435 Konstantin Nikolaevich Zjabrev (peasant) — see Letter N° 63, Note 36.
436 See Letter N° 117, Note 424.

sitting on the barrel, I began to think about the division of labour,[437] which was fine. But when it came time to fill [the barrel], I suddenly realised I didn't have a pail, and so I went to fetch a pail, and [headed to the well] once again. Upon my return, I obtained a *pood* of whole wheat flour from Filip, and began kneading it according to Frey's method, and the pancake-shaped loaf turned out to be quite tasty. Later, after taking coffee with Fejnerman and Aleksandr Petrovich,[438] I got down to work and sat there working from 9 to 2. Then I had dinner: borshch and a marvellous oat *kissel*. Then I rode over to Bibikov's to find out about Fejnerman's salary, and then to Kozlovka to fetch letters — I got yours[439] as well as one from Chertkov.[440] Tomorrow I'll post [a letter] myself. I'm sorry to have missed Kramskoj. Farewell, dear friend. In any case, if I'm still alive, I'll be there soon. — I'm not disheartened, and I'm terribly eager to finish *Ivan Ilyich,* and now as I was riding along I kept thinking about him. I can't express [in words] to you how absorbed I am right now in this work which has gone on for several years and is now nearing completion. I have to clarify things for myself which were unclear before, and put aside a whole raft of questions, as happened with me [earlier] with the theological questions.

Don't get angry, my darling; be kind and friendly, the way I feel about myself in relation to you.

On the envelope: Moscow. Dolgokhamovniki Lane N° 15. Countess Sofia Andreevna Tolstaya.

N° 120 – LEV NIKOLAEVICH TOLSTOY ❧ SOFIA ANDREEVNA TOLSTAYA
[PSS 83/341]
20 November 1885. Moscow.

I wrote you [an earlier] letter today on a postcard, which will probably arrive a day ahead of this one. Yesterday I spent the whole day in Tanja's room in the heat, and the whole day there were visitors: Stakhovich,[441] a notary, an agent,[442] then came Kolichka Ge along with Mjasoedov,[443] later Verochka and Hélène;[444] then [my brother] Serëzha; but unfortunately I didn't get to see Serëzha, as I went to bed before 10 o'clock, and slept better. Now I'm completely recovered and I shan't go out — you needn't worry. — [Our son] Serëzha took the money and deposited [it]. Now it's after 1 o'clock in the afternoon. Yesterday I received a letter which greatly concerned me — I am sending you a copy and I'm asking you very, very [urgently] to

---

437 In his article What then must be done? LNT points out how 'division of labour' is used to justify the exploitation and oppression of the poor by the rich: "If some people give orders, while others obey them, if some live in plenty and others in want, that is not God's will — this [comes about] not because the state is a form of manifestation of personality, but because in societies, just as in living organisms, there occurs a division of labour necessary for the whole: some people in societies perform muscular labour, others intellectual labour. This is an article of faith underlying the prevalent justification of our age" (PSS 25: 330).

438 Aleksandr Petrovich Ivanov (1836–1912) — retired army officer who suffered from alcoholism; he served as a copyist for LNT.

439 Letter N° 118 of 22 October 1885.

440 The letter from Vladimir Grigor'evich Chertkov is dated 20 October 1885 (see PSS 85: 271).

441 Aleksandr Aleksandrovich Stakhovich (1830–1913) — equerry; a landowner in Orël, amateur actor, an old acquaintance of LNT's, who loaned LNT money for the publication of his complete collected works.

442 *an agent* — a reference to the manager of Volchaninov's printshop.

443 Grigorij Grigor'evich Mjasoedov (artist).

444 LNT's nieces Vera Sergeevna (Verochka) Tolstaja (see Letter N° 102, Note 297) and Elena Sergeevna (Hélène) Tolstaja (see Letter N° 74, Note 114).

do something to relieve this remarkable man's[445] plight. Ask Sasha Kuzminskij's advice on what to do. What actually can be done? — [One could] ask the war minister[446] and the headquarters commandant[447] to deal with Zaljubovskij according to the law — they have a law for so-called sectarians — Mennonites[448] and others — who refuse military service on religious grounds. I am [also] thinking of asking [Aleksandra Andreevna] Tolstaja. We need to definitely put a word in for him — mainly so that the authorities are aware that this man's situation and their treatment of him are known to the public at large. — I'm afraid that you have a lot on your plate, and that you will get upset with me for piling this matter on top of you. Here [in Moscow] I don't know who to turn to. I'll try Shuvalova.[449] For some reason I trust Sasha[450] will be able to help and instruct you.

I'll add a postscript later this evening. I wrote Stasov[451] with a request to do something; I wrote Shuvalova[452] and Birjukov.[453] Birjukov and Stasov may come and see you; you can show them the letter. If I knew where Mirskij[454] was, I'd write to him. Couldn't Sasha do something through Loris-Melikov?[455] The main thing they need is to keep the matter out of the public eye. If they sent him to assist in a hospital, nobody would know about it; but now, if, God forbid, they torture him or execute him, it will backfire on them. —

A postscript late at night — I've been busy with all my letter-writing and copying Za-lju-bov-skij's letter. I got Lëlja and Teplov[456] (who came to play with him) to do the writing. Everything's fine with us. My brother Serëzha was here this evening. I'm fine, but there is still [a sense of] *malaise.* — It's my usual state of ill health. I received your postcard[457] — thank you. Well, fare-well, my darling. Don't worry. Even if you don't succeed in anything, that will take nothing from the happiness of your life. Hugs and kisses to the dear Kuzminskijs and please ask [your sister] Tanja to forgive me for not carrying out her request… to proofread.[458] It's a difficult [task].

445 Anatolij Petrovich Zaljubovskij (1859–1936) — lieutenant, later lieutenant-general. His brother Aleksej Petrovich Zaljubovskij (1863–?), under the influence of LNT's writings refused military service and was sentenced to exile in a distant kraj.

446 Pëtr Semënovich Vannovskij (1822–1904) — Russian general; Minister of War (1881–98) and later Minister of Education (1901–02).

447 Nikolaj Nikolaevich Obruchev (1830–1904) — army headquarters commandant (1881–97); honorary member of the Petersburg Academy of Sciences.

448 *Mennonites* — a Dutch Protestant sect that settled in Russia in 1789 at the invitation of Empress Catherine the Great.

449 Elena Ivanovna Shuvalova (1830–1922) — a noblewoman, paternal aunt to Vladimir Grigor'evich Chertkov, married to Count Pëtr Andreevich Shuvalov (1827–1889); she was intrigued by the teachings of the English religious activist Lord Radstock and participated in the defence of persecuted sectarians. LNT's letter to her is unknown.

450 Aleksandr Mikhajlovich (Sasha) Kuzminskij (SAT's brother-in-law).

451 Vladimir Vasil'evich Stasov (librarian) — see Letter Nᵒ 61, Note 26. For LNT's letter to Stasov of 20 November 1885, see PSS 63: 300–01.

452 This letter has not been preserved.

453 Pavel Ivanovich (Posha) Birjukov (1860–1931) — a Tolstoyan who acted as a liaison between LNT and the Doukhobors, both before and after their emigration to Canada in 1899; he was also LNT's first biographer. See *My Life*, II.76. For LNT's letter to Birjukov of 20 November 1885 see PSS 63: 299.

454 Dmitrij Ivanovich Svjatopolk-Mirskij (1824–1899) — an old wartime chum of LNT's from the Caucasus campaigns during the Crimean war in 1855. In 1880 he became a member of the Russian State Council.

455 Count Mikhail Tarielovich Loris-Melikov (1825–1888) — Minister of Internal Affairs (1880–81), an acquaintance of Aleksandr Mikhajlovich Kuzminskij's.

456 Mikhail Vasil'evich Teplov (1862–1958) — artist, pupil of Nikolaj Nikolaevich Ge Sr; a friend of Lev L'vovich (Lëlja) Tolstoj's.

457 In her postcard of 19 November 1885 SAT wrote about her arrival in St. Petersburg, where she had come to clear up matters of censorship regarding her latest edition of LNT's collected works.

458 This is in reference to Tat'jana Andreevna Kuzminskaja's story *Beshenyj volk* [*The mad wolf*].

Nº 121 – SOFIA ANDREEVNA TOLSTAYA ❧ LEV NIKOLAEVICH TOLSTOY
[LSA 156]
[21 November 1885. St. Petersburg]

Dear Lëvochka, Feoktistov was here just now,[459] and I'm still very much concerned over this meeting and [my] conversations [with him]. My overall impression was a dismal one; he does not give me any opportunity to speak or present arguments; he is sending [me] to the Religious Censorship Board, and doesn't want [me] to contact any authorities. The upshot was that he took the volume and promised to do what he could. But he made frequent reference to Pobedonostsev,[460] and it appears that this is the whole source of the delay. Feoktistov promised he would give this volume to his chief censor to read and to look it over himself. This will be done by Sunday or Monday. Then he promised to take it personally to the Religious Censorship Board and possibly declare his opinion in my favour, and to give a reply pro or con by Tuesday or Wednesday. If the reply is that it is *impossible,* then I'll go to Tolstoj,[461] etc. You see, dear friend, we need to arm ourselves with patience and wait. I'm doing very well here, but it is terribly hard without my family, without any activity, just concern and anticipation and worry over all of you. May God grant you all to be healthy and safe! It's after two. I shall take the letter to the train myself, otherwise it won't go out today, and that's why once again I'm not writing much. I don't go out at all; yesterday Strakhov[462] was here to dinner; he's very sad, thin and pitiful-looking. You could at least write him some time — he likes you so much.

Still no letters from you, very sad. Today's Thursday, and I left on Monday.

To our misfortune, a few days ago in Kiev they detained a whole gang of revolutionaries; they found a [clandestine] printshop and [texts of] all your works in [the hands of] these people. Of course that's going to hurt my cause. What a shame! And here I thought these underground [revolutionaries] had dropped out of sight lately.

In any event I am not losing my strength, but it's going to be difficult for me to stay here for long. Hugs and kisses to all of you, my friends, my children, my little ones.

S. T.

Feoktistov was in such a hurry and kept talking so much that I didn't have a chance to tell him about the 'tale',[463] and I didn't give them the article about money[464] which Birjukov brought to me. But [maybe] that's for the better, not to overwhelm them all at once. As for the 'tale', will they understand right off what's wrong? Maybe it's best not to say anything about it.

---

459 SAT describes this meeting in *My Life* (IV.56): "On the 20th of November I went to the head of the [government's] press affairs department, Mr. Feoktistov, and took him the typeset and proofread copy of Volume XII of the *Complete Collected Works*. He took it and came to see me himself the following day with the reply that he would be sending Volume XII to the religious censorship board, that everything would depend on Pobedonostsev, that there was no point in my appealing to the minister, but that he (Feoktistov) himself, after consultation with his chief censor and after reading Volume XII, would personally support it before the religious censorship board." On Evgenij Mikhajlovich Feoktistov, see Letter Nº 114, Note 402.

460 Konstantin Petrovich Pobedonostsev (Synod procurator) — see Letter Nº 94, Note 238.

461 Count Dmitrij Andreevich Tolstoj (1823–1889) — Minister of Internal Affairs and Head of the Gendarmerie (1882–89).

462 Nikolaj Nikolaevich Strakhov (editorial associate) — see Letter Nº 47, Note 303.

463 The reference here is to LNT's work *A tale of Ivan the fool and his two brothers* [*Skazka ob Ivane-durake i ego dvukh brat'jakh*], first published in Volume XII of his *Complete Collected Works* (1886).

464 An excerpt from LNT's article *What then Must Be Done?* [*Tak chto zhe nam delat'?*].

Well, farewell. Hugs and kisses to you, dear Lëvochka. Strakhov yesterday cited a Russian proverb: *Vsjakoe delo siden'em stoit* [roughly equivalent to "They also serve who only sit and wait"].

And so I'm going to sit.

N° 122 – LEV NIKOLAEVICH TOLSTOY ❧ SOFIA ANDREEVNA TOLSTAYA
[PSS 83/342]
21 November 1885. Moscow.

Today is a holiday,[465] and the weather is beautiful. I got up early and spent the morning with the little ones. Sasha was taken out for a walk, and she was delighted, she's terribly precious. Then I went to work and learnt that everybody had gone to the Patriarch Ponds,[466] where they had a really good time [skating]. Alësha walked separately with Nanny, and Officer Leva-shov[467] drove him to a sweetshop and bought him candy. Il'ja, as always, was nowhere to be seen. He was either sleeping or out of the house. Now, I know, he's at the Chernjavskoe[468] to hear Ziloti[469] [play]. Tanja, Masha and Serëzha are all there as well. I sent Tanja with a letter to Shuvalova[470] about Zaljubovskij. Shuvalova was very nice to her and promised to write. A woman-teacher interfered (not exactly *interfered*, I was slow at [my own] writing [today]) with an essay [she claimed was] written by the spirit of Filaret[471] on religion (spiritualism). The essay is a strange one, but there's a lot of good in it. Then I went to do a bit of sawing and wood-chopping (I didn't go out in the morning), but I shouldn't have — my health is still not good. They sent the proofs of just one printer's sheet of the fourth book.[472] I complained to them that it had been a long time coming. I received your letter;[473] I'm sorry you have a headache. You need to work with your head, only not like a German.[474] Concerning [your sister] Tanja, I didn't understand the phrase that *everything* is finished.[475] It's now 9 o'clock in the evening; Lël-ja, Alcide, Mme Seuron and Uncle Kostja are sitting around, and I'm going to bed. Andrjusha is not behaving very well, but not terribly badly either. Misha is wonderful, as always. — I'll leave this letter unsealed so that [our daughter] Tanja can add something.[476] —

Please don't fly off to the Tsar.[477] Better not to go to see Tolstoj[478] either. If they pass it at their own initiative, then we can do it, but otherwise you'll only end up with a case of bad blood. — My general impression of the children: they're all very precious to me, except for Iljusha and to

465 On 21 November (4 December N. S.) Christians observe the feast of the Presentation of the Virgin in the Temple.

466 *Patriarch Ponds* — a favourite recreational spot for Muscovites, which includes a skating rink in the winter.

467 *Officer Levashov* — a tenant in the annexe of the Tolstoys' house in Khamovniki Lane.

468 A reference to the Usachevsko-Chernjavskoe Women's Academy at Deviche Pole in Moscow.

469 Aleksandr Il'ich Ziloti (pianist) — see Letter N° 116, Note 418.

470 Elena Ivanovna Shuvalova (Chertkov's aunt) — see Letter N° 120, Note 449.

471 *Filaret* — Orthodox Metropolitan of Moscow (secular name: Vasilij Mikhajlovich Drozdov; 1782–1867).

472 The reference here is to the *Fourth Reader [Chetvërtaja kniga dlja chtenija]*.

473 A letter dated 20 November 1885 (not included here), in which SAT described her life in St. Petersburg and complained of headaches (Letters to L. N. Tolstoy, p. 338).

474 In the first edition of LNT's A tale of *Ivan the fool*, 'Mr. Clean', who worked with his head, was a German.

475 In her letter of 20 November, SAT wrote concerning her sister Tanja's outing to buy a hat, that Tanja "asked [me] to assure you that everything is surely finished" and that no further explanation would be forthcoming (ibid., p. 338). It is not known what she had in mind.

476 There is no postscript by Tat'jana L'vovna in this letter.

477 In the same letter (20 November) SAT wrote that some acquaintances (including Birjukov) had advised her to go see the Tsar, while others advised against it (ibid., p. 338).

478 Interior Minister Count Dmitrij Andreevich Tolstoj.

a small extent Serëzha. Until [our] next letter, hugs and kisses to you and the dear Kuzminskijs. Tanja[479] can write separately. I'll send this letter to the post with Kosten'ka.

On the envelope: St. Petersburg. Nevsky [Prospekt] 75,1. Apt 12. Countess Sofia Andreevna Tolstaya.

Nº 123 – SOFIA ANDREEVNA TOLSTAYA ❧ LEV NIKOLAEVICH TOLSTOY
[LSA 157]
[23 November 1885.] Saturday 11 a.m. [St. Petersburg]

I just got up, dear Lëvochka, and I wanted to reply to your letter[480] concerning Zaljubovskij. I received it yesterday, and Birjukov also received one and came to see me right away. I don't feel at all disturbed, and I have lots of time, since I am waiting for them to read my volume. But we don't know where or who to turn to. Alexandrine has been out of the country for two months now; the Shuvalovs[481] have gone to Spain to the king's funeral;[482] Sasha [Kuzminskij] has absolutely no acquaintanceship with anyone in the military and doesn't know what to say.

Birjukov and I have decided to seek out [Zaljubovskij's] brother,[483] an artilleryman-academic. They'll be coming to see me today at one o'clock. From his brother we shall learn what has been done, and what still remains to be done — what steps to take. The only thing I can do — and will do — is to go and petition the war minister,[484] while Birjukov will go ask Grand Prince Sergej Aleksandrovich.[485] — It is difficult for me as your wife, as I am petitioning for the release of your works, to [also] petition for someone who has accepted these teachings. When I think of *what* I shall say to the minister or to whomever I ask, the only thing that comes to me is that I am asking because I have been requested to, and it is painful for me that this young man's convictions, which are probably derived from your teachings of Christ, have not led to any good — i.e. not to the result *you* intended, but to the young man's demise, and that is why I am asking to mitigate his fate. — This is the only thing I've thought of, but we shall see anon.

How is your health? Here we've had rain, thawing — such nasty [weather] that I am quite exhausted. Indoors it's been 16, 17 degrees of dry air, which has given me constant asthma, pain in my side and sleeplessness from not being able to breathe, and my being all in a sweat. The Kuzminskijs are [so] accustomed to it, that Tanja and Vera[486] are even having chills!

Yesterday I had lunch at Vera Aleksandrovna's.[487] Very tasty and very boring! In the evening the Kuzminskijs had relatives and guests over ([and a lot of] conversations!). I'm very tired

---

479 The Tolstoys' daughter Tat'jana L'vovna (Tanja).
480 Letter Nº 120 of 20 November 1885.
481 Count Pavel Andreevich Shuvalov (1830–1908) — a wartime chum of LNT's in the Sevastopol' defence, with his second wife Marija Aleksandrovna Shuvalova (née Komarova; 1852–1928).
482 Alfonse XII, King of Spain (1857–1885) died 25 November (N. S.) 1885.
483 Anatolij Petrovich Zaljubovskij — see Letter Nº 120, Note 445.
484 Pëtr Semënovich Vannovskij — see Letter Nº 120, Note 446.
485 Grand Prince Sergej Aleksandrovich (1857–1905) — brother to Emperor Alexander III; at the time, he was a colonel with the Preobrazhensk Imperial Guard regiment, later to become the Governor-General of Moscow.
486 SAT's sister Tat'jana Andreevna (Tanja) Kuzminskaja and Tanja's daughter Vera Aleksandrovna Kuzminskaja.
487 Vera Aleksandrovna Shidlovskaja (née Islavina; 1825–1910) — elder sister to SAT's mother, whose second husband was State Councillor Vjacheslav Ivanovich Shidlovskij (1823–1879). By her first marriage to Mikhail Petrovich Kuzminskij (1811–1847) she was mother to SAT's brother-in-law Aleksandr Mikhajlovich Kuzminskij.

— not from my activities, but from all the bustle. Today I'm going to ask on Nagornov's[488] behalf at the State Bank, then I shall go to the Public Library and to the Islavins,[489] where I have not yet been. I shall have dinner and [spend] the evening at home, and take a bath. Tomorrow is St-Catherine's Day, I have to go and congratulate Mme Shostak,[490] but the rest of the time I shan't be dragged out anywhere. The girls and I shall just go to the Academy [of Arts] and look at paintings. On Monday I am hoping that Feoktistov will respond, and how happy I would be if his answer is such that I am able to leave.

Have they sent you the proofs of the 4th *Reader [Kniga dlja chtenija]*? How are my [publishing] affairs? Has Nikolaj Mikhajlovich Nagornov sent you the insurance receipts?

What mood is Tanja in, depressed or happy? How are Il'ja and Lëlja doing in their studies? Is Andrjusha behaving himself and are the three younger ones healthy? Did Masha go to Chernjavskoe, and was it fun for her?

Hugs and kisses to you all. I'm waiting for [your] letters.

Nº 124 – LEV NIKOLAEVICH TOLSTOY ✎ SOFIA ANDREEVNA TOLSTAYA
[PSS 83/346]
15–18 December 1885. Moscow.[491]

For the past seven or eight years all our mutual conversations have ended after many heart-wrenching torments in one thing, at least from my point of view. I said that harmony and a love life between us cannot be realised until — I said — you come to [the same conclusions] that I have come to, either through love for me, or through an instinct which is given to everyone, or through the conviction <that you don't trust me>[492] — and will start walking together with me. I said "until you come to me" and not "until I come to you", because that is impossible for me. Impossible because what you live by is the same that I have just been saved from — from a frightful horror which all but drove me to suicide. — I cannot return to what I used to live by, to what offered me only perdition and what I recognised as the greatest evil and misfortune. But you can try to come to something you don't know yet, something that in general terms may be described as living not for one's own pleasure (I'm not talking about your life, but about the children's), not for one's own self-love, but for God or for others — which has always been considered to be the best by everyone and which resonates as such in your own conscience as well. All our arguments over the past years have always led just to this point. Indeed, it is worth pondering why this is so. And if you think [about it] sincerely and (most importantly) calmly, it will be clear to you why this is so. — You are making such valiant efforts to publish my writings, you have been petitioning so much in Petersburg and fervently defending my banned articles. And just what has been written there in these articles? In the first of these, in *A Confession [Ispoved']*,

488 Nikolaj Mikhajlovich Nagornov (husband to LNT's niece Varvara) — see Letter Nº 54, Note 348. From 1874 to 1881 he assisted LNT in the sale of his writings.

489 A reference to the family of SAT's uncle Vladimir Aleksandrovich Islavin (see Letter Nº 5, Note 31).

490 Ekaterina Nikolaevna Shostak (cousin) — see Letter Nº 108, Note 351.

491 LNT left this letter unsent in Moscow while he went off to the Olsuf'ev's Nikol'skoe-Obol'janovo estate. In *My Life* (IV.63), SAT reflected on the theme of the letter as follows: "I find it easier now to find an explanation for this difficult condition of Lev Nikolaevich's. The convictions and fervour expressed in his preaching on the harmfulness of the city, money, luxury, science and art — and his rejection of all this — were so strong that living with family members who didn't share these negative thoughts had become simply unbearable for him. He wanted to break down mankind, but he couldn't break down his own family."

492 Chevrons < > in this letter indicate interpolations by the editors of the Russian text.

which was written in 1879 but expresses thoughts and feelings which I lived with about two years before that — hence, a little less than ten years ago. This is what I wrote. I was writing not for the public; but I wrote what I endured, what I came to not for conversation or eloquent words, but came, as you know, <if you are not in [a state of] irritation,> I came to everything I came to sincerely and <seriously> in order to live the way I spoke. This is what I wrote: pages 56, 57, 58, 59 marked off…[493]

You know, after all, that all this I did not write just for the beauty of words, but that this is [the realisation] I came to in saving myself from despair. (For God's sake, don't say that this was madness, that it was impossible for you to keep up with all my fantasies, and so forth. I ask you not to say that, so as not to detract from the subject [at hand]. The subject at hand is *me* — I'll talk about *you* later — and I want to present myself in the actual condition in which I find myself, [in which] I live and shall die, harnessing all my strength to tell only the truth before God.) And so it is just under ten years ago that the <major> quarrels between us began to end the way I said: [namely,] that we would not come together until we came to a single view of life; since that time my life has gone — not just in my thinking (in my soul I have always been similarly inclined) — completely opposite to the direction in which it was going before, and is still heading further and further in the same direction both in my thoughts, which I am more and more clarifying to myself and expressing as clearly as I can, and particularly in my life's activities, which are reflecting more and more closely [the principles] I believe in. Here, in order to [continue] talking about myself, I should [also] speak about your reaction to the changes in my faith and in my life. I shall talk about you not with the thought of accusing you — I am not accusing you — I understand, it seems, <all> your motives, and see nothing bad in them, but I must describe what has happened in order that the result may be understandable; and so, my darling, in the name of all that is holy, do listen calmly to what I have to say. I am not accusing you and cannot [accuse you] of anything, and I do not want [to accuse you]; on the contrary, I desire [only] our unity and love, and so I cannot desire to hurt you, but in order to explain my situation, I must speak about those unhappy misunderstandings which have brought us to the present divergence in our togetherness — to this situation which has been tormenting both of us.

For God's sake hold back and read calmly, setting aside temporarily any thought about yourself. About you, your feelings and your situation I shall be speaking later, but right now it is vital that you understand your attitude towards me, that you understand me, understand my life as it is and not as you might wish it to be. When I tell you that my situation in the family is my constant misfortune, that is an unquestionable fact. I know that [for certain], just as people know when they have a toothache. Perhaps I myself am to blame, but the fact remains, and if it torments you to know that I am unhappy (I know that it torments you), what needs to be done is not to deny the pain, not to tell me that I myself am to blame, but to think of how to escape from it — from the pain that hurts in me and is causing you and the whole family to suffer. Pain from [the fact] that almost ten years ago I came to [the realisation] that my (or anyone's) only [hope of] salvation in life is to live not for one's self, but for others, and that our life — the life of our social stratum — is all geared to living for one's self, all built on pride, cruelty, oppression and evil, and consequently that someone in our way of life wishing to live a good life, to live with a peaceful conscience and to live joyfully, need not seek to accomplish any clever, far-off heroic deeds, but right now, right this minute, act and work hour by hour and day by day to change [our life] and advance from the bad to the good; and in this alone is [to be found] the

493 A reference to the pages of *A confession [Ispoved']*, published by Èlpidin in Geneva in 1884.

happiness and true worth of people of our circle, but in the meantime you and the whole family are heading [on a course]: not to change this life, but with the growth of the family, with the increasing selfishness of its members, to reinforce [this life's] bad aspects. This is where the pain comes from. How do I treat it? Renounce my faith? You know I can't do that. If I said in words that I renounce it, nobody, even you, would believe me, any more than if I said that 2 x 2 was not 4. What can I do? Confess this faith in words and books but act just the opposite way in life? Again, even you cannot recommend such a course. Forget about it? I can't. — What then can I do? Here's the crux of the matter, after all: this concept that I'm occupied with — perhaps one to which I am called — is an issue of moral teachings. And issues of moral teachings are different from all other subjects in that they cannot change, they can't be relegated to [mere] words, that they cannot be obligatory for one but not obligatory for another. — If one's conscience and reason require — and it has become quite clear to me *what* conscience and reason require — I cannot avoid doing what conscience and reason require and feel at peace — I cannot look at people associated with my love, people who *know* what reason and conscience require and refuse to do it, and not suffer. —

No matter which way you turn, I cannot help but suffer! living the life we live. And nobody, not even you, can say that the cause of my suffering is false. You yourself know that if I die tomorrow, the same things I say will be said by others, people's very conscience will say them, and keep on saying them until such time that people actually *do* them, or at least begin to do what their conscience requires. — And so, to do away with our discord and misfortune, you cannot take away from me the cause of my suffering, since it is not I, but she — <truth> — [who is] in the conscience of all people, she is even in you. — And that leaves one more thing to ponder: is it not possible to eliminate the discrepancy between the way we live and the requirements of conscience? Is it not possible that by changing our life-style we could eliminate the suffering which I experience and convey to you? — I said that I was saved from despair by coming to the truth. This seems a rather proud affirmation for people such as Pilate who say "What is truth?"[494] but there is no pride here. Man cannot live without knowing the truth. But I want to say that I am ready [to accept] — despite the fact that all the wise men and holy people of the world are on my side and that you also recognise what I recognise to be the truth I am willing to consider [the possibility] that what I have lived by and [still] live by may not be the truth but only my obsession, that I have fancied myself as knowing the truth and that I cannot stop believing in it and living for it, that I cannot cure myself of my obsession. I am ready to consider this, too, in which case you are left in the same position. Since nothing can take away from me what I live by and return me to the past, then [the question is:] how <to live with me in the best possible way?>, to destroy those sufferings, those experienced by me and all of you, which result from my incurable madness?

Whether you consider my views the truth or madness (it's all the same), there is only one solution for this: to grasp the essence of these views, to take a comprehensive look at them, to understand them. And, by an unfortunate coincidence (which I talked about [earlier]), not only have none of these [steps] ever been taken by you, (or by the children following [your example]), but you have accustomed yourselves to be wary of them. You have inculcated in yourselves a habit of forgetting, of not seeing, of not understanding, of not [even] admitting the existence of such views, of treating them as curious <literary> thoughts, but not as key to the understanding of mankind.

494 John 18: 38.

This is how it happened: when I experienced a spiritual upheaval within me and my inner life changed, you attached no meaning or significance to it and failed to grasp the essence of what was taking place in me; [instead,] through an unfortunate coincidence, you succumbed to the general opinion that a writer-artist like Gogol'[495] needs to create works of art and not think about his life or correct what seems to be a kind of foolishness or mental illness; you succumbed to this tendency, right away you <even> took a hostile stance against what was for me a salvation from despair and a return to life.

It turned out that all my activity along this new path — everything that was supporting me therein — you began to see as harmful and dangerous for me and the children. — So as not to come back to this later, I shall speak here about the relation of my views on life to the family and the children, — to counter the ungrounded objection — <so you don't set [it] up in your heart> — that my views on life might be all right for me, but not applicable to the children. There are various views on life — private views: one person thinks that to [achieve] happiness one must <first of all> be a scholar; another says an artist, a third — rich, or nobility, etc. These are all private views, but my views have been [basically] moral and religious, referring to what anyone should do to fulfil God's will, so that he and everybody else might be happy. Religious views may be incorrect and if so, they should be refuted, or simply not accepted, but in opposing religious views one should not say what people say (including you, sometimes) that they're all right for you, but are they all right for the children? In my view I and my life have no meaning or rights; my views are precious to me not for my sake, but for other people's happiness; and among those others it is the children who are closest to me. And so what I consider good, I consider as such not for myself, but for others and especially for my children. And so it turned out that by an unfortunate misunderstanding you did not grasp the essence of what was for me a major upheaval, changing my life <irrevocably>, but you even treated it, not exactly as something hateful, but as a disease of abnormality, though with good motives, desiring to save me and others from this obsession; and from that time on you took special effort to pull [me] in exactly the opposite direction from the one in which my new life was leading me. Everything that was dear and important to me, all of that became repulsive to you: our charming, quiet modest country life and people who participated in it, like Vasilij Ivanovich, whom, I know, you hold in high regard, but whom you at one time considered an enemy who provoked in me and the children what you saw as a false, diseased and unnatural reaction.[496] And this was the starting-point of your treating me as a mental patient, which I was very well aware of. Even before that you were bold and decisive, but now this decisiveness has become even stronger, as happens with people when they take care of patients deemed mentally ill. My darling! Remember these past years of our life in the country, when on the one hand I worked harder than I had ever worked (or will work again) in my life — on the Gospel[497] (whatever the result of this

495 Nikolaj Vasil'evich Gogol' (writer) — see Letter N⁰ 16, Note 102. This is a reference to the censorship committee's (and part of Russian society's) rejection of his work *Vybrannye mesta iz perepiski s druz'jami* [*Selected passages from correspondence with friends*] (1847). LNT's views on this work shifted 180° over time. In his youth, after reading Gogol's letters he described them in his diary as 'terrible rubbish'. But in a letter to Pavel Birjukov in 1887 he admitted: "Lately I've taken an interest again in Gogol's correspondence with his friends. What an amazing piece!" (PSS 64: 99). The following year LNT published excerpts from Gogol's work through his Posrednik publishing house.

496 The reference is to Vasilij Ivanovich Alekseev's support of LNT's desire to petition Tsar Alexander III to commute the death sentence issued to the assassins of his father Aleksander II in 1881 (cf. also Vladimir Solov'ëv's lecture described in Letter N⁰ 61, Note 29). SAT overheard Alekseev's remarks and angrily voiced her disapproval of them.

497 The reference here is to LNT's *A translation and harmony of the four Gospels* [*Soedinenie i perevod chetyrëkh Evangelij*], on which he was working in 1880–81.

work may be, I know that I put every ounce of my God-given spiritual strength into it) — and on the other hand I began to apply in life what had been revealed to me from the Gospel teachings: I renounced private property, started to give away things people asked me for, renounced vainglory <both> for myself and the children, knowing (as I knew 30 years ago what was being stifled in me by vainglory) that what you were preparing for them in the form of a refined education with French and English governors and governesses, with music, etc., were temptations of vainglory, exalting one's self over others — [this was] a millstone which we ourselves had placed around our necks. Remember that time and [remember] how you treated my work and my new life. All that seemed to you a one-sided obsession, a pitiful one at that, and the results of this obsession seemed to you to be even dangerous for the children. I'm afraid to say, and I'm not dwelling on it, but this is associated with the young age at which you married, weariness from motherly labours, ignorance of the high society which to you seemed so captivating, and you, with great decisiveness and energy, completely closing your eyes to what was taking place in me, to [the ideals] in whose name I became what I became — were pulling in exactly the opposite direction: [you sent] the children to a *gymnasium,* [you decided] to bring out [our] little girl and introduce her to society, and to create a perfect social setting. <And in this activity of yours you felt yourself completely free. Here you made an unintentional mistake.> You believed your own feeling and the general opinion that my new life was an obsession, a kind of mental illness; you failed to grasp the essence of its meaning and started to act with an unaccustomed decisiveness and at the same time great freedom, with [the result that] everything that you were doing — the move to Moscow, your setting up your life there, and bringing up the children — all that was so foreign to me that I could no longer have any voice in the matter, since all this was happening, <counter to what I believed>, in the area that I considered evil [?]. What happened in the countryside on the basis of mutual concessions, in terms of the utter simplicity of life and especially because it was 20 years old, still had some sense and meaning for me; the new, <monstrous> order of things [in Moscow], contrary to all my concepts of life, could no longer have any meaning for me other than that I should try to bear it in the best and calmest way possible. This new Moscow life was a trial for me, one I had never experienced before in all my days. Not only did I suffer every step, every minute, from the discrepancy between my and my family's life and my life in terms of luxury, depravity and poverty, in which I felt like a participant — I not only suffered, but I went mad and turned into a devil, and participated directly, deliberately in this depravity. I ate, drank, played cards, indulged in vainglory, repented, and was becoming repulsive to myself. There was one salvation — my writing, and in this I didn't find peace, but I forgot myself.

It wasn't any better in the countryside. [I felt] the same neglect, not by you alone, but also by our growing children, naturally inclined as they are to assimilate that view of me which would indulge their [own] weaknesses and tastes — as a kind, relatively benign lunatic with whom you should never discuss the specific nature of his lunacy. Life passed by me. And sometimes (you were wrong about this), you called upon me to participate in this life, you made demands on me, you reproached me for not involving myself in money matters or in the bringing up of our children, as though I were capable of handling money matters, [as though I were capable of] increasing or preserving [our] wealth, so as to increase and preserve the very evil which, in my view, was causing my children to ruin themselves. As though I could involve myself in an upbringing based on pride — isolating one's self from people, secular education and academic degrees, which were identical with what I associated with people's downfall? You, along with our growing children, were moving farther and farther in one direction, and I in quite another.

Thus years passed — one year, two years, five years. The children grew, <[you] spoilt them as [you] raised them>, while the two of us kept growing further and further apart, and my situation become more false, more difficult. I was travelling with people who had strayed down a wrong path, in the hopes of turning them around: I would travel along silently, or try to persuade them to stop and change their course, or yield to them, or get upset and try to stop them. But the farther [we went], the worse [it became]. Now inertia has set in: they travel because that is the way they have been travelling, they are already in a groove and my attempts at persuasion only irritate them. <I had only one [choice] left: to avoid pandering and keep pulling until I pulled [their] tendons in the opposite direction.> But that doesn't make things any better for me and sometimes, as in these days, I fall into despair and ask my conscience and reason what I should do, and do not hear any answer. I have three choices: [1)] Use my authority: give my possessions to those to whom they belong — the workers, give them away to somebody just to save little ones and young people from temptations and perdition; but [if I attempt to do that], it will be forcing it, and I shall provoke malice and irritation along with the same desires, only without satisfaction, which would be even worse; 2) Leave the family? — but I would be leaving them all alone — it would destroy my seemingly ineffective influence (but possibly effective and active [in the future]); I would be leaving both my wife and myself in a lonely [state] and breaking a commandment; 3) Continue to live as I have been, working out within myself the strength to fight evil lovingly and meekly. This I am doing, but I am not gaining any lovingkindness or meekness and am doubly suffering both from life and from remorse. Is that the way it has to be? Do I have to live to my dying days under such agonising conditions? Death is not that far off. And it will be difficult for me to die under a reproach for all the unnecessary burdens of the last years of my life, which I shall barely be able to suppress even before death, and [difficult] for you to bid farewell to me, doubting as to whether you could have avoided causing me those uniquely severe sufferings that I have experienced in my life. — I'm afraid that these words will cause you grief, and that your grief will result in irritation.

Imagine — if I happened to come across your diary, in which you describe your deepest feelings and thoughts, all the motivations behind your various activities — how interested I would be in reading it! Yet all my works, which have been nothing less than my life, have been and continue to be of so little interest to you that, when you come across them, you will read them [only] out of curiosity or as a literary work; while the children aren't even interested at all. You all seem to think that I exist for myself alone, and that my writings exist for themselves alone. —

My writings are *me* — through and through. In [daily] life I was not free to fully express my views, in life I make concessions to the need of co-habiting with the family; [but] I live and deny in my heart this whole [daily] life, and this whole life which is not mine is what you all consider to be my life, while my life as expressed in my writings you dismiss as mere words having no reality.

The source of all our discord was that fatal mistake, whereby eight years ago you thought the upheaval taking place in me <to be something unnatural>. This upheaval, which took me from the realm of dreams and spectres into real life, you deemed something unnatural, coincidental, temporary, fantasaical, one-sided — something which was not to be explored or deciphered but which must be struggled against with all one's might. — And you struggled [against it] for eight years and as a result of this struggle I am suffering more than ever, I'm <gasping for breath>, but not only do I not abandon my new convictions, but I keep on heading in the same direction and gasp for breath in the struggle and, through my own suffering, cause all of you to suffer, too.

What is to be done? It's strange [that I even have to] answer this, since the answer is so simple: we need to do what should have been done right from the start, what anyone does when

faced with any kind of obstacle in life: <remove the obstacle by force, or> understand where this obstacle came from and then remove it or, if we consider it to be immovable, yield to it.

[All of] you point to every [explanation] except one — namely, that [the lot of] you are the cause — the unintentional, unwitting cause — of my sufferings. —

People travel along with a bloody, suffering, dying creature trailing behind them. They feel pity and want to help, but don't want to stop. Why not try stopping?

You look for the cause — [you should] look for some kind of medicine. [Let's say] the children stop overeating (Vegetarianism). I am happy and cheerful (despite the resistance and malicious attacks). The children begin to tidy up their rooms, refrain from going to the theatre, show mercy to peasant men and women, and pick up a serious book to read — and [so] I'm happy and cheerful, and all my diseases disappear instantaneously. But, after all, this is not happening, obstinately and deliberately not happening.

A struggle for death is taking place between us — [Are we] God's or not God's. And since you have God in you, you[–][498]

It is important to grasp the essence of what motivates me and what I am expressing to the best of my abilities; this is necessary all the more so since sooner or later — judging by the spreading [popularity] and sympathy which my thoughts engender — people will have to understand them: not in the way they are assiduously misunderstood by those who find them repulsive — that I only preach that everybody should live a primitive life and plough [fields], and renounce all pleasures — but in the way that I understand and express them.

N° 125 – SOFIA ANDREEVNA TOLSTAYA ☙ LEV NIKOLAEVICH TOLSTOY
[LSA 162]
[19 December 1885. Moscow]

Dear friend, I am enclosing for you a letter Pobedonostsev wrote to me,[499] as copied by Lëlja. You can see from it that [our request] has been denied with no right of appeal, which is very disconcerting and unpleasant. But it seems that everything in my life has gone against the current, and the greater any kind of suffering, the more and more constricted I feel and the less I want to live. Now, before the holidays they could actually typeset *What then must be done? [Tak, chto zhe nam delat'?]*[500] and print the whole volume! But you have left and taken everything [with you], and I cannot undertake anything!

Please take this into consideration and, if possible, help me get out Volume XII as soon as possible. Each day brings a huge demand for the books, today [we published] 31 notices, and again I'll have to collect vouchers and send out Volume XII by *special* [shipment].

498 Sentence left unfinished.
499 During her stay in St. Petersburg, SAT met with Konstantin Petrovich Pobedonostsev — Senior Procurator of the Holy Synod (see Letter N° 94, Note 238) — in person, regarding approval for the publication of LNT's religious-philosophical writings in Volume XII of his *Complete Collected Works*. Following his promise to communicate his decision to her presently, in December 1885 he wrote her: "In view of your zeal regarding the project you mention, I don't want to leave you without an answer. Right off I ordered the proof sheets from the Synod office and read them. They will be considered by the Synod, but I can tell you frankly, just to avoid any confusion, that there is no hope of them being passed for publication. Everything that is passed is considered to be approved, and there is no way these pages can be approved. I already explained my thoughts in person to you, and now, after reading the sheets, I confirm them openly. And I urge you: do not persist, and if such rejection seem an evil to you, do not resist this evil" (Letters to L. N. Tolstoy, pp. 350–51).
500 This article was included in Volume XII with a change in title by the censors: Thoughts resulting from the census [Mysli, vyzvannye perepis'ju].

How was your trip? This morning was fine, but now in the evening it's windy and cold. Masha and Andrjusha went to the Patriarch Ponds [to skate] with the Tolstojs.[501] I've been busy all day with my own project. Ol'ga Zajkovskaja[502] had dinner here. She's filled out quite a bit. I was glad of her visit. Uncle Kostja is here; he took it upon himself to write out addresses [on the packages of books] and has been torturing me with his *instruments.*

Both Masha and I have had a sore throat since [yesterday] evening, and Lëlja has been having a headache. He didn't go to the *gymnasium* today. He had a sleep, and now he's sitting with me and copying Pobedonostsev's letter. Masha is studying. Everything's fine for now; I am impatiently awaiting news of you all.

I received a very dear letter[503] from Mikhail Stakhovich about a *peasant woman.* There's a lot to tell about her which I shan't write for lack of time.

Tanja, dear, don't fall ill, love me the way you've been loving me lately. As long as you haven't been missing us too much, I'm happy that you all are with such dear, kind, intelligent, marvellous people as the whole Olsuf'ev family, to whom I send my heartfelt regards and gratitude for you.

S. T.

19 December, evening.

Lëvochka, don't forget my request to do something to speed up the overdue volume. Write and tell me whether anything needs to be done by way of transcribing or typesetting.

Nº 126 – LEV NIKOLAEVICH TOLSTOY ❧ SOFIA ANDREEVNA TOLSTAYA
[PSS 83/348]
21 or 22 December 1885. Obol'janovo.

I have not written you for two days, dear friend, since Tanja wrote and since I had not yet regained my normal state [of health and mind].

Today I received your letter[504] with a copy of Pobedonostsev's [letter], which has interested and offended everyone. It didn't fascinate me in any way, but I was fascinated by your letter — that mood of burdensomeness and haste which you continue to find yourself in and which is very hard on you. — My manuscript, I think, will not delay anything, since between now and Christmas the printshop will not be operating, and by the 3rd day of the holiday I shall deliver the manuscript with Tanja or I shall bring it myself. — Ah, my darling, such a pity that you torment yourself this way — either that, or the projects you started are tormenting you. I comfort myself with [the thought] that physical causes will help you calm down, and am glad that I [finally] find myself in such a normal situation, that I shall not disturb or torment you as I have all *this past while.*

I was busy writing [this letter], when Lëlja and Verochka arrived. And now I just read your letter.[505] And now my heart [is constricted] and I feel the same despair and melancholy which I felt back in Moscow and which completely disappeared here. Again the same thing: "The

501 the Tolstojs — in this case, the family of LNT's sister Marija Nikolaevna Tolstaja.
502 Ol'ga Dmitrievna Zajkovskaja (friend of SAT's) — see Letter Nº 99, Note 273.
503 The letter by Mikhail Aleksandrovich Stakhovich (see Letter Nº 101, Note 287) has not been preserved.
504 Letter Nº 125 of 19 December 1885.
505 A reference to SAT's letter to their daughter Tanja, in which she complains of insomnia, under the pressure of so many concerns in her life. She adds: "Tell Papà that I read his letter — he wanted me to, but there's nothing I can say to him in reply. Indeed, does he desire a completely sincere answer?" She also expresses her concern that LNT's urging of vegetarianism might be harming his own health and the health of their children.

burden is too heavy: he never helps, I am doing everything, life doesn't wait." All these words are familiar to me and, most importantly, completely unrelated to what I am writing and saying. I was saying and am still saying the same thing, [namely,] that you need to take stock and decide what is good and what is bad, and in which direction you should go; and if you don't take stock, you shouldn't be surprised that you will suffer yourself and that others will suffer, [too].

As to the necessity of doing something right now, there is nothing to say, since people with money for shelter and food need to do nothing but think things over and live as best they can. But for now, for God's sake, let's never talk about this again. I shan't. I hope to calm my nerves and keep quiet. — Everything I experienced in Moscow came not from physical causes. After three days here of the same life I had in Moscow — without [eating] meat, with heavy physical work — here I chop and saw wood — I feel quite lively and have splendid sleeps. — But what to do? I, at least, cannot change anything — you know that yourself. There is only one thing [I can do]: and that is to work out a [sense of] inner peace and kindness, which I have little of, and that I shall try to do. Farewell, my darling. Hugs and kisses to you; I love you, and feel sorry for you. Hugs and kisses to the children!

How lonely you must be! I need to come to you as soon as possible.

On the envelope: Moscow. Dolgokhamovniki Lane. Nº 15. Countess Sofia Andreevna Tolstaya.

Nº 127 – SOFIA ANDREEVNA TOLSTAYA ✉ LEV NIKOLAEVICH TOLSTOY
[LSA 164]
(Letter addressed jointly to Lev Nikolaevich Tolstoy and Tat'jana L'vovna Tolstaja)
23 December [1885]. Night. [Moscow]

Well, I thank you, my dear Lëvochka and Tanja, that you have cheered me with [your] good letters. This evening I am at least *certainly* happy and cheerful. But [my health problems] have really got me down! I am starting to have neuralgia again in the old place in the right (painful) eye, my temple, eyebrows and my whole head. There is still hope that it won't continue for long — but there is also a nasty fear of pain, which is very sharp, so that my hands tremble when I write. This is untimely in view of my activities, which have been exhausting for me. And then there are the holidays, and everyone's bustling about, cleaning, washing busily and noisily. But it would all be fine if only nobody reproached anyone else for anything, and everybody were happy and cheerful! I shall probably be wracked by pain — no matter how brave I try to be, this *tic douloureux* is very real and since dinner it has been tormenting me worse and worse. Tomorrow Serëzha will go and take this letter, and I am also sending all Chertkov's letters along with those addressed to Tanja. Review them all, [the two of you,] as best you can and don't lose anything.

Varen'ka[506] had dinner here, along with Treskin[507] and Uncle Kostja. I went shopping before dinner.

I am writing and I feel I can't write any more: I feel a knocking in my temples, even a trembling breaking through. I needed to write something and can't remember [what].

Yes, we read over your *letter* again today,[508] together with Varja. And the letter made the same impression [on us] which you yourself make — sad, pitiful to see and hard [on us to see] you suffer. But what to do?

506 Varvara Valer'janovna (Varen'ka) Nagornova (LNT's niece) — see Letter Nº 6, Note 43.
507 Vladimir Vladimirovich Treskin (Il'ja's friend) — see Letter Nº 116, Note 417.
508 Letter Nº 124 of 15–18 December 1885.

You know, I'm actually glad that my temples are *so* painful. The physical pain distracts from the pain in my heart. Maybe tomorrow it will all be past, but today, once again, I am too tired. All these past few days I have been going to bed at 4 in the morning and getting up after 10.

Gribovskij[509] was here — what another repulsive creature he is!

He asked *me* (why?) for some of your works for *Niva*! What sort of fools! but my temples were hurting, and I got angry and made fun of him. But he's a bold fellow.

Tanja, I'm sincerely happy that you and Papà are doing well and that he is relaxing. I know, Tanja, that everything is fine in our [family] life, and that there's nothing to cry about, But tell this to Papà rather than me. *He* is the one who whines and groans, and is killing us by doing so. Why doesn't he cry at Nikol'skoe[510] over the Olsuf'evs, and over himself and you? Isn't it the same — but even wealthier — life there and all over the world? Why should *I* be the *souffre-douleur* for all his fantasies? I, who always have loved and wanted to live for others, and it cost me nothing — this has [always] been my sheer joy! — I am grateful that my children trust me. And I shall justify their trust, as now that's the only thing I have left. — But to be cheerful?! Is that possible, when you [constantly] hear a sick man's groanings right beside you? Especially a sick man you are accustomed to loving?! Just think about it. I'll say just one thing for now: yes, I want him to come back *to me,* just as he wants me to follow *him*. Mine — this is the old, happy [life] undoubtedly well lived, bright and cheerful, and loving, and friendly. *His* — that is the new, everlasting torment, tugging at everyone's heartstrings, perplexing and shocking, provoking despair not only among the family, but among his relatives, chums and friends.

It is a state of *gloom* which I will not enter, it is an affliction which will kill me. No, I shan't be tempted into that horror. It is the *new* — supposedly *redemptive*, but actually instilling the same *desire to die* — that has been torturing me so much that I hate it.

Yes, I call upon my *old*, which is *true*, and happiness will be restored only when we start living [again] the way we used to live.

It's never been this clear to me before. And it's clear that I am now very, very unhappy with such discord — but I will not and cannot destroy [my] life.

As to my 'publishing ventures', I'll simply say this: I retreat into this frightening work for intoxication; it's my *drinking house*, where I can forget myself and my strained family situation. Fancy balls and society life — these have also been my tavern. — To go off anywhere from these scenes and reproaches, from these sufferings in the name of some kind of *new good*, killing the *old happiness*, and woe to me if I, tortured and intoxicated, go off not to just some kind of tavern, but go off anywhere full stop — that is something I so often desire.

I've been writing such a long [letter] under the influence of [my] neuralgia. But at the same time it's all clear, and it's *all* — all the same. Farewell, I am not asking [you to] come home — what for? I have to suffer through my illness alone — it's easier for me, and better for you.

S. T.

---

509 Vjacheslav Mikhajlovich Gribovskij (1867–1924) — jurist, literator, who first contacted LNT while still a *gymnasium* pupil, with questions on moral and religious themes.
510 A reference to the Olsuf'evs' Nikol'skoe-Obol'janovo estate.

N° 128 – SOFIA ANDREEVNA TOLSTAYA ❧ LEV NIKOLAEVICH TOLSTOY
[LSA 165]
24 December [1885]. [Moscow]

Dear Lëvochka, my last letter, unfortunately, did not fulfil the programme you [suggested]. With the [passing] years it's been harder to withstand the tribulations of the soul and physically easier to give into a diseased condition. Yesterday my head was aching something awful; today that neuralgic pain is still there, but it's eased somewhat. It seems it's only a twenty-four hour migraine, or something like that. My work is still piling up, but *it's not the work that slows [me] down, but the [everyday] cares.* I feel at peace about you and Tanja; you're with good people [i.e. the Olsuf'evs], you have good air [to breathe], and complete mental tranquillity.

Never have holidays been so lonely for me; there's absolutely no one around, I dare not indulge in *Christmas trees* or *merriment*, and am not about to call anyone to gaze at my dismal figure. I sit at my desk with my envelopes.

Anyway, today I took the three little ones to a Christmas party at the Obolenskijs.[511] How cheerful they all were, dancing and delighting in their presents! It was all so kindhearted, hospitable — especially (as always) on the part of the hosts. Mashen'ka, [your] sister, danced the quadrille, grasping her gown with both hands and clowning around. She's very adorable when she's cheerful. Yesterday D'jakov tempted everyone, i.e. Mashen'ka, his daughter Masha, Liza and her husband [the Obolenskijs], Varen'ka and her husband [Nikolaj Mikhajlovich Nagornov], Uncle Serëzha — they all went to the Yar[512] — to hear Hungarian gipsies. I was invited, too, but what would I want with gipsies? — I just wanted to be quiet.

By contrast, a very witty and interesting letter arrived from Fejnerman[513] for you. But what a miserable fanatic [he is], with your patterns of thought — i.e. gloom. He writes that he and his wife almost came to blows, and he wants to leave her. He is [trying to] take from her only her most meagre possessions — her last piece of bread, to give it away. She won't give it, of course, and all hell has broken loose. — And that is what I am expected to strive for! No, your teachings are sheer monasticism, which people turn to when they become monks for the first time [in history].

Chertkov is at odds with his mother — he wanted to leave her. Fejnerman wants to leave his wife; you want to leave your family. — But if it weren't for that, [think] how happy we would be, how we *probably* still love each other deep in our hearts. And surely both Chertkov and Fejnerman love their families. Something I shall never understand: why the *truth* must bring with it *evil* and *dissension* — dissension not with bandits, but with quiet, *loving* people? For the first time in my life I was glad that you went away. How painful and sad that is! But, of course, I shall be even more glad when you come [home].

How are Tanja and Vera[514] doing? They are both missed at their homes — their families are longing for them. Il'ja has gone off in his most usual mood: he wants to bring in [hunting] dogs, and was asking extra money for that. Alcide and [Vladimir Fëdorovich] Orlov have gone off with him to the same place. Masha is feeling quite unwell these days. Either she has had chest

511 Elizaveta Valer'janovna (Liza) Obolenskij (LNT's niece) and her husband Leonid Dmitrievich Obolenskij — see Letter N° 40, Note 259.
512 the Yar — a popular restaurant (1826–1925) in Kuznetsky Most Street, known for its gypsy choir, and frequented over the years by a number of prominent writers (e.g. Pushkin, Chekhov, Gorky and LNT). A second restaurant by that name, on the St. Petersburg Chaussée, ran from 1909 to 1913. A current incarnation is to be found at this same location (the street now named Leningradskij Prospekt).
513 Isaak Borisovich Fejnerman — see Letter N° 115, Note 411. The whereabouts of his letter are unknown.
514 Tat'jana L'vovna (Tanja) Tolstaja and her cousin Vera Sergeevna Tolstaja — see Letter N° 102, Note 297.

pains — [for which] they applied mustard plasters, or her head aches terribly. She doesn't eat anything at all — soon it will be seen how the poor thing has been done in by vegetarianism. — But I'm not the one killing her. My job has [always] been to keep feeding the little ones, and that is a job I've done well. And whoever would interfere with *my* job, let him answer to God. Well, farewell, Lëvochka. Once again it's late and I'm going to bed.

Sonja.

My greetings to all for the holidays, and I wish health, happiness and peace to everyone that needs it. I hear the Christmas bells ringing out all over Moscow.

Nº 129 – LEV NIKOLAEVICH TOLSTOY ❧ SOFIA ANDREEVNA TOLSTAYA
[PSS 83/351]
27 December 1885. Obol'janovo.

I am writing, dear friend, in any case — i.e. in case I am somehow delayed, as tomorrow, Saturday, I was planning to go to Moscow. It is possible I shan't go because of the weather or a wretched night; another cause [for not going] might be: [if I went now,] Lëlja might miss receiving his books [on time][515] and I might miss receiving news from you.

For some time, ever since Tanja's departure [on 26 December] and your latest illness letter,[516] I haven't had any news from you. Since Christmas Day I can say that I have been feeling better and better, especially morally. They went [horseback] riding, while I took a stroll along the roads, walking and thinking, and repenting, and praying to God. I am saying this not [just] to put your mind at ease, but I sincerely realised how much I am to blame, and as soon as I realised this and specially rooted out of my heart any contrived reproaches and replaced them with love for you and Serëzha, I began to feel good, and will continue to feel good regardless of any external conditions. — As for writing, I have not got around to any. Life here is the same as before — quiet, pure and kind. Today, just now, the mummers were here, and all of us, Serëzha and Treskin, and Liza,[517] went in costume to the priest. Tanja would have been so excited, I'm sorry [she left early]. Hugs and kisses, love to you and the children.

On the envelope: Moscow. Dolgokhamovniki Lane. Nº 15. Countess Sofia Andreevna Tolstaya.

Nº 130 – SOFIA ANDREEVNA TOLSTAYA ❧ LEV NIKOLAEVICH TOLSTOY
[LSA 168]
[7 April 1886. Moscow]

Dear Lëvochka, we have just written to Lëlja at Yasnaya, in care of Kozlovka, where he went yesterday with Alcide, a detailed description of yesterday's reading,[518] which was ten times

---

515 Lev L'vovich (Lëlja) Tolstoj had accompanied LNT to Nikol'skoe-Obol'janovo.
516 Letter Nº 128 of 24 December 1885.
517 Sergej L'vovich (Serëzha) Tolstoj, Vladimir Vladimirovich Treskin and Elizaveta Adamovna (Liza) Olsuf'eva.
518 SAT had written a letter to her son Lev (Lëlja) describing a public reading of some of LNT's stories at Moscow University. Part of this description is as follows: "The auditorium was filled to overflowing. When they read How much land does a man need?, the applause was so unanimous and went on for such a long time that the emcee kept ringing his bell again and again, but couldn't stop them. That [story], apparently, appealed to them most of all. […] I'm writing all this, as I think Papà will be interested; do read him this letter" (quoted by SAT in Letters to L. N. Tolstoy, p. 363).

more solemn than the first, and so I shan't describe it to you any more [here]. There was long and unanimous applause especially for *How much land does a man need? [Skol'ko cheloveku zemli nuzhno?].* Storozhenko[519] gave a good reading and left the impression that *the style* was remarkably strict, compact, not a single unnecessary word, everything spot on, precise, in perfect harmony: a lot of content, few words, and satisfying right to the end. [Of course] you know all this yourself. There were a lot of young people, all of them students. I saw Ivanova[520] there, Urusov's sister — she's in despair over her nephew[521] and his rudeness. They didn't read *The imp and the crust [Kak chertënok krajushku vykupal],* since there the devil says: "I only gave a *muzhik* just some more of the harvest, and a beast's blood started speaking in him." As though that would stir up young people against you, and [they] wouldn't like it.

Oh, the cold and the wind! I am simply in despair over all my absent [family]: Lëlja caught cold out hunting, while when you're in the field the wind blows right through you. You perspire [even just] walking, and then the wind cools you off. Simply a calamity! Besides, I rarely get news, I know nothing about any of you. The few words [you wrote] from Podol'sk have not satisfied me in the least: Are you all soaked through? Tired? Did you get enough to eat? Where did you spend the night? — I've had no news.[522]

I have very little time, and so I shan't write you any long letters; besides, there's nothing to write about. Everything's [fine] with us, thank God. Only my heart is quite restless, and that is worst of all. If [the weather] were warm, I'd be happy about your journey, but without warm clothing it can be very dangerous in the cold north wind. You are playing with God, you are putting Him to the test; you do have good health, but you will be done in by your own fantasies. When I hear that everyone's healthy and safe, then I shall be at peace.

The Kuzminskijs are coming on Wednesday. Tomorrow I'm expecting Volume XII; I'll write to you care of Kozlovka. Hugs and kisses to you, and regards to your fellow-travellers.

Sonja.

N° 131 – LEV NIKOLAEVICH TOLSTOY ❧ SOFIA ANDREEVNA TOLSTAYA
[PSS 83/356]
9 April 1886. Yasnaya Polyana.
From Yasnaya. After 10 p.m.

I received all your letters.[523] I was very glad and grateful. — Only it's a pity you've been worrying [about me] when there's no need to. We had a splendid trek. As I had expected, I'm left with one of the best memories of my life. From beginning to end my health has been better than in Moscow — excellent [in fact]. No troubles at all. It is just like someone on dry land imagining he's on an island with the sea all round. That's how we are when we stay in cities, under our own [self-imposed] conditions. But once you venture across this sea, it [turns out to be] dry land and magnificent. Kolichka[524] and I — he was in the lead, I right behind him, in second place. Stakhovich proved to be not as strong. Kolichka [and I] were saying that this is

---

519 Nikolaj Il'ich Storozhenko (1836–1906) — professor of literature at Moscow University.

520 Adelaida Dmitrievna Ivanova (*née* Urusova) — see Letter N° 94, Note 236

521 Sergej Leonidovich Urusov (1872–1948) — son to Leonid Dmitrievich Urusov; later a State Councillor (1916).

522 On 4 April 1886 LNT had set out on foot from Moscow to Yasnaya Polyana in the company of Nikolaj Nikolaevich (Kolichka) Ge Jr (see Letter N° 115, Note 406) and Mikhail Aleksandrovich Stakhovich (see Letter N° 101, Note 287). For a description of the trek, see *My Life,* IV.73.

523 Letter N° 130 of 7 April 1886, plus 3 other letters dated 5, 6 and 8 April.

524 Nikolaj Nikolaevich (Kolichka) Ge Jr.

one of the most instructive and joyful times — we saw nothing but kindness and geniality and we ourselves showed nothing but these to anyone.[525] We sustained ourselves on tea and bread, — twice had cabbage soup and felt sprightly and healthy. We spent our nights with as many as twelve people to a hut and had a splendid sleep. I got to sleep late, but then we didn't set out that early [the next morning]. Along the way we had two rides [in wagons] — 25 versts in all. I'm very happy for you, for [getting] Volume 12 [past the censors],[526] and am happy for myself, mainly over *Ivan the Fool [Ivan-durak]*. We arrived at Yasnaya at 8 o'clock. Lëlja and Alcide were out hunting. Then they came along with [Isaak Borisovich] Fejnerman, and [we all] had tea. Lëlja and Alcide are cheerful and healthy, and are going hunting with Fomich.[527]

I thank Mme Seuron for the book and the pencil; I used them a little in connection with the stories of a 95-year-old soldier with whom we stayed overnight. I had various thoughts come to me, which I jotted down.[528]

Hugs and kisses to Serëzha — he, no doubt, is helping you; Tanja — she, no doubt, calms you down when you start worrying; Masha — she, no doubt, is also helping you; and the little ones — they, no doubt, cheer you up, — especially Andrjusha. He's been good lately. I love you very much and am constantly thinking about you. No doubt you've come to terms with Il'ja. He is generally good, when he's not snorting away. Hugs and kisses to the Kuzminskijs. They have a calming effect, too — both father and daughter. —

Don't fret that [this] letter's all jumbled. I'm writing and nodding off [at the same time]. 'Til our next meeting, darling, if God grants.

N° 132 – SOFIA ANDREEVNA TOLSTAYA ❧ LEV NIKOLAEVICH TOLSTOY
[LSA 172]
[2 May 1886. Moscow]

I gather Birjukov is with you at the moment, and [he] has probably have told you about how we live. It's quite warm today, and even though my littlest ones are coughing quite a bit, I have let them go out into the garden. Lëlja and I are quite disappointed that you are overworking yourself to your own harm. Don't make any unnecessary effort, and beware of sunstroke. After all, you don't have a worker's brain — i.e. not one like working people, but one that is tortured, sensitive and perceptive.

The Odessa girl[529] upset me greatly, but your reaction to her appearance calmed me down. I'm really disappointed that Kolichka is not coming; there is so much to be done, that it is

---

525 Again, this is in reference to the trek by LNT and his companions from Moscow to Yasnaya Polyana (see Letter N° 130, Note 522).

526 On 8 April SAT wrote her husband that "Volume XII has been passed by the censors. It will come out on Thursday. I'm very pleased" (*Letters to L. N. Tolstoy*, p. 363).

527 Mikhail Fomich Krjukov — a servant.

528 LNT used these notes as a basis for his story Nikolai Palkin [Nikolaj Palkin].

529 The Odessa girl — Elizaveta Vladimirovna Viner (married name: Dzhunkovskaja; 1862–1928). In a letter of 29–30 April 1886 (not included here) LNT wrote to his wife: "Yesterday an Odessa girl arrived with Fejnerman. She arrived here a week ago and is staying with Prokofij Vlasov in the country. I can't understand her for the life of me and shan't even try. On the contrary, I shall try to get her out of here, since all these outsiders are a great burden. […] I hope she leaves soon. In the meantime, I shall try to ignore her. If you were here, you would understand her better [than I] and could advise me" (PSS 83: 564). See also *My Life*, IV.76.

unthinkable to turn my attention to packing [books] or anything else. I feel badly that I haven't yet transcribed "Soldier"[530] for you. Your postscript I shall send to Klobskij.[531]

Serëzha's just arrived from the Olsuf'evs', and on Monday is heading to Samara. Serëzha remembered Klobskij's address. A telegram from Samara says that the Patrovskij plot [at the Samara estate] has been leased for 2,000 silver roubles.

There are still problems with money [management] — I'd [like to] arrange things in a better way, only I don't know how.

I still wanted to tell you something: Lëlja sits [every] evening on the day-bed, fretting, afraid of his exams, says that his geography preliminary is tomorrow, and so today — his spirits are really down. And here am I writing, bored because there are no letters from you. — Just this moment they brought a letter.[532] We were delighted, we read the letter, and [Lëlja] cheered up so much that he's been studying all evening, and today at the preliminary he got a 4 [out of 5], and there won't be a geography exam, which means he'll soon be free.

Do keep on writing, dear friend, you see how your letters liven up [our lives].

I am sending you the notice; you are to sign it and send it back.

Skrytnov[533] came today, and brought *What then must be done? [Tak chto zhe nam delat'?]*. He demanded [the return of] the book with the portrait of François Lasalle — I think that was it. We looked for it and couldn't find it anywhere.

Panov[534] was here, urgently demanding money, and I dealt with him severely. He's bad, he's a swindler and not reliable, it seems.

He wants to write to you, but I said it wouldn't lead to anything, and that he would receive his money from the first sales [of the edition]. Yesterday [Ge's] illustrations went to Mamontov's[535] and [the books] will come out next week.

Farewell, dear friend, be healthy and cheerful. Tomorrow I'll spend the day at Alësha's little grave.[536] I'm going to put up a marker and a fence. And another time I shall go and do all the planting. I'm drawn to his grave. My grief is pointless and powerless.

Hugs and kisses.

Sonja.

530 A reference to LNT's story The story of Yemilyan and the empty drum [Rabochij Emel'jan i pustoj baraban].

531 Ivan Mikhajlovich Klobskij (also spelt: Klopskij; 1852–1898) — a student at St. Petersburg University; a Tolstoyan.

532 A letter dated 29–30 April 1886 (PSS 83: 563–65).

533 Vladimir Ivanovich Skrytnov — a correspondent of LNT's. The portrait he was seeking was of St-François de Sales (1567–1622). This saint is mentioned by LNT in *The Kingdom of God is within you* [*Tsarstvo Bozhie vnutri vas*] and *For every day* [*Na kazhdyj den'*].

534 Mikhail Mikhajlovich Panov (1836–1894) — artist-photographer, who produced phototypes of twelve of Nikolaj Nikolaevich Ge's (Sr) illustrations for LNT's story *What men live by* [*Chem ljudi zhivy*].

535 Anatolij Ivanovich Mamontov (printshop owner) — see Letter N° 116, Note 419.

536 The Tolstoys' son Aleksej L'vovich (Alësha) died on 18 January 1886 and was buried in the Nikolo-Arkhangel'sk cemetery near Moscow. In 1932 his remains were transferred to the Tolstoy family cemetery at Kochaki. See also Letter N° 62, Note 31.

N° 133 – LEV NIKOLAEVICH TOLSTOY ❧ SOFIA ANDREEVNA TOLSTAYA
[PSS 83/361]
4 May 1886. Yasnaya Polyana.

I'm writing this morning so as not to hurry this evening. I saw off my guests[537] yesterday, and I stayed behind alone with great delight. It rained the whole day. I went for a walk in the woods — I didn't find any morel mushrooms, but I did pick some violets. At home I found many *muzhiks* who had come [to see me]. There has always been poverty, but all these years it has been on the rise and this year it has reached a frightening stage which is, like it or not, troubling to rich people. You can't even have a quiet bowl of porridge and a bun with tea when you know that right next door there are people and children you know (like Chilikin's children at Teljatinki, or Tanja's wet-nurse Matrëna) who are going to bed without bread — they ask for it but there's none. And there are so many like these. Not to mention the absence of oat seeds which threatens these people's future, since it clearly shows them that if their fields are not sown and handed over to others, they have nothing awaiting them but the sale of their last belongings and to go begging. You can close your eyes to it — just as you can close your eyes when you are skating on the edge of an abyss — but it won't change your situation. A few people used to complain about poverty, but that was rare. Now it's a whole mass groaning. On the road, in taverns, in church, in homes, everybody's talking about just one thing: destitution. You will ask: What can be done? How can one help? One can help by giving seeds and bread to those who ask for it, but that is not [real] help — it's but a drop in the ocean, and, besides, that kind of help is counter-productive. [Let's say] you've given to one or two, why not to twenty, a thousand, a million? Obviously, even if you give away everything you have, it's still not enough. What to do? What to help with?[538] With just one thing: a good and kind life. The totality of evil is not [the fact] that the rich have taken from the poor. That is just one small part of the cause. The [real] cause is that people, whether rich or middle-class or poor, live like predatory animals — each one for himself, each one trampling on [the rights of] others. This is where sorrow and poverty come from. Salvation from this comes only by introducing something else into one's own life — and, consequently, the lives of others — [namely,] respect for all people, love for them, care about others and the greatest possible [degree of] self-denial, the rejection of one's own selfish pleasures. — I am not admonishing you or preaching at you; I only write what I think — I am thinking aloud with you.

I know — and you know — everyone knows — that human evil will be destroyed by people, that this alone constitutes people's [true] goal and meaning in life. — People will be working and are working for this. Why then should we not work for the same thing?

I could go on writing forever on this, but why do I have the premonition that you will respond with some kind of cruel word? [My] hand refuses to write any more about this — The weather today is splendid, hot. Now I want to heat up the house for the night. And open it up tomorrow for the sun itself. Today already there's warm air blowing upstairs, and any moisture

---

537 Anna Konstantinovna Diterikhs (1859–1927) and Ol'ga Nikolaevna Ozmidova (married name: Spengler; 1865–?) stopped over at Yasnaya Polyana on 2 May 1886, along with Pavel Ivanovich Birjukov (see Letter N° 120, Note 453), on their way to Vladimir Grigor'evich Chertkov's estate for the summer. Anna Diterikhs was soon to marry Chertkov.
538 In a subsequent letter to her husband dated 5 May (not included here), SAT countered: "Your attitude that there is no way to help is hopeless. To bring about a change in society your thoughts and books are important, but are insignificant as an example and direction in the lives of us sinners, little people that we are. Love is all the more needed amongst humanity — it is, I would say, more important than anything else" (Letters to L. N. Tolstoy, p. 369).

is scarcely to be felt. I remember that before I left you were saying something about a key to the keys. Did you give it to me or not? If you didn't, then send it; if you did, write and tell [me where it is]. It's not here, and I'm going to order a new key. The house has been washed, and if it stays that way, in about four days I'll be able to move in. Only how are things with you? How are the little ones' coughs? Has Kolichka come? — Farewell, my dear. Last night I saw you in a dream, and you were treating me badly. This means the opposite. Let it be so. Hugs and kisses to you and the children. So good [to hear] that Il'ja and Lëva are sitting with you [in the evenings]. That's the way it ought to be. It's better [when you gather] together. Has Masha stopped crying? Has Tanja stopped hiring a horse for 5 roubles an hour? 5 roubles could feed bread to children for a month instead of just crusts. I'm afraid that this is hard to understand [when you're] in Moscow. And I'm waiting, waiting for all of you to come here as soon as you can. Thank you for the oranges and apples (you shouldn't have!). Overall, you worry a lot about me. But I'm perfectly healthy. There's nothing I'm missing, it's all here. You've provided for everything.

I received your letter.[539] Your attack on the girls was without cause. They are confused, but they are very kind and pure. I, too, heard about Orlov[540] this year. It's very sad.

On the envelope: Moscow. Dolgokhamovniki Lane. 15. Countess Sofia Andreevna Tolstaya.

Nº 134 – SOFIA ANDREEVNA TOLSTAYA ❧ LEV NIKOLAEVICH TOLSTOY
[LSA 178]
[3–4 January 1887. Moscow]

I've just got back with the little ones and Masha from the Obolenskijs',[541] where they all went dancing (with piano accompaniment), and I received two telegrams: one from Savina[542] (which I enclose) and one from you. Both were of concern to me, especially Savina's. I'm terribly anxious to go and fight [for you] in Petersburg. Your telegram[543] is disconcerting, as I don't know where to find the variant [you asked for]. Everything was done without my knowledge: I don't know where to find what — at Sytin's,[544] at Petrov's[545] or somewhere else. Tomorrow morning I'll send the artel worker around everywhere [to look for it]. I can't guarantee that I'll be able to locate the variant before Mrs. Sizova's[546] departure. If I can't, I'll copy it out later and send it to Podsolnechnaja.[547] I dare not send the printed copy.

Everything's fine with us. Only we couldn't possibly lead a sillier or emptier life. I went calling this morning, made nine calls. Urusov[548] and Uncle Kostja took dinner with us. My brother

---

539 A letter dated 1 May 1886, not included here, expressing concern over the possible effect of Diterikhs' and Ozmidova's visit on Chertkov's mother.

540 Vladimir Fëdorovich Orlov (teacher) — see Letter Nº 71, Note 101.

541 A reference to Elizaveta Valer'janovna (Liza) Obolenskaja and her husband Leonid Dmitrievich Obolenskij.

542 Marija Gavrilovna Savina (née Podramentseva; 1854–1915) — an actress of the Aleksandrinskij Theatre in St. Petersburg. She was asking LNT for copies of his play *The power of darkness* [*Vlast' t'my*] and permission to stage a charitable benefit performance of it. The play, however, was blocked by the censorship board.

543 In his telegram of 3 January 1887, LNT asked his wife to find variants of the drama.

544 Ivan Dmitrievich Sytin (1851–1934) — printer and publisher, who published LNT's books through Posrednik.

545 Ivan Ivanovich Petrov (1861–1892) — assistant to Sytin who worked particularly with Posrednik.

546 Aleksandra Konstantinovna Sizova (?–1908) — a children's writer.

547 *Podsolnechnaja* — a railway station close to the Olsuf'evs' Nikol'skoe-Obol'janovo estate.

548 Probably a reference to Prince Sergej Semënovich Urusov (see Letter Nº 40, Note 258).

Sasha[549] came; he is inviting us to his wedding on the 11th. Tomorrow he's having dinner with me. In the evening we went to the Obolenskijs': Masha, Lëva, me, Alcide, and two little ones. We danced there until midnight — the *cotillon* and others. It was hilarious to watch my little ones try so hard to imitate the grown-ups, dancing the quadrille, the mazurka, the waltz, and pretending they could do everything.

A huge lot of people are inviting themselves to hear your drama, Lëvochka. I promised only Auntie[550] and Masha Sverbeeva and Varja Nagornova that I would read the drama [to them] on Monday. That is always pleasant for me. But suddenly today I began to receive requests from all sides. Where do they find out about it all from? Urusov, Ermolova, Lopatin,[551] Lev Ivanovich Polivanov through Lopatin. People who are all total strangers to each other. I got frightened, but then a sense of boldness overcame me — I said: "Well then, come, all of you!" I don't know how my reading will turn out and what will come of it. Curious!

I hesitate to write about the censorship; so much anger is boiling up inside me that I'm ready to do anything, even take extreme measures, and I shall no doubt get all burnt up with this anger and not do anything. Tomorrow I shall write a letter to Feoktistov[552] — I shall be most curious as to how my letter turns out. I didn't dare write him today — it would have turned out badly.

Thank you for wiring me about your health and your [safe] arrival. You should both take care of yourselves and write when you can. I wish you both cheer and good living. My regards to all your dear hosts, and I regret that I have never had the occasion to enjoy their hospitality. I have almost no business left now to do. But so much the worse — I just keep on chattering and muddling about.

Il'ja is meek; Lëva and Masha are cheerful; the mood at home is good; no word from Serëzha.

Hugs and kisses to Lëvochka and Tanja. It's night-time now, I'm tired and writing whatever comes to my tired mind. But you will make proper sense of it all.

Farewell. I am sending along everything that I have received since you left.

S. T.

3–4 January 1887.
Night.

No 135 – LEV NIKOLAEVICH TOLSTOY ✍ SOFIA ANDREEVNA TOLSTAYA
[PSS 84/371]
7 January 1887. Nikol'skoe-Obol'janovo.

This morning, the 7th [of January], we received your letter[553] in which you write about the reading. As to how you prepared for it, — i.e, [your] preceding letter[554] — that hasn't come yet. I'm happy that things are fine at home, judging by your two letters. Probably someone will

---

549 Aleksandr Andreevich (Sasha) Behrs (see Letter No 4, Note 13) was about to get married for the second time, to Anna Aleksandrovna Mitrofanova, daughter of the director of the Dvorjanskij Bank in Orël. For more on their wedding, see *My Life*, IV.100.
550 Vera Aleksandrovna Shidlovskaja.
551 Prince Sergej Semënovich Urusov, Ekaterina Petrovna Ermolova, philosopher Lev Mikhajlovich Lopatin (1855–1920).
552 Evgenij Mikhajlovich Feoktistov (press supervisor) — see Letter No 114, Note 402.
553 SAT's letter of 6 January 1887 (not included here), informing her husband that the reading of LNT's play *The Power of Darkness* [*Vlast' t'my*] at her Moscow home was a great success.
554 Letter No 134 of 3–4 January 1887.

come tonight bringing me your letters and those you are enclosing.[555] Things are fine here, the way you might expect them to be.

Among [my] guests [here] were [Aleksandra] Sizova (she got [your] letter too late and couldn't stop in to see you) and Kovalevskij.[556] Today Tatarinov[557] arrived.

Tanja is quiet and reserved, neither listless nor happy. Everyone is very much *aux petits soins* with her. Today she began drawing a portrait of the nanny. When I feel the spirit move me, I work on the narrative[558] I started, which I spoke to you about. I haven't been very well the whole time here, and am in a depressed mood, and with no spiritual energy, but [otherwise] splendid. I've been having stomach aches, chills and constipation, but this morning I started to feel better, only I went for a walk in the frosty air, and once again have begun to not feel quite myself. I don't feel like going to see the Vsevolozhskijs;[559] I feel like going home. But neither do I feel like arguing with Tanja. I'll try to do as she wishes. Today I received your letter,[560] as well as Stakhovich's[561] on the drama — I'm forwarding it to you along with the article from *Novoe vremja*.[562] It's being talked about everywhere. Weren't you a little too hard on Feoktistov? It's important not to get angry; even better to avoid being concerned at all. [Our] correspondence here is very indefinite; I know little about you all, and I miss [hearing about you]. There was a Christmas tree here in the Manège.[563] Everything here is somehow languid and strained. They're all good people, but the boys[564] are the best of all. — Well, farewell, darling. I'll write again tomorrow after receiving your letters. Both your letters [today] were so good, delightful, calm and substantial. Hugs and kisses to you and all the children; regards to Mme Seuron and [English governess] Miss Martha.

On the envelope: Moscow. Dolgokhamovniki Lane. 15. Countess Sofia Andreevna Tolstaya.

Nº 136 – SOFIA ANDREEVNA TOLSTAYA ✍ LEV NIKOLAEVICH TOLSTOY
[LSA 181]
[10 January 1887. Moscow]

I'm sending you, dear Lëvochka, Birjukov's letter and another, which is rather mysterious, besides. Apart from these there are some rather uninteresting letters: from Èsfir' Fejnerman,[565] who is complaining about her fate and her husband; a whole notebook from an unknown lady;

---

555 Letters from Il'ja Efimovich Repin, Vladimir Grigor'evich Chertkov, Isaak Borisovich Fejnerman and others.

556 Maksim Maksimovich Kovalevskij (1851–1916) — Moscow University professor of constitutional law.

557 Ivan Vasil'evich Tatarinov (1862–1903) — regional Nobility representative for Novotorzhok; a friend of Sergej L'vovich Tolstoj's.

558 A reference to LNT's story *Walk in the light while ye have light* [*Khodite v svete, poka est' svet*].

559 Mikhail Vladimirovich Vsevolozhskij (1860–1909) and his sister Sof'ja Vladimirovna Vsevolozhskaja (1859–1923), who married Ivan Vasil'evich Tatarinov. The Tolstoys' daughter Tanja was about to pay a visit to their Talozhnja estate in Tver' Gubernia.

560 Again referring to Letter Nº 134 of 3–4 January, which finally arrived.

561 Aleksandr Aleksandrovich Stakhovich's letter was dated 28 December 1886, and was concerning LNT's drama *The Power of Darkness*.

562 The reference here is to a review of *The power of darkness* published in *Novoe vremja* on 5 January 1887 by Aleksej Sergeevich Suvorin (1834–1912) — a prominent journalist, playwright and theatre critic in St. Petersburg, also the owner and editor of *Novoe vremja*. His review was entitled "Po povodu dramy grafa Tolstogo" [On Count Tolstoy's drama].

563 *Manège* (exhibition hall) — see Letter Nº 74, Note 113.

564 Mikhail Ada-mov-ich Olsuf'ev (1860–1918) — regional nobility representative — and his brother Dmitrij Adamovich Olsuf'ev (1862–1937) — a member of the Horse Guard, later a deputy of the State Council.

565 Esfir' Borisovna Fejnerman (second married name: Varshavskaja) — wife to Isaak Borisovich Fejnerman.

20 sheets from an unknown [person named] Voevodin, and so forth. I don't think I can send all these. It's a bit upsetting to me that we shan't see each other until the 16th, but what to do? — we have to let the young people live [their own life], too. Today I received a letter from Tanja,[566] where she writes about leaving. I was very interested in the letters regarding [your] drama. Tanja also wrote that [(a)] it was read at Obolenskaja's (D'jakova's); [(b)] it will be read at Alexandrine Tolstaja's,[567] with [several] grand princes in attendance; and [(c)] everyone's talking about it, all ecstatically. Today a pupil in Polivanov's[568] *gymnasium* was saying that Polivanov excitedly told his pupils about the drama in class and added that it will [prove to] be one of the most outstanding works of Russian literature. What the censorship board will do [about it], I have no idea. I know one thing, that I need to go to Petersburg and shall probably do so. Possibly this is also evident from the letter (I am enclosing) by this unknown lad, but his whole letter is strange and not reassuring. Why does he write that *terrorists are starting to count you as one of their own*? Only an idiot could fail to understand that everything you preach is diametrically opposed to terrorism, and that makes you terror[ism]'s worst enemy. What nonsense can be heard in Petersburg [these days] on both sides!

I'm *not feeling well* today, and my spirits are low. Then there's [my brother] Sasha's wedding which is confusing [me]. It will be tomorrow. For some reason Sasha has invited Arkadij Dmitrievich Stolypin[569] to give away the bride. The wedding is illegal,[570] [taking place] in the barracks, and here he's asking the corps commander to give away the bride! I call that tactless. But I'm taking the opportunity of petitioning for Grisha,[571] who will be one of the ushers. He arrived yesterday from Suwałki[572] specifically to find out about a job. Sergej Nikolaevich will also be coming soon, no doubt.

These days are very busy ones for me. The proofreading has accelerated. It's being done by anyone I can catch — if not Il'ja, then I go the Shidlovskijs', or [even] visitors. Then there has been a lot to do regarding the edition [of Volume XIII]. So many old tangles to unravel. Add to that my visits, a lot of pattern-cutting, arranging for undergarments and dresses — all quite a bother, and I'm very tired. It's high time for that idler Kolichka to return — or [at least] write [me] that he's not returning — or else my duties will become too much for me.

Things are not going all that well with the Englishwoman. I changed my tone with her and became strict, which is very hard [on me]. The children are mostly with me or Madame Seuron. — We get along with Il'ja, Lëva and Masha, we feel each other out, and that's quite good.

566 Tat'jana Andreevna (Tanja) Kuzminskaja (SAT's sister). Her letter of 7 January 1887 from St. Petersburg is only partly preserved. An excerpt follows: "The other day Aleksandr Aleksandrovich Stakhovich Sr read Lëvochka's play at the Obolenskijs' [Princess Aleksandra Andreevna Obolenskaja (sister to D. A. D'jakov and wife to Prince Andrej Vasil'evich Obolenskij)]. [Dmitrij Alekseevich] D'jakov introduced him and I listened; there were a lot of people there (all scholars). Well, it was such a delight, that I had never read anything like that before… Obolenskaja was jumping up and down in her seat with excitement. All the scholars could be heard simply exclaiming 'Ah, ah! What [force of] language, what artistry!', and Stakhovich's reading was a delight [to listen to]. ¶Sasha [my husband] was out hunting and didn't hear it, but Stakhovich has promised to read it [again] at our place. Well, what can I say more, it was so good, so powerful, so true, and never mind the [characters'] coarse morals, that was my [overall] impression" (Manuscript Division, State L. N. Tolstoy Museum).
567 Aleksandra Andreevna (Alexandrine) Tolstaja (LNT's great aunt).
568 Lev Ivanovich Polivanov (headmaster) — see Letter N° 82, Note 176.
569 Arkadij Dmitrievich Stolypin (LNT's wartime chum) — see Letter N° 42, Note 269.
570 A subsequent annotation on this point by SAT reads: "My brother Sasha married his second wife while his first, née Princess [Matrona Dmitrievna (Patti)] Èristova, was still living, and she herself had married [Sergej Aleksandrovich] Pisarev" (Letters to L. N. Tolstoy, p. 385). On Èristova and Pisarev, see Letter N° 99, Note 8.
571 Grigorij Sergeevich (Grisha) Tolstoj (LNT's nephew) — see Letter N° 6, Note 44.
572 *Suwałki* — a Polish town near the Russian border.

Tomorrow, as long as there's no snowstorm, I shall go skating with all my children, and then to the wedding in the evening. What are you busy with? And why do you call what you are writing a *narrative*? Keep on working, your fame has now ballooned to the *maximum*, and I'm delighted. I hope you are healthy and taking care of yourself. I'm writing [just] to you, and not to Tanja, since she's probably left [by now]. Regards to everyone, hugs and kisses to Tanja, and to you, too. I'll write another postcard. Farewell.

S. T.

10 January 1887. Evening.

Nº 137 – SOFIA ANDREEVNA TOLSTAYA ❧ LEV NIKOLAEVICH TOLSTOY
[LSA 186]
[11 April 1887. Moscow]

My terribly busy day today is finally over! I'm frightfully tired, and [my visitors] Stolypin and Vera Shidlovskaja, [along with] Serëzha, Tanja and Lëva are still here, playing vint. Last night I was doing proofreading until 3 a.m. Every day I get up right at 9 o'clock and manage to take tea with the children. This morning I went out shopping and on [other] errands, then at three o'clock the children of (Mitasha) Obolenskij,[573] those of the Sverbeevs,[574] the Nagornovs[575] and our own, all got together to roll [Easter] eggs. I made for them two huge *Van'ka-Vstan'kas* [weighted dolls], and the competition generated tremendous excitement. Our [daughter] Sasha managed to hit one of them, and Katja Sverbeeva the other, and there was no envy [involved] — the egg-rolling was very good-natured, cheerful and lively.

Then everybody had dinner, and in the evening we all gathered at Tanja's: Sonja Samarina,[576] Liza Obolenskaja,[577] Beklemisheva,[578] Rachinskaja,[579] various young people, [all in all] a huge crowd. — Vera Aleksandrovna [Shidlovskaja], Petja,[580] our Liza[581] and others played vint; I was terribly listless and exhausted, I sat there yawning and, as always, comforted myself with the thought that it would all, of course, stop some time. Tomorrow there won't be anyone around; I want Lëva's day to be completely free of distraction before his studies, and I am persistently refusing all visitors.

On Tuesday of this coming week I'm going to Grot's[582] lecture, and on Wednesday to the exhibit.[583] Those will be *my* two pleasures.

573 A reference to the children of Dmitrij Dmitrievich (Mitasha) Obolenskij (see Letter Nº 13, Note 79).

574 The children of Mikhail Dmitrievich Sverbeev (see Letter Nº 81, Note 170).

575 The children of Varvara Valer'janovna Nagornova (LNT's niece) and her husband Nikolaj Mikhajlovich Nagornov (see Letter Nº 54, Note 348).

576 Sof'ja Dmitrievna (Sonja) Samarina — daughter to regional nobility representative Dmitrij Fëdorovich Samarin (1831–1901) and Varvara Petrovna Samarina (*née* Ermolova).

577 Elizaveta Dmitrievna Kazenbek (*née* Obolenskaja).

578 Elizaveta Fëdorovna Beklemisheva — daughter to Fëdor Andreevich Beklemishev (?–1906) and Dar'ja Aleksandrovna Beklemisheva (*née* Koshelëva).

579 Marija Konstantinovna Rachinskaja (1865–1900) — the future wife (as of 1895) of the Tolstoys' son Sergej L'vovich (Serëzha) Tolstoj.

580 Pëtr Andreevich (Petja) Behrs (SAT's brother).

581 Elizaveta Valer'janovna (Liza) Obolenskaja (LNT's niece).

582 Nikolaj Jakovlevich Grot (1852–1889) — philosopher, chairman of the Psychological Society. On 14 April 1887 SAT attended his public lecture on philosophy entitled "On spirit and matter".

583 SAT took her children Marija, Andrej and Mikhail to an exhibit of Itinerant artists (see Letter Nº 117, Note 423).

Tomorrow Serëzha goes back to Tula; there's some kind of performance going on there, to which he was called. Il'ja's gone hunting for the day, once more to Krjukovo. Masha, the little ones and Lëva are all well and healthy.

Den[584] showed up today, he's very pleased with his stay at Yasnaya, and told about his stay in detail, what you did, what you ate, the warm [weather], and so forth.

You write that you would like to take a trip to see Khilkov[585] — and I happened to say this in front of Masha Sverbeeva; and she says that she had been talking about him yesterday with his auntie, who told her that Khilkov has gone off somewhere to wander, or *walk*, as she put it; that he apparently took his drunk and dissolute father into his home, but it turned out his father had an illegitimate family [on the side] who had all moved to his mother's estate — it was actually [Khilkov's] farmstead, but still on his mother's estate. Khilkov himself keeps a peasant woman whom he calls his wife, but since he is a *Doukhobor*, he doesn't recognise the church or marriage. — What a fine kettle of fish this is! Everyone calls everything *as they see it*, and everyone lives in line with: "*Don't go against my nature!*" — This is a very sad state of affairs: the victims are always the same — i.e. women and children. Sometimes it's mothers, as in Khilkov's case, sometimes it's wives, like with Fejnerman, sometimes it's daughters… A dark, dark people! Morally sick and miserable!

As for bidding adieu to Kolichka, I think he will get there without you, and if you really want to go somewhere, I think in this weather it is very dangerous for someone to travel if they are not in good health; in any case it is better to wait for a warm [day]. We hear about pneumonia everywhere, and people continue to die from it.

[Your] letter to Popov[586] in prison was sent through Mikhail Nikolaevich Lopatin during Holy [Week].

If after a period of intense intellectual labour you feel the need of taking a trip, you don't have to ask me. It's up to you. Only you wouldn't want to make the trip and not find Khilkov [at home].

Well, farewell, Lëvochka; again, it's after two [in the morning]. Your letters, too, are impersonal. There's nothing in them of an intimate nature, and nothing relating specifically to me. Only one thing is clear there — how confident you are that I am still living apart and do nothing but worry about you and your well-being. I await the promised written explanation of why you reproached me for not loving you *the way I ought to*… What if [I loved you] in no way? That would be undoubtedly more calming for you, and as for me — I don't know, maybe more calming and cheerful for me, too. So send me this explanation, though after twenty-five years [I think] it's too late to learn *how* one ought to love. Now, of course, to be a little calmer [about it] is best of all.

I shan't move to Yasnaya Polyana any earlier than the 20th of May. The prospect of sharing my family life with Fejnerman is so difficult that [in a way I'd rather] not go at all. As to your living your life apart from us, I look at it this way: if you are healthy, contented and happy, that's

584 Vladimir Èduardovich Den (1867–1933) — first a student at Moscow University (1885–90) and later a professor of economic geography; married to Natal'ja Nikolaevna Filosofova (1872–1926), sister to Sof'ja Nikolaevna Tolstaja.

585 Prince Dmitrij Alekseevich Khilkov (1858–1914) — a Lieutenant-Colonel of the Guard, married (common-law) to Tsetsilija Vladimirovna Viner (1860–1922), sister to Elizaveta Vladimirovna Viner (see Letter Nº 132, Note 529). In 1898 Khilkov became involved in the Doukhobors' emigration to Canada (see Woodsworth 1999: 121–64, 199–204).

586 Ivan Ivanovich Popov (1860–1925) — a statistician in Voronezh Gubernia; he was arrested on political grounds in October 1886 and in November 1887 was exiled to Petropavlovsk near Omsk (see PSS 63: 370). The whereabouts of LNT's letter are unknown.

good enough. The children aren't longing for the countryside either; evidently last summer[587] has long lain like a heavy stone on everybody's heart.

Today the girls are saying: "Let's do everything the opposite of the way we did it last year, and it'll be fine."

Please, continue to take care of yourself, or you'll start to feel worse again, and you can't drink the [mineral] water — [the weather's too] cold. Today I was at Ferrejn's,[588] I declined to have any water until May; oh and they also said that there had been no delivery of fresh water until now.

I'll write [and ask for] the Posrednik books to be sent to Yasenki.

Hugs and kisses. I'm sleeping alone upstairs, and these nights are very wretched.

11 April 1887. Night.

Nº 138 – LEV NIKOLAEVICH TOLSTOY ❧ SOFIA ANDREEVNA TOLSTAYA
[PSS 84/382]
13 April 1887. Yasnaya Polyana.

Today I received your most recent letter,[589] dear friend, and I was very sad to hear that you are feeling neither peace nor joy. I know this is temporary, and I'm almost certain that tomorrow I'll receive a good letter from you which will be in a different tone altogether. Yesterday was the first day that I haven't written to you and I did not go to Kozlovka. The other evening I went to Kozlovka with Kolichka, and we trudged back from there in the mud, in such darkness that you couldn't see past the nose on your face; very good. At the crossroads of the highway and the old road we saw a light flickering and happy women's voices. Gipsies, we thought. When we came closer, [it turned out to be] children with sticks, girls, a man, and in the lead was Pelageja Fëdorovna,[590] with a lantern; she was seeing off Sonja's[591] fiancé to Kozlovka. — Upon reaching home, we found Alëkhin[592] who had arrived [in the meantime] — you remember, the chap in the spectacles? He's on his way to buy some land and stopped in. We went to bed. Yesterday morning I did quite a lot of work — I was working on a whole new chapter on suffering, — pain.[593] We went for a stroll, and had dinner. Also in the morning Sytin's brother[594] came; he's come from Moscow to look for somewhere to live and work in the countryside; he went off to see Marija Aleksandrovna,[595] and Alëkhin left. During the evening visitors came: Daniil,[596]

---

587 *last summer* — a reference (most probably) to the physical labour in the field the children were engaged in, along with the peasant workers, during the summer of 1886.

588 A reference to a pharmacy belonging to Vladimir Karlovich Ferrejn (1834–1918).

589 Letter Nº 137 of 11 April 1887.

590 Pelageja Fëdorovna Suvorova — the Tolstoys' laundress.

591 Sof'ja Vasil'evna (Sonja) Suvorova (married name: Larionova) — daughter to Pelageja Fëdorovna Suvorova and Vasilij Vasil'evich Suvorov.

592 Arkadij Vasil'evich Alëkhin (1854–1908) — a Tolstoyan who founded agricultural communes but subsequently became disenchanted with LNT's teachings.

593 At the time LNT was working on Chapter 35 of his treatise *On life* [*O zhizni*].

594 Sergej Dmitrievich Sytin (1863?–1915) — an alcoholic brother to Ivan Dmitrievich Sytin (see Letter Nº 134, Note 544).

595 Marija Aleksandrovna Shmidt (1844–1911) — a friend and kindred thinker to LNT; a former schoolmistress in a Tula diocesan school.

596 Daniil Davydovich Kozlov (1848–1918) — a peasant and former pupil at LNT's Yasnaya Polyana school.

Konstantin;[597] we read "*Khvoraja*" [The sick woman] by Potekhin.[598] Fejnerman wasn't there. He was in Tula petitioning for a divorce, for which there was a whole heap of obstacles [to overcome]. Today just Kolichka and I took tea and coffee: then I wrote, he transcribed and stoked [the stove for] the bathhouse. We had dinner; then came the slightly drunk Pëtr Tsyganok[599] and had a lot of good things to tell me. Just now I was at the bathhouse and wanted to take some tea. It's the second day of spring — the lungwort and nut-trees were in blossom, and the flies, bees and ladybugs woke up and were buzzing and swarming about. The nighttime is even better: quiet, warm, starry — you don't feel like going indoors. I also worked well today. First [I] did some reviewing and correcting. I really wanted to translate everything into [a kind of] Russian that everybody could read — down to the least literate peasant.[600] And how compact and self-explanatory it all becomes then. When you talk with professors you get verbosity, gobbledy-gook and abstruseness, while *muzhiks* express themselves with conciseness, linguistic beauty and clarity. — I received letters from Chertkov,[601] Birjukov,[602] Simon[603] — all good, delightful letters. — My health is good. Now *I hope.*[604] Oh, and I shan't go see Khilkov. *I hope* that you are not getting weighed down by the proofreading, and that the workdays have calmed everyone down, and that only the grass in the garden is trembling and giving joy. *I hope* that Il'ja is behaving himself, that the little ones are healthy, and that Tanja and Masha are in a good mood, and that Lëva is not playing vint. Fejnerman saw [our son] Serëzha today in Tula: he was trying to decide whether to come to Yasnaya or not. I think he'll come tomorrow, most likely, and with hunters. The very best [time] for hunting. — Well, farewell, dear friend. Hugs and kisses to you and the children.

L. T.

On the envelope: Moscow. 15. Dolgokhamovniki Lane. Countess Sofia Andreevna Tolstaya.

N° 139 – SOFIA ANDREEVNA TOLSTAYA ❧ LEV NIKOLAEVICH TOLSTOY
[LSA 189]
[14 April 1887. Moscow]

I wanted to describe and summarise for you Grot's lecture,[605] but I shan't be able to — it's long, wordy and impossible to follow, he read it so quickly. Now I understand why people come down on him for [trying to] serve two masters — evidently his aim is to reconcile materialism with idealism. To this end he assigns the *former* to the realm of science, and the *latter* to the realm of religion. He frankly rejects categorising philosophy as *science* and said so today. I did not care for the way he began his lecture. It's the old chestnut of the diseased and abnormal

---

597 Konstantin Nikolaevich Zjabrev (peasant) — see Letter N° 63, Note 36.

598 Aleksej Antipovich Potekhin (1829–1908) — author of stories of peasant life. His story "The sick woman" was originally published in *Vestnik Evropy* (1876, N° 2), and then republished as a separate edition by Posrednik in 1887.

599 Pëtr Dmitrievich (Tsyganok) Novikov — a Yasnaya Polyana peasant carpenter; his nickname *Tsyganok* means 'little gypsy'.

600 In the original letter, LNT uses the name of Tit — i.e. Tit Ivanovich Polin (a.k.a. Pelagejushkin; 1867–1932), one of the Tolstoys' servants — as a symbol of his 'least literate peasant'.

601 The letter from Vladimir Grigor'evich Chertkov was dated 9 April 1887 (see PSS 86:45–46).

602 In the Manuscript Division of the State L. N. Tolstoy Museum there are three letters from Birjukov addressed to LNT dated April 1887, dealing mostly with the Posrednik publishing house.

603 Fëdor Pavlovich Simon (1861–after 1916) — a student at the Forestry Institute who was attracted to LNT's ideas.

604 The words *I hope* are given in English in the original letter (in all three instances in this paragraph).

605 *Grot's lecture* — see Letter N° 137, Note 583.

moral and political state of Russian society, as infected by Europe. Then [he made] the comparison: just as the grape phylloxera which was brought in from Europe devastated Russian vineyards, so, too, society must become devastated by moral phylloxera. This was followed by an historical philosophical survey with a brief summary of the teachings of each individual philosopher, comparing Plato with Descartes and Aristotle with Kant.

The second part of the lecture was devoted to an analysis of matter and spirit in the personality of each individual and proving the presence of this spirit and its relation to God and Nature.

I was quite tired, and towards the end [of the lecture] could not follow it all that well. Besides, he was in a hurry and frightfully agitated [in his presentation]. He was mainly disappointed that there were so few people [in attendance]. When Solovёv spoke,[606] the hall was completely full. But Grot was applauded, while Solovёv was not, [not even] once.

I received your rather lengthy letter[607] and was surprised [to learn] that the dark people found you even there. Today I heard concerning [Ivan Dmitrievich] Sytin's brother [Sergej] from the words of Bulygin,[608] who continues to wander, and Gerasimov[609] is quite fond of [Sergej] and praises him, — and Ivan Dmitrievich wrote to our office about his brother Sytin, [saying] that we should under no circumstances give him either books or money, that he has [already] forged two counterfeit promissory notes in his brother's name and he is both a drunkard and a debaucher (his [Ivan's] very words). Ivan Dmitrievich Sytin is in despair — evidently he doesn't know what to do with [his brother], and has sent him away. As to where all these good-for-nothings go, they get sent to you. Decent people are either going about their business or living in families. You'll again say that I'm angry; while I'm not angry, but to my misfortune I have a coarsely down-to-earth view of people, and I can't close my eyes, the way you do, to what exists. Your head and imagination are filled with *types,* not people. And by compensating for their deficiencies and casting off what doesn't fit, you categorise everyone under these types, spiritualising and idealising them. But this is not the way it is in life, and I see and judge people in life.

Serёzha came and was sorry he didn't go see you yesterday [at Yasnaya]. Tomorrow I am forwarding to you letters and manuscripts: from Chertkov, Jagn[610] and Timashev-Bering[611] — c/o *Yasenki.* You can send for them in a couple of days. Also the artel worker asked to tell Kolichka that he has sent something to Tula. Ask Kolichka how to enter payments from the old edition into the little [account] book: neither I nor Gerasimov understand the significance of the Roman numerals, or, [indeed], of this whole complex record. Perhaps he will be able to decipher it.

Tanja's leg is better; tomorrow I'll take Masha and the little ones to the exhibit.[612] For some reason I can't quite figure out Il'ja and Lёva — what kind of mood they're in — a lackadaisical one, it seems. When I dropped in today on the Tolstojs[613] to collect Masha, where she was

---

606 *When Solovёv spoke* — see Letter N° 61, Note 12.

607 Letter N° 138 of 13 April 1887.

608 Mikhail Vasil'evich Bulygin (1864–1943) — a former officer of the Guard, who shared LNT's views; he owned the Khatunka farmstead 15 *versts* from Yasnaya Polyana.

609 Osip Petrovich Gerasimov (1863–1920) — writer, tutor to the Tolstoys' children; later Minister of Education (1905–08 and 1917).

610 Aleksandr Nikolaevich Jagn (1818?–1900) — a doctor from Saratov Gubernia who sent LNT his article *Naprasnye bedstvija i stradanija ljudej* [*People's unnecessary poverty and suffering*].

611 Vladimir Alekseevich Timashev-Bering (1854–1905) — a notary; a writer of stories and poetry; son of a former Moscow police chief and deputy governor Aleksej Aleksandrovich Timashev-Bering (1812–1872).

612 See Letter N° 137, Note 583.

613 A reference to the family of LNT's brother Sergej Nikolaevich Tolstoj.

supposed to be playing four-handed piano with Varja, I was dismayed to find that Vera[614] and Mar'ja Mikhajlovna[615] were not there, but Il'ja and Sonja,[616] Orlov[617] and Nata, all red-faced; apparently these *rendez-vous* are arranged at the Tolstojs, when convenient, as, for example, today, since Sof'ja Alekseevna[618] had gone to see the dying Alësha Bobrinskij,[619] and [Sonja's] father[620] is ill; the girls arranged this [get-together] themselves. Tanja will write Sonja a letter tomorrow; she, too, is outraged over the impropriety of such behaviour.

Our garden, too, has been getting greener, and the children run around all day. Today both Fomich[621] and the cook Semën were all playing on the swings and having fun, just like in the country. The whole household was outdoors all day long. Some people are packing books. Vas'ka[622] from the artel is proudly taking the dogs for walks; the cook, Annushka — they're all working outdoors; the nanny and Masha the maid are sewing on little benches in the garden. I alone am coping with dusty packages and writing full tilt. Today I almost went without dinner. I had to check whether they had made the proper corrections based on my [previous] proofreading, and the courier waited while I worked; everybody had dinner, and I had a bite to eat afterwards, even though I felt [almost] too tired to eat. This morning I spent at the State and the Merchant Banks. I have a hurt in the pit of my stomach and my back, I just feel like crying. If only I could die sooner! I'm fed up with work, but it's impossible to stop a machine once it's started. If the machine breaks down, the work stops of necessity, or they will bring another machine and again it starts! Gerasimov is clever and a good man; but he will be a poor worker: he has neither the health nor the energy, but already shows signs of fatigue and a reluctance to work, because of previous difficulties in earning his daily bread. Kolichka works unevenly: either too much or too little, and not skilfully.

Instead of the fiction [I was] hoping for, you've started to write about suffering.[623] That's a pity. Anyway, the question does interest me. When will you have this article finished? It would be good if you divided it into chapters and named each chapter according to its contents. That always helps [readers] understand! For example: "On pain", "On the joy of life", "On labour", "On the soul", etc.

Well, farewell. This letter has turned out to be longer than I had expected. May God save you from disease, sorrow, dark people and any sort of deception or misfortune. Hugs and kisses.

Sonja.

14 April 1887

---

614 Vera Sergeevna Tolstaja (Sergej's daughter) — see Letter № 102, Note 7.

615 Mar'ja Mikhajlovna (Masha) Tolstaja (*née* Shishkina; 1832–1919) — a gypsy woman who married Sergej Nikolaevich in 1867.

616 Sof'ja Nikolaevna (Sonja) Filosofova (1867–1934) — fiancée to the Tolstoys' son Il'ja L'vovich, whom she would marry in 1888.

617 Mikhail Nikolaevich Orlov (1866–1907) — a jurist; a friend to Il'ja L'vovich Tolstoj; here together with Natal'ja Nikolaevna (Nata) Filosofova (1872–1926) — younger sister to Sof'ja Nikolaevna Filosofova.

618 Sof'ja Alekseevna Filosofova (*née* Pisareva; 1847–1901) — mother to Sof'ja and Natal'ja Nikolaevna Filosofova.

619 Count Aleksej Alekseevich (Alësha) Bobrinskij (1864–1909) — nephew to Sof'ja Alekseevna Filosofova.

620 Nikolaj Alekseevich Filosofov (1838–1895) — vice-president of the Academy of Arts; husband to Sof'ja Alekseevna Filosofova.

621 Mikhail Fomich Krjukov (a servant).

622 Vasilij Sevast'janovich Makarychev — see Letter № 103, Note 304.

623 See Letter № 138, Note 593.

Nº 140 – LEV NIKOLAEVICH TOLSTOY ❧ SOFIA ANDREEVNA TOLSTAYA
[PSS 84/388]
1 May 1887. Yasnaya Polyana.

You must be quite dissatisfied with me, dear friend, over my letters. They probably turned out [rather] gloomy, since my soul has felt gloomy these past two, or one-and-a-half, days. Gloomy doesn't mean unwell, but physically languid. Probably something in my liver. But now since last evening, I feel fine once again. And today I've been doing a lot of work and feel like doing even more. I've had so many [ideas] come to me for my writing that I soon shan't be able to count them on my fingers, and it seems that I could just sit down and write something. Whatever God shows me after I finish writing *On Life and Death [O Zhizni i Smerti]*. After all, there will be an ending. But not yet. It's a serious subject, and so I want to write about it as best I can. You think it's worse, but that's not how it seems to me. Yesterday Serëzha arrived and moved in with Filip,[624] that is, downstairs in the annexe — especially since he moved with his furniture, and he claims he feels so much at home there that he would like to stay there the whole summer. — It's after five now, and we just had dinner, and I shall take [this] letter to Kozlovka and probably receive one from you. It will be too bad if I don't see Chertkov.[625] You ask:[626] Why did I leave? Of course, in many respects it is better and more joyful [for us] to be together, but from the point of view of [my] work — and I don't have that much more [to finish at the moment] — it's a lot better here. And loneliness is productive. Keep that in mind — and [I know that] you have [it in mind]. — Yesterday I picked violets, and they are now in front of me on my desk. — How strange it was a couple of evenings ago, after [Tomáš] Masaryk's[627] departure, that I was overcome by such a physical bout of melancholy as I had at Arzamas.[628] And back then the most frightening aspect of this was the thought of death. This time, on the contrary, as soon as I began to feel melancholy, I started to think: What do I need? What am I afraid of?

How do I stop this from happening? And all I needed to do was to think about death as I understand it [now], and immediately any sense of melancholy disappeared and a very calm, even pleasant, state set in.

Today is a fine, warm day; the windows are open and they're washing at the Kuzminskijs'.[629] They'll be stoking [the stoves] in the annexe tomorrow.

624 Filip Rodionovich Egorov (coachman) — see Letter Nº 73, Note 110.

625 On their way from St. Petersburg to Vladimir's mother's estate in Voronezh Gubernia, Vladimir Grigor'evich Chertkov and his wife Anna Konstantinovna Chertkova made a stopover in Moscow and had lunch with SAT at her home.

626 In a letter to her husband dated 27 April 1887 (not included here), SAT wrote: "God knows why you left, and I felt so sorry for you!" (Letters to L. N. Tolstoy, p. 409).

627 Tomáš Garrigue Masaryk (1850–1937) — at the time, a professor of philosophy at the University of Prague, later the founding President of Czechoslovakia (1918–35). He was a guest at Yasnaya Polyana 27–29 April 1887, on the recommendation of Nikolaj Nikolaevich Strakhov (see Letter Nº 47, Note 303).

628 A reference to an experience of LNT's during an overnight stop at Arzamas on his way to Penza Gubernia in 1869. On 4 September 1869 he wrote in a letter to SAT (not included here): "The other day while I was spending the night at Arzamas, something unusual happened to me. It was around 2 a.m., I was frightfully tired, I wanted to sleep, and nothing was aching. But all of a sudden I was overcome by such a feeling of longing, fear and terror as I had never experienced before…" (PSS 83: 168). It was an extreme fear of death, which LNT later described in his story Notes of a madman [Zapiski sumasshedshego] — see PSS 26.

629 The Kuzminskij family (of SAT's sister Tat'jana Andreevna Kuzminskaja) would be soon arriving to spend the summer (as usual) in the Yasnaya Polyana annexe.

What have you decided about [your] departure and how are you doing? I feel fine being alone [here], but of course I shall be even happier when you come.

I shan't seal the envelope for now — I may add a postscript at Kozlovka.

[Kozlovka:] I received your two letters[630] about Misha. It's probably gone by now, or you would have let me know. Hugs and kisses to all. — An amazing evening. I'm sitting [here] at Kozlovka.

On the envelope: Moscow. 15. Dolgokhamovniki Lane. Countess Sofia Andreevna Tolstaya.

Nº 141 – SOFIA ANDREEVNA TOLSTAYA ❧ LEV NIKOLAEVICH TOLSTOY
[LSA 195]
[18 April 1888. Moscow]

They told me that yesterday you started your trek[631] so cheerfully, dear Lëvochka. I'm glad that the weather is so fine, and that you [and your fellows] didn't start out the day before. I can only imagine how cheered you must have been when after pavement and stones and cities you set foot on *soft [ground],* as my sister Tanja puts it, and walked across the grass, with wide open space before you, and that space infinite. From my little cage it seemed so joyous; however, when I think of staying overnight, the meals and the people [you meet], I wouldn't want to do it myself.

I hope this trek wakes you up a bit, and that its result will not be a *Palkin,*[632] but something more poetic, soft and artistic. It all comes down to *I hope.*[633]

Here after you left yesterday we were inundated with a crowd of eighteen people, and just before noon they all headed in boats to the Vorobëvy Hills. And they took my little ones with them. They all had a very good time, and in their absence I entertained Petja and his wife,[634] both Shidlovskijs — Vera Aleksandrovna and Ol'ga — and Masha Sverbeeva,[635] and Ermolova,[636] and the two Olsuf'ev brothers[637] — so [you see] I was a little exhausted. In the evening Buturlin[638] was here, along with Uncle Kostja.[639] Buturlin is a pathetic creature, but [somehow] he continues to appeal to me. Tomorrow he is going to the exhibit with our family and see Polenov's[640] picture, and later he'll come and take dinner with us.

---

630 SAT's letters dated 28 and 29 April 1887 (not included here) concerning the illness of their youngest son Mikhail (Misha).

631 On 17 April LNT, along with Nikolaj Nikolaevich (Kolichka) Ge Jr and a close friend, Aleksandr Nikiforovich Dunaev (1850–1920), began a trek on foot from Moscow to Yasnaya Polyana. For more details, see *My Life,* IV.130.

632 LNT used notes from his earlier trek as a basis for his story Nikolai Palkin [Nikolaj Palkin] (see Letter Nº 131).

633 *I hope* — Again, these two words appear in English.

634 See Letter Nº 59, Note 14.

635 SAT's aunt Vera Aleksandrovna Shidlovskaja (see Letter Nº 123, Note 487) with her two daughters: Ol'ga Vjacheslavovna Shidlovskaja (married name: Severtseva; see Letter Nº 30, Note 4) and Marija Vjacheslavovna (Masha) Sverbeeva (née Shidlovskaja; see Letter Nº 81, Note 4).

636 Ekaterina Petrovna Ermolova — see Letter Nº 106, Note 329.

637 Mikhail Adamovich Olsuf'ev and Dmitrij Adamovich Olsuf'ev — see Letter Nº 135, Note 564.

638 Aleksandr Sergeevich Buturlin (1845–1916) — a doctor; a revolutionary member of the 'People's Will' party, who served three years (1883–1886) in exile in Simbirsk Gubernia.

639 Konstantin Aleksandrovich (Kostja) Islavin (SAT's uncle) — see Letter Nº 47, Note 301.

640 Vasilij Dmitrievich Polenov (1844–1927) — prominent Russian realist landscape painter. The specific reference here is to his 1888 painting *Khristos i greshnitsa* [*Christ and the sinner*], which was shown for the first time at the XVI Itinerant artists' exhibit held at the Moscow School of Painting, Sculpture and Architecture from 17 April to 8 May 1888.

The little one[641] and I slept better, and I feel fresher [than before]. Write me more often; it will be a great source of strength in these moments of nervousness.

The girls have gone shopping, Serëzha is getting ready [to head off to] Nikol'skoe, tomorrow, it seems. The younger ones are diligently going to church of their own free will; I am happy to let them come to everything on their own without clumsy or over-mature interference.

Regards to Kolichka; I'm sorry I didn't say good-bye to him properly. Where did he put Mamontov's bill,[642] and what did he find out about it?

Farewell, dear friend. I am teaching Misha[643] and am hastening to send off this letter. They were really fussing around me this morning: the girls with their purchases, and the artel worker, and the baby, and others.

Hugs and kisses to you; it's not my usual handwriting; for some reason my hand is not obeying me [today].

S. T.

N° 142 – LEV NIKOLAEVICH TOLSTOY ✿ SOFIA ANDREEVNA TOLSTAYA
[PSS 83/398]
23 April 1888. Yasnaya Polyana.

Lëva[644] has already told you, dear friend, about yesterday, and how we arrived [home] and how I, drooping from fatigue, fell asleep almost as early as 10 o'clock. Your letter[645] saddened me, very much so. I promised you that I would write you the whole truth about myself, not hiding [anything], and I would ask you the same and I hope that you will do it. I was sad to learn from your letter that you are despondent in your soul, besides being not well in your body, but I was glad to learn and feel that I know the whole, the most complete truth about you. I hope that [your troubles] have passed; if not, write and tell me what you are thinking and feeling, and I shall come at once if I see that's needed. From what I said about getting tired during ploughing, the same as I did when travelling, and in conjunction with Birjukov's letter,[646] you deduce that I want to torment and kill myself in any way possible. This is completely uncalled for, since I always insist that a person should do everything just for his own good. Only the point is this: that getting tired, even extremely tired in the spring air, [either] when travelling or ploughing, is a positive benefit in every respect and, vice-versa, the absence of labour fatigue is an evil. I feel splendid. Our young people[647] are very dear, and my fellow trekkers — i.e. [Aleksandr Nikiforovich] Dunaev, are nicer and more refined than I had expected. I spent the whole morning today in my study, cleaning out all the dust and putting everything in order so that if the occasion presents itself tomorrow, I can [actually] sit down and do some writing, which would be [both] possible and pleasant. This morning I took a walk to the village to see Tit Borisov.[648]

641 Ivan L'vovich (Vanechka) Tolstoj (1888–1895) — the Tolstoys' youngest son (and the dearest to his mother's heart), born 31 March 1888.

642 Mamontov's bill — for printing LNT's drama *The power of darkness* [*Vlast' t'my*] in the printshop of Anatolij Ivanovich Mamontov (see Letter N° 116, Note 419).

643 Mikhail L'vovich (Misha) Tolstoj — the Tolstoys' seventh surviving child (born 1879).

644 Lev L'vovich (Lëva) Tolstoj had just arrived in Moscow that very day from Yasnaya Polyana.

645 A letter dated 19 April 1888 (not included here), in which SAT complained of illness after giving birth to Vanechka.

646 The whereabouts of Pavel Ivanovich Birjukov's letter are unknown.

647 Il'ja L'vovich Tolstoj with his new bride (as of 28 February 1888) Sof'ja Nikolaevna (Sonja) Tolstaja (*née* Filosofova).

648 Tit Borisovich Borisov (1828–1888) — a Yasnaya Polyana peasant.

But he's no longer there, he died. Now I'm riding over to Yasenki to fetch mail and take this letter to the post.

Today I took down [the storm windows and] opened the windows in all the rooms. I'll see to Tanja's balcony. Please write and tell me what is needed: I shall be very glad to take care of everything. Hugs and kisses to you and to our daughters who are helping you and probably want [to do] only that, and enjoy doing it, and to the boys, and Sasha[649] (Ivan included in the boys).

L.

Nº 143 – SOFIA ANDREEVNA TOLSTAYA ✷ LEV NIKOLAEVICH TOLSTOY
[LSA 200]
[1 May 1888. Moscow] [Preceded by SAT's Nº 7U, 27 April 1888]

My breast-feeding [of Vanechka] is not going at all well, dear friend. One breast has become so painful that after every feeding I'm all in a sweat, and am almost ready to break into hysterics, and can't hold back my tears. What hellish pains [I am experiencing] and how unnaturally everything in the world is constructed! Tanja happened to notice how I was breast-feeding, and started to repeat emphatically: "You'd better hire a wet-nurse". But I'm still not ready for a wet-nurse and I pray to God for patience. I don't have much milk; the baby has such frail little legs, and he is all — both his little face and his whole little body — so frail, and I feel so sorry for him! This time the pity set in earlier than six weeks; it's been later in the past. This shows the weakness and tenderness of old age towards the very young and helpless.

Since I can't even move on account of the pain, nor work, nor do anything with my right hand (it's painful even to write), I spend my time sitting motionless and have a terrible case of melancholy, as I cannot see any end to my sufferings. And how did this happen so quickly, all of a sudden, without any [apparent] cause? — How is your own health, and how are you getting along? I haven't had a letter from you for two days now, and that in itself makes us all concerned. We were thinking perhaps you could send the coachman Mikhail at my request, and with him a letter, too, tomorrow morning. Konstantin[650] left today, and we are without a coachman.

Today your sister Mashen'ka and Uncle Kostja took dinner with us, and later all the children and the grown-ups ran or went for a walk in the garden. I saw Maslova[651] and Gubkina[652] through the window, but nobody came in to see me on account of my ill health, which I was very glad of. A little drama took place over dinner. Serëzha whispered to Andrjusha that his hands were dirty. Masha overheard it and everybody came down on him and he broke into tears, left the room and wouldn't eat, and sobbed for a long time, more from being shamed in front of Kolja Obolenskij and Borja Nagornov.[653] I didn't interfere, my nerves were too far shot, and I felt so sorry for him and wanted to cry myself. Later it all worked itself out: he ran off to play, and at 7 o'clock he got some salt beef from the cupboard and ate with great gusto. I went down to him, Lëva didn't know I was doing this, and he went first [among the children]

---

649 Aleksandra L'vovna (Sasha) Tolstaja and baby Ivan L'vovich (Vanechka) Tolstoj — the Tolstoys' two youngest children at the time.
650 *Mikhail, Konstantin* — no further details available.
651 Varvara Ivanovna Maslova (1839–1905) — a Moscow acquaintance of the Tolstoys'.
652 Anna Sergeevna Gubkina (1857–1922) — tutor to Marija L'vovna (Masha) Tolstaja.
653 Nikolaj Leonidovich (Kolja) Obolenskij (1872–1934) and Boris Nikolaevich (Borja) Nagornov (1877–1899) — grandsons to LNT's sister Marija Nikolaevna Tolstaja.

to comfort him. He's very dear, Lëva, only he shouldn't have bought a balalaika — his exam [preparations] might suffer [as a result].

Farewell, Lëvochka, hugs and kisses. Lessons begin tomorrow, and I'm glad about that, otherwise the children would do nothing but run around and often get bored from inactivity.

If my breasts are not better, I don't know how we can move. I can't undertake anything in my present condition and, without a push from me, my whole household machine cannot be set in motion. And this grieves me. — Lëva asked me yesterday: "Mamà, are you happy?" I was very surprised, didn't know what to say at first, but then I responded: "Yes, I consider myself happy." And he said: "Then why do you look like a martyr?" I didn't say anything in reply, and I think it comes from my cares and fatigue over sleepless nights, as well as from pain. But he notices everything, and he needs all of us to be doing well.

You and I are a lot closer in our letters than in our lives. In a letter we remember everything and write down anything that might be of interest, even just a little, while in life we see little of each other, *dark* people take possession of you, and it's always shameful to somehow talk about the trifles of everyday life, while in a letter everything seems interesting.

Well, farewell again; don't keep us too long without news. Hugs and kisses.

S.

1 May.
Hurry up with the work on the house, so you won't make us wait.[654]

654 In a letter dated 5 May (not included here) LNT replied: "The whitewashing of the house is a rather difficult task, [we want] to avoid breaking or getting the paint on the furniture. Yesterday, for example, we caught the painters sleeping on our beds and chased them out. I'll try not to mess up anything and get the work done soon" (*Letters of Count L. N. Tolstoy to his wife*, p. 329).

PART III

LETTERS 1889–1910

INTRODUCTION TO LETTERS, PART III

The correspondence between Lev Nikolaevich Tolstoy and his wife over the last two decades of their married years certainly reflected the drama of their life itself. Tolstoy's return to fiction writing had been accomplished with such masterpieces as *The Death of Ivan Ilyich [Smert' Ivana Il'icha]* (1886) and *The Kreutzer Sonata [Krejtserova sonata]* (1889). He would be active on the belletristic scene well into his advanced years: his novel *Hadji Murat [Khadzhi Murat]* was finished in 1904, although published only posthumously, together with some of his other later works. In time, however, this artistic endeavour became a source of deepening family discord with Tolstoy's public renunciation in 1891 of copyright on all his works published after 1881.

In the meantime, Tolstaya continued producing one edition after another of her husband's ever-popular *Complete Collected Works [PSS]*. However, she kept encountering more and more difficulties with censorship in respect to his later offerings, which were often controversial thanks to their deliberate — and even emphatic — conflict with official political and religious values of the time. Initially this involved *The Kreutzer Sonata*, but later included some of his theatrical plays such as *The power of darkness [Vlast' t'my]*. In 1891, Sofia Andreevna obtained a personal audience with Emperor Alexander III and a compromise was achieved.

In the following years, Lev Nikolaevich became a kind of cult figure in both his home country and the world at large. While he remained, of course, a great artist, it was his philosophical and religious works (often crossing into the realm of burning social issues) that gained him many new followers. He was being seen more and more not so much as a famous writer but as a kind of guru with a devoted following of 'Tolstoyans'. His vocal opposition to what he viewed as hypocrisy and intolerance in the official Russian Orthodox Church eventually led to his formal ex-communication in 1901. Sofia Andreevna, by contrast, remained a devoted adherent of the church and its traditional practices, even while considering her husband's ex-communication as an unwarranted punitive measure.

All this signalled a deepening rift between husband and wife. Certain events brought them brief periods of reconciliation, such as their joint efforts in famine relief (1891–93) and (to a lesser extent) in the relocation of the Doukhobors to Canada (1898–99). Another unifying emotional experience was the birth — and (only seven years later) death — of their last child Ivan (Vanechka) (1888–1895). As a family they did manage to come to an amicable agreement (1891) concerning the division of the inheritance among the surviving children. But these occasional moments of respite could not compensate indefinitely for the widening gulf between them in their philosophical and moral worldviews. Tolstoy rejected the idea of personal property and gave his wife full power-of-attorney over his financial affairs, but not without expressing continual disapproval of the very fact that she (and the rest of the family) dealt with 'earthly' issues, while he was devoting his whole attention to 'spiritual' seekings.

The rift was exacerbated even further by Sofia Andreevna's striking up a second platonic friendship in the mid-1890s (the first had been with philosopher Leonid Urusov at the end of the 1870s), this time with composer and concert pianist Sergej Taneev. This relationship grew out of her passionate love for Taneev's musical talent, which proved a great comfort to her following her beloved Vanechka's death (1895). But the attachment sparked repeated fits of jealousy on the part of her husband, even to the threat on several occasions of leaving the marriage.

During this whole period Tolstaya was adding to the store of her own artistic talents — including painting, photography and writing. She began publishing her own stories, such as *The rescued dachshund* (which she said was "dictated" by Vanechka) in 1895, and culminating

in a whole book collection (1910), under the title *The skeleton-dolls and other stories*. She also began penning two autobiographies, the more extensive of which, entitled *My Life*, was not published (in either its original Russian or an English translation) until the early twenty-first century.[1]

In the meantime, the arts in Russia as a whole were continuing to flourish. On the music scene, the decades around the turn of the century brought to prominence not only Taneev, but composers such as Sergei Rakhmaninoff, Alexander Scriabin and Igor Stravinsky; moreover, the revolutionary modernism of the latter two paved the way for such twentieth-century notables as Sergei Prokofiev and Dmitri Shostakovich. Russian theatre was celebrating the likes of director Konstantin Stanislavsky, producer Vladimir Nemirovich-Danchenko and actor Leopold Sullerzhitsky ('Suller' was instrumental in escorting two parties of Doukhobors to Canada at LNT's request). Russian literature, in turn, featured the rise of novelist Maxim Gorky and playwright/storyteller Anton Chekhov, both of whom visited the Tolstoys at Yasnaya Polyana and were photographed in Lev Nikolaevich's company by Sofia Andreevna. At the same time, Russian poetry was entering upon its so-called Silver Age, which came to include the works of Anna Akhmatova, Osip Mandelstam, Boris Pasternak and Marina Tsvetaeva, all well known both within Russia's borders and far beyond.

1   University of Ottawa Press, 2010

N° 144 – LEV NIKOLAEVICH TOLSTOY ❧ SOFIA ANDREEVNA TOLSTAYA
[PSS 84/408]
24 March 1889. Spasskoe.

I'm having an excellent stay here to date.[1] Yesterday I took a long walk through the surrounding villages, but didn't write anything. I read and chatted with Urusov and Posha.[2] Posha left last night. Urusov is very precious, at home with his old, God-fearing and equally upperclass Gerasim and his sister.[3] He gets up at 4 o'clock and drinks tea and writes some kind of mathematical essay which I can't understand. They were making tea for me when I rose at 9, but later I declined [this courtesy]. He takes dinner at 12 with tea, which coincides with my breakfast, and has supper with tea at 6.

He eats Lenten fare with fish and with oil and is very concerned about healthy food for me — they bake apples for me every day. Today is Friday — tomorrow they'll send [my] letter but I am writing you today. I kept myself busy this morning;[4] then I listened to Urusov [reading] his essay.[5] Just as in all his writings, there are some new thoughts, but [his essay] is strange and unproven. Though he *is* touching. He lives with no conflict with anyone around him, helps others and prays to God. For example, before dinner he will walk up and down the path in front of the house. I did approach him, but I saw I was bothering him, and he admitted to me that while walking he reads the "'Hours"[6] and the Psalms. — In my view he's aged quite a bit.

Like everywhere else in Russia, the country life around here is deplorable. The priest runs what passes for a school and has four boys, but in the neighbouring villages, half a verst distant, there are more than thirty boys who are [altogether] illiterate. And they don't go [to school], since the priest does not teach them, but makes them work [instead].

Some *muzhiks* are coming — eleven of them — from somewhere. "From where?" [I ask them.] [It turns out] they were being sent to the village Elder over their quit-rent, sent to the Police Superintendent. I struck up a conversation with one elderly peasant woman: she told me that all the girls, including from her own house, were [working] at a [fabric] factory 8 versts away — [a scene of] total debauchery, as Urusov puts it. At the church is a guard without a nose. [But] there's a pub and tavern — a splendid building with a fat *muzhik* [who owns it]. It's the same sadness everywhere: people are abandoned to their own devices, without the slightest help from the strong, the rich or the educated. On the contrary, a kind of hopelessness. As though it is assumed that everything is set up perfectly and cannot and should not be messed with; [as though] it were offensive to some, a Don Quixote [attitude]. [As though] everything were [already] set up [perfectly] — church, school, state administration, industry, entertainment — and we, the upper classes, needed to care only about ourselves. But if we take a closer look at ourselves, our classes are in an even more deplorable situation: we're stagnating.

1   LNT arrived for a stay at Sergej Semënovich Urusov's (see Letter N° 40, Note 258) estate on 22 March 1889.
2   Pavel Ivanovich (Posha) Birjukov (LNT's biographer) — see Letter N° 120, Note 453.
3   Gerasim Pavlovich (former servant to Urusov) and his sister Dar'ja Pavlovna (no further details available).
4   LNT was busy reading *Zapiski* [Notes] by Nikolaj Nikolaevich Muravëv-Karskij.
5   Urusov's unpublished essay was entitled "*Filosofija soznanija very*" [The philosophy of confessing one's faith]. LNT described this reading in his diary: "There are some good thoughts, for example, that the Mohammedans are close to us and would be even closer were it not for their rejection by the Church; and even better are his three criteria for [determining] authenticity: the Book of Revelation, the Book of Nature and the Book of the Human Soul. That is true. We need all three criteria in order to have authenticity and truth" (PSS 50: 57).
6   "*Hours*" — one of four brief prayer services of the Russian Orthodox Church marking the cycles of the day (daybreak, mid-morning, mid-day, mid-afternoon).

I wanted to give Prince [Urusov] *On life [O zhizni].* If you have a copy, send me the Russian version, if not, the French.[7]

Hugs and kisses to you and all the children.

Send me the letters.

L. T.

On the envelope: Moscow. Dolgokhamovniki Lane, Nº 15. Countess Sofia Andreevna Tolstaya.

Nº 145 – SOFIA ANDREEVNA TOLSTAYA ♪ LEV NIKOLAEVICH TOLSTOY
[LSA 205]
[26 March 1889. Moscow]

Even though my hands are aching from writing to you, I cannot live apart from you and not have any communication at all — that would be too miserable. Along with that, why and *what* should I write? Now [I've heard] the violin and piano played by the Mamonovs,[8] the Gerasimovs,[9] Lenochka,[10] and Golokhvastova[11] was here, too, — you have no sympathy for any of that. The children have tried cabinet-making, they visited the D'jakovs[12] and the Severtsevs,[13] — you don't care; — they did cabinet-making for exercise, not for their daily bread. I was dealing with proofreaders and printers, and sewing clothes for my children — and you have no sympathy even for this — the former will bring in money, the latter you consider simply superfluous.

My breast is giving me frightful pain, worse than it was at the start; yesterday Vanechka was sucking, and blood from my breast was streaming across his lips. The hurt I feel from those tiny wounds pierced by twelve sharp little teeth — you simply can't imagine. — Perhaps if, beyond those principles, you have even a little of your former heart, you would have at least a wee bit of sympathy for this.

I would really love to know how your stay went with the prince[14] — Are you healthy? Are you able to work? Do you walk a lot? What physical work have you thought up for yourself? — on the whole I do care about everything that concerns you, and the only thing that always worries me is what might bring you evident harm — either physically or morally. Such elements, unfortunately, have multiplied [of late].

Write me a good letter so that I can get a feel for you. I shan't write you in kind: apart from intolerable physical pain, these days I have to cope with disturbing letters — accusatory reports

7   LNT's book *On life* was translated into French by SAT in collaboration with Edmond Tastevin and his brother; it was published in Paris in 1888 by Charles Marpon and Ernest Flammarion (publishers of works by Émile Zola and Alphonse Daudet).

8   Sof'ja Èmmanuilovna Dmitrievna-Mamonova (1860–1946) and Aleksandr Èmmanuilovich Mamonov — Moscow friends of the Tolstoys.

9   Osip Petrovich Gerasimov (1863–1920) — writer, educator; and his wife Anna Andreevna Gerasimova (*née* Linberg).

10   LNT's niece Elena Sergeevna (Lenochka) Tolstaja (married name: Denisenko) — see Letter Nº 24, Note 161.

11   Ol'ga Andreevna Golokhvastova (*née* Andreevskaja; 1840–1897) — writer; wife of folk musicologist Prince Pavel Dmitrievich Golokhvastov (1838–1892).

12   LNT's friend Dmitrij Alekseevich D'jakov and his family.

13   Ol'ga Vjacheslavovna Severtseva (*née* Shidlovskaja) and her family.

14   Prince Sergej Semënovich Urusov.

regarding [our] foremen from Samara and Yasnaya about drunkenness, dishonesty, disorders and other vexing situations. This is something I have absolutely *no* feeling for, yet these appeals to me make me look as though I'm responsible [for doing something about it].

Lëva is very frail and despondent. He's trying to wind himself up — doing a lot of walking and drinking milk, but none of this has been of much help. As always, a lot of hope [rests] on the summer [ahead].

Farewell, dear Lëvochka, it's already after 1 a.m., time to go to bed. Hugs and kisses to you and regards to the prince and Pavel Ivanovich [Birjukov], if he hasn't left already.

S. T.

Sunday evening.

N° 146 – LEV NIKOLAEVICH TOLSTOY ✍ SOFIA ANDREEVNA TOLSTAYA
[PSS 84/412]
1 April 1889. Spasskoe.[15]

Since my last writing, I have received your letter[16] plus a lot of letters through the post and brought by Americans.[17] As before, I'm doing quite well indeed. Today I had a bit of a stomach ache. I attribute this to the fact that I ate sturgeon yesterday, and possibly to the fact, too, that I overexerted myself yesterday, chopping and sawing and hauling timber. It's melting here, too, and becoming more like spring. Yesterday I corrected the proofs [of my article] *On art [Ob iskusstve]*[18] and there were a lot of changes to be made (Urusov found a deacon's son who is now transcribing), and did some chopping and sawing in the woods with the *muzhiks* who were working there. It was a very pleasant [task] to fell large firs and saw fragrant, resinous lumber. And I came across a very nice father with his son. (Not all gloomy scenes.) All the previous days I was wanting to finish the comedy[19] and today I finished the 4th and final act, but it's so bad up to this point that I feel ashamed even giving it to you to transcribe. At least now it's out of my hands. And if I feel like going back to it at another time, I shall work on correcting it [then].

Tomorrow I'm heading off to the Troitse;[20] [hopefully] there will be some news from all of you. Depending on [your] letter I shall decide when to get ready to return home. I do want to see you, but I'm not doing too badly here, either. —

---

15 *Spasskoe* — the name of Sergej Semënovich Urusov's estate at Spass-Torbeevo. During his 1889 visit here, LNT took many long walks through the surrounding countryside and villages. He was especially delighted to meet Urusov's wife, Princess Tat'jana Afanas'evna Urusova (*née* Nesterova; 1829–?).

16 A letter written 28 March 1889 (not included here; see *Letters to L. N. Tolstoy*, p. 432–33).

17 On 30 March, at the recommendation of Aleksandra Andreevna Tolstaja, three Americans came to see LNT at Spasskoe. One of them, Episcopalian pastor William Wilberforce Newton (1843–1914) wrote a book which was published in 1894 entitled *A run through Russia. The story of a visit to Count Tolstoi.*

18 LNT first intended to publish his article on art in the journal *Russkoe bogatstvo*, and was going over the proofs when he became disenchanted with his article and decided to postpone its publication. He continued to work on it and it eventually appeared under the title *What is art? [Chto takoe iskusstvo?]*.

19 A reference to what he first called *Themselves outwitted [Iskhitrilas']* and eventually became *The fruits of enlightenment [Plody prosveshchenija]*.

20 A reference to the Troitse-Sergiev Monastery [Troitse-Sergieva lavra] located at Sergiev-Posad, not far from Spass-Torbeevo. However, the trip never materialised.

I would be most interested to know what you thought of my last letter.[21] I didn't read it over again, but I know that I wrote not only what I thought then or still think sometimes, but what I always feel. And it's strange — your last letter — even though it expresses some kind of strange and illicit aversion to just about anything Russian (as you put it) — your last letter[22] I found especially delightful, as it was, in a way, an answer to my letter, which you hadn't [yet] received. I wish I knew what tomorrow has in store for us; the main thing is that you are not tortured by physical pain. — Yesterday I wanted to cross over to the Troitse, but I couldn't because of the stream overflowing [its banks] and [so] I went into the woods. — The prince [Urusov] is very nice. He gets up at 3 or 4 [in the morning] and puts on the samovar; he takes some tea, smokes and does his calculations. After dinner and all day long it's the same, except for naps, [games of] *patience* and walks. I'm afraid that all these computations are unnecessary. He has this cloudiness of thought, [a habit of] self-deception, whereby it seems to him that he has found a solution to the problem he was wanting to solve. I'm afraid [his mind] is further clouded by *papirosas*,[23] an occasional vodka, in small portions, and tea. But his simplicity and aspirations to virtue are genuine, and therefore I get along well with him. His roses are in bloom — a lot of them, and he suggested I enclosed some leaves in my letter. Well, farewell for now, hugs and kisses to you and Tanja and Lëva (how is he getting along with his studies at the *gymnasium*?). And to Andrjusha (is his throat not [any better]?), and to Masha and Sasha and Vanechka. My respects to [governess] Kate and [tutor] Lambert.

L. T.

On the envelope: Moscow. Dolgokhamovniki Lane, Nº 15. Countess Sofia Andreevna Tolstaya.

Nº 147 – SOFIA ANDREEVNA TOLSTAYA ❧ LEV NIKOLAEVICH TOLSTOY
[LSA 213]
[25 October 1889. Moscow]

So I have spent my first busy day in Moscow. How did all of you spend it at Yasnaya — I hope [you are] well and healthy. The train trip was so unbearably hot that sleep was impossible; I was constantly jumping out of bed and heading out to the open platform. I arrived in the morning and found Lëva still in bed. He has a head cold, but generally, he still has his same cheerful [disposition], though he's worried about his exams, which are still in the distant future.

At 10 o'clock we drove out on business, as well as to Sof'ja Alekseevna Filosofova.[24] She's coughing terribly and gasping for air; today Nikolaj Alekseevich[25] went to see Zakhar'in[26] and, if it turns out to be necessary, she will go abroad [for treatment]. The poor thing — she can't speak or breathe at all, a truly wretched [case].

---

21 A letter written 29 March 1889, written in response to SAT's letter (Nº 145 of 26 March) in which she complained of her husband's indifference to her activities and concerns.
22 A reference to SAT's letter of 28 March.
23 A *papirosa* is a type of Russian cigarette.
24 Sof'ja Alekseevna Filosofova — see Letter Nº 139, Note 618.
25 Nikolaj Alekseevich Filosofov (her husband) — see Letter Nº 139, Note 620.
26 Dr. Grigorij Antonovich Zakhar'in — see Letter Nº 34, Note 210.

Then I saw Storozhenko,[27] did a bit of shopping, and went with Lëva for dinner at the D'jakovs'[28] with Liza, Varja and Masha,[29] and had a good time. I left *The Kreutzer Sonata*[30] for them, and right away went to see the Shidlovskijs[31] nearby. There I saw Masha Sverbeeva[32] with Katja, Verochka, Ol'ga[33] and Uncle Kostja; there was food and vint. I stayed there a bit, [then] went back to fetch the manuscript from D'jakov, finished reading the ending [aloud], and now Lëva and I are home, and he's already gone to bed, while I am writing to you. I was sorry to leave home[34] yesterday, and what a wonderful ride we had to Kozlovka! I wonder who picked up the letter for me today, which I am expecting tomorrow evening. I didn't get much done today — just couldn't, for lack of sleep. My head aches, partly because of the thawing [going on here] and the bad odour in the Moscow [air].

How are all my little ones doing? [How are] the older children's lessons, Vanechka's walks and Sasha's taking care of him?

The Kreutzer Sonata made a big impression on everyone. Varja and her husband[35] praised it. Masha Kolokol'tsova[36] was unhappy about something, D'jakov was puffing and panting; all he said was: "[Lev Nikolaevich Tolstoy] suffered through it all, as we all did…" Lisa had nothing special to say. On Saturday we are sending it to Petersburg.[37]

Farewell, my dears, stay healthy all of you, cheerful and prosperous. I am refraining from worrying about you all. My regards to everyone; hugs and kisses to you, Lëvochka, the girls and the children.

S. T.

25th [October]. Night.

Nº 148 – SOFIA ANDREEVNA TOLSTAYA ❧ LEV NIKOLAEVICH TOLSTOY
[LSA 215]
[29 March 1891. Moscow]

Dear friends, I arrived safely, though I am tormented by nightmares in sleep and Vanechka's illness when awake. I joined Lëva over tea and talked with him about the property division.[38] He, too, was concerned about it and has already written something to Il'ja. Lëva, too, is strongly

---

27 Nikolaj Il'ich Storozhenko (professor) — see Letter Nº 130, Note 519.

28 Dmitrij Alekseevich D'jakov and his family.

29 LNT's nieces: Elizaveta Valer'janovna (Liza) Obolenskaja and Varvara Valer'janovna (Varja) Nagornova, as well as the Tolstoys' daughter Marija L'vovna (Masha) Tolstaja (married name [as of 1897]: Obolenskaja).

30 A transcribed manuscript copy of *The Kreutzer Sonata [Krejtserova sonata]*.

31 Vera Aleksandrovna Shidlovskaja (see Letter Nº 123, Note 487) and her family.

32 Marija Vjacheslavovna Sverbeeva (*née* Shidlovskaja; see Letter Nº 81, Note 170) with her daughter Ekaterina Mikhajlovna (Katja) Sverbeeva (married name: Zvegintseva).

33 Vera Vjacheslavovna (Verochka) Shidlovskaja (see Letter Nº 108, Note 354) and her sister Ol'ga Vjacheslavovna Shidlovskaja (see Letter Nº 30, Note 181).

34 *home* — in this case, Yasnaya Polyana.

35 LNT's niece Varvara Valer'janovna Nagornova and her husband Nikolaj Mikhajlovich Nagornov.

36 Marija Dmitrievna (Masha) Kolokol'tsova (see Letter Nº 51, Note 328).

37 On 28 October 1889 the manuscript of *The Kreutzer Sonata [Krejtserova sonata]* was sent to the Kuzminskijs in St. Petersburg, who held a reading by Anatolij Fëdorovich Koni (1844–1927) — a St. Petersburg court judge and a respected member of the Petersburg Academy of Sciences.

38 For a more detailed description of the property division, see Parts v and vi of *My Life* (specifically: v.68, v.71, v.79, v.80, v.97, v.99, v.106, v.108, v.116, v.123; also vi.32, vi.36, vi.38, vi.57, vi.116).

in favour of the division, to make a reliable transition to a more modest life, and know what each one has.

I visited the State Bank as well as the Merchant Bank, and got everything done on time. Now it's two hours until the train [leaves]; Lëva and I are chatting and I am writing letters.

The telegram hasn't come yet.[39] I am awaiting it impatiently. Be sure to wire Petersburg tomorrow. God grant you are all still healthy! I wish the girls cheerfulness and prosperity.

In Moscow all the talk is about Grand Prince Mikhail Mikhajlovich, who was discharged from his regiment and stripped of all his rights — poor thing, all over his marriage to Mlle Dubbel't,[40] a mere mortal with no royal blood.

Farewell. I'm off to Petersburg with no energy and with none of the ardour needed for the cause, and oh, how I'd like to return home! But, apparently, this is my destiny — *la fatalité*, as they put it better in French, and possibly all jumbled up in my head.

Regards to everyone at home. Hugs and kisses to Papà and the children.

S. T.

Around 1 p.m., 29 March.

Nº 149 – LEV NIKOLAEVICH TOLSTOY ❧ SOFIA ANDREEVNA TOLSTAYA
[PSS 84/437]
1 April 1891. Yasnaya Polyana.

Everything would be fine with us if it weren't for Vanechka's chicken pox. Andrjusha was right when he wrote you (from my words) that no new marks have formed, and the former ones are drying up. There is one on his forehead that is larger than the others: [dimensions given] and the rest this size: [dimensions given] or less. He sustains himself largely on milk, which is very good; he does most of his sleeping in people's arms; the nanny doesn't sleep at night, but she is very cheerful and tender with him. At his request, we sometimes carry him around in a blanket, but [otherwise] he spends all his time in bed. It's now ten o'clock, and he's already in bed and asleep. —

Serëzha will take this letter. I'll be quite insistent that he doesn't forget. He is very kind-hearted. From Sergievskoe I received a reply today about a sick *muzhik;* they're accepting him conditionally [as a patient], provided he is not chronic, and that is why I've decided to take him to Tula. Rudnev[41] promised to take him and give him his attention. The boys are very precious, especially Andrjusha. — We've been reading in the evenings *A family chronicle [Semej-naja khronika].*[42] There have been no especially interesting letters of late. My work is turning out more successfully, which I'm very happy about. I'm entirely, quite healthy. I am not writing

---

39 SAT was planning to go St. Petersburg to petition Emperor Alexander III for permission to publish *The Kreutzer Sonata*, and was waiting for a telegram confirming that she would be granted an audience with His Imperial Majesty. For further details, see *My Life*, v.84.

40 On 26 February 1891 Grand Prince Mikhail Mikhajlovich (1861–1929), while abroad, entered into a morganatic marriage with Sof'ja Nikolaevna Dubbel't (*née* Countess Merenberg; also spelt Duppel't; 1858–1927) — granddaughter to the poet Aleksandr Sergeevich Pushkin.

41 Dr. Aleksandr Matveevich Rudnev (1842–1901) — Chief Physician at the Tula Gubernia Hospital, who treated members of the Tolstoy family on a number of occasions. In 1891 he founded a clinical research laboratory and in 1894 was elected chairman of the Society of Tula Physicians.

42 A book by writer Sergej Timofeevich Aksakov (1791–1859).

about the girls, to spare their modesty, since they will be reading this letter. Stakhovich[43] has not managed to receive the letter yet. [My] letter is about Losinskij,[44] who submitted a petition to the Tsar about adoption, so that [we] need to ask someone to set this matter in motion. Use Petersburg as best you can so that those who are with you will feel as pleased as possible. The business isn't that important. Give a kiss from me to dear Aleksandra Andreevna[45] if you see her again, and, of course, [your sister] Tanja and the Kuzminskijs. Sasha[46] had some stomach trouble, but she's better now. She's healthy and precious. Hugs and kisses.

L. T.

On the envelope: Petersburg. 77, Nevskij Prospekt. S. A. Tolstaya c/o Tat'jana Andreevna Kuzminskaja.

N° 150 – LEV NIKOLAEVICH TOLSTOY ❧ SOFIA ANDREEVNA TOLSTAYA
[PSS 84/440]
4 April 1891. Yasnaya Polyana.

I was going to write to you and, in searching for an envelope, I found this one — with this paper enclosed, probably prepared by Lidia[47] along with Vanechka and Sasha. — Today only Sof'ja Dmitrievna Sverbeeva[48] came with her little Ljuba and, she, it seems, received as good an impression from us as we did from her. Everybody, including Vanechka, is completely healthy. Yesterday we received Strakhov's article.[49] I agree with you that it exaggerates my importance to the point of immodesty, but it seems that, regardless of how it flatters me, I am not mistaken when I say it is a remarkably good article — not only well written and intelligent, but sincere and heartfelt. To understand the essence of Christianity is something only a true Christian, or rather, a disciple of Christ, can do. Tell that to Nikolaj Nikolaevich. I shall be writing him.[50] Your news I do not find pleasant. You didn't need to write to the Tsar[51] and you didn't have to request anything of him. That can only cause harm to everyone and provide an additional excuse for irritation. — We were very happy to see Lëva. He keeps complaining about his health, but he looks well. Hugs and kisses.

L. T.

On the envelope: Petersburg. 77, Nevskij [Prospekt]. S. A. Tolstaya c/o Tat'jana Andreevna Kuzminskaja.

43 Mikhail Aleksandrovich Stakhovich (poet) — see Letter N° 101, Note 287. LNT's letter to him was dated 1 April 1891 (PSS 65: 283).

44 Semën Alekseevich Losinskij — stationmaster at Yasenki, who was attempting to adopt his premaritally conceived son.

45 LNT's great aunt Aleksandra Andreevna (Alexandrine) Tolstaja.

46 A reference to the Tolstoys' youngest daughter Aleksandra L'vovna (Sasha) Tolstaja.

47 *Miss Lidia* — governess and English tutor to the Tolstoy children.

48 Sof'ja Dmitrievna (Ljuba) Sverbeeva (1842–1903) — sister to Tula Deputy Governor Dmitrij Dmitrievich Sverbeev (1845–1921), with her niece L'jubov' Dmitrievna Sverbeeva (1879–1958).

49 A reference to Nikolaj Nikolaevich Strakhov's article "Tolki o Tolstom" [Rumours about Tolstoy], published in *Russkoe obozrenie* (1891, N° 2, pp. 287–316).

50 For LNT's letter to Strakhov of 7 April 1891 see A. Donskov, *Leo Tolstoy and Nikolaj Strakhov: complete correspondence*, vol. II, p. 865.

51 On 31 March 1891 SAT wrote a letter to Emperor Alexander III asking for an audience. An English translation of this letter is given in *My Life*, v.84.

Nº 151 – SOFIA ANDREEVNA TOLSTAYA ✉ LEV NIKOLAEVICH TOLSTOY
[LSA 218]
[9 September 1891. Moscow]

Today, dear friends, I am especially sad all alone here without you, and I'm yearning to go home [to Yasnaya Polyana]. I can picture you all so vividly — all of you together and each one in particular. But I still don't know when I shall come — I'm not completely well, yet — and it's hard for me to leave the [younger] children. Yesterday Andrjusha pleaded so plaintively with me not to go just yet. But last night Lëva arrived and today was already participating in all the children's lessons and activities; it seems he really wants to be helpful. Lëva told me some things about the house [at Yasnaya Polyana], and one thing worries me a little — that it is only 12 degrees in the salon and that there's absolutely no heat in the house; dampness will set in and everybody will start to feel ill. See that they heat the house from time to time, even just a little. Here we're heating every day, and it's still cold at that. — The children are healthy and have been improving, though Andrjusha is not a good pupil. Yesterday he went with *Monsieur*[52] and Mitrokha[53] to the Zoological Gardens; I didn't let them go to the exhibit — too cold. I shut up the house and sat all by myself, reading and making corrections on Volume XIII for the new edition.[54] Then I set the table, brought a pail of water from the well, and the children came to dinner. After dinner three of us went to see Grot.[55] His mother[56] and sister[57] were there. The children at once set about playing, and a little girl[58] climbed into his lap. From there we went to the D'jakovs'. I took my work with me and chatted with Dmitrij Alekseevich, while the children played as a foursome, took tea and talked about the *gymnasium*. We returned home shortly after 9 and found out about Lëva's arrival. When he didn't find us at home, he headed off to the Raevskijs';[59] by the time he came back, the children were already asleep. Starting this morning, again, a lot of fuss: the winter window-frames were being installed; they were washing the doors and windows; a carpenter was making minor repairs, and Sasha's room was being wallpapered. The dirt and the chaos are frightful.

I bought Tanja everything she needed, and got back by 4 o'clock. I found all three children[60] had come home from the *gymnasium* and Vera[61] was there with the three younger ones.[62] In the evening I made some notes, spent some time again reading from Volume XIII; the children kept busy, and towards 8 o'clock Natasha Filosofova[63] and [Aleksandr Nikiforovich] Dunaev arrived.

---

52 Monsieur Lambert (tutor to the Tolstoys' children).

53 Mitrofan Filipovich (Mitrokha) Egorov — son to the Tolstoys' coachman Filip Rodionovich Egorov (see Letter Nº 73, Note 110).

54 Two editions of Volume XIII ("Writings of recent years") of LNT's Complete Collected Works were published in 1891.

55 Nikolaj Jakovlevich Grot (philosopher) — see Letter Nº 137, Note 582.

56 Natal'ja Petrovna Grot (*née* Semënova; 1824–1899) — mother to Nikolaj Jakovlevich Grot.

57 Natal'ja Jakovlevna Grot (1860–1918) — sister to N. Ja. Grot; an artist.

58 *a little girl* — one of Grot's daughters.

59 The Tolstoys' sons were friends with the sons of Ivan Ivanovich Raevskij (see Letter Nº 69, Note 76): Ivan Ivanovich Raevskij Jr (1871–1931) and Pëtr Ivanovich Raevskij (1873–1920).

60 A reference to the Tolstoys' sons Lev, Andrej and Mikhail.

61 SAT's niece Vera Aleksandrovna Kuzminskaja (see Letter Nº 43, Note 281).

62 The specific reference here is unknown.

63 Natal'ja Nikolaevna Filosofova (see Letter Nº 137, Note 584).

We took tea, Lëva told us about the Caucasus and Masha's wedding.[64] Dunaev and Natasha talked about the famine victims[65] and again my heart gave a leap, and I wanted to forget and close my eyes to this, but it was not possible; there's no way to help — too much is required. And how invisible it all is here in Moscow! Everything's still the same, the same luxuries, the same horses trotting by, the same stores, and everybody buying and neatly and tastelessly arranging (just like me) their own corners, from where we shall look off into the distance to people dying of starvation. If it weren't for the children, I myself would go this year to help with the famine [relief], and feed as many people as I could with what I could obtain by any means; anything's better than looking and torturing one's self and not being able to do anything.

I still have about three days' work left to do here. Lëva says that things are so much the better at home without me, and I believe that; but I need to come back at some point; and this miserable [question of property] division has to be resolved. Nothing will go forward without me. — Tanja, buy some grapes and watermelons in Tula and give them to the little ones; they're better than pastries. Everything here is terribly cheap. And fruit is healthy. And if it's cold, stoke the stoves and put [storm] windows in where needed. How are Auntie Tanja, Vera and their and our little ones doing? Hugs and kisses to all.

S. T.

Nº 152 – LEV NIKOLAEVICH TOLSTOY ☙ SOFIA ANDREEVNA TOLSTAYA
[PSS 84/459]
27 September 1891. Yasnaya Polyana.

Upon her return, Vera[66] told us how disturbed and disappointed you were as regards our plan[67] and this greatly upset us — not because our wishes will not be carried out, but because all of this upsets you. I repeat what I wrote you about the deposition: the main thing for me is not to violate [our] love and harmony. Let's go for a time, set things up and come back, and let us do everything to make sure your peace and happiness are taken into account. Everyone's healthy and cheerful here, especially me. Yesterday, as you were leaving,[68] I felt lethargic, but today, quite the contrary, I had a marvellous sleep, did a lot of writing and a lot of walking and I rode to Yasenki and back. I began writing an article about the famine,[69] but didn't finish it and I'm afraid of spoiling it. — Sof'ja Alekseevna[70] is passing through tonight, and all three girls decided to ride over to Kozlovka, from which they'll take the mail train to Yasenki, and from Yasenki back at 1:30 p.m. to Kozlovka. Sof'ja Alekseevna and Sasha[71] will probably get this letter to you.

---

64 In October 1891 SAT's niece Marija Aleksandrovna (Masha) Kuzminskaja (1869–1923) married Ivan Egorovich Èrdeli (1870–1939) — later a cavalry general and a participant in the so-called "White Movement" which fought against the Bolsheviks in the Russian Civil War (1917–1923).

65 Because of poor harvests, a number of Russian gubernias experienced an extended famine in the years 1891–93.

66 SAT's niece Vera Aleksandrovna Kuzminskaja.

67 A reference to a plan for organising famine relief efforts.

68 On 26 September 1891 SAT left for Moscow together with her sister Tanja's family (who had been summering at Yasnaya Polyana); in Moscow she collected her *gymnasium*-pupil sons Andrej and Mikhail and returned to Yasnaya Polyana on 28 September (see her *Diaries* I: 212).

69 LNT eventually submitted this article to the journal *Voprosy filosofii i psikhologii*, but it was rejected by the censorship committee.

70 Sof'ja Alekseevna Filosofova (see Letter Nº 139, Note 618) with her two daughters and Vera Alekseevna Kuzminskaja.

71 Here a reference to Aleksandra Nikolaevna Filosofova (1878–1897), sister to Sof'ja Nikolaevna Filosofova (Il'ja's bride).

I hesitated [at first], but then I let the girls go. Vanechka is especially dear and unfailingly cheerful. — What have you all decided? Hugs and kisses to you and the children.

L. T.

I received Grot's letter[72] at Yasenki.

[Also] Feoktistov's letter[73] to you saying that *The Kreutzer Sonata* is allowed only in my *Complete Collected Works* and so, if by my order it is printed separately, they won't let it pass. And since that would be a waste, wouldn't I state that I am allowing everything to be printed except *The Kreutzer Sonata*? —

I am ready to state that I am informed that *The Kreutzer Sonata* will not be passed by the censorship board; but in this form my declaration will not pass; but I cannot write that I will not allow it to be printed, since that is not the truth. I think it is better simply not to reply.

Nº 153 – SOFIA ANDREEVNA TOLSTAYA ❧ LEV NIKOLAEVICH TOLSTOY
[LSA 220]
[25 October 1891. Moscow]

Lëva's leaving,[74] too; the snowstorm today and the fearful cold and all these departures and our life apart, of course, are worst of all for miserable me, sitting as though chained to my drawing rooms and without any other purpose than worrying about everybody. The famine victims are undergoing physical torture, but for us sinners there is a worse torture — a moral one. Somehow, I guess, we'll get through this difficult time for all, but it won't pass without victims.

I am sending my fur coat to [our daughter] Masha, and I bought one for you, Lëvochka, a cheap one. You won't last 30 versts [in the sleigh] without two fur coats. I am sending you 500 roubles, along with the previous 600; Lëva is taking 200, Serëzha 100 for the famine victims; that's a total of 900 roubles. Then I'll see what more can be done. — I haven't yet managed to read your article [on the famine], Lëvochka; Grot brought it round today, but didn't find me in, and so I have not seen him up 'til now. Yesterday Sonja Mamonova and Alik[75] were here, and later [Aleksandr Nikiforovich] Dunaev. I haven't seen anyone else; today I went for Lëva's fur coat and yours, Lëvochka, and shopping for household needs in general. The famous Muir & Mirrielees[76] will deliver groceries to our home less expensively than others, which avoids any suspicion as to dishonesty on the part of [our] cooks, and consequently it will be easier dealing with them. — Thank you all for writing so many letters: I received three. My health is better — i.e. for two nights now there has been no fever or perspiration. But the melancholy I am

---

72 A letter dated 19 February 1891.

73 Evgenij Mikhajlovich Feoktistov's (see Letter Nº 114, Note 402) letter of 25 September 1891 was in response to LNT's declaration of 16 September 1891 renouncing his copyright to all his writings published after 1881, including *The Kreutzer Sonata [Krejtserova sonata]*. For further details, including the text of LNT's copyright renunciation, see *My Life*, v.122.

74 Lev L'vovich (Lëva) Tolstoj has left for Samara Gubernia to help organise famine relief efforts among the peasant population there.

75 Sof'ja Èmmanuilovna (Sonja) Dmitrieva-Mamonova and her brother Aleksandr Èmmanuilovich (Alik) Dmitriev-Mamonov — see Letter Nº 145, Note 8.

76 *Muir & Mirrielees Trade Company* — the largest department store in Moscow at the time, co-founded in St. Petersburg in 1857 by British merchants Andrew Muir (1817–1899) and Archibald Mirrielees (1797–1877). It was nationalised during the 1917 revolution and was eventually named *TsUM* (the Russian initials for "Central Department Store").

struggling with is terrible; it won't let up. Just as soon as night falls, everything is gloomy; I keep wanting to cry; I am literally physically and morally cut off.

I hope your cold has gone, Lëvochka, otherwise it could be the start of influenza. The old man Gattsuk[77] died of influenza. Today it is –10°, with a fearful wind as well as snow. The coachmen are using sleighs. If you are so cold, I'd hesitate about going out.

And our potatoes and apples — all frozen! I've just received the receipt.

Vanechka wakes me up every morning at 7 o'clock, and plaintively begs for his soother. We've never given it to him, and he doesn't drink milk [by itself], rather tea with milk, and he eats precious little. But he is cheerful; Sasha and the boys, too. If only all of them were healthy! Misha is not a good pupil — all twos.[78] Andrjusha is much better. Yesterday they were both playing the violin: [here] Misha is better. — I'm not fixing up the house, none of it is in order; I just can't bring myself to such a trivial activity; it's a shame to pay out money, we have to skimp everywhere, and I do everything myself with Fomich.[79] The servants are all despondent, not cheerful either. Upstairs they don't light [the lamps] and barely stoke [the stoves]. We all crowd together downstairs, each one doing his own thing. Farewell, my dears, don't forget me and write at every opportunity — give me all the details of how you are getting along. And Lëva is drowning in this sea of the Samaran steppes; I miss him the most, but there's no way I can hold him back.

Now in a few days I'll write to Dankov Uezd,[80] [where you'll be] by that time.

S. T.

25 October 1891.

Nº 154 – SOFIA ANDREEVNA TOLSTAYA ❧ LEV NIKOLAEVICH TOLSTOY
[LSA 221]
26 October 1891. Night. [Moscow]

Thank you for your letter,[81] dear Lëvochka. And so, you are leaving tomorrow, and probably Lëva, too. It will be very interesting [to see] what will come of your attempts to help. In my opinion — and I stand by my own [opinion] — you have all been going about this the wrong way right from the start. Anyway, it's too late now. I shall live with the hope and the expectation that at some point these difficult times will pass, that everybody will come home and the famine will blow over. Now everyone is saying that the situation is far worse than anyone could have anticipated. What a heavy weight on the soul from the hopelessness of providing help in this natural disaster! Lëva's trip worries me no less than yours. He's taken nothing with him, hasn't given thought to anything; he has no idea what is involved in a long-distance trip in the countryside, especially through the steppes; his whole mental state is one of agitation, despair and uncertainty — [i.e.] run as fast as you can whatever betides — and nothing more.

Today I spent the whole day at home, the wallpaperers were hammering and Fomich was agitated. Andrjusha and Misha bought some warm fur hats, gloves and galoshes, and got twos

---

77　Aleksej Alekseevich Gattsuk (1832–1891) — publisher of a newspaper and the *Cross Calendar* (since 1875).

78　A two (out of a possible five) was a very low mark.

79　Mikhail Fomich Krjukov (a servant).

80　*Dankovskij Uezd* — the location of Ivan Ivanovich Raevskij's Begichevka estate, where LNT went with his daughters Tat'jana (Tanja) and Marija (Masha) to organise famine relief efforts.

81　A letter dated 24 October 1891 (not included here) — see PSS 84: 88.

[on their tests]. Sasha had her first French lesson with Monsieur [Lambert] and had a great time laughing loudly. Then she and [Miss] Lidia kept repeating French words, giggling all the while, and went for a walk just to the postbox, since it is very cold out. I didn't let Vanechka go out [at all]. He is healthy for the moment and very precious, and really misses his soother. He says himself: "Vanja's outgrown now", and he's started to drink more milk, and is eating better. Mitasha Obolenskij[82] came for dinner and told me about you. But he got me worried, saying that you look ill and weak, that you've grown thin and aged a lot. [I can just imagine] how well you will look when you come back from Dankovskij Uezd! — He also got me worried when he said that his wife[83] has a great deal of sympathy for me; she even pitied me after reading your declaration on the *17th of September*.[84] She thought (as everybody probably thought — I anticipated this) that you were angry with me and deliberately published this declaration behind my back on my name-day. And what a coincidence: on the 17th of September I was given and [then] deprived of [your] story: *The death of Ivan Ilyich [Smert' Ivana Il'icha]*. — This is all very painful, and for so long now everything — everything has been painful.

My health is better, the fever's gone and probably won't return.

After dinner [Aleksandr Nikiforovich] Dunaev came, and later [Nikolaj Jakovlevich] Grot. At the same time Protas'ev[85] showed up to collect his money for the paper. Grot was very agitated. *Moskovskie vedomosti* raised a huge alarm over Solov̈ev's reading,[86] and here [in Moscow] was Pobedonostsev,[87] and the editor of *Moskovskie vedomosti*[88] and his staff were reporting to Pobedonostsev that — just look and see what evil is coming from that. At this point they illegally cancelled the whole November issue on orders from Petersburg. Your article is considered less harmful and they promise to let it through, while most of the attack was directed at Solov̈ev. If they don't retract the cancellation soon, Grot will go to Petersburg.

Obolenskij wrote an article (it will appear as an editorial) on his [projected] edition of a special album in aid of the famine victims, and in it he mentioned that you were contributing your story. Which one? He even says that you *gave him your word* that you would write or contribute something. He read his article to us aloud. — I finished the evening alone, since the children were at the Severtsevs',[89] and it is nighttime now. I am anxiously awaiting news from Dankovskij Uezd; how are you all getting along there? I hope that [our daughter] Tanja will take good care of you all; all my hope is pinned on her; I just hope nobody takes ill in this dry cold. How have my fur coats been received? Farewell, dear Lëvochka; you take care of the girls, too, and let them take care of you.

Hugs and kisses to you all.

S. T.

---

82   Prince Dmitrij Dmitrievich (Mitasha) Obolenskij (jurist) — see Letter N° 17, Note 112.
83   Princess Elizaveta Petrovna Obolenskaja (*née* Vyrubova) — see Letter N° 74, Note 116.
84   A letter regarding LNT's renunciation of copyright on his post-1881 writings (see Letter N° 152, Note 73).
85   Ivan Evlampievich Protas'ev (1867–1920) — co-owner of a writing-paper manufacturing business founded by his grandfather, Ivan Aleksandrovich Protas'ev (1802–1875), in 1858.
86   On 19 October 1891 Vladimir Sergeevich Solov̈ev (see Letter N° 52, Note 333) read his paper "*O prichinakh upadka srednevekovogo mirosozertsanija*" [On the causes of the fall of the Middle Ages world-view] at a meeting of the Psychological Society.
87   Konstantin Petrovich Pobedonostsev (Synod procurator).
88   Sergej Aleksandrovich Petrovskij (1846–1917) — journalist, editor of the paper *Moskovskie vedomosti* (1888–96).
89   Ol'ga Vjacheslavovna Severtseva (*née* Shidlovskaja) and her family.

Nº 155 – LEV NIKOLAEVICH TOLSTOY ✉ SOFIA ANDREEVNA TOLSTAYA
[PSS 84/463]
29 October 1891. Begichevka.

Oh, how I wish that this letter might find [you] in a good mental state, my friend. I shall hope that this is so, and tomorrow, when the post arrives, I shall wait and open your letter with great anticipation. — You write that you are all alone, miserable, and I feel sad for you. But enough of that. I shall write about us. We all took a wagon ride in fine weather: Lëva, Popov[90] and the five of us[91] including Mar'ja Kirillovna. At the station we met Ivan Ivanovich [Raevskij], who went with us. At the station, as everywhere, there were [a whole lot of] common people heading out [to look] for work and returning after a fruitless search — it's a bottomless pit.

We had tickets for 3rd class but they put us in 2nd class. Here we found Kern[92] and later Bogojavlenskij.[93] The heat was terrible, and were simply dazed by it. At Klekotki we bade farewell to Lëva and Popov[94] and found two troikas with sleighs [which had been sent] for us. We decided not to go on, because a blizzard was blowing, and we spent quite a good night in a poor but relatively clean hotel.

The girls are taking such good care of me, they did all the packing so meticulously; they are so conscientious that one can only wish them a reduction rather than an increase in their duties. All this is your own care for me expressed through them, and I do appreciate it, even though I don't actually need it, or so it seems to me. We rose early this morning, but did not set out until 10. We had a fine trip and kept ourselves warm. At one point I put on my sheepskin coat — and we arrived at 2 o'clock. The house was warm and heated — everything had been beautifully prepared [for us]. Ivan Ivanovich put me in his magnificent study. The girls have two rooms with a special entranceway. There is a large general-purpose room for *repas*. [Ivan Ivanovich] himself moved into Aleksej Mitrofanovich's[95] little room, together with his Fedot.[96] Today I insisted that we switch places and that he move back to his study. And now I've moved, and I'm doing just fine; it's warm and cozy, and Fedot sleeps behind a partition. Dinner is simple, neat and filling; there's milk a-plenty.

After dinner I took a nap. Our things arrived. The girls unpacked them; in the evening Ivan Ivanovich's son-in-law Mordvinov[97] came; [he is] the district council head, and is all absorbed in looking after the people. After he left, and everyone dispersed at 9 o'clock, I sat down to write an article about how frightening it is not to know whether Russia will or will not have enough food to feed [her people],[98] and I continued writing until 11 o'clock. Then I had an excellent

90 Evgenij Ivanovich Popov (1864–1938) — a Tolstoyan characterised by LNT as "very pleasant, … kind and serious" in a letter to SAT dated 3 May 1889 (not included here; PSS 84: Letter 413).
91 Accompanying LNT were his daughters Tat'jana (Tanja) and Marija (Masha), his niece Vera Kuzminskaja, along with Marija Kirillovna Kuznetsova (1867–?) — a maid and seamstress to SAT and her household.
92 Èduard Èduardovich Kern (1855–1938) — botanist and forester, who had worked on the *Zaseka* preserve (see Letter Nº 80, Note 163).
93 Dr. Nikolaj Efimovich Bogojavlenskij (tutor) — see Letter Nº 61, Note 23.
94 Lev L'vovich (Lëva) and Evgenij Ivanovich Popov were on their way to Samarà Gubernia to help with famine relief.
95 Aleksej Mitrofanovich Novikov (1865–1927) — the Raevskij family's tutor; from 1889 to 1890 he lived at the Tolstoys'.
96 Fedot Vasil'evich Afanas'ev — cook at the Raevskijs'.
97 Ivan Nikolaevich Mordvinov (1854–1917) — husband to Ivan Ivanovich Raevskij's daughter Margarita Ivanovna Raevskaja (1856–1912).
98 A reference to LNT's article *A frightful question [Strashnyj vopros]*, published in *Russkie vedomosti*, Nº 306, 6 November 1891.

sleep. In the morning I went on with the article. By and by I chatted with Ivan Ivanovich, and the girls' activities became more focused. I'm urging Tanja to organise spinning and weaving work, that would provide an income [for the famine victims in the region]. Masha will [take charge] of the soup-kitchens and bakery. Just now I visited three villages, in two of which I found places for soup-kitchens which in each case would accommodate up to 50 people. — There are no easy words to describe the poverty and neglect these people [have suffered]. But it is good and healthy to see them, if only we can be of service to them in some way, and I think we can. You probably know from Grot that my article was among the others taken to Petersburg, to the censorship board, and they will probably ban it. And I'm glad. I'll write another and rework this one. It should have a kinder [tone], but it is hard to be both truthful and kind. If I do write it, I'll send it to you. You and Grot should look it over and send it to *Russkie vedomosti*. — Well, farewell for now. Hugs and kisses to you and the children — petite and precious, as Fet put it, and to you, who are not petite but still precious. Ivan Ivanovich has gone to see Pisarev[99] and will probably bring him back with him.

L. T

Nº 156 – LEV NIKOLAEVICH TOLSTOY ❧ SOFIA ANDREEVNA TOLSTAYA
[PSS 84/464]
2 November 1891. Begichevka.

We haven't received any letters [from you] yet, dear friend, and I'm concerned about you. I hope we shall receive one tomorrow, and that there will be good news from you. Our activity here is most joyful, if one can call activity joyful which stems from human misfortune. Three soup-kitchens are open and operating. It is touching to see how little is needed to render help and, more importantly, to call forth feelings of kindness. Today I was at two [kitchens] at the times of gathering and dinner. There were around 30 people each time. These included a priest's widow and a sexton's wife. Today I made the observation that upon taking a close look at the sufferings, even the tremendous deprivation and suffering are not surprising, since worse [calamities] can be seen all around. And the sufferers themselves see it, too. Our girls are all very busy, they are helpful and sensitive to this. We are not expanding our activity so as not to exceed our means, but if anyone wanted to assist others, here is a wide open field. And it's so easy and simple. The setting up of soup-kitchens, for which we are indebted to Ivan Ivanovich [Raevskij], is an amazing thing. The people take to it like something innate, natural, and look on it all as something that ought to be this way and cannot be otherwise. I'll describe this in more detail at another time. Ivan Ivanovich is very dear to all of us. Warm-hearted, intelligent and serious. We all [find ourselves] loving him more and more. We are getting along splendidly. It's too luxurious and comfortable. Pisarev was here yesterday, and today she[100] was supposed to come. Tomorrow Tanja is planning to go see her. Natasha[101] is very dear, energetic and serious. Bogojavlenskij[102] was here twice. I wrote that article.[103] I read it to Pisarev and Raevskij;

99 Rafail Alekseevich Pisarev (1850–1906) — a Tula landowner and regional nobility representative for Epifan' Uezd in Tula Gubernia.

100 A reference to the wife of Rafail Alekseevich Pisarev: Evgenija Pavlovna Pisareva (*née* Baranova; ?–1936).

101 Natal'ja Nikolaevna (Natasha) Filosofova (married name: Den; see Letter Nº 137, Note 584) took an active part in famine relief.

102 Dr. Nikolaj Efimovich Bogojavlenskij — see Letter Nº 61, Note 23.

103 A reference to LNT's article *A frightful question [Strashnyj vopros]* — see Letter Nº 155, Note 98.

they approved, and it seems it might be helpful. There's no eloquence there, and no room for it, but there is something which is precisely needed and is tormenting everyone. Send it as soon as you can to *Russkie vedomosti*, and if they offer, accept money from them, the more the better, for our soup-kitchens. If they send some, fine, but if not, that's fine, too. Payment is not necessary, but if they send it, we'll find a use for it here.

I'm writing this, and am afraid myself. I'm afraid lest this money and any money contributed might throw us off and lead into activities beyond our capabilities. People are needed most of all. — Write me more specifically about yourself, your health and the children. Hugs and kisses to you, dear friend, and the children. The girls will probably add something [to this letter].

Ask Aleksej Mitrofanovich [Novikov], to whom I am grateful for his fine letter, to take a look at the article and correct the punctuation and even phrases where there may be some inaccuracies, under your supervision; I'm sure you'll take a look at the proofs. Regards to [tutor] *Monsieur* Borel.

Well, farewell for now.

Nº 157 – SOFIA ANDREEVNA TOLSTAYA ❧ LEV NIKOLAEVICH TOLSTOY
[LSA 224]
4 November 1891. [Moscow]

This evening, dear friend Lëvochka, I received your article [*A frightful question*]; I sent it and your letter at once with Aleksej Mitrofanovich [Novikov] to Sobolevskij,[104] editor of *Russkie vedomosti*, asking him to come and see me. Tomorrow morning at 11 o'clock he will come with the article already typeset, and if the censorship board lets it pass, Aleksej Mitrofanovich and I will carefully proofread it. Did you read my letter to the editor in *Russkie vedomosti* dated 3 November?[105] In just twenty-four hours it brought me in around 1,500 roubles. Write *soon* about where to send the money. I'll send you, Serëzha and Lëva 500 roubles each. People will probably be sending in even more.

It's very touching [how] the money's coming in. One person crossed themselves upon entering [the house] and contributed silver roubles; another (an elderly man) kissed my hand and said through tears: "Most gracious Countess, accept my gratitude and what I can afford by way of a donation." He gave 40 roubles. Several lady teachers contributed, and one of them said: "I wept yesterday over your letter." And then a natily attired gentleman came on his horse and met Andrjusha at the door. He asked: "Are you Lev Nikolaevich's son?" "Yes." "Is your mother at home? Give [this] to her." And he left. In the envelope was 100 roubles. Children came and contributed 3, 5 or 15 roubles [each]. One lady brought a bundle of old pieces of clothing. One well-dressed young woman was beside herself, saying: "Oh, how touching a letter you wrote! Here, take this — it's my own money: Papà and Mamà don't know that I'm giving it away. But I'm so happy to!" In the envelope was 101 roubles 30 kopeks. Brashnin[106] brought 200 roubles.

I don't know how all of you will look at my actions. But I find it tiresome just sitting by without participating in your efforts, and since yesterday I even feel my health has improved; I record [all my transactions] in a notebook, make out receipts, express my thanks, talk with the

104 Vasilij Mikhajlovich Sobolevskij (1846–1913) — a political commentator.
105 SAT's letter was published in *Russkie vedomosti*, Nº 303, 3 November 1891; it reads in part: "I have decided to appeal to anyone who can and wishes to help, to support my family's efforts financially. All donations will go directly to the feeding of children and the elderly at the soup-kitchens set up by my husband and children."
106 Ivan Petrovich Brashnin (1826–1898) — a Moscow merchant who shared LNT's views.

public, and I am glad that I can help in the expansion of your cause, even if it is through other people's donations. Uncle Serëzha, who is visiting me, has a sympathetic attitude; Ekaterina Fëdorovna Junge[107] was here and enthusiastically supports my plan. Everybody is in favour, what do you all say? As soon as I receive the money from the Theatrical Directorate,[108] I shall again send you money, only I would urge you to keep a strict tally of what is bought with this money and where, who is fed, in what places, in case I need to publish an account of donations.

Just now I received a telegram from [Nikolaj Jakovlevich] Grot to the effect that your article,[109] Lëvochka, was passed [by the censorship committee] with some minor omissions. I am very much afraid for this latest one;[110] it awakened within me a sense of despair, and despair is harmful to the whole spirit of all Russian society and the people.

Nagornov and Varja[111] are sitting here [with me], and Nagornov says that the amount of foodstuffs in Russia is known precisely. That there is *certainly* not enough *rye*, but that there is a great abundance of oats, corn, wheat and potatoes; from the Caucasus they will bring 35 million poods of all sorts of foodstuffs, and 20 million will remain there which cannot be brought in, since there are not enough railway carriages or ships for transport, and so in any case the extra amounts will need to be sold abroad. How true all this is, I don't know. — Tomorrow I shall write more about what Sobolevskij says.

Everybody's healthy here. It's –11° out, and the little ones are all staying at home. Andrjusha and Misha are at the *gymnasium*. I am teaching Sasha every day, I'm working and sitting quietly as advised by the doctor, and I feel a lot better today. — There's no news from our sons, not even one of them, and now I am especially concerned about Lëva. — Dear Lëvochka, keep watching out for yourself, eat better and more — you need all the strength for your body. — Your letters are very joyful and interesting to me; write a bit more often. My regards to Ivan Ivanovich [Raevskij]; today [my brother] Petja was with me and read a few of your letters with great enthusiasm.

Hugs and kisses to Masha, Vera, Tanja and to you. Stay healthy and may God help you. When shall we see each other?! I dare not even imagine lest I be overcome with impatience.
Farewell.

S. T.

Nº 158 – SOFIA ANDREEVNA TOLSTAYA ✍ LEV NIKOLAEVICH TOLSTOY
[LSA 231]
13 November 1891. [Moscow]

I am sending you the receipt for the lentils and peas for your soup-kitchens. Too bad we have to pay for shipping; if I had some Red Cross forms, we could send it free of charge. I don't know

---

107 Ekaterina Fëdorovna Junge (*née* Countess Tolstaja; 1843–1913); second cousin to LNT; daughter to artist Fëdor Petrovich Tolstoj (1783–1873), vice-president of the Imperial Academy of Arts.
108 A reference to the author's honorarium for the staging of LNT's play *The fruits of enlightenment [Plody prosveshchenija]*.
109 A reference to LNT's article *On the famine [O golode]* that he wrote for the journal *Voprosy filosofii i psikhologii*.
110 *this latest one* — referring this time to *A frightful question*.
111 Nikolaj Mikhajlovich Nagornov and his wife Varvara Valer'janovna Nagornova (LNT's niece).

with whom I can send the various pieces of cotton fabric donated by Morozov.[112] I am waiting for complimentary shipping. According to all the data I have received from all of you and from other people, I see that everything's melting, as though a piece of sugar were tossed into a barrel of water, and that charitable aid not only does not save the people, but confuses them, and you look at the whole situation more and more gloomily.

Grot was with me today; he said that the article *A frightful question [Strashnyj vopros]* aroused disapproval on the part of the government. — "He's confused us with this article," said the Minister of Internal Affairs. From the Theatrical Directorate I haven't yet received either money or news. — However, after the article *A frightful question,* [the authorities] immediately sent out a communication and gave an order to count all the foodstuffs [in Russia] by 20 November. They say that there will be a Supreme decree to all food-growers to sell their produce to the government at a certain rate. I think it is high time that happened. — I have around 10,000 [roubles now]. I gave Pisarev 3,000 for your disposition, Lëvochka. He suggested buying rye; the two of you should come to some arrangement. We have to decide on the best possible apportionment of what everybody is giving me with such love. I am receiving [the most] touching letters.

Sasha's taken ill, she has an extremely high temperature and a sore throat. The same old disease. She's had swollen cheeks, and now influenza. I'm quite exhausted, but I'm not sick.

Today I'm writing a letter to the Minister of Internal Affairs[113] regarding the articles in *Moskovskie vedomosti*. The way I see it, they are inciting revolution with their articles, comparing Tolstoy, Grot and Solovëv to some kind of revived (in their opinion) liberal party which exploits a national calamity for achieving some kind of political end. All this rubbish is difficult to describe. Pick up a copy of *Moskovskie vedomosti* from the 9th and 11th of November[114] and read [for yourself]. The thought I want to convey to the minister is this: if the revolutionaries are made aware of this supposed support from the best representatives of the *intelligentsia* and their moral influence on society, they will believe their own luck and rise again. And at the present time this is terrible and even dangerous. — Just yesterday I found out that two of the leading activists at *Moskovskie vedomosti*[115] were zealous revolutionaries but have now put on a mask of government and Orthodox [loyalty]. — And how transparent they are under this mask!

I received your letters, dear Lëvochka and Tanja;[116] they arrived for some reason with Nikita's[117] wife, whom Ivan Aleksandrovich[118] sent along as a cook for [our] servants. Apparently he was on his way to the post office when he handed them over to her for faster delivery. Ivan Aleksandrovich writes, too, that you are all healthy and very cheerful: that you play and

112 Vikula Eliseevich Morozov (1829–1894) — a member of the famed Morozov family of entrepreneurs. In a letter dated 19 November 1891 (not included here), LNT wrote to his wife: "The contributions you have collected are very good. The 1,500 arshins of fabric are amazing. [...] Today I saw a widow with her children positively naked. Only one boy can go out [of their house]. Never before have I seen such poverty" (PSS 84: 101).

113 Ivan Nikolaevich Durnovo (1834–1904) — Minister of Internal Affairs (1889–95).

114 A reference to the editorial "Count L. Tolstoy's plan" (*Moskovskie vedomosti*, № 310, 9 November 1891); also the articles "A word to social mischief-makers" and "Caught on the spot" (*Moskovskie vedomosti*, № 312, 11 November 1891) in response to LNT's article *A frightful question*.

115 Lev Aleksandrovich Tikhomirov (1852–1923) — writer and philosopher; Jurij Nikolaevich Govorukha-Otrok (pseudonym: Jurij Nikolaev; 1854–1895) — writer and literary critic. Both were former members of the revolutionary "People's Will" [*Narodnaja volja*] party but later went over to a conservative viewpoint.

116 A letter from daughter Tanja with a postscript by LNT, dated 11 November 1891 (for LNT's postscipt see PSS 84 :97).

117 Nikita — a peasant servant with the Tolstoys'.

118 Ivan Aleksandrovich Berger (1867–1916) — nephew to Ivan Ivanovich Raevskij; manager at Yasnaya Polyana in the early 1890s.

sing, that all of you at the Mordvinovs,[119] even Lev Nikolaevich, are playing at *petits jeux*. How cheerful it all is apart from one's *direct* obligations! If you only could stay as I did with feverish and capricious children for ten days, you wouldn't call it a fun time. And I myself am not completely healthy. — I think you have become accustomed to the spectre of famine, while to me here, as to all in Moscow, [the situation] seems very bad. — I am happy that all of you are free from the influenza and the oppressive Moscow atmosphere. I realise now how with passing years it is more and more difficult to change one's way of life and adapt to [changing] circumstances. That's the way it's always been with you, Lëvochka. I never go anywhere at all, either by carriage or on foot; I haven't even cleaned the house; it's as though I am heading off somewhere. — Maybe to the next world? — Anyway, I am saying this even though I'm not really ill, and may be troubling you for no reason. Farewell, write *in all truthfulness* what your plans and intentions are for the future. One thing I ask: don't go a single step out of your way and don't change anything *for me*. My spirit and nerves are not strong enough to endure silent reproaches when you come. I am fairly sensitive to that. Farewell! Father Ioann Kronshtadtskij[120] sent me 200 roubles. [I received] a postcard from Lëva at Bibikov's[121] farmstead. That's where real horrors are taking place — in Samara Gubernia. Hugs and kisses to all.

S. T.

Nº 159 – LEV NIKOLAEVICH TOLSTOY ✍ SOFIA ANDREEVNA TOLSTAYA
[PSS 84/475]
28 November 1891. Begichevka.

You already know about the terrible happening.[122] Now at 12 o'clock on the night of the 27th[–28th], the house is full of relatives who have come: Pisarev, Dolgorukaja,[123] Davydova, Nikolaj Vasil'evich Davydov[124] and various acquaintances besides. Now it's been thirty-six hours since he died. He died peacefully, without suffering, from pneumonia. Vanja[125] found him, but he was already unconscious. Elena Pavlovna is a pitiful sight, so are the children. Just now I received both your letter and news from Aleksej Mitrofanovich.[126] — We are all quite healthy and would like to stay here for several days after the funeral, so as not to give the impression to the famine victims that the whole cause has been disrupted and abrogated with the death of Ivan Ivanovich. I say "would like to", but it will all depend on your courage. I realise that this is terribly frightening for you, but at the same time I cannot help but see that there are

---

119 Margarita Ivanovna Mordvinova (*née* Raevskaja; 1856–1912) — sister to Ivan Ivanovich Raevskij — and her husband Ivan Nikolaevich Mordvinov (1859–1912).
120 Ioann Kronshtadtskij (secular name: Ioann Il'ich Sergiev; 1829–1908) — archpriest of St-Andrew's Cathedral at Kronstadt; a staunch opponent of LNT's views. See: P. V. Basinskij: *Svjatoj protiv L'va. Ioann Kronshtadtskij i Lev Tolstoj: istorija odnoj vrazhdy* [A Saint versus a Lion. Ioann Kronshtadskij and Lev Tolstoy: the story of a feud].
121 Aleksej Alekseevich Bibikov (foreman for the Tolstoys' Samara farmstead). Lëva's message spoke of the dire conditions and panic being experienced by the population in that area as a result of the famine.
122 Ivan Ivanovich Raevskij (see Letter Nº 69, Note 76) passed away on 26 November 1891.
123 Rafail Alekseevich Pisarev (see Letter Nº 155, Note 99) and his sister Lidija Alekseevna Dolgorukova (*née* Pisareva; 1851–1916).
124 Ekaterina Pavlovna Davydova (*née* Evreinova; 1845–1913) — sister to Ivan Ivanovich's wife Elena Pavlovna Raevskaja (*née* Evreinova; 1840–1907); married to Nikolaj Vasil'evich Davydov (see Letter Nº 90, Note 212), who was the first chairman of the Tolstoy Society.
125 Ivan Ivanovich Raevskij Jr (1871–1931) — son of Ivan Ivanovich Raevskij (Sr).
126 Aleksej Mitrofanovich Novikov (tutor) — see Letter Nº 155, Note 95.

absolutely no grounds for worry. — Everything will take care of itself. I know one thing, that I love you with all my heart and can't wait to see you and comfort you.

Today your sister Tanja is writing Vera[127] about a rumour circulating that we are leaving, and there are whispers abroad that we shouldn't be abandoning the cause for which so many sacrifices have been made. — And indeed, we should not. Now Matvej Nikolaevich[128] will remain here for a time; but he cannot cope with the work alone. But in any case we shall discuss the situation together calmly and lovingly. —

I am sending you [my] article about the soup-kitchens.[129] I didn't want to offend Gajdeburov,[130] who has also sent donations from his newspaper and modestly wrote to Tanja: why has your dad forgotten me? But I am ready to agree with you and send it to *Russkie vedomosti*. Do read it, correct it, transcribe (you can go without transcribing), make a list of your donations and Tanja's and include them. If something doesn't go right or if there is a delay for any reason, then we'll come and I'll make the correction. I am hastening to write, so that I can send off this letter with Pisarev. I feel terribly sorry for him. I really, really liked him [Raevskij]. And I can't forgive myself for not understanding him earlier. But, on the other hand, what a joyful and youthful time we had, often triumphantly being and working together this last while. I've started to write a few words about him for publication, but then I had second thoughts.[131] In any case, I don't know. —

Well, good-bye, hugs and kisses to you and the children. Thanks to Lëva for writing. I hope his toothache has passed. Today Iljusha returned from Grodno. [Nikolaj Vasil'evich] Davydov saw him on the train. They were just leaving as he arrived.

L. T.

On the envelope: Moscow. Khamovniki Lane, N° 15. Countess Sofia Andreevna Tolstaya.

N° 160 – SOFIA ANDREEVNA TOLSTAYA ✿ LEV NIKOLAEVICH TOLSTOY
[LSA 244]
6 February 1892. Thursday. [Moscow]

I wrote to Klekotki and I'll write again to Chernava so that you don't worry. Tanja and Vera[132] will leave tomorrow night and go straight to you. Vera has swollen glands, and this is Tanja's first day of being completely healthy. Posha and Repin[133] have arrived. Mikhail [Aleksandrovich] Stakhovich stayed here last night until three o'clock in the morning. I've been

---

127 Tat'jana Andreevna Kuzminskaja and her daughter Vera Aleksandrovna Kuzminskaja.
128 Matvej Nikolaevich Chistjakov (1854–1920) — sent by Vladimir Grigor'evich Chertkov to assist LNT in famine relief.
129 LNT's article *On the means of aiding famine victims [O sredstvakh pomoshchi naseleniju, postradavshemu ot neurozhaja]*, published in the collection "Help for the hungry" as an insert in *Russkie vedomosti*.
130 Pavel Aleksandrovich Gajdeburov (1841–1893) — editor of the newspaper *Nedelja* (as of 1876).
131 LNT's obituary of Ivan Ivanovich Raevskij was published only after LNT's death, in the magazine *Ogonëk* (N° 17 (56), 1924).
132 The Tolstoys' daughter Tat'jana L'vovna (Tanja) Tolstaya and SAT's niece Vera Aleksandrovna Kuzminskaja.
133 Pavel Ivanovich (Posha) Birjukov (see Letter N° 120, Note 453) and artist Il'ja Efimovich Repin (see Letter N° 59, Note 11).

tormented by rumours about the article in *Moskovskie vedomosti*.[134] Tanja writes[135] that a committee of ministers was assembled in Petersburg and they decided to send you into exile abroad, but that the Tsar vetoed that and said: "He betrayed me to my enemies", and as though he were quite annoyed: "And [to think] I received his wife, I didn't do that for anybody [else]." — You will ruin us all with your provocative articles: where is [your] *love* and *non-resistance* [to evil]? And you do not have the right, when you have nine children, to ruin me and them. Maybe [you're on] Christian soil, but [your] words are not good. I am very alarmed and don't yet know what I shall do, but I can't leave things as they are. I shall be cautious and gentle — you can be sure of that. Hugs and kisses to you and Masha.

S. T.

Nº 161 – LEV NIKOLAEVICH TOLSTOY ✿ SOFIA ANDREEVNA TOLSTAYA
[PSS 84/486]
12 February 1892. Begichevka.

The weather is superb and we want to take advantage of it to visit Bogoroditskij Uezd: — myself, Tanja, Natasha[136] and Lëva. The trip will probably take about four days. To the Bobrinskijs' [in Bogoroditsk] is 50 versts, from there [another] 20 to Uspenskoe.[137] — If the weather's bad, we shan't take the sleigh, but will return by rail. We shall be very careful. —

I feel bad, dear friend, that you're so troubled by the silly rumours regarding the articles in *Moskovskie vedomosti,* and that you went to see [Grand Prince] Sergej Aleksandrovich.[138] Nothing new has happened, after all. What I wrote in the article on the famine [has been written] many times, and in far stronger terms. What is new here? It is all a matter of a crowd, and the hypnotising of a crowd, and it is growing like a snowball. I did write a refutation.[139] But, I beg of you, my friend, do not change a single word, do not add anything, and do not let anyone else change it. I have considered every word carefully and told the whole truth and nothing but the truth, and I completely refuted the false accusation.

The students were of a great help to me.[140]

Hugs and kisses to you and the children.

L. T.

---

134 In an editorial in the paper *Moskovskie vedomosti* (Nº 22, 22 January 1892) there was condemnation of LNT's "Letters on the famine" which he had sent to the journal *Voprosy filosofii i psikhologii.* Having become acquainted with the piece in English translation (it was banned in Russia), the paper accused the writer of inciting peasants to protest against the authorities.

135 A reference to a letter from SAT's sister Tanja dated 4 February 1892.

136 Natal'ja Nikolaevna (Natasha) Den (*née* Filosofova) — see Letter Nº 137, Note 584.

137 *to Uspenskoe* — i.e. to the home of Vasilij Nikolaevich Bibikov (see Letter Nº 6, Note 45).

138 Grand Prince Sergej Aleksandrovich, by now Governor-General of Moscow — see Letter Nº 123, Note 485. On 10 February 1892 SAT described her visit to the Grand Prince in a letter (not included here) in part as follows: "I asked that he order my refutation [to the articles in *Moskovskie vedomosti*] in the papers. He was very much interested in the case, but he is unable to help me in any way. Apparently, as he told me, they are waiting for a refutation from you, Lëvochka, in *Pravitel'stvennyj vestnik,* over your signature; other papers are prohibited from accepting it…" (*Letters to L. N. Tolstoy,* p. 492).

139 See LNT's letter to the editor of *Pravitel'stvennyj vestnik* of 12 February 1892 (PSS 66:160–62).

140 In her letter to LNT of 10 February 1892 (not included here), SAT wrote about two St. Petersburg students who had written to LNT expressing their bewilderment over the *Moskovskie vedomosti* articles.

N° 162 – SOFIA ANDREEVNA TOLSTAYA ✆ LEV NIKOLAEVICH TOLSTOY
[LSA 248]
[16 February 1892. Moscow]

Do not read aloud.

Thank you, dear friend Lëvochka, for sending the letter to *Pravitel'stvennyj vestnik*.[141] Though [Grand Prince] Sergej Aleksandrovich himself said that it would be desirable for you to write a refutation to *Pravitel'stvennyj vestnik*, as this would *calm [people's] minds and completely satisfy the Tsar*, but God knows whether they would print it. In response to *my* objection that I sent in, Sluchevskij,[142] editor of *Pravitel'stvennyj vestnik*, wrote that *Pravitel'stvennyj vestnik* does not accept polemical articles. Istomin,[143] however, said it was the *law*. Which Grand Prince Sergej Aleksandrovich might not have known. Anyway, it's all the same. Sheremeteva[144] will show the Tsar the letter I wrote to her. This is what Aleksandra Andreevna[145] asked Pavel Ivanovich [Birjukov] and also the Kuzminskijs to convey to me. Today I received a letter from Durnovo[146] in response to mine, saying that *my* refutation, in view of additional rumours, could not be printed. I've calmed down now. Moscow society has taken the tone: "*La pauvre comtesse, comme elle est dérangée*", and so forth. Yesterday I was told that the Grand Duchess[147] had great sympathy for me and said to tell me that I should not worry, *qu'il n'y a rien, rien à craindre*. The second *rien* was particularly emphasised. This [was the message] Olsuf'eva[148] asked to convey to me. I was at Ermolova's[149] at her Saturday [reception] and there were a lot of people there. — Now tomorrow is [the beginning of] Lent, and I shall happily retreat once more into my shell, from which I would not have emerged at all this year if it were not for this silly story. — But does peace and quiet [ever] last for long? These days you always live with a moral shudder; at any moment something will start knocking at you.

Tanja told someone in Moscow: "How *tired* I am of being the daughter of a famous father!" — Well, *I* might say, how tired I am of being the *wife* of a famous husband!

You're probably angry, Lëvochka, over my telegrams.[150] But how could I not get nervous again? I receive a letter in the hand of Aleksej Mitrofanovich [Novikov], unsigned and with the words to the effect that you make your admission "in inverted commas"; but in the inverted

141 In a different letter dated 12 February 1892 (other than Letter N° 161 above), LNT claims that the excerpts from his 'letters' on the famine quoted in *Moskovskie vedomosti* were inaccurate by virtue of being translated back into Russian from a published English translation (see PSS 66 :161–62).

142 Konstantin Konstantinovich Sluchevskij (1837–1904) — poet, editor-in-chief of *Pravitel'stvennyj vestnik* (as of 1891) wrote to SAT on 11 February 1892: "Articles of a polemic nature are not permitted in *Pravitel'stvennyj vestnik*, and your refutation of the article in Issue N° 22 of *Moskovskie vedomosti*, cannot be printed [in our paper]" (cited in S. A. Tolstaja, *Letters to L. N. Tolstoy*, p. 502).

143 Vladimir Konstantinovich Istomin (writer) — see Letter N° 47, Note 299.

144 Elena Grigor'evna Sheremeteva (*née* Stroganova; 1861–1908) — daughter to Grand Duchess Marija Nikolaevna and granddaughter to Nicholas I.

145 LNT's great aunt Aleksandra Andreevna Tolstaja.

146 Minister of Internal Affairs Ivan Nikolaevich Durnovo. His letter to SAT dated 13 February 1892 reads in part as follows: "Even though we might wish to fulfil your request, I hesitate to allow the publication of the refutation you sent me on the grounds that, since by its very nature it will raise quite legitimate protestations, and will undoubtedly provoke further controversy, which is by no means desirable in the interests of maintaining civil order" (cited in S. A. Tolstaja, *Letters to L. N. Tolstoy*, p. 492).

147 Grand Duchess Elizaveta Fëdorovna (1864–1918) — wife to Grand Prince Sergej Aleksandrovich.

148 Anna Mikhajlovna Olsuf'eva, *née* Obol'janinova — see Letter N° 109, Note 364.

149 Marija Nikolaevna Ermolova (1853–1928) — prominent Russian stage actress with Moscow's Maly Theatre.

150 A reference to SAT's telegrams to LNT concerning his sending a refutation to *Pravitel'stvennyj vestnik*.

commas is the lie itself, as in the words: "the importantest question", etc. I was really horrified that you might have sent it from [Begichevka, without further editing]. And how could your clever 'nanny' Tanja have overlooked that? That idiot, Aleksej Mitrofanovich, if *he* transcribed it, could have at least given it [to you] *to sign*! What kind of people [are we dealing with]?! Thank God, [we] have got it all corrected now, [we] have come to [our] senses. I sent [your] letter to *Pravitel'stvennyj vestnik* just today, and received an acknowledgement; I very much approved of the letter.

Now to something else: please take care of the following [for me]: as I was leaving, there was a parcel addressed to *me*, sent by [our daughter] Tanja. It contained Lëva's letters, which I pleaded to have sent to me, and no one has done this [to date]. There were also some *foreign translations* there. Not the ones you sent to me through Sof'ja Alekseevna; *those* I've sent off, but the ones Tanja sent, addressed to me.

Please be more careful; it shouldn't be like that. Masha probably received [all of] these, as soon as I had left. Where did everything go? I'm asking Tanja to let this be known, and to keep me informed, and to send me what should be coming to me.

I'm also troubled by Masha's insistently contriving to go to Chernava herself. Has she been in secret correspondence with Petja?[151] This is most undesirable. Who knows what will come out of it? She spends all her time in these secret romances, which will burst just as surely as children's balloons, and she'll be marked with indelible spots and rebukes of conscience — if she has a conscience, which I doubt, since people with conscience *do not deceive,* but do everything openly and honestly. — If I'm mistaken [in believing] that she is corresponding *secretly*, I ask her forgiveness but, after all, she has already deceived me so many times!

Pavel Ivanovich [Birjukov][152] will be taking this letter. I feel sorry for him now and I still like and respect him as before. What are you assigning him to? Is he not carrying out your plan for the soup-kitchens in Samara? It would be good if he could take Lëva's place, and Lëva could get down to preparing for his university exams and not quit university.[153] But, let's face it, it's hopeless: [he's] got off track. I really don't know or understand anything about Lëva or his plans.

Your trip continues to concern me, as to what its consequences will be. Posha and I sighed when we read that you "had eaten *bliny*" [Russian pancakes]. You almost died from eating them one February [1890], after all. [This is] the worst month for colic diseases. I myself have been unwell since [visiting] Begichevka; I've often felt sick in the pit of my stomach; please don't let yourself go, take care and watch what you eat.

I've been sending you [things], sending you everything, now I'm not sending anything. Tanja is not writing [to tell me] what you need, though there will be a chance on Thursday — Boratynskaja[154] is coming your way; she's been called to Saratov, and is getting ready to go there, unless you find there's something she can do for you. I suggest you do precisely that — i.e. persuade [her] to go to Saratov. You've got lots of people [where you are], but there are [only]

151 Marija L'vovna [Masha] Tolstaja was attracted to Ivan Ivanovich's son Pëtr Ivanovich (Petja) Raevskij (1873–1920). LNT was doubtful it was anything serious, and had the impression whatever there was would soon fade.

152 Pavel Ivanovich [Posha] Birjukov and Masha also had romantic feelings for each other and even considered marriage plans, but it didn't work out. Instead, Masha would marry Nikolaj Leonidovich (Kolja) Obolenskij in 1897.

153 Lev L'vovich (Lëva) enrolled in Moscow University's Faculty of Medicine in September 1889. A year later he transferred to the Faculty of Philology. On 12 October 1892 he quit university for good and voluntarily joined the Guard.

154 Ekaterina Ivanovna Boratynskaja (*née* Timirjazeva; 1859–1921) — a translator who helped with the Posrednik publishing house; first wife to Moscow Deputy Governor Lev Andreevich Boratynskij (1848–1907).

a few there. Nothing has resulted with Stebut.[155] In my opinion, these Stebuts are extremely unpleasant [to deal with], and they be best left alone. We wanted to help his region, but he not only refuses to help Ekaterina Ivanovna find a place to live, but is creating all sorts of complexities besides.

Vanechka kept running around looking for something to send 'the ladies'. He had some pistachio nuts, laid them all out and then asked me for something more and had me write: "From Vanja to the ladies". Don't let them overlook his little box and his consideration.

Yesterday we had a dance lesson, and the children eagerly learnt the mazurka. After dancing at the Sverbeevs, Misha's simply crazy about dancing; he keeps doing [all sorts of] steps, and Andrjusha looks at him with some degree of envy, [imagining] that he's *missed out* on something. Andrjusha has had a red throat now for five days. There's no fever, but he can't go out of the house and is very bored. — They [both] have good moral thoughts for Lent: studying well, obtaining *excellent* [marks for] behaviour, eating Lenten fare, and so forth. — Sasha is healthy, Vanja, too. He sings all morning, plays and enjoys life. Until you give me precise instructions as to what Kolechka Ge and I are to do about provisions, I hesitate to undertake any further steps. I sent 1,500 roubles for two railway wagons of peas, along with a money order for 10,000 roubles, promising to send another 5,000 during the first week of Lent — i.e. 16,500 roubles to Kolechka Ge; I shall have 6,500 roubles left of charity money left in the bank, 2,000 roubles from [the sale of contributed] diamonds and 1,600 roubles at home — about 10,000 silver roubles in all. I don't advise you to open any further [soup-kitchens], as contributions have completely dried up.

Zinov'ev[156] was here; he said that they are issuing firewood for the soup-kitchens. We need to write to Glebov[157] (Vladimir Petrovich, Tula, Petersburg Hotel), [asking him] to give permission to take wood from the forest plot which you designate. The peasants have to be paid for [their] work, [as well as] those who process the wood; those who transport it, too, shouldn't have to do it for free. The wood is moist as it's fresh from the trees. Well, that's everything. Hugs and kisses to all; don't forget me, dear friends, and do answer my questions which I am writing out [below].

S. Tolstaya.

16 February 1892

MY QUESTIONS:

1) Where has the package gone which was addressed to me and [where are] the foreign translations?
2) Send me Lëva's letters.
3) Am I wrong about Masha?
4) Why is Lëva staying at Begichevka for two months and is he needed there?
5) Who will replace him in Samara?
6) Where are you assigning Pavel Ivanovich [Birjukov]?
7) Shall I send another 5,000 roubles to Kolechka Ge after sending 11,500 roubles?

---

155 Ivan Aleksandrovich Stebut (1833–1923) — professor at the Petrovskaja Agricultural Academy; author of a series of articles "On the famine of 1891" published in *Russkie vedomosti* (1891, N° 335, and 1892, N° 13 & N° 17).
156 Nikolaj Alekseevich Zinov'ev (1839–1917) — Governor of Tula (1887–93).
157 Vladimir Petrovich Glebov (1850–1926) — a Tula landowner; regional nobility representative for Epifan Uezd.

8) What are the 600 roubles that Sof'ja Alekseevna[158] was telling me about?

9) Did you receive the onions and cabbage?

10) Why is Sof'ja Alekseevna not paying me the 1,000 roubles and saying that Tanja or Papà received 50 pounds sterling addressed to her from England, and that you still owe her for the soup-kitchens?

11) What shall I send by way of supplies?

12) How is Bogojavlenskij's[159] health?

Please, dear Tanja, answer all these questions of mine point by point. It would be better if you didn't get mixed up with Sof'ja Alekseevna. She has had nothing good to say about you all, and when I went to see her, she let out such a malicious poisonous flood of condemnations, curses and silly and crazy nonsense that I shan't go see her any more. Everyone in Moscow is afraid of her, the way they're afraid of a mad dog that's got loose and is attacking everyone. I've experienced this now personally.

In any case, you should know that Natasha[160] has been sent three railway wagons of peas and five of rye, and I have received only 4,000 roubles.

Tanja, you need to do a better job taking care of Papà. How could you have given him *bliny*? Hugs and kisses to you.

S. T.

Nº 163 – LEV NIKOLAEVICH TOLSTOY ♂ SOFIA ANDREEVNA TOLSTAYA
[PSS 84/494]
28 February 1892. Begichevka.

We've been living through these snowstorms in complete silence and isolation; yesterday, the 27th, (as Tanja knows) I rode once again to Rozhnja, but once again didn't make it. The snow was piling up in mountains, and there were no roads [to be discerned] anywhere. I went to Kolodezi and another village [to see] about firewood and shelters for the children; then did some blacksmithing with the *muzhiks* and got home at 5. At home I found Ekaterina Ivanovna Boratynskaja with a letter from the Swede.[161] At that moment Vysotskij[162] arrived, a friend of Vladimirov's,[163] then towards evening two Alëkhin brothers,[164] Skorokhodov[165] from Poltava, along with their chum Sukachëv. I would have been glad to meet them each individually, but everybody at once was too much. Vysotskij is leaving today and he will take this letter. Skorokhodov and Sukachëv will go to the horses at Kurkino. Mitrofan [Vasil'evich] Alëkhin will go with Posha to Orlovka [to oversee] the distribution [for famine relief] and to run the Orlovka soup-kitchens and do all the bookkeeping for us, which he is a master at. He is very likeable — not like [his brother] Arkadij. — Now about food.

---

158 Sof'ja Alekseevna Filosofova (*née* Pisareva) — see Letter Nº 139, Note 618.

159 Nikolaj Efimovich Bogojavlenskij — see Letter Nº 61, Note 23.

160 Natal'ja Nikolaevna (Natasha) Filosofova — see Letter Nº 137, Note 584.

161 Ionas Stadling (1847–1935) — Swedish writer, author of a series of books and articles on Russia and on Tolstoy, including "With Tolstoy in the Russian famine" (published in New York in 1893).

162 Kapiton Alekseevich Vysotskij — farmstead owner, who (like others mentioned below) assisted LNT in famine relief.

163 Nil Timofeevich Vladimirov, landowner from Kaluga Gubernia.

164 Mitrofan Vasil'evich Alëkhin (1857–1935) and Aleksej Vasil'evich Alëkhin (1859–1934) — along with their elder brother Arkadij Vasil'evich Alëkhin (1854–1918) — all shared LNT's views.

165 Vladimir Ivanovich Skorokhodov (1861–1924) and Evgenij Andreevich Sukachëv (?–1905) — two other Tolstoyans.

In my latest letter, if I remember correctly, I explained to you the significance of Kolichka handling [my] order for 22 railway wagons, and I didn't understand what that meant. Now everything's fine. Have him place the order. Only I don't know whether he has [governor's] authorisations. He writes now,[166] sending a detailed account, that he needs 24 authorisations. Did you send those to him? If not, then do send them, if you can, or (you, Tanja)[167] obtain them and send them. It will be easier and faster for you all from Moscow to make contact with the [various] governors. And confirm with Kolichka that he placed the order, if there's time.

Concerning Grot, I wrote [earlier], and he would also write a letter and issue a hectographed press release for sending to newspapers and journals. I've signed it all and am despatching it. — For God's sake, dear friend, don't you worry about this. According to dear Aleksandra Andreevna's letter,[168] they're taking the tone that I've incriminated myself in some way and that I must justify myself to someone. This tone should be rejected. I write what I think, and for twelve years [I've been writing things] that cannot please either the government or the upper classes, and I write not haphazardly but deliberately, and not only do I not intend to justify myself in this, but I hope that those who want me to justify myself will endeavour not to justify themselves, but at least to purge themselves of what not I but all life itself accuses them of.

In this particular case the following is happening: The government establishes the censorship board, awkward and illegitimate as it is, preventing people's thoughts from appearing in their real light, forcing these things to appear in a distorted form abroad. The government becomes agitated and instead of taking an open and honest look at the situation, it again hides behind the censorship board, and also takes offence in some way, allowing itself to put the blame on others rather than itself. What I wrote in the article on the famine is part of what I have been writing and saying at every turn for the past twelve years, and shall continue saying it until the day of my death; and this is what is said not only by me, but by everything that is enlightened and honest in the whole world, what is said by the heart of every uncorrupted human being, what is said by the Christianity that is confessed by the very people that stand aghast [at what I teach]. I ask you kindly not to take on the tone of an accused. This is a complete reversal of roles. One can remain silent. If one does not remain silent, one must accuse not [so much] *Moskovskie vedomosti*, (which is not at all [an] interesting [step to take]), and not individual people, but those living conditions that allow everything to be possible that is possible with us. I've been wanting to write this [to you] for a long time now. And early this morning, with a clear head, I am outlining what I think about this. — Notice along with this that my views are laid out in my writings, which appear in 10,000 copies in various languages. And all at once, through the aid of some mysterious letters which have appeared in the English papers, everyone has suddenly realised what kind of bird I am! That's funny, after all. Only those ignorant people, the most ignorant of whom are members of the [Imperial] court, are incapable of knowing what I wrote and think that such views as mine may one day suddenly change and become revolutionary. All of that is funny. And to reason with such people for me is both humiliating and insulting.

I fear that you will curse me for these diatribes, dear friend, and accuse me of pride. But that would not be fair. It's not pride. But those principles of Christianity by which I live cannot be bent to the demands of non-Christian people, and I am not asserting *myself* nor do I feel insulted for *myself*, but for those principles by which I live.

166 Nikolaj Nikolaevich (Kolichka) Ge Jr's letter is dated 16 February 1892.
167 A reference to the Tolstoys' daughter Tat'jana L'vovna (Tanja) Tolstaja.
168 A letter dated 19 February 1892.

So I have written and signed the declaration, since, as dear Grot justifiably notes, truth always needs to be restored, if that is the case. — For those who tear up portraits, it was quite pointless to have had them in the first place.[169]

Just look at how I have sounded off before breakfast! And I'm afraid that I shan't answer some essential [question] or say what needs saying. If so, I shall write to Chernava the day after tomorrow. I received Ivan Aleksandrovich's letter[170] to Lëva and read it. It gave me some concept of their work there. — I shall send Posha to see him. Hugs and kisses to him and Tanja. Today I hope to receive some news of her. Bogojavlenskij is terribly weak, but no worse [than before]. Thanks to dear Vanechka [for his letter].[171] I hope that his disease has passed. Otherwise you would have written [about it].

Ekaterina Ivanovna [Boratynskaja] is heading off to see [Ivan Aleksandrovich] Stebut.

Big hugs and kisses to you.

L. T.

On the envelope: Sofia Andreevna.

№ 164 – LEV NIKOLAEVICH TOLSTOY ❧ SOFIA ANDREEVNA TOLSTAYA
[PSS 84/547]
7 November 1892. Yasnaya Polyana. [Preceded by SAT's № 8U, 25 April 1892 and № 9U, 11 May 1892]

I'm writing to you both for you and for myself. I've got accustomed each evening to communicating with you — both writing and receiving. Posha will tell you all what happened yesterday.[172] It's been a rather difficult time with our guests, but we, it seems, did nothing to offend them. The only thing was that we [might have] tired them out with walking.

Yesterday we received your distressed letter[173] regarding [our daughter] Tanja. She, it seems, wrote one letter when she was not in a good mood, and held it back, but not a second one. But all this is so silly when you see, as I can see as an onlooker, that you love each other. I saw how Tanja suffered yesterday when she found out she had hurt you, — and so neither you nor any one [of us] should get angry or offended at one another, especially in trying to justify ourselves. We are all such weak and pitiful [creatures] that if we are to understand each other, we can only show mercy and love, and in no way get angry. I feel terribly sorry about your autumn melancholy, not only that, but you are in Moscow and not well. My only comfort is [knowing] that the more quickly it comes upon you, the more quickly it will pass.

Last night I also had a visit from the 'dark' fellow, Anatolij Butkevich,[174] whom you are afraid of, but who is kind, meek and a pitiful sight. Yesterday he told me that once when he was 9 years old, he was running after his brother, aiming a curtain-rod like a pretend rifle; as he was heading through a door, the rod hit the door-frame [by mistake] and [its other end] pierced him in the eye. The eye bled, and he was a hair's breadth from madness or death. And now his other

---

169 In a letter to her husband dated 22 February 1892 (not included here), SAT cited reports that some disorderly young people who had doubts about LNT had torn up his portrait (*Letters to L. N. Tolstoy*, p. 506).

170 The whereabouts of Ivan Aleksandrovich Berger's letter to Lev L'vovich Tolstoj are unknown.

171 On 21 February 1892 little Vanechka (Ivan L'vovich Tolstoj, now almost four years old) wrote his father a letter.

172 Pavel Ivanovich (Posha) Birjukov stopped over at Yasnaya Polyana to see LNT, on his way from Begichevka to Moscow.

173 The whereabouts of these letters are unknown.

174 Anatolij Stepanovich Butkevich (1859–1942) — beekeeper and scholar, who shared LNT's views.

eye has started to hurt. How can you get angry and condemn a 9-year-old like that, or a 32-year-old, for that matter?

Yesterday I received a letter[173] from Lëva. God grant that he come through this experience as quickly as possible, in a way that he will look back on it with joy and not with shame.[175] — This morning Popov[176] (also pitiful, timid, meek, desirous of being as good as possible) and Butkevich went to see Bulygin.[177] And shortly after noon [our daughter] Tanja[178] went to Tula on some sort of business — about a blind girl on Mordvinova's[179] [estate], then about firewood, and was afterwards going to go to Mamonova's.[180] She'll return on Tuesday. It's always hard to let her go. But she went. Sonja Mamonova always travels alone and showed her how to make enquiries and to whom. So Masha and I had dinner just the two of us. What do you think of Masha's trip to the Don [River]?[181] I, too, find it very hard to let her go, but travel is useful now for [our] cause, in Posha's absence. Hugs and kisses to you and the children.

L. T.

Masha will take this letter now (10 o'clock) to Kozlovka. Will there be anything from you?

On the envelope: Moscow. Khamovniki, 15. Sofia Andreevna Tolstaya.

Nº 165 – SOFIA ANDREEVNA TOLSTAYA ❧ LEV NIKOLAEVICH TOLSTOY
[LSA 278]
[9 November 1892. Moscow]

For the very first time, dear Lëvochka, you wrote me a letter[182] in which I could feel your heart, and I at once felt light and cheerful, as though my whole life were once again turned radiant. You were quite right that none of us should feel angry towards one another, especially us oldsters. We need to treat everything calmly and remember that the basis of our relationship is a solid love for one another, — and that's the main thing. — There's no way I can separate myself from all sorts of physical influences. My fright over Vanechka's illness, my quarrel with Tanja — all that has had an effect on my women's complaints. The past two days I have been doubled over with pain in my loins, then I didn't sleep the whole night, and then [my period] *came* way ahead of time. All of this has produced such melancholy, agitation and unrest that it's simply a tragedy. — Your letter today sobered and comforted me. Granted, I can very quickly switch from one mood to another, but in essence, it is true, I love you all fervently, and it's all just a matter of words — while in actuality I always try to do what is best for you all. Except when I am unable to cope with my physical disorders, which often throw me off track.

175 A reference to Lëva's service in the Guard at Tsarskoe Selo.
176 Evgenij Ivanovich Popov (a Tolstoyan) — see Letter Nº 155, Note 90.
177 Mikhail Vasil'evich Bulygin (a Tolstoyan) — see Letter Nº 139, Note 608.
178 A reference to the Tolstoys' daughter Tat'jana L'vovna (Tanja).
179 Margarita Ivanovna Mordvinova (sister to Ivan Ivanovich Raevskij) — see Letter Nº 158, Note 119.
180 Sof'ja Èmmanuilovna (Sonja) Dmitrieva-Mamonova and her brother Aleksandr Èmmanuilovich [Alik] Dmitriev-Mamonov — see Letter Nº 145, Note 8.
181 In a letter dated 8 November 1892 (not included here) SAT wrote her husband: "I feel bad that our girls' lives are absorbed by their obligations [to others]. Will they never be able to live *their own* personal lives? … See, Tanja's gone, and Masha is dying to dash over to Begichevka — apparently there's something unbearable for them [at home]" (*Letters to L. N. Tolstoy*, p. 548).
182 Letter Nº 164 of 7 November 1892.

Yesterday I wrote you literally blaming you over the girls' [behaviour], and I'm very sorry if I hurt you. But I suddenly felt terribly sorry for them, and fearful for their future.

Everybody's healthy here, it's snowing out and some people have gone out sleighing. I've been staying at home for four days now because of illness; it's better not to move and stay healthy rather than to be out and about, shopping, etc., and suffer an abnormal condition. Now I hope that I shall get better [soon]: the peak of the autumn season has passed. Come some autumn I shall either die or kill myself. It's a kind of periodic madness.

Amiel[183] says there are times when we should live quite idly and have fun. — [We] should try to live this way. — A terrible snowstorm is blowing. What's going on with you? The snowstorm here has lasted three days already. Please confirm Tanja's arrival at least by telegram. I, too, am disturbed by her leaving in weather like this. And nobody's written [to tell me] just where Tanja gets off [the train] and how many versts their estate[184] is from the railway. Hugs and kisses to you and Masha and Tanja, if she's returned. Don't let Masha travel in a snowstorm, and when she does go, remind her of our general rule: never try to move anywhere in a snowstorm. God keep you all healthy and safe.

S. Tolstaya.

9 November 1892.
Today Lëva's account[185] has been published but in a greatly abridged [form].

Evening.

Evgenij Ivanovich's mother[186] has come. Without my request, she has been allowed [to open] an eating-house, and she's very satisfied and happy. She's a good woman as she passionately loves children; she's full of energy and works for their benefit. But what a strange environment! Nothing is clearly understandable. She came to me to see whether there were any possibility of sending a fur coat to her son at Yasnaya. Unfortunately there is nobody [who could take it]. Liza's husband[187] was here, too. He is a very serious chap and is involved in questions of thought-distraction, hypnosis, etc. How are you all getting along, how's Tanja? I love you all so much and constantly think of you all.

Nº 166 – LEV NIKOLAEVICH TOLSTOY ❧ SOFIA ANDREEVNA TOLSTAYA
[PSS 84/556]
3 February 1893. Yasnaya Polyana.

We received two letters from you,[188] though yesterday there were none; but thank you all the same. But the more often and the more details you write, the more pleasant it is for us. It's good

---

183 Henri-Frédéric Amiel (1821–1881) — Swiss moral philosopher; professor of æsthetics and moral philosophy at the University of Geneva. The Yasnaya Polyana library contains his two-volume *Fragments d'un journal intime* (1877), which LNT read, making copious marginal notes. In 1893 LNT wrote a foreword to the Russian edition.
184 A reference to the estate of the Dmitriev-Mamonovs, whom Tanja was visiting near Dmitrievka (Kaluga Gubernia).
185 Lev L'vovich (Lëva) Tolstoj's account of the distribution of funds collected for famine relief, published in *Russkie vedomosti*.
186 Anna Pankrat'evna Popova (*née* Novakovich; 1844–1914) — mother to Evgenij Ivanovich Popov.
187 Prince Leonid Dmitrievich Obolenskij — husband to LNT's niece Elizaveta Valer'janovna Obolenskaja (*née* Tolstaja).
188 Letters dated 30 & 31 January 1893 (not included here) — see *Letters to L. N. Tolstoy*, p. 554.

that Lëva came and is cheerful. You write that you had visits from Ge,[189] Solovëv,[190] Stolypin,[191] Sukhotin,[192] [our son] Serëzha, Kasatkin,[193] — all dear people, but everybody all at once is too much for me to take in. This is the inconvenience of the city. *Two is company, three is none.*[194] I should like to see each of them individually, but [when they come] all together, an intelligent and interesting conversation is probably impossible. And you're all [immersed] in proofreading again.[195] I'm afraid that you will completely fray your nerves, and I would advise you hand this work to a proofreader. — We shall go when Tanja arrives. Tomorrow I shall be meeting with the new District Council head, Tulubl'ev[196] and discuss what should be done here. Yesterday I went to Yasenki, today to Tula, [where] I saw L'vov[197] at Davydov's.[198] There are no [governor's] authorisations left, and Posha writes that there is little firewood and it's very much needed. Could it not be obtained from Petersburg, from the Heir's committee,[199] and through Aleksandra Andreevna or someone else? Find out from someone, and if [the answer is] yes, have Tanja write. [My] work is going well. After dinner Masha and I corrected [her translation of] Amiel.[200] [Amiel] is very good. Gertsog's[201] letter is lying on my desk [in Moscow]. Have Tanja bring it [to me]. We are completely well. [I] only [wish] all of you were the same.

Hugs and kisses to all. We are eating splendidly and having wonderful sleeps. It's terrific weather outdoors, warm in the house.

On the reverse side: Moscow. Khamovniki Lane, House N° 115. Countess Sofia Andreevna Tolstaya.

N° 167 – SOFIA ANDREEVNA TOLSTAYA ❧ LEV NIKOLAEVICH TOLSTOY
[LSA 291]
25 February, evening. 1893. [Moscow]

Today I received news from you, dear Lëvochka, that you are coming on Saturday, and I do look forward to seeing you. I hope that nothing will get in the way [of your arrival], and that you are all healthy. — Yesterday Lëva brought you news from us;[202] but listening to the fearful

---

189 Nikolaj Nikolaevich Ge Sr (artist) — see Letter N° 117, Note 423.

190 Vladimir Sergeevich Solovëv (philosopher) — see Letter N° 52, Note 333.

191 Aleksandr Arkad'evich Stolypin (1863–1925) — son of LNT's wartime chum Arkadij Dmitrievich Stolypin — see Letter N° 42, Note 269.

192 Mikhail Sergeevich Sukhotin (1850–1914) — Tula landowner, son of LNT's old-time acquaintances; in 1899 he would marry the Tolstoys' daughter Tat'jana L'vovna (Tanja) Tolstaja.

193 Nikolaj Alekseevich Kasatkin (1859–1931) — artist of the Itinerant school.

194 This sentence is given in English.

195 In 1893 SAT was working on preparing the ninth edition of LNT's collected works.

196 Ivan Vasil'evich Tulubl'ev (1838–?) — a Tula landowner and head of the local *zemstvo* (administrative council).

197 Prince Georgij Evgen'evich L'vov (1861–1925) — politician, who served as Chairman of the Provisional Goverment following the February 1917 revolution.

198 Nikolaj Vasil'evich Davydov (Tula District Prosecutor) — see Letter N° 90, Note 212.

199 On 18 November 1891 a "Special Committee of the Heir, Czarevich Nikolaj Aleksandrovich" (i.e. the future Tsar Nicholas II) was struck to appeal to the Russian public to assist in famine relief, either personally or financially.

200 A reference to Marija L'vovna's (Masha's) Russian translation of Henri-Frédéric Amiel's *Fragments d'un journal intime* — see Letter N° 165, Note 183.

201 Aleksandr Aleksandrovich Gertsog.

202 In January 1893 Lev L'vovich (Lëva) Tolstoj left his military service on account of illness and came to Moscow, and later proceeded to Yasnaya Polyana. LNT informed his wife of Lëva's arrival in a letter also dated 25 February 1893 (not included here), mentioning that Lëva was still experiencing ill health (*PSS* 84: 188).

howling of the wind, I worried about him all night, as to how his trip was. A terrible snowstorm has been blowing for the past twenty-four hours, with a temperature of −10°. For Lëva with his frail physical frame any disease is dangerous; I hope he hasn't caught cold and that you will all take good care of yourselves to the end [of your stay]. — [Our daughter] Tanja has embraced her Moscow life quite eagerly, it seems. She has told me little about Begichevka and the situation there, and I am waiting for the news from you. Tanja was invited by the Mamonovs for tea at three o'clock today, and from there she went to [art] school. On Saturday she and Sonja[203] are organising a children's party and some sort of game; they've invited about twenty children, and I'm very afraid you will not find it a pleasant [experience] arriving amidst this bustle and crowd of children with their parents. But there's no way we can cancel it; besides, our children have gone visiting so many times that it is our turn to host [people] here. Anyway, it's all been organised by Tanja and Sonja themselves.

My life goes on in the same old world — [the world] of *War and peace [Vojna i mir]*, in which I find great pleasure. Only my eyes have finally given out and have somehow started hurting from [all] the proofreading, so yesterday I decided not to work through the night. How silly I was when you were writing *War and peace* and how smart you were! How delicately — cleverly, with such genius — *War and peace* was written. — Only one thing: when [I re-read] *Childhood [Detstvo]* I often wept; with *Family happiness [Semejnoe schast'e]* my nose twitched, but with *War and peace* you spend the whole time marvelling, admiring, dumbfounded — but you don't cry. We shall see how it goes with *Anna Karenina*.

The children are healthy; they didn't go out today; but yesterday Tanja took Sasha and Vanja and accompanied them to the Martynovs'[204] and the Sukhotins',[205] while I made some necessary calls. Tomorrow is the Tsar's [birth]day, and the children will be excited, but will hardly be able to undertake anything in this weather. As far as writing more, "nothing comes to me", as our Samara foreman put it to me. I am sitting down to do proofreading, and shall continue until nightfall. You haven't been writing anything about Masha's cough. I hope that [if] you are having a day like [ours here], you will be taking good care of each other. Hugs and kisses; I shan't write anything more [until you come].

S. Tolstaya.

I don't know why, but what *touches* me most in *War and peace* is always the old prince and Princess Marya, and all the Bolkonskys in general, and not the Rostovs at all.

Nº 168 – LEV NIKOLAEVICH TOLSTOY ❧ SOFIA ANDREEVNA TOLSTAYA
[PSS 84/577]
15 September 1893. Yasnaya Polyana.

Yesterday I didn't manage to get off a proper letter to you.[206] —
Today Vanechka came to tea, and I told him that you were unwell. I saw how this upset him. He asked: And what if she becomes really sick?. I said: Then we'll go see her. He said: And we'll

---

203 Sof'ja Èmmanuilovna (Sonja) Dmitrieva-Mamonova — see Letter Nº 145, Note 8.
204 Viktor Nikolaevich Martynov (1858–1915) and Sof'ja Mikhajlovna Martynova (*née* Katenina; 1858–1908), whose children were friends with the Tolstoys' children.
205 Mikhail Sergeevich Sukhotin and his family.
206 On 14 September 1893 LNT just added a one-sentence postscript to a letter from his daughter Tanja to SAT.

take Rudnev[207] with us. Then Lëva showed up and sent [Vanechka] to Tanja to ask for yesterday's mail. You have to see how he understood everything, and with what joy he ran to carry it out, how upset he was that Lëva thought that he conveyed the wrong message. He is very dear — more than dear — good. Yesterday the weather was marvellously fresh, and I went on foot to Tula. [In Tula] I wanted to see Bulygina[208] and [Nikolaj Vasil'evich] Davydov, and to go to the post office. I had an easy and pleasant walk [to Tula]; Davydov and I actually crossed paths, but we didn't recognise each other. But upon learning at his flat that he had gone to see us, I hurried and took a cab to Rudakova Hill; here I met a driver from Kaznacheevo who offered to give me a lift. At Zaseka I met Davydov and took him back to Yasnaya. He's very nice; he told me that an excerpt from my latest book *The Kingdom of God Is Within You* [*Tsarstvo Bozhie vnutri vas est'*] about conscription was published in *Figaro*. This is a little disconcerting. It's also disconcerting to me that Masha has once more got involved with Zander.[209] She turned him down sharply, too sharply, it seems. He replied to her in a letter, which touched even me. I wrote him a letter[210] taking pity on him, and thought that was the end of it. But she had written quite a different reply to his letter, saying she was not turning him down, that everything remained as it was before he left, i.e. that [he should] wait until the new year. I feel very sorry for her. I hope she will come to her senses. But we have to wait for this to take place within herself and her relations with him. External pressure might only prevent a good and rational solution. She has not talked about this with either Tanja or Vera, but told me on condition that I not tell them. I advised her today to write to you. But she said that she already wrote you yesterday and will write again today. Don't be too cross with her. It's quite a pitiful situation, but if she's in an ill mood, she can be helped only through tenderness and kindness. What you write about the Raevskijs,[211] that's hard, too. After Petja Raevskij and Posha to choose Zander! — We'll talk about it when we see each other. The main thing is: neither she nor we should take any action. I am telling her this, but she has written another letter. She [acts] as though she's ill. I [can only] imagine how this is upsetting you — God grant, to a lesser degree than me. Hugs and kisses to you and the children.

L. T.

On the envelope: Moscow, Khamovniki Lane, House N° 15. Countess Sofia Andreevna Tolstaya.

N° 169 – LEV NIKOLAEVICH TOLSTOY ❧ SOFIA ANDREEVNA TOLSTAYA
[PSS 84/588]
28 January 1894. Grinëvka.

We are living here very quietly and well. — Only today we had a visit from the Ivanovs;[212] Treskin's sister with her children and husband. They are simple, ordinary people. I do my writing in the morning, the rest of the time I read or go for a walk. Yesterday I walked over to Nikol'skoe; admired [my brother] Serëzha's house and the *intérieur*. His assistant coachman

---

207 Dr. Aleksandr Matveevich Rudnev (hospital physician) — see Letter N° 149, Note 41.

208 Anna Maksimovna Bulygina (*née* Ignat'eva; previous married name: Slavinovskaja; 1862–1909) — wife of Mikhail Vasil'evich Bulygin (a Tolstoyan) — see Letter N° 139, Note 608.

209 Nikolaj Avgustovich Zander (1868–?) — violin teacher for the Tolstoys' sons; later a physician.

210 In a letter of 3 August 1893 LNT declined Zander's proposal of marriage to his daughter Marija L'vovna (Masha).

211 A reference to SAT's letter to LNT dated 12 September 1893 (not included here) — *Letters to L. N. Tolstoy*, p. 571.

212 Natal'ja Vladimirovna Limont-Ivanova and Andrej Ivanovich Limont-Ivanov with their four sons. Natal'ja Vladimirovna — sister to Il'ja L'vovich's friend Vladimir Vladimirovich Treskin — see Letter N° 116, Note 417.

brought me home on a jet-black mare; Aleksandr Afanas'evich[213] was in Mtsensk. I'm cough-ing rather little — much less than in Moscow; however, there is some sort of pain — or, rather, uncomfortableness — in my chest, but mainly it's weakness, a loss of physical and emotional energy that has manifested itself with this illness. Perhaps it is a new phase of old age which I am not accustomed to yet. I have to adapt. Today I received Lëva's letter and yours.[214] His trip to Paris was quite pleasant. Only he's terribly susceptible to new impressions. His parting ways with the doctor[215] (I don't get the impression from his letter that their relations have deterio-rated) is very good. I've never approved of this doctor's presence — not for my own sake, but for Lëva's. Everyone must tread their own special and ever new path. And Lëva's path is of interest to me. What will come of all this nobody can tell. His health does not concern me very much. I'm somehow confident — God forbid I'm mistaken — that it will be restored in its own good time independently of doctors and climate, provided, of course, nothing out of the way occurs. I am interested in his spiritual life and his inner workings. Now I want to write to him, too.

From Il'ja there were two letters from Berlin.[216] Sonja is writing to him, and we are con-fident that even without a letter or telegrams they won't miss each other in Paris, since they have points of contact in Dimer Bobrinskij[217] and Salomon.[218] Tanja isn't her usual cheerful self — it's either her stomach, or she's freezing. Anyway, she's better today. In the morning she does drawing and goes for walks, and in the evenings she meticulously transcribes for me. — I've been reading *Michel Tessier*.[219] How mediocre! How artificial it all is! One does not see the passion which prompted him to ruin everything, and even less of his (Tessier's) talent. Along with this I've been reading [Alexandre] Duma-père's old novel *Sylvandire*. What a difference! Fast-paced, cheerful, clever and talented, and *sobre*, and without pretensions. But this chap pompously puts on the charm and passes himself off as a psychologist… Hugs and kisses to the children. I cannot think of Andrjusha without unpleasant associations over his silly speeches about killing Germans with a bayonet. I try to forget, and shall forget, but [it is still] unpleasant. Farewell, hugs and kisses to you. What about Posha — has he arrived? Forward any letters to me [which come to Moscow]. Sometimes there are important ones. Besides, if you don't send them, too many pile up.

N° 170 – SOFIA ANDREEVNA TOLSTAYA ❧ LEV NIKOLAEVICH TOLSTOY
[LSA 303]
31 January 1894. [Moscow]

Dear Lëvochka, thank you for writing me your long letter;[220] the one thing that bothers me is your loss of energy, which I have been noticing this past while, and that frightens me. In part it's your less-than-serious but persisting state of ill-health, partly your strict Lenten diet — in addition, the winter thaw may be having its usual bad effect on you. How will you all be living there at Yasnaya? It must be very uncomfortable there. I am happy this time that you all have

213 Aleksandr Afanas'evich Uspenskij (?–1900) — manager of Sergej L'vovich's Nikol'skoe estate.
214 These letters have not been preserved.
215 Dr. Vladimir Nikitich Gorbachëv, who accompanied Lev L'vovich on his trip abroad.
216 Il'ja L'vovich went abroad with Vladimir Nikolaevich Filosofov (1874–1938), brother to Sof'ja Nikolaevna (Sonja) Tolstaja (*née* Filosofova; see Letter N° 139, Note 616). The letters have not been preserved.
217 Count Vladimir Alekseevich (Dimer) Bobrinskij (1867–1927) — a Tula landowner.
218 Charles Salomon (1862–1936) — translator, professor of Russian in Paris.
219 A reference to the novel *La Vie de Michel Tessier* by French novelist Édouard Rod (1857–1910).
220 Letter N° 169 of 28 January 1894.

gone, and I am not complaining about my loneliness. This was needful for you; as for us [in Moscow], we have had a rest from the crowd from which you do not wish and do not know how to free yourselves.

I am sending Lëva's letter;[221] it is not very comforting. It is apparent that once again he is frightened of being alone and misses the family. He will probably come with Il'ja; and earlier [than usual], in the spring, he will head off to Yasnaya, where we shall, I think, order some koumiss to be sent. It's silly to think of it as harmful, but it must be taken in moderation. I am asking Tanja to bring me back Lëva's letters. What's this about her catarrh of the stomach developing, too? I feel very sad that she is deliberately doing harm to herself, and I consider this mustard-seed oil to be harmful. They say it is the most fatty of all Lenten foods. — I wrote Lëva what you wrote about him, and that will comfort him. Yesterday I read Chekhov's "*Chërnyj monakh*".[222] Very well written, but how painful! What a gruesome literary mood it presents! — I also read "*Zarnitsa*" by Veselitskaja.[223] Beautifully written, though little in the way of substance so far. But the [overall] tone is noble, and the mood is not gloomy — something to be grateful for, at least! Now I want to read "Life" *[Zhizn']* by Potapenko.[224] — I am addressing this letter to Kozlovka already; by tomorrow you all should be at Yasnaya, but it's annoying that letters are going astray. Berger[225] writes that he did not receive my letter in which I wrote out all my instructions for him clearly.

The Denisenkos[226] came yesterday; they are friendlier to each other and happier than ever. Lenochka looks especially well; his legs still ache with rheumatism. Tomorrow they will be dining with me, along with Lizan'ka,[227] and Masha Maklakova and her husband.[228] They will be staying until the 10th of February, right up to the time that you will be returning from the countryside, and that is upsetting to them.

I am constantly living with the children and not managing to do much else. I take them to the rink, or visiting, or they go shopping with me, or to a dance class. And at home I'm busy with them, reading to them, teaching them conscientiously. I haven't gone anywhere without them yet, except for three visits. It's warm all the time here, only just now a light frost has set in, about 2 degrees' [worth]. The boys watered the rink for Sasha, and had a really fun time. Serëzha's gone off with Kolja[229] to the Tolstojs'[230] to see Lenochka; the little ones are playing in the salon with *Mademoiselle*.[231] It's very pleasant having Serëzha here, and I shall miss him a lot when he leaves.

221 The whereabouts of Lëva's letter are unknown.

222 Anton Pavlovich Chekhov (1860–1904), "*Chërnyj monakh*" [The black monk], published in the journal *Artist* (1894, N° 33).

223 Lidija Ivanovna Mikulich-Veselitskaja (1857–1936), "*Zarnitsa*" [Summer lightning], published in *Severnyj vestnik* (1894, N°N° 1–4).

224 Ignatij Nikolaevich Potapenko (1856–1929), "*Zhizn'*" [Life], a drama.

225 Ivan Aleksandrovich Berger (Yasnaya Polyana manager) — see Letter N° 158, Note 118.

226 LNT's niece Elena Sergeevna (Lenochka) Denisenko (see Letter N° 24, Note 160) and her newlywed husband Ivan Vasil'evich Denisenko (1851–1910).

227 LNT's niece Elizaveta Valer'janovna (Lizan'ka) Obolenskaja.

228 Marija Leonidovna (Masha) Maklakova (*née* Princess Obolenskaja; 1874–1949) — Elizaveta Valer'janovna's daughter, married to Nikolaj Alekseevich Maklakov (1871–1918), later Minister of Internal Affairs (1912–15).

229 Nikolaj Leonidovich (Kolja) Obolenskij — see Letter N° 143, Note 653.

230 *the Tolstojs'* — in this case to visit LNT's sister Marija Nikolaevna Tolstaja and her family.

231 Mademoiselle Detraz — French governess to the Tolstoys' younger children.

Have you received the parcel of letters from Chern'? Tanja wrote not to send them, but too late, while earlier you asked me to forward them to Grinëvka. Tomorrow I'll send off another parcel to Yasenki, addressed to Tanja. What a mass of all sorts of useless correspondence!

I wanted to say to you that if things aren't working out for you intellectually, maybe your work in its present form (I have no idea what you're writing) is not what you should be working on. Take a pause, have a rest, step back from it, do something else, but don't fret that it's not working out. I can see you smiling ironically, but that doesn't make any difference. It's so troubling and painful to me that everybody is out of sorts, everyone's listless and drained of energy. I'm not accustomed to seeing that in you. God grant you bounce back, and if it's better for you in the countryside, don't think about me, do what is good for you; only live a reasonable life, [all of you].

Hugs and kisses to you and our daughters. What kind of mood is Tanja in? Masha, apparently, is quite content.

S. Tolstaya.

N° 171 – LEV NIKOLAEVICH TOLSTOY ✿ SOFIA ANDREEVNA TOLSTAYA
[PSS 84/592]
3 February 1894. Yasnaya Polyana.

Dear friend Sonja,

Today at 2 o'clock I rode over to Yasenki to fetch parcels. I took the letter for you from Tanja, to which I added a few words;[232] but I was in a hurry at Yasenki and forgot to hand the letter in; and I remembered it only on my way back, as I was passing a shop; I didn't feel like going all the way back, and so I gave the letter to a groundskeeper and asked him to hand it in to the post office. He promised he would; but he does not inspire my confidence, and since Ivan Aleksandrovich [Berger] is now heading to Kozlovka, I decided to write you once again. We arrived safely; I was very sorry to leave Sonja[233] and her [two] children, now that I have come to know and love all three of them, especially Sonja. — I am no longer coughing at all and feel very sprightly again. We've settled in here beautifully: I am in Tanja's room. Tanja is in [our daughter] Masha's, while Masha and Marija Aleksandrovna [Shmidt] are in the women-servants' room. They are stoking [the stove in] the vault room, but it's still only 12° there, and we use it just for meals. I received your letter yesterday[234] as well. Everything is fine with all of you, along with Serëzha's care for you and the way he is mentoring Andrjusha. — Nothing has a greater influence than the mentoring of a brother. The only bad thing is your sleepless nights. Try to spend more time in the fresh air. Especially during such marvellous days as we're having right now. In addition to the letters you forwarded, I received at Yasenki two interesting letters: one from [Reverend William] Battersby, along with articles written by various *Reverends*[235] regarding excerpts from *The Kingdom of God* which appeared in a certain journal,[236] and the other from a publisher asking for the Russian text from which to produce a third translation

232 LNT wrote the following postscript (to his daughter Tanja's letter) upon his arrival at Yasnaya Polyana from his son Il'ja's Grinëvka estate: "I received your letter here yesterday, saying that everything's fine except for your sleepless nights. Hugs and kisses" (PSS 84: 209).
233 Sof'ja Nikolaevna (Sonja) Filosofova, Il'ja's wife. Her two children up to this point were Anna Il'inichna Tolstaja (1888–1954) and Mikhail Il'ich Tolstoj (1893–1919).
234 The whereabouts of this letter are unknown.
235 This term is given in English. The reference is to articles by clerical representatives of the Church of England.
236 These appeared in the February 1894 issue of *The New Review* — an issue devoted to LNT's teachings.

and edition.[237] You ask: What am I writing? The same so-called *Toulon*,[238] in which I have got involved in explaining the issue of 'patriotism', and this is very interesting and, I think, new and necessary — i.e. proof of the falsity and harm that comes from this patriotism. You write that in Moscow it is possible to construct a solitude: I desperately desire this and am trying to construct it and be as strict as possible in this. Both girls are completely well. Khokhlov[239] is here, who had come on foot from Moscow to see Mar'ja Aleksandrovna even before we arrived. This was not pleasant. Tomorrow he'll be off to see Bulygin. Finally, the most interesting news for both me and you about Lëva. I find his letter[240] upsetting. His health is still not improving. Whether he's in Paris rather than Cannes makes no difference. It's frightening that he's so far away from us. Let's wait and hope it all gets better. I wrote him one long letter from Grinëvka.[241] Farewell, hugs and kisses to you and the children, Serëzha in particular. Regards to Pavel Petrovich[242] and Mlle Detraz.

Pëtr Vasil'evich[243] has arrived. He really wanted [the job], saying he was bored. And today he's drunk.

On the envelope: Moscow. Khamovniki Lane, House N⁰ 15. Countess Sofia Andreevna Tolstaya.

N⁰ 172 – SOFIA ANDREEVNA TOLSTAYA ❧ LEV NIKOLAEVICH TOLSTOY
[LSA 307]
11 May. Evening. 1894. [Moscow]

There are peals of thunder but no rain, it's hot, and I am languishing after the bath-house, but I still feel like writing to you. We feel orphaned without Lëva and mentally escorted him to Yasnaya with Kolja[244] and Andrjusha. At the bank I ran into Dunaev,[245] who was very upset that he did not see Lëva prior to his departure. His garden [work] has exhausted him: he gets up at 4 o'clock in the morning, does some watering and replanting, and has even grown thinner from [all] his labour. From the bank I stopped into the Slavjanskij Bazaar hotel[246] to take my card to Mr. Crosby[247] as a recommendation, as per his request to Papà.[248] How did you like Mr. Crosby? I'm ecstatic about him. He's clever, refined, educated and well-mannered. Add to that his marvellous looks and tremendous seriousness. He showed me pictures of his wife and children.

I went to see Polivanov[249] (this should interest Lëva); without the least hesitation he agreed to a re-examination of Misha on his Latin and designated Friday at 1 p.m. But Misha took

---

237 A letter by E. G. Ribblewhite, editor of *The Weekly Times* in London, dated 10 February (N. S.) 1894.
238 *Toulon* — A reference to LNT's future article *Christianity and patriotism [Khristianstvo i patriotizm]*.
239 Pëtr Galaktionovich Khokhlov (1864–1896) — a Tolstoyan; a student at the Moscow Imperial Technical Institute.
240 Lev L'vovich's (Lëva's) letter from Paris is dated 26 January (or 7 February N. S.) 1894. See Lev L'vovich Tolstoj, *Opyt moej zhizhi*, pp. 284–85.
241 LNT's letter to his son Lev L'vovich is dated 28 January (or 9 January N. S.) 1894. See *ibid.*, pp. 285–86.
242 Pavel Petrovich Kandidov (1867–?) — tutor to the Tolstoys' sons Andrej and Mikhail; for a time he also served as SAT's secretary for publishing affairs.
243 Pëtr Vasil'evich Bojtsov — cook for the Tolstoys'.
244 Nikolaj Nikolaevich (Kolja) Kolokol'tsov (1886–1918).
245 Aleksandr Nikiforovich Dunaev (LNT's close friend) — see Letter N⁰ 141, Note 631.
246 *Slavjanskij Bazaar hotel* — see Letter N⁰ 62, Note 32.
247 Ernest Howard Crosby (1856–1907) — American social activist, writer and reformer. His books were published through Posrednik.
248 *Papà* — i.e. LNT.
249 Lev Ivanovich Polivanov (headmaster) — see Letter N⁰ 82, Note 176.

this quite indifferently and isn't preparing himself at all — evidently he's already thoroughly bored by all this! Polivanov asked a lot about Lëva and his affection for him is quite evident; I myself was surprised and I am at pains to repeat the flattering phrases he used to describe Lëva. Among other things he said: 'I read his article about the Salvation Army followers[250] — how dear that was, after all, how fairly described, clever and well written. He certainly has talent; please let him know my opinion, and tell him that I believe in his future, [that I urge him] not to stop writing — it is definitely his calling.'

In the *lycée* everything is official, proper and unfriendly. Andrjusha's[251] exams are set for the 23rd up to the 28th. On the 29th he will come to Yasnaya.

I was at the house where the Olsuf'evs[252] lived, to ask about the German woman. I didn't find her in, but I saw Neradovskij.[253] Misha[254] didn't leave until Sunday the 8th of May; Mitja is in Saratov. On the 17th everyone's coming back from abroad.

Neradovskij took me to see the Zubova girls.[255] [Their mother] the Countess herself had gone to Petersburg, where [her sister-in-law] Countess Gejden[256] had suffered a sudden decease. When the maid entered Countess Gejden's room in the morning, she found her on her knees on the floor beside the bell-pull, dead. At her head lay a photographic portrait which had fallen off the wall and showed a group of nurses. But how instantaneous her death must have been when her head had not even flinched enough to knock a small, light-weight portrait away from her head. Nevertheless, Ol'ga Zubova's wedding will go ahead [as planned] on the 10th of June in Moscow. All the Olsuf'evs, the Mejendorfs[257] and so forth are coming. They're even hiring a huge hall for the wedding. — In the evening Vanja Raevskij[258] came, as well as Natasha,[259] who is staying with me overnight. Her room at the Raevskij's is being occupied by some ill student with his mother — they live on their premises. Petja[260] and Aleksej Mitrofanovich [Novikov], along with Grisha[261] are sitting and studying assiduously. — Tomorrow I shall spend the morning at Flërov's,[262] and the afternoon at the Rumjantsev Museum,[263] and then my *business* will be finished. I am waiting for [your] answers to my questions: should I

250 Lev L'vovich Tolstoj, "Letters from Paris" — published in *Severnyj vestnik*, 1894, N° 5.

251 Andrej L'vovich (Andrjusha) Tolstoj transferred from Polivanov's *gymnasium* to Katkov's *lycée*, but did not graduate, and in 1895 joined the Russian army voluntarily. Cf. a similar move on the part of his brother Lev L'vovich (Lëva) in 1892 (Letter N° 162, Note 153).

252 Count Adam Vasil'evich Olsuf'ev (see Letter N° 81, Note 172) and Anna Mikhajlovna Olsuf'eva (see Letter N° 109, Note 364).

253 Pëtr Ivanovich Neradovskij (1875–1962) — art critic.

254 Mikhail Adamovich (Misha) Olsuf'ev (1860–1918) and his brother Dmitrij Adamovich (Mitja) Olsuf'ev (1862–1927) — sons to Adam Vasil'evich Olsuf'ev and Anna Mikhajlovna Olsuf'eva.

255 Marija Nikolaevna Zubova (1868–1939) — future wife of Sergej L'vovich Tolstoj — and her sister Ol'ga Nikolaevna Zubova (1870–1930), who in June 1894 was to marry the Tolstoys' Moscow neighbour Dmitrij Vasil'evich Olsuf'ev (1871–1915). These were daughters to Count Nikolaj Nikolaevich Zubov (1832–1898), nobility representative for Kovno Gubernia, and Aleksandra Vasil'evna Zubova (*née* Olsuf'eva; 1838–1913).

256 Elizaveta Nikolaevna Gejden (*née* Countess Zubova; 1833–1894) — sister to Count Nikolaj Nikolaevich Zubov; wife to Count Fëdor Logginovich Gejden (1821–1900).

257 Baron Fëdor Egorovich Mejendorf (1842–1911) and Countess Marija Vasil'evna Mejendorf (*née* Countess Olsuf'eva), sister to Count Adam Vasil'evich Olsuf'ev — with their family.

258 Ivan Ivanovich (Vanya) Raevskij Jr — see Letter N° 159, Note 125.

259 Natal'ja Nikolaevna (Natasha) Den (*née* Filosofova) — see Letter N° 137, Note 584.

260 Pëtr Ivanovich (Petja) Raevskij — see Letter N° 162, Note 151.

261 Grigorij Ivanovich (Grisha) Raevskij (1875–1905) — brother to Ivan (Jr) and Pëtr.

262 Dr. Fëdor Grigor'evich Flërov (1838–1910) — a doctor who treated the Tolstoy family.

263 From 1887 to 1904 LNT's manuscripts were held in the Rumjantsev Museum (see Letter N° 32, Note 192) at SAT's request.

borrow books and, if so, which ones? Should I borrow the Maupassant?[264] Should I take 3,000 roubles from a stranger for the poor? Someone will be coming for a reply on Saturday. If you don't respond by letter, send me a wire. I am glad that you are all healthy and cheerful. This is the most beautiful time [of year] and the weather is marvellous. Girls, take good care of Lëva in my absence, so that he doesn't have any trouble with bathing [treatment], eating, etc. This is the most opportune time for treatment. Do hire the Gipsy[265] to put in a changing-house [by the pond] as soon as possible. I hope that you have started giving Vanechka salt baths. They must be 27° and 2 funts of salt per six pails [of water]. Hugs and kisses to you all; be healthy, cheerful and friendly. —

S. Tolstaya.

Nº 173 – LEV NIKOLAEVICH TOLSTOY ❧ SOFIA ANDREEVNA TOLSTAYA
[PSS 84/606]
12 May 1894. Yasnaya Polyana.

I was going to write you a better and longer letter, dear friend Sonja, but it turned out I didn't get around to it: Crosby[266] — I went for a walk with him and got soaked, and feel tired and weak. Yesterday I received your letter. I certainly had nothing left in me the evening you departed;[267] I only [wanted] you to have no unkind or gloomy thoughts, which, by the way, are quite natural in your present situation of loneliness and in the city, along with your worry over Andrjusha and Vanechka. We can comfort ourselves knowing it is not for long, and we shall barely have time to look around before we're together again and living in harmony and thus cheerfully.

Today they brought some timber and placed it in the meadow, in front of the balcony. At first we were all upset and blamed Vasilij Ivanovich,[268] but after analysing the situation, I realised there was nowhere else to put it, and here it takes up not much room. Crosby, like all Americans, is decent and far from stupid, though rather superficial. [I guess] the main thing is that I'm tired of speaking English.

Farewell, hugs and kisses to you and the children.

L. T.

On the envelope: Moscow. Khamovniki Lane, Nº 15. Countess Sofia Andreevna Tolstaya.

Nº 174 – SOFIA ANDREEVNA TOLSTAYA ❧ LEV NIKOLAEVICH TOLSTOY
[LSA 310]
11 September 1894. [Moscow]

I have not yet once written to you personally, dear Lëvochka, in my letters, but that makes no difference: when I write, I generally think equally about everyone, and am grateful that you are all writing to me, and often. Today there was a letter from Sasha and Tanja, along with

---

264 At the time LNT was working on a Foreword to a Russian edition of Guy de Maupassant's writings, published by Posrednik.

265 *the Gipsy* — Pëtr Dmitrievich Novikov (see Letter Nº 138, Note 599).

266 American writer Ernest Crosby was a guest at Yasnaya Polyana.

267 In her letter to her husband of 9 May 1894 (not included here), SAT had written: "I'm very sorry that my stay at Yasnaya seemed to leave you with something unpleasant and difficult; now this unpleasantness has gone together with me, and I hope the bad impression will wear off before my return" (Manuscript Division, State L. N. Tolstoy Museum).

268 Vasilij Ivanovich — foreman at Yasnaya Polyana.

a postscript from you about bricks.[269] Pity I didn't know that Ivan Ivanovich Gorbunov[270] was going to see you, or I would have sent something with him, or at least written to you. Sasha[271] wrote me a very nice and interesting letter. I think a lot about you, Lëvochka, all the time; I am happy, of course, that you are cheerful and sprightly, but I am interested in the story you have thought up.[272] For some reason it seemed to me from your attitude that it will be *genuine* — i.e. extremely good. How strange they are, these artistic flashes! Just as a beautiful woman over the years appears less and less beautiful, so artistic beauty sparks forth with increasing rarity and fades more quickly. And that's too bad: we need to cherish these glimmerings, as we now cherish the rare rays of the sun in the autumn rainy season. I cannot forswear my love for your *artistic* works; and today I suddenly had the clear realisation that this is because I experienced it during the best years of my life together with you — i.e. simply in my youth. And [our] daughters in *their* youth are experiencing another side of your literary activity, and will love it above all else.

All these reasonings, perhaps, are unpleasant for you, in which case I'm sorry to have written them; I simply wanted to have a conversation with you.

Despite the constant rain and cloud-covered sky, Lëva seems to have improved — that is, he's groaning less and is more lively in his talk and walk. He drinks sour milk which Faddeevna[273] prepares very poorly, but is not getting better; he applies compresses to his stomach, and has given up all medication. He doesn't exercise; today he tried playing the violin a bit.

Manja Rachinskaja[274] was here; she brought a large bouquet as well as a small one — of beautiful dahlias. She stayed about two hours, but was tired and sleepy. There was also Aleksej Maklakov,[275] Kholevinskaja,[276] who gave me an interesting account of the (Nizhnij Novgorod) fair and the women there. Now the children are studying: Lëva is dictating to Pavel Petrovich[277] a translation from Coppée.[278] Another visitor was Pavel Ivanovich [Birjukov]; he arrived yesterday from Kostroma with Dushan[279] and Popov.[280] Dushan's hand is hurting; he cut it and even went to bed. Pavel Ivanovich did a lot of work in the ground, he has a tired and despondent appearance. Things are apparently going differently with you. Sasha writes that it was frosty and clear, while we have had neither frost nor sunshine, but a light rain has been falling, almost constantly.

---

269 This collective letter was dated 11 September 1894.

270 Ivan Ivanovich Gorbunov-Posadov (1864–1940) — an associate of Posrednik, who headed the publishing house as of 1897.

271 Aleksandra L'vovna (Sasha) Tolstaja (the Tolstoys' youngest daughter).

272 On 6 September 1894 LNT wrote in his diary: "This morning in bed after a rotten night I thought up a lively short story about a master and his servant" (PSS 52: 137). This is the first mention of his story *Master and Man [Khozjain i rabotnik]* (1894–95).

273 Avdot'ja Fadeevna — the Tolstoy's cook.

274 Marija Konstantinovna Rachinskaja (Sergej L'vovich's wife as of July 1895) — see Letter Nº 137, Note 579.

275 Aleksej Alekseevich Maklakov (1872–1918) — oculist, later professor at Moscow University and director of the University's eye clinic; a Tolstoy family friend; brother to Nikolaj Alekseevich Maklakov (see Letter Nº 170, Note 9) and Vasilij Alekseevich (Vasja) Maklakov (1869–1957), a lawyer.

276 Marija Mikhajlovna Kholevinskaja (council doctor) — see Letter Nº 104, Note 310.

277 Pavel Petrovich Kandidov (tutor) — see Letter Nº 171, Note 242.

278 François Édouard Joachim Coppée (1842–1908) — French poet and novelist.

279 Dr. Dushan Petrovich Makovitskij (1866–1921) — a Tolstoyan who served as LNT's personal physician (1904–10). He first visited Yasnaya Polyana in 1894.

280 Evgenij Ivanovich Popov (Tolstoyan) — see Letter Nº 155, Note 90.

Today I went to see both headmasters.[281] Andrjusha needs to take a maths tutor; he will never solve a single problem [on his own]. I asked whether Misha might be allowed to study French at home, but Polivanov refused outright. — I feel very sorry for poor Tanja, over how ill she is; God grant this will not be repeated. — Last night I was with Vera Aleksandrovna,[282] she's staying alone with Lëlja, and was very happy to see me. I wanted to take another sheet of paper, but there's nothing more to write about. So, until tomorrow then. Write me again, dear friend, some kind of good letter, and not just about tiles. Hugs and kisses to you and my dear daughters, and my little ones, whom I often miss. My respects to Miss Welsh[283] and to the nanny[284] with Dunjasha.[285]

S. Tolstaya.

I'm in Misha's [room]: he is doing his lessons; I was doing proofreading, and now I am writing letters.

Nº 175 – LEV NIKOLAEVICH TOLSTOY ❧ SOFIA ANDREEVNA TOLSTAYA
[PSS 84/618]
18 September 1894. Yasnaya Polyana.

I have not experienced the slightest discomfiture over your writing[286] about your reaction to my works and the current reaction of the girls' as well. I consider that quite legitimate and have only pleasant feelings as I think back to the time of my work in fiction. Now I've written out a draft of a rather uninteresting story,[287] but it has occupied me for quite a while. I don't really have any desire to revise it, at least not at the moment. I am constantly digging into my [other] work.[288] Why don't you write anything about Urusov?[289] I'm very sorry that I shan't see him. Give him my very best wishes. After all, we haven't seen each other for quite a long time. Has he changed? We have postponed a trip to Pirogovo for the time being. But I also want very much to see my brother Serëzha so that he can chew me out. We don't have too many times left for that. —

I was very glad [to receive] Lëva's letter.[290] Hugs and kisses to him.

L. Tolstoy.

281 Lev Ivanovich Polivanov, headmaster of Polivanov's *gymnasium* (see Letter Nº 82, Note 176) and Vladimir Andreevich Gringmut (1851–1907), headmaster of the Katkov *lycée*.
282 Vera Aleksandrovna Shidlovskaja — see Letter Nº 123, Note 487.
283 Miss Anna Welsh (known in Russia as Anna Lukinichna Vel'sh) — proprietor of a small music school in Moscow, who spent her summers at Yasnaya Polyana tutoring the Tolstoys' daughter Aleksandra L'vovna (Sasha).
284 *the nanny* — Anna Stepanovna Sukolenova (1828–1917), a peasant from the village of Sudakovo.
285 Evdokija (or Avdot'ja) Nikolaevna (Dunjasha) Bannikova (maid) — see Letter Nº 5, Note 37.
286 See the preceding Letter Nº 174.
287 A reference to *Master and man [Khozjain i rabotnik]*.
288 A reference to *A catechesis [Katekhezis]*, later to be called *Christian teachings [Khristianskoe uchenie]*.
289 Sergej Semënovich Urusov (LNT's wartime chum) — see Letter Nº 40, Note 258.
290 In a letter to his father dated 14 September 1894, Lev L'vovich (Lëva) describes his mental state and his ongoing efforts for self-improvement, including better relations with his family, in the face of challenging circumstances. See L. L. Tolstoj, *Opyt moej zhizni*, p. 306.

Nº 176 – SOFIA ANDREEVNA TOLSTAYA ❧ LEV NIKOLAEVICH TOLSTOY
[LSA 312]
27 October 1894. [Moscow]

Your letter, dear friend Lëvochka, greatly comforted me yesterday, especially since yesterday was extremely difficult. Lëva's enmity towards me is quickly increasing, and is so incomprehensible that nobody could actually find any cause for it. Even what [he might] call [my] *bothering* [him] with [my] cares and endearments — there is absolutely none of that now. I can't possibly describe all the details of his nitpicking, but yesterday when I took your letter to him in the annexe, he drove me to tears; I fled, so that he wouldn't be able to say, on top of everything else, that I was making a scene with him. — Now he's come [to me], subdued, in a pitiful [state] — he is so caught up in his sufferings, poor thing, that he is no longer sensitive, as he was before, to everything around him. Yesterday he dined not with us, but in the annexe, and told me he [had to] get out of the house, away from me. Now he will take dinner in the annexe, alone once again — [the rest of] us have already had our dinner. — Andrjusha is quite confined to bed; his cuts from his opened abscesses are painful; he cannot sit down, add to that: diarrhœa, for which he was prescribed opium, so as to avoid infectious cuts in his anus.

Misha hasn't had dinner either; he has a severe cough, and today it's –10° with a strong north wind.

I'm very much afraid for Lëva — he keeps walking about in this frost.

Did Masha see Vera Petrovna[291] on her trip to the country? For some reason I haven't written to Masha for some time, but I think of her with love, and often picture to myself her tender (as it has seemed lately), animated and even cheerful face — i.e. not listless or unhappy — for which I am always glad. How is Tanja coming along with her mandolin? — Dear Varin'ka[292] came by today; she, too, has been ill with severe cramps and diarrhœa, and has been very frightened that she might have a miscarriage; now, [however,] she is healthy [again]. She more than anyone has calmed my fears regarding Limontikha.[293] She says that [Limontikha] has been almost unbearable of late; that she has so repulsively latched on to Serëzha, that Sonja[294] even told her about that; that she is a morphine addict, and that she had not four, but eight children; that Serëzha didn't think about her, but that *she* was unbearably obtrusive [with him]. — I have been seeing practically no one — I'm too lazy to move — and so I know nothing of what is going on in the world or [even] in our Moscow. Only Pavel Petrovich [Kandidov], the artel worker[295] and the nanny[296] have shared various preposterous rumours, for example, that Zakhar'in[297] has poisoned himself, which means he is guilty of poisoning the Tsar, that the windows in his home have all been smashed. Apart from that, there are rumours from the

---

291 Vera Petrovna Severtseva (married name: Istomina; 1870–1900) — daughter to SAT's first cousin Ol'ga Vja-che-sla-vov-na Severtseva (see Letter Nº 30, Note 181).

292 LNT's niece Varvara Valer'janovna (Varin'ka) Nagornova — see Letter Nº 6, Note 43.

293 Natal'ja Vladimirovna Limont-Ivanvova (sister to Il'ja's friend Vladimir Vladimirovich Treskin) — see Letter Nº 169, Note 212.

294 Sof'ja Nikolaevna (Sonja) Tolstaja (Il'ja's wife).

295 *the artel worker* — Matvej Nikitich Rumjantsev, who maintained a warehouse of LNT's books for SAT in a section of the carriage-house at the Tolstoys' Moscow home.

296 *the nanny* — Anna Stepanovna Sukolenova (see Letter Nº 174, Note 284).

297 Dr. Grigorij Antonovich Zakhar'in — see Letter Nº 34, Note 210.

Raevskijs that Klejn[298] (a Moscow professor) did the post-mortem on the Tsar[299] and found precisely what Zakhar'in said: adiposis, or, rather lipomatosis of the heart; the kidneys are not diseased, but only slightly shrivelled. — Today Varin'ka said further that at the university many [students] refused to swear the oath [to the new Tsar] on religious grounds, that they [the university authorities] are trying to hush it up, but evidently these [students] will be expelled. Also someone, I don't remember who, suggested that you, Lëvochka, wrote some sort of manifesto of your own and read it at Khamovniki. All-in-all, there is some kind of alarming heightening of tension [in the air]; as always, people expect something of a new sovereign, and of course not everybody is going to be calmed down that quickly.

On Saturday they're expecting the arrival of the [late] Tsar's body. Troops are stationed everywhere, guards are on duty everywhere — at everybody's gates, at the churches, palaces — enhanced security. Who are they guarding against? Surely nobody would take it into their head to create any kind of disorder over the deceased's body, unless such a possibility were planted in thought by these enhanced security measures. — I shall probably not see any of the funeral ceremonies, for [a number of reasons:] laziness, and the fact that I am not in the best of health — my right temple still hurts, as well as my right arm — probably connected with the nerves, too; but mainly I have no energy; all I feel like doing is sitting down, nothing interests or excites me, or gives me joy. — Mightn't you all have caught cold there at Yasnaya in that biting north wind and frost? Please take care of yourselves, all of you, including Marija Aleksandrovna[300] — and don't take sick.

Lëvochka, maybe I don't need to tell you this at all, but please don't write anything about the new Tsar's reign for the English or American or any other foreign papers. I know all your thoughts and actions are always based on pure Christianity, but now [the press] takes particular delight in finding fault with everything and interpreting it in its own way, and [interpreting] every word you utter in the shallowest [possible] sense (as with *Moskovskie novosti*). The late Tsar knew you and understood you, I could feel that, but as for this poor fellow, God knows!

I'm very sorry [to hear] that once again you are not satisfied with your work, and that you want to start everything over from scratch.[301] This must weigh heavily on you. But perhaps God does not want this [kind of work], and that is why you do not feel drawn to it and are unable to finish it. Perhaps your spiritual forces are needed for some other kind of work. It's good that you are healthy and cheerful; I've quite forgotten how to be either [healthy or cheerful] here. Hugs and kisses to you, Tanja and Masha. What about Annushka[302] — will she come or not? She may do herself out of a job. Give me an answer on this, as Strakhov has already asked me twice about it. Farewell, dear friend; thank you for comforting me with your words of love, at least in my old age; this is especially precious to me precisely in [my] *old age*. Without you and the girls I feel very lonely in the world, although Vanechka is so loving and tender, that it is even touching.

Your Sonja Tolstaya.

---

298 Ivan Fëdorovich Klejn (1837–1922) — professor of pathology at Moscow University.

299 Emperor Alexander III passed away 20 October 1894 in the Crimea.

300 Marija Aleksandrovna Shmidt (kindred thinker to LNT) — see Letter Nº 138, Note 595.

301 In a letter dated 25 October 1894 (not included here) LNT wrote to his wife: "My statement of faith I shall put aside for now. I really want to start again and differently" (PSS 84: 229). This is in reference to his treatise *Christian teachings* [*Khristianskoe uchenie*] on which he worked from 1894 to 1896 (see Letter Nº 175, Note 288).

302 Anna Petrovna (Annushka) Deeva (1869–?) — the Tolstoys' cook (as of 1891); wife to Nikita Evdokimovich Deev.

N° 177 – SOFIA ANDREEVNA TOLSTAYA ❧ LEV NIKOLAEVICH TOLSTOY
[LSA 314]
[31] October 1894. [Moscow]

This day has been full of events on the occasion of the removal of the Tsar's body from Moscow. The children were terribly eager to watch this whole procession, but since nobody knew of the exact day and hour of its departure for Petersburg, there was no clamouring to see it. But various boys gathered here last night: from the Sukhotin,[303] Behrs, Kolokol'tsov and D'jakov [families] and then all at once Dostoevskaja[304] arrived with her daughter.[305] She stopped by on her way [home] from the Crimæa in the hopes of seeing the whole family together. The mother is very kindhearted and boisterous, while the daughter is quite intellectual, very much like her father; she is well-read and very knowledgeable, lively, something like Rossa Del'vig[306] in character. — Anyway, the Dostoevskys found out that the children wanted to see the procession and promised to secure us seats at the Historical Museum.[307] — All of a sudden this morning at 7 o'clock [we could hear] the bells ringing. I hear *this same* young lady[308] coming and saying: "Get ready quick, at 10 o'clock they will already be starting to take the body back." I jumped out of bed, threw on a robe and started waking the children. It was half-past seven by the time everyone was up, the carriage was harnessed in a moment and we left. [The younger] Dostoevskaja took Andrjusha in her carriage, to his great delight, as he was quite attracted to this young lady, and he was in uniform, and with his mourning garb and clean gloves he looked immaculate. But his face had become frightening: yellowed, thin, tormented. His abscesses had passed, but his general condition was still pretty poor. — At the Historical Museum we were allotted a window directly on the Iversky side. Our seats on the scaffolding were very nice and comfy; Dostoevskaja had sent a whole basket of *pirozhki*[309] with hot meat; the children ate [as they] waited, full of anticipation.

Finally the procession came. When the coffin approached, everything stopped at the Iversky [chapel]. An icon draped in black was hoisted onto the porch. There were flowers on the icon, the clergy was [dressed] in white robes, and candles were burning. As soon as everyone had stopped, the young Tsar[310] climbed up to the porch, knelt down and kissed the icon, and did this twice. The Prince of Wales,[311] corpulent, red-faced, sporting a hat with copious plumage, stood in place and waited. Then the [new] Tsar's younger brother Mikhail[312] came up to kiss [the icon]. A thinnish youth just a little taller than the Tsar. The young Tsar is quite lean, even

303 From the families of Mikhail Sergeevich Sukhotin, Aleksandr Andreevich Behrs, Nikolaj Apollonovich Kolokol'tsov and Dmitrij Alekseevich D'jakov.

304 Anna Grigor'evna Dostoevskaja (*née* Snitkina; 1846–1918) —an early Russian stenographer and one of the first philatelists in Russia; second wife to writer Fëdor Mikhajlovich Dostoevsky (1821–1881 — by this time his widow). She also edited and published her husband's works and was a freqent correspondent of SAT's.

305 Ljubov' Fëdorovna Dostoevskaja (1869–1926) — daughter to Anna Grigor'evna Dostoevskaja.

306 Rossa Aleksandrovna Del'vig (married name: Levitskaja; 1859–1922) — niece to Anton Antonovich Del'vig (see Letter N° 23, Note 155).

307 The Historical Museum is situated between the Kremlin walls and the Iversky [Iberian] Gate which Alexander III's funeral cortège was to pass through.

308 Ljubov' Fëdorovna (Dostoevskaja's daughter).

309 *pirozhki* — small bun-sized pastries with meat, vegetable or other kind of filling.

310 Emperor Nicholas II (1868–1918). The coronation would take place 14 May 1896.

311 A reference to Prince Edward, Prince of Wales, a cousin to Nicholas II, who would serve as King Edward VII of Great Britain from 1901 to 1910.

312 Grand Prince Mikhail Aleksandrovich (1878–1918).

lanky, has an unwholesome look; his face is handsome and timid. I got a splendid look at him. He was wearing a simple grey coat and a sheepskin cap. His hair is rather dark. No women or girls were to be seen. The Tsarina,[313] as well as the Tsar's fiancée[314] and everyone [else], rode in funereal carriages and did not show themselves.

After the procession had passed, the Dostoevskys led us to the Dostoevsky Museum. A small, very bright, octagonal-shaped room [within the Historical Museum] with bookshelves, many busts, portraits and manuscripts along with Dostoevsky paraphernalia. Such a cheerful, neat and nice corner devoted to him, and his wife is constantly bringing and contributing new letters, papers, etc.

We went home to have breakfast. It was warm outside; the sun kept peeping in and out. Lëva came, and we told him all [about the procession], but he treated us with irony and said that what was important was not our stories, but that [students] at the university had refused to swear an oath [to the new Tsar], that there was a protest meeting at Deviche Pole, that more than a hundred students had been arrested, and that the university was closed for three days. — However, I saw in this not a kind of movement, but simply half-drunk boys rebelling without cause. [Lev Nikolaevich Tolstoy's nephew] Kolja Obolenskij is of the same opinion.

At two o'clock I took the horse-tram to the Devichij Nunnery.[315] I had read in the papers that all monasteries and nunneries would be providing dinners for the poor for two days, and that interested me. As I approached the monastery I was struck, as usual, by the vast expanse of space — the fields, river, forest and empty space. From the tram stop I went on foot to the gates of the nunnery. I saw a huge crowd of all sorts of women — with nurslings and little ones, old women, poor women, cheerful and even fancily dressed maidens in red shawls, others in rags. Indeed, it was a crowd of people such as you might see waiting at night-time shelters, but this one was made up only of women. The gatekeeper was letting them through the gates approximately two hundred or more at a time, making a rough count as they entered. At first they were admitted to the monastery courtyard, and then right into the low stone church, where the dinner was held. I was asked who I was, and I was admitted, even with respect. They might have suspected that I was sent to observe. In the low church there were long, long tables set with white tablecloths, and benches just as long. To one side there was a table stacked with pies and bread, pots of cabbage soup and cups with *kissel*.[316] Young novices ran around carrying baskets (the size of laundry baskets) filled with bread and large, beautiful cabbage pies made with white flour. Everything was served in the proper order. First of all, spoons were given out to everyone. Before eating, everyone rose, and the priest, along with a choir of nuns, read a requiem for Tsar Alexander III — "may he rest with the saints", "in eternal memory". The Mother Provisor handed out copper coins, as well as 5 kopeks[317] each in the name of the Mother Superior. Then they served a glass of beer or mead to everyone. Everything was done quietly and in order, without a sound from the crowd. On the right there was a separate table just for the children. [It seemed] the children were having a more jolly time, and were especially happy to have kissel with milk. In the corner a young nun was reading, breaking the silence with a loud and distinct rendition,

313 *The Tsarina* — i.e. Alexander III's widow, Empress Marija Fëdorovna (see Letter N° 30, Note 178).

314 Victoria Alisa Elena Luiza Beatrisa, Princess of Hessen-Darmstadt (1872–1918) married Nicholas II on 14 November 1894.

315 This description of her visit is reproduced in *My Life*, VI.100.

316 *kissel* [Russian: *kisel'*] — a popular Russian dessert made of thickened sweet juice or milk, to which fruits may be added.

317 The 5-kopek copper coin was introduced by Peter the Great in 1723.

in a high soprano voice, of one of the *Lives of Saints*[318] — it was the Life of St-Isidore,[319] I think. After the plates were taken away, once again prayers were read. Everyone rose and thanked the two elderly nuns, who kissed each woman in turn, saying: "Now you are full, thank God, and may God be with you" and so forth. The women crossed themselves, gave thanks once again and went out through a gate, and through a different gate the next lot of two hundred women were admitted. Everyone was in a hurry, they pushed each other and climbed over each other in the gateway. I chatted with the nuns, and one of them, about fifty years old, cried whenever I asked her about anything, and kept repeating: "My heart has turned to stone, I have so many sins, and oh, my sins lie heavy on me. I've been praying for thirty years, and I shall never pray them all away, my heart has turned to stone!"

I went home for dinner, again taking the tram; Sulerzhitskij[320] arrived; again I recounted everything to him and Lëva. For some reason L'vov was angered by Suller and had expelled him from the school. An uproar ensued, they wanted to attack both L'vov and the glass [windows]. Some students [from other institutions] came to them, i.e. to the pupils of Mjas-nits-kaja School; the students offered to help them protest. I promised Suller I would go to see L'vov tomorrow and intercede on his behalf. I asked him to quickly inform his colleagues about this and stop the unrest. Suller himself did not want any protest; he promised to stop his colleagues and wait [to hear] what L'vov would say to me. Now a lot depends on [the success of] my diplomatic eloquence with L'vov. Suller was punished for somehow arbitrarily changing some kind of background. Farewell. Misha Sukhotin[321] and Ekaterina Ivanovna[322] have arrived. Everybody's healthy here, everything is as it was before. Hugs and kisses to all of you.

S. Tolstaya.

N° 178 – LEV NIKOLAEVICH TOLSTOY ✿ SOFIA ANDREEVNA TOLSTAYA
[PSS 84/633]
26 April 1895. Moscow.

Today we received a brief letter[323] from Il'ja, saying that you have all safely reached Orël. — We are counting the hours down to your arrival in Kiev.[324]

I hope, Sonja my dove, that this trip will be very good for you. We have to live, dear friend, if God commands, and if we are to live, then we should live as well as possible, the way He wishes us to. You asked Him, I know, sincerely and fervently, to show you how, and He will certainly

---

318 *Lives of saints* [Russian: *Zhitija svjatykh*] — biographies of Christian saints and others canonised by the Christian church, beginning with the early Christian martyrs in the Roman Empire, and including a number of Slavic saints canonised by the Russian and other Eastern Orthodox churches.

319 SAT was evidently mistaken here, as St-Isidore would not correspond to the Orthodox calendar for this particular day.

320 Leopol'd Antonovich (Suller) Sulerzhitskij (also spelt: Sullerzhitskij; 1872–1916) — theatre director who assisted Konstantin Sergeevich Stanislavsky (1863-1938) at the Moscow Art Theatre, and was a good friend to LNT, Chekhov and Gorky. In 1899, at LNT's behest, he escorted two boatloads of Doukhobors on their journey from the Caucasus to Canada (see Donskov 1998). At this time, however, he was a pupil at the School of Painting, Sculpture and Architecture, where the headmaster was Aleksej Evgen'evich L'vov (1850–1937).

321 Mikhail Sergeevich Sukhotin (future husband of the Tolstoys' daughter Tat'jana L'vovna) — see Letter N° 166, Note 192.

322 Ekaterina Ivanovna Boratynskaja (translator) — see Letter N° 162, Note 154.

323 The whereabouts of Il'ja's letter are unknown.

324 On 24 April 1895 SAT left with her daughter Marija L'vovna (Masha) for Kiev, to pay a visit to her sister Tat'jana Andreevna (Tanja) Kuzminskaja. The journey took them through Orël. The visit was intended to take SAT's mind off the recent death of her youngest and dearest child Ivan L'vovich (Vanechka), who passed on with scarlet fever on 23 February.

show you. A change of place and travel have always had an effect on me, giving rise to new views on things and a new order of thoughts and intents, and increased my liveliness. I am confident that they will have the same effect on you.

Yesterday, the day of your departure, the following happened — seemingly an insignificant event, but one which greatly touched me, almost the same way as [the incident with] Andrjusha's teeth,[325] which still makes me smile. After breakfast I went into Tanja's room. There was Manja.[326] I thought she was in the process of getting dressed, so I excused myself and was about to shut the door. "No, you're not in the way," she said, and at this point an embarrassed Serëzha stepped away from the wall; he, too, declared that I was not bothering them. They both looked so embarrassed that I was sure [Serëzha had proposed], but unfortunately, when I went back to see them after my bicycle ride, Serëzha told me that she would be leaving today, and when I enquired about what had happened [between him] and Manja, he said it was a ticklish conversation. Today she left for England. Tanja went to have dinner with her and see her off. Znamenskij[327] told Andrjusha that two teeth [needed to be] implanted, and now the roots must be protected. I don't remember the details of what he plans to do; it seems he will be going to see Iljusha.

I took dinner just with Kolja[328] and Dunaev,[329] who came to the Manège. After dinner I went with [our daughter] Sasha to [my brother] Sergej Nikolaevich's and to Vygodchikov's[330] for honey. Sergej Nikolaevich was in very low spirits and not dressed to go out. I wanted very much to help them, but I don't know how. In any case I shall try. Tanja and Misha went to see them. Sasha is sleeping. I'm home alone. — My mental state is far from active, but it's not bad. I think of you with love and pity. Masha should come home all pink and plump. Hugs and kisses to her, Vera[331] and all the Kuzminskijs. I am very grateful to [your sister] Tanja for coming and taking you off [to Kiev]. I forgot to tell her. — Tanja [our daughter] has now arrived from the Tolstojs;[332] she says Uncle Serëzha is very irritated. How sorry I feel for him!

L. T.

On the envelope: Kiev. Shuljavskaja 9. S. A. Tolstaya c/o Tat'jana Andreevna Kuzminskaja.

Nº 179 – SOFIA ANDREEVNA TOLSTAYA ∫ LEV NIKOLAEVICH TOLSTOY
[LSA 317]
26 April 1895. Kiev.

Dear friend Lëvochka, I am constantly haunted by the feeling as to why I left you and all of you and my precious memories of Vanechka, and sometimes I feel like hurrying back home at once. But my sister Tanja, and Sasha, and Vera, and the boys are so solicitous, taking such good care of me, so tenderly attentive to my sorrows, that I cannot help but feel comforted and grateful the whole time. Masha, of course, would be frightfully upset if I were to leave soon. Nevertheless, we are leaving on Sunday, and with the express train we shall be in Moscow on Monday, if nothing changes either with you or with us. I never stop thinking of you, or Tanja,

325 At the end of March Andrjusha injured his teeth against a cast-iron fence while playing in the yard. See *My Life*, VI.113.
326 Marija Konstantinovna (Manja) Rachinskaja (Sergej L'vovich's wife 1895–1900) — see Letter Nº 137, Note 579.
327 Dr. Nikolaj Nikolaevich Znamenskij — a dentist.
328 Nikolaj Leonidovich (Kolja) Obolenskij (LNT's grand nephew) — see Letter Nº 143, Note 653.
329 Aleksandr Nikiforovich Dunaev (close friend of LNT's) — see Letter Nº 141, Note 631.
330 *Vygodchikov's* — a grocery store on Moscow's famed Arbat.
331 Vera Aleksandrovna Kuzminskaja (SAT's niece).
332 A reference to LNT's brother Sergej Nikolaevich (Serëzha) Tolstoj and his family.

or Andrjusha's teeth, or Sasha's fingers, or Misha's exam. With a frightened soul I am afraid of everything and await whatever comes from Fate. My health, it seems, is improving; this evening Sasha persuaded us to visit the Botanical Gardens. This has made the best impression [I've had] to date: a huge garden, all in the mountains, allées [lined with] chestnut trees, a whole garden with young green [leafage], not yet shady, and nightingales in every corner. Of course, all this beauty and joy of vernal Nature has called forth, like everything [else] these days, [only] despair and tears. I feel sorry for [my sister] Tanja, who all the time weeps with me; I try to hold back, and go out to the little garden with Mitja.[333] I feel sorry for Sasha, but I am no longer in control of myself, and no circumstance in the world, I realise clearly now, will either cure or even relieve my sorrow.

Masha runs around everywhere, excited. Today she visited the Lavra[334] and admired the Dnieper, which now makes almost the same impression as the Volga; but Masha says that even last night she broke out in a sweat and experienced a feverish state. I hope it will pass by Monday. Vera[335] is travelling with us to Moscow, which will make the trip a lot easier; she is cheerful and compassionate, and has greatly matured. Mitja keeps asking me about Vanechka, caresses me, takes me by the hand and looks out for me. When I tell him about Vanechka, he keeps responding: "yes, yes" and sighs. He venerates Vanechka's memory. Today we bought a frame, a little vase and fresh violets; we put a card with Vanechka's [picture] into the frame and put the violets in front of it on Mitja's desk. And yesterday I gave him Vanechka's little bronze dog, and when he went to bed, he put this little dog on the pillow beside him, and covered it with a small cloth. He and I sit around a lot and reminisce about happier times. — I still feel myself weak, but of course my body is recovering, but not my soul. God might at least give me less suffering [to deal with]! There hasn't been any letter from you yet, but there couldn't be. How are you doing, dear Lëvochka? How is [our daughter] Tanja, and what kind of mental state is she in? How sorry I am for all of you, that you are not able to enjoy such a garden, nightingales and freshness of air and nature as we have been enjoying [here] this evening! I realise how good it is to live here with these gardens, the Dnieper and the warm climate. Huge and tender hugs to all of you. Have Manja and Vera[336] gone to England? Has there been no news from Lëva?[337] A lot can happen in a week; after all, Vanechka was taken away in two days! Well, farewell, my friend. Do not forget me.

S. Tolstaya.

Nº 180 – LEV NIKOLAEVICH TOLSTOY ❧ SOFIA ANDREEVNA TOLSTAYA
[PSS 84/637]
3 October 1895. Yasnaya Polyana.

The other day Tanja wrote you[338] and yesterday I wanted to write you, but missed the [postal collection] time; today I definitely want to communicate with you, dear friend. I hope [this

---

333 Dmitrij Aleksandrovich (Mitja) Kuzminskij (1888–1937) — son to Tat'jana Andreevna Kuzminskaja and Aleksandr Mikhajlovich Kuzminskij, born in the same year as SAT's beloved Vanechka.

334 A reference to the Kievo-Pecherskaja Lavra, a major monastery situated on the banks of the Dnieper River.

335 Vera Aleksandrovna Kuzminskaja.

336 Marija Konstantinovna (Manja) Rachinskaja and Vera Petrovna Severtseva (see Letter Nº 176, Note 291).

337 Lev L'vovich (Lëva) was at this time taking treatment at a sanatorium near Moscow from neuropathologist Dr. Mikhail Petrovich Ogranovich (1848–1904), an acquaintance of LNT's.

338 Tat'jana L'vovna's (Tanja's) letter to her mother (not included here) was dated 1 October 1895 and is to be found in the Manuscript Division of the State L. N. Tolstoy Museum in Moscow.

letter] will reach you in your challenging solitude in Tver'.[339] Everybody's healthy here. I did have some sort of fever, resulting in a rash on my lip, and for two days after you left I wasn't myself, but today I'm completely back to normal. Vera and Sasha have gone to Tula and we are expecting them back at any moment ([it's] 3 o'clock). Today Il'ja arrived. Sonja[340] is concerned about Andrej[341] and is taking him to see Rudnev.[342] Tomorrow she'll be in Tula. Sultan [the horse] is lying with [paralysed] legs in the apple [storage] tent and dying a natural death.

That's all about us. I constantly think of you. How hard and lonely and alarming it must be for you in Tver'! I can recommend only one thing to you — something I recommend to myself in difficult and challenging moments: *Fais ce que doit, advienne que pourra.*[343] If you have done what you consider your duty and what you are able to do, you can demand nothing more of yourself, and then all you need do is calm down, rest and pray. There is a state in which you feel that you can't do anything further of substance, that any attempt to continue to work in such a state of fatigue, bustle or irritation will only hurt your cause instead of advancing it. And then you must stop, not get flustered, and rest. In order not to be anxious, you need to pray. You know this, because you yourself are praying right now. Only I prefer praying not from a book, not with somebody else's words, but with my own. Prayer I consider to be thinking about one's situation not in the context of any earthly events, but in the sight of God and death, i.e. the transition toward Him or into another of His realms. This greatly calms and supports me when I vividly realise and admit that I am here only for a time and to carry out some task that is required of me. If here I carry out this task according to my own abilities, then what unpleasant situation can await me, either here or hereafter? I know that for you the chief sorrow is your parting from Vanechka. But even here [you can] still [find] the same salvation and comfort: by drawing nigh to God, and through God to him. It is through this that in our sorrow of losses and deaths we turn to God, that we feel that our connection with them is only through Him. I write, saying that I think of you. I fear for your state of alarm in your loneliness and I say what I think may [help you] calm down. Hugs and kisses to Andrjusha. God help him find the way that brings him closer to Him. Mainly, let him have pity on and preserve his immortal, Divine soul, and not becloud it. Tender hugs and kisses to you.

Sasha and Vera have just arrived [home from Tula].

L. T.

On the envelope: City of Tver'. Hotel Evropejskaja. Countess Sofia Andreevna Tolstaya.

Nº 181 – SOFIA ANDREEVNA TOLSTAYA ✍ LEV NIKOLAEVICH TOLSTOY
[LSA 319]
12 October 1895. [Yasnaya Polyana]

These past days I have been walking around with a stone in my heart, but I dared not bring it up with you, fearing not only that it would upset you but would also drive me into the same

---

339 The Tolstoys' son Andrej L'vovich (Andrjusha) was doing his military service in Tver'. SAT had gone to visit him there. See *My Life*, VI.122.

340 Sof'ja Nikolaevna Tolstaja (*née* Filosofova), wife to Il'ja L'vovich Tolstoj.

341 Andrej Il'ich Tolstoj (1894–1920) — son to Il'ja L'vovich and Sof'ja Nikolaevna.

342 Dr. Aleksandr Matveevich Rudnev (physician) — see Letter Nº 149, Note 41.

343 *Fais ce que doit, advienne que pourra* [Do what must be done, come what may] — LNT's favourite saying, which he wrote in his diary just before his death.

condition which I was in last winter in Moscow. But I cannot help but tell you (for the last time — and I shall do my best to see that it *is* the last time) what causes me such terrible suffering. Why do you always treat me so spitefully when you mention my name in your diaries? Why do you wish future generations and our own grandchildren to vilify my name as a *flighty, evil* wife who makes you unhappy? After all, if [you think] it enhances your glory to be a *victim,* [have you ever considered] how that will ruin me?! If you simply swore at me or even beat me for everything I do which you deem bad, that would be incomparably easier for me — that would pass, but this will all remain.

After Vanechka's death — (remember [he said]: "Papà, don't ever hurt my mama"), you promised me you would cross out those spiteful words referring to me in your diaries. But you didn't do that — quite the opposite. Or are you in fact afraid that your posthumous glory will be less if you don't portray me as a torturer and yourself as a torture victim, bearing the cross in the person of [your] wife?

Forgive me if I stooped so low as to read your diary.[344] I was pushed into it quite by chance. In cleaning your room and brushing the dust off your desk and the cobwebs from underneath, I [happened to] knock down a key. The temptation to peer into your soul was so great that I ended up doing it. And my eye lit, for example, upon words such as these: "S[onja] arrived from Moscow. She thrust herself into a conversation with Bool',[345] flaunting herself. She's become even *flightier* after V[anechka's] death. I must needs *bear my cross* to the end Help me, Lord." and so forth…

When you and I are no longer alive, each one will interpret that [word] *flightiness* in their own way, and each one will throw mud at your wife thanks to your provoking this with your own words.

And this is all on account of [the fact] that I have lived my whole life only for you and your children, that I have loved you alone more than anyone else in the world (except for Vanechka), that I have not behaved myself with *flightiness* (as you are telling future generations) and that I shall die in body and soul only as *your* wife. I know that this [word] *flightiness* relates to religion, but who [else] is going to understand that?

I try to hold myself superior to the suffering which is so tormenting me at the moment; I am trying to face only God and my own conscience, to humble myself before the spitefulness of my beloved and, more than anything else, to remain in communion only with God, to "love them that hate us", "as we forgive our debtors", and "grant us to see *our own* wrong-doings and not to condemn my brother", and to turn the right cheek when struck on the left… and God grant that I may indeed attain this exalted attitude.

344 A reference to a diary entry LNT made under 6 October 1895. At his wife's request he crossed out (with a thick pen) seventeen lines (*PSS* 53: 59). On 13 October 1895 he wrote in his diary concerning SAT's letter of 12 October 1895 (Letter N° 181): "All these past days I've noticed that something was troubling Sonja. I found her poring over a letter. She said she would tell me later. This morning the explanation came out. She read me malicious words about her written [by me] in the heat of the moment. I had got irritated somehow, wrote that down right off and forgot about it. In the depths of my soul I had the lingering feeling that I had done something wrong. And so she read it. And, poor thing, she suffered horribly and, precious woman that she is, instead of getting angry she wrote me this letter. Never before have I felt so guilty and humbled. Oh, if only this could bring us even closer together! If only she could free herself from faith in trifles and had faith in her soul, her mind. Looking over my diary, I found the place — there were several — where *I renounce those malicious words I wrote about her.…* I have often become irritated with her for her quick, thoughtless temper but, as Fet said, every man has that wife which is needful to him. I can already see that she is the one needful for me…." (*PSS* 53: 61).
345 Klara Karlovna Bool' — governess to the Dunaev family.

But if it is not too difficult to do, — delete from all your diaries every spiteful reference to me. After all, this will just be a *Christian* [act]. To love me — that's something I cannot ask of you, but to spare my name, if it's not difficult, do this; however, it's all up to you, even in this. Once again I am attempting to appeal to your heart. I am writing this with pain and tears. I shall never be able to speak it. Farewell. Every time I go away, I can't help but think: will we see each other again?

Forgive me, if you can.

S. Tolstaya.

Nº 182 – SOFIA ANDREEVNA TOLSTAYA ❧ LEV NIKOLAEVICH TOLSTOY
[LSA 324]
29 October 1895. [Moscow]

I have just arrived from Korsh's [Drama Theatre], where they put on *The power of darkness*.[346] But so much depends on the performance and a sympathetic audience, as in Petersburg.[347] Here the performance was mediocre, the audience cool, and I was only [able to] find comfort with the elderly Stakhovich,[348] who was literally burning with enthusiasm for the play. He was there with his wife and his daughter Ogarëva. I received your little letter[349] just before I left. It is brief, but again one that lets me feel the whole of you very close to me, and reachable, and kind, and understandable. Besides, I feel quite ashamed and sorry to tell you this, but for some reason I find joy in the fact that you have become disenchanted with your narrative.[350] I've felt all along that it was *contrived*, and that it did not well up from the depths of your heart and talent. It was something you *composed*, but did not *live*. I would like something from you in which I can rejoice approvingly at every word of your piece, the way Akim[351] delights in the confession and repentance of his son. How I would like to lift you higher so that when people read you, they might feel they, too, need wings to fly to you, so that their heart might melt, and so that whatever you wrote would offend no one, but make things better, and so that your work might have an *eternal* character and fascination.

Here is a whole one-page recipe which you can follow in your writing. [Your] *Childhood [Detstvo]* was written according to this recipe. I shall be delighted now to read it over again in the proofs. I shall include it in an edition for children.

Today I went with the nanny in a hired carriage to visit Vanechka's and Alësha's graves. Perhaps I would not have gone [today], but, in the first place, my longing for Vanechka these days has quite overwhelmed me and, secondly, I had some business there. Kamolov[352] urgently

---

346 LNT's play *The power of darkness [Vlast' t'my]* was written in 1886 but prohibited by the censors from being performed on stage until 1895, when it had its first authorised performance in Moscow at a private theatre owned by Fëdor Adamovich Korsh (1852–1923).

347 SAT attended the performance of *The power of darkness* at the Alexandrine Theatre in St. Petersburg on 18 October 1895.

348 Aleksandr Aleksandrovich Stakhovich (equerry) — see Letter Nº 120, Note 441. His wife was Ol'ga Pavlovna Stakhovich (née Ushakova; 1827–1902). His daughter was Nadezhda Aleksandrovna Ogarëva (née Sta-kho-vich; 1854–1919), married to Major-General Aleksandr Nikolaevich Ogarëv (1839–?).

349 A letter dated 28 October 1895 (not included here; PSS 84: 243).

350 In his letter of 28 October, LNT wrote: "Today, the 28th, I did some good thinking, some writing, and finally abandoned the narrative I started. A wretched piece" (PSS 84: 243). The work in question was an early draft of *Resurrection [Voskresenie]*, which LNT laid aside temporarily.

351 *Akim* — a character in *The Power of Darkness*.

352 *Kamolov* — a peasant, former valet to SAT's grandfather Andrej Evstaf'evich Behrs.

asked me to petition for his son, who has [just] been conscripted, [to be allowed to] remain in Moscow. Nagornov[353] promised [to help], but tomorrow is the final deadline, and Kamolov was to have been informed of it today. I went there for this purpose, and I'm very glad I went. It is always good for me to get out of the city to these quiet, solemn little graves, where I have buried everything that was precious to me in this world. It is good to remember [one's values], although it is painful; and so I raise myself in my heart up to the world whereto my boys have departed. It's strange, but every time I go, no matter how overcast the day, during those few minutes I spend there, the sun peers through even for just a moment. And that's how it was today. And the fields are all white, covered with snow, as it was on the day of the funeral, only, of course, a lot less. The little graves are also snow-covered, from under which bright and strong flowers peer out caught by the frost in full bloom.

Tanja is unwell today, but did go to the theatre, and Vera Tolstaja,[354] too. The boys are all right, they're bearable. Misha was bad yesterday, but when I left and lay down, exhausted by the quarrel with him, he repented and asked forgiveness.

Farewell, dear friend. Tanja will tell you all about what's happening; I simply wanted to have a heart-to-heart talk with you. Thank you, too, for the diaries;[355] thanks, too, for the mental composure you have now given me. If only it could last forever! Hugs and kisses.

S. Tolstaya.

Nº 183 – LEV NIKOLAEVICH TOLSTOY ❧ SOFIA ANDREEVNA TOLSTAYA
[PSS 84/642]
2 November 1895. Yasnaya Polyana.

I sent the telegram. I very much would have liked to avoid all this fuss,[356] but I can't refuse. Your health is important. Why did you abandon treatment — baths, etc.? For God's sake, don't give them up. Nothing is important if you're suffering bodily and mentally.[357] Wouldn't you like me to come to you? Everything is so insignificant in comparison with your health. Of course you should not receive any [visitors]. And for God's sake wire me, and I'll come to you at once. What you write about the boys is sad, but I'm not expecting anything else. And that's all to the good.

For God's sake, my dove, don't hold anything in, don't think about others, only of yourself. I would be happy to give up a lot for you, but unfortunately I don't need to give up anything here, since coming to see you will be a joy [for me]. — The whole of the past two days I have been re-reading my diaries so as to delete what is untrue, and I found only one place, but even that is not nearly as dastardly as the ones that upset you.[358] Hugs and kisses, my dove, and I await [your] letter.

L. T.

353 Nikolaj Mikhajlovich Nagornov (husband to LNT's niece) — see Letter Nº 54, Note 348.
354 Vera Sergeevna Tolstaja (daughter to LNT's brother) — see Letter Nº 102, Note 297.
355 In his diaries of 1888–89 LNT crossed out or cut out thirty-three excerpts; in the ones for 1890–95 — twelve excerpts (see S. A. Tolstaya: *Letters to L. N. Tolstoy*, p. 627).
356 LNT's telegram dated the same day reads: "LET THEM COME I'M WRITING" (PSS 84: 243). This is in regard to granting the request of Moscow's Maly Theatre company to come to Yasnaya Polyana to hear LNT read his drama *The power of darkness [Vlast' t'my]*.
357 In her letter of 31 October 1895 (not included here) SAT complained of ill health and mentioned having to turn away visitors, that the constant stream of visitors was proving too much for her nerves. She also confessed her concern that their son Andrej was having a bad influence on his younger brother Mikhail. (*Letters to L. N. Tolstoy*, pp. 628–29).
358 See Letter Nº 181, Note 344.

N° 184 – LEV NIKOLAEVICH TOLSTOY ❧ SOFIA ANDREEVNA TOLSTAYA
[PSS 84/648]
22 February 1896. Nikol'skoe-Obol'janovo.

I am sitting down to write letters, and first of all I want to write to you, dear friend; otherwise I might not have enough strength left in me after [writing] the others. I feel very good, quite healthy; though I don't know why — whether it's a reaction to the nervous excitement of Moscow or simply old age — [I'm] weak, flaccid, I don't feel like either working intellectually or moving around physically. True, today, the 22nd, I spent the morning, if not writing, then at least contemplating with interest and making notes…[359] I don't want to admit that I'm old and finished [with writing], but I probably ought to. I am trying to get to this [thought], and not overexert myself and damage my [health]. That's enough about me. Still, I am very well, I'm enjoying the quiet and the kindness of my hosts. — How are you? Are Serëzha and Manja coming to see you from time to time? Has Masha left?[360] How are your eyes? How are you spending your nights? Are you sleeping well? When we arrived here, there was nobody around but the old people[361] and Matil'da Pavlovna Mollas.[362] Liza was actually in Dmitrov at the *gymnasium* there, where she is a trustee. Yesterday she arrived [here]. — How is Mashen'ka [my] sister? When will she leave? I thought of her since right now I am experiencing the coldness of religious feelings I talked with her about. [You see,] for us oldsters who are close to death, this feeling of coldness is very unpleasant, especially when you know it is a feeling of the expansion of life beyond the borders of birth and death, and something you recently experienced. — I asked that Grot be told that in two places in the published letter[363] where it says "*be true in word and deed*" the words "*in thought*" be added, so that it comes out as: "*in thought, word and deed*". I forgot Lëvshin's article[364] and photographs; please forward them. Please send [any] letters, too, and anything else you consider important from the brochures and books we have received. And do send Aicard's[365] *Notre Dame d'Amour*, along with some English novels that were together with it. None of these are really necessary, and so if you don't locate them right away, not to worry. Farewell for now, hugs and kisses to you and the newlyweds,[366] [along with] Misha and Sasha. How's Andrjusha? I hope he's not a bother to you?

L. T.

On the envelope: Moscow. Khamovniki. Countess Sofia Andreevna Tolstaya. Private house.

359 LNT was working on his drama *And the light shines in darkness [I svet vo t'me svetit]*.
360 On 23 February Marija L'vovna (Masha) left for the Crimea.
361 A reference to Adam Vasil'evich Olsuf'ev and Anna Mikhajlovna Olsuf'eva, owners of the Nikol'skoe-Obol'janovo estate, where LNT was a guest — see Letter N° 109, Note 364.
362 Matil'da Pavlovna Mollas (1857–1921) — a teacher of French for women's higher-education courses in Moscow and a family friend of the Tolstoys'; a close friend to Elizaveta Adamovna (Liza) Olsuf'eva (see Letter N° 112, Note 386).
363 A reference to LNT's letter to governess P. K. Novitskaja (a native of Bessarabia; 1874–?) dated 11 December 1894, which was published in the journal *Voprosy filosofii i psikhologii* (1894, N° 32) under the editorship of Nikolaj Jakovlevich Grot (see Letter N° 137, Note 582). LNT's request for the word change was honoured in publication. The letter touched upon LNT's views on the meaning of life.
364 A reference to one of a number of articles published in the journal *Kolos'ja* between 1887 and 1879.
365 Jean Aicard (1848–1921) — French novelist, poet and playwright; his novel *Notre-Dame d'Amour* was published in 1896.
366 On 9 July 1895 the Tolstoys' eldest son, Sergej L'vovich (Serëzha) Tolstoj, married Marija Konstantinovna (Manja) Rachinskaja (see Letter N° 137, Note 579).

Nº 185 – SOFIA ANDREEVNA TOLSTAYA ❧ LEV NIKOLAEVICH TOLSTOY
[LSA 331]
26 February 1896. Evening. [Moscow]

Dear Lëvochka, thank you for the long, good, frank letter;[367] it is always precious for me to know exactly what kind of mood you are in, though this time it upset me: you write that you are listless and weak both physically and spiritually, that [you're in] a cold religious mood, and even the natural surroundings and peaceful quiet of the country has evidently not cheered you up. Winter in the country always seems to me not so much 'all right' as majestic and peaceful, especially in the woods. I hope you will awake to life and not give in any longer. You yourself said that there is no such thing as old age, — so don't you give in, that way it won't happen. Perhaps it will not please you to hear that I, on the other hand, whether from fasting, or remembering the sacred event of Vanechka's death... — but all this week of my strict fast I have felt remarkably well, quietly in harmony with religion. I've been to the church from two to four times a day. [I have heard] wonderful Lenten prayers, and the church service is something special. We don't have any singers in our church,[368] and I like it better when the vicar reads in a monotone — it reminds me of my childhood. At home I read the Gospel and prayer books. I kept thinking that Vanechka was joining me from that heavenly realm, and on the eve of Communion Day I saw him in a dream, only sad — for some reason I always picture him as sad. — On Communion Day I rose at 6 o'clock in the morning and went to mass. They started the service early since at 9 o'clock the priests were called to give their blessing to the Snegirëv Clinic.[369] At 9 I came home and slept until 11:30. I seemed to see my whole communion mass as though it had been a dream. When I got up, Sasha and the servants — everyone greeted me — though I didn't understand at first what the occasion was. — Throughout the week of my fast I hardly saw anyone; both my eyes hurt fearfully, and I walked to church with a bandage on my eye and a lotion-soaked cloth in my pocket. And so I did little writing or reading, and sometimes felt quite bored, pacing the room without purpose, people or [fresh] air. I could not go out in the wind and bright sunshine. I did go to see Krjukov[370] and he gave me silver nitrate and mercuric chloride in a cloth. Now [the condition] has all passed, and Sasha and I are going skating tomorrow, although this is not entirely prudent; I am not completely free of women's complaints — [my period] was three weeks late. It was back at Tver'[371] that I fell ill, [the period] stopped, but now I feel quite free and physically well; my head has stopped hurting.

Tomorrow it will be a whole week that you have all been gone. Please stay healthy and cheerful, so that your trip is completely successful. My life is not at all difficult; I'm very busy, with lots of friends; I'm not at all bored at the moment, only definitely do write to me. [For my part,] I am to blame for writing so rarely, but brief telephone messages[372] are somehow not satisfying, and only provoke disappointment that I am not hearing your genuine heartfelt voice.

---

367 Letter Nº 184 of 22 February 1896.
368 Church of the Sign of the Blessed Virgin at Deviche pole [Maidens' Field] in Moscow.
369 *Snegirëv Clinic* — a clinic established in 1889 by an early pioneer in Russian gynæcology, Vladimir Fëdorovich Snegirëv (1847–1916).
370 Aleksandr Aleksandrovich Krjukov (1849–1908) — an oculist, Deputy Chair of the Moscow Oculists' Society, with whom SAT took treatment for her eyes.
371 In January of 1896 SAT went to Tver' for a visit with the Tolstoys' son Andrej, who was engaged in his military service there at the time.
372 LNT had a 'telephonogramme' connection with Moscow from Nikol'skoe-Obol'janovo.

Many letters have come all at once, and I am sending them on. I am sending you the book *Notre dame de l'amour*, please bring it back with you. Mme Junge[373] borrowed the English novel and hasn't returned it yet. Nothing terribly interesting has come. Still no letters from Lëva.[374] Read the letter [I wrote] to Tanja; it will complement what I have written here. In the meantime, hugs and kisses; I am still transcribing your narrative, but my eyes have held me back. There are fewer than three chapters left [to copy]. Well, farewell, dear friend; give everyone my regards, especially Anna Mikhajlovna,[375] whom I sincerely thank for [hosting] all of you.

Your Sonja Tolstaya.

Nº 186 – LEV NIKOLAEVICH TOLSTOY ❧ SOFIA ANDREEVNA TOLSTAYA
[PSS 84/651]
3 March 1896. Nikol'skoe-Obol'janovo.

It is now Sunday evening, 3rd March, and we have received another letter from you,[376] dear Sonja. I knew that when I wrote reproaching you,[377] my reproach would be unfounded and that you would [indeed] write. I see that everything is well with you, both outwardly and inwardly. I wanted to tell you that your tendency to forget yourself, though quite natural, is not sound enough in that, when you forget yourself, you only put off answering the question, but the same question remains, and still has to be answered — [if] not in this world, then in the next, i.e. after the death of the flesh. As the spiritualists say, if you kill yourself, you will still have to deal with the same life as in this [world]: you cannot avoid answering the question of life and death for yourself and your loved ones — you won't get away from that. I wanted to tell all this to you, but I'm not saying it, because you yourself will have to experience all this and come to this [same realisation]. One thing I'll say: that it is an amazingly good [sensation] when you not so much understand clearly but, [rather,] *feel* clearly, that life is not limited to this [earthly life], but is infinite. And so right away you have a different evaluation of all things and feelings, like coming out from a confined prison into the light of God, the true light. I [feel] more sprightly and got a bit of work done today, I want to go for a walk and keep drinking in the silence and freedom from human demands. Tanja, it seems, is also doing well. Lëva is very touching;[378] I want to write to him again. Hugs and kisses, dear, and to Sasha and Masha.

L. T.

On the envelope: Moscow. Khamovniki. Countess Sofia Andreevna Tolstaya.

---

373 Ekaterina Fëdorovna Junge (LNT's second cousin) — see Letter Nº 157, Note 107.

374 On 26 February 1896 (9 March N. S.) Lev L'vovich (Lëva) Tolstoy, in Sweden for medical treatment, became engaged to Dora Westerlund (1878–1933), daughter to his physician, Dr. Ernst Westerlund (1859–1924). Their wedding would take place in May 1896.

375 Anna Mikhajlovna Olsuf'eva — see Letter Nº 109, Note 364.

376 A letter dated 1 March 1896 (not included here; *Letters to L. N. Tolstoy*, pp. 643–44).

377 In a letter of 27 February 1896 (not included here), LNT wrote: "Your letter [Nº 185 of 26 February] is not comforting. The main thing is [your] restraint and, it seems, not so much discontent, but sadness. Please write nicely, with a nice, bright disposition" (PSS 84: 252).

378 Lëva's letter to his sister Tanja of 26 February 1896 (describing his marital relations with his young wife Dora) had been forwarded to LNT.

Nº 187 – SOFIA ANDREEVNA TOLSTAYA ❧ LEV NIKOLAEVICH TOLSTOY
[LSA 334]
5 March 1896. [Moscow]

Dear friend Lëvochka, today Countess Miljutina[379] came by and didn't find me in; I was at a music lesson, and now I shall take all the letters to her myself. An awful lot of books have come, too, but I am not forwarding them. I [received] a postcard today saying that you are returning on Saturday, and I got frightened [to think] that possibly I was the one who was calling for you with my question. Please, my dear, if you feel better and work more easily in the countryside, don't hurry [home] for me. I am living well and am very busy; it's just that occasionally, when I stop my feverish activity and come to my senses all alone by myself, with my memories, my old age and fear for the future, I suddenly have this unbearable feeling of longing. But that is a weakness, and generally I feel buoyant. Only when people marvel over my *energy,* so-called, I feel ashamed, and I know within myself that not only do I not have any energy, but I am weak — so weak that very quickly I can revert to last year's February madness, which I mulled over in horror the other day when I was at the requiem for Nagornov,[380] at the same [Novo]devichij convent which has been so strongly etched into my memory. — And see, I keep going on about myself — that's a weakness, too.

Manja[381] is sitting here with me and reading your narrative which I am just finishing transcribing. Serëzha and Vasja Maklakov[382] are playing a four-handed Mendelssohn overture which I bought. Sasha has just come in from the garden where she was skating; Misha was out riding and has now got down to his studies. [I have just received] a very anxious and fussy letter from Lëva with instructions on sending documents, and questions about who's coming to the wedding,[383] with particulars as to where and when it will take place (1 June N.S.). I'll take care of everything for him, but as this event draws nearer, I'm getting just a little fearful and excited. Marriage is a big step.

You were writing me[384] that the question of life and death needs to be answered now and not put off, and there should be no attempt to forget it. But the whole point is not in answering the question: as far as I'm concerned, it was already answered a long time ago in the same sense in which you yourself are answering it — i.e. in the sense of eternity and infinite life in God. But it is very hard to stay at the height of this attitude, and the sensations of painful loss, the joys of earthly temptations and feverish activity — and all purely earthly sensations in general — try to snare [us] in a trap on all sides, and this is where my much-touted energy might help me, but I don't have enough of it, and as a result [I feel] melancholy and frustration.

[Aleksandr Nikiforovich] Dunaev has come; Manja and Serëzha are leaving, no more time to write. Hugs and kisses to you, my dear friend. To Tanja, too; I still haven't managed to write

---

379 Countess Ol'ga Dmitrievna Miljutina (1846–1926) — daughter to war minister Dmitrij Alekseevich Miljutin (1816–1912).

380 Nikolaj Mikhajlovich Nagornov (husband to LNT's niece Varvara Valer'janovna Tolstaja; see Letter Nº 6, Note 43) passed away on 23 January 1896. Two days later LNT wrote in his diary: "The main event these past couple of days has been Nagornov's death, ever new and meaningful — death. I thought: death is portrayed on stage at the theatre. Does it produce even one ten-thousandth of the impression produced by the closeness of a real death?" (PSS 53: 78).

381 Marija Konstantinovna Tolstaja (*née* Rachinskaja), Sergej L'vovich's wife, was reading a draft of LNT's *Resurrection.*

382 Vasilij Alekseevich (Vasja) Maklakov (family friend) — see Letter Nº 174, Note 275.

383 The wedding of Lev L'vovich (Lëva) Tolstoj and Dora Westerlund (see Letter Nº 185, Note 374) took place in Sweden on 15 May 1896 (this was actually 27 May N. S.; SAT was evidently mistaken about the N. S. date).

384 Letter Nº 186 of 3 March 1896.

her, but I think of her a lot, and often miss her, in spite of her strictness towards me. Farewell — if you come on Saturday, I shall be very happy; if not, God be with you. Only don't travel in a snowstorm or when you're not completely healthy. Let me know if you cancel your trip. Why on Saturday, when there may be [a lot of] visitors? In any case, I would dissuade [you], even though I myself am afraid I might not see you for a long time.

Your Sonja Tolstaya.

Farewell, you'll be back soon now.

Nº 188 – SOFIA ANDREEVNA TOLSTAYA ✖ LEV NIKOLAEVICH TOLSTOY
[LSA 337]
9 September 1896. [Moscow]

Dear friend Lëvochka, I just saw Stasov[385] off, who brought me your letter. And your letter would have prolonged my meek, loving mood and attitude to you, if it were not for what [Stasov] told me about the articles you read to him. My whole soul clouded over at once and I was overwhelmed by a dreary sense of despair. Even though Stasov strongly and overly loudly praised your speech and your boldness, along with everything you write, yet I got the impression from it all, including your letter to Van der Veer[386] (it seems) and your letter to the liberals,[387] that this is a provocative challenge: "Just try and touch me!"

And this challenge (especially from the Christian point of view) is not only [not] helpful to anyone, but is in itself harmful, unkind and dangerous. Besides, it is some kind of boyish tomfoolery, bravado. It turns an artist, or philosopher, or serious religious teacher into a cockamamie hack. If you only knew how such antics and articles (as Stasov outlined for me in detail) tear me apart and frighten me, and how much they diminish my love and respect for you! All at once I cease to believe in your heart and your teachings, and I see [only] that youngster full of untempered zeal, vices and pride that you used to be, judging by your [early] diaries, in your youth. Throw off your zeal, don't send these letters, for God's sake, I beg of you. You won't change anything in people's lives. Let your writings live on as your legacy, but don't aggravate anyone, don't torment me, or put all our lives and peace at risk.

I have never asked anything of you this urgently before. At least wait until I come on Saturday and show me what you want to write. You should write your catechesis[388] and be meek and humble; [think] how much better and worthy that would be. It's time to calm down and love people, and not provoke them.

Farewell. I am very upset and worried, and on account of my pain I cannot love you today.

S. Tolstaya.

385 Vladimir Vasil'evich Stasov (librarian; see Letter Nº 61, Note 26) had just visited LNT at Yasnaya Polyana before coming to see SAT in Moscow. He brought SAT a letter from LNT dated 7 September 1896 (not included here) in which he said of Stasov: "In him there's a lot of kindness and genuine love and understanding of art" (PSS 84: 255, there dated 9 September 1896).

386 Johannes Kœnraad van der Veer (1869–1928) — a Dutch Tolstoyan and Christian anarchist. For his refusal to do military service he was sentenced to three months of solitary confinement.

387 LNT's *Letter to the liberals* (like his letter to Van der Veer, eventually published in England in Chertkov's bulletin *Svobodnoe slovo* in 1898) was in response to a letter he received from writer and pedagogue Aleksandra Mikhajlovna Kalmykova (*née* Chernova; 1849–1926) concerning the closure (in November 1895) of the St. Petersburg Literacy Committee, created in 1861 to facilitate public education, and its merging with the Free Economic Society.

388 *catechesis* — see Letter Nº 175, Note 288.

N° 189 – LEV NIKOLAEVICH TOLSTOY ☙ SOFIA ANDREEVNA TOLSTAYA
[PSS 84/658]
September 1896. Yasnaya Polyana.

This morning, dear friend Sonja, I received your brief letter,[389] and was a little upset by your weakness, but then I was delighted to see that you had overcome it. You have a great deal of strength — not only physical but moral, too — only you are still missing something little and the most important, which will still come, I am confident. I shan't be anything but sad in the next world, when all this will come about after my death. Many are upset that glory will not come to them until after death; I have no reason to desire that; — I would give up not just a lot, but *any* glory if only you could agree with my heart during my lifetime the way you will agree with it after my death. The day after your departure I thought of you and wanted to respond to your claim that you have nothing to live for.[390] Perhaps I shall write at some point or tell you my thoughts on this. It's better to write, since I can think things through better. Well, enough of that. I am quite healthy; not only healthy, but my spirit is far more cheerful than it has been in a long time; I have been working splendidly and, it seems, I have completed my rough draft of my outline of faith, at least to the point that, if I should die without correcting it, people will still understand what I wanted to say. Now I want to write something different, and I've [already] begun. Not only am I healthy in body but I am completely at peace in spirit, not the way I was during your previous absence. Tanja arrived early this morning cheerful and sprightly, and happy with her trip.[391] Kolasha[392] and Andrjusha also arrived. The Japanese [visitors] have been here since this morning. Very interesting: fully educated, original, smart and free-thinking. One[393] is the editor of a magazine, evidently very rich and a [Japanese] aristocrat, getting along in years; the other, a younger chap, is his assistant, likewise a writer. They had a lot to talk about, and now they are leaving. It's too bad that you weren't [here] to see them, too. The weather is still fine. [People] are playing tennis, and taking horseback rides. Yesterday I went to Tula, but Davydov wasn't there and I returned at once. Hugs and kisses to you and [our son] Misha. I am very glad for him, if the transition to the *lycée* will help him become more conscientious. — Though I don't accept the need to rely on external change to [bring about] inner change, but I admit that it can sometimes be useful. God grant. Oh, how good it would be if he really changed a great deal, especially if he could understand that people are not predestined to be served by [others], but to serve [others], and that your joy in life is not in what you take from people but what you give them. That is undoubtedly how our lives are structured, and one would have to be a real dimwit not to see that. Only children up to [our] grandson Misha's age are forgiven for not seeing it. Hugs and kisses to you both.

L. T.

26th, evening. With the Japanese [visitors].

---

389 A letter dated 24 September 1896 (not included here; see S. A. Tolstaja, *Letters to L. N. Tolstoy*, p. 653).

390 SAT wrote a comment on his letter (PSS 84: 260), saying "The whole time I kept missing my deceased Vanechka and there was no way I could fill the emptiness left in my life by his death."

391 The Tolstoys' daughter Tat'jana L'vovna (Tanja) had paid a visit to her friends the Stakhoviches on their Pal'na estate in Orël Gubernia.

392 LNT's nephew Nikolaj Leonidovich (Kolasha) Obolenskij (see Letter N° 143, Note 653).

393 Intiro Tokutomi (pseudonym: Sokho; 1863–1957) — Japanese journalist, historian and social activist, who ran the Japanese magazine *Kukumin-Shimbun* [Friend of the people]; he was accompanied by an assistant named Fukaj.

Nº 190 – LEV NIKOLAEVICH TOLSTOY ❧ SOFIA ANDREEVNA TOLSTAYA
[PSS 84/667]
31 October 1896. Kozlova-Zaseka.

I wanted to write you today, dear friend, but I initially fell asleep, then in the evening I went for a walk in the snow, and so I became exhausted, and didn't manage to [get around to it]. Now I've come to meet Tanja at Kozlovka (how grand it is in a two-horse sleigh [travelling] through deep, soft snow). Upon reaching there, I borrowed a piece of paper from the station manager and am writing you. I have just received your wire[394] about [Vasilij Alekseevich] Maklakov's arrival, and hence, if there is no letter from you on the Moscow train, which is late and hasn't arrived either, Maklakov will bring one, and I shall hear news from you. I never cease living with you in thought. Yesterday I received your letter to Tanja.[395] All this past while I have not been in good health — a weak stomach and despondency and dullness of thought — no work [is getting done].

Yesterday I received letters from Chertkov[396] and Tregubov[397] with descriptions of the calamities being suffered by the Doukhobors. One of them, they write, was whipped to death in a disciplinary battalion, while their families, as they write, have been driven to destitution, and are dying out from homelessness, famine and cold. They have written an appeal[398] for help from society, and I have decided to send them a thousand roubles out of our charitable fund. This money will find no better use, and they will thank you that you solicited these funds contrary to my will. So when you come, you can bring this money, or wait until I confer with Chertkov as to where to send it. It will probably be forwarded through Princess Nakashidze,[399] who has already forwarded funds to them from the Quakers.

This news is the main event for me at this time. I have also written a letter to the Head of a Caucasus battalion.[400] The train is coming. Hugs and kisses, dear friend. I await all good and joyful news from you. Our people here are healthy. Dora is disappointed that she will have to wait another month before she can have children.[401]

L. T.

31 Oct. 1896.

On the envelope: Moscow. Khamovniki. Countess Sofia Andreevna Tolstaya. Private house.

---

394 The telegram has not been preserved.
395 A letter to their daughter Tat'jana L'vovna (Tanja) dated 28 October 1896 (Manuscript Division, Tolstoy Museum).
396 Vladimir Grigor'evich Chertkov (kindred thinker) — see Letter Nº 97, Note 257.
397 Ivan Mikhajlovich Tregubov (1858–1931) — a Tolstoyan closely involved (like Chertkov) in the emigration of the Doukhobors to Canada in 1899.
398 The appeal, entitled "Pomogite!" [Help!] called upon the public to help the persecuted Doukhobors emigrate abroad; it was signed by Chertkov, Tregubov and Pavel Ivanovich Birjukov, with an Afterword added by LNT.
399 Princess Elena Petrovna Nakashidze (1868–1943) — sister to one of LNT's kindred thinkers, a Georgian political commentator and social activist named Il'ja Petrovich Nakashidze (1863–1923).
400 A letter to Lt-Colonel Morgunov of the Ekaterinodar Disciplinary Battalion, asking him to show mercy on the Doukhobors in his battalion who refused military service.
401 Dora was still suffering from complications arising from an earlier miscarriage and was waiting for her doctor's prognosis. The couple went on to bear nine children between 1898 and 1914.

Nº 191 – LEV NIKOLAEVICH TOLSTOY ❧ SOFIA ANDREEVNA TOLSTAYA
[PSS 84/669]
12 November 1896. Yasnaya Polyana.

12 November, morning.

I haven't written to you for a whole day, dear friend, and I'm already missing you. Writing is better than thinking, it only brings us closer. I received your little letter[402] in which you write about being exhausted and in ill health, and not getting to sleep until 4 o'clock [in the morning]. That's all very bad. And this is the hardest thing that torments me when I am away from you. Everything here is fine and peaceful. I shan't say it is especially cheerful, but it is not bad. Kolja and Mar'ja Aleksandrovna Dubenskaja[403] are visiting. In my view, even though they are not a bother, they are still superfluous, and it's better without them. The girls have been very busy and this makes life here more interesting for them. But they work a lot, and I am always delighted in them. — I heard from Ivan Mikhajlovich Tregubov and [Vladimir Grigor'evich] Chertkov as to where to send money to the Doukhobors, as well as details of their calamitous situation. I'm enclosing this letter. I think that very soon there will be an outpouring of sympathy for them, along with help, and it would be good to get started. The money is to be sent as follows: Tiflis, Malo-Karganovskaja [Street], Nº 11. Prince Il'ja Petrovich Nakashidze, and inside the envelope, on the paper the money is wrapped in, to write: for E. P. N. — E. P. N. is Elena Petrovna Nakashidze, and she gave this address. Please send these funds. They are needed. I think I told you about a particular precious ink-pot which they wanted to send me as a gift from some club in Barcelona. I sent them [a letter] through Tanja, saying that I would prefer the money designated for this be used for a good cause. And here they reply that, after receiving my letter, they opened a subscription in their club and collected 22,500 francs, which they are offering to me to use at my discretion. I am writing them[404] that I am very grateful, and have just the occasion to use this money — to help the Doukhobors. What will become of this, I don't know. It's very strange. And the ink-pot, they say, has [already] been ordered, and "we shall send it in any case, you can sell it and use the money as you wish".

I feel entirely healthy and buoyant. I go riding after lunch. Yesterday I went to see Gil',[405] and petitioned on behalf of a mother whose son perished in a mine, as well as for those who are being sued for legal costs — 270 roubles from one and 250 from the other — for one having broken his back and the other his leg. And it seems my petitions have not been without success.

My works — I write in the plural, since there be many that I have started[406] — are not going too successfully, but not badly either.

I finished a rough draft of my article on art, and once Masha finishes transcribing it, I shall try to edit it into its final form. — Why do you write so little about [our] mysterious [son] Misha? I've been thinking about him all day long. How it's all changed! For me in my youth

---

402 A letter dated 9 November 1896 (not included here; Manuscript Division, Tolstoy Museum).

403 Nikolaj Leonidovich (Kolja) Obolenskij (LNT's nephew and future son-in-law) and Marija Aleksandrovna Dubenskaja (*née* Tsurikova; 1854–1924), an acquaintance of the Tolstoys'.

404 A reference in particular to LNT's letter of 11 November 1896 to Demetrio Zanini (1868–1922), a stamp- and autograph-collector in Barcelona.

405 Richard Richardovich Gil' — owner of a colliery and brick factory in Moscow.

406 In November 1896 these would have included: *Christian teachings [Khristianskoe uchenie]*, *What is art? [Chto takoe iskusstvo?]* and *O vojne [On war]*.

life away from home, at boarding school, would have seemed something terrible, but *he* enjoys it.[407] How is he? Hugs and kisses to all three of you.

L. T.

N° 192 – SOFIA ANDREEVNA TOLSTAYA ❧ LEV NIKOLAEVICH TOLSTOY

[LSA 346]
13 November 1896. [Moscow]

Dear Lëvochka, it's been so long since I've received any letters, and then the other day I received three letters all at once: yours[408] — a good long one, like the ones I love because I feel you [in them], then one from Lëva, and the other from Masha.[409] I, too, feel like writing you a good letter but I shan't be able to, since I am very much in a cranky mood these days (today is better); I'm weeping, running up to four hours [at a time] through the streets to the point of exhaustion (there's always some business [to take care of]) and having fitful sleeps. Yesterday I cried ever since morning, as they were watering the rink and I had especially vivid recollections of Vanechka, and on top of that Liza and Varja[410] were talking about him, and I was quite beside myself. This can go on for days, especially when I am unable to play or listen to music. Yesterday's concert was cancelled on account of Gol'denvejzer's[411] illness and, despite my whiny mood, yesterday was especially pleasant for me: Lizan'ka and Varichka and Masha Kolokol'tsova[412] came for dinner, along with Masha Maklakova and her husband[413] (such dear young and joyful people, so much in love with each other), as well as Masha Tolstaja.[414] Misha also asked for leave from the *lycée* to attend the dinner, so there ended up being more guests than ever. Most of the time there are just the four of us: Mlle Aubert,[415] Sasha, Jusha[416] and I. Jusha moves the day after tomorrow; his mother was here the other evening, and at the same time Sergej Ivanovich Taneev[417] was here, and later [Aleksandr Nikiforovich] Dunaev came. Taneev, Dunaev and I analysed, that is, together read over and discussed Solovëv's article,[418] and Dunaev cried out with a loud voice, trying to put his *own* interpretation on everything

---

407 By this time the Tolstoys' son Mikhail L'vovich (Misha) had abandoned the *gymnasium* and entered the Tsarevich Nicholas Lycée (a Moscow boarding school).

408 Letter N° 191 of 12 November 1896.

409 A letter from Lev L'vovich (Lëva) and one from Marija L'vovna (Masha) — both dated 11 November 1896 (Manuscript Division, Tolstoy Museum)

410 LNT's nieces Elizaveta Valer'janovna (Liza, Lizan'ka) Obolenskaja and Varvara Valer'janovna (Varja, Varichka) Nagornova.

411 Aleksandr Borisovich Gol'denvejzer (a.k.a. Alexander Goldenweiser; 1875–1961) — pianist and composer; professor at the Moscow Conservatory. A close friend of LNT's, he published a number of reminiscences on the writer.

412 Marija Dmitrievna (Masha) Kolokol'tsova (D'jakov's daughter) — see Letter N° 51, Note 328.

413 Marija Leonidovna Maklakova (Masha) and her husband Nikolaj Alekseevich Maklakov — see Letter N° 170, Note 228.

414 Marija Sergeevna (Masha) Tolstaja (married name: Bibikova; 1872–1954) — daughter to LNT's brother Sergej Nikolaevich Tolstoj.

415 *Mlle Aubert* — Swiss governess employed by the Tolstoys to tutor Sasha.

416 Jurij Nikolaevich (Jusha) Pomerantsev (1878–1933) — a pupil of Sergej Ivanovich Taneev's (later a composer and conductor), who had been living with the Tolstoys in Moscow.

417 Sergej Ivanovich Taneev (also spelt: Taneyev; 1856–1915) — prominent Russian pianist and composer, professor (and later Director) of the Moscow Conservatory. He was also one of the first Esperanto users in Russia, writing several romances in Esperanto. For his relationship to SAT, see *My Life*, VI.117.

418 An article entitled "*Nravstvennaja organizatsija chelovechestva*" [*The moral organisation of mankind*] by philosopher Vladimir Sergeevich Solovëv (see Letter N° 52, Note 333).

and saying that I didn't understand Solovëv's underlying thought and that I was putting my *own* interpretation on everything — this he could agree with if that's how it actually was with Solovëv. — We took tea upstairs; Sergej Ivanovich played shuttlecock with Sasha, Misha and Jusha, but didn't play the piano; the children also chased whirligigs. Sergej Ivanovich and Dunaev left quite early, at the same time.

Today I took my music lesson with Miss Welsh, and all day I'll be staying at home; but this evening I shall go to the Shidlovskijs,[419] whom I have not visited yet. Yesterday Verochka Severtsova[420] was here with Miss McCarthy[421] and reproached me for not visiting my relatives'. Tomorrow there will be a concert by Igumnov,[422] and perhaps I shall take Sasha, if her teachers are happy with her [school performance]. Misha, too, wanted to come; tomorrow is a royal holiday,[423] and he will be spending the whole day at home; I don't know whether they would release him for the evening, too.

Yesterday morning I was awakened by Andrjusha; he was on his way to the Kursk Railway Terminal [in Moscow], apparently to see his girlfriend again. Terribly sad — why on earth do they let him out on leave?! Only for two days; he travelled fourth class, won't sleep for three days, he's thin and pale. I feel I should write to the regiment [and tell them] not to allow him leave — though I don't know whether that would be any better — what do you think? It was his arrival yesterday that drove me into this nervous mental state, but today I feel easier, though I am again waiting to see him on his way back.

None of you have said anything yet about [your] arrival, and I have no opinion whatsoever about that. If it is better for you [personally], and it's probably better for the girls, then don't think about me; somehow [my mind] has been dulled to everything, except [to make sure] all *my loved ones* are fine. Are you working, [Lëvochka,] and how are your spirits, and how is your health? I don't remember whether I wrote you about Posha, how he was here and went to Petersburg. Petja Raevskij also came once to see me. Tomorrow I shall be paying return visits to some ladies. Yesterday I was at Mme Junge's; she's still ill, like Marija Aleksandrovna,[424] and really pitiful. I was at Varichka's, she has her hands full, doesn't know how to do anything and is worried. Something was stolen from her — a new dress — and she's very upset. Well, dear friend, forgive my detailed letter; [I wrote it] so that you would understand my life and feel [the real] me. Hugs and kisses to you and the children.

S. T.

Andrjusha has just returned but keeps mum about his trip. Terribly sad!

---

419 A reference to the family of SAT's aunt, Vera Aleksandrovna Shidlovskaja (*née* Islavina).

420 Vera Petrovna (Verochka) Severtsova (married name: Istomina; 1870–1900) — SAT's first cousin, once removed.

421 Miss McCarthy — governess to the Kuzminskij family.

422 Konstantin Nikolaevich Igumnov (1873–1948) — pianist, professor of the Moscow Conservatory.

423 A reference to the birthday of the Empress-Mother Marija Fëdorovna (14 November 1847) as well as the wedding of Emperor Nicholas II to Aleksandra Fëdorovna (14 November 1894).

424 Marija Aleksandrovna Shmidt (Tolstoyan) — see Letter N° 138, Note 595.

Nº 193 – LEV NIKOLAEVICH TOLSTOY ❧ SOFIA ANDREEVNA TOLSTAYA
[PSS 84/673]
1 February 1897. Nikol'skoe-Obol'janovo.

1 February, evening.

Dear friend Sonja,
Tanja wrote you[425] about our trip and how we are living [here], the outward [events], whereas I want to write you about what [really] interests you — about my inner mental state.

I was sad when I left, and you could feel this and so you came, but your [presence] did not dissipate my heavy feeling but, rather, increased it. You spoke to me to calm me down, then said that you weren't going to the rehearsal.[426] For a long time I couldn't understand: which rehearsal? and had never thought about this. And this was all painful. Unpleasant — actually, more than unpleasant — to know that, despite the amount of time you were deliberating and deciding when to go to Petersburg, it ended up that you are going just at the wrong time. I know that you did not do this on purpose — it was all done unconsciously, as always happens with people obsessed with a single thought. I know that nothing [untoward] will happen on account of your trip, but you are unconsciously playing on this, you are working yourself up, and you're also being worked up by my reaction to it. And you are playing on this. This game (I admit) is terribly tormenting to me (and humiliating and frightfully exhausting on a moral level). You will say that you had no alternative in planning your trip. But if you think about it and analyse it for yourself, you will see that is not true: in the first place, there was no special reason for the trip; secondly, you could have gone either before or after Lent.

But you do this unconsciously all by yourself. It is terribly painful and humiliatingly shameful that a complete stranger[427] — whom we don't need at all and is of no interest [to us] — is governing our lives, poisoning the last years or [even the very last] year of our life [together] so humiliatingly and tormentingly that we have to take stock of when and where he is going and what rehearsals he is playing.

It is terrible, terrible, repulsive and shameful. And it is coming right at the end of our lives — lives lived well, cleanly, and just when we were drawing closer and closer together, despite everything that could divide us. This coming together began a long time ago, even before Vanechka's death, and was becoming tighter and tighter, especially in recent times, and then all of a sudden, instead of such a natural, good and joyful conclusion to our life of 35 years [together], this repulsive filth put its horrid stamp on everything. I know that it is hard for you and that you are suffering, too, because you love me and want to be good, but up to now you haven't been able to, and for me (it is all repulsive and shameful and) I feel terribly sorry for you, because I love you with the very best love, which is not from the flesh nor from reason, but from my very soul.

Farewell and forgive, dear friend.
Hugs and kisses.

L. T.

425 The whereabouts of this letter are unknown.
426 A reference to the rehearsal for a St. Petersburg concert featuring Sergej Ivanovich Taneev. SAT attended the concert itself on 8 February 1897. She and LNT arrived in St. Petersburg the day before to bid farewell to Vladimir Grigor'evich Chertkov and Pavel Ivanovich Birjukov, who were both being exiled abroad.
427 A veiled reference to Sergej Ivanovich Taneev, with whom SAT had a platonic relationship; her attraction to Taneev and his music helped alleviate the feeling of depression she experienced following the death of her dear son Vanechka (see Editor's Introduction, "Music and Sergej Ivanovich Taneev").

Destroy this letter.

In any case, write me and write more often.

Why do I write? In the first place, to express myself and relieve myself; the other reason — the main one — is to tell you and remind you about the whole meaning of those insignificant acts which constitute what is tormenting us, to help you save yourself from the terrible hypnotised condition in which you are living.

This can end all by itself through someone's death, — in any case, that would be a terrible end for both the one who dies and the one left behind, or it can end freely, through an inner transformation taking place in one of us. This change cannot take place in me: I cannot stop seeing what I see in you, since I see your condition very clearly; neither can I be indifferent to this. In that case — [i.e. if I were] to be indifferent — I would have to erase our whole past life [together] and rip out of my heart all those feelings I have for you. And this is something I am not only unwilling to do but incapable of doing. Hence just one solution is left, namely that you awaken from this fearful state of somnambulance you find yourself in, and return to a normal natural life. May God help you in this! I am ready to help you with all my strength — just teach me how [I can help].

For you to drop in on the way to Petersburg — I think you'd better not. It's better to come and see me on the way back. We saw each other quite recently, and I cannot help having negative feelings in connection with your trip. And I'm feeling weak and am afraid of myself. Better for you to drop in on the way home. You always say to me: "Be calm", and that insults and upsets me. I trust your honesty completely, and if I desire to know [something] about you, it's not because I don't trust you — I just want to determine how bound or free you are.

On the envelope: Moscow. Khamovniki Lane. Countess Sofia Andreevna Tolstaya. Private house.

Nº 194 – SOFIA ANDREEVNA TOLSTAYA ❧ LEV NIKOLAEVICH TOLSTOY
[LSA 347]
16 February 1897. [Moscow]

If I could have yesterday, during my departure, written you everything that I thought about you and our relationship, you would have clearly understood what is taking place in my heart. Now, however, I can neither remember nor say anything; I have been suddenly overwhelmed by life from all sides with its practical demands, and this letter will be but a piece of paper from me (it makes me feel very sorry), rather than thoughts and feelings.

I am glad that you've finally admitted that I live by feelings alone. You keep appealing to my reason and I well know that whatever I have not been able to think through with my reason has [always] been re-arranged by my heart. — Before you exhausted me with this latest unpleasant conversation,[428] I wrote our children a very heartfelt [letter] about how, when you have been cut off from so many friends,[429] we should be as close to you as possible and try to lessen the pain of their absence for you. And how many times it's happened in my life, that the more fervently I have approached my heartfelt relationship to you, the more coldly and painfully you

428 The conversation in question concerned Taneev. On 16 February 1897 LNT wrote in his diary: "Sonja [= SAT] left today after a conversation which upset her. Women do not hold themselves responsible and are unable to act according to the demands of reason. For them this sail is not set. They proceed using oars with no rudder" (PSS 53: 137).
429 A reference to the exiled Chertkov and Birjukov, among others.

thrust me aside. There was nothing particularly insulting in your words, but the animosity in your tone of voice, the reproaches which could be felt in everything, betrayed a lot of spiteful bitterness, which at once fell upon my tender heart and immediately cooled it. And what a shame that is!

How have you been spending this whole day, how is your health? I didn't want to leave you alone, and now I urge you to send me news of yourself more often. I have 26 printer's sheets of proofs to go through,[430] a mountain of letters [to read] and instructions [to give], Sasha's costume, other people's requests — there is so much to be done that I don't know how I am going to cope. — Again, life will be rushing along at frightening speed and leaving [a trail of] emptiness behind it. Tanja will tell you various stories, like Tanja Nagornova's wedding[431] and so forth. —

When I was on the train, a man jumped out the window of a 3rd-class carriage while the train was in motion and ran off so quickly that no one could catch up to him. I was very frightened, when suddenly they stopped the train.

I got a desperate letter from Andrjusha:[432] he is not allowed leave and his commander is displeased with him, and I see he is in despair. I already wrote to the commander, asking that [Andrjusha] be given leave for three days; I don't know whether they will release him [or not]. Farewell, dear friend, hugs and kisses to you. I await your letter.

Sonja.

Nº 195 – LEV NIKOLAEVICH TOLSTOY ✍ SOFIA ANDREEVNA TOLSTAYA
[PSS 84/675]
17 February 1897. Nikol'skoe-Obol'janovo.

My letter went out yesterday.[433] I am writing what I think and, most importantly, what I feel. Today is Tuesday — I got up listless, not cheerful, but healthy, and I hope [I can] work. If only I could return to the condition I was in back before Petersburg. — For God's sake, don't blame yourself for anything, since neither do I think to blame you; I blame only myself and very much in relation to you. Well, farewell for now, hugs and kisses, and, the main thing, take care of yourself, don't wear yourself out with proofreading, and be sure to summon me if you're not feeling well. — Write more details about the children; I don't know anything but yesterday's old postcards. So that's it.

L. T.

I want to write more to you following our conversation on the telephone. Sad, sad, terribly sad. I feel like weeping. There's probably a great deal of physical weakness involved, but still it's sad. There's nothing I want to do or can do. But don't think you were the cause of anything. The very reason I am writing is because in this feeling there is not the slightest hint of reproach or condemnation of you; [and besides,] there's absolutely no reason for anything like that. On the contrary, there is much in you — [for example,] your attitude toward Chertkov and Birjukov

---

430 In 1897 SAT was working on the tenth edition of LNT's collected works (in 14 volumes).

431 A reference to the marriage of Tat'jana Nikolaevna (Tanja) Nagornova (daughter to LNT's niece Varvara Valer'janovna Nagornova; 1879–?) to Grigorij Èmmanuilovich Vol'kenshtejn (1875–?).

432 SAT was exaggerating here; their son Andrej L'vovich (Andrjusha), doing his military service at Tver', was actually describing a very mild punishment, which did not seem to bother him very much.

433 In his letter of the day before (16 February 1897, not included here), LNT expressed his regret that their conversation was so heated, assuring her that he had nothing but loving feelings for her and that his resentment toward her had passed.

— that gladdens me. I have said that there is no way to influence you with logic, as [is true for] women in general, and logic irritates you [women], like some kind of illegitimate invasion. But it would be unjust to say that one cannot communicate with women through logic; one should say, [one cannot communicate with women] through logic alone or through basing one's demands for them on logic. One cannot put logic ahead of feelings; one must, on the contrary, put feelings first. In any case I know nothing; I know [only] that it is painful to me that I have caused you pain, and I would like there to be none of this, and, apart from physical causes or together with physical causes, this makes me very sad. This [mood] will pass from me. And if it should [haunt] you, write [to me], my dear, and I shall have the great joy of feeling that I'm needed. That's it. I'm being called to dinner.

L. T.

On the envelope: Moscow. Khamovniki. Countess S. A. Tolstaya. Private house.

Nº 196 – SOFIA ANDREEVNA TOLSTAYA ✌ LÉV NIKOLAEVICH TOLSTOY
[LSA 354]
6 May 1897. [Moscow]

Though Masha will be telling you, dear friend, everything about our day-to-day life, I know in myself how pleasant it is to receive a letter when someone comes, and so I'm writing to you.

I spent a marvellous day today as I was with the children and Nature: with children both living and dead. This morning I took the tram to the Arbat Gates, hired a carriage and went to the graves of my children with Sasha,[434] Sonja Kolokol'tsova[435] and our Verochka.[436] Along the way, at Vsesvjatskoe, we bought a whole bunch a flowers (bedding plants) and I brought them all to the graves. There, as usual, a great number of [local] little girls gathered around me and together with our girls they hauled earth and water to make a flower-bed and water the flowers which we planted. Then I took five snapshots of the graves. Then we went to our Kamolovs'[437] for tea and eggs; we gave the children candy, gingerbread and pieces of [coloured] fabric, and then went to Pokrovskoe[-Streshnevo] to have a walk. At Pokrovskoe it was sad to see the hostility of the estate owner[438] [manifest] everywhere: everything is fenced off by barbed wire; everywhere there are hostile guards, and the only place to go for walks is along wide, dusty roads. In the morning as we were leaving [home], Sergej Ivanovich came to tutor Misha,[439] and we left him to work with Misha, for whom Sergej Ivanovich provided great encouragement.

Now it's after eight, we've returned and just had dinner. Sonja Kolokol'tsova and Verochka say that this has been the happiest day of their lives [to date] this year. I can't get over how joyful they were! It was good for me, too; I heard the nightingales, saw and felt only the children, and today it was as though my heart returned to its normal place, while last night I felt an unbearable longing, as though something inside me had gone completely off track, but today things once again hummed along smoothly and calmly.

434 Marija L'vovna (Masha) Tolstaja; Aleksandra L'vovna (Sasha) Tolstaja (the Tolstoys' daughters).
435 Sof"ja Nikolaevna (Sonja) Kolokol'tsova (also spelt: Kolokol'tseva; married name: Perfil'eva).
436 Vera Sergeevna (Verochka) Ljapunova (*née* Arbuzova; 1882–1975) — daughter to the Tolstoys' servant Sergej Petrovich Arbuzov (see Letter Nº 4, Note 15).
437 *Kamolovs* — the family of Andrej Evstaf'evich Behrs' (SAT's father's) valet.
438 Princess Evgenija Fёdorovna Shakhovskaja-Glebova-Streshneva (1846–1924) — owner of the Pokrovskoe-Streshnevo estate.
439 Mikhail L'vovich (Misha) Tolstoj was taking piano lessons from pianist Sergej Ivanovich Taneev.

I wanted to go to Yasnaya, but I held back. I very much want to see you — [I know that] I'm missing something in this marvellous spring, something that can never be brought back, ever. In any case, I want again and again to layer this feeling of spring onto the feeling of Yasnaya Polyana — of Nature so familiar, beloved and full of memories.

There is a huge amount of proofreading to be done,[440] of even horrific proportions. Now I shall be reading together with Marija Vasil'evna,[441] who had gone to Serpukhov, and came back this afternoon.

I am sending Lëva 50 roubles. Masha took care of some other requests. That miserable Sukhotin —he has no pity for his wife,[442] even as a human being. A dry, miserable soul! He is only interested in chasing girls. At some point I shall *love* him in my own way, as he takes such pains to flatter me, to pull the wool over my eyes. But he will never deceive my true sense, and I still hate him.

But, apart from that, big hugs and kisses to you and Tanja, as well as to Lëva and Dora. I very much want to see you all.

S. Tolstaya.

N° 197 – LEV NIKOLAEVICH TOLSTOY ❧ SOFIA ANDREEVNA TOLSTAYA
[PSS 84/681]
12–13 May 1897. Yasnaya Polyana.

Read by yourself.

How was your trip and how are you doing now, my friend? Your arrival left such a strong, cheerful and good impression, too good even for me, since I am missing you [now even] more strongly [than before].

My awakening and your appearance — this is one of the strongest, happiest experiences I have ever had, and that at 69 years from a 53-year-old woman.

Yesterday I sent several Molokans off with a [special] letter and [some other] letters.[443] Methinks this letter should not insult the Tsar. What I read to you and you found risky, I threw out. Twice today we had a marvellous thunderstorm and downpour. Summer is in a hurry to come to life — the lilacs are already fading, the lime-trees are flourishing [in preparation for the bees], turtle-doves and orioles [can be heard] in the thick foliage in the depths of the garden, and the nightingale under the window is amazingly melodious. And now it is night, the stars are clear as though sprinkled [by water], and there is a fragrance of lilac and birch leaves after the rain. Serëzha arrived the same evening you left; he knocked at my window, and I joyfully cried out "Sonja!". No, [it was] Serëzha. We are all getting along, and everyone's delighted. My work is coming along not too badly. This evening I feel pretty peppy and my head almost doesn't hurt at all. Perhaps my illness is simply old age. Today Marija Aleksandrovna [Shmidt]

440 In a letter dated 3 May (not included here) LNT had written: "Please, please, do not get carried away with work, i.e. don't sit up nights. That's terribly bad for you. Take a trip out of town, walk around the garden".
441 Marija Vasil'evna Sjas'kova — a copyist for the Posrednik publishing house; a tutor to the Tolstoys' children.
442 A reference to Mar'ja Mikhajlovna Sukhotina (*née* Bode) first wife of Mikhail Sergeevich Sukhotin (see Letter N° 166, Note 192); she would pass on the following month. In November 1899 Sukhotin married the Tolstoys' eldest daughter Tat'jana L'vovna (Tanja).
443 On 10 May 1897 LNT wrote several letters in defence of the Molokans (a Christian sect similar in beliefs to the Doukhobors, but who accepted literacy and the reading of the Bible). For more on the Molokans, see: A. Donskov, *Leo Tolstoy and Russian peasant sectarian writers*, pp. 44-59. One of LNT's letters was addressed to Emperor Nicholas II, another to his childhood tutor, Englishman Charles Heath (1826–1900).

was here. Masha and Tanja are going to Tula tomorrow. If *Russkie vedomosti* carries Bulanzhe's[444] article on the Doukhobors, please send it.

Farewell, hugs and kisses to you — and Masha,[445] and [our son] Misha — how's Misha doing? Has he calmed down? If he is in love and his love is returned, he must have been studying very well, since he [should feel] calm and cheerful.

Well, that's all. It's now after midnight on the 13th.

L. T.

On the envelope: Moscow. Khamovniki 21. Countess Sofia Andreevna Tolstaya.

Nº 198 – LEV NIKOLAEVICH TOLSTOY ❧ SOFIA ANDREEVNA TOLSTAYA
[PSS 84/683]
19 May 1897. Yasnaya Polyana [Letter not received by SAT].

19 May. Night.

My dear and precious Sonja.

Your closeness with Taneev is not simply unpleasant for me — it's frighteningly tormenting. By continuing to live in such conditions, I am poisoning and shortening my life. It's been a year now that I have not been able to work and have not been living, but constantly tormenting myself. You know that. I have said this to you with irritation, and with entreaties, and for the last while I haven't said anything at all. I've tried everything, and nothing has helped: [your] closeness [with Taneev] continues and is even increasing. I can see that that's how it will go on right to the end. I can't take it any more. Initially upon receiving your latest letter, I decided I would leave [you]. And over the course of three days I lived with this thought and re-lived it, and decided that no matter how hard separation from you would be, I would at least be delivered from that terrible situation of humiliating suspicions, jerkings and heartwrenchings and would be in a condition to live [as I wish] and to do what I feel I need to do [at least] at the end of my life. And I decided to leave, but when I thought of you — not of how painful it would be for me to be apart from you, painful as that might be, — but of how it would upset and torment you, how you would suffer, I realised that I can't do this, I can't leave you without your agreement.

The situation is like this: to go on living the way we are living now is almost impossible for me. I say 'almost' impossible, since moment by moment I feel as though I am losing self-control and at any moment I might go astray and do something bad: I can't think without horror about carrying on with these almost physical sufferings which I am experiencing and cannot help experiencing.

You know this, maybe you've occasionally forgotten, or wanted to forget, but knew, and you are a good woman and you love me; nevertheless you did not want to — [though] I still think you could have [if you had wanted to] — save either me or yourself from these unnecessary, horrible sufferings.

What to do? Decide for yourself. Think it over yourself and decide what to do. Ways out of this situation seem to me to be the following: 1) the best would be to cease any kind of relations

---

444 Pavel Aleksandrovich Bulanzhe (a.k.a. Paul Boulanger; 1864–1925) — an Orientalist who espoused LNT's views; his works on Oriental religions were published by Posrednik. While he did help facilitate the Doukhobors' emigration to Canada, this particular article was not published in *Russkie vedomosti*.
445 LNT's sister Marija Nikolaevna (Masha) Tolstaja.

— and not gradually but without imagining how this might appear to others and in such a way as to free ourselves completely and immediately from this terrible nightmare which has been strangling us for a whole year now. No meetings, no letters, no little boys, no portraits, no mushroom[-hunting] with Anna Ivanovna,[446] no Pomerantsev,[447] but complete liberation, as Masha liberated herself from Zander[448] and Tanja from Popov.[449] That is one [option] and the best. [2)] A second solution would be for me to go abroad and completely part ways with you, and each of us live a life independently of the other. This solution would be the most difficult, though it is nevertheless feasible and, in any case, a thousand times easier for me than continuing with the life we have been living this [past] year.

[3)] A third solution would be [for you] to cease all relations with Taneev, and you and I both go abroad and live there until what has been the cause of all [our troubles] blows over.

[4)] The fourth is not a solution but the most frightening choice, which I cannot [even] think of without a sense of horror and despair; it would be to continue to live as we have this [past] year, assuring ourselves that this will pass and that there is nothing [happening] of any significance. You yourself, not being conscious of this, would seek out all means of getting together [with Taneev], while I would look on, observe, guess and torment myself — not with jealousy — maybe there is that feeling, too, but it's not paramount. The main thing, as I told you, is shame for you and for myself. It's the same feeling I had regarding Tanja's [relationship] with Popov, [her flirtation] with [Mikhail Aleksandrovich] Stakhovich, only a hundred times more painful. [5)] The fifth solution is the one you were proposing: that I should stop looking at the situation the way I do and wait for everything to blow over on its own, if there is anything [to blow over], as you put it. I've [already] tried this fifth solution and am convinced that I am unable to destroy in myself this feeling that torments me, as long as the incidents provoking [such a feeling] continue.

I've been experiencing this over the course of a year, and have tried with all my heart and soul and could not, and I know I cannot. On the contrary, the blows [I have suffered], all hitting one and the same spot, have brought pain in the extreme. You write[450] that it is painful for you to see Gurevich,[451] despite [the fact] that the feeling [you imagined I had for her] was completely unfounded and in any case [our working relationship] lasted [but] a few days. How should I feel after two years of distractions with very evident foundations, when you, after all that happened, set up, in my absence, daily rendezvous?[452] — if they weren't [always] daily, that wasn't your doing.

And in the same letter you write out what amounts to a programme of our future life, one that will not hinder you in your activities or joys — when I know what they are all about.

Sonja, my dove, you are a good, kind and just woman. Put yourself in my position and realise that to feel differently from the way I feel — i.e. tormenting pain and shame, is impossible, and think, my dove, of the best way to save us — not so much to save me from this, as to save

---

446 Anna Ivanovna Maslova (1844–1925) — She and her family were good friends of Sergej Ivanovich Taneev's, who often spent his summers on their Selishche estate in Orël Gubernia, occasionally inviting SAT to visit him there.

447 Jurij Nikolaevich Pomerantsev (Taneev's pupil) — see Letter № 192, Note 416.

448 Nikolaj Avgustovich Zander (violin teacher) — see Letter № 168, Note 209.

449 Evgenij Ivanovich Popov (a Tolstoyan) — see Letter № 155, Note 90. LNT was opposed to Tanja's brief relationship with Popov, whom he considered simply a womaniser.

450 A reference to SAT's letter of 14 May 1897 (not included here).

451 Ljubov' Jakovlevna Gurevich (1866–1940). SAT was disturbed that LNT had given his story *Master and man [Khozjain i rabotnik]* to Gurevich for publication in the journal which she co-edited, *Severnyj vestnik*.

452 From 1 to 20 May 1897 SAT saw Taneev five times.

yourself from even worse torments which will most certainly come in one form or another if you do not change your view on this whole affair or don't [even] make an effort. — I am writing you this third letter.[453] The first letter[453] was full of irritation, the second one I am enclosing. It will give you a better picture of my former mood. I have gone to Pirogovo to give you, and myself, the freedom to better think this over and not fall into irritation or false reconciliation.

Consider it [all] carefully before God and write me [your answer]. In any case, I'll come [to see you] soon, and we shall try to discuss everything calmly. Only we can't just leave things as they are; there could be no worse hell for me. Perhaps that's what I deserve. But you probably don't. True, there are two other solutions — your death or mine, but either one is terrible if it happens before we succeed in undoing our sin.

I am opening the letter to add this: If you choose neither the first, the second nor the third solution, i.e. if you will not completely sever all relations, will not let me go abroad with the aim of cutting off all relations, or go with me abroad for an indefinite time — of course, taking Sasha with us — but choose the muddled and unfortunate solution that we must leave everything as it was and it will all blow over, then I would ask you never to talk with me about this again. I shall keep mum, as I have this past while, waiting only for death, which is the only thing that can save us from this torture.

Another reason I am leaving,[454] is that, having gone almost five nights with no sleep, I feel my nerves are extremely weak, that if I didn't control myself, I would [simply] burst into tears, and I'm afraid I might not survive a meeting with you and everything that might come out of it.

I cannot [simply] attribute my condition to physical ill health, since I have felt extremely well this whole time without any stomach or gall trouble.

Nº 199 – LEV NIKOLAEVICH TOLSTOY ❧ SOFIA ANDREEVNA TOLSTAYA
[PSS 84/684]
8 July 1897. Yasnaya Polyana. [Letter unsent] [455]

Dear Sonja,

For some time now I have been troubled by the discrepancy between my life and my beliefs. [I] was not able to make any of you change your life, or your habits, which I myself accustomed you to, neither have I been able to leave you up to now, thinking that I would be depriving the children, while they were small, of what little influence I might have on them, and would upset you all. Neither can I go on living the way I have lived these [past] sixteen years, either struggling and irritating the lot of you, or else falling victim to those temptations to which I am accustomed and by which I am surrounded. And so I have decided now to do what I have wanted to do for a long time — *to leave*: first, because this life is becoming more and more difficult for me in my advancing years, and I feel more and more the desire for solitude and, secondly, because the children are [now] grown, my influence in the home is no longer needed, and you all have more lively interests for yourselves, which will make my absence less noticeable to you.

453 A reference to LNT's letter of 18 May 1897 (PSS 84: 284). The whereabouts of the second letter are unknown.
454 LNT was leaving to visit his brother Sergej Nikolaevich at the latter's Pirogovo estate; this letter was not delivered to SAT.
455 This letter arose out of Sergej Ivanovich Taneev's visit to Yasnaya Polyana at the beginning of July 1897, which provoked heightened arguments between LNT and his wife. As the situation eventually ended with a reconciliation, LNT did not give the letter to SAT at the time. He kept it under the seat of his chair in his study. It was given to SAT only after the writer's death in 1910.

The main thing is this: just as when the Hindus, approaching 60 years, go off into the woods, just as any elderly religious person wants to devote the final years of his life to God rather than to jokes, puns, rumours [or] tennis, so I, upon entering my 70th year, desire this quietude and solitude with all my heart, and [would like to have,] even if not full agreement, at least no crying discrepancy between my life and my beliefs, or my conscience.

If I were to do this openly, there would be requests, condemnations, arguments, complaints, and I would become weak, and might not carry out my decision, which should be fulfilled. And therefore, please forgive me if my actions cause all of you pain, [I would ask] especially you, Sonja, to release me voluntarily in your heart and not come looking for me, nor fret over me, nor condemn me.

My leaving you, [Sonja,] does not mean that I have been displeased with you. I know that you could not, literally could not and cannot see and feel the way I do, and hence could not and cannot change your life and give up something for the sake of something you are not conscious of. And so I do not blame you but, rather, think back with love and gratitude on the long 35 years of our life [together], especially the first half of this period, when you so firmly and energetically bore [the tasks] to which you felt yourself called, with the maternal self-sacrifice that was inherent in your nature. You gave to me and to the world what you could give, and gave a great deal of maternal love and self-sacrifice, and I can't help but appreciate that. But in the latter period of our life [together], in the last 15 years, we have drifted apart. I cannot think that I am to blame [for this], as I know that I have changed not for myself, not for people, but because I couldn't help it. Neither can I blame you for not following me, but I am thankful and remember, and will remember, with love what you have given me. Farewell, dear Sonja.

Lovingly yours, Lev Tolstoy.

8 July 1897.

Nº 200 – SOFIA ANDREEVNA TOLSTAYA ❧ LEV NIKOLAEVICH TOLSTOY
[LSA 363]
19 November 1897. [Moscow]

It is surprising that yesterday I was expecting a letter[456] from you *for certain*, dear Lëvochka. It should have arrived yesterday, but for some reason they brought it [only] this morning. And [now] you are responding to the very same questions which I sent you only last night, and which you could not possibly have received yet. That is, *what* are you writing? at what stage is your article on art? and about your arrival. — The question as to whether I'm angry that you're not coming is always a difficult one for me to answer. You are quite right when you say that you need solitude for your work, that you quite possibly have not that long to live and that you cherish both your time and your leisure hours. The whole world — indeed, the whole of mankind whom you serve through your writing — will discover that you are completely right.

But as an individual, as your wife, I am obliged to make a tremendous effort to admit that whether something is written slightly better or worse, or whether the number of articles you have written is lesser or greater — is more important than my personal life, my love for you, my desire to live with you and find happiness in *this* and not *somewhere else*.

456 A probable reference to LNT's letter of 17 (or 18) November 1897 (not included here), in which he excuses himself for not coming to see her, hoping she will understand his need for "quiet solitude".

I am writing this to you as reasoning, not as a challenge. I have now accustomed myself both to leading a good life without you and to not letting myself get bored. Often it even seems to me that when we are physically apart, we are more together in spirit, while when we come together materially, it is as though we drift emotionally apart. — You make the argument that there may not be that much time left to live, and I could turn that to my advantage and say: all the more reason to spend our remaining time *together*. But lately, especially after reading Beethoven's biography,[457] I've finally awakened to the realisation that people who serve mankind and receive for this the greatest gift — namely, *fame*, are no longer able to resist this temptation and cast aside anything that stands in the path to this fame or interferes with this service. Beethoven, fortunately, did not have a family — and so he was right.

All this I am mulling over as well as experiencing first-hand. You wanted to *feel* me, and I'm afraid that you will not like what I write. But somehow we have to cope with all of life's circumstances, and you will not put a stop either to the workings of your thought nor to the struggle of different feelings.

I live carefully in respect to both myself and others. Ever since we parted, right up to the present moment, I have had no feelings of spitefulness or vexation towards anyone, and I have not been — and am not [now] — angry in the least that you are not coming. Stay [at Yasnaya] for as long as it seems necessary and pleasant to you; everything here would be vexing to you, and that is harder than separation.

For example, I am again doing a lot of playing on the piano — sometimes as much as five hours [at a time]; I go to bed around three [a.m.] every night; today I didn't go out of the house, except in the evening I went to see Auntie Vera Aleksandrovna [Shidlovskaja] for a couple of hours — I had not been to see her [lately]. Boris [Vjacheslavovich] Shidlovskij came from Yalta and said that Tanja, perhaps, is leaving today, Wednesday, [to return home], and that [our] little [grandson] Andrej[458] is better. — Strange, today I tried telling my own fortune with cards, and twice I received the *death* card. We shall see!

But I am still alive, and I send you hugs and kisses. I often think of you, and feel all your days and thoughts and interests passing by me — I see them going off into articles and narratives, to England, to Chertkov's letters and so forth. Before, your writings would blend with me, and I felt as though I were omnipresent. — Your supplies must surely be running out, and you have no dates or dry breads — nothing. Is there anything I can send [you]? Farewell.

S. T.

Nº 201 – LEV NIKOLAEVICH TOLSTOY ❧ SOFIA ANDREEVNA TOLSTAYA
[PSS 84/700]
26 November 1897. Yasnaya Polyana.

Tanja passed through yesterday, and spent one day here. She left me with a joyful impression that she had liberated herself from her obsession.[459] God grant that she maintain that free state of mind she is [currently] in, and that she find her true heart as well as some good work.

---

457 Taneev had given SAT Ludwig Nohl's biography of Beethoven, *Beethovens Leben*, originally published between 1864 and 1877. The three-volume Russian translation, *Betkhoven, ego zhizn' i tvorenija* [*Beethoven, his life and works*] was published in 1892.
458 Andrej Il'ich Tolstoj (1895–1920) — son to Il'ja L'vovich Tolstoj and his first wife Sof'ja Nikolaevna (*née* Filosofova).
459 A reference to Tat'jana L'vovna's obsession with Mikhail Sergeevich Sukhotin, whom she later married.

Today I received your letter addressed to Dora,[460] from which I see that you are experiencing difficulties and ill health. And that is very painful for me, especially since I am unable to help you. — Your reasoning[461] that it is much more important and necessary for me to be with you in Moscow than for something to be written a little better or worse is patently unfair. First, the question is by no means what is more important; secondly, I am living here not just because some essay might turn out to be a little better written; thirdly, my presence in Moscow, as you very well know, could not prevent either Andrjusha or Misha from living badly, if that's what they want. Not even the strictest father in the world can stop people with full beards from living the way they feel is best; fourthly, even if the question lay in what is more important — writing what I write or what I at least think and hope (otherwise I wouldn't [bother to] work [at all]) will be read by millions and may have a good influence on millions [of people], or living in Moscow without any purpose there, in vanity, nervously and in poor [moral] health, then anyone would decide the question in favour of not going to Moscow.

This does not mean that I do not want to come to Moscow, nor that I do not wish to do all I can to make your life better, nor simply that I do not desire to be with you. On the contrary, this is something I very much desire. In fact, it means that your reasoning is very unfair, as is your reasoning (derived from Beethoven's biography) that the goal of my [literary] activity is *fame*. — Fame may be the goal of a youngster or a very empty person. For a serious person, though, especially an older person, the goal of one's activity is not fame, but the very best use of one's abilities. We are all called to live and act like a horsecar. Whether we are going to the Slavjanskij Bazaar,[462] or digging for iron ore,[463] or playing the piano, we are all obliged to do something. Any person who is not stupid and is experienced in life — and I count myself among such — cannot help but see that the only good approved by one's conscience is the carrying out of that work which he is best qualified to do and which he considers acceptable to God and beneficial to people. That is the motive which guides me in my work. As for fame, I have long asked myself: would I work in just the same way if I never knew whether people would accept my work or not, and I sincerely answer: it stands to reason that I would work in just the same way. I am not saying that I am indifferent to [other] people's approval — I enjoy such approval, but it is not the cause or motive of my activity. I am writing this in particular because I have wished for you, dear Sonja, this same kind of activity, the kind of activity that you knew was the very best you could do, and which would give you peace before God and people. You did have such activity: raising children, which you did unselfishly and did well, and you know the consciousness of a duty fulfilled, and so you know that it was by no means fame which prompted you to [engage in] such activity. You see, this is the kind of activity I desire for you — [something] I passionately desire, and would pray for if I believed that prayer could do this. What specific activity this would be, I don't know and cannot tell you, but the activity is one that is peculiar to you and important, and worthy, such that one may stake one's whole life upon, as is such activity for anyone, and this activity for you is certainly not in playing the piano and going to concerts.

460 Dora Westerlund, married to the Tolstoys' son Lev L'vovich (Lëva). The whereabouts of SAT's letter to Dora are unknown.
461 See Letter Nº 200 of 19 November 1897.
462 *Slavjanskij Bazaar* (Moscow restaurant) — see Letter Nº 62, Note 32.
463 On 12 November 1897 LNT wrote in his diary: "Lëva has found some iron ore and finds it quite natural that people will stay underground where their lives are in danger, while he makes a profit" (PSS 53: 160).

How I wish, dear Sonja, that you would accept this letter with the same unselfish love and utter self-forgetfulness, and with the sole desire for your happiness, which I am now experiencing. — Once again, my work [at the moment] is in correcting [my treatise] *On art*. I need to send it to Maude[464] and to Grot.[465] I'm thinking over something. I am quite healthy, and just now I was skating with Lëva and the village boys. And [it was] great! The whole of the Great Pond is like a mirror, after all. Why aren't you skating? I am certain it would be very good for you. But going to bed at 3 [a.m.] is very bad. Big hugs and kisses.

L. T.

Today an important point in *On art* was clarified which seemed worthless before.

On the envelope: Moscow. Khamovniki Lane, House N° 21. Countess Sofia Andreevna Tolstaya.

N° 202 – LEV NIKOLAEVICH TOLSTOY ❧ SOFIA ANDREEVNA TOLSTAYA
[PSS 84/703]
22 March 1898. Moscow.

Sunday, 4 [p.m.]

Sasha wrote you yesterday, dear Sonja, and today it's my turn. Everything's fine with us. Yesterday a mass of people [visited us]. It was probably Tanja who invited them: there were the Sollogubs[466] and the Trubetskojs,[467] and a regiment of little boys, who sang and played leap-frog.

There is nothing new in my life [at the moment]. I have finished all [my] letters and made some notes, but haven't got around to any detailed work. This morning Dunaev[468] came with the news that Brashnin[469] was dying and wanted to say farewell. I went to see him. He'll probably die any day now — the dropsy has already taken over his ribs. — And we bade our glorious, serious, simple and touching farewells, "see-you-soons".

Yesterday an American came to see me, a rich, young cotton merchant and a gentleman.[470] He is close to the American Secretary of the Interior[471] and promised to find out and let me know about the conditions for the re-settlement of the Doukhobors. — Any news from Ukhtomskij?[472] Will he decide? How are you doing? Are things fine for you? I was very worried

464 Aylmer Maude (1858–1938) and his wife Louise Maude (*née* Shanks; 1855–1939) — LNT's principal English translators during his lifetime. Louise Maude was born in Moscow, and she and her husband were friends of the Tolstoy family. They also assisted in the 1899 Doukhobor emigration to Canada.

465 Nikolaj Jakovlevich Grot (philosopher) — see Letter N° 137, Note 582.

466 A reference to the daughters of the artist Fëdor Lʹvovich Sollogub (see Letter N° 96, Note 253): Elena Fëdorovna Sollogub (1874–1933) and Vera Fëdorovna Lëvshina (*née* Sollogub; 1875–?).

467 A reference to the sisters of philosophy professor Prince Sergej Nikolaevich Trubetskoj (1862–1905): Elizaveta Sergeevna Osorgina (*née* Trubetskaja; 1865–1935) and Varvara Sergeevna Lermontova (*née* Trubetskaja; 1870–1933).

468 Aleksandr Nikiforovich Dunaev (close family friend) — see Letter N° 141, Note 631.

469 Ivan Petrovich Brashnin (1826–1898) — a Tolstoyan; a Moscow merchant, friend of Dunaev's.

470 No further details are known.

471 A reference to Cornelius Newton Bliss (1833–1911), who served as the U. S. Secretary of the Interior from March 1897 to February 1899.

472 Prince Èsper Èsperovich Ukhtomskij (1861–1921) — diplomat, poet, translator and specialist in Oriental studies, editor of the paper *Sankt-Peterburgskie vedomosti*, who supported LNT's move to help the Doukhobors emigrate to Canada. However, LNT at first accepted but then later rejected his initial suggestion that the Doukhobors be relocated to Mongolia (see Donskov 2005: 22). In the next sentence LNT asks whether Ukhtomskij will decide to publish his (LNT's) letter appealing for aid to the Doukhobors. The letter was not published in Ukhtomskij's paper.

about your travel at night with your nervous condition. Sometimes rail travel can make it worse, and sometimes it acts as a soporific.

How have things been with you? Hugs and kisses, farewell for now.

L. T.

On the envelope: Petersburg. Nadezhdinskaja [Street], Nº 18, Behrs flat. Countess S. A. Tolstaya.

Nº 203 – SOFIA ANDREEVNA TOLSTAYA ✿ LEV NIKOLAEVICH TOLSTOY
[LSA 369]
28 April 1898. Yasnaya Polyana.

Dear Lëvochka, I have not felt so sorry and sad for a long time at parting from you as on this occasion,[473] apart from that concern about leaving you that is constantly with me.

But at Yasnaya it is so intoxicatingly good, such beauty, so majestically calm (even though real spring is slow in awakening) that I am constantly in [a state of] wonder and ecstasy.

Why is it always better at Yasnaya than anywhere else? The grass is already green, the greenery is rich, the meadow is full of dark violets, and there are already little leaves [on the trees]. At Grinëvka I never saw any grass, and Nature is so desolate there. At Grinëvka [my] whole charm and joy are the little children, while in both places the older children ([our] sons and daughters-in-law) are very dear and hospitable to me.

Yesterday I was dashing about [all day], first with Dora and Lëva, and later alone. I ran about the garden, Chepyzh, and the flower-beds; I had great fun picking sweet *medunichka* apples; today I did some house-cleaning, and was overcome several times by a fretful mood. The visiting boys left quite a number of chamber-pots unemptied, [there was also] dirt, paper and boxes [lying around], and the main thing: in searching for his boots, Misha somehow broke the door lock to my room. Such impudence, it almost drove me to tears. There were screws to take out, repairs to be made, etc. The bottom of your unemptied new wooden pail got warped, and it's no longer good for anything; there was a large piece of ice [left] in it, which started to melt! — But these are all little annoyances from people, while from God [there is] Nature, warmth and spring — all that is charming! You can move here whenever you wish; today I changed the window [frames] and cleaned your room, which in two or three days will be nice and warm and dry.

I really hope you've written me a letter at Moscow. You were depressed all the time and it seems you had even more to say, and it made me feel like I constantly had a stone on my heart. If only I could, how much I would *like* to cheer you, make you happier, help you in your work, help you to be joyous, healthy and at peace! Apparently I no longer have the ability or capacity to do that, and that is a [source of] great suffering for me. If only you knew how [hard] I always *try* to do it with all my heart and soul!

There is no news from home, and I doubt that this letter, too, will reach you. I wrote to Andrjusha at Bastyevo, [but] he didn't receive the letter; Sasha wrote me, [too,] and I didn't receive it. Yesterday Lëva sent you some spinach and apples at Bastyevo care of a trainman. This evening I am going to Moscow; there's no need for me to go to Tula. The lawsuit has been settled[474] and

473 LNT and SAT were visiting their son Il'ja L'vovich and his wife Sof'ja Nikolaevna on their Grinëvka estate. Towards the end of April 1898 SAT left for Yasnaya Polyana while LNT stayed on at Grinëvka.
474 The Tolstoys' neighbour Vladimir Aleksandrovich Bibikov (see Letter Nº 68, Note 73) wanted to take back some land they had purchased from his father and launched a lawsuit, which he subsequently lost (according to an annotation by SAT, *Letters to L. N. Tolstoy*, p. 684).

now they are going to send a court official here to summon witnesses concerning the land ownership, and that will be the end of it.

I am now dashing out for a walk and to do some planting; I really don't want to leave here. And it's very nice staying on with Lëva and Dora, because they, too, like to plant, decorate and clean, and we would work marvellously [together].

How are you getting along with the soup-kitchens? Dearest, please don't tire yourself out and do take care of yourself. Hugs and kisses to you and to everyone at Grinëvka. Write me a good, *sincere* letter, not a contrived one.

Your Sonja Tolstaya.

Nº 204 – LEV NIKOLAEVICH TOLSTOY ✍ SOFIA ANDREEVNA TOLSTAYA
[PSS 84/705]
30 April 1898. Grinëvka.

Dear Sonja,

I wrote a few words to you at Yasnaya, along with a postcard from Sasha, but that was probably too late to reach you. Yesterday I received your kind letter[475] from Yasnaya. — I feel fine — not so weak as I was when you saw me, but not so cheerful as I would like and as I sometimes am. Have written almost nothing. Yesterday I went to Nikol'skoe,[476] where I finished setting up some soup-kitchens, and to see Varen'ka.[477] She bustles about with her house-cleaning. Her Tanja[478] sits in her own room and reads. Serëzha and I sat for more than an hour, but she still didn't come out. Her husband is here, but wasn't at home; he'd gone to the village to buy kerosene and nails. Varen'ka is clear-headed enough, but her children are just the opposite.

When Protashinskij[479] protested against the soup-kitchens the other day, Iljusha went to a Red Cross meeting at Mtsensk, and yesterday he went to Orël to see the Governor,[480] from whom he received permission for the soup-kitchens. I saw Stakhovich,[481] who wants to come here on Saturday. Today he went off to a fair with Andrjusha. Sonja[482] is seriously trying to help, but not altogether efficiently, so that for the sake of the conscientious carrying out of these relief efforts in the eyes of the donors, I'm glad I came.

The other day I was in Lapashino, where we also need to open soup-kitchens. Now I'll go through Bastyevo, where I'll hand over this letter, again in the direction of Spasskoe,[483] where I shall set up soup-kitchens. We haven't purchased any flour yet. I'm waiting for a reply from Voronezh.

Here I am doing fine in all respects. Everybody's nice to me, both the grown-ups and the children. Iljusha is much better when he's at home than when he's away from it.

I don't have any [news] from Moscow. It's been more than a week, it seems. And it's [probably] better this way. I'd just like to know more about the children, especially our daughters, at

475 Letter Nº 203 of 28 April 1898.
476 A reference to Sergej L'vovich [Serëzha] Tolstoj's Nikol'skoe-Vjazemskoe estate.
477 LNT's niece Varvara Valer'janovna (Varen'ka) Nagornova, whose estate was located about 9 versts from Grinëvka.
478 Tat'jana Nikolaevna (Tanja) Vol'kenshtejn (Varvara Valer'janovna's daughter) and Tat'jana's husband Grigorij Ėmmanuilovich Vol'kenshtejn — see Letter Nº 194, Note 431.
479 Aleksej Alekseevich Protashinskij — a landowner in Mtsensk.
480 Aleksandr Nikolaevich Trubnikov (1853–1922) — governor of Orël Gubernia (1894–1901).
481 Mikhail Aleksandrovich Stakhovich (poet) — see Letter Nº 97, Note 258.
482 Sof'ja Nikolaevna (Sonja) Tolstaja (*née* Filosofova; wife to the Tolstoys' son Il'ja L'vovich Tolstoj).
483 A reference to Spasskoe-Lutovinovo, Turgenev's estate (see Letter Nº 24, Note 160).

least about their teeth. Now *you* will be writing [from there]. This morning I wrote letters, dealt with old ones, fearing that there might be new demands for replies.

Well, it seems I've written everything of importance. My requests to you are the following:

1) The oblong address book on the table — please send it as soon as you can. 2) There should be a book [there, called] *Dvadtsat'-pjat' let na Kavkaze* [*Twenty-five years in the Caucasus*], Part 2 by Ziserman.[484] It should be on the bookshelf. 3) Tell Ivan Ivanovich Gorbunov[485] that if the lady who wants to come can pay her own expenses, let her come. There will be a lot to do, and I don't feel like asking Andrjusha [to help]. He wouldn't refuse, but he would not do it willingly. 4) Misha promised me he would go to the photographic shop in Tverskaja [Street], near Filippov's, and ask the retouch artist Krasnov[486] for [copies of] my book *The Kingdom of God [Tsarstvo Bozhie]*, and have Sasha[487] bring it to Yasnaya. Well, you see how many requests I have made!

Hugs and kisses to you. I hope they are not bothering you and that you aren't getting flustered, and are sleeping well, and retiring early. Don't sit up nights. This is terribly harmful, especially to you. —

My letter is not the one you were wishing for, but I can't do any differently; by my handwriting I see that I am not in strong spirits.

On the envelope: Moscow. Khamovniki Lane, 21. Countess Sofia Andreevna Tolstaya.

Nº 205 – LEV NIKOLAEVICH TOLSTOY ♨ SOFIA ANDREEVNA TOLSTAYA
[PSS 84/728]
19 October 1898. Yasnaya Polyana.

I'm terribly ashamed, dear Sonja, that I have not written to you in such a long time. Lately I have had a cold — either one left over from the last time, or a new one — and I felt sluggish and didn't get around to it, or someone interfered. Now it is warm and my cold has gone, but my head aches — from stove fumes, apparently. My work[488] is having its ups and downs. It's more clear in my imagination, but not yet on paper. I don't feel myself in full possession of my [creative] forces which are needed for this [work]. We had a visitor — an Englishman from the Hawaiian Islands[489] — to negotiate the resettlement of the Doukhobors there. Unfortunately [he came] too late. He captivated us all with his description of these marvellous islands. The only other visitor was Andrjusha,[490] who also captivated us ([at least] me) with the transformation which is undoubtedly taking place in him. The Gospel is so right in saying that one sheep

---

484 Arnol'd L'vovich Ziserman (1824–1897) — a book LNT needed for his work on the story *Hadji-Murat [Khadzhi-Murat]*.

485 Ivan Ivanovich Gorbunov-Posadov (Posrednik publisher) — see Letter Nº 174, Note 270.

486 Vasilij Filippovich Krasnov (1878–?) — peasant writer who served as a photographic retouch artist.

487 The Tolstoys' daughter Aleksandra L'vovna (Sasha) Tolstaja.

488 LNT was working on his novel *Resurrection [Voskresenie]*.

489 On 20 October 1898 LNT wrote to Chertkov: "I received a letter from a Mr. Marlsden *[sic!]* from Petersburg, saying he was an agent [facilitating] relocation to the Hawaiian Islands and that he had come to Russia specifically to talk with me about the relocation of 3000 (he knows only about the 3000 that have been granted [the right to] relocation).... I considered it my duty, despite the fact that negotiations with Canada had already progressed quite far, to invite him. He came yesterday and I was impressed by the comparative advantage of the terms of relocation to the Hawaiian Islands" (PSS 88: 137). This meeting was also described by SAT in *My Life* (VII.50), although there researchers identified the visitor in question (from external sources) as Nicholas Russel (a.k.a. Nikolaj Konstantinovich Sudzilovskij; 1850–1930). No further information is known concerning a "Mr. Marlsden", whose name LNT gives in this English spelling.

490 The Tolstoys' son Andrej L'vovich (Andrjusha) Tolstoj.

lost and found is worth more than 99.[491] Then there came a remarkable elderly chap from Simbirsk Gubernia, a Christian and a rationalist who is quite remarkable if you understand him. I have news of you through [what I have heard from] Anet[492] and it seems you are, if not in a completely peaceful mental state, at least not in a disturbed state. Our girls are good, even good-looking; I wish the same for you. I'm joking, that's not what I wish at all. I wish you tranquillity and stability which will keep you satisfied. It always frightens and troubles me when you talk of your instability. — Don't believe you are weak, but believe that you are omnipotent, and you will be omnipotent in the spiritual realm.

Lately I have not stepped out of the house nor gone horseback riding. We are having marvellous autumn weather.

Farewell, my dear, hugs and kisses to you, our dear, laughing Sasha, and Misha, who has the capacity to be dear.

L. T.

N° 206 – SOFIA ANDREEVNA TOLSTAYA ❧ LEV NIKOLAEVICH TOLSTOY
[LSA 382]
9 November 1898. [Moscow].

It is true, dear Lëvochka, that you are now writing me more often, for which I'm grateful. Archer[493] was here today and brought your letter[494] and he was brought here by a young lady [named] Jenken,[495] and it was difficult to hold conversation with Archer: you'd ask him a question and he would answer, and then again silence. These English are strange birds! So Serëzha has up and left with Suller?[496] Poor Serëzha, with no family! *All* [my] children pull at my heartstrings, each in their own way; if there is no real acute unhappiness, at least each is unhappy in their own way.

I made copies[497] for the censorship board, and last night I read to a few people your superb and touching excerpt. I really enjoyed it, as did everyone else. And when the excerpt ended, we were desperate to know: *what* comes next — there is such a strong desire to peer more deeply into the life and soul of this mother, who instantly touches a chord. On Saturday I took one copy right off to the censorship board, then gave another copy to the school trustee for his approval, and then I still had to pass it by the police. It's simply beastly what they put us through — just to read a fictional story, and have to pass it through a dozen ordeals [to get it published].

Read my letter to Masha; I described there Misha and Sasha. As regards myself I shall only offer this: I remember your saying there is a senior age when you stop and begin to hesitate about which way to go: uphill, i.e. to moral perfection, or downhill, i.e. to an empty,

---

491 See Luke 15: 7.
492 Anna Aleksandrovna (Anet) Behrs, wife to SAT's brother Aleksandr Andreevich (Sasha) Behrs.
493 Herbert Archer — a young Englishman; an associate of Chertkov's English "Svobodnoe Slovo" publishing house. He subsequently spent several years in Canada with the Doukhobors.
494 A letter dated 2 November 1898 (not included here; PSS 84 :333–34).
495 Natal'ja Aleksandrovna Ienken (Dutch name: Jenken; 1863–1927) — an artist of Dutch descent who shared LNT's views.
496 Leopol'd Antonovich Sullerzhitskij (actor who escorted Doukhobors to Canada) — see Letter N° 177, Note 320.
497 A reference to LNT's unfinished story *Mother (Notes of a mother)* [Mat' (Zapiski materi)], which he began in 1891.

meaningless material life. You cited Vasen'ka Perfil'ev[498] as an example of this sudden moral fall. And here I am feeling with horror that I am rapidly heading downhill. Sometimes with tears and torment in my heart I feel the desire to rise, to learn again how to pray and be wise, and I can't; right now I am experiencing a terrible longing and I seek out entertainment, and then I repent for having sewn a [new] dress or gone to the theatre, or chattering nonsense, — and it gets worse and worse. Could it be that this is incorrigible? Yesterday, partly from boredom, partly to make Sunday entertaining for the children, I — didn't invite [her myself] but — agreed to Lavrovskaja's[499] offer to sing for me. And she sang the whole evening, and [Sergej Ivanovich] Taneev played, and I read your excerpt. Besides these two musicians, there was my brother Sasha and his wife, Uncle Kostja, Marusja with her brother,[500] and Pomerantsev,[501] who turned the pages. We spent a very fine and serious evening — all in art. [Our daughter] Sasha has not been going out anywhere these days and was in ecstasy; my brother Sasha, too. Have you ever heard Lavrovskaja [sing]? She has a marvellous voice, but she is a pitiful woman, devastated by suffering, 50 years old, but when she sings, she comes completely alive; she has a fantastic understanding of music. She paid a visit to me [this] autumn, a visit which I then returned, and afterwards we would meet at concerts, and she said she wanted to do me some kind of favour in return for my tenderness towards her; and so I called upon her to entertain [us], and that was very nice. The guests left before 12 o'clock, and Misha has never gone anywhere astray these days; he's always either stayed at home or come home early, and been very nice to me.

Why don't you write anything about Tanja? I'm terribly disappointed in Masha; I feel frightened for her, since her life is not going at all the way it should be. And her husband is not serious, and her child and her health and her situation[502] — it seems as though it is all just *temporary*, and will be better *later on*. But in the meantime it only gets worse and worse.

I'm delighted at being with you again. But it couldn't be as good a second time as on this [past] occasion. It was so naturally joyful, easy and loving. — Well, we can [certainly] hope that it will be this good again, and maybe even better. I await your directions concerning [my] trip — where [am I] to go? Hugs and kisses, dear friend.

Yours, S. Tolstaya.

Today half my head was aching terribly. Imagine, I sleep only three hours every night, from 3 to 6. It's got to the point of driving me completely mad. Just these past two nights. You have snow, and we haven't had even a single flake. Only it feels like frost is in the air, while the sky is clear.

498 Vasilij Stepanovich (Vasen'ka) Perfil'ev served as Governor of Moscow (1878–87); he was married to LNT's second cousin Praskov'ja Fëdorovna Tolstaja (see Letter Nº 16, Note 94). LNT used him as one of the prototypes for Stiva Oblonskij in *Anna Karenina*.

499 Princess Elizaveta Andreevna Tserteleva (*née* Lavrovskaja; 1845–1919) — opera singer and singing teacher.

500 Marija Alekseevna (Marusja) Maklakova (1877–?) with her brother Vasilij Alekseevich Maklakov (see Letter Nº 174, Note 7).

501 Jurij Nikolaevich Pomerantsev (pianist) — see Letter Nº 192, Note 416.

502 On 2 June 1897 the Tolstoys' daughter Marija L'vovna (Masha) Tolstaja married her second cousin, once removed, LNT's grand nephew Prince Nikolaj Leonidovich Obolenskij (see Letter Nº 70, Note 893), who was penniless and jobless. She had just had a stillbirth.

Nº 207 – SOFIA ANDREEVNA TOLSTAYA ❧ LEV NIKOLAEVICH TOLSTOY
[LSA 388]
9 February 1899. [Kiev]

Well, now I've arrived [at Kiev] and I don't know quite what to say about Tanja's situation;[503] I don't really know what's so dangerous about such diseases; [but] we're all already fearful — [we can] clearly imagine how it could actually be dangerous, and how the end might very well be near — and so we all cheer each other up and don't allow ourselves to jump to any conclusions.

The bad thing is that the inflammation has today turned out to be creeping, i.e. after yesterday's crisis, manifested in extreme perspiration, [Tanja's] temperature had risen to higher than 39° by nightfall; but this morning it was 37.6, and right now it's 38.1. That means the inflammation has not yet run its course, and nobody can predict what the result will be. The young doctor is staying close to Tanja, and a professor comes three times a day. The professor administering the treatment recommended only Chirkov,[504] whom we [too] very much wanted, but he is still suffering from an injured lung (not his arm [as was earlier rumoured]), and even though he is now out of danger, he could not be called to participate in the consultation.

Tanja was delighted [to see] me; she repeated several times: "I'm happy, how happy I am [to see] you." Both yesterday and this morning she kept talking about me and asking that I be called [to her side]. I am terribly glad that I came; [Tanja's husband] Sasha wept when he saw me. Yesterday, they say, during the time of crisis, Tanja called her husband and all her children together and started to say her farewells; the other day they administered communion and confession to her. Today she says to me: "If I am dying, tell me, and I'll know and prepare myself; I'm not afraid of death but I want to know." To Masha[505] she said: "I'm not afraid of death, but I don't want to die." — In general, she is still relatively strong; for example, she writes her wishes on paper so as to avoid talking; it is difficult for her to talk and breathe. Her appearance is similar to that of any ill person; only her eyes are quite dimmed and pitiful-looking. Oh, how painful it is for me to look at her! I know all her thoughts, her emotions; I know how she feels about me, the children, her husband, about life — and all at once you sense this wall, which always pops up between the importance and seriousness of dying and the flightiness of our everyday life. Even if Tanja manages to lift herself out of this disease, nevertheless now, at this moment, her condition is closer to non-life than to life; she is so weak, so concentrated on her disease, listening to what is going on inside her.

[Her daughter] Masha is here, she is efficient, takes good care of her mother and is very precious. Sasha is feeling very tense; he is either crying, or running out to buy her some cotton wool, or talkative and even laughing. The young boys do not feel stressed at all and all four of them[506] are continuing to look out for their own interests.

Vera[507] is disturbed most of all. She is frightfully exhausted, and talks despairingly about the possibility of her mother's death. Of course for her, as well as for Sasha, this would be a terrible misfortune, it would leave them without a single shred of hope or comfort.

---

503 SAT went to Kiev to visit her sister Tat'jana Andreevna (Tanja) Kuzminskaja, who was seriously ill with pneumonia.
504 Dr. Vasilij Vasil'evich Chirkov (1846–1907) — Kiev University professor, whom the Tolstoys had got acquainted with in Moscow as assistant to Dr. Grigorij Antonovich Zakhar'in (see Letter Nº 34, Note 210).
505 Marija Aleksandrovna (Masha) Èrdeli (*née* Kuzminskaja; second daughter to SAT's sister Tanja) — see Letter Nº 151, Note 64.
506 The Kuzminskijs' four boys: Mikhail (1875–1938), Aleksandr (1880–ca1930), Vasilij (1882–1933), Dmitrij (1888–1937).
507 Vera Aleksandrovna Kuzminskaja (third daughter to SAT's sister Tanja) — see Letter Nº 43, Note 281.

What do I think? I don't know, at the moment. I'm frightened by Tanja's estrangement from everyone, by her vomiting of the medicine she took. Another bad thing is that her hearing has started to go; that happened to Nastja Safonova[508] on the eve of her death. — Well, God's will be done!

I had a good trip with the through-train service; I met some very pleasant ladies. Lëva is doing very well;[509] he was very nice to me. But my head is going rather wild, and the trip and tension of anticipating what I would find, and Tanja's appearance — all that did something to me, which I haven't yet been able to sort out in my mind. Take care of yourself while I'm gone, and do write. Hugs and kisses to all; I'll be keeping you posted.

S. Tolstaya.

Nº 208 – LEV NIKOLAEVICH TOLSTOY ❦ SOFIA ANDREEVNA TOLSTAYA
[PSS 84/741]
15 February 1899. Moscow.

It's very difficult [for me], dear Sonja, to write to you, [as] I don't know what situation [you're in]. Just now I received your 3rd letter[510] — a letter on the verge of hopelessness, and [we] would be in despair if it were not for your encouraging telegram the other day. I cannot read through your letter[511] without shedding tears. I also feel how extremely tense your situation is, and my only regret is that I cannot personally be with you. All our news [here] is so pale in comparison with what is going on with all of you. How good and true she[512] was in saying that religious feeling grows in those moments when you come face to face with God. If only we could get accustomed to summoning this increasing faith at times other than death! [Our daughter] Tanja's caught a cold and has the sniffles. Misha's been ill. The headmaster[513] was here; I spoke with him, trying to support his favourable approach to Misha. My spine hurts, and I am experiencing considerable weakness and a runny nose — I am not going out. Nothing special has been happening. No news from Serëzha. Bakunin[514] has arrived [back] from Canada. He didn't see Serëzha.[515] I only know from an English newspaper clipping which Chertkov sent that they have been released from quarantine and have gone to Winnipeg. Serëzha asked you to write to him in New York, where I wrote him today, along with Crosby,[516] who, I hope, will give him a good reception there.

We are really looking forward to receiving a telegram. If it doesn't come tomorrow, I'll make an enquiry. I'm not writing anything [at the moment]. [At the moment] I'm feeling disgusted

508 Anastasija Vasil'evna (Nastja) Safonova (1883–1898) — daughter to pianist and conductor Vasilij Il'ich Safonov (1852–1918), who was a Moscow acquaintance of the Tolstoys'.
509 SAT saw her son Lev L'vovich (Lëva) at Yasnaya Polyana, where she stopped en route.
510 The whereabouts of this letter, as well as of the telegram mentioned, are unknown.
511 Letter Nº 207 of 9 February 1899.
512 A reference to SAT's sister Tanja Kuzminskaja.
513 Lev Aleksandrovich Georgievskij (1860–after 1917) — future Headmaster of the Katkov Lycée (1906–08).
514 Dr. Aleksej Il'ich Bakunin (1874–1945) — surgeon; nephew to anarchist Mikhail Aleksandrovich Bakunin (1814–1876); deputy representing Tver' Gubernia in the Second State Duma. He accompanied the first boatload of Doukhobors to Canada, along with actor Leopol'd Antonovich Sullerzhitskij.
515 Sergej L'vovich (Serëzha) Tolstoj accompanied the second boatload of Doukhobors a few weeks later, leaving Batoum on 23 December 1898 and arriving at Halifax on 15 January (27 January N. S.) 1899 (see Donskov 1998: 278–81).
516 Ernest Howard Crosby (American social activist) — see Letter Nº 172, Note 247. For LNT's letter to him, see PSS 90: 308–09.

with my work. I have just finished all my letters, along with a very simple article with an accounting of how the funds were distributed.[517]

Still no rest from visitors. — You see, it's impossible to write to you, as I don't know the current state of your affairs, or of your mental state.

In any case I offer you tender hugs and kisses and I share all your feelings in my heart. Hugs and kisses to [Tanja's daughters] Masha, Vera and everyone.

L. T.

On the envelope: To give to Countess S. A. Tolstaya.

N° 209 – SOFIA ANDREEVNA TOLSTAYA ♠ LEV NIKOLAEVICH TOLSTOY
[LSA 396]
23 September 1900. [Moscow]

I just got up, and the first thing I wanted to do was to write to you, dear Lëvochka, and remember that day[518] that united us for these many years we have spent together. I feel very sad that we are not together today, but still I look upon you and the reminiscences of our life together all the better, all the more deeply and tenderly, and I do want to thank you for the happiness which you gave me in times past, even while I regret that it has not continued throughout the rest of our life so strongly, fully and peacefully.

It's terribly disappointing that [our daughter] Sasha did not write me; I am worried about your health; she probably forgot to send it care of the artel worker or didn't post it in time. How are your furuncles? How has the shift to cold weather affected you?

There's a lot of boring, fussy work here; I'm coping little by little. For two days I dined at the Maklakovs',[519] [another] two days at my brother Sasha's. In the evenings I feel so tired that I stay home, take care of my accounts and notes and play a little on the piano. Yesterday I was invited over by Elena Pavlovna Raevskaja,[520] and I spent a very pleasant evening with her, her sister Davydova and two of the Samarins: Aleksandra Pavlovna and Pëtr Fëdorovich. I came home at 11 p.m. since it is hard for the nanny to wait up for me. Today once again I shall be at home, only I wanted to go to mass at the palace church where we got married; I don't know whether I shall manage that. Back home at Yasnaya I felt bold enough to make plans to go to the theatre, but here I am so exhausted, I'm simply not up to any entertainment.

I went to see Krjukov;[521] he says that my *vision* has improved, but that the black spot will not soon go away, as the inner eye has little communication with the organism, and so the exchange of matter within the eye proceeds frightfully slowly. He gave me some ointment to massage my eyes; some drops [to apply] when the eyes are inflamed.

---

517 LNT's account of the distribution of funds collected for the Doukhobors (as of 15 February 1899) was published in *Russkie vedomosti* (1899, N° 62, 4 March 1899).
518 23 September 1862 was the Tolstoys' wedding day; they were married in the Church of the Nativity of the Blessed Virgin in the Moscow Kremlin. SAT always tried to take a picture of herself with LNT on their wedding anniversary.
519 A reference to one of the families related to Aleksej Nikolaevich Maklakov.
520 Elena Pavlovna Raevskaja (*née* Evreinova; wife to Ivan Ivanovich Raevskij) and her sister Ekaterina Pavlovna Davydova (*née* Evreinova; wife to Nikolaj Vasil'evich Davydov) — see Letter N° 159, Note 124. Their other sister, Aleksandra Pavlovna Samarina (*née* Evreinova; 1836–1905) was married to Pëtr Fëdorovich Samarin (1830–1901), the nobility representative for Tula Gubernia in the latter half of the 1870s and an old acquaintance of LNT's.
521 Dr. Aleksandr Aleksandrovich Krjukov (oculist) — see Letter N° 185, Note 370.

Tomorrow I want to go to Petrovskoe-Razumovskoe with Marusja[522] to have a look at my grandson. Tomorrow is Sunday, and so no work is permitted. Also tomorrow morning, I shall be going to the shelter.[523] As for the evening, I still don't know what I shall be doing. On Monday I'll be doing some shopping and probably Tuesday evening I'll head home to Yasnaya. Send [a carriage] for us Wednesday morning to Kozlovka, for 8:30.

How are my projects doing at Yasnaya? How are the diggers? In any case work is more joyful in the country than in the city.

I hope, dear Lëvochka, that you will write me at least once for old times' sake.

Hugs and kisses to you; take care of yourself and let us live longer and better together.

Yours, Sonja Tolstaya

N° 210 – LEV NIKOLAEVICH TOLSTOY ❧ SOFIA ANDREEVNA TOLSTAYA
[PSS 84/768]
31 December 1900. Moscow. [Preceded by SAT's N° 10U, 28 December 1900]

31 Dec.

I'm very sorry, dear Sonja, that because of the holidays my letters and telegrams didn't reach you on time. I made special efforts, knowing your concern, to keep you apprised right away of everything I knew. But because of a series of co-incidences, you left Yasnaya without receiving anything. Yesterday I got your brief letter[524] from Arkhangel'skoe — at least I know where you are. Yesterday I went to meet the express train, hoping to find Westerlund,[525] but he wasn't on it. I only hope that Tanja's situation[526] continues to improve, and that you don't catch cold in the move; I'm glad you are at Kochety and are resting from the difficult feelings you experienced at Yasnaya. We are completely healthy [here]. Sasha was at the Martynovs'[527] yesterday. Misha is here. This evening during the New Year's celebrations at the Glebovs'[528] his engagement to Lina was announced. It's good that I have no lingering superstitions left. The fact that we are greeting the New Year apart doesn't bother me in the least, as long as we are close in spirit. Hugs and kisses to you and our dear clever Tanja.

L. T.

On the envelope: Orlov-Grjazskaja Railway. Arkhangel'skoe Station. Tat'jana L'vovna Sukhotina.

---

522 SAT was planning to go with Marija Alekseevna (Marusja) Maklakova (see Letter N° 206, Note 500) to the Rachinskijs' Petrovskoe-Razumovskoe estate (owned by Sergej L'vovich's in-laws) to see her grandson Sergej Sergeevich Tolstoj (1897–1974).

523 SAT was a trustee of a children's shelter in Moscow.

524 A postcard dated 29 December 1900 (Manuscript Division, Tolstoy Museum).

525 Dr. Ernst Westerlund, father of Lev L'vovich's (Lëva's) wife Dora (see Letter N° 185, Note 374), who was coming from Sweden (through Moscow) to Yasnaya Polyana to comfort his daughter and Lëva after the death of her two-year-old firstborn son Lëvushka (1898–1900); this was a devastating blow for the young couple.

526 The Tolstoys' daughter Tat'jana L'vovna (Tanja) experienced a stillbirth. Her sick husband Mikhail Sergeevich Sukhotin was taking medical treatment abroad, and so SAT went to comfort her daughter at the Sukhotin's Kochety estate.

527 On 30 December 1899 the Tolstoys' daughter Aleksandra L'vovna (Sasha) visited Viktor Nikolaevich Martynov and his wife Sof'ja Mikhajlovna Martynova (see Letter N° 167, Note 204).

528 Vladimir Petrovich Glebov (1850–1926) — member of the State Council (as of 1906), and his wife Sof'ja Nikolaevna Glebova (*née* Princess Trubetskaja; 1853–1936) — both Tolstoy family acquaintances; major landowners in Tula and Moscow. Their daughter Aleksandra Vladimirovna (Lina) Glebova (1880–1967) married the Tolstoys' son Mikhail L'vovich (Misha) Tolstoj on 31 January 1901. She wrote a book of memoirs of LNT.

N° 211 – SOFIA ANDREEVNA TOLSTAYA ❧ LEV NIKOLAEVICH TOLSTOY
[LSA 402]
22 April 1902. Sevastopol'.

Our trip to Balaklava was extraordinarily easy and we were there before we knew it. The Baydar Valley was such a delight to our gaze with its fresh spring greenery; it was green everywhere, and gave our eyes a real rest from the grey, heavy rocks of our Gaspra.[529] From Balaklava on a warm wind blew, and through the Sevastopol' barrens, as well as in the city itself, my face and head were literally burning. We've got our tickets and are leaving in an hour. I am concerned about everything that is happening in Gaspra; I worry, but I try not to lose my self-control in this regard.

Hugs and kisses to all. Has Sasha[530] sent my telegrams?

N° 212 – LEV NIKOLAEVICH TOLSTOY ❧ SOFIA ANDREEVNA TOLSTAYA
[PSS 84/777]
2 May 1902. Yasnaya Polyana.

It is with great pleasure that I am keeping my promise — to write to you, dear friend Sonja, all the more so since I am able to give you good news about myself and all of us. I am in much better health than when you [last] saw me, though, as always, I have a weak stomach. The weather is damp — I don't do much walking so as not to get soaked. I'm working[531] and reading. Last night I had a good chance to work through my longstanding inner thoughts on the definition of life.[532] Now I am going to take tea with Lëva, Sasha, Julija Ivanovna[533] and the doctor,[534] whose voices I am [now] hearing in the salon. Today [I received] a dear letter from Naryshkina.[535] How is Boris Nikolaevich[536] doing? Send him my regards through Serëzha.

Farewell, hugs and kisses to you.

L. T.

N° 213 – SOFIA ANDREEVNA TOLSTAYA ❧ LEV NIKOLAEVICH TOLSTOY
[LSA 404]
8 October 1903 2 p.m. [Moscow]

This morning I received your telegram, dear Lëvochka, saying that all is well and that Abrikosov[537] has arrived. Thank God you are healthy. As I suspected, to get everything done in three

---

529 In early October 1901 the Tolstoys left Yasnaya Polyana for the Crimea, where they had been invited to spend the winter at the Gaspra estate of Countess Sof'ja Vladimirovna Panina (1871–1957), a family friend. During their stay there SAT made one trip back to Moscow and Yasnaya Polyana (in April 1902, through Sevastopol') with an unidentified companion.
530 A reference to the Tolstoys' daughter Aleksandra L'vovna (Sasha).
531 LNT was working on his novel *Hadji-Murat [Khadzhi-Murat]* between 1896 and 1904.
532 LNT's diary for 1903 contains many notes on the "definition of life" (see PSS 54).
533 Julija Ivanovna Igumnova (1871–1940) — an art student, who often stayed with the Tolstoys at Yasnaya Polyana.
534 Dr. Dmitrij Vasil'evich Nikitin (1874–1960) — LNT's personal physician (1902–04).
535 Aleksandra Nikolaevna Naryshkina (*née* Chicherina; 1839–1919) — lady-in-waiting.
536 Boris Nikolaevich Chicherin (1828–1904) — philosopher, historian; a long-time acquaintance of LNT's; brother to Aleksandra Nikolaevna Naryshkina.
537 Khrisanf Nikolaevich Abrikosov (1877–1957) — a kindred thinker and assistant to LNT. In 1905 he married LNT's grandniece Natal'ja Leonidovna Obolenskaja (1881–1955) — sister to Nikolaj Leonidovich Obolenskij (see Letter N° 206, Note 502).

days is impossible. A day and a half has gone by already, and I've not managed to get much done. Yesterday I was detained for a long time at the bank, where I met Aleksej Maklakov,[538] who persuaded me not to go back to Krjukov, but to come to *him*, right here in Vlas'evskij Lane. I shall go, and, by the way, he has invited me to dinner at their home tomorrow.

After the bank (it was already past 3 o'clock) I did some shopping for Ol'ga[539] and myself. I took dinner with Varvara Ivanovna and Fëdor Ivanovich[540] and went to the [Moscow] Art Theatre to see *Julius Cæsar,*[541] beginning at 7:30. I was freezing in the orchestra seats and was bored at times, but I cannot deny that the production and the performance were magnificent. I'll tell you the details when [I see you]. For part of the play I sat with the elderly Strekalova[542] and [her granddaughter] Princess Liven in the director's box. I spent the whole morning today going over accounts with the artel worker and [a young lawyer named] Makarenko and from 3 o'clock on we'll be doing the same thing. We should finish by evening and, if I have time, I shall go see Auntie.[543] So that's my whole day today. Tomorrow I need to choose the wallpaper for the house, drop in there and pick up things.[544] I shall have to see Maklakov about my eyes, which have become quite inflamed again; I have some shopping to do, and [I'll be meeting with] Mjasoedova[545] and so forth. — It will be impossible to get all that done [on time] and so I shall probably arrive *Saturday morning,* so send [a carriage to Kozlovka] for me [then]. If for some reason I manage to get it done [earlier], I'll wire you. Naturally, if you are ill or I am needed at home, I'll drop everything and come [at once].

The Maslovs are extraordinarily dear people, and apart from them I also saw [Aleksandr Nikiforovich] Dunaev at the bank, [but] nobody else. Hugs and kisses to you and my regards to Julija Ivanovna [Igumnova], and Pavel Aleksandrovich [Bulanzhe] and Khrisanf Nikolaevich [Abrikosov].

Yours, Sonja.

N° 214 – SOFIA ANDREEVNA TOLSTAYA ✍ LEV NIKOLAEVICH TOLSTOY
[LSA 406]
10 January 1904. Night. [Moscow]

I am writing you once again, dear Lëvochka. I received your reassuring telegram and am happy, but for some reason it seems to me, and I'm afraid, that boredom and loneliness will prompt you to go to [to our daughter] Masha's or [daughter-in-law] Ol'ga's. Today it's warm with wet snow. How is your health? I'd like to know more details.

Sasha began her dental treatment today, and they said she would require treatment and fillings for a whole week. She and Annochka[546] are healthy and cheerful; they went to look at

---

538 Aleksej Alekseevich Maklakov (oculist) — see Letter N° 174, Note 275.

539 Ol'ga Konstantinovna Tolstaja (*née* Diterikhs; 1872–1951) — first wife to Andrej L'vovich Tolstoj; sister to Anna Konstantinovna Chertkova (*née* Diterikhs; see Letter N° 133, Note 537).

540 Varvara Ivanovna Maslova (see Letter N° 143, Note 651) and her brother Fëdor Ivanovich Maslov (1840–1915) — jurist, friend to composers Tchaikovsky and Taneev.

541 This performance of Shakespeare's tragedy in Russian featured the celebrated actor Konstantin Stanislavsky as Brutus.

542 Aleksandra Nikolaevna Strekalova (*née* Princess Kasatkina-Rostovskaja; 1821–1904) — prominent Moscow philanthropist. Her granddaughter was Princess Aleksandra Andreevna Liven (1862–1914).

543 Vera Aleksandrovna Shidlovskaja (*née* Islavina) — see Letter N° 123, Note 487.

544 SAT and family were probably staying at the Maslovs' while their own house was being renovated.

545 Julija Sergeevna Mjasoedova — distant cousin to LNT. Several of her letters to LNT have been preserved, containing requests to help her find work in an almshouse or widows' home.

546 Anna Il'inichna (Annochka) Tolstaja (1888–1954) — daughter to Il'ja L'vovich Tolstoj and his wife Sof'ja Nikolaevna.

paintings in the Historical Museum, and in the evening we all went to a concert: Sasha, Anno-chka, myself, Serëzha, Andrjusha and [Pavel Aleksandrovich] Bulanzhe, and we were all in ecstasy over Chaliapin[547] and were pleased with the whole concert. We had a fun time at home [afterwards] drinking tea and now everyone is asleep.

The three of us[548] took dinner at the Maslovs, and Fëdor Ivanovich[549] — as it turned out, a sole chevalier in the midst of six ladies — made great efforts to attract the girls' attention and told them jokes.

Today I was at the Rumjantsev and Historical Museums, where I decided to take [your] manuscripts;[550] but first I want to look at the room [they will be kept in]. Prince Shcherbatov[551] has given me an appointment on Monday at 12:30 for an inspection of the room, and then on Tuesday I shall take over the boxes.

My impression of the administration at the Rumjantsev Museum, headed by Tsvetaev,[552] was quite negative, while at the Historical Museum Shcherbatov and especially his dear wife and daughter[553] and the elderly Zabelin[554] left me with a very positive impression.

Serëzha, Fëdor Ivanovich [Maslov] and Pavel Aleksandrovich [Bulanzhe] all advise me to hand over the manuscripts to the Historical Museum for safekeeping.

Of the books in the Rumjantsev Museum they are sending you the following at my request:

1) The works of Saint Basil the Great. Parts 3 and 5.
2) The works of Saint John Chrysostom. Volume III. Books 1 and 2.
3) Selected moral principles of Saint Basil the Great.
4) Sayings of the Holy Fathers about the preservation of soul and body in the purity of chastity.

That's all they sent. Apparently, without Fëdorov[555] there, nobody knows anything, and Fëdorov has been replaced by some young man.

Well then, farewell, dear friend, time to go to bed; tomorrow all day I shall be going over accounts with the artel worker and I don't know myself where we'll be having dinner or [spend-ing] the evening.

We wanted to go see my brother Sasha, but we didn't let him know; tomorrow morning I'll send and ask him.

547 Feodor Chaliapin (Russian: Fëdor Ivanovich Shaljapin; 1873–1938) — prominent Russian bass opera singer, who was featured in a special concert together with the Moscow Conservatory Orchestra on 10 January 1904, under the aus-pices of the Russian Musical Society.

548 *The three of us* — i.e. SAT, her daughter Aleksandra (Sasha) and her granddaughter Annochka.

549 Fëdor Ivanovich Maslov (see Letter N° 213, Note 540).

550 A reference to nine boxes of LNT's writings plus his earlier diaries.

551 Prince Nikolaj Sergeevich Shcherbatov (1853–1929) — director of the Historical Museum in Moscow, to which SAT decided to transfer LNT's manuscripts from the Rumjantsev Museum, where they had been stored for safekeeping.

552 Ivan Vladimirovich Tsvetaev (1847–1913) — philologist and archæologist, professor at Moscow University and Director of the Rumjantsev Museum (1901–10). In her diary (*Dnevniki* II: 99) SAT expressed her disgust at Tsvetaev's apparent disregard for the importance of LNT's manuscripts.

553 Princess Sof'ja Aleksandrovna Shcherbatova (*née* Apraksina; 1852-1919) and her daughter, Princess Marija Nikolaevna Shcherbatova (married name as of 1911: Countess Chernyshëva-Bezobrazova; 1886–1975), lady-in-waiting.

554 Ivan Egorovich Zabelin (1820–1908) — historian, assistant to the Chairman of the Historical Museum (since 1879).

555 Nikolaj Fëdorovich Fëdorov (1828–1903) — philosopher; librarian at the Rumjantsev Museum.

My greetings to your 'bodyguards'.[556] I'm thinking of returning Thursday morning; there are various projects I shan't be able to deal with before then.

Yours, Sonja Tolstaya.

N° 215 – SOFIA ANDREEVNA TOLSTAYA ❧ LEV NIKOLAEVICH TOLSTOY
[LSA 408]
17 February 1904. [Moscow]

I didn't write you yesterday, dear Lëvochka, because I was out of sorts. Il'ja was after me all day long, asking for money; he is in debt to everyone, with endless schemes, and expenses, too. I gave him 400 roubles, and he promised to leave. And in the evening, after dinner with Serëzha, Marusja[557] came to see me, and soon there came that same young lady[558] that [Il'ja] has been attracted to, and then followed all sorts of clownishness, jokes and scurrying about the house. I went off to a Wagner concert,[559] which was not pleasurable: some annoying, self-absorbed Germans singing off-key, coarsely, repulsive music; it was boring and I'm tired.

But my main concern at the moment has turned out well and successfully: I have settled Sasha's financial affairs; for two days in the museum we have been sorting and recording objects, papers, portraits and letters. The elderly librarian Aleksej Ivanovich Stankevich[560] is sorting everything smartly and with love, and has laid them out in a magnificent display case, locks everything away, and is meticulous to the point of pedanticism. The Maslovs have known him for some time and commend him highly.

Pavel Aleksandrovich[561] took everything straight from the railway terminal to the museum, which was already open, as we hadn't hurried [along the way]; besides, the train was late. After washing my hands I went out into the lounge carriage, Buturlin[562] and Pavel Aleksandrovich were having a leisurely tea, and later we all rode together [to the museum], but with three cart-loads of boxes. Tomorrow I shall be once again at the museum, from 11 to 3, and tomorrow [we'll do] the sorting of the letters and making a record of them — a most difficult [task]. Today in Mjasnitskaja [Street] I ordered four busts and Robecchi[563] said that he would make a bronze [copy of] Troubetzkoy's[564] bust (similar to ours) for 80 roubles — very inexpensive. — I don't foresee any music these days and that is sad. Today I took dinner at the Maslovs. [I spent] the evening at home alone, weary, and now I'm writing to you. It is very quiet; the only [sound is] the clock ticking in the dining room. At the museum a Mr. Salomon[565] came to see me; Serëzha

556 *'bodyguards'* — SAT is jokingly referring to Julija Ivanovna Igumnova (see Letter N° 212, Note 533) and Dr. Grigorij Moiseevich Berkengejm (1872–1919) — the Tolstoys' family physician at the time.

557 Marija Alekseevna (Marusja) Maklakova — see Letter N° 206, Note 502.

558 A reference to Margarita Mikhajlovna Naryshkina (1881–1920) — later married to Vladimir Afanas'evich Afanas'ev (1851–?). Il'ja depicted his relationship with Naryshkina in his story "*Pozdno*" [Late], published in *Vestnik Evropy* (April 1914).

559 *Wagner concert* — a reference to excerpts from Wagner's opera *Die Meistersinger von Nürenberg* performed by guest artists from abroad under the direction of Dutch conductor and violinist Willem Kes (1856–1934)

560 Aleksej Ivanovich Stankevich (1856–1922) — historian, bibliographer, translator; senior librarian at the Historical Museum.

561 Pavel Aleksandrovich Bulanzhe (Orientalist) — see Letter N° 197, Note 444.

562 Aleksandr Sergeevich Buturlin (doctor) — see Letter N° 141, Note 638.

563 Carlo Robecchi — Italian bronze master, proprietor of a bronze foundry in Moscow.

564 Pavel Petrovich (Paolo) Trubetskoj (also transliterated: Troubetzkoy; 1866–1938) — sculptor who executed a bust of LNT in 1898.

565 Charles Salomon (1863–1936) — a translator of LNT's writings into French.

and Stakhovich[566] had breakfast with him at the Slavjanskij Bazaar. Misha Stakhovich is going with the Red Cross, as the representative of the Russian nobility, to the war.[567] The Maslovs told how they saw off the hospital train, with 60 young ladies, many of them from the upper echelons [of Russian society], going as nurses; [there were also] doctors, paramedics, and so forth. The train was huge, and its departure was marked by dead silence, despite the enormous crowd. There is a general sense of gloom about the war; there's something unspoken, unclear. The cabmen, just like the *muzhiks*, have strong faith in a Russian victory.

So farewell, dear friend, hugs and kisses to you and Sasha, and my regards to everyone.

S. Tolstaya.

N° 216 – LEV NIKOLAEVICH TOLSTOY ❧ SOFIA ANDREEVNA TOLSTAYA
[PSS 84/785]
14 August 1904. Pirogovo.

I shall be here, dear Sonja, for another two or three days. Don't know myself [how long exactly]. I don't feel like leaving, as I think I may be useful to him[568] in the most important respect, i.e. his mental state, although it is very difficult to be with him and feel my own powerlessness to help him. I am dismissing [the coachmen with his] horses, as Masha[569] has promised to take me [back to Yasnaya]. In any case, I shall stay here no longer than three days, counting from today, the 14th.

His situation is deplorable in that he does not see — or does not want to see — his [real] situation and he excites himself and acts up with everything, on top of his [actual] sufferings. He's terribly weak: he can't walk without stumbling, but still he [manages to] dress himself properly and walk around.

Please tell Julija Ivanovna[570] that Chertkov writes that, after receiving everything that was sent, he still has not yet received [my] foreword to [his] article on revolution.[571] Apparently it has been intercepted. Could she please send another with a return [acknowledgement of] receipt?

Farewell, hugs and kisses to you.

I had a severe case of heartburn; now it's better, and the weather is marvellous.

L. T.

I forgot my notebook on the table; do [be sure to] hide it.
I am still working on my *Calendar [Kalendar']*.[572] It is easy and pleasant work.

566 Mikhail Aleksandrovich (Misha) Stakhovich (1861–1923; poet, political activist) — see Letter N° 97, Note 258.
567 The Russo-Japanese war began 27 January 1904 (9 February N. S.) and lasted until 23 August 1905 (5 September N. S.).
568 On 11 August 1904 LNT went to the Pirogovo estate to see his brother, Sergej Nikolaevich Tolstoj (1826–1904), who was dying of cancer.
569 Marija Mikhajlovna (Masha) Tolstaja (*née* Shishkina; wife to Sergej Nikolaevich Tolstoj) — see Letter N° 15, Note 86.
570 Julija Ivanovna Igumnova (art student) — see Letter N° 212, Note 533.
571 LNT had written a foreword to Chertkov's article "*Nasil'stvennaja revoljutsija ili khristianskoe osvobozhdenie?*" [*Violent revolution or Christian liberation?*].
572 This was also known as *A cycle of readings [Krug chtenija]*, defined as "thoughts of many writers about the truth of life and [about] behaviour, selected, compiled and arranged for every day by Lev Tolstoy", published by Posrednik (1906–07).

Nº 217 – SOFIA ANDREEVNA TOLSTAYA ❧ LEV NIKOLAEVICH TOLSTOY
[LSA 412]
15 January 1905. [Moscow]

In Moscow everything is calm,[573] dear Lëvochka. Several factories have gone on strike, but even those have started to work [again]. Bakhrushin[574] and Morozov[575] have told their workers that there would be no deduction for the days they spent on the picket line, and they began to experience remorse over their action and returned to work. The newspapers came out today. Posha Birjukov still hasn't come. I tried contacting Pavel Aleksandrovich by telephone for a whole half-hour but couldn't wait [any longer]. Serëzha, it seems, is in a good mood; he's gone to have dinner with the Maklakovs, while I'm getting ready to go to a concert.

I was at the bank today and saw [Aleksandr Nikiforovich] Dunaev; today he's on his way to the countryside for a rest. He's quite exhausted and is terrified by what happened in Petersburg. I myself feel quite good, though weary; nobody can be peaceful or happy these days anywhere.

Stay healthy, hugs and kisses to you, Sasha,[576] Julija Ivanovna [Igumnova] and Vera [Aleksandrovna Kuzminskaja], regards to Dushan Petrovich.[577]

And how is Il'ja Vasil'evich?[578]

Yours, Sonja.

Nº 218 – LEV NIKOLAEVICH TOLSTOY ❧ SOFIA ANDREEVNA TOLSTAYA
[PSS 84/791]
16 January 1905. *Yasnaya Polyana.*

Everything's fine here with us, dear Sonja. Yesterday Nazhivin[579] was here with his wife. They are both nice people, as well as Orlov.[580] Il'ja Vasil'evich [Sidorkov] is still under the weather, and he looks terrible, although Dushan [Petrovich Makovitskij] sees no particular danger.

Zhozja[581] is here, and yesterday came Vera[582] and Nadechka Ivanova.[583] I am healthy, but very old, which, despite Avdot'ja Vasil'evna's[584] opinion to the contrary, doesn't bother me.

573 The First Russian Revolution took place from January 1905 to June 1907, set off by the mass demonstrations of "Bloody Sunday" (9 January 1905; 22 January N. S.) when Imperial troops opened fire on hundreds of protesting workers led by priest and union organiser Georgij Apollonovich Gapon (1870–1906). SAT was in Moscow at the time, while her son Lev L'vovich (Lëva) was in St. Petersburg. In his autobiographical memoirs (*Opyt moej zhizni*, p. 64) he lamented the absence of any real leader "capable of leading Russia onto the bright path of order and renewal". And later he added, from the point of view of an eye-witness (*ibid.*, p. 85): "In [just] one fine morning the priest Gapon managed to raise a whole Petersburg crowd and set it marching on the [Tsar's] Winter Palace."
574 Aleksej Aleksandrovih Bakhrushin (1865–1929) — head of a leather and fabric manufacturing concern, announced a two-week closure of his factory, during which time his workers would still receive their wages.
575 *Morozov* — one of the members of the wealthiest and most prominent industrial family dynasties of the period.
576 Aleksandra L'vovna (Sasha) Tolstaja (the Tolstoys' youngest daughter).
577 Dr. Dushan Petrovich Makovitskij (LNT's personal physician) — see Letter Nº 174, Note 279.
578 Il'ja Vasil'evich Sidorkov — the Tolstoys' servant, who had recently fallen ill.
579 Ivan Fëdorovich Nazhivin (1874–1940) — writer, with his wife Anna Efimovna Nazhivina (*née* Zusman).
580 Nikolaj Vasil'evich Orlov (1863–1924) — an artist.
581 Iosif Konstantinovich (Zhozja) Diterikhs (1868–1932) — brother to Ol'ga Konstantinovna Tolstaja (see Letter Nº 213, Note 539) and Anna Konstantinovna Chertkova (see Letter Nº 133, Note 537).
582 SAT's niece Vera Aleksandrovna Kuzminskaja — see Letter Nº 43, Note 281.
583 Nadezhda Pavlovna (Nadechka) Ivanova (?–1926) — a merchant's daughter; a friend to Aleksandra L'vovna (Sasha) Tolstaja.
584 Avdot'ja Vasil'evna Popova — housekeeper for the Tolstoys.

Yesterday I received a letter from your admirer Bourdon,[585] who is coming to Russia again. [We are having] a severe snowstorm, but I still took my usual two outings close to the house. How are you enjoying [your] music? The other day this thought about music came to me: Music is the stenography of feelings. When we speak, we use rising or falling [intonation] and volume, as well as fast or slow sequencing of sounds to express those feelings associated with what we say — the thoughts, images, events we express in words. On the other hand, music conveys just the combinations and sequencing of these feelings without the thoughts, images or events. — This explains to me what I experience when I listen to music. Do write. Farewell. Hugs and kisses to you and [our] sons.

L. T.

Nº 219 – SOFIA ANDREEVNA TOLSTAYA ❧ LEV NIKOLAEVICH TOLSTOY
[LSA 413]
19 January 1905. [Moscow]

I was quite delighted to receive your letter, dear Lëvochka, and today I was waiting for Mr. Davitt,[586] who promised he would come and see me on his way back from Yasnaya, but for some reason he didn't come. Serëzha and I really liked your definition of music, that it is the *stenography of feelings*. Unfortunately there won't be any music all this week, only the opera with Chaliapin on Friday,[587] and I am planning to go. Every day Pavel Aleksandrovich and I go to the museum; he is there from 11 to 3, and I go at 12, since in the morning I am torn to bits by various activities. Now there is almost nothing left to be done. There is utter chaos in the museum; three boxes with manuscripts have deteriorated, and on one of them the bottom even fell out. We had to hoist the manuscripts onto a shelf, hand over the boxes to be repaired, and I want to order an extra set of shelves for the boxes.

Everywhere in Moscow there are meetings, gatherings and discussions going on. Tomorrow the nobility elections[588] open and two contradictory messages have been compiled: those of Samarin[589] and Trubetskoj,[590] and all the talk is about who will defeat whom. There was also a gathering and a meeting today at Posrednik, and another at Maklakov's, and Serëzha went to yet a third.

I have considerable pain in my mouth, tongue, throat and palate — everything's all puffed up, with a burning [sensation]. I know how to treat it, but there's no prescription here and it is extremely bothersome.

Andrjusha has left for Petersburg after having fun [here] for three days. I didn't even see him. I don't see Lina and Misha either; I've only been to their place once. Today I had dinner at

---

585 Georges Bourdon (1868–1938) — a French journalist who, after visiting Yasnaya Polyana in 1904, published a book in Paris entitled *En écoutant Tolstoï*, with flattering descriptions of SAT. In a letter of 9 January 1905 (22 January N. S.), Bourdon asked permission to visit Yasnaya Polyana once more.

586 Michael Davitt (1846–1906) — Irish Labour MP, journalist, founder of the Irish National Land League.

587 On Friday 21 January 1905 Chaliapin performed the title role in Mussorgsky's opera *Boris Godunov* in Moscow's Bolshoi Theatre.

588 These were held every three years to elect representatives and officials of the nobility at various administrative levels, including the gubernia and the uezd.

589 Aleksandr Dmitrievich Samarin (1866–1932) — Collegiate Councillor (from 1905), State Council member (from 1912).

590 Sergej Nikolaevich Trubetskoj (1862–1905) — a liberal-inclined philosopher.

home with Serëzha and the two Marusjas: Maklakova[591] and Naryshkina.[592] Our gathering this evening was attended by: Lizan'ka, Natasha, Khrisanf,[593] my brother Sasha, Marusja, Katerina Fëdorovna Junge with her son,[594] Anna Aleksandrovna Gorjainova,[595] Gol'denvejzer[596] with his wife — and once again the talk was about the state of affairs in Russia. We sat chatting until 2 o'clock, and now it is 3 a.m.

Tomorrow morning I'm going to the Tret'jakov Gallery, then to the [Historical] Museum; I shall take dinner at home, and in the evening a violinist is coming to play with me. I really want to leave [here] Friday evening and arrive home [at Yasnaya] Saturday morning; I don't know if I shall manage to, since Posha and I will still not have finished our work at the museum. In that case I shall probably be [home] Sunday.

You complain of old age; I myself feel it in the extreme, and on these snowstorm days it is particularly severe. And I agree with Dunjasha,[597] whereas you do not (that whatever is old cannot be good). — How are you all doing? How is Il'ja Vasil'evich? How are the snowstorms — has anyone been hurt by them? I hope that you are taking care of yourself. Hugs and kisses to you, my greetings to everyone.

Yours, Sonja T.

N° 220 – SOFIA ANDREEVNA TOLSTAYA ❧ LEV NIKOLAEVICH TOLSTOY
[LSA 418]
14 May 1906. Moscow

I've [just] come from the graves of my children;[598] I'm sitting alone in my house and somehow started to feel sad, and worried about all of you, since I haven't heard any news of you yet, and today a frightful cold came on, along with a north wind. What I feared came to pass: Lëva and his family moved house in bad weather, missing the whole charming, warm spring.

From the gravesite I dropped into see the *stanovoj*[599] at Vsesvjatskoe, asking him to issue a warning to the populace of Nikol'skoe, since Vanechka's headstone has once again been damaged by rock-throwing. He turned out to be a very pleasant, clever old chap (and *stanovojs*, too, can be good people). He told me that they've been expecting all day and are still expecting — it's now 8 p.m. — considerable unrest. The Sumsk regiment has been returned from their [summer] camps; all the police and groundskeepers are armed; there are so many police that they group together in fours. And the artel worker's children informed me that starting tonight there will again be a general political strike, that everywhere there's going to be a commotion the likes

---

591 Marija Alekseevna (Marusja) Maklakova — see Letter N° 206, Note 500.

592 Marija Mikhajlovna (Marusja) Naryshkina (married name: Bel'skaja; 1881–?).

593 Elizaveta Valer'janovna (Lizan'ka) Tolstaja, Natal'ja Leonidovna (Natasha) Obolenskaja, Khrisanf Nikolaevich Abrikosov.

594 Marija Alekseevna (Marusja) Maklakova, Katerina (Ekaterina) Fëdorovna Junge (*née* Tolstaja; see Letter N° 157, Note 107) with her son Aleksandr (or Fëdor) Èduardovich Junge.

595 Anna Aleksandrovna Gorjainova (*née* Princess Golitsyna-Prozorovskaja; 1851–1921) — great-granddaughter to friends of LNT's grandfather's (Nikolaj Sergeevich Volkonskij): Sergej Fëdorovich Golitsyn and Varvara Vasil'evna Golitsyna.

596 Aleksandr Borisovich Gol'denvejzer (pianist; see Letter N° 192, Note 411) with his wife Anna Alekseevna Gol'denvejzer (*née* Sofiano; 1881–1929).

597 Avdot'ja (Evdokija) Nikolaevna (Dunjasha) Bannikova — see Letter N° 5, Note 37.

598 Two of the Tolstoys' sons — Aleksej (Alësha; 1881–1886) and Ivan (Vanechka; 1888–1895) were buried at the Nikolo-Arkhangel'sk Cemetery near Moscow. In 1932 their remains were transferred to the Tolstoy family plot at Kochaki.

599 *stanovoj* — a local police official.

of which have never been seen before. Discipline has completely disappeared from the schools; here in Zemledel'cheskaja, at the Smolensk market, there's practically a riot.

The *stanovoj* said that if it weren't for Dubasov,[600] they would immediately have ransacked all of Moscow and a certain Fidling[601] would be established as governor. All in all, it's very alarming, and you can feel revolution in the air. Nobody trusts the Duma; these very same children — of the artel worker and Il'inichna's — were sounding as though [Dmitrij Fëdorovich] Trepov[602] would be a dictator and then they would secure their control over everyone, and disband the Duma. The cabman [who drove me] from the station was saying to me angrily that Trepov had been appointed commander of all the troops; that it was a disgrace: could a policeman really be appointed for such a position? It turns out [the cabman] is a soldier, who served in the Turkish as well as the latest, the Japanese war[603] and was saying: "Look what [kind of] generals we had in the [last] war! They brought in women and girls, lived in luxury, took cognac all day, while we soldiers in the field were dying of cold and starvation. Here I served with Skobelev;[604] he was practically a father to us: when we went hungry, he went hungry with us; we were cold, and he froze along with us. Wherever the soldiers went, he was there, too." He doesn't believe in the Duma either, says they'll disband it, and won't allow the land to be given to the *muzhiks*. — Everyone has their own point of view, but one and the same theme: "they will disband".

Yesterday we had dinner at the Metropol' [hotel]: Konstantin Aleksandrovich Rachinskij,[605] [our] son Serëzha and grandson Serëzha, Miss Genzh[606] and myself. Then grandson Serëzha accompanied me home, looked all around, and piped up: "Oh, how cozy, how great! I would like to live at Yasnaya Polyana and here with Papa."

In the evening we had a gathering here: Anna Ivanovna Maslova, [her cousin] Julija Afanas'evna Jurasova, Baroness Taube[607] with her eldest son, a sailor who has just returned from the war and had a lot to say about the chaos of orders from the [military command] and the government, as well as those from Rozhdestvenskij.[608] They're all on trial, these sailors.

All Friday long I waited in [various] banks, did some shopping, took dinner at the Maslovs', and in the evening went to see Auntie,[609] who was busy making preparations for her move into our house and today sent [her servant] Tat'jana to see us.

---

600 Fëdor Vasil'evich Dubasov (1845–1912) — admiral, adjutant-general, Governor-General of Moscow (1905–06), in charge of repressing the December 1905 uprising in Moscow.

601 *Fidling* [sic] — Ivan Ivanovich Fidler (1864–1934) — headmaster of the Fidler (non-classical) secondary school in Moscow, who made his premises available for revolutionary gatherings. He was arrested and served several months in the Butyrka Prison. In 1906 he emigrated to Switzerland, and later moved to France.

602 Dmitrij Fëdorovich Trepov (1855–1906) — Governor-General of St. Petersburg (as of January 1905). In May 1905 he was appointed to the post of Deputy Minister of Internal Affairs in charge of the police, as well as commanding a separate branch of the *gendarmerie*.

603 A reference to the Russo-Turkish War (1877–78) and to the Russo-Japanese War (1904–05).

604 Mikhail Dmitrievich Skobelev (1843–1882) — infantry general, a hero of the Russo-Turkish War.

605 Konstantin Aleksandrovich Rachinskij (1838–ca1909) — Director of the Moscow Agricultural Institute; father to Marija Konstantinovna Tolstaja (*née* Rachinskaja; wife of Sergej L'vovich (Serëzha) Tolstoj).

606 *Miss Genzh* (transliterated from the Russian variant; English spelling unknown) — possibly governess to grandson Serëzha.

607 Baroness Sof'ja Arturovna Taube (*née* Countess Këller; 1855–1936), wife of Senator Nikolaj Èrnestovich Taube (1847–1920); her eldest son was Georgij Nikolaevich Taube (1877–1948) — later a rear admiral.

608 Zinovij Petrovich Rozhdestvenskij (1848–1909) — vice-admiral commanding the Second Squadron of the Pacific Fleet during the Russo-Japanese War; he was routed at Tsushima, seriously wounded, and was taken captive along with his Fleet.

609 Vera Aleksandrovna Shidlovskaja (SAT's aunt) — see Letter Nº 123, Note 487.

Yesterday I went through the accounts regarding the sale of books and [we] finished today. Friday night, at 3 o'clock Saturday morning I was awakened by severe stomach pains; [mild] diarrhœa, and I took strong measures: opium, mint [tea], fasting — and the trouble passed, although I [still] don't feel well. And my tooth, too, has been causing a lot of pain during the last hours of its life. The dentist won't do anything until Monday (tomorrow), he is so busy, and so tomorrow my fate will be decided as to how long I have to stay here [in Moscow]. Apart from my teeth and some spring cleaning, which I wasn't able to do because of the rain, I've got everything done. I don't believe in the strike — nothing can repeat itself in exactly the same way. Did we get any rain at Yasnaya?

Well, that's it. I hope to have some news from you all at least by tomorrow. I was feeling sad at leaving everyone, especially our new grandchildren, and at not being able give them any help or attention. God grant we can live together [for a while] longer. [Even] if my teeth keep me [here in Moscow] at the moment, I still shan't [have to] move anywhere [from Yasnaya Polyana] before August — what happiness!

Hugs and kisses to everyone. I'm writing to everyone no specific addressee, as in my heart I am appealing to everyone.

Your combined wife, Mama, mother-in-law, grandmother and so forth.

S. Tolstaya.

(Like the tsar writes: Emperor of All Russia, Tsar of Poland, Grand Prince of Finland, etc., etc. — I would echo that.)

Nº 221 – LEV NIKOLAEVICH TOLSTOY ✎ SOFIA ANDREEVNA TOLSTAYA
[PSS 84/799]
4 April 1907. Yasnaya Polyana.

I am very happy to be writing to you, dear Sonja, since you say it pleases you. Everything's fine here with us. I am quite recovered from my bout of ill health; today I walked over to the forester's to talk with Andrjusha[610] by telephone, but there was no answer. I wanted to ask him whether the woman who came to see me whose husband was killed by *gendarmes* at Zhitovo — where they were dragging merchandise from crumpled freight wagons[611] — could count on receiving any [financial] assistance. We took dinner today at Tanja's. A cheery letter came from Sasha.[612] As usual, I've been teaching the children,[613] and still hope that some kind of benefit will come from this. This kind of contact calls forth one's best thoughts and feelings. We are awaiting news from you; to date we know [little or] nothing. We received today a [financial] contribution from [North] America.[614] Please send the artel worker to collect these funds and

---

610 The Tolstoys' son Andrej L'vovich (Andrjusha) Tolstoj, who was then serving as a special commissioner in the Tula Governor's office.

611 On 19 February 1907 LNT's doctor Dushan Petrovich Makovitskij noted in his *Jasnopoljanskie zapiski* [*Notes from Yasnaya Polyana*]: "A few days ago two trains collided between Yasenki and Zhitovo. The freight wagons were left for several days unguarded, and people began dragging out of them [sacks of] flour, grain, oranges, copper [coins]. A few days later gendarmes showed up; they started shooting and killed two people" (cited from PSS 84: 377).

612 A reference to Aleksandra L'vovna's (Sasha's) letter from Yalta dated 3 April 1907.

613 In the evenings LNT would give lessons to the children of Yasnaya Polyana peasants.

614 On 10 April 1907 LNT received a donation of $5,000 from the Doukhobors in Canada (see PSS 56: 441–42).

bring them [to me]. I have decided to keep them with me and hand them over to the poor. Farewell. Hugs and kisses to you and Serëzha and Masha.[615]

Nº 222 – LEV NIKOLAEVICH TOLSTOY ✿ SOFIA ANDREEVNA TOLSTAYA
[PSS 84/806]
16 May 1908. Yasnaya Polyana.

I am writing these lines on the morning of the 16th only to ask you not to give my letter to Koni[616] but to tear it up. It is impossible, unseemly and shameful for me to make [such] a request, *c'est une contradiction criante*. In any case, dear Sonja, I'm glad of the opportunity to think of you and give you news of us, even though it's been only one night. It's now 9 o'clock; I am starting in on some cheerful work.[617] I feel so good in my heart, it's even shameful.

Hugs and kisses to you.

L. T.

Tell Koni that I very much liked his "Reminiscences",[618] especially his account of Pisemskij.[619]

Nº 223 – SOFIA ANDREEVNA TOLSTAYA ✿ LEV NIKOLAEVICH TOLSTOY
[LSA 423]
18 June 1909. [Yasnaya Polyana]

Dear Lëvochka, we are living without you here at Yasnaya like a body without a soul. There are no visitors, but lots of beggars, and you can never have enough change for all of them. We are all safe, but I have found two of our children, Lëva and Sasha, to be nervous and morose. Lëva is doing a sculpture[620] of Sasha in peasant dress; he has spoilt your bust a little, in my opinion. He is awaiting your return so he can work on it more from life, and doesn't want to leave without seeing you.

He's let out his Petersburg house[621] for two years and has decided — now definitely, since there will be nowhere for him to stay — not to return to Petersburg during this period.

Today is Sasha's birthday, and she left this morning by troika for Tula with Varvara Mikhajlovna[622] and I inadvertently insulted her by not ordering a special breakfast which she

---

615 A reference to Sergej L'vovich (Serëzha) Tolstoj and his second wife Marija Nikolaevna Tolstaja (*née* Zubova; 1867–1939), whom he married in 1906.

616 In his letter to Senator Anatolij Fëdorovich Koni (a judge; see Letter Nº 147, Note 37) of 15 May 1908, LNT petitioned on behalf of one of his followers, Vladimir Ajfalovich Molochnikov (1871–1936), a locksmith from Novgorod, who had been sentenced to a year of incarceration for distributing banned LNT articles. He also requested Koni to help find a position for his son. On second thought, however, he judged the latter request to be inappropriate and so asked SAT to withhold the letter. Still, she did not tear it up but decided to preserve it for posterity (see PSS 78: 141).

617 LNT was working on his article *I cannot be silent [Ne mogu molchat']*.

618 Koni's "*Otryvki iz vospominanij*" ["Reminiscences" (excerpts)] was published in *Vestnik Evropy* (1908, Nº 5).

619 Aleksej Feofilaktovich Pisemskij (1821–1881) — Russian writer and dramatist, personally acquainted with LNT since 1856.

620 Beginning in 1908 Lev L'vovich (Lëva) became interested in sculpture. The following year he went to Paris to study with French sculptor Rodolphe Julian (1839–1907) and even took lessons with the famous Auguste Rodin (1840–1917).

621 After receiving the Tolstoys' Khamovniki Lane house in Moscow as his inheritance in 1891, Lev L'vovich sold it to his mother (SAT) and bought a house in St. Petersburg, which he let out as flats.

622 Varvara Mikhajlovna Feokritova (1875–1950) — a companion to Aleksandra L'vovna (Sasha) Tolstaja.

was anticipating, as I thought she wouldn't be returning home in time for breakfast. And I felt sorry for her, and her rude reaction was hard to take. Well, I'm used to that by now!

I've started in on household tasks, and I can see that a lot of things went badly while I was away. And it's simply true that when you return home after being away, everything's more noticeable, and you tackle it all the more energetically.

I am still cherishing my memories of Kochety[623] and I can still hear Tanjushka's little voice, and it seems that I should be busying myself with taking care of you.

The road to Blagodatnoe seemed far easier and shorter this time.

Mamontov[624] was saying that it's impossible to go to Mtsensk; [people] are making huge detours, finding themselves stuck in river fords, getting delayed and becoming frightfully exhausted from the long journey and terrible roads. It was raining today, too.

[On the train trip] from Orël to Zaseka one can get some sleep, arrive at dawn and then lie down again, and get a full rest. I recommend going through Blagodatnoe, but, in any case, it's up to [the lot of] you to decide.

Hugs and kisses to Tanja and our granddaughter and you, and my greetings to all. How is your health?

Yours, Sonja Tolstaya.

Nº 224 – LEV NIKOLAEVICH TOLSTOY ❧ SOFIA ANDREEVNA TOLSTAYA
[PSS 84/812]
23 June 1909. Kochety.

Today I received your letter to Tanja,[625] dear Sonja. I'm doing quite nicely here, but I do want to come home, too — for your sake, and for Lëva's, and for Sasha's (since she is not coming here), and for my own sake as well. I don't like specifying a time in advance, but I think it will be soon. Today I received a letter from Chertkov[626] enclosing a copy of [his] letter to you. He suggests I give the story *The devil [D'javol]* to the *Literary Collection*,[627] which has been asking for it. I haven't yet made up my mind.

I don't really like the story. I'll have to read it again. It's pretty quiet here, far quieter than at Yasnaya, in terms of visitors. Today Mikhail Sergeevich [Sukhotin]'s son Misha[628] came. I'm feeling fine. I'm working on something,[629] and there's so much that I want [to accomplish] that these are clearly the commonplace unrealisable dreams of an old man. I just want not to waste my remaining months, days and hours, when so much that used to be obscure and concealed

---

623 SAT was a guest at the Kochety estate of her daughter Tat'jana L'vovna (Tanja) Sukhotina and son-in-law Mikhail Sergeevich Sukhotin, whose own daughter Tat'jana Mikhajlovna (Tanjusha) Sukhotina was born in 1905.

624 Vsevolod Savvich Mamontov (1870–1951) — son of fabric manufacturer and philanthropist Savva Ivanovich Mamontov (1841–1918).

625 SAT's letter to her daughter Tanja is dated 22 June 1909 (Manuscript Division, Tolstoy Museum).

626 Vladimir Grigor'evich Chertkov's letter to LNT is dated 19 June 1909 (see PSS 89:123–24). In his enclosed letter to SAT he replies to her request regarding the date LNT wrote *The devil [D'javol]*. (The novella was written in 1889, supplied with an alternative ending in 1909, but not published until the year after LNT's death.)

627 A reference to an anthology marking the 50th anniversary of the Society for Aid to Needy Literators and Scholars. But *The devil* was not offered to this anthology.

628 Mikhail Mikhajlovich [Misha] Sukhotin (1884–1921) — stepson to the Tolstoys' daughter Tat'jana L'vovna (Tanja) Sukhotina.

629 At the time LNT was working on an article entitled *The one commandment [Edinaja zapoved']*.

has now become clear. Yesterday Natasha Abrikosova[630] was here. I repeat my advice not to give too much importance to household tasks, but rather — as you rightly say yourself[631] — to be a good person. That's the only thing that's needed. And the proof that it's the only thing that's needed is the fact that it is the one thing that is always possible.

Hugs and kisses to you, Sasha and Lëva, and greetings to Varvara Mikhajlovna [Feokritova].

L. T.

Nº 225 – SOFIA ANDREEVNA TOLSTAYA ❧ LEV NIKOLAEVICH TOLSTOY
[LSA 425]
24 June 1909. [Yasnaya Polyana]

Yesterday I received your letter[632] with the instructions: *give as little attention to household tasks as possible*, as well as: *good feelings towards others are incomparably more important than anything else*. There's a lot to say about this in reply. Good *feelings* [merely] in words, but not in deeds, have no value whatsoever. I do my own housework only because I have no desire to offend anyone; [I want] to get things done fairly and without judging others as much as I can. For three days in a row *muzhiks* kept coming to see me from Grumont. They comprise fifteen households in all, and I wrote a letter to the elder, saying that the 37 *desjatinas* I am giving them must be distributed equally. The village elder and the boldest *muzhik*, Grigorij Matrosov, were dividing the land through nepotism, and reserved for themselves a far greater portion than for the poor. They were completely unwilling to do it by my method, i.e. equally. Then after I said I would not hand over the land at all, they were left with no other choice — they distributed it my way, and the poor came and thanked me [personally].

That's one example. There are many others: They don't accept coupons from the poor for paying their rent, they reserve a part of the pasturelands, so they can give them later to someone more convenient, and those who offer bribes … There's too many stories to count, let alone the various simple, logical household procedures.

The whole day yesterday was difficult. Andrjusha came, he'd got entangled in his debts. He needed eight thousand [roubles], wept and begged forgiveness; the debts are old, and the lenders were unwilling to wait [any longer]. I refused, and he said: "the only thing left is to kill myself" and sobbed. That's [the state] he departed in. And you know how distressing this has been over my whole life.

While we were having dinner on the *terrasse*, a young woman approached and requested help for her one-year-old child: [the baby] had fallen [and struck his head] on a window, there was a terrible cut on his head, right to the bone; it was frightful to look at. Sasha took her to the nurse at the Chertkovs',[633] but she could do nothing [for him], and tomorrow they're taking the baby to Tula. The absence of a doctor is very much felt here; they're accustomed to receiving help from us, and everyone comes [to us]. Later, after dinner, to cap off everything, a letter

630 Natal'ja Leonidovna (Natasha) Abrikosova (*née* Obolenskaja) — daughter to LNT's niece Elizaveta Valer'janovna Obolenskaja and her husband Leonid Dmitrievich Obolenskij (see Letter Nº 213, Note 537).
631 A reference to SAT's letter of 22 June 1909 (not included here; Manuscript Division, Tolstoy Museum).
632 Letter Nº 224 of 23 June 1909.
633 In 1907 Chertkov bought a plot of land at Teljatinki, not far from Yasnaya Polyana, on which he built a house. He wanted to live closer to LNT.

from Dima,[634] saying that Chertkov was at Stolypin's,[635] who decisively refused him permission to return home [to Tula Gubernia]. Chertkov asked if he could visit his wife,[636] who was ill, to which Stolypin replied that it was up to the police. What hideous despotism!

All this served to upset Lëva and me; he told me: "I'm off to Sweden as soon as I can." And so you've gone, [dear Lëva,] — you're living and enjoying yourself; whereas I've long forgotten what is meant by the joy of life. My heart is always hurting from something, and I keep feeling a pressure on my shoulders, which are [already] so weary with life. Well, farewell, be healthy and cheerful.

S. Tolstaya.

N° 226 – SOFIA ANDREEVNA TOLSTAYA ❧ LEV NIKOLAEVICH TOLSTOY
[LSA 428]
13 December 1909. 12 p.m. [Moscow]

Dear Lëvochka, I am joyfully fulfilling your request and am writing to you. I am completely safe and am now on my way to a day-time concert in honour of Haydn[637] — just of his works, and Wanda Landowska[638] will be at the keyboard. Yesterday I was terribly tired, mainly from a sleepless night and an overheated railway carriage. My little book[639] comes out tomorrow at 9 a.m., and the artel worker will be taking it round to bookshops. I've been told that a review has already appeared in *Russkie vedomosti*; I couldn't find it, but they say it came in for a good deal of praise. Still, I was far more delighted when, for example, I read my story *Vanechka* aloud just now to [my] little [grandson] Serëzha. He simply melted over it and kept repeating: "How precious!"; the same with Stëpa's son,[640] who bears a striking resemblance to his father.

Now, listen, Lëvochka. I'm asking *you*, as I don't feel like writing a separate letter to Sasha. All of Serëzha's family and two of [my] Behrs [relations] will be coming for the entire [Christmas] holiday season. Do ask Il'ja Vasil'evich [Sidorkov] to start heating the annexe right away; I have arranged with the foreman as to which worker should be detailed for this and which wood to use for heating. Sorry for the bother. The frosts can be heavy, and if we don't start heating now, the walls will freeze through and then it will be all the more difficult to heat the house.

Everything's fine here; of the people I know, the only one I've seen (at the bank) is [Aleksandr Nikiforovich] Dunaev, who is flourishing. I've got rather little done, it's very hard [to take] extremely warm rooms after [being out in] a biting wind and frost, and wearing a heavy fur coat.

Hugs and kisses to you all; I constantly think of you all and worry about you, [Lëva]. Take care of yourself, dear friend.

Your old [wife] Sonja.

---

634 Vladimir Vladimirovich (Dima) Chertkov (1889–1964) — son to Vladimir Grigor'evich Chertkov.

635 Pëtr Arkad'evich Stolypin (see Letter N° 42, Note 269) was (as of 1906) Minister of Internal Affairs and Chairman of the Council of Ministers (in effect, Prime Minister).

636 Anna Konstantinovna Chertkova (*née* Diterikhs) was at Teljatinki.

637 A reference to a memorial concert in honour of the centenary of the composer Haydn's passing (31 May 1809 N. S.), held at the Great Hall of the Moscow Conservatory, under the baton of Sergej Nikiforovich Vasilenko (1872–1956).

638 Wanda Aleksandra Landowska (1879–1959) — Polish-French harpsichordist, who became a naturalised French citizen in 1938, although with the onset of World War II she went to America. In 1933 she became the first musician to record Bach's *Goldberg variations* on the harpsichord. She was a friend of the Tolstoys' and visited Yasnaya Polyana in 1908.

639 A reference to *The skeleton-dolls and other stories [Kukolki-skelettsy i drugie rasskazy]*, which was about to be published.

640 Nikolaj Stepanovich Behrs (1889–?) — SAT's nephew, son to her brother Stepan Andreevich (Stëpa) Behrs.

Nº 227 – LEV NIKOLAEVICH TOLSTOY ❧ SOFIA ANDREEVNA TOLSTAYA
[PSS 84/824]
14 June 1910. Otradnoe.

I am taking advantage of Dimochka's[641] departure to write to you, dear Sonja. Sasha[642] wrote to you about our journey and our arrival. The only bad news since then is that Sasha has somewhere caught a strong case of sniffles, but no cough, and she is fine and in good spirits. I'm quite healthy [myself]. I'm living exactly the way I lived at Yasnaya Polyana, the only difference being the absence of visitors and petitioners — which is very pleasant. This is such an interesting region with its unusual *zemstvo*[643] activity. Just three versts from here there is a huge psychiatric hospital with 700 beds, and another, government-run, with 1,500 beds, also psychiatric; [also] a prison [and] a hospital for political prisoners; besides that, recovering mental patients are distributed among the villages. Today I visited one such village, where there are 50 [recovering patients]. I talked with quite a few of them, and one [in particular] is very interesting. Until now I have not been working on anything special. I still keep digging into old stuff.[644] But I hope to take advantage of [this] leisure time. — However nice it may be to go visiting, home is still better. And I shall come, as I've planned, now no later than the 24th,[645] if everything is going well with me and with you. How are you and how are your activities both in publishing[646] and at home? Not too bothersome for you? That's the important thing — more important than all material affairs. I'm very sorry that [my son] Il'ja did not find me. How is he?

Farewell, my dear old wife. Hugs and kisses. 'Till we meet again, I hope.

Your husband
L. T.

14th, evening.

---

641 Vladimir Vladimirovich (Dimochka) Chertkov — son to Vladimir Grigor'evich Chertkov, who at the time was living on his Otradnoe estate in Podol'skij Uezd, Moscow Gubernia. The son took the letter to SAT.
642 Aleksandra L'vovna (Sasha) Tolstaja (the Tolstoys' youngest daughter).
643 *zemstvo* — a system of local government instituted by Tsar Alexander II during a period of liberal reforms in the latter half of the nineteenth-century.
644 At the time LNT was correcting the Preface to *For every day [Na kazhdyj den']* and working on *The path of life [Put' zhizni]* — see PSS 45.
645 *Now no later than* is underlined twice by SAT in both ink and red pencil; the previous sentence and a half are similarly marked with red pencil, which she used to note in the margin, in an apparent fit of hysteria: "It's all a lie, and I am dying alone at home, 22 June 1910".
646 SAT was busy preparing the 12th edition of LNT's collected works.

Nº 228 – LEV NIKOLAEVICH TOLSTOY ❧ SOFIA ANDREEVNA TOLSTAYA
[PSS 84/831]
14 July 1910. Yasnaya Polyana.

14 July 1910.

1) My current diary I shall not give to anyone; I am keeping it to myself.[647]
2) My old diaries I shall take back from Chertkov and keep myself, probably at the bank.
3) If you are worried by the thought that my diaries, [especially] those passages written under the influence of the moment concerning our disagreements and confrontations, might be used by future biographers who are prejudiced against you, then, apart from the [fact] that such expressions of temporary feelings either in your diaries or mine cannot possibly convey a true concept of our actual relations — if this worries you, I am happy for the opportunity to express in [my] diary, or simply through this [present] letter, my attitude towards you and my appraisal of your life.

My attitude towards you and my appraisal of you are as follows: just as I have loved you from [our] youth, [I can say] that, despite various reasons for the cooling [of our relationship], I have loved you without ceasing and [still] do love you. These reasons were (I am not speaking about the termination of our marital relations — such termination could only erase deceptive expressions of a false love) — the reasons were, [1)] firstly, my greater and greater distancing from the interests of secular life and my feeling of repulsion towards them, while you did not wish to and were not able to part with them, not having in your heart those principles which led me to my convictions, which is quite natural and for which I do not blame you. That's first. [2)] Secondly (forgive me if I tell you something you may find unpleasant, but what is now taking place between us is so important that we must not fear to tell and to hear the whole truth), secondly, your nature over the past few years has become more and more irritated, despotic and unrestrained. The manifestation of these character traits could not help but cool — [if] not the feeling itself, [then at least] its expression. That's second. Thirdly, the main cause [of our difficulties] has been disastrous, for which neither you nor I are to blame — it is our diametrically opposite understanding of the meaning and purpose of life. Everything in our conceptions of life has been diametrically opposite: our ways of life, our attitudes to others, our means of life — property, which I have considered a sin and which you [treat] as a necessary condition of life. So as to avoid a parting of our paths, in my own way of life I have subjected myself to what are to me burdensome conditions, while you have taken these as concessions to your views — [as a result of which] the misunderstanding between us has kept growing more and more. There have been other causes of the cooling [of our relationship], for which we are both to blame, but I shall not bring them up, as they are not germane to the issue [at hand]. The thing is that, despite all [our] former misunderstandings, I have [never] stopped loving or appreciating you.

---

647 SAT added the following comment on this letter: "Lev Nikolaevich's letter, written to me at the time of my illness brought on by my despair over Chertkov stealing all [LNT's] diaries since 1900, which he hid from both me and Lev Nikolaevich. This drove me to desperation, and I was ready to kill myself if Chertkov did not return the diaries and [if] my husband's love [for me] did not return." SAT was greatly troubled by the question of LNT's diaries. She had given his diaries from 1847 to 1900 to the Rumjantsev Museum for safekeeping, while pianist Aleksandr Gol'denvejzer (see Letter Nº 192, Note 411) was keeping his later diaries in a Moscow bank safe. SAT wanted to preserve his diaries for all these years to use at her own discretion.

My appraisal of your life with me is as follows: I, as a licentious person, extremely sexually profligate, long past his first [stage of] youth, married you, a pure, good and clever 18-year old girl and, despite my dirty, profligate past, you have lived with me almost 50 years, loving me, in a laborious, difficult life, bearing children, feeding, educating, caring for them and for me, and not giving in to those temptations which could so easily take hold of any strong, healthy and beautiful woman in your situation. But you have lived [your life] in such a way that I have nothing to fault you for. I cannot and do not blame you for not following me in my unique spiritual movement, since each person's spiritual life is a secret between them and God, and one cannot demand it of others. And if I have demanded this of you, then I have been mistaken and am quite at fault in this.

So this is a true description of my relationship to you, and my appraisal of you. As for what may turn up in my diaries, I only know that there is nothing to be found there that is rude or contrary to what I am writing now.

So that is point 3), concerning what might — and ought not — to trouble you concerning my diaries.

[Point] 4) is this: that if at the moment you are disturbed by my relationship with Chertkov, I am prepared to stop seeing him, although I will say that this is not as unpleasant for me as it is for him, knowing how difficult that will be for him. But, if you wish, I shall do it.

Now [to point] 5): if you do not accept these conditions of mine for a good and peaceful life, then I take back my promise not to leave you. I shall leave — I shall definitely not go to Chertkov's. I shall even make it a firm condition that he not come and live in my vicinity, but I shall certainly go away, since to go on living the way we are living now is impossible.

I could continue living this way if I were able to patiently put up with your sufferings, but I can't. When you left yesterday you were distraught and anguished. I was going to lie down, but began — not so much to think — as to 'feel' you; I couldn't sleep and stayed alert until one or two [in the morning], then would wake up again and listen and see you in a dream — or almost in a dream. Give it some quiet thought, dear friend, listen to your heart, feel it, and everything will work out as it should. As for myself I will say that for my part I have worked everything out in such a way that *I cannot, cannot* act otherwise. My dove, stop the torture — not torturing others, but yourself, because you are suffering a hundred times more than anyone else. That's all.

Lev Tolstoy.

14 July, morning.
1910

Nº 229 – SOFIA ANDREEVNA TOLSTAYA ❧ LEV NIKOLAEVICH TOLSTOY
[LSA 432]
15 July 1910 at Yasnaya Polyana.

Lëvochka dear, I am writing to you (rather than telling you) since after a sleepless night it is difficult for me to speak, and I am overwrought and could easily upset everyone again.[648]

---

648 SAT added a comment on this letter as follows: "The letter was delivered in person. After Lev Nikolaevich's stay with Chertkov his [attitude] towards me greatly changed. He threatened to leave and upset my bodily system, taxed as it was with difficult work, even more.… This letter was written as a result of Chertkov's unpleasantness and rudeness towards me, and my eyes were opened to [the fact] that Lev Nikolaevich, under his despotic influence, subjected himself to him, and completely lost his head over his love to this person, casting me aside and abandoning his love for me without cause."

But I want to, *terribly* want to be quiet and clear-headed. I was going over it all last night in my thought, and it became painfully clear to me that you have been caressing me with one hand while showing me a knife with the other. This knife is a threat, and a very poignant one — a threat to go back on your promise and to secretly leave me if I don't change my ways. So what am I to believe if you can go back on your word the very next day?

The way I am, as of now — I am undoubtedly *ill*, and after losing my spiritual equilibrium I am suffering as a result. That means, each night like last night I shall be listening [to hear] whether you have gone off somewhere. Each time you go, even if it's just for a slightly more extended period, I shall worry terribly that you might have left [me] forever. Just think, dear Lëvochka: after all, this [contemplated] departure and [your] threat are tantamount to a threat of murder. How can I live without you? How can I survive if you, without any provocation on my part, abandon me senselessly in my misery — me, who loves you dearly more than ever before? How can I now recover my health under such a threat, afraid day and night that you are abandoning me? And again I'm constantly weeping, and right at the moment I'm shaking all over, and my whole body, my whole body is hurting. Don't be in haste to go away; after all I'm hoping that I myself will soon pass on; the Lord will indeed be looking down on me. Right now I am suffering for my sins.

Then in Chertkov's letter, which somehow provoked you to tears, he apparently hopes that you will hand your diaries over [to him] when you are ready, for [his future] work.[649] Again I feel torn apart day and night by [the thought] that you will hand them over *behind my back*. My one hope is that you will give me for safekeeping the paper and key to the safety deposit box at the bank.[650] Give [them to me], my dove. After all, there's nothing I can really do; everything will be in your name. Relieve me of these two extreme fears which are constantly eating away at me: 1) that you will leave me *behind my back*; 2) that you will once again give Chertkov the diaries *behind my back*. After all, truly, I am telling you in all sincerity that I am still quite ill — [you] have to recognise that, there's no alternative — [if] you think I have temporarily taken leave of my senses, forgive me and help me! I shall not come to say hullo to you, so as not to irritate you with my presence. I shall not say anything more; I am afraid of myself and feel terribly *sorry* for you, my poor dear, my beloved, taken away from me, torn out of my heart — my husband! And this is a huge wound which hurts! The most painful part of it is that by suffering I am tormenting you. I am the one who needs to leave, and perhaps I *shall* leave, [at least] for a while!

S. T.

---

649 On 7 July 1910 Chertkov wrote to SAT: "I indicated to you that to date I have never abused my close acquaintance-ship with the intimate side of your family life, that I have never made any *indiscrétions* in this direction and I shall not do so in the future, *despite* [emphasis: Chertkov] the fact that I already have sufficient data to harm you here if I wanted to" (Sofia Tolstaya Archives).
650 See Letter № 228, Note 647.

N° 230 – SOFIA ANDREEVNA TOLSTAYA ❧ LEV NIKOLAEVICH TOLSTOY
[LSA 433]
24 night–25 July 1910 [Yasnaya Polyana]

Farewell, Lëvochka![651] I thank you for my *former* happiness. You have abandoned me for Chertkov; the two of you have made some kind of secret agreement, and [this] evening you said that you are determined to allow yourself freedom of action and will be totally without scruples. What does that mean? What kind of *freedom* [are you talking about]?

The doctors have advised me to go away and, now that I have left,[652] you are quite free to keep any secrets à parte and rendez-vous with Chertkov. I can't look on any of this any longer, I [simply] can't… I am tired of jealousy, suspicion and the sorrow that you have been taken away from me forever. I tried coming to terms with my unhappiness, [I tried] to meet with Chertkov, and I can't. — Humiliated by my daughter [Sasha],[653] rejected by my husband, I am forsaking my house as long as my place is occupied by Chertkov, and I shall not return until he has left the scene. If the government [decides] to let him stay at Teljatinki, I shall probably never return. Be healthy and happy in your *Christian* love for Chertkov and all mankind, which for some reason excludes your unhappy wife.

N° 231 – LEV NIKOLAEVICH TOLSTOY ❧ SOFIA ANDREEVNA TOLSTAYA
[PSS 84/833]
1 September 1910. Kochety.

I was hoping for a letter from you today, dear Sonja, but thank you at least for the brief one you wrote to Tanja.[654]

I constantly think about you, and feel your [presence], despite the distance. You care about my physical condition, and I am grateful to you for that, while I am concerned about your mental state. How is it? May God help you in that work which I know you are zealously undertaking for your soul. Even though I am more occupied by spiritual concerns, I still would like to know about your [current] physical health. As for me, if it weren't for the alarming thoughts

---

651 This letter was written before SAT left Yasnaya Polyana on 25 July. She describes her departure in her diary: "In the morning I decided to leave home, at least for a time. Firstly, to avoid seeing Chertkov and avoid getting upset at his presence, his secret conspiracies and his whole underhandedness, and then suffering as a result. Secondly, simply to have a rest and give Lev Nikolaevich a rest from my presence and my suffering soul. — I haven't decided yet where I shall live…. At the railway terminal [in Tula] I ran into [Andrjusha = Andrej L'vovich Tolstoj], and thought, after accompanying him to Yasnaya, to travel to Moscow that evening. But Andrjusha, realising the condition I was in, stayed with me, resolved not to let me alone even for a moment. What could I do? I agreed and returned with him to Yasnaya…. Travelling to and fro, and the excitement — all that quite tired me out, and no sooner had I climbed the stairs than I lay down, fearful of meeting my husband with his jeering comments. But, something quite different happened — something unexpected and quite joyful. He came to me with a kind and touching attitude. Through tears he started thanking me for coming back…. And he embraced me, kissed me, pressed me to his frail chest, and I cried, too, and told him how I loved him as fervently and forcefully as though I were a young woman again, and what happiness I felt in snuggling up to him." (*Dnevniki*, II.157–58).

652 LNT's doctor Dushan Petrovich Makovitskij wrote on this day, 25 July: "Sofia Andreevna left at 2 o'clock in the afternoon. She bade us farewell as though she were leaving for good and had no intention to return. In one pocket she carried a pistol, and had some opium with her. She made the sign of the cross over her daughter [and] Ol'ga Konstantinovna [wife to Andrej L'vovich Tolstoj]. She asked me to forgive her if she was to blame for anything…" (quoted by SAT in *Dnevniki* II.158).

653 Aleksandra L'vovna (Sasha) Tolstaja nearly always took her father's side in family conflicts.

654 In his *Diary only for myself [Dnevnik dlja odnogo sebja]* LNT commented on his letter to SAT of 1 September 1910 as follows: "I wrote a letter to Sonja which [simply] flowed forth from my heart" (*PSS* 3: 135).

about you, which will not leave me, I would be quite content. My health is good; as usual every morning I take my walks, which are most precious to me, during which I jot down fresh thoughts which delight me, then I do reading and writing at home. Today for the first time I started continuing the article[655] I began writing long ago about the causes of the immoral life which everybody in our time is living. Then I went for an outing — partially on horseback, but mostly on foot. Yesterday Dushan and I rode over to see Matveeva,[656] and I got worn out, not so much from the ride over — she brought us home in a carriage — as from her very unintelligent chatter. But I don't regret my trip. I found it interesting and even instructive to observe this environment — coarse, base, rich — [an island] amidst the [general] indigent population. The other day Mavor[657] was here. He fascinated me with his tales of China and Japan, but I got worn out with him from the pressure of speaking a language[658] I am not accustomed to and have little [conversational] familiarity with. Today I took a walk. It's evening now. I am responding to letters, first of all to yours.

How are you making use of your time? Are you going to Moscow and when? I don't have any definite plans, but I want to do what would be pleasing to you. I hope and trust that I will feel just as fine at Yasnaya as here.

I await a letter from you. Hugs and kisses.

Lev.

1 Sept. 1910.

Nº 232 – SOFIA ANDREEVNA TOLSTAYA ✒ LEV NIKOLAEVICH TOLSTOY
[LSA 437]
11 September 1910. Kochety.[659]

Dear Lëvochka, I wanted to say a few words to you before we part. But you get so irritated by your conversations with me that it would pain me to upset you.

I would ask you to realise that all my — not *demands*, as you put it, but *desires* — have had one source: my love for you, my desire to be apart from you as little as possible, and my annoyance at the invasion of an external influence, highly unfavourable to me, on our long, definitely loving, intimate marital life.

Now that this is out of the picture — while you, unfortunately, regret it, I am infinitely grateful for the great sacrifice which will return to me happiness and life — I swear to you that I shall make every effort peacefully, caringly and joyfully embrace your spiritual and whole life.

---

655 A reference to LNT's article *On madness [O bezumii]* (PSS 38).
656 Varvara Dmitrievna Matveeva — a landowner and neighbour to the Sukhotins, married to the nobility representative for Mtsensk Uezd.
657 James Mavor (1854–1925) — a professor of political economy at the University of Toronto, who served as a Canadian intermediary for the resettlement of the Doukhobors to Canada. It was Mavor who, at the request of a Russian anarchist then living in Canada — Prince Pëtr Alekseevich Kropotkin (1842–1911) — had contacted the Canadian government in support of the Douhkobors' immigration and later helped make arrangements for their settlement on the Canadian prairies. Mavor had previously visited Yasnaya Polyana in August 1899 at the invitation of Sergej Lʹvovich Tolstoj, who had met him while escorting the Doukhobors to their new home in Canada earlier that year. See his two-volume work *My windows on the street of the world* (Mavor 1923).
658 LNT had a good reading command of English, but not much practice in speaking it.
659 The Tolstoy couple were staying with their daughter Tatʹjana Lʹvovna (Tanja) Sukhotina, who lived with her husband Mikhail Sergeevich Sukhotin (see Letter Nº 166, Note 192) on their Kochety estate. She left Kochety on 11 September, leaving this letter with Sukhotin to give to LNT.

After all, there are hundreds of wives that really *demand* of their husbands a lot: "Let's go to Paris to the fashion shows, or for gambling, accept my lovers, don't dare go to the club, buy me diamonds, legitimise the child I had with God knows who, etc., etc."

The Lord hath delivered me from all sorts of temptations and *demands*. I was so happy that I have had no wants, and [for that] I can only give thanks to God.

For the first time in my life I have not demanded [anything], but I have still suffered terribly from your cooling attitude towards me and from Chertkov's interference in our life, and for the first time I have *desired*, with all my suffering heart, quite possibly the impossible — [i.e.] a restoration of what we had before.

The means [I employed] to achieve this, of course, were the most vile, awkward, unkind and tormenting for you, even more for me, and it gives me considerable grief. I don't know whether I was self-willed; I think not; everything about me weakened: my will, my heart and soul, and even my body. Rare glimpses of your former love made me incredibly happy all this time, and my love for you, which serves as a basis for all my actions, even those which smack of jealousy or insanity, has never waned, and it shall be with me until the end of my life. Farewell, dear, and don't get angry over this letter.

Your wife, and yours for ever, just Sonja.

Nº 233 – SOFIA ANDREEVNA TOLSTAYA ⬥ LEV NIKOLAEVICH TOLSTOY
[LSA 438]
14 October 1910. [Yasnaya Polyana]

It seems that every day you are asking me with concern about my health, about how I slept, and every day there are new attacks which burn my heart; they are shortening my life and constantly tormenting me, and I cannot stop myself from suffering.

This new blow, [your] evil action regarding the denial of copyright [protection] to your many descendants,[660] Fate deemed me worthy of discovering, although your accomplice in this told you not to convey it to me or the family.

He [Chertkov] threatened to *play a dirty trick on* me[661] — me and the family — and he carried out this [threat] brilliantly, tricking you into [signing] the paper renouncing [your copyright]. The government, which you and he have excoriated and lambasted in every which way in all your leaflets — will now *legally* take away from your heirs their last piece of bread and hand it over to the Sytins and various rich printshop owners and swindlers, while at the same time Tolstoy's grandchildren will die of hunger thanks to [Chertkov's] evil and vainglorious volition.

And the government, the *State* bank will not permit Tolstoy's *wife* to have access to his diaries.

Step by step, through its various actions, *Christian love* murders the person closest to one (in my sense, not yours) — one's wife, on whose part there have never, ever, been any evil *actions*, and there are none now, apart from the most acute sufferings. I still feel even now various threats hanging over me. And so, Lëvochka, [when] you go praying on your walks, as you

---

660 On 22 July 1910 LNT signed a secret will giving over the whole of his literary legacy to the public domain. His youngest daughter Aleksandra L'vovna (Sasha) Tolstaja was appointed executrix. An explanatory note regarding the will expressed LNT's desire that all "compositions, literary works and writings of any kind published anywhere, as well as those still unpublished, after his death should *not become anyone's private property*, but could be published or republished by anyone who wished to do so". SAT guessed that he had made such a will, and this greatly disturbed her. In his *Diary just for myself* LNT wrote (under 2 August 1910): "I am very, very cognisant of my mistake. I should have called all my heirs together and declared my intention, and not in secret."
661 See Letter Nº 229, Note 649.

pray, think hard about what you are doing under pressure from this evildoer: snuff out evil, open your heart, awaken love and good rather than malice and wrongdoing, or the vainglorious pride (in regard to your copyright), hatred towards me, to the person that, in loving you, has given you her whole life and love…

Should you happen to suppose that I am being motivated by *self-interest*, then I am personally, officially, willing, like our daughter Tanja,[662] to relinquish my rights to my husband's inheritance. What would I need it for? It is evident that I shall soon depart from this life one way or another. I am terrified, if I should survive you, of the evil that could arise over your grave and in the memories of our children and grandchildren. Snuff it out, Lëvochka, while you're still alive! Awaken and soften your heart, awaken in it God and the love which you preach with such vehemence to mankind.

S. T.

N° 234 – LEV NIKOLAEVICH TOLSTOY ✿ SOFIA ANDREEVNA TOLSTAYA
[PSS 84/837]
28 October 1910. Yasnaya Polyana.

My departure will upset you.[663] I am sorry about that, but understand and believe that I could not act any other way. My situation at home is becoming, has become, unbearable. Apart from everything else, [since] I can no longer live in these conditions of luxury in which I have been living, I am doing what elderly people of my age generally do: give up on worldly life and go off to spend the final days of their lives in solitude and quietude.

Please understand this and don't come after me, even if you [happen to] find out where I am. Your arrival on the scene will only worsen your situation and mine, but will not affect my decision. I thank you for your 48 years of honest life with me, and I ask you to forgive me for everything for which I am to blame in your sight, just as I forgive you with all my heart for everything for which you might be to blame in my sight. I advise you to come to terms with these new circumstances in which my departure places you, and don't harbour any unkind feelings towards me. If you wish to communicate with me, do it through Sasha; she will know where I am and will forward to me whatever is necessary. She cannot tell you where I am, since I have her word that she will tell this to no one.

Lev Tolstoy.

28 Oct.
I have tasked Sasha with collecting my things and manuscripts and sending them to me.

L. T.

On the envelope: To Sofia Andreevna.

662 Tat'jana L'vovna (Tanja) Sukhotina relinquished her rights to an inheritance from her husband in favour of his children by his first marriage.
663 This letter was written on the day of LNT's secret departure from Yasnaya Polyana. He left the house at dawn in the company of his physician Dushan Petrovich Makovitskij, having informed only his youngest daughter Aleksandra of his plans. LNT first went to see his sister Marija Nikolaevna at the Shamordino convent. He planned to take a small house in the country and live in peace. Along the way he stopped by the Optina-Pustyn' monastery and spent the night in its guest house. He walked over to the priory where his sister's spiritual confessor, Father Iosif, lived, but decided not to go in to see him.

Nº 235 – SOFIA ANDREEVNA TOLSTAYA ❧ LEV NIKOLAEVICH TOLSTOY
[LSA 439]
[29 October 1910. Yasnaya Polyana]

Lëvochka, my dove, come back home, my dear, save me from another suicide [attempt].[664] Lëvochka, my lifelong friend, I shall do everything you wish; I shall renounce luxury altogether; the two of us shall be on friendly terms with your friends; I shall take treatment, I shall be meek; come back, my precious, my precious! After all, you must *save* me; after all, it says in the Gospel, too, that one must not forsake one's wife under *any circumstance*. My precious, my dove, my soul-friend, save me, come back, come back at least so that we can say farewell to each other before we part for eternity.

Where are you? Where? Are you healthy? Lëvochka, don't torment me so, my dove; I shall serve you with love and with my whole heart and soul, come back to me, come back, for God's sake, for the sake of that love of God which you proclaim to everyone; I shall give you that same meek and self-sacrificing love! I sincerely and solemnly promise, my dove, and we shall simplify everything on friendly terms; we shall go away, wherever you wish; we shall live as you wish.

Farewell, forever, perchance forever.

Yours, Sonja.

Have you really left me *forever*? You know I shall not survive this misfortune, you know you will kill me [by this]. Precious, save me from sin; after all, you cannot be happy and at peace if you kill me.

Lëvochka, my dear friend, don't conceal from me *where* you are, and allow me to come and see you, my dove; I shall not upset you, I give you my word; I shall treat you meekly, and with love.

Here are all my children, but they will not help me with their self-confident despotism; I need but one thing, I need your love; it is *vital* that I see you. My friend, allow me at least to say farewell to you, and tell you for the last time how much I love you. Summon me, or come to me yourself. Farewell, Lëvochka, I am still seeking you and calling you. How my soul is in torment!

Nº 236 – SOFIA ANDREEVNA TOLSTAYA ❧ LEV NIKOLAEVICH TOLSTOY
[LSA 440]
30 October 1910. 4 a.m. [Yasnaya Polyana]

I have yet no news from you, my dear Lëvochka, and my heart is being torn apart from suffering. My dove, do you not feel its resonance in yourself? Can it be that my one stupid gesture will bring ruin to my whole life?[665] You sent a message to me through Sasha that my suspiciously rummaging through your papers that night was the last straw which precipitated your departure. That night I was carrying my letters downstairs; the yellow dog chased after me, and I hastened to close all the doors [behind me] so that it wouldn't wake you up, and I honestly

---

664 Upon learning of her husband's departure, SAT threw herself in the pond, but was rescued by LNT's alert secretary, Valentin Fëdorovich Bulgakov (1886–1966), along with several servants, who rushed to the scene.

665 SAT commented on this sentence with the following explanation: "The gesture was this: in the night, while taking my letter and proof sheets to the post bag, I went into Lev Nikolaevich's study to close the door on the new dog which was chasing me. I *did not rummage* through any papers (there weren't any to begin with). The only thing I touched was a diary locked in a briefcase, just to make sure it hadn't been taken by Chertkov" (cited in S. A. Tolstaja, *Letters to L. N. Tolstoy*, p. 802).

don't know what prompted me to go into your study and just *touch* your diary, which I used to do but have not done for some time — [just] to make sure it was in its place.

It wasn't out of suspicion that I sometimes looked at you, but, often, simply to gaze on you with love. My silly jealousy of Chertkov, prompting me to sometimes try and ascertain how much you love him, and obtain proof of this, has started to fade away. On several occasions I wanted to tell you this, but felt ashamed, as though it might be humiliating for you if it were up to *me* to allow [you] such rendez-vous.

Lëvochka, my friend, when you come to think of it, everything you wrote that is great, artistic and spiritual — all that, you wrote while living with me. If my nervous disease has prevented you lately from working, forgive me, my dove. Yesterday I began intensive treatment; daily, twice for a whole hour, I am to sit in a warm bath with cold compresses on my head and stay in bed most of the day. I shall behave, especially since I was driven into such a horrible state [of mind] by your action — i.e. your departure — you've no doubt heard the rumours — that the minute Sasha told me that you had left *for good*, I didn't even finish your letter[666] before I ran off and threw myself into the Middle Pond, flat on my back, so as to prevent any escape.

And how is it that I, who am ever alert, did not hear you leave? When I ran away, I must have looked quite a fright, since Sasha immediately called [Valentin Fëdorovich] Bulgakov, Vanja[667] and the cook[668] and they came after me. But I had already reached [the pond], the water covered me completely, and I felt with great delight that here it was — the end of my mental agony — for ever. But it did not please God to allow you and me to be touched by this sin; poor Sasha and Bulgakov plunged, fully clothed, into the water and managed to pull me out with the help of Vanja and the cook, and carried me home.

You, no doubt, will be angered to hear this, but at the time, as now, I was beside myself with despair. I sleep in your room, that is, I sit and lie at night, and water your pillows with my tears and I pray to God and you to forgive me, to return you to me. — The kind Marija Aleksandrovna[669] sleeps next to me on the sofa, coughing all night long. Poor Sasha has caught cold and has a severe cough. *All* the children have taken pity on me, bless them, and have come to heal and comfort me. Tanechka[670] is so thin! She'll be coming again at the beginning of November and spend a month with us, along with her husband and little girl. Couldn't you come then, too? When Misha and Il'ja saw me, they shed such sorrowful tears, hugging me and looking at my agonised face, that I felt joy at their love. The same with Serëzha.

Lëvochka, dear, have you really left us for good? Did you not love me before? You write that elderly people retreat from the world. But where did you see this? Elderly peasants live out their final days [by sleeping] on the stove,[671] and within the circle of their family and grandchildren, and this latter is the same whether in lordly or any other kind of surroundings. Is it natural for a weak old man to abandon the care, concern and love on the part of his children and grandchildren around him?

Come back, my dear, precious husband. Come back, Lëvochka, my dove. Don't be cruel, allow [me] at least to visit you, once I'm feeling a little better after my treatment.

---

666 Letter N° 234 of 28 October 1910.
667 Ivan Osipovich (Vanja) Shuraev — a Yasnaya Polyana peasant.
668 Semën Nikolaevich Rumjantsev (1867–1932) — son of Nikolaj Mikhajlovich Rumjantsev (see Letter N° 5, Note 27).
669 Marija Aleksandrovna Shmidt (family friend) — see Letter N° 138, Note 595.
670 The Tolstoys' daughter Tat'jana L'vovna (Tanja, Tanechka) Tolstaja.
671 A large masonry stove (which could also be termed an oven or furnace) was a central feature of Russian peasant homes. Not only did it serve for heating the house and cooking, but provided a warm place to sleep on cold winter nights.

Don't torment me even further by not telling me — especially me — where you are. You may say that my presence will interfere with your writing. But can you work, knowing how agonisingly I am suffering?

You know, it says in the Gospel: "Love thy neighbour as thyself."[672] And nowhere does it say to love some sort of writings more than a human being. If only you could feel how I love you, how I am willing with my whole being to make any kind of concessions, to do anything to serve you. Lëvochka, forgive me, come back to me, *save* me! Don't think these are all just words, *love* me, take pity [on me] once again in your heart, pay no attention to what people will write or say about you — hold yourself superior to that — after all, there is nothing in this world that is superior to *love*, and let us live out the final days of our life *together* in holiness and love! How many times you have conquered your passions! How many times, in love to me, you have stayed with me, and we have lived a long life together in friendship and love! Could my guilt be so great now that you are unable to forgive me and come back to me? After all, I was, indeed, ill.

Dear Lëvochka, your concessions, your living together with me, have to date not lessened or diminished your greatness or glory. And your forgiveness and love for me will elevate your soul in God's sight. They will elevate it also through your *saving* me, your wife — simply saving a human being and ignoring your desire for glory and good *for yourself*. If you could see me [the way I am] now, if you could peer into my soul, you would be horrified at the sufferings I am experiencing — the tearing apart of my whole spiritual and physical being! I already wrote to you, my precious Lëvochka; I don't know whether my letter reached you. Andrjusha took it to send off by some means — I don't know.

Read this letter carefully; I shall not be writing any further about my feelings. For the last time I am appealing to you, my husband, my friend, my precious, beloved Lëvochka; forgive me, save me, *come back* to me.

Yours, Sonja.

Nº 237 – LEV NIKOLAEVICH TOLSTOY ❧ SOFIA ANDREEVNA TOLSTAYA
[PSS 84/839]
30–31 October 1910. Shamordino.

Our meeting together and especially my return are now completely impossible.[673] This would be, as everybody says, harmful in the highest degree for you, while for me it would be an [absolute] horror, since my current situation, thanks to your agitation, irritation and diseased condition would become, if such a thing is possible, even worse. I advise you to come to terms with what has happened, adjust to your new temporary situation, and, most importantly, take treatment.

Even if you don't actually love me, but simply not hate me, then you should be able to appreciate my situation, even if just a little. And if you can do that, you will not only not condemn me, but you will try to help me find that peace, the possibility of some kind of [decent] human life, help me through your own inner efforts and no longer desire my return yourself. Your

672 Mark 12: 31.

673 This is LNT's last letter to his wife. Aleksandra (Sasha) Tolstaja arrived at Shamordino from Yasnaya Polyana and reported to LNT that her mother had a guess as to where he was, and might come. It was decided that he should move on, but with no firm plan as to where. LNT caught cold on the train, fell ill, and was obliged to get off the train at the Astapovo station on the Rjazan'-Ural railway line. He was put to bed in the quarters of the stationmaster, Ivan Ivanovich Ozolin (1872–1939?), where he passed away at 6:05 a.m. on 7 November 1910.

current mood, your desire and your attempts to commit suicide, show — more than does anything else — your loss of self-control, and make my return unthinkable now. Nobody but you alone can save your loved ones, me and, especially yourself, from experiencing agony. Try to direct all your energies not to bring about everything you desire — namely, my return — but to come to terms with yourself, your soul, and you will have what you desire. I have spent two days at Shamordino [Nunnery] and Optina [Pustyn' Monastery] and am about to leave. I shall post this letter along the way. I shan't tell you where I am going, since I consider this separation necessary for both you and myself. Don't think I left because I don't love you. I do love you and I have pity for you with all my heart, but I cannot act in any other way. As to your letter, I know it was written in all sincerity, but you do not have the power to carry out everything you desire. And the [important] thing lies not in fulfilling any wish of mine, but rather in your equanimity, your calm and rational approach to life. And as long as those [qualities] are absent, life with you is unthinkable for me. To come back to you [now] when you are in such a state would mean for me an abdication of life. And I don't feel I have a right to do that. Farewell, dear Sonja, may God help you. Life is not a joke, and we do not have the right to toss it about at will, and to measure it by length of time is likewise irrational. The remaining months we have left to live are quite possibly more important than all the years we have lived heretofore, and we have to live them well.

L. T.

Nº 238 – SOFIA ANDREEVNA TOLSTAYA ⚘ LEV NIKOLAEVICH TOLSTOY
[LSA 441]
1 November 1910. [Yasnaya Polyana]

I received your letter;[674] have no fear that I shall now come in search of you. I am so weak that I can hardly move, and I have no wish to force anything. Do what is best for you. It is a terrible misfortune, your departure — [it teaches] me the lesson that if I should survive and you join together with me, I shall make every effort in the world to make sure that everything is good for you.

But for some reason I get the impression that we shall not see each other again! Lëvochka, dear, I am writing this in full awareness and sincerity and shall definitely carry it out. Yesterday I made peace with Chertkov; today I shall confess my sin of [attempted] suicide, with which I was hoping to bring an end to my sufferings!

I don't know what to write to you, I have no knowledge of what is to come. Your saying — that if you met with me it would be *disastrous* for you — has convinced me that it is impossible. But how meekly, gratefully and joyfully I would meet with you! My precious, have pity on me and the children, put an end to our sufferings!

Serëzha has gone, Andrjusha is here and just now Misha arrived. Tanja is so exhausted that right now she wants to leave. Lëvochka, [just] awaken the love within yourself and you will see how much love you will find in me.

I can't write any more, I've somehow grown extremely weak. Hugs and kisses to you, my dear old friend, who used to love me. There's no sense in expecting that something new *will*

674 Letter Nº 237 of 30–31 October 1910. At the end of the letter we find this comment by SAT: "The following letter (Nº 239) of 2 November did not reach Lev Nikolaevich; it is also unfinished. At 7:30 a.m. we received a telegram from [the paper] *Russkoe slovo*, saying that Lev Nikolaevich had fallen ill at the Astapovo station with a temperature of +40° [i.e. 3 degrees above normal]. At Tula we boarded a special train and headed there. On 7 November 1910 Lev Nikolaevich passed away" (cited from S. A. Tolstaya, *Letters to L. N. Tolstoy*, p. 803).

begin in me. Already right now in my heart there is such love, such meekness, [such] a desire for your joy and happiness, that time will not create anything new. Well, God be with you, take care of your health.

Sonja.

Nº 239 – SOFIA ANDREEVNA TOLSTAYA ❧ LEV NIKOLAEVICH TOLSTOY
[LSA 443]
2 November 1910. 5:30 a.m. Yasnaya Polyana [Letter unsent][675]

Before we part, possibly forever, I want to — not justify, but only — *explain* to you my conduct which you accused me of in your letter to Sasha.[676]

If I watched you through the balcony door as you were playing *patience*, if I met you and saw you off on your ride or wanted to come across your path on a walk, or if I ran into the salon when you were just coming in or having breakfast, none of that was ever out of suspicion, but out of some kind of crazy, passionate feel for you which I've been having lately. I must have had a premonition of what was going to happen. I would look through the window and think: "Oh, there's my Lëvochka, still here with me, God bless him!" After seeing you off on a ride, on entering the house I would often cross myself and say: "God bless him, bring him safely home." I cherished each minute with you, I was so happy when you would ask me for something, or simply call out: "Sonja!" Every day I would be resolved to tell you what I wanted — that you would see Chertkov, but somehow felt ashamed to again, as it were, *allow* you to do something. And you became gloomier and more austere; in my presence you would hold out your cup and ask others to pour you tea or offer you strawberries; you would no longer talk with me. And you took cruel revenge on me for your friend. And I had a painful premonition of this.

As for your diary, I acted out of a silly habit: if I happened to be [in your study], I would feel to check whether the diary were there or not; but, you see, I did it without making a sound. On that terrible final night I closed the door to shut out the yellow dog which had come upstairs, so that it wouldn't waken you. I peeked into your office after taking the letters downstairs, and out of a stupid habit I *touched* the diary just with my hand. I did not *rummage* through anything, I wasn't searching for anything, I didn't read anything, and right away I realised I had made a stupid mistake.

But you would have left all the same; I had a premonition of this and was greatly afraid.

I am getting treatment and taking baths; there's nothing else to do. It's hard to stand the presence of other people — a very stupid doctor and a chatterbox of a nurse. But the children want them, and I dare not object, though it's even shameful how little there is left for them to do. I try

675 Again, SAT commented: "I did not manage to finish this letter, and it was not sent. I am copying it to show what kind of mood I was in at the time" (cited from S. A. Tolstaya, *Letters to L. N. Tolstoy*, p. 805).

676 On 29 October 1910 LNT wrote to his daughter Aleksandra L'vovna (Sasha) from the Optina Pustyn' monastery: "I am very much counting on a good influence on the part of Tanja and Serëzha. The main thing is that they understand me and try to make her [i.e. SAT] realize that with all this spying, eavesdropping, endless reproaches, treating me according to her whim, her endless controlling, her contrived hatred to the person *closest* and most needful to me, with this obvious hatred towards me and her pretensions of love — such a life is not [just] unpleasant for me, but downright impossible, and if anyone is drowning [as a result], it's by no means her, it's me. I just desire one thing — to be free of her, of this lie, pretension and malice which have infused her whole being. Naturally, they cannot make her realize this, but they can make her see that all her behaviour towards me does not only not express love, but seems to indicate a clear goal of killing me, which she will achieve, since I hope that with this third heart attack that is threatening me I shall rescue her and myself from this terrible situation in which we have been living and to which I do not want to return" (*PSS* 82: 218).

to keep busy a little, but it's hard. Yesterday I started to eat a little — the children are so touch-ingly happy at this — I exhausted my precious ones: Tanechka and Andrjusha; but to put a stop to my emotional agonies is not within their power. That's not what can save me! I keep thinking day and night about whether you're healthy, where you are, what you are thinking, what you are doing. Can it be easy for you to tear me apart like this? How quickly and joyfully I would improve, how [willingly] I would give you my word never to chase after you, not read anything and not touch anything if you didn't want me to, and [just] do everything you wanted [me to]… But I feel we shall never see each other again, and that kills me! At least, even if we didn't *live* together for the time being, we could just see each other! I would come for a few hours and promise to leave. Fear not, I shan't come without your permission, besides I have to achieve a little better state of health. Do not be afraid of me: it would be better to die than to see the *horror* on your face upon my arrival…

II-1. Lev Nikolaevich Tolstoy with his daughter Alexandra L'vovna, 1906.
Photo by V. Chertkov, from the collection of Igor Jascolt

11-2. Lev Nikolaevich Tolstoy with his sister Marija Nikolaevna Tolstaja at
Yasnaya Polyana, 1908.
Photo by Karl Karlovich Bulla

11-3. Lev Nikolaevich Tolstoy and Sofia Andreevna Tolstaya on the eve of his 80th birthday, August 1908, at Yasnaya Polyana.
Photo by Vladimir Grigor'evich Chertkov

Левъ Толстой. 23 Мая, 1908.

11-4. The only known colour photograph of Lev Nikolaevich Tolstoy, taken 28 May 1908 by Sergej Mikhajlovich Prokudin-Gorskij, who served as photographer to the Tsars. He had developed a high-quality colour-processing technique that was far ahead of its time.

II-5. Lev Nikolaevich Tolstoy (right) with his brother Sergej Nikolaevich Tolstoy (left), 1902.
Photo by Marija L'vovna Obolenskaja (the Tolstoys' daughter)

11-6. Lev Nikolaevich Tolstoy with his granddaughter Tat'jana Mikhajlovna (Tanjushka)
Sukhotina, daughter of Tat'jana L'vovna Sukhotina (née Tolstaja), Yasnaya Polyana, 1908.
Photo by Vladimir Grigor'evich Chertkov

II-7. Lev Nikolaevich Tolstoy at work in his Yasnaya Polyana study in 1909.
Photo by Sofia Andreevna Tolstaya

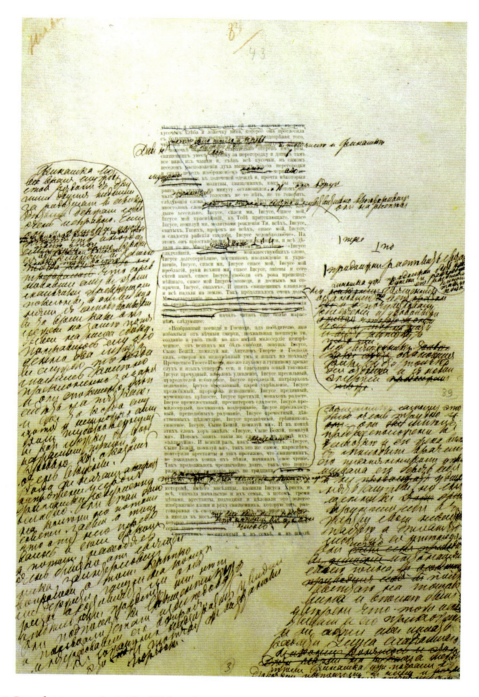

II-8. Page from an early draft of Tolstoy's novel *Resurrection* [*Voskresenie*], showing deletions by the censors and the author's revisions in the margins (1899).

11-9. Lev Nikolaevich Tolstoy, followed by his personal physician Dushan Petrovich Makovitskij, passing through the gates of Yasnaya Polyana, January 1910.

Photo by A. I. Savel'ev

11-10. Lev Nikolaevich Tolstoy standing in front of his Moscow house
in Khamovniki Lane, 1899.
Photo by Il'ja L'vovich Tolstoj

II-11. Lev Nikolaevich Tolstoy's last letter to his wife, dated 31 October 1910, written from Shamordino. See Letter № 237.

не успѣла послать.

2 Ноября 1910
5½ часовъ утра

Прежде чѣмъ намъ разойтиться можетъ быть на вѣки, я хочу не оправдаться, но только объяснить тебѣ мое то поведеніе, въ которомъ ты меня обвинялъ въ письмѣ къ сыновьямъ или вскорѣ послѣ.

Если я сердилась на тебя и ... тихонько вечеромъ подсмотрѣла, если я встрѣчала тебя и провожала на верховую ѣзду и хотѣла встрѣтить на прогулкѣ, или бѣжала въ залу когда ты приходилъ завтракать,

11-12. Sofia Andreevna Tolstaya's last letter to her husband, dated 2 November 1910, written from Yasnaya Polyana, but not sent. See Letter № 239.

II-13. Lev Nikolaevich Tolstoy on his deathbed at Astapovo Station, 7 November 1910.

11-14. Last will and testament of Lev Nikolaevich Tolstoy, dated 22 July 1910.

II-15. Sofia Andreevna Tolstaya at her husband's grave, 1912.
Photo by Sofia Andreevna Tolstaya

II-16. Stamp commemorating the 25-year
anniversary of Lev Nikolaevich Tolstoy's death.
From the collection of Igor Jascolt

PART IV

ELEVEN UNPUBLISHED LETTERS
(1864–1905)

These eleven letters are but a small sampling of the 201 hitherto unpublished letters written by Sofia Andreevna Tolstaya to her husband. Unlike Tolstaya's other letters in Parts I, II and III, the original Russian versions of these eleven letters are not available anywhere else to the reading public. As it did not seem proper for them to be released in their translated form first, we decided it was only right to show the translation side by side with the original Russian text. All these letters were entrusted to the Slavic Research Group at the University of Ottawa, no doubt in recognition of the group's close collaboration over the past twenty years with the Russian Academy of Sciences and the Tolstoy Museums in Moscow and Yasnaya Polyana, along with our many joint publications, most recently Sofia Tolstaya's extensive autobiographical work *My Life* (2010), also published by the University of Ottawa Press.[1]

---

1 In Parts I, II and III, the unpublished letters are referenced at the beginning of the subsequent published letter. Thus letter N° 1*U* of the unpublished letters is mentioned in the header for letter N° 17 in Part I as follows: [Preceded by SAT's unpublished letter N° 1*U*, 1 December 1864].

Nº 1U – SOFIA ANDREEVNA TOLSTAYA ❧ LEV NIKOLAEVICH TOLSTOY

1 декабря 1864 г. Ясная Поляна

1-го декабря, вечером.

Я, признаюсь, ужасно рада, милый друг мой Лёвочка, что ты велел мне всякий день посылать в Тулу. Самой бы мне было страшно гонять человека и лошадь, а по твоей воле я смело посылаю всякий день. Теперь живу, живу целый день и думаю, а вечером Лёвочке напишу — это моя рекреация и мое утешение. Твои письма я боюсь ждать. Слишком я радуюсь всегда и слишком грустно, когда не привозят. Нынче опять жду. У нас всё хорошо, всё весело — если б только ты был тут. Сережа поправляется, хотя тихо. Понос прошел, сыпь еще не знаю, как, потому что ручки забинтованы, он очень дерет их. К ночи мы развяжем, и я тебе напишу тогда, как его оспа. У девочки подсохло, она чудо какая, даже страшно. И животик даже никогда не поболит. Мое горло тоже прошло от летучей мази, и я нынче не утерпела, соблазнилась хорошей, даже чудесной, погодой и пошла опять с Лизой гулять. Уж мы так с ней наслаждаемся, так хорошо, скоро и бодро мы с ней ходим. Она хотела описать тебе подробно наши прогулки, пускай ее, она это делает лучше меня. А как мне ты везде, везде недостаешь. Мы с Лизой всё говорим: вот кабы еще Лёвочка с нами был. На днях мы отправимся с ней на порошу. Я непременно, во что бы то ни стало, хочу сойти след и хоть одного зайца да спугнуть. Это ужасно весело; право, и во мне, и в Лизе есть охотничья кровь. Лёвочка, приезжай к нам, милый, скорей, мы будем вместе ходить на порошу. Я так теперь бодра, здорова, легка и сильна. Мы с девочкой ладим очень хорошо. Что-то бедная Машенька какая всё мрачная, грустная. Так жаль ее. Ты мою Таню всё жалеешь и видишь ее грустной, я твою Машеньку точно так же. Я ее спрашивала, что она такая, отчего, а

1 December 1864. Yasnaya Polyana

1 December, evening.

I must admit I am terribly happy, my dear friend Lëvochka, that you asked me to send a letter to you through Tula every day. I would be fearful of despatching a horse and rider at my own initiative, but at your behest I am taking the liberty of sending you [a letter] every day. Now I am alive, I live all day long in anticipation of writing Lëvochka in the evening — this is my recreation and my comfort. I'm afraid to look forward to your letters. I am always overly joyful [when they come] and overly saddened when they do not. Today I'm waiting again. Everything's fine and cheery here — all that's missing is you. Serëzha's getting better, albeit gradually. His diarrhœa has passed; I'm not sure about the rash, since his little arms are bandaged, he scratches them awfully. By nightfall we shall take off the bandages and I shall write you then as to how his smallpox is. [Our] little girl's [skin condition] has dried up, she's such a miracle — it's even frightening! And her little tummy does not get sick — ever. My throat is also better from [applying] liniment, and today I couldn't wait, tempted as I was by the good — yea, marvellous — weather and went out for another walk with [your niece] Liza. She and I have such a delightful time together — our walks are good, sprightly and brisk. She wanted to describe our walks in detail to you — I'll leave that to her, [as] she can do it better than I can. How I miss you, no matter where I am! Liza and I keep saying: If only Lëvochka were with us! In the next day or so she and I shall take a walk in the fresh snow. I definitely want to go hunting [in the snow] and flush out at least one hare. That's terribly exciting — both Liza and I must surely have hunting in our blood. Lëvochka, come to us, my dear, just as soon as you can, and we can take an outing in the fresh snow together. Right now I feel so cheerful, healthy, easy

она говорит: «Я всегда такая, мне всегда грустно». Как посмотришь, сколько
несчастных на свете, поневоле совестно
станет за свое счастье. За что мне всё, а
им ничего. И болезни детей, и рука твоя,
и наша разлука, и всё это проходящее,
а вот Машеньке, Тане — плохо. Всё еще
не воротился Кондратий, хотя уже 8-й
час. Я так жду письма твоего. Может
быть, нынче я получу от кого-нибудь из
кремлевских подробности об операции,
которую тебе делали. Дай Бог, я так этого
жду и в такой до сих пор тревоге, как это
всё было. Надеюсь, что всё благополучно,
а то ты, верно, дал бы мне знать, я уже
надеюсь, милый мой Лёва, что ты и вперед
ничего не будешь от меня скрывать.
Напиши, когда ты надеешься вернуть-
ся. Т. е. вели написать, ты, верно, уже не
владеешь рукой, так как она забинтова-
на. Как жаль, что уже не ты будешь мне
писать. Это много, много у меня отнимет
утешения и радости. Того через других
не напишешь, что написал бы сам мне.
У меня мало интересного писать тебе о
нашей жизни. Всё оно же и то же. Сегодня
утром уехал Сережа в Пирогово. Он всё
очень мил и весел. Примерял нынче твой
дворянский мундир, который берет, чтоб
ехать на выборы. Зачем у тебя вдруг такая
паясническая одежда? Я очень удивилась,
на что тебе мундир. Сережа из Пирого-
ва приедет уже к выборам, конечно, не
минует нас. С девочками он читает вслух,
шутит с ними, а со мною всё церемонии
ужасные, даже тяжело. Нынче же утром
приехал Ив[ан] Ив[анович] Орлов. Он
завтра тебе напишет подробности дел в
Никольском. Он заплатил 1000 в Опек[ун-
ский] совет и 1000 дохтуровского долга.
Денег у него нет ничего. Еще он сам занял
250 р. с[еребром], чтоб доплатить долг.
Ждет твоих приказаний, что продавать,
вообще, он напишет обстоятельно. А мы
живем покуда Машенькиными мило-
стями. Я денег ниоткуда не получала; к

and strong. [Our] little girl and I get along
very well. For some reason poor Mashen'ka
seems all sad and morose. I feel so sorry for
her. You keep commiserating with my [sister]
Tanja and see her sorrowing, while I see your
[sister] Mashen'ka in exactly the same way.
I asked her how come she's that way, and she
answers: "I'm always that way, I'm always
sad." When you see how many miserable
people there are in this world, it can't help but
make you feel ashamed to be happy yourself!
Why is it that I have everything and they
have nothing? The children's diseases, your
arm, and our being apart — that's all fleeting,
but Mashen'ka and Tanja have it really bad.
Kondratij hasn't returned yet, even though it's
getting on towards 8 o'clock. I am so looking
forward to your [next] letter. Perhaps today
I shall receive from [a family member in] the
Kremlin some details about your operation.
God grant — I've been waiting so long for
news, and have been in such a state of worry
up to now as to how it all went. I hope it all
went safely; otherwise you would have no
doubt let me know, and I am already hoping,
my dear Lëva, that in future, too, you will not
keep anything back from me. Write and let
me know when you hope to return [home].
That is, ask someone to write for you; you are
probably no longer able to use your arm, since
it's all bandaged up. What a pity you won't be
the one [actually] writing me any more! This
greatly detracts from my comfort and joy. You
won't write through others what you would
write directly to me. I have nothing much of
interest to tell you about our life. It's all pretty
much the same. This morning [your brother]
Serëzha left for Pirogovo. He is always very
nice and cheerful. Today he measured your
court uniform which he is taking to go to
the [nobility representative] elections. Why
have you all of a sudden got such a clownish-
looking outfit? I was very surprised — what
do you need a uniform for? Serëzha will be
coming from Pirogovo just in time for the
elections; of course, he won't pass up a visit to

Николину дню все пристают дать жалова-
нья, придется раздать хоть немного. Ну, да
это всё сообразим при свидании. Я очень
стараюсь быть экономна, насколько могу
и умею. Сейчас глядели ручки Сережи. Всё
подсыхает, и всё гораздо лучше. Оспа при-
нялась и уже подживает. Еще дня два, три,
и всё пройдет. Это меня радует. Нынче я
всё пишу тебе о житейских делах, милый
Лёва. Может быть, тебе скучно. Теперь
иду кормить, а после, по возвращении
Кондратия, напишу еще. —

Сейчас получила письмо Тани, опи-
сание твоей операции, милый мой Лёва.
Видно, не так легко это было, как я думала.
Ты, бедный, очень страдал и, верно, до сих
пор еще не поправился, всё, верно, больно.
Господи, отчего нет меня с тобой, отчего
не я хожу за тобой. Мне это очень грустно,
но всё-таки, слава Богу всё, слава Богу,
вправили. Читала письмо, а на сердце Бог
знает, что делалось, а только вспомню, что
уже всё прошло и была телеграмма, что
здоров, а рука на месте, сделается и весело,
и хорошо. Ты, друг милый, не спеши
теперь домой, я буду писать всю правду
и всякий день. А так как у нас теперь всё

us. As for the girls, he reads aloud to them and
jokes with them, but with me it's all perfunc-
tory, a ceremony — even hard to take. Just this
morning Ivan Ivanovich Orlov came. Tomorrow he'll be writing you in detail about how
things are at Nikol'skoe. He paid 1,000 [rou-
bles] to the Board of Trustees and 1,000 to the
Dokhturov debt [owed by LN's deceased elder
brother Dmitrij to Major Fëdor Nikolaevich
Dokhturov]. He hasn't any money. He himself
borrowed 250 silver roubles to pay the debt.
He is awaiting your instructions as to what to
sell; in any case, he will write [you] in detail
[about it]. For the moment we are living off
Mashen'ka's generosity. I have not received
money from anywhere. By St-Nicholas' Day
everybody will be asking for their wages, and
[we'll] have to pay out at least a little. I'm sure
we'll work it all out when we see each other.
I am very much trying to be frugal, to the
extent that I am able and capable. Just now we
looked at Serëzha's arms. Everything's drying
up, and everything's a lot better. The vaccination has taken and the healing has begun.
Two or three more days and it will all have
passed. I'm glad of that. Today I'm writing
you all about day-to-day affairs, dear Lëva.
Perhaps you find that boring. Now I'm going
to breast-feed [our baby girl], and afterwards,
when Kondratij comes back, I'll write some
more. —

Just now I received [my sister] Tanja's letter
with the description of your operation, my
dear Lëva. Apparently it did not go as easily
as I had imagined. You, poor thing, went
through a lot of agony, and are by no means
completely recovered yet; you must still be
in quite a bit of pain. Lord, why am I not the
one there at your side, caring for you? This is
very sad for me, but, in any case, all thanks to
God, thank God that they [managed to] re-set
the bone. I read the letter, and God knows
what was going on in my heart; but as soon as
I remembered that everything had gone well
and I'd got the telegram saying that you were
healthy, and the arm was in place, then all

хорошо и благополучно, то тебе нечего и спешить. Береги, душенька, свою руку, ради Бога, думай больше о себе, нервы свои совсем не раздражай, они так раздражены хлороформом и операцией. Спасибо Тане, что написала мне, и вперед благодарю за намерение писать мне о тебе. Я ей завидую, она за тобой ходит, видит тебя, а я еще не скоро увижу тебя. Ну, да это всё переживется, только бы теперь рука была на месте и ты сам был бы здоров. Лёвочка, не забывай только меня, люби по-прежнему, мы ведь еще не скоро увидимся. Еще почти 2 недели. Ты будь благоразумен, ради Бога, не приезжай, пока совсем не будешь благополучен. То-то мы опять заживем с тобой хорошо. Точно молодые будем, только что повенчавшиеся. Ведь будет же когда-нибудь это благополучие. Лёвочка, голубчик мой, пришлось тебе много помучиться, бедный, не думала я, что это всё будет иметь такие последствия. Прощай, мой друг, завтра пошлю это письмо, а вечером опять буду писать тебе. Смотри, не падай духом, будь весел, благоразумен; у нас теперь повернуло к лучшему, и, верно, к твоему приезду все будут молодцами. Целую тебя, мой милый. Не забывай меня.

was well and cheerful. Now, my friend, don't hurry to get home; I shall write you the whole truth and [I shall write it] every day. And since we are all good and safe here, there's no reason for you to hurry [home]. Take care of your arm, my darling, for God's sake, think more about yourself, don't do anything to excite your nerves; they are excited enough by the chloroform and the operation. My thanks to Tanja for writing me, and I am grateful to her in advance for thinking to write to me about you. I envy her, she is caring for you, she sees you, while I shan't be seeing you for some time. But we shall get through all this; the only thing now is that your arm be in place and that you yourself be healthy. Only don't forget me, Lëvochka, love me as before; after all, we shan't be seeing each other for a while. Almost two weeks to go. Be sensible, for God's sake, don't come until you are quite healed. Just think how well we can start living together again. We'll be, you know, like newly-weds. This state of well-being will surely come, after all. Lëvochka, my dove, you've had a lot of torment to go through. Poor thing, I didn't think all this would have such consequences. Farewell, my friend; I'll be sending this letter tomorrow, and I'll be writing you again [tomorrow] evening. Take care that you keep your spirits up; be cheerful and sensible. Everything here has taken a turn for the better and, by the time you come, everyone will be in fine fettle. Hugs and kisses, my precious. Don't forget me.

№ 2U – SOFIA ANDREEVNA TOLSTAYA ❧ LEV NIKOLAEVICH TOLSTOY

12 августа 1866 г. Ясная Поляна *12 August 1866. Yasnaya Polyana*

Суббота.   Saturday.

Нынче в таких попыхах пишу тебе, милый Лёвочка. Боюсь, что письмо мое пойдет слишком поздно. Максимовна уехала в Тулу, я осталась с Илюшей, и всё утро не выберу свободной минутки. Теперь уж скоро 12 часов. Вчера брала

I am writing you in such a hurry, dear Lëvochka. I'm afraid my letter will be sent off too late. Maksimovna has gone to Tula, I have stayed behind with [baby] Iljusha, and I haven't had a moment free all morning. Now it's almost 12 o'clock. Yesterday I took a bath

ванну и легла очень поздно, благода-ря больше Танюше, которая не спала и была чудо как мила. Просила всё: «Дай ужинать», «дай курятинки», просилась в кроватку, и когда няня спросила, зачем, она говорит: «Я буду шалить». Так она была оживлена и шаловливо мила. А Сережа день не спал и лег очень рано. Теперь мы с тетенькой пьем чай на балко-не, и хотя свежо, но, слава Богу, ясно. Где ты провел нынешнюю ночь, был сильный дождь, уж не в дороге ли? Я никак не сооб-ражу до сих пор твой маршрут. Должно быть, нынче ты у Дьяковых. Хотела бы написать тебе, что груди лучше, но, к несчастью, могу только сказать, что хуже. Левая так велика ранка, просто такая скука. С камином так возились, без тебя беда, ничего не сообразим. Даже хотели отправить печников, да уж решились сде-лать по-своему. Михаил Алекс[???] совсем растерялся с камином. Он вчера ездил ночью на охоту и загнал 30 лошадей, в том числе и наших, за что, конечно, оштрафо-вали работников. Нынче мне что-то очень скучно и даже завидно, досадно, что я не с вами там. Ужасно бы хотелось, ничто бы мне не доставило такого удовольствия. Воображаю, как тебе все рады были и как ты приятно время провел. Как бы я рада была, если б ты завтра приехал, но, верно, не приедешь. Прощай, милый, тетенька нынче исповедуется на дому, у нас, дети гуляют, а главное — все здоровы. Целую тебя крепко.

and went to bed quite late, thanks mostly to [our daughter] Tanjusha, who couldn't sleep but was incredibly cute. She had all sorts of requests: "Can we have supper?", "Can we have chicken?" She asked to go to bed, and when the nanny asked why, she said: "I'm going to be naughty." She was so lively and so mischievously nice. As to Serëzha, he didn't sleep all day and went to bed quite early. At this moment Auntie and I are taking tea on the balcony, and while [the air] is cool, thank God the sky is clear. Where did you spend this past night? There was a heavy rain. You weren't still travelling? I still can't ever figure out your itinerary. If I'm not mistaken, today you are at the D'jakovs'. I was hoping to write and tell you that my breasts felt better, but [now] I can only say they are worse. The wound in the left one is so great, it's extremely annoying. We spent great effort trying to cope with the stove, [but] without you it's a disaster, we can't figure out anything. We even con-sidered dismissing the stove-setters, but then we thought to dare suggest our own solution. Mikhail Aleks[???] got quite distraught [try-ing to fix] the fireplace. Last night he took a party out hunting and [they] overworked 30 horses, including ours, for which, of course, the workers were fined. Today I feel rather out of it and even envious, [or at least] disap-pointed, that I am not there with you lot. I'd terribly like to [be there]; nothing would give me greater pleasure. I can only imagine how pleased everyone was to see you and the fun time you must have had. How happy I would be if you came tomorrow, but probably you won't come. Farewell, dear. Auntie is today saying confession here at home, our children are out walking, but the main thing is that everybody's well. Hugs and big kisses.

№ 3*U* – SOFIA ANDREEVNA TOLSTAYA ❧ LEV NIKOLAEVICH TOLSTOY

13 ноября 1866 г. Ясная Поляна

13-го ноября.
Воскресенье вечер.

Мне следовало бы тебе писать по утрам, милый мой Лёвочка, потому что утром, когда я встану, я и энергична, и бодра, и на что-нибудь способна, а по вечерам я чувствую себя до того усталой, бесполезной и одинокой, что не могу весело писать тебе. От англичанки у меня остается то впечатление, что, взяв помощницу, у меня никогда не было так много дела и никогда так мало времени, как, например, весь нынешний день. Объясняюсь я с ней довольно хорошо и с помощью диксионера, когда не знаю слова, но с детьми беда, они всё сидят со мной, Таня даже не отходит от меня; конечно, всё это и может быть, образуется, но как? И не потеряем ли мы с этой молоденькой Ханной терпение? Она всё болтает по-английски, а иногда, видно, ей станет грустно, и она замолчит. Я даю ей книгу читать, книга ее очень заинтересовала, но зато она детей совсем уже предоставила мне. Гораздо лучше будет, если дети совсем перейдут в ее комнату, она сама этого очень желает. А теперь всё так еще неопределенно, так трудно это переходное время, и детей жалко почему-то, а верно, жалеть нечего, и им ничуть не тяжело. Я думала нынче, что только третий день как ты уехал, а мне уже так давно, давно кажется, и просто сил в себе не чувствую, как я проживу еще эти 4 или 5 дней, это просто ужас. Я не не в духе, ни на кого не сержусь, ни к чему не придираюсь, я думаю, оттого что если б я хоть одним словом дала высказаться своей тоске, то я сейчас бы расплакалась, как и теперь, жалуясь тебе. Во мне всё так сжалось, и так я не живу, а только боюсь всё чего-то и жду всё ночи, потому что тогда, слава Богу, день прошел. Вот что значит, без тебя, милый мой Лёвочка. И

13 November 1866. Yasnaya Polyana

13 November.
Sunday evening.

It would actually be better for me to write you in the mornings, my dear Lëvochka, since when I get up in the morning I feel both sprightly and full of energy and capable of doing anything, while in the evenings I feel weary, useless and alone, to the point where I cannot write you a cheerful letter. I got the impression from the Englishwoman that, after hiring an assistant, I never had so much to do and never so little time to do it as, for example, this whole day today. We understand each other quite well — and with the help of a dictionary, when I don't know a word — but it's a disaster with the children, they still stay close to me, Tanja will not leave my side; of course, all this will possibly work itself out, but how? And won't we lose patience with this young Hanna? She keeps chattering away in English, though sometimes, apparently, she will become sad and fall silent. I gave her a book to read; the book very much interested her, but now she's left the children completely up to me. It would be better if the children moved into her room; she herself would like that very much. Right now this transition time is still all so uncertain, and for some reason I feel sorry for the children but, on the other hand, there is nothing to be sorry about, and they are not inconvenienced at all. I was thinking today that it's only been three days since you left, but to me it seems so long, long ago, and I simply haven't any strength left in me to get through these next four or five days — it is simply a fright! It's not that I feel out of sorts, I'm not angry at anybody, and I don't find fault with anything — I think, for the reason that if I were to express my melancholy even in a single word I would break into tears right away, as [I'm doing] at the moment, complaining to you. Everything feels so tight in me, and I'm not really living, but am only

нельзя этого изменить, и опять ты будешь уезжать, а я оставаться и опять буду проживать такие мучительные дни, как теперь. Мне кажется, если б ты написал мне, что пробудешь еще несколько дней в Москве, я бы сейчас уложилась и поехала бы со всем семейством в Москву. Не надо, не надо тебе уезжать от меня. От тебя еще письма не было, оттого еще скучней, верно, завтра получу. Я всё пишу тебе о себе, а это менее всего интересно в настоящую минуту. — Дети здоровы, только Таня всё ничего не ест, а Илюша по утрам кашляет. Я слышу сейчас, как Сережа рассказывает Ханне, что «папаша меня называет Сергулевич, а Таню — Чурка, плаво!» А Таня такая прелесть, нынче всё за англичанкой повторяла слова, а та приходила в восторг. Таня до того считала своей обязанностью повторять английские слова, что уже русские стала повторять за мной. Теперь ей это надоело, и она всё гоняет от себя Ханну. Пожалуйста, не забудь привезти детям книги с картинками, они с утра до вечера об этом толкуют и очень огорчатся, если ты не привезешь. Они часто о тебе спрашивают, и Таня вдруг, юродствуя, стала глядеть под скамейку и искать тебя: «Папаша, папаша!» Вообрази, сижу у своего письменного стола. И мою свечку задувает, так дует из балконной двери. У нас холод страшный, я целый день из пледа не выхожу, дрова — какой-то мелкий хворост, а морозы и особенно ветер очень сильны. Ты, когда приедешь, верно, изменишь это. А рамы твои еще не полированы и без стекол, я видела нынче. У тебя там такой холод, что там и думать нечего жить и сидеть, пока не будут рамы и хорошие дрова. — Переписываю я тебе мало, всё время нет. Но авось до твоего приезда перепишу всё, что ты оставил. Поиграла нынче «Дон-Жуана», но ничего не весело. Я даже дохожу до такой слабости, что думаю — зачем я выписала эту англичанку, не зная языка. Потом я начну

afraid of something all the time, and keep waiting for the night-time since then, thank God, the day is over. That's what [life] without you means [for me], my dear Lëvochka. And there's no way of changing this, and once again you'll leave, and I'll stay behind and once again live out days of torment, like right now. It seems that if you were to tell me you'll be spending several more days in Moscow, I'd right off pack up everything and go with the whole family to Moscow. You shouldn't, you shouldn't leave me [at all]. There haven't been any letters from you yet, and this makes me miss you even more: I'll probably get a letter tomorrow. I am writing you about myself, though that is what is the least interesting at the moment. — The children are healthy, only Tanja still isn't eating anything, while Iljusha coughs every morning. At the moment I can hear Serëzha telling Hanna that "Papasha calls me *Sergulevich*, and Tanja [he calls] *Churka* [Poppet], [I'm telling the] *tluth*!" And Tanja is such a charmer — today she keeps repeating words after the Englishwoman, and [Hanna] has been going into ecstasy! Tanja felt so obliged to repeat English words that she's now started to repeat Russian words after me. Now she's got tired of that and keeps shooing Hanna away. Please don't forget to bring picture books for the children; from morning to night they constantly talk about this and get very upset if you don't bring them [any]. They often ask about you, and one time Tanja began clowning around, and started looking for you under a bench, [calling out:] "Papasha, Papasha!" Imagine, I'm sitting at my desk, and my candle goes out in a gust of wind blowing from the balcony door. It's frightfully cold here; I don't come out from under the blanket the whole day; we have only light brushwood for firewood, and the frosts and especially the wind are extremely severe. When you come, you will no doubt adjust that. But your frames are not polished and have no glass in them — I noticed that today. It's so cold there in your [study] that there is

бранить себя за такой нравственный упадок, а потом начну плакать. Ты меня, Лёвочка, пожалуйста, прости за мое малодушие, я при тебе буду опять нравственно воскресшая из мертвых, а теперь не могу, хотя вижу всё безобразие своего состояния. Всё-таки как будто дело делаешь, да и занят благодаря неразборчивости твоего писания. Будешь ли ты в состоянии заниматься, писать. Я думаю, если тебе будут вправлять руку, то не сделалось бы с тобою общего физического расстройства. Лёвочка, милый, я ужасно тебя люблю, и теперь без тебя я ни хорошая мать, ни хозяйка, ничего, ничего. Мне кажется, что без тебя ничего не нужно, и если я на что и способна, только благодаря твоему нравственному влиянию.

У нас всё то же. Наверху ужинают, тетенька всё говорит: «Поешь, поешь», а я всё отвечаю: «Merci, ma tante». Машенька и дети скучны, а я в душе бодрюсь и только буду говорить: «Ну вот, еще день прошел, слава Богу». Прощай, Лёва, мне не надо писать тебе по вечерам, я слишком усталая и сонная, и мысли путаются. Целую тебя, милый, будь здоров и бодр. Всякий день писать не буду, потому что в Тулу посылать нельзя же всякий день.

Твоя Соня

no way you can live or even spend time there until you've got windows and some good firewood. I've not been doing much transcribing for you [of late] — there's been no time. But hopefully before you come I shall manage to transcribe everything you left. Today I played a little of *Don Juan,* but nothing can cheer me up. I'm even reaching the point of weakness where I'm starting to wonder why I sent for that Englishwoman, not knowing the language. Then I'll start cursing myself for such moral decay, and then I'll start to cry. Please, Lëvochka, you'll have to forgive me for my [spiritual] weakness. Once I am with you again I shall be again morally raised from the dead, but right now I can't, although I see the whole ugliness of my condition. While doing [the transcribing, I] at least can feel that I am doing something useful, and it also keeps me busy — thanks to the utter illegibility of your handwriting. Will you be in a condition to do any work, to write? I worry that if you decide to get your arm straightened, it might cause you some general physical disruption. Lëvochka, dear, I love you terribly, and right now when you're not here I am neither a good mother nor a housekeeper; I'm nothing, [just] nothing. It seems that, without you around, nothing has any point to it, and if I am capable of anything, it is only thanks to your moral influence.

Everything's going along here as usual. Upstairs they're having supper, and Auntie keeps saying: "Eat! Eat!", and I keep replying: "*Merci, ma tante.*" Mashen'ka and the children are bored, while I am trying to cheer myself in my heart and can only repeat: "Well, another day's gone by, thank God." Farewell, Lëva, I shouldn't be writing you in the evenings; I'm too tired and sleepy, and my thoughts get muddled. Hugs and kisses, dear, be healthy and cheery. I shan't write every day, since I can't send [mail] to Tula every day.

Yours, Sonja

Напиши, что [???] хотя и просить нече-го, сам, верно, напишешь. Целую их всех.

Write [me at least] something, though there is no need [for me] to ask — you'll probably write in any case. Hugs and kisses to all [the Behrs family].

Nº 4U – SOFIA ANDREEVNA TOLSTAYA ❧ LEV NIKOLAEVICH TOLSTOY

24–25 июня 1871 г. Ясная Поляна

24–25 June 1871. Yasnaya Polyana

24-го июня
1871.

24 June
1871.

Что же это, Лёвочка милый, какое унылое письмо я получила вчера от тебя. И писано-то оно так давно, еще 14-го, а нынче уже 24-е, стало быть, 10 дней прошло. Как и что изменилось в это время? Главное, что меня очень поразило и огорчило, это то, что ты кумыса еще не нашел. Я предвидела всё — только не это. Теперь я утешаюсь тем, что если б ты до сих пор не нашел кумыса, ты был бы давно дома. Твои бессонницы и унылое расположение духа не оттого, что ты уехал, а вспомни, то же самое было дома. А теперь, по крайней мере, есть причина быть унылым, ты нас не видишь, а дома та же тоска была без причины. Всё это обойдется, как только ты вольешь в себя известное число ведер хорошего кумыса; но нашел ли ты его наконец, вот что меня с вчерашнего дня страшно мучает.

What is going on, Lëvochka dear — what a cheerless letter I received from you yesterday! And it was written some time ago, back on the 14th, and today is the 24th already; which means 10 days have passed. What has changed during this time, and how? The main thing that struck me and upset me is that you haven't found any koumiss yet. I could have imagined anything except this. Now I am comforting myself with [the thought] that if you hadn't found the koumiss up to now, you would have been home a long time ago. Your sleepless nights and gloomy disposition do not stem from your going away — remember, it was the same at home. Whereas now, at least, you have cause for your gloom: you do not see us, while at home the same melancholy was without cause. This will all work out once you imbibe a few barrels of good koumiss; but if you haven't finally found it, that's what has me so frightfully worried since yesterday.

Конечно, если б твоя тоска стала продолжаться и дошла бы до высшей степени, то и кумыс пользы не принесет; я тебе говорила, что лучше б всего было мне ехать с тобой. Сегодня как подумаю о том, что ты уныл, почувствую такой прилив нежности к тебе и так мне кажется, что я бы тебя и утешила, и устроила, и развеселила. Но ведь я ничего не могла этого сделать, когда ты был тут, а только сама заражалась твоим унынием. Если ты занимаешься греками, то брось их. Наверное, это на тебя больше всего действует. Брось,

Of course, if your melancholy were to continue to the extreme, the koumiss wouldn't afford you any benefit; I told you that it would have been better for me to go with you. Today as I think about how gloomy you are, I [can't help] feel such an influx of tenderness toward you, and it seems to me that I might [be in a position to] comfort, make you feel at home, and cheer you up. But after all, I wasn't able to do anything like that while you were here, but only ended up infecting myself with your gloominess. If you are busy studying Greek, give it up. That's probably what's affecting you

пожалуйста, верь Урусову, верь Фету, верь моей глупой голове и любящей душе, что эти занятия тебе вредны.

Авось это письмо мое найдет тебя уже более веселым, более здоровым, чем ты был, когда писал то письмо, а главное — пьющим кумыс.

У нас всё идет хорошо, все здоровы, ничего особенного не случилось. Сегодня утром приехала к мама Надежда Алекс[ан-дровна] Карнович с своей девочкой. Она очень смешна, но добра. Дети наши нынче целый день с Славочкой и Соней Карно-вич играли на лугу палками, на которые ловят кольца, и им эта всем очень игра нравится, особенно Сереже. Таня малень-кая вся погружена теперь в грибы и ягоды. Они уже принесли из Чепыжа белых гри-бов и в большом восторге. Ханна теперь здорова, нынче в первый раз купалась. С Варей мы в большой дружбе, по вечерам философствуем, и с ней единственной я могу и люблю о тебе говорить, высказы-вать свои беспокойства и выслушивать утешенья.

Завтра тетенька Полина дня на три едет в Тулу; мы с ней так дружны, как нельзя лучше. Завтра же мы ждем Дьяковых и Оболенских, которые теперь дня четыре как уехали в Крапивну. Тогда я тебе опять напишу, когда уедут Дьяковы; а нынче пишу скорей, оттого что боюсь, что засуе-чусь с гостями. Я вчера еще хотела скорей писать, так смутилась твоим письмом, да хорошо, что отложила, а то нынче мое волнение улеглось, и я не напишу тебе тех глупостей, которые бы написала вчера.

Бедная Таня опять в страшном вол-нении. Нынче ее няня объявила ей, что ходить за Верочкой она не согласна, что ей с большими детьми расстаться жалко, проплакала всё утро, глядя, как немка с

most of all. Please stop, trust Urusov, trust Fet, trust my silly mind and loving heart, [which say] that these studies are harmful to you.

If only this letter of mine might find you already more cheerful and healthy than you were when you wrote that [last] letter, and especially drinking koumiss.

Everything's going well with us, everyone's healthy, nothing out of the ordinary has hap-pened. This morning Mamà had a visit from Nadezhda Aleksandrovna Karnovich and her little girl. She's very funny, but kind. Our children have been playing in the meadow with Slavochka and Sonja Karnovich. They catch rings on sticks and they all really like this game, especially Serëzha. Little Tanja is now completely immersed in mushroom and berry [picking]. She's already brought mushrooms from Chepyzh [forest] with great delight. Hanna is now recovered, and today she went swimming for the first time. Varja and I are good friends; in the evenings we talk about philosophy, and she is the only one with whom I can talk about you — and enjoy doing this — as I share my anxieties and receive some comforting.

Tomorrow Auntie Polina goes to Tula for a few days; she and I are getting along better than ever. Tomorrow we are expecting the D'jakovs and Obolenskijs, it's been about four days now since they left to go to Krapivna. I'll write you again when the D'jakovs have left; today I am hurrying to get this letter written, as I'm afraid that [otherwise] I may get bogged down with guests. I wanted to write you a quick note yesterday, but I got so distracted by your letter that it's just as well that I put it aside, since today my degree of concern has lessened and I shan't write you the stupidities I would have expressed to you yesterday.

Poor [sister] Tanja is frightfully upset again. Yesterday her nanny told her that she was unwilling to look after [baby] Verochka, that it was too terribly sad for her to part from the older children; she wept all morning,

детьми обращается, и наотрез отказалась ехать, если ей не ходить за старшими. Между тем немка объявила, что больше, чем на два года, она инее поедет, а потом чтоб ее отправили на их счет, так что Таня решилась взять няню за большими детьми, а немке отказать. Ее сейчас же наняла тетенька Карнович. Но Таня расстроена, жалеет немку, которая оказалась прекрасная, а делать нечего, так как еще без няни и Трифовна ни за что не поедет, нынче сама сказала. Вот и труды твои пропали, жаль.

Хотела еще тебе сказать, что к удивлению своему замечала, что к своей маленькой Маше стала как-то особенно болезненно привязываться. Я теперь без особенного грустного чувства не могу слышать ее жалкого крика и видеть ее болезненную фигурку. Всё вожусь с ней, и так хочется ее получше выходить.

Постройка наша идет хорошо, теперь плотники работают, и третьего дня тут был архитектор. Алексей хозяйничает, кажется, хорошо, нынче сено возили, только не очень зелено, его дождем помочило на рядах. Погода у нас теперь чудная. Жарко, но не душно и не знойно. Пиши мне, милый Лёвочка, побольше и подлиннее письма. Ты мне написал такие две записочки коротенькие, не поймешь того, что так хотелось бы знать и что особенно близко к сердцу. Что тебе делать, ведь нечего, и неужели тебе скучно писать ко мне. Ты знаешь, как мне приятно получать и читать твои письма; я по нескольку раз их перечитываю. Если ты уныл, жалуйся, пиши всё, что думаешь и чувствуешь, только пиши больше и подробнее. Прощай, милый, нынче больше писать нечего; и поздно, и кормить надо. Целую тебя

watching how the German woman treated them, and flatly refused to go if she couldn't look after the older ones. In the meantime the German lady announced that she would not go [with the family to the Caucasus] for longer than two years, and demanded they send her home after that at their expense. And so Tanja decided to take along her [current] nanny for the bigger children, and dismissed the German lady — who was immediately hired by Auntie Karnovich. But Tanja is upset; she feels sorry [to lose] the German woman, who turned out to be a very good governess indeed, but there's nothing to be done, since even [the housekeeper] Trifovna would absolutely not go without the nanny — she said so herself today. So your efforts are in vain, more's the pity.

I was also going to tell you that to my surprise I noticed that I'm starting to feel an especially acute attachment to my little Masha. I can no longer take her plaintive crying and her emaciated little figure without a particular feeling of sadness. I'm constantly caring for her, and really want to see her looking a bit better.

Our construction is going along nicely; the carpenters are now at work, and a couple of days ago the architect was here. Aleksej is looking after the estate — quite well, it seems; today they were gathering the hay, only it isn't very green; it was moistened by the rain in the field. Now the weather is simply marvellous. It's hot, but not stifling or sweltering. Write to me, Lëvochka, more letters and longer ones. You wrote two such brief notes; you don't understand what I most want to know and what is especially dear to my heart. What [else] is there for you to do? — [Quite possibly,] nothing. Can it be that you find it boring to write to me? You know how delightful it is for me to receive and read your letters; I read each one several times over. If you are despondent, complain [to me], write down everything you are thinking and feeling, only write more and in greater detail.

крепко, поцелуй Степу, спасибо ему, что тебя развлекает.

Твоя Соня

25-го утром. Приписываю, потому что думаю, что тебе приятно будет знать, что и 25-го у нас всё было хорошо. Сейчас мне принесли ягоды, и я в первый раз начинаю варить варенье. Нынешний год особенно не хочется. Нынче всю ночь видела тебя во сне, и так рада хоть во сне-то. Что за праздник будет — увидать тебя опять. Ты всё мне точно осветишь на свете. Да и всегда так было.

Farewell, dear, today there is nothing more for me to write; it's late, and I have to go feed [the baby]. Big hugs and kisses to you and [my brother] Stëpa; I thank him for keeping you entertained.

Yours, Sonja

25th, morning. I'm adding a postscript, since I'm thinking you'll be happy to know that on the 25th, too, everything was fine here. Just now they've brought me berries, and for the first time I've started to make jam. This year I especially didn't feel like doing it. All night I've been seeing you in my dreams, and I'm so happy, at least in my dreams. What a celebration it will be to see you again! You literally light up the whole world for me. And it's always been that way.

№ 5U − SOFIA ANDREEVNA TOLSTAYA ❧ LEV NIKOLAEVICH TOLSTOY
28 мая 1877 г. Ясная Поляна

28 May 1877. Yasnaya Polyana

Исполняю твое желание, милый друг, и пишу, чтоб послать завтра на Козлов-ку, хотя почти уверена, что письмо это пропадет. Теперь, когда ты решительно уехал, беспокойство мое прошло, а то если б волноваться, как вчера, то я бы умерла через два дня. Ночью так было страшно, везде будто ходили и шуршали, что я позвала в 3-м часу няню и положила ее в гостиную. Мальчики на свою предпола-гаемую рыбную ловлю не ходили, было холодно, и ветер после грозы всё-таки был сильный. Но купаться ездили сначала дамы, потом мальчики все трое с Mr. Rey и Александром Григорьевичем. Препода-ватель Рожд[ественский] еще не являлся и, верно, теперь исчезнет на некоторое время.

Обе Танины девочки лежат в постелях в легком жару, а Миша совсем здоров. Думаю, что и девочки завтра встанут, Таня уж очень с ними осторожна. Наши все благополучны. У меня от вчерашней росы,

I am carrying out your wishes, dear friend, and I am writing to send this letter tomorrow to Kozlovka, although I'm almost certain that it will go astray. Now that you've definitely left, my anxiety has passed; otherwise, if I got worried the way I did yesterday, I would [probably] die within two days. It was so frightening [last] night — it seemed as though people were pacing and shuffling about eve-rywhere — that between 2 and 3 o'clock in the morning I summoned the nanny and moved her into the drawing room. The boys did not go on their planned fishing trip; it was cold, and the wind after the thunderstorm was still quite strong. But they went swimming — at first the ladies, then all three boys with Mr. Rey and Aleksandr Grigor'evich. The teacher Rozhdestvenskij hasn't appeared yet, and now will probably disappear for some time.

Both of Tanja's girls are lying in bed with a light fever, while Misha is quite healthy. I think the girls will be getting up tomorrow. Tanja is really very careful with them. Our [children] are all safe. I have a strong case of

когда гуляли, сделался сильный насмо-рк. Мальчики вечером ходили гулять на пчельник, а мы, дамская компания, ходили на деревню и кругом через Заказ домой. Нас застал дождь, но мелкий, и мало промочил.

Иду с Таней пить чай и всё думаю, где ты проведешь сегодняшний вечер, и не могу представить.

Теперь скоро 10 часов, дети сейчас идут спать; они ведут себя хорошо. Как я жду тебя или известий о тебе, чтобы успоко-иться насчет твоего спокойствия. Меня, право, твое всякое дело больше за душу тянет, чем тебя самого.

Прощай, душенька, если и получишь письмо, то за несколько часов до твоего приезда домой.

Соня

Понедельник. 10 час[ов] вечера. 1877. Май.

№ 6U – SOFIA ANDREEVNA TOLSTAYA ❧ LEV NIKOLAEVICH TOLSTOY
Октябрь 1884 г. Москва

Всякий вечер я напряженно жду тебя около 8-го часу. Мне всё кажется, что ты приедешь. Потом это время пройдет, я успокоюсь, и как раз в это время прино-сили письма, а сегодня утром принесли, — пожалуй, вечером не будет. Иногда мне досадно бывало и больно, что тебе жить без нас не скучно; это по старой памяти, это не новое чувство, а прежнее, неспра-ведливое; я знаю, что скучно тебе, но что нужно иногда одиночество. Дети по отношению к тебе — мне кажется, по чув-ству идут непосредственно за мной. Тоже доверие, что это нужно так быть врозь, что тебе в деревне лучше и что всё-таки все так любовно и дружелюбно смотрят и на тебя, и на меня (хотя меньше на меня).

sniffles from yesterday's walk in the [morn-ing] dew. In the evening the boys went for a walk to the beehives, while we ladies walked over to the village and took the roundabout way home through the *Zakaz*. We were caught in the rain, but it was more of a drizzle and didn't actually soak us.

I am going with Tanja now to have some tea and I keep wondering how you are spend-ing this evening, and have no idea.

Now it's almost 10 [p.m.], the children are on their way to bed; they are behaving well. How I'm waiting for you or [at least] for news about you, to calm myself down concerning your mental state! All your affairs, it is true, are much more heart-wrenching for me than for you.

Farewell, darling. If you do actually receive this letter, it will be only a few hours before your arrival home.

Sonja

Monday. 10 p.m. May, 1877.

October 1884. Moscow

Every evening I anxiously wait for you around 8 o'clock. It still seems to me that you will come. Then the time goes by, I calm down, and just at this time they bring the post, and they brought it this morning — it looks like there won't be any evening delivery. Sometimes I get annoyed and hurt that you can live apart from us without missing us; that's a feeling from the past; it's not a new feeling, but an old one, and no longer fair. I know that you miss us, but sometimes you need solitude. In terms of how they feel about you, it seems to me the children are directly in line with me. [They have] the same trust that we need to be apart, and that you do better in the countryside; still, they all look upon both you and me with equal love and friendliness (although less upon me).

Прощай, милый друг, я всё жду, что ты напишешь: «Это мое последнее письмо». Но этого ты еще не писал. Не будь в унынии, милый, что унывать, так всё хорошо и весело, если не создавать себе горя. Целую тебя и жду.

[Рукой Т. Л. Толстой:]

Ты хоть велел some more, и мне это очень приятно, но сегодня вечером ничего не пишется, и событий никаких не было. Утром копировала, и очень было легко и весело писать, — если бы всегда так, я живо бы докончила. Дядя Сережа едет в Крапивну и думал заехать к тебе. Тетя Маша и Лиза Оболенская часто о тебе спрашивают и желают видеть. Прощай, целую тебя. Часто жалею, что тебя нет, чтобы помочь мне, — подумай, я каждый день просыпаюсь без десяти двенадцать, и никто меня не срамит.

Таня

Farewell, dear friend, I am still waiting for you to write: "This is my last letter." But you haven't written that yet. Don't be despondent, my dear. Why despair, if everything is good and cheerful, if [we] don't manufacture [our] own sorrow [in the meantime]. Hugs and kisses, and I'm waiting for you.

[In Tat'jana L'vovna Tolstaja's hand:]

Even though you did ask for *some more* — and I'm very happy to oblige — this evening there is nothing to write, and there haven't been any events [to write about]. This morning I did some transcribing, and it was a very easy and cheerful [task] to write — if it were always like this, I would finish it very quickly. Uncle Serëzha is going to Krapivna and has been thinking of dropping in to see you. Aunt Masha and Liza Obolenskaja often ask about you and want to see [you]. Farewell, hugs and kisses. I often regret that you are not here to help me — just think, I wake up every morning at ten minutes to twelve, and there is nobody to chide me [for it].

Tanja

№ 7U – SOFIA ANDREEVNA TOLSTAYA ❧ LEV NIKOLAEVICH TOLSTOY
27 апреля 1888 г. Москва   *27 April 1888. Moscow*

Милый Левочка, сегодня получила твое письмо к Тане, и какая-то судьба моих длинных и более хороших писем — не доходить до тебя, как серпуховское и другое еще, на Козловку. Ну, да всё равно, иногда устала, не в духе, чем-нибудь расстроена в моем сложном механизме жизни, ну и отзовется в письме к тебе; а ведь ты твердо должен знать, что ты всегда первый и главный и на уме у меня, и в сердце, что самое больное место в душе моей — это та рознь, которая сделалась между нами, и что огорчительнее всего для меня опять-таки твоя же болезнь. Жду и радуюсь тому времени, когда мы будем опять вместе, а пока прошу тебя, береги

Dear Lëvochka, today I received your letter to Tanja, and it must be some sort of fate that my longer and better letters do not reach you — like the one [I sent] to Serpukhov and another one to Kozlovka. Well, no matter, sometimes I feel weary, out of sorts, upset by something in the complex mechanism of my life, which is echoed in my writing to you. After all, you should know absolutely that you are always first and foremost in my mind and heart, and that the most painful spot in my soul is the gulf that has formed between us, and that, once again, what upsets me most of all is your own disease. I am expectant and look forward to the time when we are together again, and in the meantime I beg of you

себя как можно больше, ведь частые боли и погрешности в диете прямо изнашивают и организм, и больной желудок. Не надрывайся также в работе физической — это вредно тебе.

Третий день меня огорчает малое количество молока и более болезненное состояние сосков. Мальчик жалкий, да еще с утра начал кашлять, и так его жалко, грудка надрывается, сосать нечего; я ему вчера молока коровьего давала, да он еще не умеет справляться с рожком, зажмет в рот и уставится удивленными глазами.

Сегодня у нас обедали все Оболенские наши и тетя Маша с Елен, а теперь приехали к Тане Соня Самарина, Ольга Трубецкая, Мамоновы, Рачинские; и наши дети, и Оболенские девочки, и большие — все катают в зале яйца, это все-таки для всех занятие — легче с гостями.

Утром был Tastevin, принес письмо к издателю в Париже для «О жизни». Я уж переписала его и послала сегодня. Tastevin обещал еще мне гувернера, очень его хорошо рекомендует, но еще неизвестно, пойдет ли; я его не видала, а жду к себе. Был еще Столпаков, и я его приняла для Сережи. Он многое мне сообщил по поводу той службы в банке, которую хочет взять Сережа. Он еще не возвращался от Олсуфьевых.

Я думаю, тебе стало более одиноко без молодых. Да и позаботиться о тебе так, как могут свои, теперь некому. Количка добр, но он своим вегетарьянством и аскетизмом сбивает и тебя с толку. Дунаев все-таки очень чуждый человек, несмотря на то, что он готовит обед. Вот

to take care of yourself as much as possible. After all, frequent pains and abnormalities in one's diet directly erode both the system and a sick stomach. Don't strain yourself with physical exertion — it is harmful to you.

For the third day already I'm concerned over my small quantity of milk and the increasingly painful condition of my nipples. The little boy [Vanechka] is in a pitiful state; he started to cough from early morning, and it is so bad that his chest is being overworked with no [milk] to suck. Yesterday I gave him some cow's milk, but he still can't cope with a bottle — he jams it into his mouth and stares at me wide-eyed.

Today all our Obolenskijs, as well as Aunt Masha and Elen, took dinner with us, and now Tanja has had visitors: Sonja Samarina, Ol'ga Trubetskaja, the Mamonovs and the Rachinskijs. Our children and the Obolenskij girls — along with the older ones —have all been rolling [Easter] eggs in the salon; it's been a source of entertainment for everyone — it makes it easier having guests.

[French translator Edmond] Tastevin was here this morning; he brought [me the French translation of] a letter [I had written] to a publisher in Paris concerning *On life [O zhizni]*. I copied it out and sent it off today. Tastevin also promised [to put me in touch with] a governor [for my children], one whom he highly recommends, but it's not clear yet whether [this gentleman] will actually accept [the position]; I haven't seen him [yet], but am expecting a visit from him. Stolpakov came, too, and I received him on behalf of Serëzha. He told me a lot about the position in the bank which Serëzha is interested in. He [Serëzha] has not yet returned from the Olsuf'evs'.

I think you may be lonelier now without the young people around. Now there is nobody around to care for you the way our own family can. Kolechka [Ge] is kind, but he ends up leading you astray with his vegetarianism and asceticism. Dunaev is still a very strange person, despite the fact that he can

от таких поваров и живот-то болит! А ты бы лучше позвал Николая Михайловича, устроился бы получше, тогда бы и писать мог; чем отбиваться так усиленно от всех неудобств и время всё убивать на матерьяльные заботы.

Так как ты, по словам Лёвы, в Москву больше не вернёшься, то не прислать ли тебе твои вещи багажом на Козловку. Мы бы уложили в корзинку и прислали. Напиши об этом. Да напиши, какие книги тебе будут нужны. Хоть времени у всех нас совсем мало, но мы для тебя найдем. Девочки очень замучились. Малыши совсем с цепи сорвались: по утрам голые бегают по коридору, встают рано и ложатся друг к другу в постель. Вчера Андрюша влез на крышу конюшни, сорвался и покатился — спасибо, о жолубь удержался, а то бы разбился. Авось Бог на меня оглянется, и ничего не случится, что бы могло меня убить; а подчас в горле спазмы от слез и тревоги, а вместе с тем чувство бессилия и невозможности что-либо сделать. — Теперь до Ясной недолго; только бы молоко совсем не пропало от этого нервного (послеродового) состояния, и тогда я буду вознаграждена за терпение. Девочки, особенно Маша, напряженно и прекрасно смотрят за детьми, но подчас в отчаянии и они. Сейчас все так веселы и оживлены, что и мне весело их слушать. Лева тоже катает яйца и очень весел, как ребенок.

Когда кончила тот лист, я вдруг почувствовала, что писать больше нечего; что-то в голове защелкнулось. В конце концов, я опять точно на что-то жалуюсь, а в сущности всё слава Богу.

cook dinner. Cooks like that can make your stomach hurt! But wouldn't it suit you better to call upon Nikolaj Mikhajlovich, then you could make better arrangements and [get to your] writing — this would be better than making such horrendous efforts to free yourself from all the inconveniences and wasting time on material cares.

Since, according to Lëva, you are not returning to Moscow any more, perhaps we should send your things by freight to Kozlovka. We could put them in a basket and send them. Write me about this. And write, too, about any books you need. Even though none of us have much time to spare, we shall find time for you. The girls are quite exhausted. The younger boys have gone in for some rather wild behaviour: in the mornings they run naked through the hallway, they get up early and play with each other in their beds. Yesterday Andrjusha climbed onto the roof of the stable, lost his balance and started rolling down — thank goodness he caught himself on the edge of the gutter or he would have been done for. May God watch over me, and let nothing happen that could take my life, though sometimes I have spasms in my throat from tears and worry, along with feelings of helplessness and powerlessness to do anything. — It won't be long now 'til [I move to] Yasnaya [for the summer]; if only my milk doesn't disappear entirely as a result of this nervous (post-natal) condition, and then I shall be rewarded for my patience. The girls, especially Masha, are doing a fine, intense job of looking after the younger ones, though sometimes they, too, are in despair. At the moment they are so cheerful and lively that I, too, feel cheered by listening to them. Lëva is also rolling eggs with all the enthusiasm of a child.

When I finished the previous page, I suddenly had the feeling that there was nothing more to write; something snapped in my head. The upshot is that I am again complaining about something, while in fact all is thanks to God.

Была еще нынче история, кучер просит расчет, Фомич с няней кричали до исступления, все перессорились и пережаловались. Но мое хладнокровие и презрительное отношение к их разлившейся от разговенья желчи — подействовали, кажется, на всех отрезвляющим образом. — вчера вечером Таня, Маша и Лева ездили с Северцовыми в театр смотреть «Лес», но приехали унылые и что-то не особенно довольные. И Андреев-Бурлак их не прельстил. Сегодня малыши ездили с Северцовыми же на передвижную выставку, и Андрюша восхищался, и Миша — картиной «На войну». Я тоже собираюсь, но не раньше следующей недели.

Сейчас отрывали меня кормить, и потому кончаю письмо. Прощай, милый друг, пиши получше, посылаю тебе марку и конвертик, а то у тебя, может быть, нет. Есть ли у тебя деньги? Когда-то я тебя получу опять на свое попечение! Целую тебя и еще прошу беречь себя.

С. Т[олстая]

27 апреля 1888.

№ 8*U* – SOFIA ANDREEVNA TOLSTAYA ❧ LEV NIKOLAEVICH TOLSTOY
(Письмо в адрес Льва Николаевича и Марии Львовны Толстых)

25 апреля 1892 г. Москва

Милый друг Левочка, сегодня переписала твой отчет и хотела его послать, но Таня и Дунаев задержали, хотят по газетам справиться о последнем русском отчете Тани, чтоб не было разногласия в показаниях; и еще Таня говорит, что она с Величкиной послала тебе такие документы, по которым может оказаться ошибка в

Another incident occurred today: the coachman asked to be paid, Fomich and the nanny were yelling at the top of their lungs, everybody was quarrelling and complaining to each other. But my equanimity and disregard for their rancour, which was [no doubt] spilling over from breaking their fast, had a sobering effect, it seems, on everyone. Last evening Tanja, Masha and Lëva went to the theatre with the Severtsovs to see [Aleksandr Ostrovskij's play] *The forest*, but arrived [home] despondent and for some reason not really satisfied. And [the Russian actor Vasilij Nikolaevich] Andreev-Burlak did not particularly stand out to them. Today the boys went with the Severtsovs to an exhibition of the Itinerant [artists], and both Andrjusha and Misha were excited by [Konstantin Savitskij's] painting *To the war*. I'm also planning to go, but not before next week.

Right this moment I've been called away to breast-feeding duties, and so I'll close this letter. Farewell, dear friend, write something better; I'm sending you a stamp and envelope, in case you don't have them. Do you have money? Who knows when I shall have you back in my care! Hugs and kisses, and I ask you again to take care of yourself.

S. Tolstaya

27 April 1888.

(Letter addressed jointly to Lev Nikolaevich Tolstoy and Marija L'vovna [Masha] Tolstaja)
25 April 1892. Moscow

Dear friend Lëvochka, today I made a copy of your report [on the funds collected for famine relief] and was going to send it [to the publisher], but Tanja and Dunaev held it back; they want to check with the newspapers about Tanja's latest report in Russian, so that there be no discrepancy in [our] accounts; and Tanja also says that she sent you documents

твоем отчете. Как тебе, должно быть, трудно было и долго составлять этот отчет! Но это хорошие, полезные для всех сведения, и я очень буду огорчена, если почему-либо откажут напечатать этот отчет. Если не примут в «Русск[их] вед[омостях]», я пошлю в «Новое время».

Тане сегодня гораздо лучше, вообще она бодрей, но поправка ее идет очень медленно. Только что ревматизм лучше, сделался насморк, зубная боль. — Вчера была тут Лиза Олсуфьева и Маша Зубова, а теперь нашло на Таню беспокойство ехать в Никольское к Олсуфьевым. Эта мысль ее неотвязно преследует, и я вижу ясно, что если она не съездит посмотреть на косого, она не успокоится и уедет неудовлетворенная в Бегичевку. Я ничего не говорю и не советую, боюсь только, что она себя расстроит опять и физически, и морально. Собирается она в понедельник на три дня, а потом, около 4 мая, в Бегичевку. Ек[атерина] Ив[ановна] Баратынская тоже собирается. — Сегодня были тут Раевские, Петя четыре экз[амена] выдержал, Ваня еще не держал. Были и Мамоновы, и Екат[ерина] Ив[ановн]а, и Дунаев. У Грота жены всё жар, и жалко на него смотреть: и суетится, укладывается, и опять отчаивается, а она всё слабеет. Просто горе смотреть на них! — Вот я всё здоровею, давно я не чувствовала себя такой бодрой, сильной и здоровой, как теперь. Даже совестно, но, видно, это на что-нибудь нужно. И портрет мой очень хорош. Дети все тоже здоровы. Взяла я с 10 мая гувернера нового, вегетарианца — без яиц и молока, лет сорока пяти, рекомендован Поливановым, на вид солидный, а кто его знает! В молодости бывал гувернером, теперь приехал в Россию изучать язык, немец, живший во Франции тринадцать лет, знает и по-английски. Скучно с гувернерами, но и с Митькой нельзя оставлять детей, а я не вездесуща.

with Velichkina which might have resulted in a mistake in your report. How difficult it must have been for you and how long it must have taken to compile this report! But this is good and useful information for everybody, and I shall be very upset if for any reason they refuse to publish it. If they don't accept it at *Russkie vedomosti*, I'll send it to *Novoe vremja*.

Tanja's feeling much better today, she's definitely more cheerful, but her healing is going quite slowly. Just as soon as her rheumatism started improving, she came down with the sniffles and a toothache. — Yesterday Liza Olsuf'eva was here, along with Masha Zubova, and now Tanja is just dying to go to Nikol'skoe with the Olsuf'evs. She is constantly haunted by this thought, and I can see clearly that if she doesn't go and see the cross-eyed chap [Mikhail Adamovich Olsuf'ev, to whom she was attracted], she will find no peace and will head off to Begichevka unsatisfied. I am not saying or advising anything; it's just that I'm afraid that she will upset herself once more both physically and morally. She is planning to go Monday for three days, and then, around the 4th of May, to Begichevka. Ekaterina Ivanovna Baratynskaja is also planning on going. — The Raevskijs were here today, Petja passed four exams, Vanja hasn't had his exams yet. The Mamonovs were here, along with Ekaterina Ivanova, and Dunaev. Grot's wife still has a fever, and it's pitiful to look at him: he fusses, does some packing, and plunges again into despair, while she continues to grow weaker. Simply painful to look on them! — And here I keep on improving; I have not felt this sprightly, strong and healthy for a long time. Almost shameful, though apparently, serving some purpose. And my portrait has turned out very well. The children, too, are all healthy. Since the 10th of May I have employed a new governor [for the children], a vegetarian — no eggs or milk, about 45 years of age, recommended by Polivanov, decent enough looking, but who can tell?! He served as a governor in his younger

Вчера вечером ездила я с Мишей, Лидой, Сашей и Ваней в Кунцево. Как там красиво! Высокие обрывы над Москвой-рекой, тишина, никого мы не видали и очень наслаждались. Пили чай под березками, совсем в одиночестве, ели апельсины, дети ловили майских жуков и рвали цветы. Но больше всех я была довольна. Домой ехали в 9 часов. Ваничка заснул. Завтра, воскресенье, едем все в Останкино с завтраком, до обеда, и Мамоновы с нами. Я очень радуюсь быть опять за городом и вывезти туда детей. Таня тоже поедет.

Сегодня была сильная гроза, ливень, и ясный, теплый вечер. Так и тянуло в деревню. Я всё себе стараюсь втолковать, что это блажь одна, что я такая во всем счастливая, и вдруг не могу в городе чувствовать себя хорошо, но ничего не помогает, и я весь день в суете, и только одна мысль — убежать из города.

Не знаю, писала ли я тебе, что было письмо от Левы и телеграмма из Самары 22-го апреля. Он просил 3000 р. на семена, и мы ему уже их послали. От старших сыновей известий не было.

Попроси Машу мне написать, всё ли тебе было впору, и если нет, то перешила ли Мар[ия] Кир[илловна], чтоб годилось. Как довезла Вера Михайловна 1000 рублей?

Здоровы ли вы все и как духом себя чувствуете? Мне иногда кажется, что вы оба что-то невеселы и труднее вам живется, чем прежде. Дай Бог только, чтоб здоровье было хорошо, чтоб ничего не случилось. Какими способами вы

days, and has now come to Russia to study the language; he's a German, who lived thirteen years in France, knows English, too. It's tedious [working] with governors, but I can't leave the children with Mit'ka, and I can't be everywhere at once.

Last evening I went with Misha, Lida, Sasha and Vanja to Kuntsevo. How beautiful it is there! The high cliffs overlooking the Moskva River, the quiet — we didn't see a soul and had a wonderful time. We took tea beneath the birches, in complete solitude, ate oranges; the children hunted maybugs and picked flowers. But more than anyone else I was happy. We went home at 9 o'clock. Vanechka fell asleep. Tomorrow, Sunday, we'll all go to Ostankino with our breakfast, before dinner, and the Mamonovs [will go] with us. I'm very glad to be out in the countryside again and to take the children there. Tanja will be going, too.

Today we had a severe thunderstorm, quite a downpour, and a clear, warm evening. I felt such a longing for the countryside. I am still trying to tell myself that it's just a one-time fantasy, that I do feel happy about everything [here], but then all at once I can't seem to feel so good in the city, and nothing helps, and I'm so busy the whole day that I have only one thought — to escape from the city.

I don't know if I told you, but I received a letter from Lëva and a telegram from Samara on the 22nd of April. He asked for 3,000 roubles for seeds, and we already sent this to him. There's been no news from our older sons.

Ask [our daughter] Masha to write to me and tell me whether everything fits you, and if not, has Marija Kirillovna made the alterations, so that you can use it? How did Vera Mikhajlovna deliver the thousand roubles?

Are you all healthy and are you all in good spirits? It sometimes seems to me that both of you are somehow less than cheerful and that you are finding life more difficult than before. God only grant that you are healthy and that nothing happens. How do you get about?

передвигаетесь? Не утомляй себя, Левочка, слишком ездой, и не рискуй, Маша, Доном. Без привычки и без знания реки можно и утонуть. Береги папа и заботься получше и поразнообразнее его кормить. Как ведет себя Петр Васильевич? Не нужно ли что послать? Сегодня справлялись об экипаже, обещали к среде.

Ну, прощайте, милые друзья, кланяйтесь сотрудникам и сотрудницам. Чистяков-то так и не приехал? Очень жаль.

Целую вас обоих. Пишу на Клекотки, а то в Чернаву долго еще почта.

С. Толстая

25 апреля, вечер. 1892.

N° 9U – SOFIA ANDREEVNA TOLSTAYA ❧ LEV NIKOLAEVICH TOLSTOY
11 мая 1892 г. Москва

Ты, может быть, меня осудишь, милый друг, что я деньги посылаю с артельщиком. Но послать пять тысяч по почте стоит тоже много денег, и мы с Таней разочли, что ты больше недели не получишь денег, а деньги вам очень нужны, и вы должны скорей кончать свои дела и приезжать в Ясную. Посылаю Маше своих 100 рублей на домашние расходы и поездку. Сегодня же едет Софья Алексеевна, я была у нее, но так ее и не видала, а она ко мне не приехала. Как я рада буду слышать от артельщика по его возвращении о здоровье твоем и о вас вообще! У нас сегодня невозможный хаос. С утра укладываются. Фомич кричит, бегает, Дуняша с узелками, няня, все в азарте. Передняя загромождена ящиками и сундуками. На дворе плотники строят забор, клозет, кроют крышу, человек десять рабочих.

Don't wear yourself out, Lëvochka, with too much horseback riding, and Masha, don't risk [bathing] in the Don [River]. Unless you have experience and a good knowledge of the river you could even drown. Take care of Papà and try to feed him better and with more variety. How is Pëtr Vasil'evich behaving himself? Is there anything you need sent? Today they're finding out about the carriage; it's promised for Wednesday.

Well, farewell, dear friends; my regards to your fellow-workers [on the famine relief]. Has Chistjakov still not arrived? That's too bad.

Hugs and kisses to you both. I am sending [this letter] to Klëkotki; the mail takes longer through Chernava.

S. Tolstaya

Evening, 25 April 1892.

N° 9U – SOFIA ANDREEVNA TOLSTAYA ❧ LEV NIKOLAEVICH TOLSTOY
11 May 1892. Moscow

You may possibly reproach me, dear friend, for sending money with the artel worker. But to send five thousand [roubles] by post also costs a lot of money, and Tanja and I calculated that you would not receive it for over a week, and you all need the money badly so that you can finish up your [relief] work as soon as possible and come to Yasnaya. I am sending [our daughter] Masha my 100 roubles for household expenses and travel. Also today Sof'ja Alekseevna is to go [to Begichevka]; I went by her place but still didn't see her, and she didn't come to see me. How glad I'll be to hear from the artel worker, upon his return, about your health and all of you in general! Today we are in [a state of] incredible chaos. People have been packing since this morning. Fomich is yelling and running around, Dunjasha is busy with some bundles, the nanny and everyone else are all excited. The front hallway is overflowing with

Ко мне всё ходят с разными счета-
ми, лежит корректура четвертой книги,
конверты с почты и пр. об экзаменах
детям ничего не говорят, и Миша боится,
что провалился из латыни, и Андрюша
тоже; сегодня был экзамен. — Таня была
у доктора, он говорит, что у ней похоже
на нервное состояние, велел брать ванны
всякий день соленые, пить опять Эмс, и
очень одобряет, что она едет в Ясную на
покой. Сегодня она выразила мысль, что
ты, верно, подозреваешь ее в обмане или,
вернее, в преувеличении ее нездоровья.
Мне даже смешно стало; она очень худа и
бледна стала, ты увидишь, когда приедешь.

Поступил вчера Фольхерт, говорит
по-немецки, по-французски и по-английски, классик и вегетарианец, понравился
Гроту. Грот приводил мне сенатора
Семенова, своего дядю, который очень
интересно мне рассказывал о разных
госуд[арственных] проектах по поводу
народного благосостояния. Он горячий
и умный человек, но он будет одинок, как
все умные люди. Наш новый гувернер
48 лет, плешивый, и, думаю, понравится
тебе. К пище относится, похоже, как швед.
Что-то он? Тут идет дождь, и сыро. И
пасмурно, что-то у вас?

Приехали сегодня утром Вера и Маша
Толстые зубы чинить. И проведут со мной
дня три. А время идет, ближе к тому, когда
увидимся и будем в Ясной. Праздник моей
жизни сократился, трудовой период уве-
личился для всех нас. Целую тебя и Машу,
которая была мне очень мила: светлая,
кроткая и приятная. Надеюсь, что мы в
конце концов будем очень нежно и прочно

boxes and trunks. Outdoors, carpenters are
building a fence and an outhouse, along with
covering the roof; there must be around ten
workers in all.

People keep coming up to me with various
bills, the proofread fourth book is lying [on
my desk], along with envelopes and stamps,
etc., nobody is saying a word to the children
about their exams, and Misha is worried that
he failed Latin, Andrjusha, too; today was the
exam. — Tanja was at the doctor's; he says
she has something like a nervous condition;
he told her to take salt baths every day, and
to drink Ems water again, and he strongly
encourages her to go to Yasnaya for a rest.
Today she expressed the thought [to me]
that you may well suspect her of deception
or, rather, of exaggerating her illness. It even
seemed funny to me; she has become very
thin and pale — you'll see for yourself when
you come.

Fol'khert started work yesterday [as the
children's governor]; he speaks German,
French and English. He's a classicist and a vegetarian, and he appeals to Grot. Grot brought
his own uncle, Senator Semënov, to see me.
He gave me an interesting account of various
state projects related to national welfare. He
is a passionate and intelligent fellow, but he
will be lonely, as all intelligent people are. Our
new [children's] governor is 48 years old, bald,
and I think you will like him. He apparently
approaches food like that Swede [Abraam von
Bunde]. I wonder where *he* is now. It's raining here, and damp. And cloudy. What's the
weather like where you are?

[LN's nieces] Vera and Masha Tolstaja
came [to Moscow] this morning to have their
teeth fixed. And they'll be staying three or
so days with me. But the time is going by,
and getting closer to our seeing each other
at Yasnaya. The holiday [period] of my life
has been cut short, and the work period has
increased for all of us. Hugs and kisses to you
and Masha, whom I liked very much: bright,

любить друг друга, когда она уравновесится, а я ее пойму с ее хорошей стороны. Ну, прощайте.

Так и вижу вашу пыльную, безотрадную Бегичевку, но мне было оба раза там хорошо.

11 мая 1892 г.

meek-hearted and pleasing. I hope that she and I shall finally express some tenderness to each other and really love each other when she finds her equilibrium and I catch her from her good side. Well, farewell.

[Even now] I can picture your dusty, dreary Begichevka, but I had a good experience there both times.

11 May 1892.

Nº 10*U* – SOFIA ANDREEVNA TOLSTAYA ❧ LEV NIKOLAEVICH TOLSTOY
28 декабря 1900 г. Ясная Поляна   *28 December 1900. Yasnaya Polyana*
28 декабря 1900 г.   28 December 1900.

Письма от тебя не было, милый друг Левочка, и я только сейчас узнала от Вестерлунда, что Таня родила мертвую девочку. Сегодня в ночь я еду к ней; вероятно, Андрюша меня проводит, мы ждем его к похоронам, к 12 часам, теперь 11 утра.

У меня такое чувство, что «бейте меня, ну, еще и еще», всё как-то застыло во мне от всего тяжелого, что приходится переживать.

Одно утешенье, что и здесь, и у Тани мое присутствие приятно и даже нужно было. Какое счастье, что у Тани был и Сережа, и Дунаев! Всё ей легче было при них, да и помогли, вероятно, вовремя.

Бедная Таня! Ребенка нет, и сознание того, что этот эгоист, ее муж, ее оставил, что у него не хватило любви пожертвовать своей противной жизнью для нее, хотя бы ему и вредно было остаться в России.

Береги себя, милый Левочка, и Сашу. Я пробуду с Таней, пока всякая опасность послеродового периода минует и, может быть, ее противный муж вернется. Себя я буду беречь, ты обо мне не тревожься, буду беречься, потому что еще кому-нибудь пригожусь, а уж самой как не хочется, как скучно жить и знать, что

There hasn't been any letter from you [lately], dear friend Lëvochka, and I just now learnt from [Dr.] Westerlund that Tanja had a stillbirth. I'm going to see her tonight. Probably Andrjusha will go with me; we are expecting him at the funeral, by 12; it's now 11 a.m.

I have the feeling that I am saying: "Hit me again and again"; everything's numb in me from all the challenges I've been obliged to endure.

One comfort here is that both here and at Tanja's my presence has been welcome and even needed. What luck that Serëzha and Dunaev were both at Tanja's! At least things went easier for her when they were there; their help seemed most timely.

Poor Tanja! She has no child, and the realisation that this egotist of her husband left her [and went abroad for medical treatment], that he did not have enough love to give up his repulsive life-style for her, even if it might have been harmful [to his health] to remain in Russia.

Dear Lëvochka, take care of yourself and Sasha. I shall stay with Tanja until any danger connected with her post-natal period passes and, perhaps, her unpleasant husband returns. I shall take care of myself — you need not worry about me — I shall take care of myself, as I may be useful to someone else, though I really don't want to live such a dull

много еще увидишь страданий тех, кого любишь.

О Тане мы здесь знали одно: она пишет письмо Леве и Доре сочувственное о смерти Левушки, а в 5 часов утра 26-го приписывает, что ей кажется, что начинаются роды. Мы вчера сейчас же ей телеграфировали запрос о здоровье и до сих пор не получили ответа; праздники — везде беспорядки, может быть, не до нас, столько всякой заботы о Тане.

Сейчас будут увозить Левушку, у меня вся внутренность дрожит, как всё стало тяжело!

Целую вас, прощайте. Пишите мне в Архангельское и *непременно* всякий день, пожалейте меня, всё легче, когда хоть письмами общаешься.

Кажется, приехал сейчас Андрюша, слышу его кашель.

Сам ты, Левочка, ради Бога, никуда не езди, прошло то время, и ушли уж твои силы.

Целую вас всех. Пишите *не на* мое имя, а Наташе [Сухотиной], а то назад ушлют.

С. Толстая

life, knowing that I shall see many more sufferings on the part of those I love.

As for Tanja, we here knew one thing: she was writing a letter to Lëva and Dora expressing her condolences on the death of Lëvushka, and at 5 o'clock on the morning of the 26th added a note that it seemed her labour was starting. Yesterday we immediately wired her a question on her health but haven't received any reply up to now. [After all,] the holidays everywhere are in chaos or, perhaps, they are too busy caring for Tanja to [contact] us.

Now they'll be coming to take Lëvushka's [body] away, and my whole inner body is trembling — how terribly difficult has it all become!

Hugs and kisses to [all of] you. Write me at Arkhangel'skoe, and *be sure* to write every day. Have pity on me: it's always easier when we can at least communicate through letters.

I think Andrjusha has just arrived — I can hear him coughing.

For God's sake, Lëvochka, don't take any trips; that time has passed, and your strength is not what it was.

Hugs and kisses to all of you. Address [your letters] *not to* my name, but to Natasha Sukhotina, otherwise they'll send it back.

S. Tolstaya

Nº 11*U* – SOFIA ANDREEVNA TOLSTAYA ❧ LEV NIKOLAEVICH TOLSTOY
11 мая 1905 г. Москва　　　　*11 May 1905. Moscow*

11 мая 1905 г.　　　　　　　　　　　　11 May 1905.

Разумеется, что я завтра не успею выехать, так как дела очень много, а сил очень мало. Сегодня убирали и сушили с Афанасьевной все вещи: ковры, платья, полости и проч. Очень было хлопотно. Вторую половину дня занималась книжными делами. Завтра дела дома с типографиями и проч. И в 3-х банках, и вечером поеду на могилки. Послезавтра дела окончу и покупки. И вот прошу выслать за мной

Naturally, I shan't be able to leave tomorrow, as I have so much to do and so little strength. Today Afanas'evna and I cleaned and dried everything: rugs, dresses, bedding, etc. It kept us very busy. The afternoon I spent working on [forthcoming] editions. Tomorrow I'll be working at home with [representatives of] the printshops, etc. I'll also [be going around] to three banks. In the evening I shall visit [our children's] little graves.

в субботу утром. Здоровье всё то же, всё кашель и слабость, и плохое пищеварение. Но ничего, живу и работаю.

The day after tomorrow I shall finish my business affairs and do some shopping. And so I would ask you to send [a carriage to pick me up at Kozlovka] on Saturday morning. My health is still the same, constant coughing and weakness, and poor digestion. But never mind, I'm alive and working.

Целую вас всех. Жаль весны и скучно.

Hugs and kisses to you all. I have been missing [our] spring [at Yasnaya]; [life here is] dull.

С. Толстая

S. Tolstaya

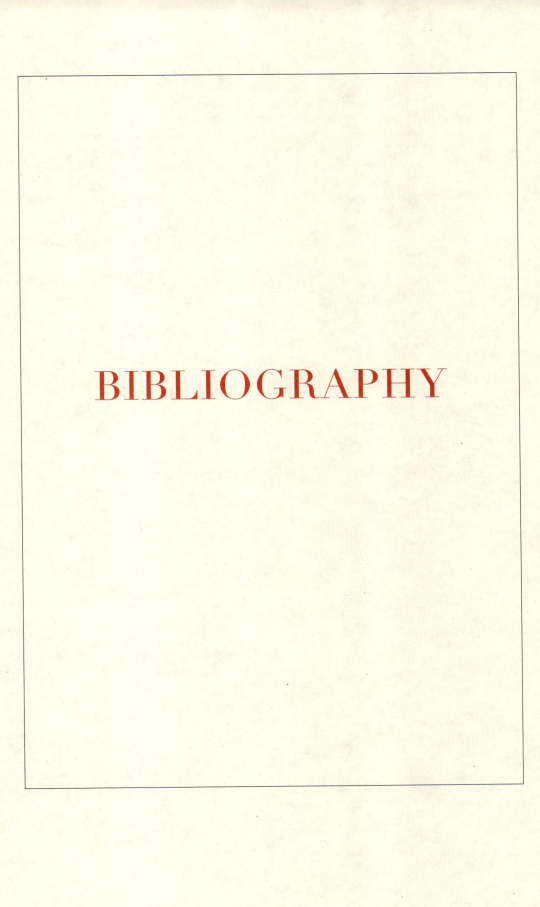

BIBLIOGRAPHY

Asquith, Cynthia. *Married to Tolstoy.* Boston: Houghton-Mifflin, 1961.

Bajkova [= Shumikhina], Ju. G. "Sof'ja Andreevna Tolstaja kak literator" [Sofia Andreevna Tolstaya as writer]. Dissertation for the degree of Kandidat filologicheskikh nauk, Uljanovskij gosudarstvennyj universitet, Uljanovsk, 2007.

Bartlett, Rosamund. *Tolstoy: a Russian life.* Boston: Houghton Mifflin Harcourt, 2011.

Basinskij, Pavel. *Lev Tolstoj: begstvo iz raja* [Leo Tolstoy: flight from Paradise]. Moscow: Astrel'/AST, 2010.

— *Svjatoj protiv L'va. Ioann Kronshtadtskij i Lev Tolstoj: istorija odnoj vrazhdy* [A Saint versus a Lion: Ioann Kronshtadtskij and Lev Tolstoj: the story of a feud]. Moscow: AST, 2013.

Belov, S. V. & Vladimir Tunimanov. *F. M. Dostoevskij–A. G. Dostoevksaja: Perepiska* [Correspondence]. Moscow: Akademija Nauk SSSR, 1979.

Birukoff, Paul [= P. I. Birjukov]. *The Life of Tolstoy.* London: Cassel & Co., 1911.

Cain, Thomas G. S. "Tolstoy in letters". *Queen's Quarterly* 86 (1979): 273–80.

Chertkov, Vladimir. *Ukhod Tolstogo* [Tolstoy's departure]. Moscow: Komitet imeni L. N. Tolstogo po okazaniju pomoshchi goludajushchim, 1922.

Christian, Reginald F. (ed. & trans.). *Tolstoy's letters.* 2 vols. New York: Scribner's, 1978.

—. *Tolstoy's diaries.* 2 vols. London: Athlone, 1985.

Donskov, Andrew (ed.). *Mixail Lentovskij and the Russian theatre.* East Lansing (Mich., USA): Russian Language Journal, 1985.

— (ed.). *L. N. Tolstoj—P. V. Verigin: perepiska.* St. Petersburg: Izd. Dmitrij Bulanin, 1995. Also published together with an English translation by John Woodsworth: *Leo Tolstoy—Peter Verigin: correspondence.* Ottawa: Legas, 1995.

— (ed.). *L. N. Tolstoj i M. P. Novikov: perepiska* [Correspondence]. Munich: Verlag Otto Sagner, 1996.

— (ed.). *L. N. Tolstoj i T. M. Bondarev: perepiska* [Correspondence]. Munich: Verlag Otto Sagner, 1996.

— (ed.). *Sergej Tolstoy and the Doukhobors: a journey to Canada.* Comp. Tat'jana Nikiforova. Trans. John Woodsworth. Ottawa: Slavic Research Group at the University of Ottawa & Moscow: State L. N. Tolstoy Museum, 1998.

— (ed.). *L. N. Tolstoj i F. A. Zheltov: perepiska* [Correspondence]. Comp. L. Gladkova. Ottawa: Slavic Research Group at the University of Ottawa & Moscow: State L. N. Tolstoy Museum, 1999. English edition: *A Molokan's search for truth: the correspondence of Leo Tolstoy and Fedor Zheltov.* Trans. John Woodsworth. Ed. Ethel Dunn. Berkeley (Calif.): Highgate Road Social Science Research Station & Ottawa: Slavic Research Group at the University of Ottawa, 2001.

— (ed.). *L. N. Tolstoj i S. A. Tolstaja: perepiska s N. N. Strakhovym / The Tolstoys' correspondence with N. N. Strakhov.* Comp. L. D. Gromova & T. G. Nikiforova. Ottawa: Slavic Research Group at the University of Ottawa & Moscow: State L. N. Tolstoy Museum, 2000.

— (ed.). *L. N. Tolstoj—N. N. Strakhov: polnoe sobranie perepiski / Leo Tolstoy & Nikolaj Strakhov: complete correspondence.* 2 vols. Comp. L. D. Gromova & T. G. Nikiforova. Ottawa: Slavic Research Group at the University of Ottawa & Moscow: State L. N. Tolstoy Museum, 2003.

—. *Leo Tolstoy and the Canadian Doukhobors: an historic relationship.* Ottawa: Centre for Research on Canadian-Russian Relations, 2005.

—. *L. N. Tolstoj i N. N. Strakhov. Èpistoljarnyj dialog o zhizni i literature* [Epistolary dialogue on life and literature]. Ottawa: Slavic Research Group at the University of Ottawa & Moscow: State L. N. Tolstoy Museum, 2006.

—. *Leo Tolstoy and Russian peasant sectarian writers: selected correspondence.* Correspondence trans. John Woodsworth. Ottawa: Slavic Research Group at the University of Ottawa, 2008.

—. *Leo Tolstoy and Nikolaj Strakhov: a personal and literary dialogue.* Ottawa: Slavic Research Group at the University of Ottawa & Moscow: State L. N. Tolstoy Museum, 2008.

— (ed.). *Sofia Andreevna Tolstaya: My Life.* Trans. John Woodsworth & Arkadi Klioutchanski. Ottawa: Ottawa University Press, 2010.

—. *Sofia Andreevna Tolstaya: Literary works.* Ottawa: Slavic Research Group at the University of Ottawa & Moscow: State L. N. Tolstoy Museum, 2011.

—. *V. F. Bulgakov: Kak prozhita zhizn': Vospominanija poslednego sekretarja L. N. Tolstogo* [How a life was lived: Reminiscences of L. N. Tolstoy's last secretary]. Comp. L. V. Gladkova, J. Woodsworth, A. A. Klioutchanski. Ottawa: Slavic Research Group at the University of Ottawa & Moscow: RGALI and State L. N. Tolstoy Museum, 2012.

—. *V. F. Bulgakov: V spore s Tolstym* [In discussion with Tolstoy]. Comp. A. Donskov, L. V. Gladkova, A. A. Klioutchanski. Ottawa: Slavic Research Group at the University of Ottawa & Moscow: RGALI and State L. N. Tolstoy Museum, 2014.

Donskov, Andrew, Galina Galagan and Lidija Gromova. *Edinenie ljudej v tvorchestve L. N. Tolstogo / The Unity of people in Leo Tolstoy's works*. Ottawa: Slavic Research Group at the University of Ottawa; St. Petersburg: Insititute of Russian Literature (Pushkin House), Russian Academy of Sciences; Moscow: Gorky Institute of World Literature, Russian Academy of Sciences, 2002.

Edwards, Anne. *Sonya: the life of Countess Tolstoy*. London: Hodder & Stoughton, 1981.

Feiler, Lily. "The Tolstoi marriage: conflict and illusions". *Canadian Slavonic Papers* 23: 3 (1981): 245–60.

Gladkova, L. V. Preface and commentaries to: *Ob otluchenii L'va Tolstogo: po materialam semejnoj perepiski* [On the excommunication of Lev Tolstoy: from family correspondence]. *Oktjabr'* 9 (1993): 184–90.

— (ed.). *Ukhod L'va Tolstogo* [The departure of Lev Tolstoy]. Tula: IPO "Lev Tolstoj", 2011.

— "On i ona. Istorija knigi i ljubvi" [He and she. The story of a book and of love]. *Moskva* 5 (2011): 178–85.

— (ed.). "On i ona (Lev Tolstoj i Sof'ja Tolstaja)" [He and she (Lev Tolstoy and Sofia Tolstaya)]. *Katalog materialov iz fondov Gosudarstvennogo muzeja L. N. Tolstogo. K stoletiju so dnja rozhdenija L. N. Tolstogo* [Catalogue of materials from the collections of the State L. N. Tolstoy Museum. For the centenary of L. N. Tolstoy's birth]. Tula, 2011.

Golinenko, O. A. et al. (eds.). *S. A. Tolstaja. Dnevniki v dvukh tomakh* [S. A. Tolstaya. Diaries in two volumes]. Intro. S. A. Rozanova. Moscow: Khudozhestvennaja literatura, 1978.

—. *The diaries of Sophia Tolstoy*. Trans. Cathy Porter. Intro. R. F. Christian. New York: Random House, 1985. Republished with a Foreword by Doris Lessing. London: Alma Books, 2009.

Gruzinskij, A. E. (ed.). *Pis'ma grafa L. N. Tolstogo k zhene* [Count L. N. Tolstoy's letters to his wife]. Moscow, 1913.

Gryzlova, I. K. "Zhizn' sem'i Tolstykh v pis'makh S. A. Tolstoj i T. A. Kuzminskoj" [The life of the Tolstoy family in the letters of S. A. Tolstaya and T. A. Kuzminskaja]. In: Vladimir Tolstoj i Ljudmila Gladkova (eds.). *Druz'ja i gosti Jasnoj Poljany. Materialy nauchnoj konferentsii, posvjashchennoj 160-letiju S. A. Tolstoj* [Friends and guests of Yasnaya Polyana. Papers of an academic conference marking the 160th birthday of S. A. Tolstaya]. Tula: Izd. dom «Jasnaja Poljana», 2006: 125–39.

Gusev, Nikolaj Nikolaevich. "K istorii semejnoj tragedii Tolstogo (po neizdannym istochnikam)" [On the history of Tolstoy's family tragedy (from unpublished sources)]. *Literaturnoe nasledstvo 37–38: L. N. Tolstoj* [Literary heritage 37–38: L. N. Tolstoy]. Moscow: Akademija Nauk, 1939: 674–97.

—. *Letopis' zhizni i tvorchestva L. N. Tolstogo* [Chronicle of the life and works of L. N. Tolstoy]. *1828–1890*. Moscow: Khudozhestvennaja literatura, 1958.

—. *Letopis' zhizni i tvorchestva L. N. Tolstogo. 1891–1910* [Chronicle of the life and works of L. N. Tolstoy. 1891–1910]. Moscow: Khudozhestvennaja literatura, 1960.

Hamburg, G. M. "Tolstoy's spirituality". Ed. D. T. Orwin, *Anniversary essays on Tolstoy*. Cambridge: Cambridge University Press, 2010: 138–58.

—. "Marriage, estate culture and public life in Sofia Andreyevna Tolstaya's «My Life»". *Tolstoy Studies Journal*, 22 (2010): 122–35.

Hoogenboom, Hilde. "The Tolstoy family: conflicts in the literary field at home". Paper delivered at the ASEEES conference, San Antonio (Texas), 22–23 November 2014. 13 pp.

Katz, Michael. *The Kreutzer Sonata variations: Lev Tolstoy's novella and counterstories by Sofiya Tolstaya and Lev Lvovich Tolstoj*. New Haven: Yale University Press, 2014.

Keller, Ursula & Natalja Sharandak. *Sofja Andrejewna Tolstaja: Ein Leben an der Seite Tolstojs* [Sofia Andreevna Tolstaya: a life at Tolstoy's side]. Frankfurt/Main & Leipzig: Insel Verlag, 2009.

Komarova, T. V. "Pometki S. A. Tolstoj na jasnopoljanskom èkzempljare *Pisem grafa L. N. Tolstogo k zhene 1862–1910 gg.*" [Notes by S. A. Tolstaya on the Yasnaya Polyana copy of «Letters of Count L. N. Tolstoy

to his wife 1862–1910».] *Jasnopoljanskij sbornik 1998* (Tula: Izdatel'skij dom "Jasnaja Poljana", 1999): 155–58.

Koteliansky, S. S. & Virginia Woolf (trans.). *Tolstoy's love letters*. London, 1923.

Kuzminskaya, T. A. *Tolstoy as I knew him: my life at home and at Yasnaya Polyana*. Trans. Nora Sigerist et al. Intro. E. J. Simmons. New York: Macmillan, 1948.

Mavor, James. *My windows on the street of the world*. 2 vols. London & Toronto: J. M. Dent & Sons, 1923.

McLean, Hugh. "Claws on the behind: Tolstoy and Darwin". *Tolstoy Studies Journal* 19 (2007): 15–33.

—. "The Tolstoy marriage revisited — many times". *Canadian Slavonic Papers* 53 (2011): 65–80.

Medzhibovskaya, Inessa. *Tolstoy and the religious culture of his time: a biography of a long conversion, 1845–1887*. Lanham, Md: Lexington Books, 2008.

Metelitsyna, P. N. *God v batrachkakh* [A year as a farm labourer]. *Otechestvennye zapiski* 9 (September), 1880.

Modzalevskij, B. L. (ed.). *Perepiska L. N. Tolstogo s N. N. Strakhovym* [Correspondence of L. N. Tolstoy with N. N. Strakhov]. *1870–1894*. St. Petersburg: Obshchestvo tolstovskogo muzeja, 1914.

Newton, William Wilberforce. *A run through Russia. The story of a visit to Count Tolstoi*. Hartford: Student Pub. Co., 1894.

Nikiforova, T. G. "Pis'ma A. G. Dostoevskoj k S. A. Tolstoj" [A. G. Dostoevskaja's letters to S. A. Tolstaja]. In: M. Shcherbakova & M. Mozharova (eds.), *Mir filologii*. Moscow: Nasledie, 2000: 290–306.

Nikitina, N. A. *Sof'ja Andreevna Tolstaja*. Moscow: Molodaja gvardija, 2010.

Orekhanov, Georgij Leonidovich. *Russkaja pravoslavnaja tserkov' i L. N. Tolstoj. Konflikt glazami sovremennikov* [The Russian Orthodox Church and L. N. Tolstoy. The conflict through the eyes of contemporaries]. Moscow: Izd. Pravoslavnogo svjato-tikhonovskogo gumanitarnogo universiteta, 2010.

Paperno, Irina. "Leo Tolstoy's correspondence with Nikolai Strakhov: the dialogue of faith". In: Donna T. Orwin (ed.): *Anniversary essays on Tolstoy*. New York: Cambridge University Press, 2010: 96–119.

Parini, Jay. *The last station: a novel of Tolstoy's final year*. New York: Anchor Books, 2009.

Polner, Tichon [= Tikhon Polner]. *Tolstoj und seine Frau. Die Geschichte der Liebe* [Tolstoy and his wife. The story of love]. Berlin, 1928.

Polner, Tikhon. *Tolstoy and his wife*. New York, 1945.

Popoff, Alexandra. *Sophia Tolstoy: a biography*. New York: Free Press, 2010.

Popov, Pavel. "Pis'mo Tolstogo k S. A. Tolstoj (novoe o semejnykh otnoshenijakh L. N. Tolstogo)" [Tolstoy's letter to S. A. Tolstaya (new materials on L. N. Tolstoy's family relations)]. *Literaturnoe nasledstvo 37–38: L. N. Tolstoj* [Literary heritage 37–38: L. N. Tolstoy]. Moscow: Akademija Nauk, 1939: 665–73.

Rancour-Laferriere, Daniel. *Tolstoy's quest for God*. Piscataway, N. J.: Transaction Publishers, 2007.

Seuron, Anna. *Graf Leo Tolstoi von Anna Seuron*. Berlin, 1895.

Shcherbakova, Marina I. (ed.). *I. S. Aksakov — N. N. Strakhov: Perepiska / Ivan Aksakov — Nikolaj Strakhov: Correspondence*. Ottawa: Slavic Research Group at the University of Ottawa & Moscow: Institut mirovoj literatury imeni M. Gor'kogo, 2007.

Shirer, William L. *Love and hatred: the troubled marriage of Leo Tolstoy*. New York: Simon & Shuster, 1994.

Smoluchowski, Louise. *Lev and Sonya: the story of the Tolstoy marriage*. New York: G. P. Putnam's Sons, 1987.

Stadling, Ionas. "With Tolstoy in the Russian famine." *The Century* (New York, 1893; new series: vol. 24, pp. 249–63).

Tolstaja, Aleksandra L'vovna. *Dnevniki* [Diaries] *1903–1920*. Comp. N. A. Kalinina, S. D. Novikova. Ed. L. V. Gladkova. Moscow: Kuchkovo pole, 2014.

Tolstaja, Sof'ja Andreevna [= Sofia Andreevna Tolstaja]. [Stories written for L. Tolstoy's *Novaja azbuka* [New primer] and published in Tolstoy's PSS (Vol. 21)]: "Byla zima, no bylo teplo" [It was winter, but it was warm, 21: 27]; "Spala koshka na kryshe" [A cat was sleeping on the roof, 21: 27]; "Khodili deti po lesu za gribami" [The children were gathering mushrooms in the woods, 21: 48]; "K Mashe prishli v gosti devochki" [Little girls visiting Masha, 21: 56]; "Orekhovaja vetka" [The nut-tree branch, 21: 80–81]; "Kak tëtushka rasskazyvala o tom, kak ona vyuchilas' shit'" [How Auntie told about how she learnt to sew, 21: 108]; "Rasskaz muzhika o tom, za chto on starshego brata ljubit" [A peasant's tale

about why he loves his elder brother, 21: 159]; "Kak tëtushka rasskazyvala o tom, kak u neë byl ruchnoj vorobej — Zhivchik" [How Auntie told about her pet sparrow named Zhivchik, 21: 160–61].

— (comp.). *Tolstoj, L. N. Pis'ma k zhene. 1862–1910* [L. N. Tolstoy. Letters to his wife. 1862–1910]. 2 vols. Izd. 1-e. Ed. A. E. Gruzinskij. Moscow: A. A. Levenson, 1913.

— (comp.). *Tolstoj, L. N. Pis'ma k zhene. 1862–1910* [L. N. Tolstoy. Letters to his wife. 1862–1910]. 2 vols. Izd. 2-e, ispravlennoe i dopolnennoe [2nd ed., corrected and enlarged]. Moscow: Tipo-litografija I. N. Kushnerev, 1915.

—. *Avtobiografija grafini S. A. Tolstoj* [The autobiography of Countess S. A. Tolstaya]. Ed. V. S. Spiridonov. *Nachala*, 1 (1921): 131–85. English translation by S. S. Koteliansky & Leonard Woolf. London (Richmond): Hogarth Press, 1922.

—. *Dnevniki S. A. Tolstoj. 1860–1891* [Diaries of S. A. Tolstaya. 1860–1891]. Ed. S. L. Tolstoj. Intro. M. A. Tsjavlovskij. Moscow: Izdatel'stvo M. i S. Sabashnikovykh, 1928. Series "Zapisi proshlogo".

—. *Dnevniki S. A. Tolstoj. 1891–1897. Chast' vtoraja* [Diaries of S. A. Tolstaya. 1891–1897. Part II]. Ed. S. L. Tolstoj. Intro. M. A. Tsjavlovskij. Moscow: Izdatel'stvo M. i S. Sabashnikovykh, 1929. Series "Zapisi proshlogo".

—. *Dnevniki S. A. Tolstoj. 1897–1909* [Diaries of S. A. Tolstaya. 1897–1909]. Ed. S. L. Tolstoj. Moscow: Sever, 1932. Series "Zapisi proshlogo".

—. *Dnevniki S. A. Tolstoj. 1860–1891* [Diaries of S. A. Tolstaya. 1860–1891]. Ed. S. L. Tolstoj. Moscow: Sovetskij pisatel', 1936. Series "Zapisi proshlogo".

—. *Pis'ma k L. N. Tolstomu 1862–1910* [Letters to L. N. Tolstoy. 1862–1910]. Ed. A. I. Tolstaja & P. S. Popov. Intro. P. S. Popov. Moscow & Leningrad: Academia, 1936.

—. "Pis'ma k V. F. Bulgakovu 1911–1918" [Letters to V. F. Bulgakov 1911–1918]. In: V. F. Bulgakov. *O Tolstom*. Tula, 1964: 280–312.

—. *Dnevniki v dvukh tomakh* [Diaries in two volumes]. 2 vols. Comp. N. I. Azarova, O. A. Golinenko, O. A. Pokrovskaja, S. A. Rozanova, B. M. Shumova. Intro. S. A. Rozanova. Series: "Serija literaturnykh memuarov". Moscow: Khudozhestvennaja literatura, 1978.

—. *Moja zhizn'* [My Life]. Ed. Vitalij Remizov. 2 vols. Moscow: Kuchkovo pole, 2011.

—. *My Life*. Trans. John Woodsworth & Arkadi Klioutchanski. Ed. & intro. Andrew Donskov. Ottawa: University of Ottawa Press, 2010.

Tolstoj, Lev L'vovich. *Arkhiv L. L. Tolstogo* [Archive of L. L. Tolstoj]. F303. 674–94.

— *Opyt moej zhizni. Perepiska L. N. i L. L. Tolstykh* [My life experiences. The correspondence of L. N. Tolstoy and L. L. Tolstoj]. Comp. L. V. Gladkova, E. V. Neljubina, S. D. Novikova. Ed. L. V. Gladkova. Moscow: Kuchkovo pole, 2014.

Tolstoj, Lev Nikolaevich [= Leo Tolstoy]. *Polnoe sobranie sochinenij*. Jubilejnoe izdanie [*Complete Collected Works*. Jubilee Edition = PSS]. Moscow: Goslitizdat, 1928–1958. [Vols. 83 (1938) & 84 (1949) contain Tolstoy's letters to Sofia Andreevna]

—. *Perepiska s russkimi pisateljami* [Correspondence with Russian writers]. 2 vols. Comp., intro. & commentaries by S. A. Rozanova. Moscow: Khudozhestvennaja literatura, 1978.

—. *Perepiska L. N. Tolstogo s sestroj i brat'jami* [L. N. Tolstoy's correspondence with his sister and brothers]. Comp., commentaries by N. A. Kalinina, V. V. Lozbjakova & T. A. Nikiforova. Intro. L. D. Opul'skaja [= Gromova-Opul'skaja]. Moscow: Khudozhestvennaja literatura, 1990.

—. *L. N. Tolstoj i A. A. Tolstaja: Perepiska 1857–1903* [Correspondence 1857–1903]. Comp. N. I. Azarova, L. V. Gladkova, O. A. Golinenko, B. M. Shumova. Ed. L. D. Gromova-Opul'skaja & I. G. Ptushkina. Moscow: Nauka, 2011.

Tolstoj, S. L. *Ocherki bylogo* [Sketches from the past]. Ed. K. Malysheva. Moscow: Khudozhestvennaja literatura, 1956. See esp. "Konchina moej materi" [The passing of my mother]: 272–76.

Tunimanov, Vladmir. "Dostoevskij, Strakhov, Tolstoj (labirint stseplenij)" [Dostoevsky, Strakhov, Tolstoy (a labyrinth of connections)]. *Russkaja literatura,* 3 (2006): 38–97.

Zhdanov, V. A. *Ljubov' v zhizni L'va Tolstogo* [Love in Leo Tolstoy's life]. Moscow: Planeta, 1993.

Zverev, Aleksej & Vladimir Tunimanov. *Lev Tolstoj*. Moscow: Molodaja gvardija, 2006. See esp. chapters: "Semejnye stseny. «Krejtserova sonata»" [Family scenes: «The Kreutzer Sonata»], "Vanechka.

Strannaja ljubov' Sof'i Andreevny" [Vanechka. The strange love of Sofia Andreevna]; "Udirat', nado udirat'" [Escape, must escape].

For more on the epistolary section of the Tolstaya archive, see Andrew Donskov (ed.), *My Life,* pp. 1046–56 and Andrew Donskov, *Sofia Andreevna Tolstaya: Literary works,* pp. 487–521. For additional English sources on Tolstoy's works, see: David Egan & Melinda Egan, *Leo Tolstoy: an annotated bibliography of English language sources to 1978* (New Jersey & London: Scarecrow Press, 1979) and: David Egan & Melinda Egan, *Leo Tolstoy: an annotated bibliography of English language sources from 1978 to 2003* (New Jersey & London: Scarecrow Press, 2005).

SELECTED CHRONOLOGY

OF EVENTS IN THE TOLSTOY FAMILY LIFE

The chronology is based primarily on Leo Tolstoy's Diaries and letters, and Sofia Tolstaya's *My Life* [*Moja zhizn'*] (as the most recently published source of pertinent information) and her *Diaries* [*Dnevniki*], as well as her letters. As with any other chronology, the aim here is to give the reader a broad idea of the overall course of the couple's years and, as much as possible, from their viewpoint and in their own words. The writings of Nikolaj Gusev (1882–1967), personal secretary to Tolstoy (1907–1909), furnished another most useful source. In the selection process an attempt was made to re-create the times, the milieu and the activities of the Tolstoys, including visits to and from other people. All dates are Old Style (O. S.) unless otherwise indicated (see "From the Editor").

1828

28 August — Lev Nikolaevich Tolstoy [LNT] is born on the family estate of Yasnaya Polyana, near Tula (central Russia, about 200 km south from Moscow) into the family of a retired cavalry colonel Count Nikolaj Il'ich Tolstoy (1794–1837) and Countess Marija Nikolaevna Tolstaja (*née* Princess Volkonskaja; 1790–1830). Yasnaya Polyana was the Volkonsky family estate. LNT is the fourth child and has three elder brothers: Nikolaj (1823–1860), Sergej (1826–1904), Dmitrij (1827–1856).

1830

2 March — The Tolstoys' fifth child, daughter Marija (1830–1912) is born.
4 August — Death of Marija Nikolaevna, LNT's mother.

1833

LNT is under tutoring of his elder brothers' tutor Fëdor Ivanovich Ressel (?–1845).

1837

10 January — LNT's family moves to Moscow.
21 June — Death of LNT's father.
Late June — The Tolstoy children come under the guardianship of their aunt, N. I. Tolstoy's sister Countess Aleksandra Il'inichna von der Osten-Saken (*née* Tolstaja; 1795–1841). They are under direct care of Tat'jana Aleksandrovna Ergol'skaja (1792–1874), a distant relative living in the Tolstoy family from her childhood.
Late June — The Tolstoy boys are given a new tutor: Prospère Saint-Thomas (1812–1881).

1838

25 May — Death of LNT's grandmother Countess Pelageja Nikolaevna Tolstaja (*née* Princess Gorchakova; 1762–1838).
6 July — The Tolstoy children are separated. The two eldest boys (Nikolaj and Sergej) stay in Moscow under the instruction of Prospère Saint-Thomas while Dmitrij, Lev and Marija move to Yasnaya Polyana together with T. A. Ergol'skaja. Except for brief visits to Moscow, LNT will spend most of the time between summer 1838 and autumn 1841 on the estate.

1841

22 August — Death of LNT's aunt Aleksandra Osten-Saken.
October — Pelageja Il'inichna Jushkova (*née* Tolstaja; 1797–1876) — another sister of LNT's father's — and Aleksandr Sergeevich Voejkov (1801–?) — a nearby landowner — are appointed new guardians of the children.

November — all the Tolstoy children move to Kazan', where P. I. Jushkova lives. Nikolaj Tolstoy is transferred from Moscow University to Kazan' University.

1844

May–June — LNT fails entrance exams at Kazan' University.

22 August — Sofia Andreevna Tolstaya [SAT] is born Sofia Andreevna Behrs in the village of Pokrovskoe Glebovo-Streshnevo (near Moscow) into the family of a court physician (a doctor of the Moscow Court Administration and Supernumerary Physician to Moscow Theatres), Andrej Evstaf'evich Behrs (1808–1868) and Ljubov' Aleksandrovna Islavina (1826–1886). She has one elder sister, Elizaveta (1843–1919).

September — LNT is admitted to Kazan' University (Faculty of Oriental Languages) after petitioning the Rector.

1845

Summer — LNT spends summer holidays at Yasnaya Polyana. He studies philosophy.

September — LNT transfers to the Faculty of Law.

1846

LNT spends the summer at Yasnaya Polyana.

29 October — Tat'jana Andreevna Behrs (SAT's younger sister, 1846–1925) is born.

1847

17 March — LNT begins his first Diary (makes entries until 16 June).

April — LNT receives his part of the family inheritance (the Yasnaya Polyana estate and a few nearby villages) and immediately leaves the university on grounds of "ill health and domestic circumstances".

1 May — LNT returns to Yasnaya Polyana. He devotes himself to his estate and the welfare of his serfs.

1849

Early February — LNT moves to St. Petersburg. He intends to enter public service, but experiences heavy debts and disillusionment.

Autumn — LNT opens a school for peasant children on his estate.

1850

LNT devotes much time to piano practice; he resumes writing his Diary.

30 December — LNT is assigned the lowest civil service rank of *kollezhskij registrator* (14th class according to the Russian Table of ranks, equivalent to *praporshchik* (ensign), the lowest officer rank in the army).

1851

LNT's first serious attempts at writing, along with heavy gambling (at cards).

29 April — LNT leaves for the Caucasus with his brother Nikolaj, travelling through Kazan' and the lower Volga.

June — LNT takes part as a Cossack volunteer in a raid against a Caucasus village.

LNT continues working on the early drafts of his story *Childhood [Detstvo]*. He retires from the civil service and requests admittance to military service.

1852

January — LNT joins the Russian army as a cadet, serving in the Caucasus. At one point he is nearly killed by a grenade.

LNT spends most of the year at the Cossack outpost Starogladkovskaja, involved in military duties, reading, writing and gambling.

4 July — LNT sends *Childhood* to editor Nikolaj Nekrasov at the journal *Sovremennik*.

September — *Childhood* appears in *Sovremennik* N° 9 (1852), and is well received by both literary circles and the general public.

1853

February–March — LNT takes part in a campaign against Chechens. Questioning justifications of war, he contemplates withdrawing from military service.

March — LNT's story *The raid [Nabeg]* appears in *Sovremennik* N° 3 (1853).

October — Turkey and Russia declare war on each other.

1854

9 January — LNT receives a military commission with the rank of *praporshchik*. He is transferred to Bessarabia (now Moldova).

6 September — LNT is promoted to the next military rank of *podporuchik* (sublieutenant), and is subsequently transferred to the Crimea.

October — LNT's story *Boyhood [Otrochestvo]* appears in *Sovremennik* N° 10 (1854).

7 November — LNT arrives at Sevastopol', where he takes up military service in various positions in and around the city.

1855

LNT serves on the Crimea front.

January — LNT's short story *Notes of a billiard marker [Zapiski markëra]* appears in *Sovremennik* N° 1 (1855).

25 January — Sofia Andreevna's paternal grandmother, Elisaveta Ivanovna Behrs (*née* Vul'fert; 1789–1855), dies of cholera at age 66.

18 February — Emperor Nicholas I (1796–1855) dies in St. Petersburg after a thirty-year reign.

June — LNT's story *Sevastopol' in December [Sevastopol' v dekabre]* appears in *Sovremennik* N° 6 (1855).

4 August — LNT is present during the Battle of the Chernaya (*Srazhenie u Chërnoj Rechki*), although his detachment does not take active part in the hostilities.

28 August (9 September) — Sevastopol' is taken by the Coalition forces. LNT witnesses the last battle.

September — *Sevastopol' in May [Sevastopol' v mae]* (although heavily censored) and the short story *The wood-cutting [Rubka lesa]* appear in *Sovremennik* N° 9 (1855).

19 November — LNT returns to St. Petersburg, where he frequents local literary circles, meeting Ivan Turgenev, Nikolaj Nekrasov, Ivan Goncharov, Aleksandr Ostrovsky and other writers.

Late November — LNT meets his great aunt Countess Aleksandra Andreevna Tolstaja (1817–1904), daughter of LNT's paternal uncle Andrej Andreevich Tolstoj (1771–1844), appointed lady-in-waiting at the Imperial Court in 1846; they develop a friendship which will last for many years.

1856

January — LNT's story *Sevastopol' in August 1855* [*Sevastopol' v avguste 1855 goda*] appears in *Sovremennik* N° 1 (1856).

March — LNT's story *The snowstorm* [*Metel'*] appears in *Sovremennik* N° 3 (1856).

26 March — LNT is promoted to the next higher military rank of *poruchik* (lieutenant).

May — LNT's story *Two hussars* [*Dva gusara*] appears in *Sovremennik* N° 5 (1856). LNT begins his acquaintance with a prominent Russian poet Afanasij Afanas'evich Fet (real surname: Shenshin, 1820–1892) that will later grow into a lifelong friendship.

26 May — LNT and SAT's uncle Konstantin Aleksandrovich Islavin (1827–1903) visit SAT's mother Ljubov' Aleksandrovna Behrs in Pokrovskoe-Streshnevo. From LNT's Diary: "The children waited on us. Such kind, cheerful girls!" (*PSS* 47: p. 76).

27 May — LNT leaves Moscow for Yasnaya Polyana.

Summer/Autumn — LNT lives at Yasnaya Polyana often going visiting (including Ivan Turgenev at Spasskoe-Lutovinovo in May and July) and hunting. He devotes himself to intense reading and equally intense writing (working on *Youth* [*Junost'*] and *The Cossacks* [*Kazaki*], also beginning work on the novel *The Decembrists* [*Dekabristy*], two comedies and other writings). He becomes infatuated with Valerija Vladimirovna Arsen'eva (1836–1909), over whom he had been appointed guardian, and contemplates marriage. His friendship with Turgenev cools, along with (gradually) his feelings for Arsen'eva. He is unsuccessful in his attempt to free his serfs.

26 August — Alexander II (1818–1881) is crowned Emperor of Russia; he reigns until his assassination in 1881.

Late September — A separate edition of LNT's *War stories* [*Voennye rasskazy*] is published.

Autumn — LNT sends an official request for withdrawal from military service, which is refused three weeks later. A second request is granted by the end of the year.

Early October — A separate edition of LNT's *Childhood* [*Detstvo*] and *Boyhood* [*Otrochestvo*] is published.

12 December — LNT breaks off relations with Arsen'eva.

1857

January — *Youth* [*Junost'*] appears in *Sovremennik* N° 1 (1857).

Late January–July — LNT's first trip abroad to France, Switzerland and Germany. He visits Paris, Dijon, Versailles, including theatres and museums, and public lectures at the Sorbonne.

25 March [6 April N.S.] — LNT witnesses a public execution in Paris; under the shock of this, he decides to spend the next few months in Switzerland (also visiting northern Italy and Germany, returning home by the end of July.

1 December —The first short biography of LNT is published in N° 34 of *Russkij khudozhestvennyj listok*, together with his lithographed portrait. He continues working intermittently on several stories (including *The Cossacks* [*Kazaki*], *Albert* [*Al'bert*] and *Lucerne* [*Ljutsern*]).

1858

January–February — Tolstoy takes an interest in two women: Ekaterina Fedorovna Tjutcheva (1835–1882; daughter of the famous Russian poet Fedor Ivanovich Tjutchev) and, briefly, in Princess Praskov'ja Sergeevna Shcherbatova (1840–1924).

9 April — LNT leaves Moscow for Yasnaya Polyana.

April — LNT's intensive work on *The Cossacks* [*Kazaki*].

May–September — While farming at Yasnaya Polyana, LNT begins a two-year affair with married peasant woman Aksin'ja Bazykina (*née* Sakharova, 1836–1919; the Bazykin family was also known by the surname Anikanov).

15 September — In Moscow LNT meets E. F. Tjutcheva, of whom he writes the next day in his Diary: "I was almost ready to marry her quietly and without love but she was deliberately cold towards me" (*PSS* 48: p. 17).

22 December — LNT is nearly killed by a bear while hunting.

1859

1 January — LNT confides to his Diary: "I have to marry this year or never" (*PSS* 48: p. 20).

January — LNT's story *Three deaths [Tri smerti]* appears in *Biblioteka dlja chtenija* N° 1.

May — LNT's story *Family happiness [Semejnoe schast'e]* appears in N° 7 & N° 8 of *Russkij vestnik*.

Late October — LNT founds a school for peasant children at Yasnaya Polyana.

1860

January–June — LNT continues teaching at his school for peasant children at Yasnaya Polyana.

May — LNT writes about his relationships with Aksin'ja Bazykina: "It even frightens me how dear she is to me" (Diary, 25 May, *PSS* 48: p. 25) and likens his feelings for her to those "of a husband for his wife" (Diary, 26 May, *loc. cit.*)

20 June — LNT writes to Fet: "…[this] solitary life, i.e. the absence of a wife, and the thought that it is becoming [too] late … disturbs [me]" (*PSS* 60: N° 174).

End of June — LNT visits the Behrs family in Moscow.

July–August — On his second and final trip abroad, LNT studies educational theory and practice in Germany and Switzerland, revisits Paris, meets Turgenev, and in December moves to Italy.

20 September — death of LNT's brother Nikolaj Tolstoj. On 13 October LNT writes in his Diary: "Nikolen'ka's death [has been] the strongest impression in my life" (*PSS* 48: p. 30).

October–November — LNT remains in the Southern France, visits some schools in Marseille, tries to work on the novel *The Decembrists [Dekabristy]*.

1861

Winter — LNT travels through Europe: Italy, France, England (where he meets Aleksandr Gertsen, attends a lecture on education by Charles Dickens and hears Prime Minister Henry Temple (Viscount Palmerston) speaking in the House of Commons), Belgium (where he meets Pierre-Joseph Proudhon, known as the 'father of anarchism') and Germany; returns to Russia on 13 April.

19 February (3 March) — Emperor Alexander II proclaims the abolition of serfdom in Russia.

6 May — After a visit to the Behrs family LNT writes in his Diary: "But I dare not marry Liza" [SAT's elder sister] (*PSS* 48: p. 37).

April–May — LNT returns to Yasnaya Polyana and resumes teaching at his Yasnaya Polyana school.

May–June — LNT is appointed and confirmed an Arbiter of the Peace (a post from which he resigns the following year).

Late May — LNT quarrels with Turgenev and challenges him to duel.

22–23 September — In Moscow LNT confides to his Diary: "Liza Behrs is tempting me; but it won't work out. Reason alone isn't enough — there's no feeling" (*PSS* 48: p. 38).

November — Several students arrive to help LNT in his teaching work at the schools he has founded in and around Yasnaya Polyana (twelve by 29 November 1862; see *PSS* 60: N° 299).

In 1861 Sofia Behrs passes the Moscow University Home Teachers' examination.

Early 1860s

Sofia Behrs writes a story entitled "Natasha".

1862

SAT begins writing her Diaries [*Dnevniki*], which she continues up until 1910, albeit with significant gaps. There are practically no entries for the following years: 1868, 1880–1881, 1883–1884, 1888–1889, 1893–1894, 1896, 1905–1907, 1909. LNT continues teaching (21 schools by 26 January; *PSS* 60: N° 230). He starts an educational magazine entitled *Jasnaja Poljana [Yasnaya Polyana]* (twelve issues appear in 1862–63), with contributions by himself, his teachers and pupils.

Early February — LNT suffers significant losses in a card game. In urgent need of income, he sells his *Cossacks* (dubbed "the Caucasian novel") to the editor of *Russkij vestnik,* M. N. Katkov, who offers him 1,000 roubles in advance.

15 May — LNT released from his post as Arbiter of the Peace.

14–19 May — In Moscow LNT visits, amongst others, the Behrs family.

May — LNT travels to the Samara region for *koumiss* [mare's milk] treatment, returning by the end of July.

6–7 July — Police raid Yasnaya Polyana during LNT's absence, search through his papers and correspondence.

5–6 August — On their way to their grandfather's (A. M. Islen'ev) country estate of "Ivitsy" (Tula Gubernia), Ljubov' Behrs and her three daughters (Elizaveta, Sofia and Tat'jana) visit LNT and stop over at Yasnaya Polyana.

Mid-August — L.A. Behrs and her three daughters visit Yasnaya Polyana again on their way back to Moscow. LNT makes a momentous decision and travels to Moscow with them.

26 August — Sofia Behrs shows her story "Natasha" to LNT, who recognises himself in the ugly elderly hero Dublitskij. (The text is not extant, as SAT destroys the manuscript before the wedding.)

14 September — LNT writes a proposal to Sofia Behrs.

16 September — Sofia Behrs agrees to marry LNT.

23 September — LNT marries Sofia Andreevna Behrs. After their wedding at the Nativity of the Most Holy Mother of God Church in Moscow, they travel to Yasnaya Polyana.

Late 1862 — LNT starts work on a novel which will become *War and Peace [Vojna i mir]*. He decides to end his involvement in his schools as well as to stop publishing his pedagogical journal (*Yasnaja Poljana*) and to return to literary pursuits.

1863

January — SAT makes the acquaintance of an old friend of LNT's, the poet Fet, who over his lifetime will dedicate several poems to SAT.

February — *The Cossacks [Kazaki]* appears in *Russkij vestnik* N° 1 (1863).

25 February — SAT writes to her sister Tat'jana that LNT has started work on a new novel (apparently, the future *War and Peace*).

March — LNT's story *Polikushka* appears in *Russkij vestnik* N° 2 (1863).

28 June — the Tolstoys' first child, Sergej L'vovich [Serëzha] Tolstoy (1863–1947), is born.

5 August — LNT's Diary: "Her [SAT's] character deteriorates every day... injustice and calm egotism frighten and torment me..." (*PSS* 48: p. 56).

October–November — LNT briefly renews his teaching of peasant children at Yasnaya Polyana.

1863–1864

SAT's sister Tat'jana Andreevna [Tanja] carries on a romance with LNT's elder brother, Sergej Nikolaevich Tolstoy (1826–1904); he, however, is also in love with a gypsy named Marija Mikhajlovna [Masha] Shishkina (1832–1919; see 7 June 1867 below).

1864

22–26 April — During his brother Sergej's and his sister Marija's absence, LNT visits their estate Pirogovo in order to curry the necessary inspection and work. This is the subject of a brief correspondence with SAT.

7–13 August — LNT goes on a hunting and visiting trip in the region without SAT.

August–September — A two-volume set of LNT's *Collected works [Sobranie sochinenij]* is published.

4 October — The Tolstoys' second child, Tat'jana L'vovna [Tanja] Tolstaja (1864–1950), is born.

21 November — After having no success with doctors in Tula, LNT goes to Moscow to consult with doctors there regarding a shoulder injury received from a fall from his horse. SAT is greatly concerned and writes almost daily letters to her husband.

25 November — SAT writes in a letter to her husband concerning her ongoing transcribing of *War and Peace*: "What you have left me to transcribe — how good it all is!.." By the time the novel is finished, she will have transcribed many parts of it several times.

1865

February–March — The novel *The Year 1805 [1805-j god]* (roughly corresponding to the first book of *War and Peace*) appears in two issues of *Russkij vestnik* (Chapters 1–28 in N° 1 and Chapters 29–38 in N° 2).

17 February — Fet and his wife visit Yasnaya Polyana.

18 May — LNT, SAT and their children go to Pirogovo, from where LNT makes a brief trip over the next few days.

26 June — The Tolstoys go to Nikol'skoe-Vjazemskoe and then to Pokrovskoe, from where LNT takes several brief trips.

Autumn — LNT works intensively on *War and Peace*; SAT's equally intensive copying.

1866

Early January — LNT is in Moscow preparing an apartment for his family's move there.

March–May — The second part of *The Year 1805* (roughly corresponding to Book Two of *War and Peace*) appears in three issues of *Russkij vestnik* (Chapters 1–9 in N° 2, Chapters 10–14 in N° 3 and Chapters 15–24 in N° 4).

Mid-April — LNT visits Nikol'skoe (see letter to SAT, *PSS* 83: N° 47)

22 May — The Tolstoys' third child, Il'ja L'vovich [Iljusha] Tolstoy (1866–1933), is born.

July–August — the house at Yasnaya Polyana is expanded.

August — LNT writes several short plays for domestic performance at Yasnaya Polyana.

29–31 October — Tolstoy and his sister-in-law Tat'jana Andreevna Behrs visit Cheremoshnja and Nikol'skoe (see letters to SAT, PSS 83: N° 51 & N° 52).

10–18 November — In Moscow, LNT meets artist Mikhail Sergeevich Bashilov (1821–1870), who is working on illustrations for *War and Peace*. He returns, for the first time, by train (on the recently opened Moscow-Kursk Railway, which passes through Tula).

1867

18–24 March — LNT visits Moscow to attend the funeral of Dar'ja Aleksandrovna D'jakova, the wife of his friend Dmitrij Alekseevich D'jakov (see letters to SAT, PSS 83: N°61, 62). During this trip, LNT signs a draft contract about the future publication of his novel, at the same time he crosses out the title *The Year 1805* and writes in: *War and Peace*.

7 June — LNT's elder brother Sergej Tolstoy marries his gypsy companion of 18 years, Marija Mikhajlovna Shishkina (1832–1919).

16–25 June — LNT travels to Moscow on business concerning the printing of *War and Peace* (see letters to SAT of 18–22 June & PSS 83: N° 65–68).

24 July — SAT's younger sister Tat'jana Andreevna Behrs marries her cousin, Aleksandr Mikhajlovich Kuzminskij (1843–1917).

End of July–early August — LNT travels to Moscow in connection with the printing of *War and Peace*; he makes subseqent trips there in late September and early November (see letters to SAT, PSS 83: N° 69 and N° 74 & N° 75).

25–27 September — LNT visits Borodino in connection with battle scenes for the novel (see letters to SAT, PSS 83: N° 70–72).

December — The first three volumes of *War and Peace* are published as a separate edition.

27–30 December — LNT travels to Moscow because of the sickness of his father-in-law, Andrej Evstaf'evich Behrs (see letter to SAT, PSS 83: N° 77).

1868

7 January — In Moscow, SAT attends the wedding of her elder sister Elizaveta Andreevna [Liza] to Gavriil Emel'janovich Pavlenkov (1824–1892). The marriage fails, and in 1877 she marries her cousin Aleksandr Aleksandrovich Behrs (1844–1921).

14 February — The Tolstoys arrive in Moscow to be near SAT's father, Andrej Evstaf'evich Behrs (1808–1868), who is dying.

March — The fourth volume of *War and Peace* is published.

30 May — Andrej Behrs, SAT's father, dies. LNT and SAT attend the funeral in early June. (See *My Life*, II.77–80)

September — In his Notebook, LNT begins sketching out a primer for peasant children (PSS 48: 167).

1869

17–19 January — LNT goes to Moscow (see letter to SAT, PSS 83: N° 79).

February — The fifth volume of *War and Peace* is published.

20 May — The Tolstoys' fourth child, Lev L'vovich [Lëva] Tolstoj (1869–1945), is born. LNT completes *War and Peace*.

Night of 2–3 August — The so-called Arzamas incident: while stopping in the small town of Arzamas, LNT suffers a sudden attack of "anguish, fear, terror" (see his letter to SAT, PSS 83: N° 82). (see his letter to SAT, PSS 83: N° 82)

December — The sixth (final) volume of *War and Peace* is published.

1870

LNT begins studying Greek. First thoughts about the future novel *Anna Karenina*. SAT begins teaching her two eldest children to read and write — she will continue seeing personally to the primary education of all her children.

14 February — SAT writes under the heading *Moi zapisi raznye dlja spravok* [Various notes for future reference]: "…it came to me that I could be of service to my descendants, who might be interested in a biography of Lëvochka [SAT's endearing name for LNT], and make an account not of his everyday doings, but of his intellectual life, so far as I am able to keep track of it…." (*Dnevniki* 1: 495). Nine years later SAT will publish a brief biography of her husband (see entry under 1879 below).

19–20(?) February — LNT visits Fet (see LNT's letter to Fet, PSS 61: Nº 302).

22 February — LNT conceives his first ideas for his future novel *Anna Karenina*. According to SAT's Diary, LNT speaks to her about "a married woman from high society who has lost herself" (i.e., her reputation).

19 March — LNT writes his first letter to his future editorial associate Nikolaj Nikolaevich Strakhov (1828–1896; see Donskov 2003, Letter 1). Over the next 25 years both Tolstoy and Tolstaya will continue an extensive correspondence with Strakhov, a prominent Russian philosopher, librarian, literary critic and long-time editorial associate.

1871

LNT continues his Greek studies. He experiences repeated bouts of illness.

12 February — The Tolstoys' fifth child, Marija L'vovna [Masha] Tolstaja (1871–1906), is born prematurely. SAT nearly dies of postpartum fever.

9 June — LNT travels to the Samara region for convalescence during the summer in Bashkiria; he is accompanied by SAT's brother, Stepan Andreevich [Stëpa] Behrs (1855–1910), and a servant, Ivan Vasil'evich Suvorov. Travels through Moscow, Nizhnij-Novgorod, by a steamer down the Volga to Samara. He arrives in Karalyk on 15 June (see his letter to SAT, PSS 83: Nº 86–88), where he will stay until 28 July (see his letters to SAT, PSS 83: Nº 89–98). He writes to SAT about his intention to buy land in Samara Gubernia.

Mid-August — Nikolaj Nikolaevich Strakhov visits Yasnaya Polyana for the first time. For his correspondence with both Tolstoys, see Donskov 2000, 2003.

18 August — See SAT's Diary under this date: "Something has come between us, some kind of shadow has divided us… Ever since this past winter, when Lëvochka and I — we were both so ill — something has been broken in our lives. I know that the strong faith in happiness and life I used to have has been broken within me" (*Dnevniki* 1: 101).

Late August — LNT visits Moscow to purchase a 2500-hectare tract of land in Samara's Buzuluk Uezd for 20,000 roubles.

September–December — LNT works on his *Primer* [*Azbuka*] for children.

November–December — A large addition to the house at Yasnaya Polyana is built.

26 December — SAT organises a Christmas costume party for her own and peasant children — a tradition which will continue over the years. (LNT dresses as a she-goat.)

1872

LNT works intermittently on his unfinished novel on Peter the Great and his times.

January–April — LNT re-opens his Yasnaya Polyana school.

4 January — A woman named Anna Stepanovna Pirogova (1837–1872), the mistress of Tolstoys' neighbouring landowner Aleksandr Nikolaevich Bibikov, throws herself under a train. After

reading about this several days later in a newspaper, LNT goes to see the woman's body. He will subsequently draw upon this incident for the ending of *Anna Karenina*.

Mid-January — LNT visits Moscow to see about the printing of his *Primer*.

1 April — SAT writes in her Diary: "The winter's been a happy one, once again we all got along famously" (*Dnevniki* 1: 102).

April — In preparation for a new baby due in June, SAT fasts at a local nunnery, accompanied by their eldest son Sergej L'vovich [Serëzha].

14–17 May — LNT visits Nikol'skoe with their son Sergej and brother-in-law Stepan Andreevich Behrs.

Late May — The main house at Yasnaya Polyana undergoes another renovation.

13 June — SAT gives birth to a son (Tolstoys' sixth child), Pëtr [Petja] (he will die within a year).

July — LNT takes another trip to the Samara steppes, stays at Tananyk (see his letters to SAT, PSS 83: №100–102). He returns earlier than planned because of problems with the publishing of his *Primer*.

Early-mid September — LNT contemplates emigration to England following legal proceedings against him for criminal negligence after a fatal injury to herdsman on his estate during his absence.

Autumn — The first two books of the *Primer* are printed in September; the third appears in October and the fourth in November. SAT has taken an active part in editing these volumes, as well as contributing several of her own stories.

27–30 October — LNT goes to Moscow to find an English governess for his children.

4–8 November — Strakhov pays his second visit to Yasnaya Polyana.

1873

January–March — LNT works on a novel about Peter the Great.

18–19 February — Strakhov pays another visit to Yasnaya Polyana.

18 March — LNT begins writing *Anna Karenina*.

28 April — Prince Sergej Semënovich Urusov (1827–1897) — a wartime chum of LNT's — visits Yasnaya Polyana.

Summer — Samara Gubernia is plagued by a famine because of a poor grain harvest. SAT successfully pleads with Grand Duchess Marija Aleksandrovna (1853–1920) for aid in famine relief. LNT writes a "*Letter to the editors of [the newspaper]* Moskovskie vedomosti" *[Pis'mo redaktoram «Moskovskikh vedomostej»]* (PSS 62: №29).

September–October — Artist Ivan Nikolaevich Kramskoj (1837–1887) paints two portraits of LNT — one for Tret'jakov's Gallery in Moscow and a second at SAT's request.

9 November — Little Pëtr [Petja] (the Tolstoys' sixth child) dies of croup.

November — Publication of LNT's *Complete Collected Works [Polnoe sobranie sochinenij]*, including a revised version of *War and Peace*. This is actually the second edition of *Collected Works* (the first edition was published in 1864), although it was called "the third" since LNT considered the publication of his works in journals as "the first".

1874

LNT continues work on *Anna Karenina* (which SAT transcribes) and compiles a *New Primer [Novaja azbuka]* and *Readers [Knigi dlja chtenija]*.

22 April — SAT gives birth to a son, Nikolaj [Kolja] (their seventh child), who dies in 1875.

20 June — LNT's 'Auntie' Tat'jana Ergol'skaja dies; after the death of her mother she had been brought up in the home of LNT's paternal grandfather, Il'ja Andreevich Tolstoj (1757–1820).

Early July — Strakhov pays another visit to Yasnaya Polyana.

July–August — LNT and his son Sergej visit the Samara estate (see LNT's letters to SAT, PSS 83: N° 107–108).

September — LNT's article *On popular education [O narodnom obrazovanii]* appears in *Otechestvennye zapiski* N° 9.

1875

14 January — LNT in Moscow.

January — Chapters 1–14 (Part I) of *Anna Karenina* appear in *Russkij vestnik* N° 1 (1875).

20 February — The Tolstoys' seventh child, baby Nikolaj [Kolja], dies of meningitis.

February — Chapters 15–27 (Part I) and 1–10 (Part II) of *Anna Karenina* appear in *Russkij vestnik* N° 2 (1875).

March — Chapters 11–27 (Part II) of *Anna Karenina* appear in *Russkij vestnik* N° 3 (1875).

May — Chapters 28–31 (Part II) and 1–10 (Part III) of *Anna Karenina* appear in *Russkij vestnik* N° 4 (1875).

June — LNT's *New Primer* is published.

12 June–mid-August — The Tolstoy family spends the summer at their Samara estate.

August–October — LNT resumes his work on *Anna Karenina,* but eventually tires of the work and becomes increasingly depressed.

Late September — Strakhov visits Yasnaya Polyana.

Early November — SAT, seriously ill with peritonitis, suffers a miscarriage in the sixth month of her new pregnancy; she gives birth to a daughter, Varvara [Varja], who dies almost immediately.

22 December — LNT's aunt Pelageja Il'inichna Jushkova (1801–1875) dies — the youngest daughter of his grandfather, Il'ja Andreevich Tolstoj.

1876

February — Chapters 11–28 (Part III) of *Anna Karenina* appear in *Russkij vestnik* N° 1 (1876).

March — Chapters 1–15 (Part IV) of *Anna Karenina* appear in *Russkij vestnik* N° 2 (1876).

March — Chapters 16–21 (Part IV) and 1–6 (Part V) of *Anna Karenina* appear in *Russkij vestnik* N° 3 (1876).

14 April — LNT writes to Count Aleksej Pavlovich Bobrinskij (1826–1894) that to live without faith as he (LNT) has been living so far "is a terrible torment" but that he is not able to fully embrace religious belief.

Spring — SAT remarks on the spring of 1876 as the beginning of LNT's 'moral transformation', first evident in a letter he wrote in mid April 1876 (14? April, PSS 62: N° 259) to Countess Aleksandra Andreevna Tolstaja. (See *My Life*, III.1). This theme occupies fully a third of their letters and runs as a unifying thread through their whole correspondence.

Summer — Strakhov pays two visits to Yansaya Polyana.

September — LNT goes to Samara to buy horses (see letters to SAT, PSS 83: N° 114–120).

October — SAT begins writing what turns out to be the first biography of LNT; she continues working on it until April 1878.

Late December — Strakhov visits Yasnaya Polyana. Chapters 20–29 (Part V) of *Anna Karenina* appear in *Russkij vestnik* N° 12 (1876).

1877

Mid-January — On a trip to St. Petersburg SAT visits LNT's great aunt Countess Aleksandra Andreevna Tolstaja, for whom she has a special affection (see *My Life*, III.15, also LNT's letters to SAT — e.g., PSS 83: N° 123).

February — Chapters 1–12 (Part VI) of *Anna Karenina* appear in *Russkij vestnik* N° 1 (1877).

March — Chapters 13–29 (Part VI) of *Anna Karenina* appear in *Russkij vestnik* N° 2 (1877), Chapters 1–15 (Part VII) in N° 3 (1877).

Early May — Chapters 16–30 (Part VII) of *Anna Karenina* appear in *Russkij vestnik* N° 4 (1877).

May — When the last part of *Anna Karenina* is published in *Russkij vestnik*, the editor, Mikhail Nikiforovich Katkov (1818–1887), makes changes to the ending (the Epilogue) without consulting LNT. LNT decides instead to publish his original ending as a separate booklet.

June–July — Strakhov spends more than a month at Yasnaya Polyana, helping LNT polish the ending of *Anna Karenina*. By this time Strakhov has developed a most amicable relationship with SAT, and is advising her on the editing of LNT's works.

14 June — In N° 463 of the newspaper *Novoe vremja*, SAT offers her explanation of why the Epilogue to *Anna Karenina* was not published in *Russkij vestnik*.

Late June — LNT and Strakhov visit Fet and other neighbours (see his letter to SAT, PSS 83: N° 126).

25–28 July — LNT and Strakhov visit the monastery Optina Pustyn' (see letter, PSS 83: N° 127, also *My Life*, III.21).

6 December — The Tolstoys' sixth surviving child, Andrej L'vovich [Andrjusha] Tolstoj (1877–1916), is born.

1878

LNT resumes his work on writing *The Decembrists [Dekabristy]*.

January — *Anna Karenina* is published in a separate edition, including the epilogue.

22–26 February — Strakhov visits Yasnaya Polyana.

4–12 March — LNT visits Moscow and St. Petersburg (see letters to SAT, PSS 83: N° 131–137).

6 April — LNT writes to Turgenev offering reconciliation.

17 April — LNT resumes his Diary after a 13-year break (entries up to 3 June).

Early May — LNT asks Strakhov to find a publisher for a new edition of his *Complete Collected Works [Polnoe sobranie sochinenij]* (see PSS 62: N° 429).

12 June — LNT leaves for Samara estate with two of his sons, Il'ja and Lev. SAT joins him there towards the end of June, Strakhov in late July. The Tolstoys return home in early August. Strakhov follows shortly thereafter for a fortnight's visit.

August–September — Turgenev visits Yasnaya Polyana twice.

Autumn — SAT makes the acquaintance of the Deputy Governor of Tula, Prince Leonid Dmitrievich Urusov (1837–1885), whom she finds herself personally attracted to and who will have a far-reaching influence on her life. She speaks of the exposure to art and culture she gains from her relationship with Urusov as constituting "the second significant period of my spiritual life" (*My Life*, III.39) — the first being her reading of LNT's *Childhood [Detstvo]* and *Boyhood [Otrochestvo]* in her youth.

11 October — Strakhov asks LNT for a portrait and brief biography in connection with the next edition of his *Collected works*, to be published in the series *Russian Library [Russkaja biblioteka]*.

October–November — Under LNT's dictation, SAT compiles facts from his life for the *Russian Library* biography. He asks Strakhov repeatedly whether the edition could be published without

the portrait and biography but later sends him SAT's compilation (see *PSS* 62: Nº 465, 472, 475 and Donskov 2003: Nº 206–209).

27 December–3 January — Strakhov visits Yasnaya Polyana. LNT tells him that he is very much immersed in his work on *The Decembrists*.

1879

First half — LNT first continues to collect historical materials for his projected novel, but then abandons *The Decembrists* and starts thinking about a novel set in the eighteenth century. SAT publishes her first biography of LNT, which is included in a volume of his works in the Russian Library series, Volume 9, under the title *Count Lev Nikolaevich Tolstoy [Graf Lev Nikolaevich Tolstoj]*.

June–August — Strakhov pays two visits to Yasnaya Polyana.

18–24(?) July— LNT visits his mother-in-law Ljubov' Behrs at her estate *Uteshen'e* (see his letters to SAT, *PSS* 83: Nº 155–156).

Autumn — LNT continues to collect historical materials for his projected eighteenth-century novel. He also starts works on *A confession [Ispoved']*, which he completes in 1882.

20 December — The Tolstoys' seventh surviving child, Mikhail L'vovich [Misha] Tolstoj (1879–1944), is born.

1880

LNT continues work on *A confession* and begins writing *A criticism of dogmatic theology* [*Issledovanie dogmaticheskogo bogoslovija*] and *A translation and harmony of the four Gospels* [*Soedinenie i perevod chetyrëkh Evangelij*]. SAT strongly disapproves of LNT's religious views and especially his penchant for proselytising.

1 January — Strakhov celebrates the New Year with the Tolstoys at Yasnaya Polyana.

17 January — In Moscow LNT negotiates a new edition of his *Collected works* (see his letter to SAT, *PSS* 83: Nº 160); the following week in St. Petersburg he has a heated discussion of religion with his great aunt Aleksandra Andreevna Tolstaja.

Early February — LNT sells the rights for the new (by his count the fourth edition of his *Collected works* (in 11 volumes)) to the Salaev Brothers' publishing house.

2–3 May — Turgenev comes for a visit to Yasnaya Polyana.

June and July — Strakhov makes two visits to Yasnaya Polyana.

7 October — LNT meets the prominent artist Il'ja Efimovich Repin (1844–1930) for the first time, with whom he will share a life-long friendship.

1881

January — SAT observes that LNT's obsession with studying the Gospels has made him "oblivious of life" (*My Life*, III.73).

28 January — Dostoevsky dies. Tolstoy writes to Strakhov about his feelings (*PSS* 63: Nº 39).

18 February — Strakhov visits Yasnaya Polyana on LNT's name-day.

1 March — Emperor Alexander II is killed by a terrorist. He is succeeded by his son, Alexander III (1845–1894). The news of the assassination saddens SAT (see *My Life*, III.76). LNT petitions the new Tsar, asking him to pardon the assassins of his predecessor (they are hanged on 3 April).

12 March — SAT writes to her sister Tat'jana Kuzminskaja about "a certain discord in the family" (State Tolstoy Museum [GMT], Gusev I: 532)

17 April — LNT resumes writing his Diary (*PSS* 49). On 18 May he makes his first entry regarding discord in the family.

6 June — Turgenev visits Yasnaya Polyana.

10–19 June — LNT makes a walking trip to the Optina Pustyn' Monastery where, on 15 June, he discusses the Gospels with the Venerable Father Ambrosius (1812–1891; see his letter to SAT, PSS 83: № 170–173).

1881: summer — SAT devises a 'letter-box' game for her household, whereby members of her family and staff deposit brief anonymous writings in a 'letter-box', to be read by everyone together, the object being to guess who wrote what (see *My Life*, III.84).

9–10 July — LNT visits Turgenev at his estate Spasskoe-Lutovinovo.

13 July–17 August — LNT and his eldest son Sergej travel to the Samara estate. LNT visits Molokan sectarians.

2 August — SAT goes to Moscow to fix up an apartment she has rented for her family in the Volkonskij house in Denezhnyj Lane.

Early September — Sergej Tolstoj becomes a student in the Faculty of Natural Sciences at Moscow University.

15 September — The Tolstoy family moves to Moscow, where tension increases over 'maternal concerns' between LNT and SAT; LNT threatens to leave.

Mid-September — The Tolstoys enrol their sons Il'ja and Lev in a private classical *gymnasium* (school) under the headmastership of Lev Ivanovich Polivanov (1838–1899), author of several books on teaching Russian language and literature.

20–27(?) September — Strakhov visits the Tolstoys in Moscow.

5 October — LNT makes a notable entry in his Diary about "the worst month of his life [since the move to Moscow]."

31 October — SAT gives birth to another son, Aleksej [Alësha], who dies of quinsy in 1886.

November — SAT takes ill.

1882

LNT begins *The death of Ivan Ilyich [Smert' Ivana Il'icha]* and *What then must be done? [Tak chto zhe nam delat'?]* — both finished in 1886. He also finishes *A confession*, which is promptly banned in Russia.

January — SAT becomes accustomed to high-society life in Moscow.

20 January — LNT publishes an article *On the Moscow census [O perepisi v Moskve]* in *Sovremennye izvestija* 19 (1882).

23–25 January — LNT takes part in a three-day Moscow census and becomes acquainted firsthand with Moscow slums.

Mid-February — Countess Aleksandra Andreevna Tolstaja visits the Tolstoys in Moscow.

Spring — In Moscow SAT becomes acquainted with another Countess Sofia Andreevna Tolstaja (*née* Bakhmetova, 1820–1895), widow of Russian novelist, dramatist and poet Count Aleksej Konstantinovich Tolstoj (1817–1875) — see *My Life*, III.111.

Late June — Strakhov visits Yasnaya Polyana.

14 July — The Tolstoys purchase the Arnautov house with a large garden in Khamovniki Lane, now a Tolstoy museum (see *My Life*, III.114).

26 August — According to an entry by SAT in her Diary (*Dnevniki* 1: 131), LNT declares his desire to leave the family. "The quarrel was a very stormy one. Lev Nikolaevich yelled that his most passionate thought was to leave the family. [...] After his bout of yelling at me, Lev Nikolaevich left and didn't come back the whole night long. I sat down without getting undressed and wept" (*My Life*, III.121).

September–October — In Moscow LNT prepares the newly bought house for the family; on 8 October the family moves to Moscow for the winter (see his letters to SAT, PSS 83: N° 213–223).

28 September–10 October — LNT continues rearranging the house (83: N° 223–229).

October–November — LNT takes up the study of Hebrew, which concerns SAT; she feels that "this harnessing of his mental forces still had a bad influence on Lev Nikolaevich's health" (*My Life*, III.125).

8 October — The Tolstoy family moves to Moscow into the newly acquired Arnautov house.

1883

LNT writes *What I believe [V chem moja vera?]*.

27–28 April — The day after the Tolstoys return to their family estate, a huge fire in the village of Yasnaya Polyana destroys 22 houses.

21 May — SAT receives a power-of-attorney from her husband and the right to publish his works written before the end of 1881. She competes with other publishers in publishing his works written after 1881. Over a period of twenty-six years (1886–1911) SAT publishes eight editions of LNT's *Complete Collected Works [Polnoe sobranie sochinenij]* as well as many of his writings in separate editions. The large print-runs and the moderately low prices contribute to the rapid circulation of LNT's works among the public at large (see 25 January 1904 below).

May–June — LNT spends more than a month at his Samara estate (see his letter to SAT, PSS 83: N° 233–242).

12–27 July — Strakhov visits Yasnaya Polyana.

3 August — SAT goes to visit her ill mother who lives with her son Vjacheslav at Rjazhsk (Rjazan' Gubernia).

22 August — Turgenev dies at Bougival, France.

24 August — LNT hears (from his friend Gavriil Andreevich Rusanov) for the first time about Vladimir Grigor'evich Chertkov (1854–1936), who will later become one of LNT's publishers and closest advisers (see *My Life,* IV.11).

28–29 September — LNT is summoned to court but refuses jury duty — on the grounds of his "religious convictions" (*My Life,* III.142; see his letter to SAT, PSS 83: N° 244).

Mid-October — LNT meets Vladimir Chertkov for the first time.

5 December — LNT's first letter to Vladimir Chertkov (PSS 85: N° 1).

December — SAT writes: "In December I came down with a serious case of neuralgia, brought on by my exhaustion and my pregnancy" (*My Life,* III.147).

1884

A set of LNT's *Complete Collected Works* is published by SAT. LNT studies oriental religions, and takes up cobbling. He makes his first attempts to leave home, under the strain of family relations.

January — Russian artist Nikolaj Nikolaevich Ge [Gay] Sr (1831–1894; the grandson of immigrants from France) paints a portrait of LNT.

14 February — *What I believe* is banned in Russia.

17 February — LNT writes to Chertkov that he would like to publish books "for the people" (PSS 85: N° 4). Over the years SAT will become increasingly concerned over what she sees as Chertkov's negative influence on LNT's life and decisions.

May — LNT continues his work on the story *The death of Ivan Ilyich [Smert' Ivana Il'icha]* for a time. The Tolstoys move to Yasnaya Polyana for the summer.

May–June — LNT makes frequent references in his Diary about the discord and misunder-standing between him and SAT.

17 June — After leaving home following a difficult conversation with SAT, LNT remembers that his wife is going to give birth to their child and returns.

18 June — The Tolstoys' eighth (and youngest) surviving child, Aleksandra L'vovna [Sasha] Tol-staja (1884–1979), is born.

18 June — LNT writes in his Diary: "The break with my wife — I don't know what's still to come, but it's complete".

October — SAT is distressed to learn of a duel between her brother Aleksandr Andreevich Behrs (1845–1918) and retired cavalry captain Sergej Aleksandrovich Pisarev (ca1855–1909), for whom Aleksandr's wife Matrëna Dmitrievna (Patti) has left him. Aleksandr seriously wounds Pisarev but does not kill him.

7 July — LNT writes about SAT in his Diary: "'Til the day of my death she will be a millstone around my neck and the children's. That's probably how it has to be. Must learn how not to drown with the millstone."

Night of 11–12 July — LNT wants to leave the family again, but changes his mind after talking with SAT.

21–26 November — Chertkov and LNT establish the publishing house Posrednik [The Interme-diary] in Moscow to publish LNT's stories.

Early December — In Moscow Afanasij Fet offers his poem dedicated to SAT, entitled *Kogda stopoj slegka ustaloj...* [When with a wearied step one passes...] (see *My Life,* final poem in Poetry Appendix).

1885

Early January — SAT takes charge of distributing LNT's published works.

19–28 February — SAT travels to St. Petersburg with her daughter Tat'jana to consult with Stra-khov and Dostoevsky's widow, Anna Grigor'evna Dostoevskaja (*née* Snitkina, 1846–1918). This is the start of a long friendship between the two writers' wives. While Tolstoy and Dostoevsky were never destined to meet in person, Tolstaya and Dostoevskaja keep in contact through cor-respondence and occasional visits. (See LNT's letter, *PSS* 83: Nº 298, also *My Life,* IV.31).

February — In St. Petersburg while visiting the Nicholas Institute (Orphanage), SAT is pre-sented to the Empress Marija Fëdorovna by Headmistress Ekaterina Nikolaevna Shostak (*née* Islen'eva, ?–1904), who is first cousin to SAT's mother. SAT petitions the Empress for permission to publish LNT's banned works, but her petition is rejected.

20–23 February — LNT is intrigued by the writings of American economist Henry George (1839–1897), who proposes the nationalisation of private land (see his letter to SAT, *PSS* 83: Nº 299–302).

March — SAT proofreads LNT's *Collected Works* (see *My Life,* IV.38) In the meantime LNT accompanies Urusov to the Crimea (see his letter to SAT, *PSS* 83: Nº 305–310).

Spring — SAT sends a portrait of herself to Fet, and in return receives his poem *I vot portret, i skhozhe i ne skhozhe...* [And here's the portrait: so like you, yet unlike you...], dedicated to SAT (see *My Life,* Poetry Appendix under IV.37).

13–20(?) June — Strakhov visits Yasnaya Polyana.

13–23 July — LNT takes ill (see *PSS* 85: Nº 75).

Summer — SAT pays a brief visit to her brother Aleksandr Andreevich [Sasha] Behrs (1845–1918) in Orël, where he has bought a dacha near Pesochnaja Station. (see *My Life,* IV.43)

Summer — A Jewish tailor named Isaak Borisovich Fejnerman (1863–1925) begins to frequent Yasnaya Polyana; his questionable devotion to LNT's views irritates SAT.

16–19 August — Vladimir Chertkov and Pavel Birjukov visit Yasnaya Polyana. Pavel Ivanovich [Posha] Birjukov (1860–1931) is a social activist and political commentator, as well as a friend, follower and biographer of LNT, who later studies the Doukhobor movement in both Russia and Canada and is instrumental in establishing the Tolstoy Museum in Moscow. (See LNT's letter to SAT, PSS 83: N° 322–325.)

August — SAT goes with her daughters Tanja and Masha to the village of Djat'kovo in Brjansk Uezd, where Leonid Dmitrievich Urusov (gravely ill) and his wife are staying with his wife's brother, Nikolaj Sergeevich Mal'tsev. Urusov takes SAT on one last ride together, before dying of illness on 23 September 1885 (see *My Life*, IV.45).

12 October — The family leaves Yasnaya Polyana for Moscow; LNT stays at Yasnaya Polyana until 1 November (see his letter to SAT, PSS 83: N° 327–339).

18 November — SAT goes to St. Petersburg, where she stays with her sister Tat'jana Kuzminskaja (see Gusev I: 619).

20 November — In St. Petersburg SAT pays a visit to the Director of the State Office of Press Affairs, Evgenij Mikhajlovich Feoktistov (1829–1898), to petition the Censorship Board to allow publication of Volume 12 of LNT's *Complete Collected Works*. She also sees the Deputy Minister of Internal Affairs, Vjacheslav Konstantinovich Pleve [also spelt: Plehve] (1846–1904). See *My Life*, IV.56.

26 November — SAT receives from Feoktistov a written refusal to allow publication of Volume XII, especially *A confession [Ispoved']* and *What I believe [V chëm moja vera?]*, and advises her to appeal to the church's censorship board. She goes for an appointment (granted the same day) with the head of the church's censorship board, Konstantin Petrovich Pobedonostsev (1827–1907), jurist, statesman and Senior Procurator of the Holy Synod of the Russian Orthodox Church from 1880 to 1905.

27–28 November — In St. Petersburg SAT has an appointment with Chief of Staff General Nikolaj Nikolaevich Obruchev (1830–1904), at which she petitions, on behalf of her husband, for a young conscientious objector named Aleksej Petrovich Zaljubovskij (1863–?), who has refused military service (see *My Life*, IV.57). Zaljubovskij will be freed in March 1887 (Gusev I: 661).

18(?) December — LNT is distressed and announces to SAT that he wants to leave her but then changes his mind and stays (see PSS 85: N° 91).

19–28 December — LNT, accompanied by his eldest daughter Tat'jana, visits the Nikol'skoe-Obol'janovo estate of his friends the Olsuf'evs (see his letters to SAT, PSS 83: N° 350–351 and *My Life*, IV.64).

End of December — The fifth edition of *Collected works* published (marked as the 1886 edition).

1886

LNT continues working on stories for the people. Finishes *What then must be done? [Tak chto zhe nam delat'?]* and *The death of Ivan Ilyich [Smert' Ivana Il'icha]*. Writes *The power of darkness [Vlast' t'my]* (banned but performed in Paris in 1888) and begins *The fruits of enlightenment [Plody prosveshchenija]*, initially under the title "Themselves outwitted" *[Iskhitrilas']* (see *My Life*, V.13).

18 January — The Tolstoys' youngest son Aleksej [Alësha] dies of quinsy (born on 31 October, 1881).

February — The writer Vladimir Galaktionovich Korolenko (1853–1921) visits LNT for the first time.

14 February — LNT finishes *What then must be done?*

4 April — With some concern, SAT sees LNT off on a trek on foot from Moscow to Yasnaya Polyana (about 200 km). He is accompanied by writer Mikhail Aleksandrovich Stakhovich (1861–1923) and Nikolaj Nikolaevich Ge Jr. He will do this twice more with different travelling companions (see his letter to SAT, PSS 83: № 353–356; also *My Life*, IV.73). See also April 1888 and May 1889 below.

Early June — Strakhov visits Yasnaya Polyana.

Early November — SAT goes to Yalta to visit her dying mother, Ljubov' Aleksandrovna Behrs (*née* Isleneva, 1826–1886), who passes away 11 November 1886 (see LNT's letter to SAT, PSS 83: № 367).

21 November — The Tolstoys move from Yasnaya Polyana to Moscow for the winter.

Late November — The sixth edition of LNT's *Collected works* is announced.

1887

LNT writes *On life [O zhizni]*.

2, 3(?) January — SAT writes a letter to the Head of Press Affairs Evgenij Feoktistov concerning the banning of LNT's drama *The power of darkness*.

Early January — LNT and his eldest daughter Tat'jana visit his friends the Olsuf'evs at their Nikol'skoe-Obol'janovo estate.

14 January — Feoktistov grants SAT permission to publish *The power of darkness [Vlast' t'my]* but expresses reservations about its public theatrical performances (see PSS 26: p. 717).

January — The sixth edition of LNT's *Collected works* begins to appear.

6 March — SAT writes in her Diary: "I transcribed [LNT's] *On life and death* and then read it through carefully. Somewhat apprehensively I looked for something new, came across some concise expressions and beautiful comparisons, but the basic underlying thought, for me, was still essentially the same — i. e., the rejection of one's personal life for the life of the spirit. One thing was impossible and unjust, as far as I was concerned, namely, any rejection of personal life should take place in the name of love for the whole world. I think that there are undoubted obligations put on us by God, which nobody has a right to reject, and in terms of the life of the spirit they are certainly not a hindrance, but actually a help." (*Dnevniki* 1: 115.)

19–29 April — Czech politician and philosopher Tomáš Masaryk (1850–1937) visits LNT in Moscow and later at Yasnaya Polyana.

20(?) April — LNT meets writer Nikolaj Semënovich Leskov (1831–1895), who visits him for the first time. Leskov's 1886 story "A tale of Fëdor the Christian and his friend Abram the Jew" [*Skazanie o Fëdorove-khristianine i o druge ego Abrame-zhidovine*] instantly attracted LNT's interest and attention.

27–29 April — Tomáš Masaryk visits LNT at Yasnaya Polyana.

May–June — The seventh edition of LNT's *Collected works* begins to appear.

Early June — A prominent St. Petersburg jurist, Anatolij Fëdorovich Koni (1844–1927), visits Yasnaya Polyana and tells LNT the true story of a woman named Rozalija Oni, a story which inspires his future novel *Resurrection [Voskresenie]*.

June–August — Strakhov pays two brief visits to Yasnaya Polyana.

25 July–4 August — Countess Aleksandra Andreevna Tolstaja is a guest at Yasnaya Polyana (Diary of SAT 1: 145).

3 August — LNT finishes his work *On life [O zhizni]*.

9–16 August — Repin visits Yasnaya Polyana, executes two portraits of LNT and sketches him ploughing.

1 September — SAT places some of LNT's manuscripts for the first time in the Rumjantsev Museum's Manuscript Division in Moscow (see *My Life*, IV.119; also May 1894 and January 1904 below). The museum housed art works originally collected by Russian diplomat Nikolaj Petrovich Rumjantsev (1754–1826). Operating from 1862 until 1925, its library served as the basis for the Lenin Library during Soviet times (now the Russian State Library [*Rossijskaja gosudarstvennaja biblioteka* / RGB], which is still the repository of many documents relating to both LNT and SAT.

23 September — The Tolstoys celebrate their silver wedding anniversary with just family present.

Early October — LNT starts working on his novel *The Kreutzer Sonata [Krejtserova sonata]*.

26–28 October — LNT visits Chertkov at Krekshino, an estate of the Pashkov family.

November — SAT starts translating *On life* into French (finishes by 6 February 1887).

Autumn — The Tolstoys are distressed to hear of the broad circulation of copies of Repin's painting of LNT ploughing in the fields (see *My Life*, IV.122).

End of December — LNT receives a first visit from Prince Dmitrij Aleksandrovich Khilkov (1858–1914); during the Russo-Turkish War of 1877–78 Lieutenant-Colonel Khilkov befriends the Doukhobors and in 1899 accompanies two of them on an exploratory mission to Canada.

1888

After several attempts over the years, LNT finally renounces meat, alcohol and tobacco. Growing friction develops between SAT and Chertkov. LNT works intensively on the land.

Early January — LNT visits Chertkov at Krekshino.

29 January — *The power of darkness* is staged for the first time in French translation by *Théâtre Libre* in Paris.

Early February — SAT finishes her translation of *On life* into French.

28 February — The Tolstoys' son Il'ja L'vovich marries Sof'ja Nikolaevna [Sonja] Filosofova (1867–1934). They settle at the family homestead Aleksandrovka in Chern' Uezd.

Late March — Tomáš Masaryk pays a third visit to LNT in Moscow (Gusev I: 692).

31 March — SAT gives birth to a son, Ivan [Vanechka], their thirteenth and last child, who soon becomes her favourite and the darling of the family. Sadly, he will die a month before his seventh birthday, on 23 February 1895.

17–22 April — Once again LNT sets out to walk from Moscow to Yasnaya Polyana, this time with Nikolaj Nikolaevich Ge Jr and Aleksandr Nikiforovich Dunaev (1850–1920) — a close friend of the Tolstoys' and director of the Moscow Torgovyj Bank. This is LNT's second walking trip (see April 1886 and May 1889; Gusev I: 694; LNT's letter to SAT, *PSS* 84: N° 396–398; also *My Life*, IV.130).

Late May — The village of Yasnaya Polyana experiences another fire; several peasant houses burn down.

October–November — LNT writes several letters to Chertkov about married life (see *PSS* 86: N° 201, 203, 205).

1 December — As a favour to Marija Aleksandrovna Shmidt's brother Vladimir, SAT buys from him a small nearby estate called Ovsjannikovo, which is eventually given to the Tolstoys' daughter Tat'jana L'vovna [Tanja].

24 December — The Tolstoys' first grandchild, Anna, daughter of their son Il'ja, is born.

1889

LNT finishes *The Kreutzer Sonata*. Begins writing both *The Devil [D'javol]* and *Resurrection [Voskresenie]*.

5 February — Composer Sergej Ivanovich Taneev (1856–1915) plays the piano at the Tolstoys' on his first of many visits to Yasnaya Polyana. SAT is infatuated with both Taneev and his music and describes her relationship to him in both *My Life* (III.39, VI.117) and her narrative *Song without words*. Her infatuation was to cost LNT years of suffering.

19 February — The writer Ivan Ivanovich Gorbunov-Posadov (1864–1940) visits LNT for the first time. Later he becomes one of the principals at the Posrednik publishing house.

Early March — SAT's translation of *On life [O zhizni]* into French is published: Comte Léon Tolstoi, "De la vie". Seule traduction revue et corrigée par l'auteur, Paris, C. Marpon et E. Flammarion éditeurs (sans date). LNT reads the published translation in March.

11 April — SAT organises a dinner for Fet's jubilee, celebrating 50 years of his literary activity; LNT disapproves.

Spring — LNT has been working on an article *On art [Ob iskusstve]*, which he does not finish, but later uses as a basis for his treatise *What is art? [Chto takoe iskusstvo?]* (1897–98).

2–7 May — LNT makes a third trek from Moscow to Yasnaya Polyana, this time with one of his followers, Evgenij Ivanovich Popov (1864–1938) — see also April 1886 and April 1888.

May — the eighth edition of LNT's *Complete Collected Works [Polnoe sobranie sochinenij]* begins to appear.

May–June — Both Strakhov and Countess Aleksandra Andreevna Tolstaja pay visits to Yasnaya Polyana.

11 July–9 August — Prince Sergej Urusov is a guest at Yasnaya Polyana.

Early December — Tat'jana Tolstaja (the Tolstoys' eldest daughter) asks LNT for permission to stage an amateur performance of *The fruits of enlightenment [Plody prosveshchenija]* at Yasnaya Polyana. LNT agrees. This takes place 30 December; three of the Tolstoys' children (Sergej, Tat'jana and Marija) are in the cast.

1890

LNT begins writing *Father Sergius [Otets Sergij]*.

10 January — *The power of darkness [Vlast' t'my]* is given an amateur performance in Russia for the first time — at the Pospelovs' house in St. Petersburg. Two days later it is staged at the *Freie Bühne* [Free Stage] *Theatre* in Germany (see Gusev I: 746).

24 January — LNT meets with Chertkov and Leskov at Yasnaya Polyana.

2–4 February — LNT and his daughter Tat'jana visit his brother Sergej at Pirogovo.

25 February–2 March — LNT pays a visit to Optina Pustyn' monastery.

10 March — Interior Minister Ivan Nikolaevich Durnovo (1834–1903) refuses to allow SAT to publish *The Kreutzer Sonata* in Volume 13 of LNT's *Collected works*.

15 April — *The fruits of enlightenment* is given two public amateur performances — one in Tula and the other at Tsarskoe selo, where the Emperor, Alexander III, himself attends, and thereafter allows the play to be staged by amateur groups only.

3–12 May — LNT and his daughter Marija [Masha] visit his brother Sergej at Pirogovo.

June–August — Strakhov pays several visits to Yasnaya Polyana.

5 August — A fire breaks out in one of the huts in the village of Yasnaya Polyana. Five houses burn down. Several members of the Tolstoy family render assistance.

8 December — SAT writes in her Diary of the horrors that still haunt her from reading LNT's diaries as a young bride (see *Dnevniki* 1: 127), describing LNT's past sexual exploits.

16 December — SAT's Diary reveals the complexity of her current life and its negative effect on her well-being: "This chaos of innumerable cares, one right after the other, often drives me mad, and I lose my equilibrium. It's easy to say, but at any given moment my attention is taken up with: children studying and ailing, my husband's state of physical and especially mental health, the older children with their activities and debts, children and [esp. military] service, the sale and plans of the Samara estate — they have to be obtained and copied for potential buyers, the new edition [of LNT's *Complete Collected Works*] and Volume XIII with the banned *Kreutzer Sonata*, the request for dividing [Tat'jana L'vovna's] property with the Ovsjannikovo priest, proofreading Volume XIII, Misha's nightshirt, sheets and boots for Andrjusha; not to postpone payments on household expenses; insurance, taxes on the estate, passports for the staff, bookkeeping transcribing, etc., etc. — all of which invariably and directly ought to concern me" (*Dnevniki* 1: 131). On this date she is also working on transcribing LNT's article *The Kingdom of God is within you [Tsarstvo Bozhie vnutri vas]*.

1891

LNT publicly renounces copyright on all his works published after 1881. He helps organise famine relief in Rjazan' Province. *The Kreutzer Sonata [Krejtserova sonata]* is banned, but SAT obtains the Tsar's personal permission for its inclusion in LNT's *Collected works*. After a poor harvest and resulting famine in several gubernias, SAT appeals in the pages of the newspaper *Russkie vedomosti* for charitable contributions from the public. Later she helps LNT open food kitchens in Tula and Rjazan' Gubernias.

January — LNT takes the first steps to divest himself of personal property and gives SAT full power-of-attorney over his financial affairs.

12 February — "I don't know how or why *The Kreutzer Sonata* has been linked with our marital life, but it is a fact, and everyone, from the Tsar on down to Lev Nikolaevich's brother and his best friend D'jakov, has expressed their sympathies for me. In any case, what do others have to offer? In my own heart I have sensed that this story was aimed directly at me. Right from the start it wounded me, humiliated me in the eyes of the whole world and destroyed the last remaining love between us. And all this time I was not to blame for the slightest violation of my marriage vows, not even a sideways glance at anyone during all my married life!" (*Dnevniki* 1: 153). This is grist for her subsequent novel *Who is to blame? [Ch'ja vina?]*.

25 February — The censorship board prohibits the publication of Volume 13 of LNT's works, including *The Kreutzer Sonata* (Gusev II: 20). In *My Life* (v.76) SAT describes her frustration at this turn of events.

13 April — SAT has a personal audience with Tsar Alexander III, where she obtains permission to include *The Kreutzer Sonata* in her edition of Tolstoy's *Collected works* (though not as a separate publication), as well as the Tsar's assurance that he will personally act as censor for LNT's future belletristic writings. She then has a separate meeting with Empress Marija Fëdorovna, conducted in French. (See *My Life*, v.92–94)

Mid-April — The Tolstoy family begin discussing the dividing of the estate between the parents and the children (Gusev II: 28). The process continues into June, when Sergej and Il'ja join the discussion. Eventually LNT approves a plan for dividing his property among his family members. (See *My Life*, v.108.)

June — Volume 13 of LNT's *Complete Collected Works* is published, including *The Kreutzer Sonata*.

25 June — We note the first mention of the famine in LNT's Diary (*PSS* 52: p. 43).

29 June–16 July — At Yasnaya Polyana, the artist Repin executes a bust of LNT, along with several portraits.

4 July — In a letter to Leskov, LNT speaks about the famine and expresses an opinion that social changes are needed more than direct donations — which partly contradicts his own future energetic actions on famine relief (*PSS* 66: Nº 1).

11–15 July — LNT writes to SAT in Moscow (*PSS* 84: Nº 453) and suggests that she publish in the newspapers (on her own and on his behalf) a letter about his renouncing copyright on all his latest works. On 15 July SAT agrees.

21 July — Following yet another difficult conversation with LNT, SAT is saved from suicide by her brother-in-law Aleksandr Mikhajlovich Kuzminskij, thanks to the latter's chance encounter with a swarm of flying ants (see *Dnevniki* 1: 201). In *My Life*, this episode is related twice, not only under 1891 (v.115) but also earlier under August 1882 (III.121).

26 July — SAT describes in her Diary (I.204) the difficulties in getting LNT's *Primer [Azbuka]* approved by the censorship committee.

29 July–1 August — Strakhov visits Yasnaya Polyana.

6 September — SAT writes to LNT about the famine.

10 September — LNT writes to the newspaper *Russkie vedomosti* renouncing copyright on his post-1881 works, including *The death of Ivan Ilyich [Smert' Ivana Il'icha]*. Two days later, he sends this letter to SAT with a request to pass it along to the editors but she does not do so. A week later LNT himself sends his letter to the paper (*PSS* 66: Nº 36), which is published on 19 September (*Russkie vedomosti*: Nº 258; also *Novoe vremja*: Nº 5588), later republished in many other papers.

19–26 September — LNT travels to various villages to see the conditions of the starving population (see Gusev II: 43–44).

27 September — *The fruits of enlightenment* is staged at the Aleksandrinskij Theatre in St. Petersburg.

October — LNT writes an article *On the famine [O golode]*.

15–26 October — SAT asks the Directorate of the Imperial Theatres to send the royalties for *The fruits of enlightenment* to LNT to be used for famine relief. Under the circumstances, they agree (Gusev II: 49–50). LNT continues his efforts on famine relief through the remainder of the year, with the assistance of his family. By the end of the year, his group has organised 70 food kitchens for the famine victims.

3 November — SAT's letter to the editor regarding the need for assistance to famine victims is published in *Russkie vedomosti* (Nº 303). Over the following week she receives the first 9,000 roubles of donations (see her Diary, II: 79; also Gusev II: 52. Later she helps LNT distribute food to famine-stricken peasants; her reports on charitable contributions to this cause appear in *Nedelja* (Nº 47 and 50 see below).

6 November — LNT's article *The terrible question [Strashnyj vopros]* is published in *Russkie vedomosti* (Nº 306).

1892

The first biography of LNT is published (in German) in Berlin: R. Löwenfeld *Leo N. Tolstoj. Sein Leben, seine Werke, seine Weltanschauung*. The Preface is dated December 1891 (Gusev II: 90).

7 January — LNT attends a production of *The fruits of enlightenment* at the Maly Theatre in Moscow.

Spring — An article entitled "Countess S. A. Tolstaya's refutation of rumours of L. N. Tolstoy's arrest" is published in *Nedelja* (N° 13).

January–March — LNT along with SAT and their daughter Marija render assistance in the famine region of Begichevka; by 11 March, 170 food kitchens have been organised, reaching 212 by mid-May (see LNT's letter to SAT, PSS 84: N° 520). In February they are visited there by the artist Il'ja Repin.

April — At LNT's request, SAT's portrait is painted by the artist Valentin Aleksandrovich Serov (1865–1911), son of two prominent composers Aleksandr Nikolaevich Serov and Valentina Semënovna Serova (*née* Bergman) — see *My Life*, VI.18.

30 April — LNT's report on the use of recently donated funds is published in *Russkie vedomosti* (N° 117).

Late June–early July — Strakhov is a guest at Yasnaya Polyana.

7 July — LNT turns all his property over to SAT and the children.

9 July — LNT leaves Yasnaya Polyana for Begichevka.

27–28 July — LNT compiles another report about the use of funds (see his letter to SAT, PSS 84 N° 532).

13 August — LNT makes notes in his Notebook and Diary about the need to leave the family.

9–13 September — LNT spends several days at Begichevka, compiling a report on the use of donated funds between April and July, which appears in *Russkie vedomosti* (N° 301).

21 November — Afanasij Afanas'evich Fet dies, with whom SAT has had a long friendship, and who has dedicated a number of his poems to her. She in turn dedicates her prose poem "Poèt" [The poet] to him. See Poetry Appendix in *My Life*, with poems translated by John Woodsworth.

1892–1893

SAT writes the story *Who's to blame? [Kto vinovat?]* in response to LNT's *Kreutzer Sonata*.

1893

LNT finishes *The Kingdom of God is within you [Tsarstvo Bozhie vnutri vas]*. SAT proofreads and publishes the 9th edition of LNT's *Collected works*. In addition to her diaries, she begins writing what she calls *Daily diaries [Ezhednevniki]* to record the most salient details of her and her husband's lives.

Early February — During Shrovetide SAT takes her children to a performance of *Ring of love [Kol'tso ljubvi]* at Moscow's Bolshoi Theatre. She pays a visit to Grand Duchess Elisaveta Fëdorovna Romanova (1864–1918) — a devout believer known for her charity work, granddaughter to Britain's Queen Victoria and wife to Grand Prince Sergej Aleksandrovich Romanov. She reads an article by philosopher Nikolaj Jakovlevich Grot (1852–1899) on LNT and Nietzsche.

6–21 February — LNT with daughter Tat'jana and Evgenij Popov check on famine relief at Begichevka.

11 April — The illegitimate daughter of LNT's sister Marija Nikolaevna, Elena Sergeevna [Lenochka] (1863–1942), marries jurist Ivan Vasil'evich Denisenko (1851–1916) at the Tolstoys' home in Moscow.

Late April — Volumes of the new Ninth Edition of LNT's collected works go on sale. SAT writes: "It was a beautiful edition, with portraits and illustrations, on high-quality paper, and meticulously corrected by N. N. Strakhov" (*My Life*, VI.66).

June — Vladimir Chertkov transfers the business of Posrednik to Pavel Birjukov and Ivan Gorbunov-Posadov.

End of July — Chertkov and Birjukov visit Yasnaya Polyana. Strakhov visits in August.

30 August — Marija Aleksandrovna Shmidt (1844–1911) settles in the village of Ovsjannikovo, 5 km from Yasnaya Polyana. She becomes a Tolstoyan and copies a number of LNT's manuscripts.

9 September — SAT takes her sons Andrej and Mikhail to a Moscow *gymnasium* [school]. She reads works by French novelist Paul Margueritte (1860–1918).

19 October — A new report by LNT and Pavel Birjukov about the use of donations to the famine relief in 1893 is published in *Russkie vedomosti*: N° 288.

1894

LNT finishes *Christianity and patriotism [Khristianstvo i patriotizm]*; *Reason and religion [Razum i religija]*; *Religion and morality [O religii i nravstvennosti]*. He writes a Preface to a Russian translation of Guy de Maupassant's works: *Predislovie k russkomu izdaniju sbornika G. de Mopassana «Na vode» [Preface to the Russian edition of Guy de Maupassant's collection «Sur l'eau»]*, published by Posrednik (1894).

23 January–2 February — LNT, tired of life in Moscow, pays a visit (with his daughter Tat'jana) to his son Il'ja's Grinëvka estate in the Tula region (see his letter to SAT, PSS 84: N° 591).

25 March–3 April — LNT (with daughter Marija) travels to Chertkov's farmstead (*khutor*) Rzhevsk in the Voronezh region, and later visits Voronezh itself.

12–13 May — SAT takes (for the second time) eight trunks of LNT's manuscripts to the Rumjantsev Museum for preservation (*My Life*, VI.90; also September 1887 above and January 1904 below).

18 May–11 August — The Chertkov family rent a house in the village of Demenka, 5 km from Yasnaya Polyana.

10 June–4 August — Strakhov is a guest at Yasnaya Polyana.

Mid-June — LNT dictates to his daughter Masha a five-act play on a peasant theme. SAT is asked to come up with and put on some kind of dramatic ending. The performance goes well: "but I should say, without boasting, that the presentation I thought up had a much greater success with the audience" (*My Life*, VI.94). SAT takes Vanechka and Misha to see her son Il'ja at Grinëvka, then to see her son Sergej at Nikol'skoe, and from there to her brother's in Orël, where the Kuzminskij family is spending the summer at their dacha near Pesochnaja Station.

13 August — A printing press ordered by Chertkov is delivered to Yasnaya Polyana. LNT's letters are systematically copied from now on.

15 August — SAT reads the 1894 story "Winter day" [*Zimnij den'*] by Nikolaj Semënovich Leskov "after which I began to dislike this writer even more" (*My Life*, VI.98). She busies herself with proofreading, sewing and housekeeping.

21–27 August — Slovakian doctor Dushan Petrovich Makovitskij (1866–1921) visits Yasnaya Polyana for the first time. He becomes LNT's personal physician in 1904.

20 October — Tsar Alexander III dies of illness, succeeded by his eldest son, Nicholas II (1868–1918), who reigns until the Bolshevik revolution of 1917.

Late December — During Chertkov's visit to Moscow, LNT has a photo of himself taken in the company of Birjukov, Gorbunov-Posadov, Popov and Ivan Mikhajlovich Tregubov (1858–1931) — a priest's son who came into conflict with the Russian Orthodox Church and then worked for Posrednik (later working with Chertkov in England). SAT dislikes the whole company and destroys the negative (see Gusev II: 162).

1895

The power of darkness [Vlast' t'my] is produced at the Maly Theatre in Moscow. LNT writes an appeal on behalf of the Doukhobors.

1–18 January — LNT and daughter Tat'jana visit the Olsuf'ev family at their Nikol'skoe estate.

January — Vanechka is ill. He dictates the story *Spasënnyj taks [The rescued dachshund]* to his mother, which is first published in the children's magazine *Igrushechka* [The Little Toy]: N° 3 (1895) and later in SAT's book *The skeleton-dolls [Kukolki-skelettsy]* (*My Life,* VI.107).

End of January–early February — SAT transcribes *Master and man [Khozjain i rabotnik]*, which LNT then submits to the journal *Severnyj vestnik,* co-published by Ljubov' Jakovlevna Gurevich (1866–1940) and Akim L'vovich Volynskij [real name: Khaim Lejbovich Flekser] (1861–1926).

6 February — SAT demands LNT give her (and Posrednik) *Master and man,* threatening to commit suicide. When LNT refuses, she attempts to make good on her threat, but is stopped by her children Serëzha and Masha. LNT begs forgiveness and agrees to hand over his story, whereupon she, Posrednik and *Severnyj vestnik* publish it simultaneously in three editions (*My Life,* VI.108).

23 February — Vanechka (born 31 March 1888) dies. He is buried on 26 February in the village of Nikol'skoe, north-west of Moscow. (In 1932 his remains are transferred to the Tolstoys' family plot beside the Nikol'skaja Church in Kochaki, not far from Yasnaya Polyana.)

Late February-March — Sergej Taneev's music and friendship help mitigate SAT's sorrow over the loss of her favourite child.

27 March — LNT writes in his Diary thoughts on his final will, leaving it to whoever survives out of SAT, Chertkov and Strakhov to manage his papers after his death. (See 23 July 1901 and 13 May 1904 below.)

3 June–27 August — Taneev rents the annexe for the summer at Yasnaya Polyana.

13 June — LNT confesses to his son Lev his impression that SAT loves him the way he was years ago, but finds his present self "strange, frightening and dangerous" (*PSS* 68: N° 103).

18 June — The Chertkovs again settle at Demenka for the summer.

28–29 June — The Caucasus Doukhobors burn their weapons and immediately experience repressions from authorities.

4 July–8 August — Strakhov spends 5 weeks at Yasnaya Polyana.

10 July — SAT (without LNT) attends the wedding of her son Sergej and Marija Konstantinovna Rachinskaja (1865–1900). In line with SAT's premonition, Marija becomes estranged from Sergej soon after the marriage and passes on within five years (see *My Life,* VI.119).

29(?) July–1 August — LNT writes a letter to British newpapers about the persecution of the Doukhobors but does not send it (*PSS* 39: N° 209–215).

4 August — Pavel Birjukov leaves for Trans-Caucasia in order to find information on the Doukhobors first hand; returns on 8 September.

8–9 August — Writer Anton Pavlovich Chekhov (1860–1904) visits LNT for the first time.

27 August–11 September — LNT's sister Marija Nikolaevna Tolstaja (1830–1912) spends two weeks at Yasnaya Polyana.

4 September — LNT writes a letter to a feminist, Nadezhda Vasil'evna Stasova (1822–1895) about the difficult work of women in poor households.

15(?)–19 September — LNT writes an article about the persecutions of the Doukhobors (entitled initially "Carthago delenda est").

October — SAT takes her children Tanja and Misha to St. Petersburg to attend two premières on 17 and 18 October: Taneev's opera *Oresteia* and the first public staging of *The power of darkness* at the *Teatr literaturnogo artisticheskogo kruzhka.* (See her letter to LNT, 22 October 1895.)

26 October — *The power of darkness* is staged for the first time in Moscow, at the Skomorokh Theatre, owned by playwright and theatre entrepreneur Mikhail Valentinovich Lentovskij (1843–1906) — also known as the *Obshchedostupnyj teatr M. V. Lentovskogo*. On 12 December LNT himself attends a performance here. (See: A. Donskov, *Mixail Lentovskij and the Russian theatre*, esp. pp. 39–48.)

28 October–3 November — At SAT's request, LNT deletes 45 passages in his 1888–1895 diaries that she finds offensive. These passages were restored where possible in *PSS* 50–53 (Gusev II: 193; also LNT's letters to SAT, *PSS* 84: N° 640, 642, 643).

21 November — LNT writes a letter to Pëtr Vasil'evich Verigin (1859–1924), the leader of the persecuted Caucasian Doukhobors, who is in exile in the town of Obdorsk.

29 November — *The power of darkness* is performed in Moscow's Maly Theatre for the first time.

December — SAT's story *Grandmother's treasure-trove: a legend [Babushkin klad: predanie]* is published in the children's magazine *Detskoe chtenie: N°* 12 (1895). See her letter to her son Lev dated 12/24 December 1895.

1895–1900

SAT writes the narrative *Song without words [Pesnja bez slov]*, considered by many as autobiographical (see Donskov 2011: 95–107).

1896

January — SAT goes to visit her son Andrej in Tver', who is serving in the armed forces.

16–24 January — SAT writes in *My Life* (VII.2) about "three deaths" during this brief period: (a) the elderly Agaf'ja Mikhajlovna [Gasha], former chambermaid to LNT's grandmother (16 January at Yasnaya Polyana); (b) Nikolaj Mikhajlovich Nagornov (1846–1896), who in 1876–81 helped LNT in publishing his *Primer [Azbuka]* (23 January in Moscow); (c) the Tolstoys' long-time editorial associate Nikolaj Nikolaevich Strakhov (24 January in St. Petersburg).

15 May — The Tolstoys' son Lev L'vovich [Lëva], in Sweden for treatment by Dr. Ernest Westerlund (1839–1924), marries Dr. Westerlund's daughter Dora Fëdorovna Westerlund (1878–1933), who subsequently accompanies him back to Yasnaya Polyana.

18 May — In Moscow SAT witnesses the aftermath of the tragedy at Khodynka Field, where a crowd of people, under pressure from a militia unprepared to handle such a gathering, stampede, and more than 2,600 people die or are wounded (see *My Life*, VII.14).

19 May–2 August — Taneev summers at Yasnaya Polyana; his friendship with SAT deepens.

6 June–31 August — The Chertkovs spend the summer at their dacha in Demenka.

Late June–early July — LNT pays visits to his son Il'ja and Il'ja's wife Sof'ja [Sonja] (with whom he feels at home), as well as to his eldest son Sergej and Sergej's wife Marija [Manja] (with whom he is disappointed). See his letter to son Lev L'vovich, 2 July 1896.

Summer — At Yasnaya Polyana LNT works on *Outline of faith [Izlozhenie very]* and *What is art? [Chto takoe iskusstvo?]*, which SAT transcribes.

18 July — LNT receives the first inspiration for his novel *Hadji Murat*.

10–15 August — SAT accompanies LNT to the Shamordino Convent to see his sister Marija Nikolaevna, afterwards visiting an elder named Father Gerasim at Optina Pustyn' (see *My Life*, VII.18).

10 October — LNT confides to his Diary: "Things are fine with Sonja; I myself am weak, but I'm struggling with love."

4 November — SAT writes in *My Life* (VII.26): "On one of my visits to Yasnaya Polyana that November I asked Lev Nikolaevich to transfer his copyright on all his writings to me, to make it easier to look after all the publishing side and spare him from having to sign documents, money orders, cheques, and such like. He gave me a flat refusal with a tone of dissatisfaction. I got upset and accused him of not being true to his principles, on the grounds that I alone was doing the work while others were reaping the benefits of my labours. I went on for quite a bit on this subject."

1897

12 January — LNT writes to daughter Marija about his estrangement from the rest of the family (see *PSS* 70: N° 6) and to Chertkov on the same matter (*PSS* 88: N° 431).

31 January — LNT (with his daughter Tat'jana) visits the home of Count Adam Olsuf'ev at Nikol'skoe-Girushki, where they are joined on 5 February by SAT.

1 February — LNT writes to SAT about her friendship with Taneev (*PSS* 84: N° 673).

6 February — SAT goes to St. Petersburg with LNT; they stay at the home of Adam Olsuf'ev's brother, Count Aleksandr Vasil'evich Olsuf'ev (1843–1907). LNT wants to see Chertkov and Birjukov, who are about to be sent into exile for their 'tolstoyan propaganda'. SAT writes to Minister of Internal Affairs Ivan Logginovich Goremykin (1839–1917), asking for an appointment to discuss censorship of future editions of LNT's *Collected works* (see *My Life*, VII.34).

13 February — LNT returns to the Olsuf'evs at Nikol'skoe-Gorushki. On the same day, Chertkov emigrates abroad while Birjukov goes into exile in Bausk in Kurland Gubernia (now Latvia), south of Riga. LNT returns to Moscow on 3 March.

1 March — SAT goes to visit her son Andrej [Andrjusha] Behrs (1878–1939) in Tver' (see *My Life,* VII.35).

Early March — The first volume of the 10th edition of LNT's collected works appears.

17 and 21 March — Aylmer Maude (1838–1938) visits LNT in Moscow; he will later become his biographer and English translator.

18 April — SAT goes with her daughter Aleksandra (Sasha) to visit the Troitsa-Sergiev Monastery [Troitse-Sergieva Lavra] about 70 km north-east of Moscow.

16–18 May — LNT makes several notes in his Diary on his sufferings over his marriage, hinting at his plans to leave home; on 20 May he goes to his brother Sergej's at Pirogovo to ponder his situation.

19 May — LNT writes to SAT about his "shame" for her and for himself, because of Taneev (see *PSS* 84: N° 683).

20 May — After five sleepless nights, LNT leaves Yasnaya Polyana and goes to his brother Sergej's at Pirogovo to think about his situation. He returns on 25 May.

June–November — SAT transcribes LNT's article *What is art?*

2 June — Marija L'vovna Tolstaja marries Prince Nikolaj Leonidovich Obolenskij (1872–1933), LNT's grand-nephew.

6–13 June — Taneev spends a week at Yasnaya Polyana. SAT confides to her Diary: "I feel so little guilt and so much in the way of quiet, peaceful joy from my pure, peaceful relations with this man that I cannot destroy them in my heart, any more than I can stop looking, breathing or thinking" (*Dnevniki* 1: 241).

8 June — SAT writes in her Diary: "Today I proofread *The Kreutzer Sonata*, and again that same weighty feeling: how much cynicism [there is] and naked exposure of the wretched human side!" (*Dnevniki* 1: 244).

19 June — SAT confesses her discomfort at her position of authority over the poor peasants carrying out illegal timber-cutting on their estate (see *Dnevniki* 1: 252).

21 June — SAT examines her motives regarding her desire to commit suicide and how her religious convictions prevent her from carrying it out; she also expresses her penchant for listening to "the most complex, harmonious music" and for harnessing her soul "to understand what the composer wanted to say through this mysterious, complex, mystical language" (*Dnevniki* 1: 254).

8 July — LNT writes a farewell letter to SAT (*PSS* 84: N° 684), but hides it inside the upholstery of an armchair in his study. Later, while seriously ill in the early 1900s, he gives the letter to his daughter Marija, instructing her to make a note on it: "To be opened fifty years after my death, if anyone is interested in this episode of my biography." After he recovers, Marija returns the letter to him. In the year following Marija's death in 1906, LNT entrusts the letter to her widower, Prince Nikolaj Leonidovich [Kolja] Obolenskij (1872–1934), instructing him to give the letter to SAT after his death. When Obolenskij witnessed SAT opening the envelope after her husband's death, he notes there are two letters in it. SAT reads them and immediately tears one of them up; its contents remain unknown.

15 July — SAT writes in her Diary: "I am passionately thirsting for music, I would like to play a bit myself. But either there is no time, or Lev Nikolaevich is working, or he's sleeping — and everything bothers him. Without the personal pleasure I now find in music, life is boring. I try to reassure myself that there is joy in the fulfilment of duty. I make myself do the transcribing, along with everything that comprises my duty, only sometimes my will breaks — I have a desire for personal joys, a personal life, my own work, and not work on someone else's writings, as it has been my whole life, and then I become weak and don't feel very well." (*Dnevniki* 1: 265)

Summer — At Yasnaya Polyana, SAT transcribes LNT's article on art, now part of *What is art? [Chto takoe iskusstvo?]* (but feels weighed down by this task). She plays the piano and continues work on her story *Song without words*, encouraged by brief visits from Taneev. She keeps on offering excruciating descriptions of her relationship with LNT.

1 October — SAT transcribes the last part of *What is art?* "For the seventh time I had to transcribe the 'Conclusion' to his article *On art*, and then I had to correct the mistakes in Chapter 10, insert excerpts from various books, as well as the decadent verses which Lev Nikolaevich hated so much" (*My Life*, VII.43).

30 October–6 November — LNT asks SAT to accompany him on a visit to his brother Sergej at Pirogovo. SAT agrees, mainly for "the chance to be with my husband for several days" (*My Life*, VII.44).

December — SAT faces difficult emotional turmoil and comes close to another suicide attempt (which afterward torments her). She wallows in her torment at the Troitsa-Sergiev Monastery (see *My Life*, VII.45).

20 December — A letter is received with a threat to kill LNT on 3 April 1898. SAT notes in her Diary: "This letter disturbs me to the point where I cannot forget it for a moment. [...] Lev Nikolaevich has shown no signs of alarm, saying that I shouldn't alert anyone and trust everything to God's will" (*Dnevniki* 1: 333). (See also *My Life*, VII.45, 48 and LNT's Diary of 21 & 28 December.)

31 December — The Minister of Internal Affairs, Ivan Logginovich Goremykin (1839–1917), gives the Doukhobors permission to emigrate from Russia on the condition that they never return.

1898

LNT decides to aid the Doukhobors, resolving to raise funds for their emigration by accepting royalties from *Father Sergius [Otets Sergij]* and *Resurrection [Voskresenie]* to raise funds. He organises aid for the starving peasants of Tula Province. He writes an article *Famine or no famine [Golod ili ne golod]*.

6 February — SAT writes in her Diary: "…I don't know where he has hid his latest diary, and I'm afraid he might have sent it to Chertkov. I'm afraid to ask him about it, too. Oh my God! My God! We have spent our whole lives together — all my love, all my youth I gave to Lev Nikolaevich. And here — the result of our lives: I'm afraid of him! Even though I have nothing to be ashamed of before him, I'm afraid of him. And when I try to analyse this feeling of fear, I stop the analysing right away. As my life has developed over the years, I have come to understand a lot of things all too well. ¶The consistency and cleverness with which he has blackened my name, elucidating only my weak points with brief, poisonous strokes of the pen, shows how cleverly he has fashioned for himself a martyr's crown, and the scourge of a Xantippe for me. ¶Lord! You alone be our judge!" (*Dnevniki* 1: 350). *Xantippe* (fifth century B.C.E.) was Socrates' wife; because of her well-known bad temper, he used her as an object-lesson for his philosophy.

March — SAT visits St. Petersburg, where she stopped over at her elder sister's — Elizaveta Andreevna Behrs (née Behrs, 1843–1919); while there, she called upon the Orientalist Prince Èsper Èsperovich Ukhtomskij (1861–1921) to ask him, on Lev Nikolaevich's behalf, to publish something about the Doukhobors and their [need for] assistance (see *My Life*, VII.51).

23 April — LNT and SAT travel to see their son Il'ja at his Grinëvka estate in the Tula region.

Late April–early June — LNT works on famine relief in the Tula and Orël regions (see his letter to SAT, PSS 84: No 704–718).

12 July — SAT travels to see her friends the Maslovs at their Selishche estate, where Taneev, who is also visiting, plays Chopin and Händel to SAT's great delight (see *My Life*, VII.57).

15–20 July — SAT visits the Kuzminskijs at their dacha near Kiev (see also August 1899).

17 July — LNT considers leaving home and moving to Finland, then a part of the Russian Empire. See his letter to the Finnish writer Arvid Aleksandrovich Ernefel't (1861–1933) — PSS 71: No 196.

Night of 28–29 July — LNT and SAT have a serious conversation about Taneev, which LNT describes in a letter to SAT's sister Tat'jana Kuzminskaja (PSS 53: 383–388).

August — SAT spends time copying Lev Nikolaevich's diaries, so that one copy may be preserved in the museum while the other remains at Yasnaya Polyana. She also transcribes *Father Sergius*, and works on the proofreading of LNT's *Collected works*. She is concerned that her husband wants to sell three of his stories — *Hadji Murat*, *Resurrection* and *Father Sergius* — at a slightly higher price in Russia and abroad and donate the money to the Doukhobors' emigration to Canada.

7 August — The first party of the Caucasus Doukhobors (1,139 people) sets sail from Batoum (now in Georgia, known as Batumi) for Cyprus, later to be relocated to Canada.

28 August — SAT organises Jubilee celebrations at Yasnaya Polyana in honour of LNT's seventieth birthday. She is overwhelmed by the number of guests (thirty-six at dinner, forty at supper).

3(?)–29 September — LNT's son Sergej travels to England to discuss the Doukhobors' emigration with Chertkov and other people involved in the process.

13 September — SAT writes in her Diary, wondering why LNT would now accept royalties (on *Resurrection*) for the benefit of the Doukhobors — complete strangers — and not to enhance the

lives of his own grandchildren (who can't even afford to eat white bread). The novel will appear in the weekly journal *Niva*, published by Adol'f Fëdorovich Marks (1838–1904) — an illustrated middle-class journal published in St. Petersburg from 1869 to 1918 (see *Dnevniki* 1: 411).

25–27 September — LNT visits the city of Orël in order to see its prison and gain first-hand impressions for his novel *Resurrection*.

23 October — SAT talks with her son Sergej L'vovich about LNT: "Serëzha says I should give away the copyright on his father's works. I say: 'Why? To reward the rich publishers? That's a lie'" (*Dnevniki* 1: 419).

9(?) November — Sergej Tolstoy, accompanied by theatre director Leopol'd Antonovich Sulerzhitskij (1872–1916), leaves for the Caucasus to assist the Doukhobors in their journey to Canada.

10 December [22 December N.S.] — The *S.S. Lake Huron* leaves the port of Batoum and sets sail for Canada with 2,140 exiled Doukhobors on board, accompanied by Leopol'd Sulerzhitskij.

22 December [4 January 1899 N.S.] — Sergej L'vovich Tolstoy sets sail from Batoum with a party of some 2,200 Doukhobors bound for Canada aboard the *S.S. Lake Superior*.

1899

Resurrection is published during the year in serial form.

8 January — The Tolstoys' son Andrej L'vovich [Andrjusha] marries Ol'ga Konstantinovna Diterikhs (1872–1951), sister to Vladimir Chertkov's wife, Anna Konstantinovna.

15 [27 N.S.] January— the *S.S. Lake Superior* with the second party of Doukhobors on board, escorted by Sergej Tolstoy, arrives in Halifax, where it is quarantined for three weeks.

26 January — SAT describes her repulsion at LNT's description of the Russian Orthodox service in his *Resurrection* (see *Dnevniki* 1: 444; also *My Life*, VII.64).

February — SAT travels to Kiev to comfort her sister Tat'jana Kuzminskaja [Tanja], who has fallen seriously ill (see *My Life*, VII.66).

February–March — SAT herself falls ill with the flu, and is confined to bed for eight days.

6 [18] April — the *Lake Superior* picks up over a thousand Doukhobors from Larnaca, Cyprus, where they had made an unsuccessful attempt to settle. It arrives in Québec City on 27 April [9 May], accompanied once again by Leopol'd Sulerzhitskij.

Late April [early May] — The fourth and final party of 2,286 Doukhobors sets sail from Batoum aboard the *Lake Huron,* arriving in Québec City in late May. They are accompanied by Dr. Vera Mikhajlovna Velichkina (1868–1918) and her future husband, Vladimir Dmitrievich Bonch-Bruevich (1873–1955), who later both serve in the Bolshevik government (Velichkina as Lenin's personal physician). See Sergej L'vovich's most interesting and touching letters to his family from Canada in Donskov 1998: 355–370; also Vera Velichkina's account (from *Russkie vedomosti*) of this journey to Canada (in English translation) in Woodsworth 1999: 165–92.

27 May — The Tolstoys' daughter Tat'jana L'vovna undergoes an operation in Vienna for frontal sinusitis (see *My Life*, VII.68).

26 June — SAT describes her husband's listlessness in her Diary (III: 120).

Early August — SAT travels to the Maslovs' Selishche estate, where she sees Taneev, afterwards visiting the Kuzminskijs in Kiev.

14 November — The Tolstoys' eldest daughter, Tat'jana L'vovna [Tanja], marries Mikhail Sergeevich Sukhotin (1850–1914). According to SAT's Diary (III: 122), LNT takes her leaving especially hard.

1900

LNT starts writing *The Living corpse* [*Zhivoj trup*] (unfinished). The International Tolstoy Society is founded (see Gusev II: 367). SAT keeps revising her novel *Song without words* throughout the year.

January — SAT begins her service as a trustee for a children's shelter, which lasts until February 1902 (see *My Life*, VIII.2).

January — SAT writes in *My Life* (VIII.4): "At that time I was unable to practise my music, since the whole house was full of guests, and instead of music I worked assiduously on my novel and finished it. But it still had to be revised. I got ready to study Italian, all on my own, and had already bought a self-instructional textbook. I was never able to survive just on practical chores and material cares, and always sought out some kind of artistic activity or philosophical reading."

13 January — The writer Maksim Gorky [birth name: Aleksej Maksimovich Peshkov] (1868–1936) visits LNT in Moscow (for the first time).

8 October — Gorky visits LNT at Yasnaya Polyana and SAT photographs them (see, for example, in Gusev II: 352, also Illustration II-45 in *My Life*).

Late October — LNT, accompanied by his daughter Tat'jana Sukhotina and her artist friend Julija Ivanovna Igumnova (1871–1940), visits the Sukhotins' Kochety estate.

24 December —The Tolstoys' grandson Lev L'vovich [Lëvushka] dies. Three days later the Tolstoys' learn that their daughter Tat'jana L'vovna [Tanja] has had a stillbirth. SAT hastens to visit both of her grieving children (see *My Life*, VIII.13).

1901

Beginning in early summer, LNT experiences several bouts of deteriorating health, including malaria, which leads to the Tolstoys' decision to spend the autumn and winter at Gaspra in the Crimea at the personal invitation of their friend, Countess Sof'ja Vladimirovna Panina (1871–1957). Literary visitors include Chekhov, Gorky and Bal'mont. See *My Life*, VIII.18.

19 January — SAT poignantly describes her frame of mind at the start of the new century in her Diary (*Dnevniki* 2: 10): "I have been busy collecting and transcribing as many of my letters as possible to Lev Nikolaevich over my whole lifetime. What a touching account these letters hold of my love for Lëvochka and my life as a mother! One of them reveals my sorrow over my spiritual and intellectual life (so typical of me), for which I was afraid to wake up, so as not to let go of my duties as a wife, mother and household manager. The letter was written under the impressions of music (a melody of Schubert's) which Lev Nikolaevich's sister Mashen'ka was learning to play at the time, as well as the sunset and religious meditations."

28 January — SAT receives news of a stillbirth from her daughter Marija L'vovna.

31 January — The Tolstoys' son Mikhail L'vovich [Misha] marries Aleksandra Vladimirovna [Lina] Glebova (1880–1967).

2 February — In a letter to German newspapers, LNT announces that he is turning over "all the negotiations with [foreign] publishers and translators" to Chertkov (*PSS* 73: № 27).

24 Febuary — *Tserkovnye vedomosti* publishes the Holy Synod's excommunicaton of LNT from the Russian Orthodox Church.

26 February — SAT writes a letter to the Senior Procurator of the Holy Synod, Konstantin Pobedonostsev and the Metropolitans who signed the decree excommunicating LNT from the Russian Orthodox Church. This letter, together with Metropolitan Antonius' response (SAT

called it "soulless"), were published in *Tserkovnye vedomosti*: N° 7 (1901) — see *My Life*, VIII.16.

23 July — LNT signs his will as copied by his daughter Marija from his 1895 Diary (see 27 March 1895 above). Later (on 28 August) SAT learns from their son Il'ja that their daughter Marija let this happen and becomes very upset. She has a difficult conversation with LNT (see Gusev II: 388).

5–8 September — The Tolstoys travel to Gaspra by way of Sevastopol'.

5 November — SAT takes a photograph of LNT with Anton Chekhov (reproduced in *My Life* as Illustration II-46). They also have visits from Maksim Gorky and Russian symbolist poet Konstantin Dmitrievich Bal'mont (1867–1942).

12 November — The Tolstoys' daughter Tat'jana L'vovna [Tanja] experiences a second stillbirth (see *My Life*, VIII.19).

2 December — In her Diary (*Dnevniki* 2: 28), SAT vents her frustration at her husband's current overall mood: "Lev Nikolaevich turned out just the way I had expected: on account of his advancing years he stopped behaving (quite recently) toward his wife as a lover, and this was replaced not what I had vainly dreamt of all my life — a quiet, tender friendship — but by utter emptiness."

7–13 December — LNT pays a visit to his daughter, Marija Obolenskaja, in nearby Yalta.

1902

LNT finishes *What is religion?* [*Chto takoe religija?*]; continues working on *Hadji Murat* and *The light shines in darkness* [*I svet vo t'me svetit*].

January–June — The Tolstoys continue their stay at Gaspra. SAT devotes her time to caring for her husband in his serious illness. Their daughter Marija L'vovna [Masha] experiences a seventh stillbirth.

16 January — LNT writes to the Tsar on the evil of autocracy and coercion and appeals to him to abolish private ownership of land.

Winter–spring — LNT experiences serious illness, almost at the point of death from pneumonia; after his health (slowly) improves, SAT visits Moscow and Yasnaya Polyana. But she returns to Gaspra in May, when LNT suffers a bout of typhoid; once again he recovers.

End of March — Dr. Dmitrij Vasil'evich Nikitin (1874–1960) arrives at Gaspra to be the Tolstoy family's personal physician (he subsequently treats Maksim Gorky and his family).

Late June — The Tolstoys return to Yasnaya Polyana, and decide to stay there for the winter. Dr. Nikitin accompanies them and later assists in copying LNT's manuscripts; he also takes photos of the Tolstoy family.

13 July — The owner of the publishing house Prosveshchenie, Natan Sergeevich Tsejtlin (1872–1930s), comes to Yasnaya Polyana and asks SAT for the rights to publish LNT's works in exchange for 1,000,000 roubles, but SAT declines (Gusev II: 420).

4–8 August — SAT visits the Maslovs at Selishche where she meets Taneev, who is visiting.

31 August — Following LNT's request, a consilium of doctors recommend he spend the forthcoming winter at Yasnaya Polyana.

2 September — SAT confides to her Diary (*Dnevniki* 2: 75): "Personally speaking, I find living in Moscow easier — there are a lot of people around whom I like, and there is a lot of music as well as amusements (both meaningful and just for fun) — exhibitions, concerts, lectures, contact with interesting people, social life. With my poor eyesight I find long evenings difficult, but life in the country is simply boring. Nevertheless, I recognise that for Lev Nikolaevich living in Moscow is unbearable with all the visitors and the noise, and so I am happy and content to live at my beloved Yasnaya, and will take trips to Moscow whenever life here wears me down."

10 October — SAT's Diary (*Dnevniki* 2: 204) records her declaration to LNT that after his passing she will *not* refuse royalties from his works.

25 November — SAT fervently expresses her extreme displeasure over LNT's legend *The destruction of hell and its restoration* [*Razrushenie ada i vosstanovlenie ego*] (*Dnevniki* 2: 80).

1903

LNT protests against Jewish pogroms in Kishinëv (in Moldova). He writes three stories — *Esarhaddon, King of Assyria* [*Assirijskij tsar' Asarkhaddon*], *Three questions* [*Tri voprosa*] and *Toil, death and disease* [*Trud, smert' i bolezn'*]) for an anthology published in Warsaw in aid of pogrom victims — as well as *After the ball* [*Posle bala*], which was not published until after his death. Also, he works on *Shakespeare and drama* [*O Shekspire i drame*].

2 January — The Tolstoys receive news from their daughter Tat'jana L'vovna of two stillborn twin boys.

January — In response to a request by Pavel Birjukov, LNT begins his *Reminiscences* [*Vospominanija*], on which he will continue working until 1906.

3 June — LNT asks his son Mikhail to copy his diaries from the 1840s and 1850s for his biography that Birjukov is compiling.

Early September — LNT works on *Shakespeare and drama*, finished in 1904 and printed abroad in 1906.

20 September — Dr. Nikitin leaves Yasnaya Polyana; his place is taken by Dr. Grigorij Moiseevich Berkengejm (1872–1919), brother to prominent Russian organic chemist Dr. Abram Moiseevich Berkengejm (1867–1938; see Gusev II: 465).

5–8 November — LNT and Dr. Berkengejm visit the Tolstoys' son Sergej at Pirogovo.

17 November — SAT confesses to her Diary (*Dnevniki* 2: 98): "Happy are those wives who live on friendly and participatory terms with their husbands right to the end! And unhappy and lonely are the wives of egotists, great people, whose wives their descendants later turn into modern Xantippes!"

22 December — LNT writes to Countess Aleksandra Andreevna Tolstaja, who is seriously ill (and will die on 24 March 1904) — see PSS 74: N° 348.

1904

LNT decides to publish no more fiction works to avoid further quarrels with SAT over copyright. He finishes *Hadji Murat,* but this work is published posthumously.

12 January — Nine boxes of materials originally presented to the Rumjantsev Museum, together with autographs, are transported to the Historical Museum, where they are kept until the end of LNT's life (see 18 December 1914 below; cf. also September 1887 and May 1894).

25 January — SAT engages a notary at Tula, Jakov Fëdorovich Beloborodov (1826–1912), to legalise the power of attorney she had obtained from LNT in 1883 (see 21 May 1883 above) in the form of a private letter.

February–May — In response to the recently started Russian-Japanese War (1904–05), LNT writes an anti-war article *Bethink yourselves!* [*Odumajtes'!*], which is published in Russian and several foreign papers in June.

13 February — Dr. Dmitrij Nikitin returns to Yasnaya Polyana to take the place of the departing Dr. Berkengejm as the Tolstoy family physician.

24 February — SAT begins work on her autobiographical memoir *My Life* [*Moja zhizn'*]. Her brief preface penned on this date reads as follows: "Last year Vladimir Vasil'evich Stasov asked

me to write my autobiography for a women's calendar. I thought that too immodest of me, and I declined. But the longer I live, the more I see the accumulation of acute misunderstandings and false reports concerning my character, my life, and a great many topics touching upon me. And so, in view of the fact that, though I myself may be insignificant, the significance of my forty-two years of conjugal life with Lev Nikolaevich cannot be excluded from his life, I decided to set forth a description of my life — based, at least for the time being, solely on reminiscences. If time and opportunity permit, I shall endeavour to include several additional details and chronological data drawn from letters, diaries and other sources. ¶I shall try to be true and sincere throughout. Anyone's life is interesting, and perhaps there will come a time when my life will be of interest to some who wonder what kind of creature was the woman whom God and destiny found fit to place alongside the life of the genius and multifaceted Count Lev Nikolaevich Tolstoy." Vladimir Vladimirovich Stasov (1824–1906) was a Russian art, literary and music critic (as well as archæologist, art historian and social activist), and an Honorary Member of the Petersburg Academy of Sciences.

March — SAT publishes a collection of nine prose poems under the general title *Groanings* [*Stony*] in the magazine *Zhurnal dlja vsekh* (N° 3) under the pseudonym *Ustalaja* [*Weary woman*]. See section "Poems in prose: Groanings" in Andrew Donskov's essay in the English translation of *My Life*.

13 May — LNT writes a letter to Chertkov about his will in respect to his papers after his death (see 27 March 1895 above).

5 August — SAT sees her son Andrej off to fight in the Russo-Japanese War.

23 August — LNT's brother Sergej Nikolaevich dies; his funeral is held at Pirogovo on 27 August.

2 August — Dr. Nikitin once again leaves Yasnaya Polyana.

18 December — Dr. Dushan Petrovich Makovitskij (see August 1894 above) arrives at Yasnaya Polyana and becomes the Tolstoys' personal physician.

1905

LNT writes several short stories, all published posthumously.

11 January — Andrej L'vovich returns from the war.

25–27(?) February — LNT writes *Alyosha the Pot [Alësha Gorshok]*.

March — After hearing rumours to the effect that she inspired the pro-war views expressed by her son Lev L'vovich (in an article in *Novoe vremja*), SAT refutes these rumours in an open letter (for publication) to Vladimir Chertkov in England, which is published in *The Times*.

24 May — Chertkov is given permission to visit Russia and visits LNT at Yasnaya Polyana after eight years of separation. He returns to England in early June.

Summer–Autumn — SAT continues to paint in oils. She copies her letters to LNT, and goes on writing *My Life*.

2–7 August — LNT visits his daughter Marija Obolenskaja at Pirogovo.

6 November — The Tolstoys' daughter Tat'jana L'vovna [Tanja] Sukhotina gives birth to a daughter of her own: Tat'jana Mikhajlovna [Tanja/Tanjusha] Sukhotina (1905–1996). After her husband Mikhail's death in 1914, Tat'jana L'vovna manages the Yasnaya Polyana estate from 1917 to 1923, and then emigrates with her daughter — first to France and later to Italy. In 1930 Tat'jana Mikhajlovna marries an Italian named Leonardo Giuseppe Albertini (1903–1960). She dies in Rome in August 1996.

December — Dr. Dushan Makovitskij takes a month-long trip to visit his home country of Slovakia (see Gusev II: 536, 539).

1906

LNT writes *What for? [Za chto?]* and *The significance of the Russian revolution [O znachenii russkoj revoljutsii]*. SAT continues her oil-painting and photography, helps look after her grand-daughter Tat'jana, continues with *My Life*, works with papers at the Historical Museum.

9–11 February — Taneev and fellow-composer Aleksandr Borisovich Gol'denvejzer (1875–1961) visit Yasnaya Polyana and play for the Tolstoys.

23 July–11 August — Chertkov pays another visit to LNT at Yasnaya Polyana.

30 July — The Tolstoys' eldest son, Sergej, marries for the second time, this time Marija Nikolaevna Zubova (1868–1939).

7–10 August — LNT, Chertkov and Dr. Makovitskij visit LNT's daughter Marija Obolenskaja at Pirogovo.

22 August — SAT takes ill, experiences severe pain on the left side of her stomach. Her Diary entry of 1 September (*Dnevniki* 2: 253) indicates she believes death to be "near at hand". On 2 September she undergoes an operation performed by Dr. Vladimir Fëdorovich Snegirëv (1847–1917), professor of gynæcology at Moscow University. He practised the methods of Dr. Grigorij Antonovich Zakhar'in, who had earlier treated SAT.

19 November — The Tolstoys' daughter Marija L'vovna [Masha] Obolenskaja takes ill with inflammation of the lungs; she dies on 27 November.

1907

January–February — SAT visits a number of art exhibits (see *Dnevniki* 2: 259, 261).

20 May — SAT receives news about the murder of her brother, St. Petersburg engineer Vjacheslav Andreevich Behrs (1861–1907), by some workers.

June — The Chertkovs arrive from England and rent a dacha for the summer in the village of Jasenki, a few kilometres from Yasnaya Polyana (see Gusev II: 589). They return to England in September.

21–29 September — Artist Il'ja Repin comes for a visit and paints portraits of LNT and SAT.

26 September — Nikolaj Nikolaevich Gusev (1882–1967) arrives at Yasnaya Polyana to take up a position as LNT's personal secretary. He is given lodging in the house of the Tolstoys' daughter Aleksandra L'vovna [Sasha] at Teljatinki (3 km from Yasnaya Polyana). On 22 October he is arrested for "Tolstoyan" activities and held until 20 December, returning to Yasnaya Polyana the following day.

26 October — LNT muses in his Diary: "It's strange that it is my lot to be silent with the people living around me and to speak only with those who are far away in time and space, who will listen to me."

17 November — The Tolstoys' son Andrej (by this time divorced) marries a second wife: Ekaterina Vasil'evna Artsimovich (*neé* Gorjainova; 1876–1959).

1908

The Diaries of S. A. Tolstaya *[Dnevniki 1860–1891]* are published by M. & S. Sabashnikov in Moscow, under the editorship of Sergej L'vovich Tolstoy.

5–6 January — Taneev and Gol'denvejzer again play for the Tolstoys.

January–March — Chertkov (visiting from England) pays two visits to LNT.

25 March — LNT writes a letter asking "all kind people" not to bother celebrating his forthcoming 80th birthday on 28 August (see *PSS* 78: N° 99). In response, a week later the Moscow organising committee abandons its celebration plans.

6 May — A difficult conversation takes place between LNT and SAT about the disposition of author's rights following LNT's death (see LNT's Diary; also Gusev II: 622).

13 May–2 June — LNT writes *I cannot be silent* [*Ne mogu molchat'*] — against capital punishment.

17 June — The Chertkovs return from England to Russia and settle at Kozlova Zaseka (not far from Yasnaya Polyana; Gusev II: 631).

2 July — LNT is uncomfortable with the fact that his Diary is read (and copied) by both his daughter Aleksandra L'vovna and Chertkov. He starts a new Diary that he calls *A diary only for myself* [*Dnevnik dlja odnogo sebja*], which he continues until 18 July (see PSS 56: № 171–174). On 6 July he writes in this new diary: "I very much want to leave. And I don't carry through. But I don't exclude it either. The main point: if I go away, am I doing this for myself? If I stay, I know that I'm not doing this for myself." And the next day: "It was a difficult time yesterday. I counted my money and figured out how to leave. I can't look at her without bad feelings. It's better now."

8 August — LNT takes seriously ill; three days later he dictates his will to Gusev (see Gusev II: 639). By 15 August he is starting to feel better.

28 August — The Tolstoy family celebrates LNT's 80th birthday.

16 September — SAT writes in her Diary (*Dnevniki* 2: 114): "I feel burdened by all the bustle of household cares, which overshadow life itself, and I have thoughts about my approaching death. It's as if everything is in preparation — what seems to be a preparation for life, but there is no life — i. e., there's no real, peaceful or leisurely life, no time for the activities which I really enjoy. This is where Lev Nikolaevich has been smart and happy his whole life. He has always worked at what he enjoys, and not because it was something he had to do. He would write whenever he wanted to. He would be out ploughing whenever he wanted to. Whenever he got tired of something, he would drop it. Would I ever try living like that? What would become of the children, or Lev Nikolaevich himself?"

18 September — After Gusev is summoned to the Tula Police Department, an uneasy conversation ensues between LNT and SAT, who fears complications with authorities (see Gusev II: 648).

20 September — SAT confides to her Diary (*Dnevniki* 2: 116–117): "I've given myself completely to household tasks. But this has been possible for me only because I've done it in conjunction with a constant communication with Nature and an admiration thereof. [...] During all this time I read articles about Lev Nikolaevich, about us, in all different languages. Nobody really knows or understands him. I know the actual essence of his nature and mind better than anybody else. But no matter what I write, people will not believe me. Lev Nikolaevich is a man of tremendous intellect and talent, a man of extraordinary imagination, sensitivity and artistic instinct. Yet he is also a man without a real heart or genuine kindness. His kindness is conceptual, not direct. [...] I am depressed and lonely in my soul; nobody loves me. Apparently, I am unworthy. There is a good deal of passion within me, an unmitigated compassion for people, — but there's not much kindness in me, either. My best qualities are a feeling of duty and motherhood."

18 December — SAT writes a letter to Gorbunov-Posadov about the need to stop publishing LNT's works written before 1881 in Posrednik (see Gusev II: 656).

1909

22 January — Regarding a priest's visit to SAT, LNT notes in his Diary: "I find it especially repugnant that he asked Sofia Andreevna to let him know when I am dying. They'll think up anything to assure people that I 'repented' before my death. And so I declare (once again, it

seems) that… *anything they may say about my deathbed confession and communion is a lie"* (italics — LNT).

30 January — In a letter, LNT gives Chertkov "full authority" [*polnoe pravo*] to publish any of his personal letters to anybody (see *PSS* 89: N° 816).

6 March — Chertkov is issued a police order to leave Tula Gubernia in three days. SAT protests in a letter published in *Russkie vedomosti*: N° 57 (11 March) and other newspapers. Subsequently, at the request of Chertkov's mother, the Tsar postpones his exile from Tula Gubernia until his health improves.

March–April — LNT suffers a bout of illness, rising from bed for the first time on 17 March, and stepping outdoors for the first time on 31 March. By 16 April he is once more riding horseback.

10–13 May — LNT makes the initial drafts of a letter to SAT to be given to her after his death — see his Diary, published in *PSS* 84: N° 840.

30 June–1 July — LNT has two meetings with Chertkov (who is forbidden to enter Tula Gubernia) in a village called Suvorovo in Orël Gubernia near Kochety (Gusev II: 697).

6 July — LNT receives an invitation to take part in the XVIII International Peace Congress in Sweden, and a second invitation three days later. On 12 July LNT accepts the invitation, but on 22 July cancels because of SAT's nervousness and opposition. When she calms down, LNT again contemplates going to Sweden, but this time SAT threatens suicide and LNT abandons the venture.

11 July — LNT is upset with SAT's intention to sue a publisher who published LNT's works without her permission (see LNT's Diary of 12 July). Two days later, however, SAT learns that she has no ownership of LNT's works and cannot go to court on his behalf. She is seriously upset.

13–14(?) July — LNT asks his sister Marija's son-in-law, Ivan Vasil'evich Denisenko (1851–1916), to prepare a document stating that he [LNT] is transferring all his works into the public domain. SAT demands ownership of his works be transferred to her (even threatening suicide), but LNT refuses. SAT suffers from neuralgia in her left hand and an inflammation of her left lung.

Late July — LNT makes repeated entries in his Diary about his overwhelming desire to leave home. On 30 July he discusses the possibility with Gusev and makes note of yet another "difficult conversation" with SAT.

3 August — The Tolstoys' daughter Aleksandra L'vovna goes to visit Chertkov and discuss plans for LNT's new will.

4 August — Gusev is arrested at Yasnaya Polyana. The following day LNT informs him of his plans to escape from Yasnaya Polyana. On 7 August LNT asks Dr. Makovitskij to clarify how he could leave Russia (Gusev II: 705, 706).

3 September — LNT (with daughter Aleksandra, Makovitskij and Sidorkov) leaves Yasnaya Polyana to visit Chertkov at Krekshino, an estate of the Pashkovs near Moscow; LNT is filmed during his trip to the railway station, and again on 17–18 September.

September–November — At Kochety LNT writes a will stating that after his death the rights to his works created after 1 January 1881 should not be in anybody's possession and that all his manuscripts should be given to Chertkov (see *PSS* 80: N° 394). On 26 October LNT learns that this will is not legally valid. LNT is upset but decides to write a new will and to transfer *all* his works to the public domain. A week later LNT signs a will conveying all rights to his works to his daughter Aleksandra for subsequent transfer to the public domain (see *PSS* 80: N° 394–395).

8 November — SAT drafts her own last will and testament, with no witnesses, and makes a list of materials for her Notes. She also writes about pain in her right eye, which is "almost completely blind" (*Dnevniki* 2: 296).

1910

SAT's collection of children's stories is published under the title *The skeleton dolls* [*Kukolki-skelettsy*] (with eight colour illustrations painted by *Peredvizhniki* ["Itinerants"] artist Aleksandr Viktorovich Moravov (1878–1951). It includes not only her stories *The skeleton dolls*, but also *Grandmother's treasure-trove* [*Babushkin klad*] and *The story of a grivennik* [*Istorija grivennika*], as well as a story composed by her youngest son Ivan, called *The rescued dachshund. Vanja's story* [*Spasënnyj taks. Rasskaz Vani*], and *Vanechka: a real occurrence from his life* [*Vanechka: istinnoe proisshestvie iz ego zhizni*].

17 January — Valentin Fëdorovich Bulgakov (1886–1966), a new secretary recommended to LNT by Chertkov, arrives at Yasnaya Polyana. He will personally prevent SAT from committing suicide after her husband's death, and will help her sort the remnant of LNT's papers. Later he will compile two volumes of his own memoirs, which have only recently been published in full (see Donskov 2012 and 2014).

29–30 March — Tomáš Masaryk visits LNT at Yasnaya Polyana (see also April 1887 & March 1888 above).

13 April — LNT writes in his Diary: "I awoke at 5 and couldn't stop thinking how to get away. And I dunno. I thought about writing. Even writing's a wretched thing, as long as I remain in this life. Talk with her? Leave? Change ever so gradually?.. It seems the latter is the only thing I can do. But it's still a challenge."

2–20 May — LNT spends three weeks at Kochety with Chertkov.

19 May — SAT: "I had a difficult conversation with Lev Nikolaevich… He reproached me for our aristocratic lifestyle and for my complaining about the difficulties in managing the household. He chased me out of Yasnaya Polyana [and said I should go] live in Odoev (a city in the western part of Tula Gubernia), or Paris, or somewhere else. I went (out of the house). It was hot, my foot was hurting, my pulse was beating fearfully, I lay down in a ditch and lay there until someone was sent with a horse to look for me. I spent the rest of the day in bed, ate nothing, and wept" (*Dnevniki* 2: 321).

23 May — LNT receives a new invitation for the XVIII Peace Congress in Sweden, scheduled for 4–6 August. On 12 June LNT declines, citing reasons of poor health (see PSS 82: Nº 58).

29 May — Another difficult conversation takes place between LNT and SAT (Gusev II: 774).

12–23 June — LNT spends two weeks visiting with Chertkov at Otradnoe near Moscow.

Late June — At Yasnaya Polyana, SAT is very nervous about LNT. She sends him several telegrams asking him to come home; he returns to find her (according to his Diary of 23 June) "worse than expected, [in a state of] hysteria and irritation … indescribable". SAT has been reading LNT's Diary, and several difficult conversations follow (Gusev II: 780–781).

26 June — SAT writes in her Diary (*Dnevniki* 2: 119): "My life with Lev Nikolaevich is becoming more unbearable by the day because of his heartlessness and cruelty toward me. And this is all the fault of Chertkov, gradually and consistently over a period of time. He has taken hold of this unfortunate old man any way he can, he has separated us from each other, he has killed the spark of artistry in Lev Nikolaevich and kindled the condemnation, hatred and denial which I have sensed in Lev Nikolaevich's articles these past few years, which he had written under the influence of a stupid evil genius."

28 June — Chertkov visits LNT. Then LNT and SAT leave to visit their son Sergej at Nikol'skoe-Vjazemskoe for his birthday.

29–30 (night) June — The Tolstoys are back to Yasnaya Polyana.

30 June — Chertkov visits Yasnaya Polyana again. SAT is nervous.

1 July — Following another visit by Chertkov, SAT writes a letter to him (as well as tells him verbally) to return LNT's diaries (*Dnevniki* 2: 127): "Chertkov peppered our whole conversation with obscenities and coarse thoughts. For example, he would cry: 'You're afraid that I will expose you through the diaries. If I wanted to, I could throw as much smut (quite an expression for a supposedly decent man) at you and your family as I liked.' […] Chertkov also snapped that if he were married to a wife like me he would have either shot himself or run off to America. Later, on coming down the stairs with our son Lëva, Chertkov maliciously said regarding me: 'I don't understand a woman who has been involved all her life in murdering her husband.' It must have been a pretty slow murder if my husband's already 82. And he persuaded Lev Nikolaevich that this was so, and that is why we are unhappy in our senior years. […] I have lost my long-time influence and love for ever, unless the Lord has mercy on me."

2 July — Chertkov's mother, Countess Elisaveta Ivanovna Chertkova (*née* Chernyshëva-Kruglikova, 1832–1922), a follower of the popular preacher Lord Radstock, visits Yasnaya Polyana.

7 July — SAT changes to a more positive tone in this diary entry (*Dnevniki* 2: 134): "Evening. No, Lev Nikolaevich has not yet been taken away from me, thank God! All my sufferings, all my energy of fervent love for him have broken the ice that was separating us these past days. Nothing can stand up to the heartfelt link between us; we are tied together by a long life and a solidly grounded love. I went up to see him as he was going to bed and said to him: 'Promise me that you will never slip away from me quietly, on the sly.' He responded: 'I have no plans to do that, and promise you that I shall never leave you; I love you' — and his voice trembled. I started crying. I embraced him, saying how afraid I was of losing him, that I fervently loved him, and despite the guilty and silly distractions over the course of my life, I never for a moment ceased loving him more than anyone else in the world, right into his old age. Lev Nikolaevich said that the feeling was mutual, and that I had nothing to worry about, that the link between us was too great for anyone to break. And I felt that this was true, and I began to feel happy. I went to my room, but returned once more to thank him for lifting the stone from my heart."

11 July — LNT writes to his daughter Aleksandra, asking her not to reproach SAT (see *PSS* 82 N° 85).

12 July — LNT sends his coachman to Teljatinki, asking Goldenvejzer to come to Yasnaya Polyana, but the coachman, by mistake, summons Chertkov instead, greatly upsetting SAT. See his letter to SAT, *PSS* 84: N° 831.

14 July — SAT notes in her diary (*Dnevniki* 2: 144–145): "Lev Nikolaevich came in, and I told him with fearful emotion that the return of the diaries hung in one side of the balance, my life in the other. It was up to him to choose. And he chose — thank God he did — to get the diaries back from Chertkov. […] For three days straight I had had nothing to eat, and that for some reason alarmed everyone, but that was the least of it… The crux of the matter was in [my] passion and strength of [my] irritation. ¶I very much regret and repent that I also irritated my children, Lëva and Tanja — especially Tanja. Once again she was so loving, compassionate and kind toward me! I love her very much. I need to allow Chertkov to visit us, even though to me he is very, very difficult and unpleasant. If I don't permit these meetings, there will be a whole litany of secret, fraternal correspondence, which is even worse."

14 July — On LNT's instructions, daughter Aleksandra goes to Teljatinki and obtains from Chertkov seven volumes of LNT's diaries for 10 years (1900–1910). SAT demands the Diaries be turned over to her, but daughter Tat'jana (Sukhotina) deposits LNT's diaries in a Tula bank under his name.

17 July — LNT visits Chertkov for the last time. He re-writes his will which, however, will turn out to contain legal inaccuracies and will need to be revised. A few days later, behind his wife's back LNT signs a codicil to his will, bequeathing his inheritance to his daughter Aleksandra. He also discusses with Aleksandra the possibility of leaving Yasnaya Polyana with her (see Gusev II: 789).

19 July — Two doctors advise LNT and SAT to separate for a while. SAT is very upset. A week later LNT writes to Chertkov about the need to stop their meetings in order to calm SAT (see PSS 89: N° 897).

26 July — SAT starts to suspect that LNT has written a new secret will. On the following day she describes in her Diary her fears of a conspiracy against her on the part of LNT and Chertkov to deprive her of her rightful inheritance (see Dnevniki 2: 159).

29 July — LNT begins a new "Diary for himself", in effect regretting the struggle he has been drawn into by Chertkov. He resolves to try a more loving approach with SAT.

2 August — LNT discusses his new will with Birjukov, who disapproves of its secrecy.

3 August — A very hostile conversation erupts between LNT and SAT (see LNT's Diary; also Gusev II: 793–94 and Bulgakov: 337–338). On the same day SAT wrote in *her* Diary: "I wanted to explain to Lev Nikolaevich the reason for my jealousy of Chertkov and showed him a page from a diary he had written in his youth, back in 1851, where he said that he had never fallen in love with women, but had many times fallen in love with men. I thought that he, like P. I. Birjukov and Dr. Makovitskij, would understand my jealousy and calm me down, but instead he went all white and displayed such a fury that I had not seen in a long, long time" (Dnevniki 2: 166).

6 August — LNT writes in his Diary: "I'm thinking of going away, leaving a letter for her. I'm afraid for her, though I think she would be better off [if I left]." Two weeks later he writes: "Now it's come to me, remembering our wedding, that there was something fateful [right then]: I wasn't ever even in love. But I couldn't help but get married."

1 September — LNT writes a letter to SAT (PSS 84: N° 833) "pouring out his heart" to her. (LNT's Diary)

2 September — At Yasnaya Polyana, SAT organises a church service in LNT's rooms in order "to expel Chertkov's spirit"; she also removes all Chertkov's portraits from LNT's bedroom.

24 September — LNT notes in his Diary: "They are tearing me apart."

25 September — The last photo of LNT and SAT together is taken.

28 September — While out riding LNT meets Chertkov accidentally. Ten days later, at SAT's invitation, Chertkov visits Yasnaya Polyana for the last time.

12 October — SAT learns about LNT's new will. She declares in her Diary (Dnevniki 2: 212–213): "Today I told Lev Nikolaevich that I knew about his arrangement. He had a pitiful, guilty look and was evasive the whole time. I said that it was wrong for him to sow evil and contention, that the children would not give up their rights without a fight. And it was painful for me to see that over the grave of a loved person could arise so much evil, reproaches, court cases and difficulties! Yes, it was an evil spirit that was arming the hand of this Chertkov — he wasn't named after the devil for nothing!" (In Russian the name *Chertkov* includes the word for 'devil' — *chert*.)

13 October — SAT expounds her feelings in her Diary (Dnevniki 2: 213–14): "The thought of suicide is growing in me again, and more forcefully than before. Now it feeds on silence. […] Life is becoming unbearable. It's like living under bombs dropped by Mr. Chertkov. […] And it is this despotism that has enslaved an unfortunate old man. Besides, back in his youth, when he wrote in his diary that he was in love with one of his chums, the main thing was he tried to please him and not irritate him. In fact one time he spent eight months of his life in Petersburg

for this very reason… He's doing the same thing now. He thinks he has to please this idiot's emotions and obey his every whim."

28 October — LNT finally leaves home (secretly, during the night) and goes first to his sister Marija in her convent in Shamordino, leaving a letter for SAT (PSS 84: N° 837). From Shamordino he pens his last letter to SAT (N° 839).

31 October — LNT leaves Shamordino; while on a train, he develops a high fever and stops at the Astapovo railway station, where the stationmaster gives him shelter in his own house.

7 November — LNT dies of pneumonia at Astapovo. Two days later he is laid to rest at Yasnaya Polyana.

9 November — SAT makes this frank declaration in her Diary (*Dnevniki* 2: 225–226): "What happened on the 26th and 27th [of October] was not recorded, but on 28 October, at 5 o'clock in the morning, Lev Nikolaevich stole out of the house along with [his doctor] D. P. Makovitskij. The excuse for his flight was that I had supposedly gone through his papers at night, and even though I did drop into his study for a moment, I did not touch a single paper; indeed, there were no papers on his desk. In a letter to me (for the whole world), his excuse was [to extricate himself from] a luxurious lifestyle and a desire to escape to solitude — to live in a hut like the peasants." LNT himself had written in his farewell letter: "I can no longer live in such luxurious conditions as I did, and I am doing what old men of my age usually do: they forsake worldly life to live out their remaining days in solitude and quietude." (PSS 84: N° 404; also *Dnevniki* 2: 509, Note 155) SAT continues: "Having learnt from Sasha and the letter of Lev Nikolaevich's flight, I threw myself into the pond in despair. Alas, Sasha and Bulgakov pulled me out. After that I did not eat for five days, but on the 31st of October at 7.30 in the morning I received a telegram from the offices of *Russkoe slovo*: LEV NIKOLAEVICH SICK AT ASTAPOVO STOP FORTY DEGREE FEVER. Our son Andrej and daughter Tanja and I went by emergency train from Tula to Astapovo. I was not permitted to see Lev Nikolaevich; they were holding him by force; they had locked the doors, tearing my heart". At this point LNT was in the company of his daughters Tat'jana [Tanja], Aleksandra [Sasha] and his son Sergej [Serëzha]. His doctor, Dushan Makovitskij — along with two colleagues — made the following statement in "Medical conclusions regarding the death of L. N. Tolstoy": "At a family consultation, in agreement with the doctors' advice, it was decided that no other relative would be allowed to see Lev Nikolaevich, since there was reason to believe that the appearance of new people would upset Lev Nikolaevich, which could have a fatal effect on his life, which was hanging by a thread." (*Dnevniki* 2: 509–510, Note 157)

10 November — SAT falls ill herself; her illness lasts until the end of November.

15 November — SAT notes in her Diary (*Dnevniki* 2: 330): "My son Serëzha, Mar'ja Aleksandrovna, Bulygin and Ge spent the day with me. [My daughter] Sasha came, and she and I got along well. I did a lot of crying. My final separation from Lev Nikolaevich was unbearable."

16 November — SAT writes in her Diary (*Dnevniki* 2: 330): "The whole village of Yasnaya Polyana — peasant men, women and children — gathered today at the grave on the fortieth day of Lev Nikolaevich's passing, which we fixed up and decorated with fir branches and wreaths. Three times they fell to their knees, doffed their caps and sang 'Eternal memory' [*Vechnaja pamjat'*]. I found myself crying and suffering a lot, but at the same time I was heartened by the people's love. And how affectionate they all were toward me. I wrote my sister Tanja, my daughter Tanja, Il'ja and Andrjusha. [I felt] lonely and burdened!"

1911

SAT publishes a twenty-volume edition of LNT's works, in which she attempts to correct a series of earlier errors by carefully checking the text against LNT's original manuscripts (*Childhood, The raid, The Kreutzer Sonata*).

January — The Tolstoys' daughter Aleksandra sends out a notarised document forbidding SAT access to the room in the Historical Museum containing family documents and ordering her to cease publication of the latest edition of LNT's works. SAT files a counter-suit. (See entry under 18 December 1914 below.)

10 May & 18 November — SAT twice petitions the Tsar with an appeal to have Yasnaya Polyana acquired as State property. In her first appeal she writes as follows: "The passing of my husband, Count L. N. Tolstoy, and his will, have so impoverished his large family, consisting of seven children and twenty-five grandchildren, that some are no longer in a position either to bring up or even to feed their children. It is with heartfelt pain that we recognise the necessity of selling the valuable estate the deceased willed to us before his death — an estate near the village of Yasnaya Polyana consisting of 885 desjatinas [1 *desjatina* = 1.09 hectares]. We no longer have any possibility of maintaining it in our family. In any case, even though selling off the land in small lots would be financially advantageous to us, we find that prospect exceedingly distasteful, as the birthplace and burial site of a man so dear to us could easily fall into obscurity. It is our fervent wish to hand over his 'cradle and grave' to the protection of the State. It is this motivation, along with our cramped financial status, that emboldens us to resort to the mercy of your Imperial Majesty in petitioning you to allow the acquisition of Yasnaya Polyana as State property. Through such mercy granted by you, Your Majesty, my many grandchildren would be afforded the opportunity to receive an education. They would grow up conscious of their undying gratitude to our benevolent Tsar who has generously extended his hand to assist them and their parents, as well as an aggrieved and impoverished widow." (T. V. Komarova, "*Angel Jasnoj Poljany*" [The angel of Yasnaya Polyana]. *Pamjatniki Otechestva* N° 28 (1992): 91.) The State declines SAT's request for purchase, but the Tsar offers her a considerable pension. See also the entry for 15-20 April 1918 below.

13 May — SAT goes to the Moscow City Duma [Council] to see council head, Nikolaj Ivanovich Guchkov (1860–1935), about selling the Khamovniki house to the city. On 28 May it is announced in the press that the Council of Ministers has decided to purchase Yasnaya Polyana for 500,000 roubles.

28 August — SAT makes special note in her Diary (*Dnevniki* 2: 355) of LNT's birthday: "There were about 300 visitors to the house and many of them at the gravesite. I didn't go. It was hard for me to see so many policemen and at the same time so little genuine feeling for Lev Nikolaevich."

7 November — SAT records in her Diary (*Dnevniki* 2: 363): "A sad day — the day Lev Nikolaevich died [one year ago]. All my sons came, except Lëva. We had a flood of reporters, members of the Tolstoy Society — about 500 visitors in all. Our peasants came to see me, and sang "Eternal memory" over the grave. My granddaughter Tanjushka Sukhotina was with me. There was a lot of bustle, talk about selling Yasnaya Polyana, and heaviness on my heart."

1912

SAT's article *L. N. Tolstoy's marriage [Zhenit'ba L. N. Tolstogo]* is published in *Russkoe slovo* (N° 219) and *Reminiscences* (on *The power of darkness*) in *Tolstovskij ezhegodnik* [Tolstoy annual]. She publishes an article "*Pervoe predstavlenie komedii L. N. Tolstogo «Plody prosveshchenija»*" [First

performance of LNT's *comedy "The fruits of enlightenment"]* in *Solntse Rossii* (N° 145). In addition, she continues her work on *My Life,* reads all the articles she can about LNT and receives visitors.

21 April — SAT sells all her unsold edition copies to Ivan Dmitrievich Sytin (1851–1934), a Russian publisher who printed books for Posrednik, a publishing firm set up in 1884 jointly by LNT and Chertkov.

28 August — In her Diary SAT once again takes note of LNT's birthday, mentioning her visit to his grave accompanied by her granddaughter Tanjushka Sukhotina as being "the best moment of the whole day" (*Dnevniki* 2: 378).

October — SAT goes to see the Minister of Internal Affairs on the matter of the official banning of the film *Ukhod velikogo startsa* [Departure of a grand old man] (also known as *Zhizn' L. N. Tolstogo* [The life of L. N. Tolstoy]) — a 1912 film directed by Jakov Protazanov and Elizaveta Thiman. SAT's son Lev L'vovich Tolstoj and her sister Tat'jana Andreevna Kuzminskaja were at the first showing in St. Petersburg; it was the first film in Russian history to be banned outright by the censors.

7 November — On the second anniversary of Lev Nikolaevich's passing, SAT notes (*Dnevniki* 2: 382): "From early morning there were all sorts of visitors to the house and the grave, [including] police, cinematographers, reporters and the general public. My son Andrjusha came, later Serëzha. Toward evening, after everyone had gone, I walked to the grave with Andrjusha. Serëzha went on his own."

13 December — SAT reprises the "very challenging" task of transcribing and editing all LNT's letters to her throughout their married life (see *Dnevniki* 2: 383).

1913

SAT prepares and publishes *Letters of Count L. N. Tolstoy to his wife 1862–1910* [Pis'ma grafa L. N. Tolstogo k zhene 1862–1910], with commentaries. A second edition appears in 1915.

SAT publishes *Four visits by Count L. Tolstoy to the Optina Pustyn' Monastery* [Chetyre poseshchenija gr. L. Tolstym monastyrja Optina pustyn'] in *Tolstovskij ezhegodnik.*

March — SAT buys from her sons the portions of Yasnaya Polyana belonging to them, amounting to 200 desjatinas.

22 March — SAT visits Gaspra (in the Crimea), accompanied by Julija Igumnova (see October 1900 above) and remarks in her Diary on the beauty of the surroundings (*Dnevniki* 2: 389; see also *My Life,* VIII.18).

July — At the request of Semën Afanas'evich Vengerov (1855–1920), Director of the *Russian Book Chamber* [Rossijskaja knizhnaja palata] and a close friend of LNT's, SAT agrees to write a short Autobiography, which she completes by the end of October 1913.

7 November — SAT once again makes a Diary entry (*Dnevniki* 2: 400) on the anniversary of LNT's death: "It's been three years now, and still painful! The day went well. As soon as I got up I went to the grave, where a variety of visitors had already gathered. Later about a hundred people came to the house, mostly young people. Four of my sons came: Serëzha, Il'ja, Andrjusha and Misha."

1914

May — SAT compiles an inventory of books and objects room by room, cupboard by cupboard, which she records in an oilcloth-covered notebook. On the inside front cover she writes in black ink: "List compiled and checked by S. A. Tolstaja, May 1914." (See also May–June 1918 below.)

Summer — SAT's daughter Aleksandra (Sasha) goes off to war as a nurse. Her son Lev becomes a Red Cross representative. Her son Il'ja becomes a correspondent for the paper *Russkoe Slovo*, while her son Mikhail goes off to war.

9 August — A telegram is received concerning the death of SAT's son-in-law Mikhail Sergeevich Sukhotin. SAT goes to Kochety to comfort her daughter Tat'jana.

18 December — SAT's access to LNT's manuscripts which were transferred to the Historical Museum in 1904 (see 12 January 1904 above) is restored by a Senate decree; access was cut off after his death as a result of a dispute which had broken out between SAT and her daughter Aleksandra L'vovna, to whom LNT had left them in his will. (See entry under January 1911 above.)

1915

28–29 January — SAT once again gives Tolstoy's manuscripts to the Rumjantsev Museum for preservation. Pursuant to her appeal to the Museum's director on 26 January and his reply the next day, SAT organises a special room in the Museum called "Tolstoy's study".

7 June — SAT receives word about the death of her composer-friend Sergej Ivanovich Taneev.

1916

11 February — SAT receives word about her son Andrej's illness. He dies on 24 February.

November — SAT's son Il'ja goes to America to give lectures on LNT; her son Lev heads to Japan for the same reason. SAT ceases writing *My Life* (which by this point has reached the end of 1901).

1917

5 March — SAT writes in her Diary (*Dnevniki* 2: 443): "A red-letter day for Yasnaya Polyana. Workers came from the cast-iron foundry at Kosaja Gora, bringing red flags and pins to do reverence to Tolstoy's house and widow. Carrying portraits of Lev Nikolaevich, they walked to his grave through deep snow and biting winds. My two Tat'janas walked with them. The workers sang, made speeches, all about freedom. In response I made a brief speech too about Lev Nikolaevich's legacy. At the grave they sang *Vechnaja pamjat'* and took snapshots."

30 April — SAT comments in her Diary (*Dnevniki* 2: 445) on the number of soldiers visitng Yasnaya Polyana, who have treated her and her daughter Tanja "very kindly", though she is concerned about running out of provisions for the family and their livestock.

Mid-to-late October — SAT records several instances of soldiers and police sent in to protect the family and the estate, in view of the widespread instances of arson in the area (*Dnevniki* 2: 452).

29 December — In a newspaper article Valentin Bulgakov (LNT's last secretary) writes: "The preservation of the historic estate is now guaranteed more than ever before. [...] The protection of Yasnaya Polyana is under the direct care of Tula political organisations, which have appointed a special constant guard to keep watch over the estate... The inhabitants of the estate are being supplied with food provisions... Just a few days ago a telephone was installed, connecting Yasnaya Polyana with Tula and Moscow... The shadow of Lev Nikolaevich is covering it and, hopefully, protecting it" (*Dnevniki* 2: 593, Note 2).

1918

15–20 April (N. S.) 146[?] — On the basis of a decision by the Council of People's Commissars [abbreviated in Russian as *Sovnarkom*] of 30 March, the Gubernia Conference on Land Apportionment adopts a resolution "on the recognition of L. N. Tolstoy's Yasnaya Polyana estate as not being subject to apportionment among the citizens of neighbouring village and its function as an historical treasure to be used only for cultural and educational purposes". At first the local peasants accept this decision, then decide to take over the land in any case, but later change their minds again (see *Dnevniki* 2: 594–595). Note that dates from this point on will be given according to the New-Style (Gregorian) calendar, adopted by the new Bolshevik régime in February 1918.

3 September — SAT writes a new will to include her daughter Aleksandra L'vovna [Sasha] among her inheritors. "I had excluded her earlier on account of her horrible treatment of me after the death of her father. I have now forgiven her" (*Dnevniki* 2: 463).

1919

1 February — SAT confides to her Diary (*Dnevniki* 2: 468–469): "I spent the whole day writing a commentary to [LNT's] *Letters of Count L. N. Tolstoy to his wife* [*Pis'ma grafa L. N. Tolstogo k zhene*]. I became very depressed reading some of the letters he had written to me, in which I could feel his sufferings caused by my reproaches, my demands for him to stay with me, and so forth. My desire not to separate from my husband grew, after all, out of my love for him! I loved him very much right to the end of my life."

2 February — SAT and her daughter Tat'jana L'vovna appeal to the board of the educational Yasnaya Polyana Society with a request to transfer the management of the estate and its buildings to this same Society. Their request is granted, and the management is entrusted to Prince Nikolaj Leonidovich [Kolja] Obolenskij (see *Dnevniki* 2: 599, Note 8). Yasnaya Polyana remains under the Society's management up until 1921, when the All-Russian Central Executive Committee [*Vserossijskij Tsentral'nyj Ispolnitel'nyj Komitet/VTsIK*] decides to nationalise the estate.

14 July — SAT writes a letter to be read after her death: "Apparently the circle of my life is closing, I am gradually dying, and I wanted to tell everyone with whom I have been living recently and before, Farewell and forgive me. ¶Farewell, my dear, beloved children, especially my daughter Tanja, whom I love more than anyone else in the world, whom I ask forgiveness for all the difficulties she had to endure on account of me. ¶Forgive me, my daughter Sasha, that I did not give you sufficient love, and I thank you for your kind treatment of me these last times.

¶Forgive me, too, my sister Tanja, for not being able, despite my immeasurable love for you, to make your life easier and comforting you in your lonely and difficult situation. I ask Kolja to forgive me for being sometimes unkind to him. No matter what the circumstances might have been, I ought to have better understood his difficult and challenging situation and treated him more kindly. Forgive me, too, all of you who have served me over my lifetime; I thank you all for your service. I have a special relationship with you, my dear, fervently beloved granddaughter Tanjushka. You made my life especially joyful and happy. Farewell, my darling! Be happy; I thank you for your love and tenderness. Do not forget your grandmother who loves you, S. Tolstaya." (*Dnevniki* 2: 600, Note 18)

8 October — In a memo to the Council of People's Commissars adopted at a special session of the Yasnaya Polyana Society, the Society warns about the danger of the estate falling into a war zone given the presence of General Denikin's army on the southern front. The Central

Executive Committee issues a corresponding order and the Red Army troops which have gathered in the village of Yasnaya Polyana are withdrawn.

4 November — SAT dies at Yasnaya Polyana from inflammation of the lungs. She is buried in the family cemetery at Nikol'skij Church in the neighbouring village of Kochaki.

LIST OF PERIODICAL TITLES

WITH THEIR ENGLISH EQUIVALENTS

Artist — Artist
Biblioteka dlja chtenija — Reader's Library
Detskij otdykh — Childhood Leisure
Detskoe chtenie — Childhood Reading
Igrushechka — The Little Toy
Kolos'ja — The Ears [i.e., of corn or wheat]
Moskovskie novosti — Moscow News
Moskovskie vedomosti — Moscow Gazette
Nedelja — Week
Novoe vremja — New Time
Obnovlenie — Renewal
Ogonёk — Spark
Otechestvennye zapiski — Notes of the Fatherland
Pamjatniki Otechestva — Memorials of the Fatherland
Pravitel'stvennyj vestnik — Government Herald
Russkaja starina — Russian Antiquity
Russkij khudozhestvennyj listok — Russian Art Bulletin
Russkoe bogatstvo — Russian Wealth
Russkoe slovo — Russian Word
Russkie vedomosti — Russian Gazette
Russkij vestnik — Russian Herald
Sankt-Peterburgskie vedomosti — St. Petersburg Gazette
Severnyj vestnik — Northern Herald
Solntse Rossii — Sun of Russia
Sovremennik — The Contemporary
Svobodnoe slovo — The Free Word
Tolstovskij ezhegodnik — Tolstoy Annual
Tserkovnye vedomosti — Church Gazette
Vestnik Evropy — Herald of Europe
Voprosy filosofii i psikhologii — Issues in Philosophy and Psychology
Zhurnal dlja vsekh — Journal for Everybody

INDEX OF WORKS

BY LEV NIKOLAEVICH TOLSTOY AND
SOFIA ANDREEVNA TOLSTAYA

All works are listed in English alphabetical order; Russian titles, where different, are indicated in brackets following the English. Unspecified numerals designate the respective **letter numbers** in which the works are mentioned, either in the text or in the footnotes. Numerals after the heading *Chr.* indicate a listing by year in the **Chronology**. Italicised numerals designate page numbers in Andrew Donskov's **Editor's Introduction**. Note that the titles of stories and articles, as well as books, by either Tolstoy or Tolstaya, are italicized throughout this volume.

*Works by Tolstaya are marked with an asterisk.

A

After the ball [Posle bala] — *Chr.* 1903
Aggej — LVI
Albert [Al'bert] — *Chr.* 1857
Alyosha the Pot [Alësha Gorshok] — *Chr.* 1905
And the light shines in darkness [I svet vo t'me svetit] — *Chr.* 1902; LV
Anna Karenina — *Chr.* 1870, 1872–78; XXXVI--XXXVIII, XLII, LIV, LVIII
*Autobiography [Avtobiografija] — XLV, XLVI

B

Bethink yourselves! [Odumajtes'!] — *Chr.* 1904
Boyhood [Otrochestvo] — 112; *Chr.* 1854, 1856, 1878; XL

C

Catechesis [Katekhezis] — see: *Christian teachings*
Childhood [Detstvo] — 5, 111, 112, 167, 182; *Chr.* 1851, 1852, 1856, 1878, 1911; E5
Chinese wisdom [Kitajskaja mudrost'] — 102
Christian teachings [Khristianskoe uchenie] — 175, 176, 191
Complete Collected Works [Polnoe sobranie sochinenij / PSS] — 112, 121, 125, 151, 152; *Chr.* 1864, 1873, 1878, 1880, 1883, 1885–87, 1889–91, 1897, 1898; XXVII, LXV, LXVI
confession, A [Ispoved'] — 77, 78, 83, 84, 86, 118, 124; *Chr.* 1879, 1880, 1882
Cossacks, The [Kazaki] — 12, 65, 118; *Chr.* 1856–58, 1862, 1863

D

death of Ivan Ilyich, The [Smert' Ivana Il'icha] — 59, 115, 154; *Chr.* 1882, 1884, 1886, 1891
Decembrists, The [Dekabristy] — 118; *Chr.* 1856, 1860, 1878, 1879
destruction of hell and its restoration, The [Razrushenie ada i vosstanovlenie ego] — *Chr.* 1902
devil, The [D'javol] — 224
*Diaries I [Dnevniki I] — 152; *Chr.* 1862, 1870–72, 1882, 1887, 1890, 1891, 1897–99, 1918, 1919; LVIII
*Diaries II [Dnevniki II] — 214; *Chr.* 1891, 1901–03, 1906–13, 1917; XXXIII (epigraph), XXXIII, XLIV, LVII
*Diaries III [Dnevniki III] — *Chr.* 1899
*Diaries of Sofia Andreevna Tolstaya, The [S. A. Tolstaja. Dnevniki 1860–1891] — *Chr.* 1908
Diary of L. N. Tolstoy [Dnevnik L. N. Tolstogo] — 2, 124, 144, 174, 180, 181, 187, 194, 201, 212, 228, 236, 239; *Chr.* 1847, 1850, 1856, 1858–61, 1863, 1878, 1881, 1884, 1891, 1892, 1895–97, 1901, 1907–10; XXXV, XLVII, LIV
diary only for myself, A [Dnevnik dlja odnogo sebja] — 231; *Chr.* 1908

E

Esarhaddon, King of Assyria [Assirijskij tsar' Asarkhaddon] — *Chr.* 1903
*Ezhednevniki [Daily diaries] — *Chr.* 1893

F

Family happiness [Semejnoe schast'e] — 12, 75, 167; Chr. 1859

Famine or no famine [Golod ili ne golod] — Chr. 1898

Father Sergius [Otets Sergij] — Chr. 1890, 1898

first distiller, The [Pervyj vinokur] — LVI

For every day [Na kazhdyj den'] — 132, 227

*Four visits by Count L. Tolstoy to the Optina Pustyn' Monastery [Chetyre poseshchenija gr. L. Tolstym monastyrja Optina pustyn'] — 50; Chr. 1913

frightful question, A [Strashnyj vopros] — 155–58; LXV

fruits of enlightenment, The [Plody prosveshchenija] — 78, 146, 157; Chr. 1886, 1889–92, 1912

G

God sees the truth, but waits [Bog pravdu vidit, da ne skoro skazhet] — LVI

Gospel in brief, The [Kratkoe izlozhenie Evangelija] — 66, 86; LXIII

*Grandmother's treasure-trove: a legend [Babushkin klad: predanie] — Chr. 1895, 1910

*Groanings [Stony] — Chr. 1904

H

Hadji-Murat [Hadzhi-Murat] — 204, 212; Chr. 1896, 1898, 1902, 1904

I

I cannot be silent [Ne mogu molchat'] — 222; Chr. 1908

K

Kingdom of God is within you, The [Tsarstvo Bozhie vnutri vas] — 132, 168, 171, 204; Chr. 1890, 1893

Kreutzer Sonata, The [Krejtserova sonata] — 147, 148, 152; Chr. 1887, 1889–91, 1897, 1911; LXV, XXXIX

L

L. N. Tolstoy and A. A. Tolstaja: Correspondence [L. N. Tolstoj i A. A. Tolstaja: Perepiska] — LVI

L. N. Tolstoy: Correspondence with his sister and brothers [L. N. Tolstoj: Perepiska s sestroj i brat'jami] — LIV, LVI

*L. N. Tolstoy's marriage [Zhenit'ba L. N. Tolstogo] — Chr. 1912

Leo Tolstoy & Nikolaj Strakhov: Complete correspondence [L. N. Tolstoj — N. N. Strakhov: Polnoe sobranie perepiski] — LXIII

Letter to the editors of Moskovskie vedomosti [Pis'mo redaktoram «Moskovskikh vedomostej»] — Chr. 1873

Letters of Count L. N. Tolstoy to his wife, 1862–1910 [Pis'ma grafa L. N. Tolstogo k zhene, 1862–1910] — 143; Chr. 1913, 1919; LXVI, LXVII

*Letters of S. A. Tolstaya to L. N. Tolstoy [Tolstaja S. A. Pis'ma k L. N. Tolstomu] — XXXIV

Living corpse, The [Zhivoj trup] (unfinished) — Chr. 1900

Lucerne [Ljutsern] — Chr. 1857

M

Master and man [Khozjain i rabotnik] — XLIII

Mother (Notes of a mother) [Mat'] (Zapiski materi) — 206

*My Life [Moja zhizn'] — 1–3, 50, 104, 108, 113, 115, 119–21, 124, 130, 132, 134, 141, 148, 150, 152, 178, 180, 192, 205; Chr. 1868, 1876–78, 1881–89, 1891–1901, 1904–06, 1912, 1913, 1916; XLIII–XLVIII, LIX, LXI, LXVI, LXVII

N

*Natasha (composed in SAT's maidenhood) — Chr. Early 1860s, 1862; XLI

New primer [Novaja azbuka] — *Chr.* 1874, 1875; *XLVII*

Nikolai Palkin [Nikolaj Palkin] — 131, 141

Notes of a billiard marker [Zapiski markëra] — *Chr.* 1855

Notes of a madman [Zapiski sumasshedshego] — 140

O

On life [O zhizni] — 138, 140, 144; *Chr.* 1887–89; *LIV, XXXIX, XLV*

On popular education [O narodnom obrazovanii] — *Chr.* 1874

On the famine [O golode] — 157, 162; *Chr.* 1891

On the means of aiding famine victims [O sredstvakh pomoshchi naseleniju, postradavshemu ot neurozhaja] — 159

On the Moscow census [O perepisi v Moskve] — 71; *Chr.* 1882

On war [O vojne] — 191

P

path of life, The [Put' zhizni] — 227

Peter the Publican [Pëtr Khlebnik] — 95; *LVI*

Polikushka — 12, 28; *Chr.* 1863; *XXXVIII*

power of darkness, The [Vlast' t'my] — *Chr.* 1886–88, 1890, 1895, 1912; *XLIII*

Preface to the Russian edition of Guy de Maupassant's collection «Sur l'eau» [Predislovie k russkomu izdaniju sbornika G. de Mopassana «Na vode»] — *Chr.* 1894

Primer [Azbuka] — 8; *Chr.* 1868, 1871, 1872, 1891, 1896; *XLII*

R

raid, The [Nabeg] — *Chr.* 1853, 1911

Readers [Knigi dlja chtenija] — 35; *Chr.* 1874

Reminiscences [Vospominanija] — *Chr.* 1903, 1912

Reply to the Synod [Otvet Sinodu] — *LXVI*

*rescued dachshund, The. Vanja's story [Spasënnyj taks. Rasskaz Vani] — *Chr.* 1895, 1910

Resurrection [Voskresenie] — 182, 187, 205; *Chr.* 1887, 1889, 1898, 1899; *XLIII, LIV, LVI*

S

Sevastopol' in August 1855 [Sevastopol' v avguste 1855 goda] — *Chr.* 1856

Sevastopol' in December [Sevastopol' v dekabre] — *Chr.* 1855

Sevastopol' in May [Sevastopol' v mae] — *Chr.* 1855

Shakespeare and drama [O Shekspire i drame] — *Chr.* 1903

significance of the Russian revolution, The [O znachenii russkoj revoljutsii] — *Chr.* 1906

*skeleton dolls, The [Kukolki-skelettsy] — 226; *Chr.* 1910; *XLVII*

snowstorm, The [Metel'] — *Chr.* 1856

*Song without words [Pesnja bez slov] — *Chr.* 1889, 1895–1900, 1897, 1900; *XLVIII*

*story of a grivennik, The [Istorija grivennika] — *Chr.* 1910

story of Yemilyan and the empty drum, The [Rabochij Emel'jan i pustoj baraban] — 132

Strider, The [Kholstomer] — 116, 118; *LVIII*

T

Teachings of the twelve apostles [Uchenie 12 apostolov] — 109; *XXXIX*

Themselves outwitted [Iskhitrilas'] — 146; *Chr.* 1886

Three deaths [Tri smerti] — *Chr.* 1859

Three questions [Tri voprosa] — *Chr.* 1903

To political activists [K politicheskim dejateljam] — *LIV*

To the Tsar and his associates [Tsarju i ego pomoshchnikam] — *LXVI*

Toil, death and disease [Trud, smert' i bolezn'] — *Chr.* 1903

translation and harmony of the four Gospels, A [Soedinenie i perevod chetyrëkh Evangelij] — 124; *Chr.* 1880; *LIX*

Two hussars [Dva gusara] — 20; *Chr.* 1856

Two old men [Dva starika] — 118

V

*Vanechka: a real occurrence from his life [Vanechka: istinnoe proisshestvie iz ego zhizni] — Chr. 1910

W

War and Peace [Vojna i mir] — 2, 4, 5, 10, 12, 16–18, 20, 22, 27, 30, 33–35, 37, 55, 78, 167; Chr. 1862–69, 1873; XXXVI, XXXVIII, XLI, XLII, XLV
War stories [Voennye rasskazy] — Chr. 1856
What for? [Za chto?] — Chr. 1906
What I believe [V chem moja vera?] — 84, 87, 88, 94, 96, 97, 114, 118; Chr. 1883–85; E10
What is art? [Chto takoe iskusstvo?] — 146, 191; Chr. 1889, 1896, 1897

What is religion? [Chto takoe religija?] — Chr. 1902
What men live by [Chem ljudi zhivy] — 68, 70, 108, 111, 132; LVI
What then must be done? [Tak chto zhe nam delat'?] — 69, 71, 101, 104, 112, 119, 121, 125, 132; Chr. 1882, 1886
*Who is to blame? [Kto vinovat?] — Chr. 1891, 1892–1893; XLV, XLVI
wood-cutting, The [Rubka lesa] — Chr. 1855

Y

Year 1805, The [1805-j god] (see also: War and Peace) — 4, 10, 16, 17, 22, 30; Chr. 1865–67
Youth [Junost'] — Chr. 1856, 1857; XL

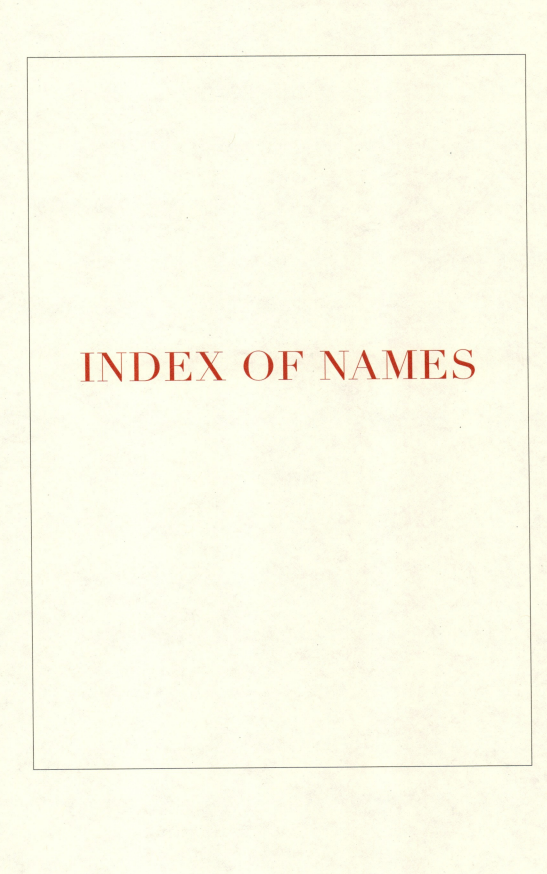

INDEX OF NAMES

Unspecified numerals designate the respective **letter numbers** in which the names are mentioned, either in the text or in the footnotes. Numerals after the heading *Chr.* indicate a listing by year in the **Chronology**. Italicised numerals designate one of the 16 sections of Andrew Donskov's **Introductory Essay**.

A

Abakumova, Ol'ga — 27

Abramovich, Marija Ivanovna (SAT's midwife) — 16, 43, 64

Abrikosov, Khrisanf Nikolaevich (Tolstoyan) — 213, 219

Abrikosov, Vladimir Alekseevich (entrepreneur) — 113

Abrikosova, Natasha — *see: Obolenskaja, Natal'ja Leonidovna*

Afanas'ev, Fedot Vasil'evich (cook to the Raevskijs) — 102, 155

Afanas'ev, Vladimir Afanas'evich — 215

Aicard, Jean (French writer) — 184

Aksakov, Ivan Sergeevich (journal editor) — 18, 22; *LXIII, XL*

Albertini, Leonardo Giuseppe — *Chr.* 1905

Alekseev, Vasilij Ivanovich (teacher) — 52, 55, 57, 64, 66, 77, 85, 102, 124

Alekseeva, Elizaveta Aleksandrovna (wife to V. I. Alekseev) — 64

Alekseeva, Marija Vasil'evna (daughter to V. I. Alekseev) — 66

Alëkhin, Aleksej Vasil'evich (brother to Arkadij Vasil'evich Alëkhin) — 163

Alëkhin, Arkadij Vasil'evich ('People's will' follower) — 138, 163

Alëkhin, Mitrofan Vasil'evich (brother to Arkadij Vasil'evich Alëkhin) — 163

Alësha (the Tolstoys' son) — *see: Tolstoj, Aleksej L'vovich*

Alexander I/II — *see: Romanov, Emperor Alexander I/II*

Alexandrine — *see: Tolstaja, Aleksandra Andreevna*

Amfilokhij, Archimandrite (secular name: Pavel Ivanovich Sergieskij-Kazantsev) — 94

Amiel, Henri (Swiss moral philosopher) — 165, 166

Anikeeva, Ol'ga Dmitrievna (*née* Gorchakova; cousin to LNT) — 35

Anke, Nikolaj Bogdanovich (professor of medicine) — 13, 16, 32, 114

Annochka (the Behrs' maid) — 20, 139, 214

Antonious, Metropolitan — *Chr.* 1901

Arbuzov, Pëtr Fëdorovich (caretaker, father to S. P. Arbuzov) — 4

Arbuzov, Sergej Petrovich [Serëzhka] (servant) — 4, 15, 19, 21, 54, 82, 92

Arbuzova, Arina Grigor'evna [Arisha] (wife to S. P. Arbuzov) — 92

Arbuzova, Marija Afanas'evna (nanny) — 16, 40, 41, 43, 69, 76, 71, 73, 79, 80, 95, 99, 104, 139

Archer, Herbert (Chertkov's English assistant) — 206

Arenskij, Anton Stepanovich (composer) — *XXXV, XL*

Aristotle (philosopher) — 139

Arkhangel'skij, Pëtr Andreevich (manager of Samara farmstead) — 85, 92

Armfel'd, Aleksandr Osipovich (professor of medicine) — 16

Arnautov family — 82; *LXI*

Arnautov, Ivan Aleksandrovich (owner of Moscow house purchased by the Tolstoys) — 81, 85

Arsen'eva, Valerija Vladimirovna — 75; *Chr.* 1856

Artsimovich, Ekaterina Vasil'evna (*neé* Gorjainova) — *Chr.* 1907

Aubert, Mlle (Swiss governess) — 192

Auerbach, Erich (German writer) — *XL*

Aurelius, Marcus (philosopher) — *XLV*

Avdot'ja Fadeevna (the Tolstoys' cook) — 174

Azarova, Natal'ja Ivanovna (biographer) — *LVIII*

B

Bach, Johann Sebastian (composer) — 226

Bakhrushin, Aleksej Aleksandrovich (manufacturer) — 217

Bakunin, Aleksej Il'ich (surgeon, nephew to an anarchist) — 208

Bakunin, Pavel (philosopher) — *XL*

Bal'mont, Konstantin Dmitrievich — *Chr.* 1901

Bannikov, Mitrofan Nikolaevich [Mitrokha] (foreman) — 71, 90, 93, 100–102

Bannikova, Anna Petrovna (farm-worker) — 19, 21

Bannikova, Avdot'ja Ivanovna [Dushka] (daughter to A. P. Mikhajlova) — 21, 26

Bannikova (Mikhajlova), Avdot'ja (Agaf'ja/Evdokija) Nikolaevna [Dunjasha] (maid, wife to A. S. Orekhov) — 16, 21, 26, 69, 71, 75, 77, 79, 90, 93, 95, 97, 103, 219; *Chr.* 1896

Bannikova, Varvara Nikolaevna (second daughter to LNT's servant Nikolaj) — 79

Baratynskij, Frants Ivanovich (lieutenant in the *Zaseka*) — 91, 107

Bartenev, Petr Ivanovich (historian and bibliographer) — 34, 39

Bartlett, Rosamund (Tolstoy biographer) — *XXXVII*

Barykova, Praskov'ja Vasil'evna — *see: Tolstaja, Praskov'ja Vasil'evna*

Bashilov, Mikhail Sergeevich (artist, son to Sof'ja Mikhajlovna Islen'eva) — 27, 32, 34; *Chr.* 1866

Basil the Great, Saint — 214

Basinskij, Pavel Valer'evich (literary critic) — 158; *E3*

Battersby, William (Church of England representative) — 171

Bazykina, Aksin'ja (*née* Sakharova) — *Chr.* 1858, 1860

Bazykina, Ol'ga Rodionovna (*née* Egorova) [Myshka] — 4, 5

Beethoven, Ludwig van (composer) — 200, 201; *E8*

Beklemishev family — 92

Beklemishev, Fëdor Andreevich (art teacher) — 92, 105

Beklemisheva, Dar'ja Aleksandrovna (wife to F. A. Beklemishev) — 105

Beklemisheva, Elizaveta Fëdorovna (daughter to F. A. Beklemishev) — 116, 137

Beloborodov, Jakov Fëdorovich (notary) — 84; *Chr.* 1904

Berger, Ivan Aleksandrovich (Yasnaya Polyana manager) — 158, 163, 170, 171

Berkengejm, Abram Moiseevich — *Chr.* 1903

Berkengejm, Grigorij Moiseevich — 214; *Chr.* 1903, 1904

Behrs family — 114; *E8*, *XLIX*

Behrs, Aleksandr Aleksandrovich (SAT's cousin) — 2; *Chr.* 1868

Behrs, Aleksandr Andreevich [Sasha] (SAT's brother) — 3, 4, 13, 20, 27, 42, 76, 81, 134, 136, 177, 206, 209, 214, 219; *Chr.* 1884

Behrs, Andrej Evstaf'evich (SAT's father) — 1, 10, 12–17, 20, 27, 28, 30, 32, 34, 182, 196; *Chr.* 1844, 1868; *XXXVIII*

Behrs, Anna Aleksandrovna [Anet] (wife to SAT's brother A. A. [Sasha] Behrs) — 205

Behrs, Elena Aleksandrovna [Lëlja] (SAT's cousin) — 43, 45, 48, 52

Behrs, Elizaveta Andreevna [Liza] (SAT's elder sister) — 2, 13, 15, 16, 18–21, 27, 30, 33, 34, 42, 47, 81, 89; *Chr.* 1843, 1861, 1862, 1868, 1898

Behrs, Elisaveta Ivanovna (*née* Vul'fert) — *Chr.* 1855

Behrs, Evgenija Petrovna (daughter to SAT's brother Pëtr Andreevich Behrs) — 47

Behrs, Ljubov' Aleksandrovna (*née* Islavina) [SAT's mother] — 14, 16, 18, 20, 27, 30, 32, 34, 39–41, 47, 48; *Chr.* 1844, 1856, 1862, 1879, 1886

Behrs, Matrëna Dmitrievna [Patti] — *Chr.* 1884

Behrs, Natalija Petrovna [Natusja] (SAT's niece, daughter to Pëtr Andreevich Behrs) — 67

Behrs, Nikolaj Stepanovich (son to S. A. Behrs) — 226

Behrs, Ol'ga Dmitrievna (*née* Postnikova; wife to SAT's brother Petja) — 67

Behrs, Pëtr Andreevich (SAT's brother) — 15–17, 20, 27, 33–35, 44, 47, 59, 62, 67, 68, 137, 139, 157

Behrs, Stepan Andreevich [Stëpa] (SAT's brother) — 16, 20, 27, 35, 39, 41, 42, 44, 45, 47, 54, 55, 226; *Chr.* 1871, 1872

Behrs, Tat'jana Andreevna — *see: Kuzminskaja, Tat'jana Andreevna*

Behrs, Vjacheslav Andreevich [Slava, Slavochka] (SAT's younger brother) — 3, 16, 20, 27, 39, 47; *Chr.* 1883, 1907; *XLIX*

Behrs, Vladimir Andreevich (SAT's brother) — 15, 20, 27, 39

Bestuzhev-Rjumin, Vasilij Nikolaevich (factory manager) — 57, 61

Bibikov family — 68, 104

Bibikov, Aleksandr Nikolaevich (illegitimate son to a landowner) — 34, 42, 45, 51, 68 , 90, 95, 99, 100, 119; *Chr.* 1872

Bibikov, Aleksej Alekseevich (son to a senator) — 56, 64, 66, 85, 158

Bibikov, Mikhail Illarionovich (son to Illarion Mikhajlovich Bibikov) — 51

Bibikov, Mikhail Mikhajlovich (son to Mikhail Illarionovich Bibikov) — 33, 34

Bibikov, Nikolaj Nikolaevich (landowner) — 6, 100

Bibikov, Vasilij Nikolaevich (landowner) — 6, 161

Bibikov, Vladimir Aleksandrovich (son to A. N. Bibikov) — 68, 203

Bibikova, Sof'ja Nikitichna (*née* Muravëva; wife to Mikhail Illarionovich Bibikov) — 33, 51

Birjukov, Pavel Ivanovich [Posha] (Tolstoyan; LNT's first biographer) — 120–24, 132, 136, 138, 142, 144, 145, 160, 162–64, 166, 168, 169, 174, 190, 192–195, 217, 219; *Chr.* 1885, 1893–95, 1897, 1903, 1910; *XXXVII, LXIV*

Bistrom, Baron Nikolaj Rodrigovich — 42

Bistrom, Baron Rodrig Grigor'evich — 42, 51, 53

Bliss, Cornelius Newton (a U. S. Secretary of the Interior) — 202

Bobrinskaja, Sof'ja Vasil'evna (Countess, wife to Viktor Fëdorovich Këller) — 70

Bobrinskij,Count Aleksej Alekseevich [Alësha] (nephew to S. A. Filosofova) — 139, 161

Bobrinskij, Count Aleksej Pavlovich — *Chr.* 1876

Bobrinskij, Vladimir Alekseevich [Dimer] (Count) — 169

Boétie, Étienne de la (French writer) — 98

Bogojavlenskij, Nikolaj Efimovich (tutor) — 61, 155, 156, 162, 163

Bojanus, Ol'ga Semënovna (*née* Khljustina) — 77, 92

Bojtsov, Pëtr Vasil'evich (cook) — 171

Bolkhin, Adrian Grigor'evich (peasant worker, coachman) — 99, 100

Bolkhin, Grigorij Il'ich (father to A. G. Bolkhin) — 79

Bonch-Bruevich, Vladimir Dmitrievich (author, political advisor) — *Chr.* 1899

Bondarev, Timofej Mikhajlovich (peasant sectarian writer) — *LVI*

Bool', Klara Karlovna (governess to the Dunaev family) — 181

Boratynskaja, Ekaterina Ivanovna (*née* Timirjazeva; translator) — 162, 163, 177

Boratynskij, Lev Andreevich — 162

Borisevich, Ivan Ignat'evich (Polish nobleman) — 95

Borisov, Ivan Petrovich (landowner) — 8

Borisov, Tit Borisovich (Yasnaya Polyana peasant) — 142

Böse, Ekaterina Egorovna (German tutor) — 20

Bossoney (tutor) — 58

Botkin, Dmitrij Petrovich (art gallery owner) — 59

Botkin, Sergej Petrovich (doctor) — 47

Boulanger (Bulanzhe), Pavel Aleksandrovich (railway employee) — 197, 213–15, 217, 219

Bourdon, George (French writer) — 218

Braddon, Mary Elizabeth (English writer) — 20

Brandt, Sof'ja Fominichna (married name: Dzhons; daughter to the Tolstoys' neighbours) — 118

Brashnin, Ivan Petrovich (Tolstoyan; Moscow merchant) — 157, 202

Bulgakov, Valentin Fëdorovich (LNT's secretary) — 235, 236; *Chr.* 1910, 1917; *LXIII, LXIV*

Bulygin, Mikhail Vasil'evich (Tolstoyan; neighbour) — 139, 164, 168, 171

Bulygina, Anna Maksimovna (*née* Ignat'eva) — 168

Butkevich, Anatolij Stepanovich (beekeeper, scholar) — 164

Buturlin, Aleksandr Sergeevich (doctor) — 141, 215

C

Chaliapin, Feodor — *see: Shaljapin, Fëdor Ivanovich*

Chekhov, Anton Pavlovich (writer) — 128, 170, 177; *Chr.* 1895, 1901, *XXXV*

Cherëmushkin, Boris Filippovich (former serf) — 4, 7

Chertkov, Aleksandr Dmitrievich (archæologist and numismatist) — 20

Chertkov, Grigorij Aleksandrovich (son to D. V. Chertkov) — 20

Chertkov, Vladimir Grigor'evich (LNT's close friend and publisher) — 105, 111, 112, 115, 118–120, 127, 128, 138–40, 159, 188, 190, 191, 193–95, 200, 205, 208, 216, 224, 225, 227–30, 232, 233, 236, 238, 239; *Chr.* 1883–85, 1887, 1888, 1890, 1893–99, 1901, 1904–06, 1908–10; *XXXV, LII, LVII*

Chertkova, Anna Konstantinovna (*née* Diterikhs; wife to V. G. Chertkov) — 133; 140, 213, 218, 225; *Chr.* 1899

Chertkov, Vladimir Vladimirovich [Dimochka] (son to V. G. Chertkov) — 225, 227

Chertkova, Countess Elisaveta Ivanovna (*née* Chernyshëva-Kruglikova) — *Chr.* 1910

Chicherin, Boris Nikolaevich (philosopher, historian) — 212

Chirkov, Vasilij Vasil'evich (doctor) — 108, 207

Chistjakov, Matvej Nikolaevich (famine relief worker) — 159

Chizh, Nikolaj Il'ich (obstetrician) — 100, 102

Christian, Reginald F. (Tolstoy scholar) — *XXXVII*

Confucius (Chinese philosopher) — 102

Coppée, François Édouard Joachim (French poet & novelist) — 174

Corneille, Pierre (French writer) — *XL*

Crosby, Ernest (American author) — 172, 173, 208

D

Dagmara — *see: Marija Fëdorovna*

Darja Pavlovna (sister to Gerasim Pavlovich) — 144

Davitt, Michael (Irish Labour MP) — 219

Davydov, Nikolaj Vasil'evich (prosecutor) — 90, 91, 159, 166, 168, 189, 209

Davydova, Ekaterina Pavlovna (*née* Evreinova; wife to N. V. Davydov) — 159, 209

Deev, Mikhail Stepanovich (merchant) — 46

Deev, Nikita Evdokimovich (husband to A. P. Deeva) — 176

Deeva, Anna Petrovna [Annushka] (cook) — 139, 176

Del'vig, Aleksandr Antonovich (brother to Anton Del'vig) — 23

Del'vig, Anton Antonovich [Antosha] (poet) — 23, 55

Del'vig, Khionija Aleksandrovna (*née* Chapkina;* friend to LNT's sister Marija Nikolaevna) — 23

Del'vig, Ljubov' Antonovna (sister to A. S. Pushkin's friend) — 10, 28

Del'vig, Rossa Aleksandrovna (married name: Levitskaja; niece to Anton Del'vig) — 177

Den, Natal'ja Nikolaevna [Natasha] (*née* Filosofova; sister to S. N. Filosofova) — 137, 156, 172

Den, Vladimir Èduardovich (professor of geography) — 137

Denisenko family — 170

Denisenko, Elena Sergeevna [Lenochka; Hélène] — *see: Tolstaja, Elena Sergeevna*

Denisenko, Ivan Vasil'evich — 170; *Chr.* 1893, 1909

Descartes, René (French philosopher) — 139

Detraz, Mademoiselle (French governess to the Tolstoys' younger children) — 170, 171

Dickens, Charles (English writer) — 4, 21; *XL*

Dikgof, Elizaveta (*née* fon-Shtal'born; Lutheran) — 39

Dikgof, Gejnrikh (Lutheran pastor) — 39

Dikgof, Lindgol'n — 39

Diterikhs, Anna Konstantinovna — *see: Chertkova, Anna Konstantinovna*

Diterikhs Iosif Konstantinovich [Zhozja] (brother to A. K. and O. K. Diterikhs) — 218

Diterikhs, Ol'ga Konstantinovna — *see: Tolstaja, Ol'ga Konstantinovna*

D'jakov family — 78, 151

D'jakov, Dmitrij Alekseevich (army major, close friend to LNT) — 16, 27, 36, 41, 42, 46, 51, 62, 74, 78, 128, 136, 145, 147, 151, 173, 177; *Chr.* 1867, 1891

D'jakova, Dar'ja Aleksandrovna (*née* Tulub'eva; wife to D. A. D'jakov) — 16, 27; *Chr.* 1867

D'jakova, Marija Dmitrievna (daughter to D. A. D'jakov) — 128

Dmitriev-Mamonov, Aleksandr Èmmanui-lovich [Alik] (Moscow friend) — 145, 153, 164

Dolgorukov, Vladimir Andreevich (Governor-General of Moscow) — 96

Donskov, Andrew — 150, 177; *Chr.* 1870, 1871, 1878, 1895, 1899, 1904, 1910; *XXXIX*

Dostoevskaja, Anna Grigor'evna (*née* Snitkina; wife to F. M. Dostoevsky) — 177; *XXXVII, XL*

Dostoevskaja, Ljubov' Fëdorovna (daughter to A. G. Dostoevskaja) — 177

Dostoevsky, Fëdor Mikhajlovich (novelist) — 47, 50, 177; *Chr.* 1881; *XXXV, XXXVII, LIV, LXII*

Droz, Gustave (French writer) — 93

Drozdov, Vasilij Mikhajlovich — *see: Filaret*

Dubasov, Fëdor Vasil'evich (admiral) — 220

Dubbel't (Duppel't), Sof'ja Nikolaevna (*née* Countess Merenberg; granddaughter to poet A. S. Pushkin) — 148

Dubenskaja, Mar'ja Aleksandrovna (*née* Tsurikova; acquaintance of the Tolstoys') — 191, 197

Dumas, Alexandre fils (son to French writer A. Dumas fils) — 92

Dumas, Alexandre père (French writer) — 92, 169

Dunaev, Aleksandr Nikiforovich (Moscow banker) — 141, 142, 151, 153, 154, 172, 178, 187, 192, 202, 213, 217, 226; *Chr.* 1888

Dunjasha — *see: Bannikova, Avdot'ja Nikolaevna*

Dupin, Amantine-Lucile-Aurore (pseudonym: George Sand; French writer) — *XL*

Durnovo, Ivan Nikolaevich (Minister of Interior) — 158, 162; *Chr.* 1890

Dushka — *see: Bannikova, Avdot'ja Ivanovna*

Dzhunkovskij, Nikolaj Fëdorovich (Tolstoyan) — 132

E

Edward, Prince [Prince of Wales] (cousin to Nicholas II) — 177

Egorov, Filipp Rodionovich (coachman) — 73, 90, 95, 99, 103, 119, 140

Egorov, Matvej Egorovich — 79

Egorov, Mitrofan Filipovich [Mitrokha] (son to F. R. Egorov) — 151

Egorova, Ol'ga Rodionovna — *see: Bazykina, Ol'ga Rodionovna*

Eliot, George (real name: Mary Ann Evans; English writer) — 107, 109

Èngel'gardt (Engelhardt), Aleksandr Nikolaevich (political commentator) — 91

Epictetus (philosopher) — *XLV*

Epishka (elderly Cossack) — 65

Èrdeli, Ivan Egorovich — 151

Èrdeli, Marija Aleksandrovna (*née*: Kuzmin-skaja; niece to SAT) — 65, 66, 68, 151, 171, 176, 207

Ergol'skaja, Tat'jana Aleksandrovna [Auntie] (second cousin to LNT's father) — 4–7, 9, 12, 22, 27, 28, 30, 34, 38, 41, 42, 69, 73, 151, 220; *Chr.* 1837, 1838, 1874

Èristova, Matrona Dmitrievna (Patti; Princess) — 136

Ermolov family — 106

Ermolov, Dmitrij Fëdorovich — 54

Ermolova, Ekaterina Petrovna (lady-in-waiting) — 106, 134, 141

Ermolova, Marija Nikolaevna (actress) — 162

Ernefel't, Arvid Aleksandrovich (Finnish writer) — *Chr.* 1898

F

Faddeevna (the Tolstoys' servant in Moscow) — 114, 174

Father Iosif (LNT's sister's spiritual confessor) — 234

Fëdorov, Nikolaj Fëdorovich (librarian, philosopher) — 71, 214

Fëdorov, Pëtr (father to S. P. Arbuzov) — 4

Fejnerman, Esfir' Borisovna (second married name: Varshavskaja; wife to I. B. Fejnerman) — 128, 136, 137

Fejnerman, Isaak Borisovich (Tolstoyan) — 115, 119, 128, 131, 132, 136, 138

Feokritova, Varvara Mikhajlovna (companion to A. L. Tolstaja) — 223, 224

Feoktistov, Evgenij Mikhajlovich (Synod press supervisor) — 114, 121, 123, 134, 135, 152; *Chr.* 1885, 1887

Fet (Shenshin), Afanasij Afanas'evich (poet) — 7–9, 40, 55, 70, 77, 112, 181; *Chr.* 1856, 1863, 1865, 1870, 1877, 1884, 1889, 1892; *XXXV, XLVI*

Féval', Paul Henri Corentin (French writer) — *XL*

Fidler, Ivan Ivanovich (headmaster) — 220

Filaret (Vasilij Mikhajlovich Drozdov; Metropolitan) — 122

Filosofov, Nikolaj Alekseevich (husband to S. A. Filosofova) — 139, 147

Filosofov, Vladimir Nikolaevich (brother to S. N. Filosofova) — 169

Filosofova, Aleksandra Nikolaevna [Sasha] (sister to S. N. Filosofova) — 152

Filosofova, Natal'ja Nikolaevna (wife to V. È. Den) — 137, 139, 151, 156, 161, 162, 172

Filosofova, Sof'ja Alekseevna (*née* Pisareva; mother to S. N. Filosofova) — 139, 147, 152, 162

Filosofova, Sof'ja Nikolaevna [Sonja] (married name: Tolstaja; wife to I. L. Tolstoj) — 139, 142, 147, 152, 169, 171, 176, 180, 200, 203, 204; *Chr.* 1888

Firekel', Ol'ga Adol'fovna (second wife to Aleksandr Nikolaevich Bibikov) — 68

Fisher, Sof'ja Nikolaevna (*née* Bogdanova; *gymnasium* headmistress) — 114

Flërov, Fëdor Grigor'evich (doctor) — 172

Fokanov, Timofej Mikhajlovich (foreman of Samara farmstead) — 7, 44

Fokanova, Marfa Evdokimovna (Yasnaya Polyana peasant) — 86

Fokht, Nikolaj Bogdanovich (teacher of ancient languages) — 78

Fonvizin, Ivan Sergeevich (Governor of Moscow) — 37

Foss (owner of an exercise gymn) — 13, 15

Frey, William (real name: Vladimir Konstantinovich Gejns; army officer) — 115, 119

Frolkova (Khrolkova), Arina (Irina) Fëdo-rovna (*née* Shentjakova) — 73, 102

Fukaj (Japanese journalist) — 189

Funk, Amalija Fëdorovna (German language tutor) — 52

G

Gaak, Fëdor Egorovich (surgeon) — 17, 18

Gachet, Mlle (Swiss governess) — 48

Gajdeburov, Pavel Aleksandrovich (newspaper editor) — 159

Galakhov, Aleksej Dmitrievich (historian) — 97

Ganja (wife to the Tolstoys' employee Grigorij Ivanovich) — 107

Gapon, Georgij Apollonovich (priest, union organiser) — 215

Garshin, Vsevolod Mikhajlovich (belletrist) — 107

Gattsuk, Aleksej Alekseevich — 153

Gauthier (bookshop owner) — 102

Ge (Gay), Nikolaj Nikolaevich Jr [Kolichka] — 114, 116, 120, 130–33, 136–39, 141, 162, 163, 166; *Chr.* 1886, 1888, 1910

Ge (Gay), Nikolaj Nikolaevich Sr — 114, 120, 132, 166, 167; *Chr.* 1884; *XXXV*

Ge, Praskov'ja Nikolaevna (illegitimate daughter of N. N. Ge Jr) — 116

Gedrojts, Romual'd Konstantinovich (chamberlain) — 34

Gejden, Elizaveta Nikolaevna (*née* Zubova) — 172

Gejden, Fëdor Logginovich (husband to E. N. Gejden) — 172

Genzh (Miss; possibly: governess to S. L. Tolstoj) — 220

Georgievskij, Lev Aleksandrovich (headmaster) — 208

George, Henry (American political economist) — 109, 110

Gerasim Pavlovich (servant) — 80, 144

Gerasimov, Osip Petrovich (writer & pedagogue) — 139, 145

Gerasimova, Anna Andreevna (*née* Linberg, wife to O. P. Gerasimov) — 145

Gerasimovna, Mar'ja (nun; godmother to LNT's sister Marija Nikolaevna) — 6, 19

Gertsog, Aleksandr Aleksandrovich — 166

Gibson (Miss; governess) — 116

Gil', Richard Richardovich (manufacturer) — 191

Gippius, Zinaida Nikolaevna (writer) — *XL*

Glazkov, Ivan Ivanovich (landowner) — 79

Glebov family — 210

Glebov, Vladimir Petrovich (landowner) — 162, 210

Glebova, Aleksandra Vladimirovna [Lina] — 210, 219; *Chr.* 1901

Glebova, Sof'ja Nikolaevna (*née* Princess Trubetskaja; wife to V. P. Glebov) — 210

Glinka, Mikhail Ivanovich (composer) — 20

Gœthe, Johann Wolfgang von (German poet) — 92; *XL*

Gogol', Nikolaj Vasil'evich (writer) — 16, 50, 124

Golitsyn, Sergej Fëdorovich (friend to LNT's grandfather) — 219

Golitsyn, Sergej Vladimirovich (brother to LNT's wartime chum) — 37

Golitsyna, Varvara Vasil'evna (friend to LNT's grandfather) — 219

Golokhvastov, Pavel Dmitrievich (folklorist) — 59

Golokhvastova, Ol'ga Andreevna (*née* Andreevskaja; writer) — 145

Golosova (headmistress) — 118

Golovin, Jakov Ivanovich (landowner) — 86

Golovina, Ol'ga Sergeevna (*née* Fëdorova; wife to Ja. I. Golovin) — 86

Gol'denvejzer (Goldenweiser), Aleksandr Borisovich (pianist) — 192, 219, 228; *Chr.* 1906, 1908, 1910

Gol'denvejzer, Anna Alekseevna (*née* Sofiano; wife to A. B. Gol'denvejzer) — 219

Goncharov, Ivan Aleksandrovich (novelist) — *Chr.* 1855; *XL*

Gorbachëv, Vladimir Nikitich (doctor) — 169

Gorbunov-Posadov, Ivan Ivanovich (editor of journal Posrednik) — 174, 204; *Chr.* 1889, 1893, 1894, 1908

Gorchakova, Princess Elena Sergeevna — 32

Goremykin, Ivan Logginovich (government official) — *Chr.* 1897

Gorjainova, Anna Aleksandrovna (*née* Princess Golitsyna-Prozorovskaja; great-granddaughter to friends of LNT's grandfather) — 219

Gorky, Maksim [real name: Aleksej Maksimovich Peshkov] (writer) — 128, 177; *Chr.* 1900–02; *XXXV, XL, XLII*

Gorstkina, Sof'ja Mikhajlovna (*née* Kuzminskaja; sister to A. M. Kuzminskij) — 5

Gotskina, Marja Fëdorovna (former servant) — 104

Govorukha-Otrok, Jurij Nikolaevich (pseudonym: Jurij Nikolaev; writer & literary critic) — 158

Gribovskij, Vjacheslav Mikhajlovich (jurist, belletrist) — 127

Grigorij (carpenter) — 12

Grigorovich, Dmitrij Vasil'evich (writer) — *XL*

Gringmut, Vladimir Andreevich (headmaster of the Katkov lycée) — 174

Grisha (LNT's cousin) — *see: Tolstoj, Grigorij Sergeevich*

Gromova-Opul'skaja, Lidija (Tolstoy scholar) — *XLII*

Grot, Natal'ja Jakovlevna (artist; sister to N. Ja. Grot) — 151

Grot, Natal'ja Petrovna (*née* Semënova; mother to N. Ja. Grot) — 151

Grot, Nikolaj Jakovlevich (philosopher) — 137, 139, 151-55, 157, 158, 163, 184, 192, 201; *Chr.* 1893; *XXXV, XLV, LXVI*

Gubkina, Anna Sergeevna (tutor) — 143

Guillod, Mademoiselle (governess) — 59, 63, 68

Gurevich, L'jubov Jakovlevna (journal editor) — 198; *Chr.* 1895

Gusev, Nikolaj Nikolaevich (LNT's secretary & biographer) — *Chr.* 1907–09

H

Haydn, Joseph (composer) — 226

Hoogenboom, Hilde (Tolstoy scholar) — *XXXVII*

Hugo, Victor (French writer) — 90; *XL*

I

Ienkin (Jenkin), Natal'ja Aleksandrovna (Tolstoyan; artist of Dutch descent) — 206

Ignatovich, Kostja (grandson to SAT's midwife) — 64

Igumnov, Konstantin Nikolaevich (pianist) — 192

Igumnova, Julija Ivanovna (art student) — 212–214, 216, 217; *Chr.* 1900, 1913

Il'ina, Ljubov' Petrovna (*née* Puzyreva; landowner) — 35

Inozemtsev, Fëdor Ivanovich (surgeon) — 11, 18

Islavin, Konstantin Aleksandrovich [Kostja] (SAT's uncle) — 17, 47, 49, 51, 70, 72, 74, 81, 89, 96, 103, 106, 108, 110, 114, 119, 122, 125, 127, 134, 141, 143, 147, 206; *Chr.* 1856

Islavin, Vladimir Aleksandrovich (SAT's uncle) — 5, 51, 53, 123

Islavina, Ljubov' Aleksandrovna (SAT's mother) — *see: Behrs Ljubov' Aleksandrovna*

Islavina (Islen'eva), Vera Aleksandrovna (SAT's aunt) — *see: Shidlovskaja, Vera Aleksandrovna*

Islen'ev, Aleksandr Mikhajlovich (SAT's grandfather) — 2, 17; *Chr.* 1862

Islen'ev, Vasilij Vladimirovich (second cousin to SAT) — 30

Islen'eva, Sof'ja Leonidovna — 108

Istomin family — 67

Istomin, Vladimir Konstantinovich (headmaster) — 47, 51, 59, 67, 162

Istomina, Natal'ja Aleksandrovna (wife to V. K. Istomin) — 67

Ivakin, Ivan Mikhajlovich (philosopher) — 63, 66, 67, 70, 102

Ivan Alekseevich (Yasnaya Polyana servant) — 14, 78

Ivanov, Aleksandr Petrovich (copyist for LNT) — 119

Ivanova, Adelaida Dmitrievna (*née* Urusova; sister to L. D. Urusov) — 94, 130

Ivanova, Nadezhda Pavlovna (merchant's daughter) — 218

Ivanova, Stepanida Trifonovna (elderly housekeeper) — 43, 45

Ivanovich, Grigorij (Tolstoy's employee) — 107

Ivanovich, Vasilij (foreman at Yasnaya Polyana) — 173

Ivanovna, Anna (widowed smallholder) — 99

Ivantsov-Platonov, Aleksandr Mikhajlovich (archpriest, theologian) — 114

J

Jagn, Aleksandr Nikolaevich (doctor) — 139

Jakov (servant) — 4

John Chrysostom, Saint — 214

Julian, Rodolphe (French sculptor) — 223

Junge, Aleksandr Èduardovich (son to E. F. Junge) — 219

Junge, Ekaterina Fëdorovna (*née* Countess Tolstaja; second cousin to LNT) — 157, 185, 192, 219

Junge, Fëdor Èduardovich (son to E. F. Junge) — 219

Jurasova, Julija Afanas'evna — 220

Jurgens, Anna Karlovna [Anetochka] (friend of SAT's) — 5, 18

Jur'ev, Sergej Andreevich (maths teacher) — 88

Jushkova, Pelageja Il'inichna [Polina] (*née* Tolstaja; LNT's aunt) — 4, 5, 41, 46; *Chr.* 1841, 1875

K

Kajutova, Nadezhda (*née* Stender) [Nadja] — 30

Kalmykova, Aleksandra Mikhajlovna (*née* Chernova; writer & pedagogue) — 188

Kamolov family — 196

Kamolov (a peasant) — 182

Kandidov, Pavel Petrovich (tutor) — 171, 174, 176

Kant, Immanuel (German philosopher) — 139

Kapnist, Count Pavel Alekseevich (school trustee) — 105

Karnitskaja, Marja Dmitrievna (wife to V. I. Karnitskij) — 68

Karnitskij, Vasilij Ivanovich (priest) — 68

Kasatkin, Nikolaj Alekseevich (Itinerant artist) — 166

Kashevskaja, Ekaterina Nikolaevna (tutor) — 102

Katkov, Mikhail Nikiforovich (journal editor) — 12, 13, 15, 18, 20, 22, 27, 30, 34, 47, 49, 100; *Chr.* 1862, 1877

Këller family — 70, 72

Këller, Gustav Fëdorovich (tutor) — 4–7, 12, 70

Keller, Ursula (German SAT biographer) — XXXVII

Këller, Viktor Fëdorovich (Major-General, Count) — 70

Kern, Èduard Èduardovich (botanist & forester) — 155

Khilkov, Prince Dmitrij Aleksandrovich (Tolstoyan) — 137, 138; *Chr.* 1887; LVI

Khitrovo, Sof'ja Petrovna (*née* Bakhmetova) — 78

Khokhlov, Pëtr Galaktionovich (Tolstoyan) — 171

Kholevinskaja, Marja Mikhajlovna (doctor) — 104, 174

Khomjakov, Dmitrij Alekseevich — 78

Khomjakov, Sergej Petrovich (Tula governor) — 61

Khomjakova, Anna Sergeevna (*née* Ushakova; daughter to S. P. Ushakov) — 61, 78

Khrolkova, Irina Fëdorovna — *see: Frolkova, Arina Fëdorovna*

Khovrina, Elizaveta [Liza] Leonidovna (friend to T. L. Tolstaja) — 112

Khovrina, Evdokija Ljubimovna (*née* Princess Engalycheva) — 112

Kireevskij, Nikolaj Vasil'evich (landowner) — 7, 9, 25, 26

Kiriakova, Ol'ga Aleksandrovna (*née* Islen'eva; daughter to A. M. Islen'ev) — 108

Kislinskij, Andrej Nikolaevich (Chairman of the Regional Government of Tula Gubernia) — 57

Klavdija (midwife) — 16

Klejn, Ivan Fëdorovich (professor) — 176

Klopskij (Klobskij), Ivan Mikhajlovich (Tolstoyan) — 132

Knertser, Nikolaj Andreevich (physician, medical inspector) — 38, 40

Kolichka — *see: Ge, Nikolaj Nikolaevich Jr*

Kolokol'tsova (Kolokol'tseva), Sof'ja Nikolaevna [Sonja] — 196

Komarova, Tat'jana Vasil'evna (researcher) — *Chr.* 1911; XXXVII, LXVII

Koni, Anatolij Fëdorovich (judge) — 147, 222; *Chr.* 1887

Korolenko, Vladimir Galaktionovich (writer) — *Chr.* 1886

Korsh, Fëdor Adamovich (theatre owner) — 182

Koshelev family — 92

Kozlov, Daniil Davydovich (pupil in LNT's school) — 138

Kovalevskij, Maksim Maksimovich (law professor) — 104, 135

Kramskoj, Ivan Nikolaevich (painter) — 117, 119; *Chr.* 1873; *XXXV*

Krasnov, Vasilij Filippovich (peasant writer) — 204

Krjukov, Aleksandr Aleksandrovich (SAT's optometrist) — 185, 209, 213

Krjukov, Mikhail Fomich (servant) — 131, 139, 153, 154

Kronshtadtskij, Ioann (secular name: Ioann Il'ich Sergiev; archpriest) — 158

Kropotkin, Prince Pëtr Alekseevich (Russian anarchist) — 231

Kryzhanovskij, Nikolaj Andreevich (Governor-General of Orenburg) — 46

Kudrin, Ivan Dmitrievich (Molokan from Patrovka) — 66

Kupfershmidt, Aleksandr Mikhajlovich (violinist) — 15, 16, 20

Kurdjumov, Evgenij (pupil) — 52

Kurnasenkova (Kurnosova), Tat'jana Ivanovna (Yasnaya Polyana peasant) — 79

Kurnosenkov, Nikolaj [Rybin] (bandit) — 99

Kushnerëv, Ivan Nikolaevich (print-shop owner) — 94

Kuvshinov Mikhail Gavrilovich (paper manufacturer) — 116, 117

Kuzminskaja, Darja Aleksandrovna [Dasha] (SAT's niece) — 38

Kuzminskaja, Marija Aleksandrovna — *see: Èrdeli, Marija Aleksandrovna*

Kuzminskaja, Sof'ja Mikhajlovna — *see: Gorstkina, Sof'ja Mikhajlovna*

Kuzminskaja, Tat'jana Andreevna (*née* Behrs; SAT's younger sister) — 2, 4–7, 9, 12–22, 24, 27–31, 33, 34, 37, 41–45, 47, 55, 61, 63, 65, 66, 68, 80–82, 85, 89, 95, 102, 104, 111, 114, 118, 120, 122, 123, 125, 136, 137, 140, 141, 149, 155, 159, 160, 162, 178, 179, 207, 208; *Chr.* 1846, 1862–64, 1863–1864, 1866, 1867, 1888, 1898, 1899, 1910, 1912, 1917; *XXXII*

Kuzminskaja, Vera Aleksandrovna (niece to SAT) — 43, 63, 65, 66, 68, 102, 111, 120, 123, 126, 128, 137, 151, 152, 155, 157, 159, 160, 168, 174, 178–180, 196, 207, 217, 218

Kuzminskij family — 108–11, 114, 120, 122, 130, 131, 140, 149, 162, 178

Kuzminskij, Aleksandr Aleksandrovich (nephew to SAT) — 63

Kuzminskij, Aleksandr Mikhajlovich (SAT's cousin, husband to T. A. Kuzminskaja) — 33, 37, 38, 40, 41, 50, 57, 63, 66–68, 81, 109, 114, 120, 123, 136, 207; *Chr.* 1867, 1891, 1894

Kuzminskij, Dmitrij Aleksandrovich [Mitja] (nephew to SAT) — 179

Kuzminskij, Mikhail Aleksandrovich (nephew to SAT) — 63, 66, 68, 123

Kuznetsov, Mikhail Ivanovich (researcher) — 104

Kuznetsova, Mar'ja (Marija) Kirillovna (SAT's seamstress & maid) — 155

Kuz'ma (gardener) — 9

L

Labourdette (French tutor to the Behrs brothers) — 16

Lake, Emmeline (Miss; English nanny) — 101

Lambert (Monsieur; tutor) — 146, 151, 154

Landovska, Wanda (Polish pianist) — 226

Lao-Tse (Laozi; Chinese philosopher) — 102

Lavrov, Vukol Mikhajlovich (journal editor) — 88

Lavrovskaja, Elizaveta Andreevna (married name: Tserteleva; opera singer) — 206

Lëlja (SAT's cousin) — *see: Behrs, Elena Aleksandrovna*

Lëlja (the Tolstoys' son) — *see: Tolstoj, Lev L'vovich*

Lentovskij, Mikhail Valentinovich (playwright) — *Chr.* 1895

Leont'ev, Pavel Mikhajlovich (philology professor) — 39

Lermontova, Varvara Sergeevna (*née* Trubetskaja) — 202

Leskov, Nikolaj Semënovich (writer) — *Chr.* 1887, 1890, 1891, 1894

Levashev, Aleksandr Ivanovich (landowner) — 51

Levashov (tenant in the annexe of the Tolstoys' second Moscow house) — 122

Lëvshina, Vera Fëdorovna — *see: Sollogub, Vera Fëdorovna*

Lidia [Lida] (Miss; tutor, governess) — 150, 154

Limont-Ivanov, Andrej Ivanovich (husband to N. V. Limont-Ivanova) — 169

Limont-Ivanova, Natal'ja Vladimirovna (sister to Il'ja L'vovich's friend V. V. Treskin) — 169, 176

Liven, Prince Aleksandr Karlovich (senator) — 30

Liven, Princess Aleksandra Andreevna (granddaughter to A. N. Strekalova) — 213

Ljapunova, Vera Sergeevna [Verochka] (*née* Arbuzova) — 196

Ljubimov, Nikolaj Alekseevich (physics professor) — 15, 20, 22, 49, 147

Lokhmacheva, Tat'jana Ivanovna (Yasnaya Polyana peasant) — 79

Lopatin, Lev Mikhajlovich (philosopher) — 134; *E2*

Lopatin, Nikolaj Mikhajlovich (singer) — 109, 112, 134, 137

Loris-Melikov, Count Mikhail Tarielovich (Minister of Internal Affairs) — 120

Losinskij, Semën Alekseevich (stationmaster at Yasenki) — 149

Löwenfeld, Rafail (German translator) — *Chr.* 1892

Lukovnikov, Pëtr Vasil'evich (bookstore owner) — 108

Lutaj (Bashkir coachman) — 56

L'vov, Aleksej Evgen'evich (headmaster) — 177

L'vov, Evgenij Vladimirovich (LNT's friend, Tula landowner) — 29

L'vov, Prince Georgij Evgen'evich (politician) — 166

L'vov, Nikolaj Aleksandrovich (amateur medium) — 78, 166, 177

L'vova, Marija Mikhajlovna (*née* Chelishcheva; wife to N. A. L'vov) — 78

M

Makarychev, Vasilij Sevast'janovich [Vas'ka] (Yasnaya Polyana peasant) — 103, 139

Maklakov, Aleksej Alekseevich (oculist; brother to N. A. Maklakov) — 174, 190, 209, 213, 217, 219

Maklakov, Aleksej Nikolaevich (oculist) — 209

Maklakov, Nikolaj Alekseevich (Minister of Internal Affairs) — 170, 174, 192

Maklakov, Vasilij Alekseevich [Vasja] (lawyer) — 174, 187, 190, 206

Maklakova, Marija Leonidovna [Marusja] (*née* Princess Obolenskaja) — 170, 192, 206, 209, 215, 219

Makovitskij, Dushan Petrovich (LNT's personal physician) — 174, 217, 218, 221, 228, 234; *Chr.* 1894, 1904, 1906, 1909, 1910

Malikov, Dmitrij [Mitja] (son to E. A. Malikova) — 66

Malikova, Elizaveta Aleksandrovna Jr (daughter to E. A. Malikova) — 66

Malikova, Elizaveta Aleksandrovna Sr (common-law wife to V. A. Alekseev) — 66

Mamontov, Anatolij Ivanovich (print-shop owner) — 116, 132, 139, 141

Mamontov, Savva Ivanovich (fabric manufacturer, philanthropist) — 223

Mamontov, Vsevolod Savvich (son to S. I. Mamontov) — 223

Marakuev, Vladimir Nikolaevich (journalist, publisher) — 94, 96, 109

Marija Aleksandrovna, Grand Duchess — *Chr.* 1873

Marija Fëdorovna, Grand Duchess (*née* Princess Marija Sofija Frederika Dagmara; — wife to Tsarevich Aleksandr Aleksandrovich — 30, 192; *Chr.* 1891

Marks, Adol'f Fëdorovich — *Chr.* 1898

Marsochnikov, Semën Nikolaevich (land-owner) — 6

Martha, Miss (English nanny) — 135

Martynov, Viktor Nikolaevich (family friend) — 167, 210

Martynova, Sof'ja Mikhajlovna (*née* Kateni-na; wife to V. N. Martynov) — 167, 210

Masaryk, Tomáš (first president of Czechoslo-vakia) — 140; *Chr.* 1887, 1888, 1910

Maslov family — 213–15, 220

Maslov, Fëdor Ivanovich — 213, 214

Maslova, Anna Ivanovna (sister to F. I. Maslov) — 198, 220

Maslova, Varvara Ivanovna (sister to F. I. Maslov) — 143, 213

Matrosov, Grigorij — 225

Matveev (husband to Ol'ga Abakumova) — 27, 231

Matveeva, Varvara Dmitrievna (landowner; neighbour to the Sukhotins) — 231

Maude, Aylmer (translator) — 201; *Chr.* 1897

Maude, Louise (*née* Shanks; translator) — 201

Maupassant, Guy de (French writer) — 90, 172

Mavor, James (political science professor in Toronto) — 231

McCarthy (Miss; governess to the Kuzminskij family) — 192

McLean, Hugh (Tolstoy scholar) — *XXXVII*

Medzhibovskaya, Inessa (Slavic scholar) — *XXXVII*

Mejendorf, Fëdor Egorovich (Baron) — 172

Mejendorf, Marija Vasil'evna (*née* Countess Olsuf'eva; sister to Count A. V. Olsuf'ev) — 172

Mendelssohn, Felix (German composer) — 187; *XLVIII*

Mengden, Elizaveta Ivanovna (*née* Bibikova; wife to V. M. Mengden) — 65

Mengden, Vladimir Mikhajlovich (landown-er) — 37, 65, 66

Meshcherskaja, Princess Mar'ja Aleksandrov-na (*née* Countess Panina) — 30; *XLIII*

Metelitsina, Pelageja Nikolaevna (landowner/farm-worker) — 86

Mezentsov, Nikolaj Vladimirovich or Pëtr Ivanovich (army officers) — 39

Michurin, Aleksandr Grigor'evich (music teacher) — 33, 55, 59

Mikhajlova, Anna Petrovna (farm-worker) — 16

Mikhajlova, Avdot'ja (Agaf'ja/Evdokija) Nikolaevna — *see: Bannikova, Avdot'ja Nikolaevna*

Mikulich-Veselitskaja, Lidija Ivanovna (writer, friend of the Tolstoys') — 170

Miloradovich, Count Grigorij Aleksan-drovich — 98

Miloradovich, Countess Vera Nikolaevna (*née* Shabel'skaja; wife to B. V. Shidlovskij) — 98

Miljutin, Dmitrij Alekseevich (Minister of War) — 187

Miljutina, Ol'ga Dmitrievna (daughter to D. A. Miljutin) — 187

Mitrofanova, Anna Aleksandrovna (daughter to bank director) — 134

Mjasoedov, Grigorij Grigor'evich (artist) — 120

Mjasoedova, Julija Sergeevna (distant relative of LNT's) — 213

Molas, Matil'da Pavlovna (teacher, friend of E. A. Olsuf'eva) — 184

Molière — *see: Poquelin, Jean-Baptiste*

Molochnikov, Vladimir Ajfalovich (lock-smith) — 222

Montagne, Michel de (French philosopher) — 97

Moravov, Aleksandr Viktorovich (artist) — *Chr.* 1910

Mordvinov, Ivan Nikolaevich (son-in-law to I. I. Raevskij) — 155, 158

Mordvinova, Margarita Ivanovna (wife to I. N. Mordvinov) — 158, 164

Morgunov (lieutenant-colonel) — 190, 191

Morozov, Vikula Eliseevich — 158, 217

Mukhalevskij, Ivan Nikanorovich (priest at Kochaki) — 99

Muravëv, Nikita Mikhajlovich (Decembrist) — 33

Muravëv-Karskij, Nikolaj Nikolaevich — 144

Mussorgsky, Modest (composer) — 219

N

Nagornov, Boris Nikolaevich [Borja] (grandson to LNT's sister M. N. Tolstaja) — 143, 182

Nagornov, Nikolaj Mikhajlovich (husband to LNT's niece V. V. Nagornova) — 54, 55, 123, 128, 137, 157, 182, 187; *Chr.* 1896

Nagornova, Tat'jana Nikolaevna (daughter to V. V. Nagornova) — 194, 204

Nagornova, Varvara Valer'janovna (*née* Tolstaja) [Varja] (niece to LNT, daughter to M.N. Tolstaja) — 6, 10, 26, 28, 40–43, 59, 69, 89, 98, 112, 127, 128, 134, 137, 139, 147, 157, 176, 187, 192, 194, 204

Nakashidze, Elena Petrovna (sister to I. P. Nakashidze) — 190, 191

Nakashidze, Il'ja Petrovich (Georgian political commentator) — 190, 191

Naryshkina, Aleksandra Nikolaevna (*née* Chicherina; lady-in-waiting) — 212

Naryshkina, Margarita Mikhajlovna (wife to V. A. Afanas'ev) — 215

Naryshkina, Marija [Marusja] (married name: Bel'skaja) — 219

Nazhivin, Ivan Fëdorovich (writer) — 218

Nazhivina, Anna Efimovna (*née* Zusman; wife to I. F. Nazhivin) — 218

Nechaev, Nikolai Vasil'evich (surgeon) — 18, 20, 22

Nekrasov, Nikolaj Alekseevich (poet & journal editor) — *Chr.* 1852, 1855

Nemirovich-Danchenko, Vladimir Ivanovich (theatre director) — *E4*

Neradovskij, Pëtr Ivanovich (art critic) — 172

Newton, William Wilberforce (pastor) — 144, 146,

Nicholas I/II, Emperor — *see: Romanov, Emperor Nicholas I/II*

Nief, Jules (real name: Vicomte de Montels; French tutor) — 51, 52, 54, 55–56

Nietzsche, Friedrich (German philosopher) — *Chr.* 1893

Nikiforov, Mikhail Illarionovich (architect) — 81, 82

Nikiforova, Tat'jana Grigor'evna (researcher) — *XXXIX*

Nikitin, Dmitrij Vasil'evich (doctor) — 212; *Chr.* 1902–04

Nikitina, Nina Alekseevna (researcher) — *XXXVII*

Nikolaev, Pëtr Petrovich (philosopher) — *LXIV*

Nikolaj Nikolaevich, Grand Prince — 80

Novikov, Aleksej Mitrofanovich (tutor) — 155–57, 159, 162, 172

Novikov, Mikhail Petrovich (peasant sectarian writer) — *LVI*

Novikov (Tsyganok), Pëtr Dmitrievich (carpenter) — 138, 172

Novosil'tsov, Ivan Petrovich (son of P. P. Novosil'tsov) — 23

Novosil'tsov, Pëtr Petrovich (Privy Councillor) — 23, 24

Novitskaja, P. K. (governess) — 184

O

Obolenskaja, Princess Agrafena Aleksandrovna [Grushen'ka] — 96, 105, 106

Obolenskaja, Aleksandra Alekseevna (*née* D'jakova; sister to D. A. D'jakov) — 136

Obolenskaja, Elizaveta (Lili) Petrovna (wife to D. D. Obolenskij) — 74, 89, 154

Obolenskaja, Elizaveta Valer'janovna (*née* Tolstaja) [Liza] (LNT's niece, daughter to M. N. Tolstaja) — 6, 10, 12, 18, 20, 26, 28, 40–43, 51, 74, 78, 89, 100, 112, 118, 128, 132, 137, 147, 165, 170, 192, 219, 224

Obolenskaja, Marija L'vovna (*née* Tolstaja; the Tolstoys' daughter) — *Chr.* 1871, 1889, 1890, 1892, 1894, 1895, 1897, 1901, 1902, 1905, 1906

Obolenskaja, Natal'ja Leonidovna [Natasha] (grandniece to LNT) — 213, 219, 224

Obolenskaja, Varvara Dmitrievna (sister to L. D. Obolenskij) — 94

Obolenskij family — 96, 105, 118, 128, 134, 136

Obolenskij, Prince Andrej Vasil'evich (husband to Aleksandra Obolenskaja) — 136; *E5*

Obolenskij, Dmitrij Aleksandrovich (Actual Privy Councillor) — 50

Obolenskij, Count Dmitrij Dmitrievich [Mitasha] (landowner) — 13, 17, 19, 137, 154

Obolenskij, Prince Leonid Dmitrievich (husband to E. V. Obolenskaja) — 40, 41, 43, 59 112, 132, 154, 165, 224

Obolenskij, Nikolaj Leonidovich [Kolja/ Kolasha] (son to Prince L. D. Obolenskij) — 70, 143, 162, 170, 177, 178, 189, 191; 206, *Chr.* 1897, 1919

Obruchev, Nikolaj Nikolaevich (army headquarters commandant) — 120

Offenberg, Baron Fëdor Ivanovich — 42

Ogarëv, Aleksandr Nikolaevich (general) — 182

Ogarëva, Nadezhda Aleksandrovna (*née* Stakhovich; wife to A. N. Ogarëv) — 182

Okhotnitskaja, Natal'ja Petrovna (poor noblewoman) — 19, 28, 30, 41

Olsuf'ev family — 82, 94, 100, 109, 111, 122, 125, 127, 128, 132, 134, 141, 172

Olsuf'ev, Count Adam Vasil'evich (son to V. A. Olsuf'ev) — 81, 109, 172, 184; *Chr.*1897

Olsuf'ev, Count Aleksandr Vasil'evich (brother to Adam Olsuf'ev) — 111; *Chr.* 1897

Olsuf'ev, Dmitrij Adamovich (brother to M. A. Olsuf'ev) — 135, 141, 172

Olsuf'ev, Dmitrij Vasil'evich (the Tolstoys' Moscow neighbour) — 172

Olsuf'ev, Grigorij Vasil'evich (son to V. A. Olsuf'ev) — 70, 172

Olsuf'ev, Mikhail Adamovich (regional nobility representative) — 135, 141, 172

Olsuf'ev, Vasilij Aleksandrovich — 72

Olsuf'eva, Anna Mikhajlovna (*née* Obol'janinova; wife to Adam Vasil'evich Olsuf'ev) — 109, 162, 172, 184, 185

Olsuf'eva, Ekaterina L'vovna (*née* Sollogub; wife to Aleksandr Vasil'evich Olsuf'ev) — 111

Olsuf'eva, Elizaveta Adamovna (friend to T. L. Tolstaja) — 112, 129, 162, 184

Olsuf'eva, Tat'jana Vasil'evna (friend to T. L. Tolstaja) — 72, 92

Orekhov, Aleksej Stepanovich (*valet de chambre*) — 5, 13, 15, 19, 20, 55, 65, 69, 71, 79

Orekhov, Fedot Terent'evich (a Yasnaya Polyana peasant) — 102

Orlov, Ivan Ivanovich (foreman) — 5, 7, 9, 100, 102, 110

Orlov, Nikolaj Vasil'evich (painter) — 218

Orlov, Vladimir Fëdorovich (revolutionary) — 71, 110, 128, 133

Orzhevskaja, Natal'ja Ivanovna (*née* Princess Shakhovskaja; wife to P. V. Orzhevskij) — 108

Orzhevskij, Pëtr Vasil'evich (senator) — 108

Osorgina, Elizaveta Sergeevna (*née* Trubetskaja) — 202

Osten-Saken, Countess Aleksandra Il'inichna (*née* Tolstaja; LNT's aunt) — *Chr.* 1837, 1841

Ostrovsky, Aleksandr Nikolaevich (playwright) — *Chr.* 1855

Ozolin, Ivan Ivanovich (stationmaster at Astapovo) — 237

P

Panina, Countess Sof'ja Vladimirovna (family friend) — 211; *Chr.* 1901

Panov, Mikhail Mikhajlovich (photographer) — 132

Pasternak, Leonid Osipovich (painter) — XL

Pavel (coachman to Marija Nikolaevna Tolstaja) — 24, 26

Pavlenkov, Gavriil Emel'janovich — 2; *Chr.* 1868

Perfil'ev, Aleksandr Sergeevich [Sasha] (cadet) — 92

Perfil'ev, Stepan Vasil'evich (general of the *gendarmerie*) — 16, 36, 51

Perfil'ev, Vasilij Stepanovich [Vasen'ka] (son to S. V. Perfil'ev) — 16, 39, 51, 59, 206

Perfil'eva, Anastasija Sergeevna (second wife to S. V. Perfil'ev) — 37

Perfil'eva, Praskov'ja Fëdorovna [Polina] (*née* Tolstaja; second cousin to LNT) — 47, 67

Perfil'eva, Varvara Stepanovna (daughter to S. V. Perfil'ev) — 16, 32

Peshkov, Aleksej Maksimovich — *see: Gorky, Maksim*

Petja (SAT's brother) — see: Behrs, Pëtr Andreevich

Petrov, Ivan Ivanovich (assistant to I. D. Sytin) — 134

Petrovskij, Sergej Aleksandrovich (journalist) — 154

Pikulin, Pavel Lukich (doctor, professor at Moscow University) — 39

Pilate, Pontius — 124

Pimenov, Kondratij (peasant, freed serf) — 4, 5, 7, 9, 15, 19

Pirogova, Anna Stepanovna — Chr. 1872

Pisarev, Rafail Alekseevich (Tula landowner) — 155–59

Pisarev, Sergej Alekseevich (retired cavalry captain) — 99, 101, 136, 155, 156, 158, 161; Chr. 1884

Pisareva, Evgenija Pavlovna (née Baranova; wife to S. A. Pisarev) — 156

Pisemskij, Aleksej Feofilaktovich (writer & dramatist) — 222

Plato (philosopher) — 139; XLV

Pobedonostsev, Konstantin Petrovich (Senior Procurator of the Holy Synod) — 94, 114, 121, 125, 126, 154; Chr. 1901; LXVI

Polenov, Vasilij Dmitrievich (painter) — 141

Polin, Tit Ivanovich (a. k. a. Pelagejushkin) — 138

Polina (LNT's aunt) — see: Jushkova, Pelageja Il'inichna

Polivanov, Lev Ivanovich (headmaster) — 82, 134, 136, 172, 174; Chr. 1881

Polivanov, Mitrofan Andreevich (major-general) — 108

Polivanova, Anna Mikhajlovna (née Paront; wife to M. A. Polivanov) — 108

Pomerantsev, Jurij Nikolaevich [Jusha] (pupil of the composer Taneev) — 192, 198, 206

Popoff, Alexandra (SAT biographer) — XXXVII

Popov, Aleksandr Petrovich (surgeon) — 13, 17, 18, 20, 22

Popov, Evgenij Ivanovich (a Tolstoyan) — 155, 164, 165, 174, 198; Chr. 1889, 1893, 1894

Popov, Ivan Ivanovich (statistician in Voronezh Gubernia) — 137

Popov, Nil Aleksandrovich (professor of Russian history) — 18

Popov, Pavel Sergeevich (husband to Anna Il'inichna Tolstaja) — XXXIV, XXXVII

Popova, Anna Pankrat'evna (née Novakovich; mother to E. I. Popov) — 165

Popova, Avdot'ja Vasil'evna (housekeeper) — 76, 99, 218

Poquelin, Jean-Baptiste (pseudonym: Molière; French writer) — XL

Postnikova, Ol'ga Dmitrievna (wife to SAT's brother Pëtr Andreevich Behrs) — 47

Potapenko, Ignatij Nikolaevich (writer) — 170

Potekhin, Aleksej Antipovich (writer) — 138

Prasekina, Elena Ivanovna [Alëna] (cook) — 83

Preobrazhenskij, Vasilij Grigor'evich (Tula physician) — 21

Protashinskij, Aleksej Alekseevich (landowner) — 204

Protas'ev, Ivan Evlampievich (businessman) — 154

Protazanov, Jakov Aleksandrovich — Chr. 1912

Prugavin, Aleksandr Stepanovich (writer) — 64

Puare, Jakov Viktorovich (owner of an exercise gymn) — 39

Pushchina, Anastasija Kondrat'evna & Evgenija Ivanovna (LNT's acquaintances) — 52

Pushkin (merchant) — 9

Pushkin, Aleksandr Sergeevich (poet) — 23, 128, 148

R

Rachinskaja, Mar'ja Konstantinovna [Manja] (first wife to S. L. Tolstoj) — 137, 174, 178, 179, 184, 187, 220; Chr. 1895

Rachinskij, Konstantin Aleksandrovich (director of the Moscow Agricultural Institute) — 220

Racine, Jean-Baptiste (French writer) — XL

Radstock, Lord Grenville (English religious preacher) — 120

Raevskaja, Elena Pavlovna (*née* Evreinova; wife to Ivan Ivanovich Raevskij) — 159, 209

Raevskaja, Margarita Ivanovna (daughter to I. I. Raevskij) — 155

Raevskij family — 151, 168, 176

Raevskij, Grigorij Ivanovich [Grisha] (brother to P. I. and I. I. Jr Raevskij)— 172

Raevskij, Ivan Ivanovich Jr (son to I. I. Raevskij Sr) — 151, 159, 172

Raevskij, Ivan Ivanovich Sr (landowner) — 69, 71, 86, 151, 153, 155–59, 162, 163, 171, 172, 209

Raevskij, Pëtr Ivanovich (son to I. I. Raevskij Sr) — 151, 162, 168, 172, 192

Rakhmetullin, Mukhamet [Romanych] (a Bashkir) — 56

Rastsvetov, Aleksandr Pavlovich (professor of medicine) — 32

Renan, Joseph Earnest (French philosopher, writer) — *LVIII*

Repin, Il'ja Efimovich (painter) — 59, 160; *Chr.* 1880, 1887, 1891, 1892, 1907; *XXXV, XL*

Ressel, Fëdor Ivanovich — *Chr.* 1833

Rey, Jules (tutor) — 46, 52

Rezunov, Sergej Semënovich (peasant carpenter) — 104

Ribblewhite, E. G. (editor of *The Weekly Times* in London) — 171

Ris, Fëdor Fëdorovich (print-shop owner) — 35–37, 49

Robecci, Carlo (Italian bronze master) — 215

Rod, Èdouard (French novelist) — 169

Rodin, Auguste (French sculptor) — 223

Romanov, Emperor Alexander II — 124, 166; *Chr.* 1861, 1881; *XXXV, LIV, LV*

Romanov, Emperor Alexander III — 61, 82, 123, 124, 148–150, 162, 167, 176, 177; *Chr.* 1881, 1890, 1891, 1894; *XXXV, LXV*

Romanov, Grand Prince Mikhail Aleksandrovich (brother to Nicholas II) — 177

Romanov, Grand Prince Mikhail Mikhajlovich — 148

Romanov, Grand Prince Sergej Aleksandrovich (Governor-General of Moscow, brother to Tsar Alexander III) — 123, 161, 162; *Chr.* 1893; *LXIV*

Romanov, Emperor Nicholas I — 37, 80, 162; *Chr.* 1855

Romanov, Emperor Nicholas II — 61, 177, 192, 197, 217; *Chr.* 1894, 1902, 1909, 1911; *XXXV*

Romanova, Aleksandra Fëdorovna (full name: Victoria Alisa Elena Luiza Beatrisa; wife to Nicholas II) — 177, 192

Romanova, Grand Duchess Elisaveta Fëdorovna (wife to Grand Prince S. A. Romanov) — 162; *Chr.* 1893

Romanova, Empress Marija Fëdorovna (wife to Tsar Alexander III) — 30, 61, 104, 108, 110, 177

Romanova, Grand Duchess Marija Nikolaevna — 162

Rozhdestvenskij, Vladimir Ivanovich (tutor) — 48

Rozhdestvenskij, Zinovij Petrovich (vice-admiral) — 220

Rudinskij, Orest Ivanovich (surgeon) — 13

Rudnev, Aleksandr Matveevich (chief physician of Tula hospital) — 149, 168, 180

Rumjantsev, Matvej Nikitich (artel worker) — 176

Rumjantsev, Nikolaj Mikhajlovich (cook) — 5, 38, 236

Rumjantsev, Nikolaj Petrovich (library organiser) — 16, 20; *Chr.* 1887

Rumjantsev, Semën Nikolaevich (cook) — 236

Rusanov, Gavriil Andreevich (friend of LNT's) — *Chr.* 1883

Russel, Nicholas (a.k.a. Nikolaj Konstantinovich Sudzilovskij; relocation agent) — 205

S

Safonov, Vasilij Il'ich (pianist & composer) — 207

Safonova, Anastasija Vasil'evna [Nastja] (daughter to V. I. Safonov) — 207

Saint-Thomas, Prospère — *Chr.* 1837, 1838

Salaev Brothers (owners of a publishing house) — 114

Salomon, Charles (translator) — 169, 215

Samarin, Aleksandr Dmitrievich (Collegiate Councillor) — 219

Samarin, Dmitrij Fëdorovich (regional nobility representative) — 105

Samarin, Jurij Fëdorovich (writer, public activist) — 34, 39

Samarin, Pëtr Fëdorovich (landowner from Epifan Uezd) — 61, 209

Samarina, Aleksandra Pavlovna (*née* Evreinova; wife to P. F. Samarin) — 209

Samarina, Sof'ja Dmitrievna [Sonja] (daughter to D. F. Samarin) — 137, 139

Sand, George — *see: Dupin, Amantine-Lucile-Aurore*

Sandoz (Swiss Tolstoyan) — 90

Sasha (SAT's brother) — *see: Behrs, Aleksandr Andreevich*

Sasha (the Tolstoys' daughter) — *see: Tolstaja, Aleksandra L'vovna*

Savina, Marija Gavrilovna (*née* Podramtseva; actress) — 134

Schiller, Friedrich (German writer) — XL

Schopenhauer, Arthur (philosopher) — XLV

Schubert, Franz (composer) — 21

Serëzha (the Tolstoys' son) — *see: Tolstoj, Sergej L'vovich*

Serëzha (LNT's brother) — *see: Tolstoj, Sergej Nikolaevich*

Sergievskij-Kazantsev, Pavel Ivanovich — *see: Amfilokhij, Archimandrite*

Serov, Aleksandr Nikolaevich — *Chr.* 1892

Serov, Valentin Aleksandrovich (painter) — *Chr.* 1892

Serova, Valentina Semënovna (*née* Bergman) — *Chr.* 1892

Seuron, Alcide (son to Anna Seuron) — 86, 114, 116, 118, 122, 128, 130, 131, 134

Seuron, Anna (*née* Weber; governess) — 86–90, 92, 95, 96, 100, 101, 104, 105, 108, 112, 114, 122, 131, 135, 136

Severtsev family — 154

Severtsev, Pëtr Alekseevich (husband to O. V. Shidlovskaja) — 30

Severtseva, Ol'ga Vjacheslavovna (*née* Shidlovskaja) — *see: Shidlovskaja, Ol'ga Vjacheslavovna*

Shakespeare, William (dramatist) — 93

Shakhovskoj, Dmitrij Ivanovich (secretary of the First Duma) — 111

Shaljapin (Chaliapin), Fëdor (Feodor) Ivanovich (singer) — 214, 219

Sharandak, Natalja (German SAT biographer) — XXXVII

Shchepkin, Mitrofan Pavlovich (political commentator) — 81

Shcherbakova, Marina Ivanovna (literary critic) — LXIII

Shcherbatov, Nikolaj Sergeevich (historian) — 214

Shcherbatova, Princess Praskov'ja Sergeevna — *Chr.* 1858

Shcherbatova, Princess Sof'ja Aleksandrovna (*née* Apraksina) — 214,

Shcherbatova, Marija Nikolaevna (married name as of 1911: Countess Chernyshëva-Bezobrazova; lady-in-waiting) — 214

Shenshin, Afanasij Afanas'evich — *see: Fet, Afanasij Afanas'evich*

Shentjakov, Pëtr Pavlovich (harness-maker) — 69

Sheremeteva, Elena Grigor'evna (*née* Stroganova; granddaughter to Nicholas II) — 162

Shidlovskaja, Ol'ga Vjacheslavovna (SAT's cousin) — 30, 141, 145, 147, 154, 176

Shidlovskaja, Vera Aleksandrovna (*née* Islavina; SAT's maternal aunt) — 16, 108, 123, 134, 137, 141, 147, 174, 192, 200, 213, 220

Shidlovskij family — 111, 136, 147, 192

Shidlovskij, Boris Vjacheslavovich (SAT's cousin) — 98, 200, 236

Shidlovskij, Vjacheslav Ivanovich (second husband to V. A. Shidlovskaja [Islavina]) — 16, 123

Shidlovskij, Vsevolod Vsevolodovich (SAT's cousin) — 78

Shirkov, Valerian Valerianovich (amateur composer) — 110

Shmidt, Marija Aleksandrovna (school teacher, Tolstoyan) — 138, 171, 176, 192, 197; *Chr.* 1888, 1893, 1910

Shmidt, Vladimir — *Chr.* 1888

Shmigaro, Sigizmund Adamovich (physician) — 5

Shostak, Anatolij L'vovich [Anatol'] (privy councillor) — 5

Shostak, Ekaterina Nikolaevna (*née* Islen'eva; first cousin to SAT's mother) — 108, 123

Shuraev, Ivan Osipovich (Yasnaya Polyana peasant) — 236

Shuvalov, Count Pavel Andreevich (a wartime chum of LNT's) — 123

Shuvalov, Count Pëtr Andreevich — 120

Shuvalova, Elena Ivanovna (aunt to V. G. Chertkov) — 120, 122

Shuvalova, Marija Aleksandrovna (*née* Komarova; wife to P. A. Shuvalov) — 123

Sidorkov, Il'ja Vasil'evich (Yasnaya Polyana servant) — 217–19, 226; *LIII*

Simon, Fëdor Pavlovich (Tolstoyan) — 138

Sizova, Aleksandra Konstantinovna (writer) — 134, 135

Sjas'kova, Marija Vasil'evna (copyist & tutor) — 196

Sjutaev, Vasilij Kirillovich (peasant preacher) — 69, 71, 72; *LVI*

Skobelev, Mikhail Dmitrievich (general) — 220

Skorokhodov, Vladimir Ivanovich (Tolstoyan) — 163

Skrytnov, Vladimir Ivanovich (a correspondent of LNT's) — 132

Slavochka (SAT's brother) — *see: Behrs, Vjacheslav Andreevich*

Sluchevskij, Konstantin Konstantinovich (poet, journal editor) — 162

Snegirëv, Dr. Vladimir Fëdorovich (gynæcologist) — 185; *Chr.* 1906

Sobolevskij, Sergej Aleksandrovich — 37

Sobolevskij, Vasilij Mikhajlovich (journal editor) — 157; *LXV*

Socrates (philosopher) — *XLV*

Sofesh — *see: Vojtkevich, Sof'ja Robertovna*

Sollogub family — 202

Sollogub, Elena Fëdorovna (daughter to F. L. Sollogub) — 202

Sollogub, Fëdor L'vovich (set decorator) — 96, 202

Sollogub, Vera Fëdorovna (daughter to F. L. Sollogub) — 202

Sollogub, Vladimir Aleksandrovich (writer) — 96

Solovëv, Ivan Grigor'evich (book distributor) — 37, 55

Solovëv, Ivan Il'ich (teacher of theology) — 114

Solovëv, Sergej Mikhajlovich (historian) — 51

Solovëv, Vladimir Sergeevich (philosopher, poet & translator) — 50–52, 61, 124, 139, 154, 158, 166, 167, 192; *XLV*

Spinoza, Baruch (philosopher) — *XLV*

Stakhovich, Aleksandr Aleksandrovich (equerry) — 120, 135, 136, 182

Stakhovich, Mikhail Aleksandrovich [Misha] (close friend of the Tolstoys') — 101, 120, 125, 130, 131, 135, 149, 160, 182, 198, 204, 215; *Chr.* 1886

Stakhovich, Ol'ga Pavlovna (*née* Ushakova; wife to A. A. Stakhovich) — 182

Stanislavsky, Konstantin Sergeevich (actor & director) — 177; *XL*

Stankovich (Stankevich), Aleksej Ivanovich (librarian) — 215

Stasjulevich, Mikhail Matveevich (publisher) — 111, 204

Stasov, Vladimir Vasil'evich (art critic, librarian) — 61, 120, 188; *Chr.* 1904; *XL*

Stasova, Nadezhda Vasil'evna — *Chr.* 1895

Stebut, Ivan Aleksandrovich (professor at Petrovsky Academy) — 162, 163

Stendhal (real name: Marie-Henri Beyle; French writer) — 91

Stëpa (brother to SAT) — *see: Behrs, Stepan Andreevich*

Stepanov, Pëtr Gavrilovich (actor) — 16

Stolypin, Aleksandr Arkad'evich (son to A. D. Stolypin) — 166

Stolypin, Arkadij Dmitrievich (general; LNT's wartime chum) — 42, 136, 137, 166

Stolypin, Pëtr Arkad'evich (Russian Prime Minister (1906–11) — 42, 225

Storozhenko, Nikolaj Il'ich (literature professor) — 130, 147

Strakhov, Nikolaj Nikolaevich (philosopher; friend & editorial associate) — 47, 49,

55, 66, 121, 140, 150, 176; *Chr.* 1870,
1871, 1873–83, 1885–87, 1889–96; *XXXV,*
XXXIX, XL, LXIII

Strauss, David Friedrich (German writer)
— *LVIII*

Strekalova, Aleksandra Nikolaevna (*née*
Princess Kasatkina-Rostovskaja; philanthropist) — 213

Sukachëv, Evgenij Andreevich (Tolstoyan)
— 163

Sukhotin, Mikhail Mikhajlovich (son to M. S.
Sukhotin) — 224

Sukhotin, Mikhail Sergeevich (husband to
the Tolstoys' daughter Tat'jana L'vovna)
— 166, 177, 196, 201, 210, 223, 224, 232; *Chr.*
1899, 1914

Sukhotin, Pavel Ivanovich (neighbour to
M. N. Tolstaja) — 24

Sukhotin, Sergej Mikhajlovich (chamberlain)
— 13, 15–17, 24, 30, 32, 78

Sukhotina, Anna Petrovna (wife to P. I.
Sukhotin) — 24

Sukhotina, Elizaveta Sergeevna (daughter to
S. M. Sukhotin) — 78

Sukhotina, Marija Mikhajlovna (*née* Baroness
Bode; first wife to M. S. Sukhotin) — 78, 196

Sukhotina, Tat'jana L'vovna [Tanja] (*née* Tolstaya, the Tolstoys' daughter) — 10, 12, 17,
22, 27–31, 33, 36, 38, 40–42, 45, 47, 52, 54, 57,
61–63, 65, 69, 71, 72, 77–79, 81, 86, 89, 92,
94–96, 98, 100, 102, 105, 106, 108, 107–109,
111, 112, 114–20, 122, 123, 126–29, 133–39,
142–44, 146, 151, 153, 155–159, 161–71, 174,
176, 178–82, 185–91, 193, 194, 196–98,
200–02, 206, 208, 210, 220–24, 232, 233,
236, 238, 239; *Chr.* 1864, 1885, 1887, 1888,
1890, 1893–95, 1897, 1899, 1901, 1903, 1905,
1910, 1914, 1917, 1919; *XLVIII, XLIX, LX*

Sukhotina, Tat'jana Mikhajlovna [Tanja/
Tanjusha] (daughter to T. L. Sukhotina) —
223; *Chr.* 1905, 1911

Sukolenova, Anna Stepanovna (peasant) —
174, 176

Sullerzhitskij, Leopol'd Antonovich [Suller]
(actor; Tolstoyan) — 177, 206, 208; *Chr.*
1898, 1899

Sushkov, Nikolaj Vasil'evich (writer) — 30

Sushkova, Dar'ja Ivanovna (*née* Tjutcheva;
wife to N. V. Sushkov) — 30

Suvorov, Ivan Vasil'evich (servant to LNT) —
41, 42; *Chr.* 1871

Suvorova, Pelageja Fëdorovna (laundress)
— 138

Suvorova, Sof'ja Vasil'evna (married name:
Larionova; daughter to P. F. Suvorova)
— 138

Sverbeev family — 137, 162

Sverbeev, Dmitrij Dmitrievich (Tula Deputy
Governor) — 150

Sverbeev, Mikhail Dmitrievich — 81, 137

Sverbeeva, Ekaterina Aleksandrovna [Katja]
(*née* Shcherbatova) — 77, 137, 147

Sverbeeva, Marija Vjacheslavovna [Masha]
(*née* Shidlovskaja; cousin to SAT) — 81,
134, 137, 141, 147

Sverbeeva, Sof'ja Dmitrievna (sister to Tula
Vice-Governor) — 148, 150

Svistunov, Pëtr Nikolaevich (cornet of the
Cavalry Guard) — 51

Svjatopolk-Mirskij, Dmitrij Ivanovich (an old
wartime chum of LNT's) — 120

Sytin, Ivan Dmitrievich (publisher, print-
shop owner) — 134, 138, 139, 233; *Chr.* 1912

Sytin, Sergej Dmitrievich (brother to I. D.
Sytin) — 138, 139

T

Tabor, Emily (English tutor) — 64

Taneev, Sergej Ivanovich (composer) —
192–194, 196, 198–200, 206; *Chr.* 1889,
1895–99, 1902, 1906, 1908, 1915; *XXXV, XL,*
XLVI–XLVIII, XLIX

Tanja (SAT's sister) — *see: Kuzminskaja,*
Tat'jana Andreevna

Tanja (the Tolstoys' daughter) — *see: Sukho-*
tina, Tat'jana L'vovna

Tarsey, Hannah (English nanny, sister to Hannah Tarsey) — 29, 31, 33, 40–44

Tarsey, Jenny (English nanny) — 28, 29, 67

Tatarinov, Ivan Vasil'evich (regional nobility
representative) — 135

Tat'jana Filippovna (nanny to the Tolstoys' eldest son Sergej) — 10, 31

Taube, Sof'ja Arturovna (*née* Këller; wife to N. È. Taube) — 220

Taube, Georgij Nikolaevich (son to S. A. & N. È. Taube) — 220

Taube, Nikolaj Èrnestovich (senator) — 220

Tchaikovsky, Pëtr Il'ich (composer) — 33, 213; *XXXV*

Teplov, Mikhail Vasil'evich (artist) — 120

Thiman, Elizaveta Grigor'evna (*née* von Mickwitz) — *Chr.* 1912

Tikhomirov, Lev Aleksandrovich (writer & philosopher) — 158

Tikhonravov, Nikolaj Savvich (philologist; rector of Moscow University) — 96

Timashev-Bering, Vladimir Alekseevich (landowner) — 139

Timrot, Egor Aleksandrovich (Samara lawyer) — 44

Tjutchev, Fëdor Ivanovich (poet) — 30; *Chr.* 1858

Tjutcheva, Ekaterina Fëdorovna (daughter to F. I. Tjutchev, lady-in-waiting) — 15, 30; *Chr.* 1858

Tokutomi, Intiro (pseudonym: Sokho; Japanese journalist) — 189

Tolstaja, Aleksandra Andreevna [Alexandrine] (LNT's great aunt) — 37, 38, 47, 53, 76, 108, 111, 120, 123, 136, 137, 146, 149, 153, 162, 163, 166; *Chr.* 1855, 1876, 1877, 1880, 1882, 1887, 1889, 1903; *XLIX, LVIII, LIX, LXII*

Tolstaja, Aleksandra L'vovna [Sasha] (the Tolstoys' daughter) — 82, 96, 100, 102, 106, 118, 122, 137, 142, 144, 146, 147, 149, 150, 153, 154, 157, 158, 162, 167, 170, 174, 178–80, 184–187, 192, 194, 196, 198, 202–07, 209–12, 214, 215, 217, 218, 221, 223–28, 233–36, 239; *Chr.* 1884, 1897, 1907–11, 1914, 1918, 1919; *LX*

Tolstaja, Anna Il'inichna (daughter to I. L. Tolstoj) — 171; 214, *Chr.* 1888; *XXXIV*

Tolstaja, Elena Sergeevna [Hélène] (daughter to M. N. Tolstaja) — 74, 120, 145, 170; *Chr.* 1893

Tolstaja, Elizaveta Valer'janovna [Liza] — *see: Obolenskaja, Elizaveta Valer'janovna*

Tolstaja, Marija L'vovna [Masha] (the Tolstoys' second daughter) — 41, 43, 47, 51, 65–68, 70, 77–9, 89, 94–96, 100, 102, 105, 109, 110, 115–17, 122, 123, 125, 128, 131, 133, 134, 136–39, 143, 146, 147, 153, 155, 157, 160, 162, 164–68, 170, 171, 176, 178, 179, 184, 191, 192, 196–98, 206, 208, 214, 221; *XLVIII*

Tolstaja, Marija Mikhajlovna [Masha] (*née* Shishkina; common-law wife to S. N. Tolstoj) — 4, 15, 139; 216, *Chr.* 1863–1864, 1867

Tolstaja, Countess Marija Nikolaevna [Masha, Mashen'ka] (LNT's sister) — 4–7, 10, 12, 18, 19, 21, 22, 24, 25, 28, 30, 35, 41, 45, 51, 62, 66, 70, 72, 74, 100, 125, 128, 143, 144, 147, 170, 176, 184, 192, 196, 234; *Chr.* 1830, 1864, 1893–96, 1901, 1909, 1910

Tolstaja, Countess Marija Nikolaevna (*née* Princess Volkonskaja; LNT's mother) — 128, *Chr.* 1828, 1830

Tolstaja, Marija Sergeevna (married name: Bibikova, daughter to S. N. Tolstoj) — 192

Tolstaja, Ol'ga Konstantinovna (*née* Diterikhs; first wife to A. L. Tolstoj) — 213, 214, 218, 228; *Chr.* 1899

Tolstaja, Countess Pelageja Nikolaevna [*née* Princess Gorchakova; LNT's grandmother] — *Chr.* 1838

Tolstaja, Praskov'ja Fëdorovna (LNT's second cousin) — 206

Tolstaja, Praskov'ja Vasil'evna (*née* Barykova; wife to A. A. Tolstoj) — 16, 53

Tolstaja, Countess Sof'ja Andreevna (*née* Bakhmetova; widow to poet Count Aleksej Konstantinovich Tolstoj) — 78; *Chr.* 1882

Tolstaja, Sof'ja Nikolaevna (Sonja; *née* Filosofova) — *see: Filosofova, Sof'ja Nikolaevna*

Tolstaja, Tat'jana L'vovna (the Tolstoys' daughter) — *see: Sukhotina, Tat'jana L'vovna*

Tolstaja, Varvara [Varja] L'vovna [the Tolstoys' non-surviving daughter] — 51; *Chr.* 1875

Tolstaja, Varvara Valer'janovna [Varja] — *see: Nagornova, Varvara Valer'janovna*

Tolstaja, Vera Sergeevna (daughter to S. N. Tolstoj) — 102, 120, 128, 139, 168, 182, 208

Tolstoj, Count Aleksej Konstantinovich
(poet) — 78, *Chr.* 1882

Tolstoj, Aleksej L'vovich [Alësha] (the Tolstoys' son) — 62, 72, 77, 78, 83, 86, 92, 105,
106, 114, 118, 122, 132, 182, 220; *Chr.* 1881,
1886, 1905

Tolstoj, Andrej Andreevich (LNT's uncle) —
Chr. 1855

Tolstoj, Andrej Il'ich (LNT's grandson) — 180,
184, 200

Tolstoj, Andrej L'vovich [Andrjusha] (the
Tolstoys' son) — 51, 53–56, 60, 63–66, 68,
70–72, 74, 80, 86, 89, 92, 95, 96, 102, 105,
106, 112, 122, 123, 125, 131, 143, 144, 146,
149, 151, 153, 154, 157, 162, 171–74, 176–80,
183–85, 189, 192, 194, 201, 203–05, 213, 214,
219, 221, 225, 228, 236, 238, 239; *Chr.* 1877,
1890, 1896–98, 1904, 1907, 1910, 1912, 1916;
LI

Tolstoj, Count Dmitrij Andreevich (Minister
of Internal Affairs) — 121, 122

Tolstoj, Dmitrij Nikolaevich (LNT's brother)
— *Chr.* 1828, 1838

Tolstoj, Grigorij Sergeevich [Grisha] (LNT's
nephew) — 4–7, 136

Tolstoj, Il'ja Andreevich (LNT's grandfather)
— *Chr.* 1874, 1875

Tolstoj, Il'ja L'vovich [Iljusha] (the Tolstoys'
son) — 27–30, 38, 40–42, 47, 51, 52, 55–57,
60, 61, 63, 65, 66, 68–70, 75–79, 81–83, 86,
89, 94, 96, 98, 100, 102, 104, 105, 109–11, 114,
116, 118, 122, 123, 128, 131, 133, 134, 136–39,
142, 146, 148, 159, 169, 170, 178, 180, 200,
203, 204, 214, 215, 236; *Chr.* 1866, 1878, 1881,
1888, 1894, 1896, 1898, 1901, 1910, 1913, 1916

Tolstoj, Ivan L'vovich [Vanechka] (the Tolstoys' youngest child) — 141, 142, 144–50,
146, 148, 150, 152–54, 162, 163, 165, 167, 168,
172–74, 176, 178–82, 185, 189, 192, 193, 220,
224; *Chr.* 1888, 1895, 1910; *XL, XLVII*

Tolstoj, Lev L'vovich [Lëlja] [Lëva] (the Tolstoys' third son) — 38, 40, 41, 43, 45, 47, 51,
52, 55–57, 60, 62, 64–66, 70, 77, 78, 80–82,
86, 89, 94, 96, 100, 102, 105, 106, 109, 110,
111, 114, 117–20, 122, 123, 125, 126, 129–34,
136–39, 141–48, 150, 151, 153–55, 157–59,

162-64, 166–72, 174–77, 179, 185–87, 192,
196, 201, 203, 207, 210, 212, 220, 223–25;
Chr. 1869, 1878, 1881, 1895, 1896, 1910–12,
1916; *XLIII, XLIV, LXII*

Tolstoj, Mikhail L'vovich [Misha] (the Tolstoys'
son) — 60, 61, 63, 64, 68, 71, 74, 77, 86, 89,
106–08, 111, 112, 118, 122, 140, 141, 143, 151,
153, 154, 157, 162, 171, 172, 174, 176, 178, 179,
182–84, 186, 187, 189, 191, 192, 196, 197, 201,
203–06, 208, 210, 219, 236, 238; *Chr.* 1879,
1890, 1895, 1901, 1903, 1913, 1914; *XLIII, LI*

Tolstoj, Count Nikolaj Il'ich (LNT's father) —
Chr. 1828, 1837

Tolstoj, Nikolaj L'vovich [Kolja] (the Tolstoys'
non-surviving child) — 51; 132, 136, 138,
Chr. 1874, 1875

Tolstoj, Nikolaj Nikolaevich (LNT's brother)
— *Chr.* 1828, 1838, 1841, 1851, 1860

Tolstoj, Nikolaj Valer'janovich [Nikolen'ka]
(LNT's nephew) — 6, 45, 46

Tolstoj, Pëtr L'vovich [Petja] (the Tolstoys' non-
surviving child) — 51; 68, *Chr.* 1872, 1873

Tolstoj, Sergej L'vovich [Serëzha] (the Tolstoys' eldest son) — 4–6, 9, 12, 14, 17, 19,
20–22, 24, 26–30, 33, 38, 41, 42, 47, 51, 52,
54, 55, 57, 60, 61, 63–66, 68, 70, 72, 77, 78,
81, 82, 85, 86, 89, 90, 93, 94, 96, 100, 102,
105, 112, 116, 117, 120, 122, 127, 129, 131, 132,
134, 136–41, 143, 149, 153, 166, 157, 170, 171,
174–76, 178, 184, 187, 197, 204, 206, 208,
209, 212, 214, 215, 217, 219–21, 226, 231, 236,
238, 239; *Chr.* 1863, 1872, 1874, 1881, 1889,
1891, 1894–96, 1898, 1899, 1906, 1908, 1910,
1912, 1913; *XLIV, LX*

Tolstoj, Sergej Nikolaevich [Serëzha] (LNT's
brother) — 4–7, 9, 10, 12, 14, 15, 19–22, 47,
61. 65, 77, 90, 93, 98, 100, 102, 105–07, 109,
112, 118–120, 128, 139, 157, 169, 171, 175, 178,
216, 221; *Chr.* 1828, 1838, 1863–1864, 1864,
1867, 1890, 1897, 1904; *LIV*

Tolstoj, Sergej Sergeevich [Serëzha] (the Tolstoys' grandson) — 220, 226

Tregubov, Ivan Mikhajlovich (Tolstoyan) —
190, 191; *Chr.* 1894

Trepov, Dmitrij Fëdorovich (troop commander) — 220

Treskin, Vladimir Vladimirovich (son of an attorney from Moscow, a friend of the Tolstoys' children) — 116, 127, 129, 169

Tret'jakov, Pavel Mikhajlovich (founder of the Tret'jakov Gallery) — 116

Trubetskoj family — 202

Trubetskoj, Nikolaj Ivanovich (Privy Councillor) — 37

Trubetskoj (Troubetzkoy), Pavel Petrovich [Paolo] (sculptor) — 215

Trubetskoj, Prince Sergej Nikolaevich (philosophy professor) — 202, 219

Trubnikov, Aleksandr Nikolaevich (Orël governor) — 204

Tsejtlin, Natan Sergeevich — *Chr.* 1902

Tserteleva, Elizaveta Andreevna — *see: Lavrovskaja, Elizaveta Andreevna*

Tsvetaev, Ivan Vladimirovich (philologist, archæologist, director of Rumjantsev Museum) — 214

Tsvetkov, Jakov Vasil'evich (hunter) — 4, 10, 12, 16

Tsyganok, Pëtr — *see: Novikov, Pëtr Dmitrievich*

Tuchkov, Nikolaj Pavlovich (aide-de-camp) — 42

Tulub'ev, Ivan Vasil'evich (landowner) — 166

Tunimanov, Vladimir Artëmovich (Tolstoy scholar) — *E3*

Turgenev, Ivan Sergeevich (writer) — 24, 28, 61, 83, 85–89 204; *Chr.* 1855, 1856, 1878, 1880, 1881, 1883; *XXXV, XXXVIII, XL*

U

Ukhtomskij, Prince Èsper Èsperovich (journal editor) — 202; *Chr.* 1898

Urusov, Prince Leonid Dmitrievich (Tula Vice-Governor, philosopher) — 57, 61, 66, 69, 71, 73, 80, 86, 97; 108, 112, 130; *Chr.* 1878; *XL, XLV, XLVI*

Urusov, Prince Sergej Semënovich (wartime chum of LNT's) — 40, 42, 81, 100, 104, 106–108, 113, 114, 130, 134, 144–46, 171, 175, 176; *Chr.* 1873, 1889

Urusova, Marija Sergeevna [Monja] (*née* Mal'tseva; wife to L. D. Urusov) — *XLVI*

Urusova, Tat'jana Afanas'evna (*née* Nesterova; wife to L. D. Urusov) — 146

Urusova, Varvara Dmitrievna (sister to L. D. Urusov) — 94, 109

Ushakova, Valentina Sergeevna (married name: Gordeeva; sister to A. S. Khomjakova) — 78

Uspenskij, Aleksandr Afanas'evich (foreman of Sergej L'vovich's estate) — 169

Uspenskij, Gleb Ivanovich (writer) — *LV*

V

Van der Veer, Johannes (Dutchman who refused military service) — 188

Vannovskij, Pëtr Semënovich (general) — 120, 123; *LXIV*

Varvara Petrovna (the Tolstoys' servant in Moscow) — 114

Varvarinskij, Iosif Vasil'evich (professor) — 30, 32

Vasilij Nikitich (peasant from Gavrilovka) — 44

Vasnetsov, Viktor Mikhajlovich (artist) — 112

Velichkina, Vera Mikhajlovna (doctor) — *Chr.* 1899

Vel'sh, Anna Lukinichna — *see: Welsh, Anna Lukinichna*

Velti (Mlle; French tutor) — 58

Vendrikh, Al'fred Fëdorovich (doctor) — 13, 18

Vengerov, Semën Afanas'evich (literary historian) — *Chr.* 1913

Verigin, Pëtr Vasil'evich (Doukhobor leader) — *Chr.* 1895; *E10*

Victoria, Queen — *Chr.* 1893

Vigand, Èduard Il'ich (doctor) — 5, 21, 43

Viner, Elizaveta Vladimirovna (wife to Tolstoyan N. F. Dzhunkovskij) — 132, 137

Viner, Tsetsilija Vladimirovna (wife to D. A. Khilkov) — 137

Vinogradov, Dmitrij Fëdorovich (teacher) — 60, 66, 90, 91, 93, 99, 101, 103

Vjazemskij, Pëtr Andreevich (censor) — 30, 37, 38

Vladimirov, Nil Timofeevich (landowner from Kaluga Gubernia) — 163

Voejkov, Aleksandr Sergeevich — *Chr.* 1841

Vojtkevich, Sof'ja Robertovna [Sofesh] (wife to D. A. D'jakov) — 46

Volynskij, Akim L'vovich (real name: Khaim Lejbovich Flekser) — *Chr.* 1895

Volkonskaja, Princess Marija Nikolaevna — *see: Tolstaja, Countess Marija Nikolaevna*

Volkonskaja, Sof'ja Vasil'evna (*née* Urusova) — 62

Volkonskij family — 82

Volkonskij, Nikolaj Sergeevich (LNT's grandfather) — 219

Volodja (SAT's brother) — *see: Behrs, Vladimir Andreevich*

Vol'kenshtejn, Grigorij Emmanuilovich (husband to T. N. Vol'kenshtejn) — 204

Vol'kenshtejn, Tat'jana (Tanja) Nikolaevna (daughter to V. V. Nagornova) — 204

Vonljarljarskij, Mikhail Alekseevich (justice of the peace) — 70

Vorob'ëv, Vlas Anisimovich (yardkeeper) — 95, 100

Vsevolozhskaja, Sof'ja Vladimirovna (wife to I. V. Tatarinov) — 135

Vsevolozhskij family — 135

Vsevolozhskij, Mikhail Vladimirovich — 135

Vygodchikov (shop-owner) — 178

Vysotskij, Kapitan Aleskeevich (farmstead owner) — 163

W

Wagner, Richard (composer) — 215

Wales, Prince of — 177

Welsh (Vel'sh), Anna Lukinichna (music school proprietor) — 174, 192

Westerlund, Dora Fëdorovna (wife to L. L. Tolstoj) — 185, 187, 190, 196, 201, 203; *Chr.* 1896

Westerlund, Ernst (Swedish doctor; father to D. F. Westerlund) — 185, 210; *Chr.* 1896

Wolff, Maurycy Bolseław (Russian: Mavrikij Osipovich Vol'f; Polish publisher & bookseller) — 102

Wood, Ellen (a. k. a. Henry Wood; *née* Price; English author) — 38

Woodsworth, John — *Chr.* 1892, 1899

Z

Zabelin, Ivan Egorovich (archæologist-historian) — 214

Zagoskin, Mikhail (writer) — 15

Zajdenshnur, Èvelina Efimovna (Tolstoy scholar) — *XLII*

Zajkovskaja, Èmilija (sister to D. D. Zajkovskij) — 30, 32

Zajkovskaja, Ol'ga Dmitrievna (SAT's childhood friend) — 99, 125

Zajkovskij, Dmitrij Dmitrievich (doctor) — 30, 32

Zakhar'in, Grigorij Antonovich (director of Moscow University's therapeutic clinic) — 34, 39, 58, 147, 176, 207; *Chr.* 1906

Zaljubovskij, Aleksej Petrovich (Mennonite) — 120, 122, 123; *LXIV*

Zaljubovskij, Anatolij Petrovich (lieutenant; brother to Aleksej Petrovich Zaljubovskij) — 120

Zander, Nikolaj Avgustovich (violin teacher) — 168, 198

Zanini, Demetro (resident of Barcelona) — 191

Zhdanov, Vladimir Aleksandrovich (Tolstoy scholar) — *XXXVII*

Zheltov, Fëdor Alekseevich (peasant sectarian writer) — *LVI*

Zhemchuzhnikov, Aleksej Mikhajlovich (poet) — 22

Ziloti, Aleksandr Il'ich (pianist) — 122

Ziloti, Vera Pavlovna (*née* Tret'jakova; daughter to P. M. Tret'jakov) — 116

Zinov'ev, Nikolaj Alekseevich (Governor of Tula) — 162

Ziserman, Arnol'd L'vovich (historian) — 204

Zjabrev, Konstantin Nikolaevich [Kostjushka]
(poor peasant) — 63, 76, 107, 119, 138

Zjabrev, Nikolaj Ermilovich (a Yasnaya
Polyana peasant) — 107

Zjabrev, Osip Naumovich (husband to LNT's
wet-nurse) — 79, 97

Zjabrev, Pëtr Osipovich (son to O. N. Zjabrev)
— 79, 97, 104

Zjabrev, Tit Ermilovich — 79

Zjabrev, Vasilij Ermilov (Yasnaya Polyana
elder) — 12

Znamenskij, Nikolaj Nikolaevich
(dentist) — 178

Zolotarëv, Aleksandr Ignat'evich (Tula landowner) — 112

Zubov, Nikolaj Nikolaevich (nobility representative) — 172

Zubova, Aleksandra Vasil'evna (née Olsuf'eva;
wife to N. N. Zubov) — 172

Zubova, Ol'ga Nikolaevna (daughter to N. N.
Zubov; second wife to S. L. Tolstoj) — 172,
221

Zubova, Marija Nikolaevna — 172; *Chr.* 1906

MARQUIS